Lecture Notes in Artificial Intelligence 7894

Subseries of Lecture Notes in Computer Science

LNAI Series Editors

Randy Goebel
University of Alberta, Edmonton, Canada
Yuzuru Tanaka
Hokkaido University, Sapporo, Japan
Wolfgang Wahlster
DFKI and Saarland University, Saarbrücken, Germany

LNAI Founding Series Editor

Joerg Siekmann
DFKI and Saarland University, Saarbrücken, Germany

Leszek Rutkowski   Marcin Korytkowski
Rafał Scherer   Ryszard Tadeusiewicz
Lotfi A. Zadeh   Jacek M. Zurada (Eds.)

Artificial Intelligence and Soft Computing

12th International Conference, ICAISC 2013
Zakopane, Poland, June 9-13, 2013
Proceedings, Part I

 Springer

Series Editors

Randy Goebel, University of Alberta, Edmonton, Canada
Jörg Siekmann, University of Saarland, Saarbrücken, Germany
Wolfgang Wahlster, DFKI and University of Saarland, Saarbrücken, Germany

Volume Editors

Leszek Rutkowski
Marcin Korytkowski
Rafał Scherer
Częstochowa University of Technology, Poland
E-mail: {leszek.rutkowski, marcin.korytkowski, rafal.scherer}@iisi.pcz.pl

Ryszard Tadeusiewicz
AGH University of Science and Technology, Kraków, Poland
E-mail: rtad@agh.edu.pl

Lotfi A. Zadeh
University of California, Berkeley, CA, USA
E-mail: zadeh@cs.berkeley.edu

Jacek M. Zurada
University of Louisville, KY, USA
E-mail: jacek.zurada@louisville.edu

ISSN 0302-9743   e-ISSN 1611-3349
ISBN 978-3-642-38657-2   e-ISBN 978-3-642-38658-9
DOI 10.1007/978-3-642-38658-9
Springer Heidelberg Dordrecht London New York

Library of Congress Control Number: 2013938841

CR Subject Classification (1998): I.2, H.3, F.1, I.4, H.4, I.5

LNCS Sublibrary: SL 7 – Artificial Intelligence

Typesetting: Camera-ready by author, data conversion by Scientific Publishing Services, Chennai, India

Printed on acid-free paper

Springer is part of Springer Science+Business Media (www.springer.com)

Preface

This volume constitutes the proceedings of the 12th International Conference on Artificial Intelligence and Soft Computing, ICAISC 2013, held in Zakopane, Poland, during June 9–13, 2013. The conference was organized by the Polish Neural Network Society in cooperation with the Academy of Management in Łódź (SWSPiZ), the Department of Computer Engineering at the Czestochowa University of Technology, and the IEEE Computational Intelligence Society, Poland Chapter. Previous conferences took place in Kule (1994), Szczyrk (1996), Kule (1997), and Zakopane (1999, 2000, 2002, 2004, 2006, 2008, 2010, and 2012) and attracted a large number of papers and internationally recognized speakers: Lotfi A. Zadeh, Igor Aizenberg, Shun-ichi Amari, Daniel Amit, Piero P. Bonissone, Jim Bezdek, Zdzislaw Bubnicki, Andrzej Cichocki, Wlodzislaw Duch, Pablo A. Estévez, Jerzy Grzymala-Busse, Martin Hagan, Akira Hirose, Kaoru Hirota, Janusz Kacprzyk, Jim Keller, Laszlo T. Koczy, Soo-Young Lee, Robert Marks, Prof. Evangelia Micheli-Tzanakou, Kaisa Miettinen, Ngoc Thanh Nguyen, Erkki Oja, Witold Pedrycz, Marios M. Polycarpou, José C. Príncipe, Jagath C. Rajapakse, Sarunas Raudys, Enrique Ruspini, Jorg Siekman, Roman Slowinski, Igor Spiridonov, Ryszard Tadeusiewicz, Shiro Usui, Jun Wang, Ronald Y. Yager, Syozo Yasui, and Jacek Zurada. The aim of this conference is to build a bridge between traditional artificial intelligence techniques and recently developed soft computing techniques. It was pointed out by Lotfi A. Zadeh that: "Soft computing (SC) is a coalition of methodologies which are oriented toward the conception and design of information/intelligent systems. The principal members of the coalition are: fuzzy logic (FL), neurocomputing (NC), evolutionary computing (EC), probabilistic computing (PC), chaotic computing (CC), and machine learning (ML). The constituent methodologies of SC are, for the most part, complementary and synergistic rather than competitive." This volume presents both traditional artificial intelligence methods and soft computing techniques. This volume is divided into four parts:

- Neural Networks and Their Applications
- Fuzzy Systems and Their Applications
- Pattern Classification
- Computer Vision, Image and Speech Analysis

The conference attracted 274 submissions from 27 countries and after the review process, 112 papers were accepted for publication. I would like to thank our participants, invited speakers, and reviewers of the papers for their scientific and personal contribution to the conference. The reviewers listed herein were very helpful in reviewing the papers.

Finally, I thank my co-workers Łukasz Bartczuk, Piotr Dziwiński, Marcin Gabryel, Marcin Korytkowski, and the conference secretary Rafał Scherer, for their enormous efforts to make the conference a very successful event. Moreover, I would like to acknowledge the work of Marcin Korytkowski, who designed the Internet submission system.

June 2013   Leszek Rutkowski

Organization

ICAISC 2013 was organized by the Polish Neural Network Society in cooperation with the SWSPiZ Academy of Management in Łódź, the Department of Computer Engineering at Częstochowa University of Technology, and the IEEE Computational Intelligence Society, Poland Chapter and with technical sponsorship of the IEEE Computational Intelligence Society.

ICAISC Chairs

Honorary chairs   Lotfi Zadeh (USA)

Jacek Żurada (USA)

General chair   Leszek Rutkowski (Poland)

Co-chairs   Włodzisław Duch (Poland)

Janusz Kacprzyk (Poland)

Józef Korbicz (Poland)

Ryszard Tadeusiewicz (Poland)

ICAISC Program Committee

Rafał Adamczak, Poland
Cesare Alippi, Italy
Shun-ichi Amari, Japan
Rafal A. Angryk, USA
Jarosław Arabas, Poland
Robert Babuska, The Netherlands
Ildar Z. Batyrshin, Russia
James C. Bezdek, USA
Marco Block-Berlitz, Germany
Leon Bobrowski, Poland
Leonard Bolc, Poland
Piero P. Bonissone, USA
Bernadette Bouchon-Meunier, France
James Buckley, Poland
Tadeusz Burczynski, Poland
Andrzej Cader, Poland
Juan Luis Castro, Spain
Yen-Wei Chen, Japan
Wojciech Cholewa, Poland
Fahmida N. Chowdhury, USA
Andrzej Cichocki, Japan
Paweł Cichosz, Poland

Krzysztof Cios, USA
Ian Cloete, Germany
Oscar Cordón, Spain
Bernard De Baets, Belgium
Nabil Derbel, Tunisia
Ewa Dudek-Dyduch, Poland
Ludmiła Dymowa, Poland
Andrzej Dzieliński, Poland
David Elizondo, UK
Meng Joo Er, Singapore
Pablo Estevez, Chile
János Fodor, Hungary
David B. Fogel, USA
Roman Galar, Poland
Alexander I. Galushkin, Russia
Adam Gaweda, USA
Joydeep Ghosh, USA
Juan Jose Gonzalez de la Rosa, Spain
Marian Bolesław Gorzałczany, Poland
Krzysztof Grąbczewski, Poland
Garrison Greenwood, USA
Jerzy W. Grzymala-Busse, USA

Vladimir Red'ko, Russia
Raúl Rojas, Germany
Imre J. Rudas, Hungary
Enrique H. Ruspini, USA
Khalid Saeed, Poland
Dominik Sankowski, Poland
Norihide Sano, Japan
Robert Schaefer, Poland
Rudy Setiono, Singapore
Paweł Sewastianow, Poland
Jennie Si , USA
Peter Sincak, Slovakia
Andrzej Skowron, Poland
Ewa Skubalska-Rafajłowicz, Poland
Roman Słowiński, Poland
Tomasz G. Smolinski, USA
Czesław Smutnicki, Poland
Pilar Sobrevilla, Spain
Janusz Starzyk, USA
Jerzy Stefanowski, Poland
Pawel Strumillo, Poland
Ron Sun, USA
Johan Suykens Suykens, Belgium
Piotr Szczepaniak, Poland
Eulalia J. Szmidt, Poland
Przemysław Śliwiński, Poland
Adam Słowik, Poland
Jerzy Świątek , Poland

Hideyuki Takagi, Japan
Yury Tiumentsev, Russia
Vicenç Torra, Spain
Burhan Turksen, Canada
Shiro Usui, Japan
Michael Wagenknecht, Germany
Tomasz Walkowiak, Poland
Deliang Wang, USA
Jun Wang, Hong Kong
Lipo Wang, Singapore
Zenon Waszczyszyn, Poland
Paul Werbos, USA
Slawo Wesolkowski, Canada
Sławomir Wiak, Poland
Bernard Widrow, USA
Kay C. Wiese, Canada
Bogdan M. Wilamowski, USA
Donald C. Wunsch, USA
Maciej Wygralak, Poland
Roman Wyrzykowski, Poland
Ronald R. Yager, USA
Xin-She Yang, United Kingdom
Gary Yen, USA
John Yen, USA
Sławomir Zadrożny, Poland
Ali M. S. Zalzala, United Arab
  Emirates

ICAISC Organizing Committee

Rafał Scherer, Secretary
Łukasz Bartczuk, Organizing Committee Member
Piotr Dziwiński, Organizing Committee Member
Marcin Gabryel, Finance Chair
Marcin Korytkowski, Databases and Internet Submissions

Additional Reviewers

R. Adamczak
M. Al-Dhelaan
S. Amari
A. Bari
Ł. Bartczuk

A. Bielskis
M. Blachnik
L. Bobrowski
P. Boguś
A. Borkowski

B. Bouchon-Meunier
W. Bozejko
T. Burczyński
R. Burduk
B. Butkiewicz

K. Cetnarowicz	J. Korbicz	E. Rakus-Andersson
M. Chang	P. Korohoda	F. Rastegar
L. Chmielewski	J. Koronacki	L. Rolka
M. Choraś	M. Korytkowski	I. Rudas
R. Cierniak	M. Korzeń	F. Rudziński
B. Cyganek	W. Kosiński	A. Rusiecki
I. Czarnowski	J. Kościelny	L. Rutkowski
J. de la Rosa	L. Kotulski	H. Safari
K. Dembczynski	J. Kozlak	N. Sano
L. Diosan	M. Kretowski	R. Scherer
E. Dudek-Dyduch	R. Kruse	P. Sevastjanov
L. Dymowa	J. Kulikowski	A. Sędziwy
A. Dzieliński	V. Kurkova	L. Singh
P. Dziwiński	M. Kurzyńński	W. Skarbek
S. Ehteram	J. Kusiak	A. Skowron
D. Elizondo	S. Lee	E. Skubalska-Rafajłowicz
A. Fanea	A. Ligęza	K. Slot
M. Flasiński	S. Litwiński	A. Słowik
M. Gabryel	I. Lovtsova	C. Smutnicki
S. Gadepally	J. Łęski	A. Sokołowski
F. Gomide	B. Macukow	T. Sołtysiński
M. Gorzałczany	K. Madani	B. Starosta
E. Grabska	W. Malina	J. Stefanowski
K. Grąbczewski	J. Mańdziuk	B. Strug
W. Greblicki	U. Markowska-Kaczmar	P. Strumiłło
J. Grzymala-Busse	A. Marszałek	P. Sudhish
R. Hampel	A. Martin	J. Swacha
Z. Hasiewicz	A. Materka	E. Szmidt
Y. Hayashi	R. Matuk Herrera	J. Świątek
T. Hendtlass	J. Mendel	R. Tadeusiewicz
Z. Hendzel	J. Michalkiewicz	H. Takagi
K. Hirota	W. Mitkowski	Y. Tiumentsev
A. Horzyk	M. Morzy	V. Torra
E. Hrynkiewicz	M. Nieniewski	B. Trawinski
D. Jakóbczak	R. Nowicki	M. Wagenknecht
A. Janczak	A. Obuchowicz	T. Walkowiak
D. Kacprzak	E. Oja	H. Wang
T. Kaczorek	S. Osowski	J. Wąs
W. Kamiński	K. Patan	M. Witczak
V. Kecman	S. Paul	M. Wozniak
E. Kerre	A. Pieczyński	M. Wygralak
P. Klęsk	A. Piegat	R. Wyrzykowski
J. Kluska	V. Piuri	J. Zabrodzki
L. Koczy	P. Prokopowicz	
Z. Kokosinski	A. Przybył	
A. Kołakowska	E. Rafajłowicz	

Table of Contents – Part I

I Neural Networks and Their Applications

II Fuzzy Systems and Their Applications

III Pattern Classification

IV Computer Vision, Image and Speech Analysis

Table of Contents – Part II

I Evolutionary Algorithms and Their Applications

II Data Mining

III Bioinformatics, Biometrics and Medical Applications

IV Agent Systems, Robotics and Control

V Artificial Intelligence in Modeling and Simulation

VI Various Problems of Artificial Intelligence

Neural Data Analysis: Ensemble Neural Network Rule Extraction Approach and Its Theoretical and Historical Backgrounds

(Invited Paper)

Yoichi Hayashi

Department of Computer Science,
Meiji University,
Tama-ku, Kawasaki 214-8571, Japan
hayashiy@cs.meiji.ac.jp

Abstract. In this paper, we first survey the theoretical and historical backgrounds related to ensemble neural network rule extraction. Then we propose a new rule extraction method for ensemble neural networks. We also demonstrate that the use of ensemble neural networks produces higher recognition accuracy than do individual neural networks. Because the extracted rules are more comprehensible. The rule extraction method we use is the Ensemble-Recursive-Rule eX traction (E-Re-RX) algorithm. The E-Re-RX algorithm is an effective rule extraction algorithm for dealing with data sets that mix discrete and continuous attributes. In this algorithm, primary rules are generated, followed by secondary rules to handle only those instances that do not satisfy the primary rules, and then these rules are integrated. We show that this reduces the complexity of using multiple neural networks. This method achieves extremely high recognition rates, even with multiclass problems.

Keywords: Ensemble, neural network, rule extraction, Re-RX algorithm, Ensemble method, Recursive neural network rule extraction.

1 Introduction

In this paper, we first survey the nature of artificial neural networks (ANNs), the origin of neural network rule extraction, incorporation of fuzziness in neural network rule extraction, the theoretical foundation of neural network rule extraction, the computational complexity of neural network rule extraction, neuro-fuzzy hybridization, rule extraction from neural network ensembles, and the background of neural network ensembles. Then we describe the three objectives of this paper.

We propose the Ensemble-Recursive-Rule Extraction (E-Re-RX) algorithm, which extracts comprehensible rules [13], [37]. In the E-Re-RX algorithm, the Re-RX algorithm [9] is an effective rule extraction algorithm for data sets that comprise both discrete and continuous attributes. The extracted rules maintain the high recognition capabilities of a neural network while expressing highly comprehensible rules.

L. Rutkowski et al. (Eds.): ICAISC 2013, Part I, LNAI 7894, pp. 1–19, 2013.

1.1 Nature of Artificial Neural Networks

ANNs attempt to replicate the *computational* power of biological neural networks and thereby endow machines with some of the *cognitive abilities* possessed by biological organisms. However, an impediment to more widespread acceptance of ANNs is the absence of the capability to explain to the user, in a human-comprehensible form, how the network arrives at a particular decision. That is, it is very difficult to discuss the *knowledge* encoded within the "*black box*" of NNs. Recently, widespread activities have attempted to revisit this situation by extracting the embedded knowledge in trained ANNs in the form of symbolic rules [14].

As a biologically inspired analytical technique, NNs have the capacity to learn and model complex nonlinear relationships. Theoretically, multi-layered feedforward NNs are universal approximators and, as such, have an excellent ability to approximate any nonlinear mapping to any degree of accuracy [6], [40]. They do not require *a priori* models to be assumed or *a priori* assumptions to be made on the properties of data [8].

Generally, ANNs consider a fixed topology of neurons connected by links in a predefined manner. These connection weights are usually initialized by small random values. *Knowledge-based networks* constitute a special class of ANNs that consider crude domain knowledge to generate the initial network architecture, which is later refined in the presence of training data. [14]

Recently, some attempts have been made to improve the efficiency of neural computation by using knowledge-based nets. Such nets help to reduce the searching space and time while the network traces the optimal solution. In such a situation, one can extract causal factors and functional dependencies from the data domain for initially encoding the ANN and later extracting refined rules from the trained network [50].

The term *rule generation* encompasses both rule extraction and rule refinement. Note that *rule extraction* here refers to extracting knowledge from the ANN while using network parameters in the process. *Rule refinement*, in contrast, pertains to extracting refined knowledge from the ANN that was initialized by using crude domain knowledge. Rules learned and interpolated for fuzzy reasoning and fuzzy control can also be considered under rule generation. In a wider sense, rule generation includes the extraction of domain knowledge (e.g., for the initial encoding of an ANN) by using nonconnectionist tools such as fuzzy sets and rough sets. [14]

1.2 Origin of Neural Network Rule Extraction [14]

Here we first consider the layered connectionist model by Gallant [15] and Saito and Nakano [16] for rule extraction in the medical domain. The inputs and outputs consist of crisp variables in all cases. Generally, the symptoms are represented by the input nodes, and the diseases and possible treatments correspond to intermediate and/or output nodes. The multilayer network described by Saito and Nakano was applied to the detection of *headache*. Headache patients respond to a questionnaire regarding the perceived symptoms and these constitute the input to the network.

In 1988, the model by Gallant [15], dealing with *sacrophagal* problems, uses a linear discriminant network (with no hidden nodes) that is trained by the *simple pocket algorithm*.

Gallant's model [15] incorporates inferencing and forward chaining, confidence estimation, backward chaining, and explanation of conclusions by IF-THEN rules. To generate a rule, the attributes with greater inference strength (magnitude of connection weights) are selected and a conjunction of the more significant premises is formed to justify the output concept.

Rule extraction techniques generally fall into two categories [44]: direct approaches and indirect approaches. We take the standpoint that indirect approaches are more promising.

In an indirect approach, a predictive model is built from training data, and rules are extracted from the model. ANNs and Support Vector Machines (SVMs) are two of the most popular algorithms used to build predictive models. Rule extraction from ANNs has been investigated by many researchers [41], [42]. SVM-based rule extraction has also been explored extensively due to the high performance of SVMs [43].

1.3   Incorporating Fuzziness in Neural Network Rule Extraction

As an illustration of the characteristics of layered fuzzy neural networks for inferencing and rule generation, the models by Hayashi [17], [18] and Hudson et al. [19] are described first. A *distributed single-layer perceptron-based* model trained with the *pocket algorithm* was used by Hayashi [17], [18] for diagnosing *hepatobiliary* disorders. All contradictory training data were excluded, as these cannot be handled by the model. The input layer consists of fuzzy and crisp cell groups while the output is modeled only by fuzzy cell groups. The crisp cell groups are represented by m cells taking on two values, $\{(+1, +1, ,..., +1), (-1, -1,..., -1)\}$. Fuzzy cell groups, however, use binary m-dimensional vectors, each taking values of $\{+1, -1\}$. Linguistic relative importance terms such as *very important* and *moderately important* are allowed in each proposition. Linguistic truth values such as *completely true, true, possibly true, unknown, possibly false, false*, and *completely false* are also assigned by the domain experts, depending on the output values. By using different linguistic truth values, a pattern belonging to more than one class can be modeled. Extraction of fuzzy IF-THEN production rules is possible by using a top-down traversal involving analysis of the node activation, bias, and the associated link weights.

1.4   Theoretical Foundation of Neural Network Rule Extraction

A fuzzy system adaptively infers and modifies its fuzzy association from representative numerical samples. Neural networks, in contrast, can *blindly* generate and refine fuzzy rules from training data. Fuzzy sets are considered to be advantageous in the logical field and in easily handling higher order processing.

Higher flexibility is a characteristic feature of neural networks produced by learning and, hence, NNs are better suited for data-driven processing [20].

In 1993, Buckley, Hayashi and Czogala [21] mathematically proved the equivalence of neural nets and fuzzy expert systems. In other words, they proved that we can describe the contents of trained neural networks by a set of linguistic IF-THEN rules. Moreover, this paper firmly established the theoretical foundation of neural network rule extraction.

Hayashi and Buckley [22] proved that 1) any rule-based fuzzy system may be approximated by a neural net, and 2) any neural net (e.g., feedforward net, multilayered net) may be approximated by a rule-based fuzzy system. This kind of equivalence between the fuzzy-rule-based system and neural networks was also studied [21],[22],[23],[24].

1.5   Computational Complexity of Neural Network Rule Extraction

A salient theoretical discovery in this area is that, in many cases, the computational complexity of extracting rules from trained neural networks and the complexity of extracting rules directly from data are both NP-hard [25].

Bologna [32] claimed that the difficulty of extracting rules is related to the dimensionality of the input samples. More precisely, the dimensionality is related to n binary valued input neurons. We could find up to 2^n rules. Generally, with large-dimensional problems, several rules may be missed. In such a situation, the degree of matching between the rules and the neutral network classification, also denoted as *fidelity*, is less than 100%.

It is also worth mentioning that Roy [26] astutely disclosed the conflict between rule extraction and traditional connectionism. In detail, the idea of rule extraction from a neural network involves certain procedures, specifically the reading of parameters from a network. Such reading is not allowed by the traditional connectionist framework on which these neural networks are based. Roy [26] indicated that such a conflict could be resolved by introducing a control-theoretic paradigm, which was supported by new evidence from neuroscience about the role of neuromodulators and neurotransmitters in the brain.

1.6   Neuro-fuzzy Hybridization

Neuro-fuzzy hybridization [51] is done broadly in two ways: a neural network equipped with the capability of handling fuzzy information [termed *fuzzy-neural network* (FNN)], and a fuzzy system augmented by neural networks to enhance some of the neural network characteristics such as flexibility, speed, and adaptability [termed *neural-fuzzy system* (NFS)].

Other kinds of categorizations for neuro-fuzzy models have been reported in related literature [28]. Buckley and Hayashi [28] classified fuzzified neural networks possessing the following: 1) real number inputs, fuzzy outputs, and fuzzy weights; 2) fuzzy inputs, fuzzy outputs, and real number weights; 3) fuzzy inputs, fuzzy outputs, and fuzzy weights. Hayashi et al. [29] fuzzified the delta rule for the *multilayer perceptron* (MLP) by using fuzzy numbers at the input, output, and weight levels.

But, the algorithm with the stopping rule has problems. Ishibuchi et al. [30] incorporated triangular and trapezoidal fuzzy number weights, and thereby increased the complexity of the algorithm. Some of these problems were overcome by Feuring et al. in [31].

1.7   Rule Extraction from Neural Network Ensemble

In the beginning of the 1990s, Hansen and Salamon [38] showed that the generalization ability of learning systems based on artificial neural networks can be significantly improved through ensembles of artificial neural networks, i.e., training multiple artificial neural networks and combining their predictions via voting. Since combining works remarkably well, it became a very popular topic in both neural network and machine learning communities [35].

In general, a neural network ensemble is constructed in two steps: training a number of component neural networks, and then combining the component predictions [36].

The rationale for considering a combination of methods is similar to that of ensemble NNs [5]. However, ensembling is more robust and mitigates the effect of one method that gives bad results and ruins the performance [52].

Although many authors have generated comprehensible models from individual networks, much less work has been done in the explanation of neural network ensembles [32].

Bologna proposed the *Interpretable Multi-Layer Perceptron* (IMLP) and the *Discretized IMLP* (DIMLP) models with generated rules from neural network ensembles [33, 34]. The DIMLP is a special neural network model for which symbolic rules are generated to explain the knowledge embedded within the connections and the activation neurons. Bologna described how to translate symbolic rules into the DIMLP and how to extract rules from one or several combined neural networks.

Rules are generated from a DIMLP network by the induction of a special decision tree and taking into account virtual hyperplane frontiers.

In [32], Bologna's rule extraction was compared to other rule extraction techniques applied to neural networks. For seven out of eight classification problems, the accuracy of his results were equal to or better than those given by other techniques.

The scale of the computational complexity of his rule extraction algorithm in polynomial time is related to the dimensionality of the problem, the number of examples, and the size of the network. Continuous valued attributes do not need to be transformed to binary attributes, as is done in many rule extraction techniques. That is a clear advantage with respect to decompositional rule extraction algorithms with high exponential computational complexity (for comparison, see Section 2.2 of [32]). In practice, the execution time of learning and rule extraction is very reasonable. For more mathematical details on the computational complexity, refer to Section 3.3 of [32] and Section 6.4 of [34].

With Rule Extraction From Neural network Ensemble (REFNE) proposed by Zhou et al. [35], attributes are discretized during rule extraction, whereas Bologna's rule extraction algorithm performs the discretization during learning through the use of staircase activation functions. Furthermore, rules generated by REFNE are limited to three antecedents, whereas DIMLP does not impose any constraints. Another important difference is that we extract unordered rules from DIMLP ensembles, whereas ordered rules are generated by REFNE. Bologna's rule extraction algorithm has no parameters; hence, it could be easier for a non-specialist in rule extraction to use the DIMLP ensemble rather than those rule extraction techniques that require several parameters be set [32].

The REFNE approach proposed by Zhou et al. is designed to extract symbolic rules from trained neural network ensembles that perform classification tasks. REFNE utilizes trained ensembles to generate a number of instances and then extracts rules from those instances. REFNE can gracefully break the ties made by individual neural networks in prediction [35].

In recent years, many approaches for rule extraction from trained neural networks have been developed. A review of these approaches can be generally categorized into two classes: function-analysis-based and architecture-based approaches. The function-analysis-based approaches extract rules by regarding the trained networks as entities that can be easily modified for extracting rules from trained ensembles instead of the networks as entities. REFNE is derived from a function-analysis-based approach, called STARE [46], for extracting rules from trained neural networks [35].

The architecture-analysis-based approaches extract rules by disassembling the architectures of trained neural networks. Such architectures are those that are relatively difficult to modify for extracting rules from trained ensembles. The reason is that even if rules could be extracted from each individual network, it is still difficult to unite them into a consistent rule set that explains the capability of the ensemble because simply gathering them together can only result in a messy hodgepodge of rules [35].

However, no matter where the approaches for rule extraction from network ensembles are derived from, they must pay attention to some specific characteristics of ensembles, e.g., the ambiguity in a prediction caused by ties made by individual neural networks [35].

Zhou et al. [35] presented a pedagogical algorithm for extracting prepositional rules from a complicated neural network system. With different configurations, the algorithm can extract rules with high fidelity but moderate accuracy, or high accuracy but moderate fidelity. A particularly interesting issue that has not been addressed appears in [35]: which configuration should we prefer? This question places us in an uncomfortable situation: to sacrifice the fidelity, or to sacrifice the accuracy. In fact, pursuing high fidelity and high accuracy may not be possible in certain situations, although this has not been recognized before [27].

Zhou et al. [36] analyzed the relationship between the ensemble and its component neural networks from the context of both regression and classification. Their work revealed that it may be better to ensemble *many* instead of *all* the available neural networks at hand. This result is interesting because most approaches ensemble *all* the available neural networks for prediction. Then, to show the feasibility of their theory, an ensemble approach named Genetic Algorithm based Selective ENsemble (GASEN) was presented. A large empirical study showed that GASEN is superior to bagging [1] and boosting [2] in both regression and classification because it utilizes far fewer component neural networks but achieves stronger generalization ability [36].

In 2012, Hara and Hayashi proposed two ensemble neural network rule extraction algorithms. The former is for two-class classification [13]. The latter is for multiple-class classification [37]. Both of these algorithms use standard MLPs and the Re-RX algorithm proposed by Setiono [9]. Their recognition accuracy is very high.

For reference, Adeodato et al. [39] showed that the ensemble of MLPs produces better results than does the single MLP solution. For this purpose, the performance of the ensemble was compared to the average of the performances of each single MLP.

1.8   Neural Network Ensembles in This Paper

In ensemble neural networks, bagging [1], boosting [2], AdaBoosting [47], averaging [48], and other techniques have been suggested as ways to split a data set and perform multifaceted analyses. Each of these studies reported classification accuracy exceeding that of individual neural networks [3], [4], [10].

Because neural network ensembles are multiple individual neural networks, they present their own problems: their complexity is greater, rule extraction is more difficult, and they use more computing resources than are necessary. In the studied neural network ensembles to date, research on methods such as weighted voting [11] and averaging [48] for integrating the output has been conducted. Algorithms that use bagging or boosting in the C4.5 algorithm have been presented, but these do not directly address the problems, because splitting the data set into parts and applying the C4.5 algorithm to them generates rules that determine the class, and so the total output is classes applied broadly based on the rules. This in turn means that the rules are numerous and redundant. Consequently, we believe that methods such as bagging or boosting cannot be assumed to extract rules from an ensemble neural network.

Nevertheless, neural networks are known to be an effective method for real-world classification problems involving nonlinear data. Contrary to the standard explanation that neural networks operate as "black boxes," many studies have been conducted on methods for rule extraction [49]. These studies can be seen as an outgrowth of the extraordinary advances that have been made in information technology (IT) and the ability of IT to easily handle massive volumes of data. Extracting rules from neural networks is not simply a matter of breaking open the black box. From the perspective of data mining, it increases the opportunities to use neural network technology as data mining technology.

In our proposed algorithm, we selected part of the learning data set , LD, and extracted a primary rule set from the learning data subset, LD'. Next, we classified our learning data subset into those instances that satisfied the primary rules and those that did not. Using the non-satisfying instances, we used the Re-RX [9] algorithm to extract a secondary rule set. The primary and secondary rule sets can be regarded as the ensemble neural network's complete rules, which have sufficiently high recognition capabilities.

We conducted experiments using the CARD data set, the German Credit data set, the Thyroid data set, and the Page block data set, which can be obtained from the UCI repository [12]. In this paper, we provide a discussion based on the results of experiments and a conclusion that states the three open questions.

2   Purpose of This Paper

This paper has three major objectives.

The first objective is to increase recognition rates. Neural networks show high recognition accuracy when used as a data mining technique, but they do not show sufficiently high recognition accuracy when using a partial data set. In most cases, multiclass problems occur where poor recognition rates are seen. In this paper, we demonstrate extremely high recognition rates, even with multiclass problems. It is understood that one cause of low recognition rates in existing methods is overfitting. In our research, we used a randomly extracted learning data subset that was arbitrarily taken from the source data set. Using a partial learning data set is effective in reducing the number of factors in the source data set that lead to overfitting.

The second objective is to extract rules from an ensemble neural network. Ensemble neural networks are extremely effective in the field of data mining due to their strong recognition capabilities, but in fields where high reliability is demanded, such as medicine and finance, the recognition capability of ensemble neural networks alone is not enough. The solution is to extract rules that express what the ensemble neural network recognizes with a high degree of comprehensibility. If the recognition results can be expressed as rules, then the technique can even be used in fields that demand a high level of reliability. This would expand the range of applications for ensemble neural networks in data mining. In our research, we used the E-Re-RX algorithm [13], [37] that we are proposing for rule extraction. This algorithm is effective for rule extraction when the data set includes both discrete and continuous attributes, and the extracted rules show a high degree of comprehensibility.

The third objective is to minimize the use of computer resources. Ensemble neural networks have typically achieved good recognition accuracy by using a large number of neural networks, but using a large number of neural networks creates the problem of creating unused neural networks. In our research, we achieved high recognition accuracy by using an ensemble neural network consisting of the smallest number of neural networks possible, which is two.

3   Structure of the E-Re-RX Algorithm

3.1   Origin of Neural Network Ensemble

A neural network ensemble is a learning paradigm, in which a collection of a finite number of neural networks is trained for the same task. The neural network ensemble originates from Hansen and Salamon's work [38], which showed that the generalization ability of a neural network system can be significantly improved by ensembling a number of neural networks, i.e., by training many neural networks and then combining their predictions.

3.2   Re-RX Algorithm

The Re-RX algorithm [9] is designed to generate classification rules from data sets that have both discrete and continuous attributes. The algorithm is recursive in nature and generates hierarchical rules. The rule conditions for discrete attributes are disjointed from those for continuous attributes. The continuous attributes only appear in the conditions of the rules lowest in the hierarchy.

The outline of the algorithm is as follows.

Algorithm Re-RX(S, D, C)

Input: A set of data samples S having discrete attributes D and continuous attributes C.

Output: A set of classification rules.

1. Train and prune a neural network using the data set S and all its D and C attributes.
2. Let D' and C' be the sets of discrete and continuous attributes, respectively, still present in the network, and let S' be the set of data samples correctly classified by the pruned network.
3. If D' has associated continuous attributes C', generate a hyperplane to split the samples in S' according to the values of the continuous attributes C', then stop. Otherwise, by using only the discrete attributes D', generate the set of classification rules R for data set S'.

For each rule Ri generated:

If support(Ri)>δ_1 and error(Ri)>δ_2, then

— Let Si be the set of data samples that satisfy the condition of rule Ri and let Di be the set of discrete attributes that do not appear in the rule condition of Ri.
— If D' has associated continuous attributes C', generate a hyperplane to split the samples in Si according to the values of the continuous attributes Ci, then stop. Otherwise, call Re-RX (Si, Di, Ci).

In the above, we define the support of (Ri) to be the proportion of samples covered by rule Ri and the error of (Ri) to be the proportion of samples it incorrectly classifies.

3.3   Ensemble-Re-RX (E-Re-RX) Algorithm [13][37]

In the proposed E-Re-RX algorithm, we first produce the learning data set LD', which is necessary for training the first neural network. LD' is the set of instances extracted at random in an arbitrary proportion from the full learning data set LD. LD' is input into a neural network having one node in its hidden layer. The neural network is trained and pruned [7], and the rules are extracted.

In this paper, we restrict ourselves to back-propagation neural networks with one hidden layer because such networks have been shown to possess a universal approximation property [6], [40]. An effective neural network pruning algorithm is a crucial component of any neural network rule extraction algorithm. By removing the inputs not needed for solving the problem, the extracted rule set becomes more concise. In addition, the pruned network also filters noise that might be present in the data. Such noise could be data samples that are outliers or incorrectly labeled. From these extracted rules, we re-extract rules in accordance with the Re-RX algorithm, and take the final rule set as the primary rules R.

We divide LD into data sets that do and do not conform to these primary rules. The set of instances that do not conform are taken as LDf, which is input into the second neural network. The second neural network is similarly trained on LDf and pruned, rules are extracted, and rules are then re-extracted in accordance with the Re-RX algorithm. These extracted rules are the secondary rules Rf.

Integrated rules are obtained from extracted rules R and Rf. In the rule integration, we focus on the primary rule and the secondary rule for attributes and values that are the same. If the attributes and values for the primary rule and the secondary rule match exactly, and the class labels are also the same, the secondary rule is integrated into the primary rule. For example, assume the following rule is obtained as a primary rule.

R: If D42=0, then predict Class 1.

The following rule is obtained as a secondary rule.

Rf: If D42=0, then predict Class 1.

In this case, all of the attributes, values, and class labels that emerge in the rules match. Therefore, these rules are integrated. Another case may appear where one rule is expressed as either a primary or secondary rule, whereas another primary or secondary rule may have some matching attributes and values. In this case, whichever rule can be encompassed by the other is integrated into the other, regardless of class labels. For example, the following is obtained as a primary rule.

R: If D42=1 and D38=0 and D43=0 and D27=0 and D24=0 and D45=0 and D2=0 and D21=1, then predict Class 1.

The following is obtained as a secondary rule.

Rf: If D24=0 and D2=0 and D45=0 and D21=1, then predict Class 2.

In this case, all of the attributes and values of the secondary rule are encompassed within the primary rule. Because the secondary rule can be encompassed by the primary rule, even though the class labels differ, the secondary rule is integrated into the primary rule. The presence of attributes in the primary rule that are absent in the secondary rule are considered to result in more accurate class identification.

With the neural network ensemble, it is possible to determine the final output by integrating the outputs of the multiple neural networks. With the E-Re-RX algorithm, it is possible to determine the overall final output by integrating the rules. This rule integration enables the reduction of the number of neural networks and irrelevant rules. The essentials of the E-Re-RX algorithm are outlined as follows.

Input: Training sets LD' and LDf

Output: Integrated rule set obtained by integration of the primary and secondary rule sets.

1. Extract at random an arbitrary proportion of instances from the learning set LD and designate this randomly extracted learning set LD'.
2. Perform training and pruning of LD' with the first neural network.
3. Apply the Re-RX algorithm [9] to the output of Step 2 to obtain the primary rules.
4. Based on these primary rules, generate the set LDf consisting of instances that do not satisfy these rules.
5. Train and prune LDf with the second neural network.
6. Apply the Re-RX algorithm [9] to the output of Step 5 to output the secondary rules.
7. Integrate the primary and secondary rules.

The composition of the two standard MLPs is shown schematically in Fig. 1.

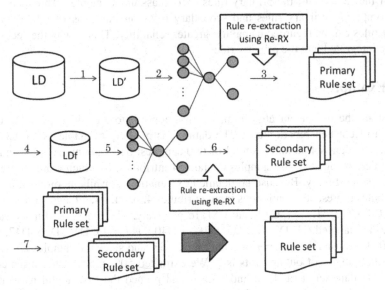

Fig. 1. Basic process for extraction of primary and secondary rules of high accuracy from two standard MLPs

3.4   Integration of Rules

Extracting rules from multiple standard MLPs is assumed to increase the number of rules, and some of these extracted rules may be redundant or irrelevant as classification rules.

The accuracy of the rules is maintained and their number is reduced by integrating the primary and secondary rules in accordance with the attributes.

In this paper, the rules extracted from the Re-RX algorithm use the decision tree formed by the J4.8 algorithm. By using the J4.8 algorithm for multiple generated rules and particularly for primary and secondary rules, the multiple attributes of the same type and value are integrated into rules having more attribute types; that is, the primary and the secondary rules are integrated into finer rules. In judgments made with a decision tree, rules having a larger number of attribute types are considered to be more accurately classified. In this paper, when rules are integrated, a reduced rule number is achieved by integration into finer rules.

That said, in some instances a primary rule will contradict a secondary rule. Here, the instance that generates the secondary rule is judged to differ depending on the hyperplane and the associated rule generated during primary rule training. Making this distinction adequately explains cases in which contradictory rules are extracted. In contradictory rules, the attributes and values are exactly the same but the class labels differ, or the class labels and attributes that appear in the rules are the same but the attribute values differ. In these cases, the rules that appear in the secondary rules are integrated into the primary rules. The decision is made based on the number of samples in the running data set. More specifically, the running data set LD' has a greater number of samples than the running data set used to generate the secondary rules for the LDf. Thus, the primary rules encompass more samples. This means that when comparing primary rules and secondary rules on the basis of reliability, the primary rules can be regarded as having greater reliability. This is why the secondary rules are integrated into the primary rules.

4   Example

To illustrate the use of our algorithm, we first apply it to a credit approval data set used in a recent benchmark study. The data set is publicly available as the CARD1 data set. The data set contains a total of 690 samples: 518 training samples and 172 test samples. Altogether, the samples contain 51 attributes, of which 6 are continuous and the rest are binary. Because no detailed explanation is available on what each of the attributes represents, continuous input attributes 4, 6, 41, 44, 49, and 51 are simply labeled C4, C6, C41, C44, C49, and C51, respectively. The remaining binary-valued attributes are labeled D1, D2, D3, D5, D7, ..., D40, D42, D43, D45, D46, D47, D48, and D50. Therefore, the number of input units is 51, and since the samples are in two groups, the number of output units is 2. We extracted 50% (259) of the instances in the CARD1 data set at random, and trained and pruned the first neural network by using the extracted set designated as LD'. From the resulting network, we extracted rules using the decision tree obtained with J4.8 and performed rule re-extraction in accordance with the Re-RX algorithm and the re-extraction threshold $\delta 1 = \delta 2 = 0.05$. The resulting primary rules are expressed as follows.

R1: If D42=0, then predict Class 1.
R2: If D42=1 and D7=0 and D19=0 and D43=0, then predict Class 1.
R3: If D42=1 and D7=0 and D19=0 and D43=1, then predict Class 2.
R4: If D42=1 and D7=0 and D19=1, then predict Class 1.
R5: If D42=1 and D7=1, then predict Class 2.

Based on these primary rules, we produced the data set for 70 instances, LDf, which was then used to train and prune the second neural network. We next performed rule re-extraction by using the same procedure applied for the first neural network. The resulting secondary rules are expressed as follows.

Rf1: If D42=0, then predict Class 1.
Rf2: If D42=1 and D13=0, then predict Class 1.
Rf3: If D42=1 and D13=1, then predict Class 2.

Comparison of the above primary and secondary rules immediately shows that R1 and Rf1 represent the same rule. Rf1 was therefore integrated into R1, and the following final rule set was the result.

R1: If D42=0, then predict Class 1.
R2: If D42=1 and D7=0 and D19=0 and D43=0, then predict Class 1.
R3: If D42=1 and D7=0 and D19=0 and D43=1, then predict Class 2.
R4: If D42=1 and D7=0 and D19=1, then predict Class 1.
R5: If D42=1 and D7=1, then predict Class 2.
Rf2: If D42=1 and D13=0, then predict Class 1.
Rf3: If D42=1 and D13=1, then predict Class 2.

The correct answer ratios obtained with the learning data set and the test data set using these rules were 96.14% and 94.19%, respectively. The value of the test data set was 5% higher than the test data set value of 89.53% reported by rule extraction with the well-known C4.5 variant as the Re-RX algorithm [9]. Moreover, the number of rules was 14 with Re-RX, but only 7 with E-Re-RX because no re-extraction was performed.

5   Results

Using the same methods, we performed all experiments on the CARD3, German Credit, Thyroid, and Pageblock data. All of this data is publicly available from the UCI repository [12].

The German Credit data set includes 56 discrete attributes and 7 continuous attributes. It has 2 classes indicating "good customer" and "bad customer." The Thyroid data set includes 15 discrete attributes and 3 continuous attributes. It has 3 classes indicating "normal," "hyper," and "hypo." The Pageblock data set includes 6 discrete attributes and 4 continuous ones. It has 5 classes indicating "text," "horizontal line," "graphic," "vertical line," and "picture." In each of these data sets, as in the CARD1 data, the attributes on each line are labeled with a D for a discrete attribute or a C for a continuous attribute.

Our experimental results are shown in Table 1, which shows the recognition rates for the data sets, and Table 2, which shows the number of rules. Our E-Re-RX results are presented with reference to Hara and Hayashi [13], [37]. Our Re-RX results are presented with reference to Setiono et al. [9]. Our results for MNNEX, PITS, Neural Network Bagging (shown as "NNBagging" in Table 1), and Neural Network AdaBoosting (shown as "NN AdaBoosting" in Table 1) are presented with reference to Akhand et al. [10].

We conducted each of the E-Re-RX experiments by setting $\delta_1 = \delta_2 = 0.05$, except for the German Credit experiments, where we set $\delta_1 = \delta_2 = 0.09$.

6   Discussion

In these experiments, we found the recognition accuracy offered by the Re-RX algorithm [9] to be more than sufficient for Card1 and Card3. We believe this can be explained by the fact that we partitioned the learning data set and worked with only part of it. In short, by working with a partial data set, we reduced the number of instances that lead to overfitting, while keeping a number just high enough for the primary rule set. Next, using only the data that did not satisfy the primary rule set, we performed another round of rule extraction, which was able to extract rules that could not have been extracted from the learning data set and produced a high recognition rate. A comparison of the number of rules showed that using an ensemble neural network sometimes increased the number of rules. However, by integrating rules, we were able to eliminate redundant rules, which seemed to hold the level of redundancy to a minimum.

Table 1. Comparison of recognition accuracy levels achieved by various methods with each data set

	E-Re-RX	Re-RX	MNNEC	PITS	NN Bagging	NN AdaBoosting
Card1	94.14%	89.53%	-	-	-	-
Card2	79.65%	86.38%	-	-	-	-
Card3(0.5)	94.77%	88.95%	-	-	-	-
Card3(0.7)	95.93%		-	-	-	-
German Credit	82.20%	80.48%	76.48%	77.52%	75.60%	75.12%
Thyroid	99.64%	-	-	94.20%	94.11%	96.72%
Page Block	95.25%	-	-	-	92.58%	96.30%

Table 2. Number of rules resulting from the E-Re-RX experiment compared to that resulting from the Re-RX experiment

	Card1	Card2	Card3 (0.5)	Card3 (0.7)	German Credit	Thyroid	Page Block
E-Re-RX	7	6	14	17	17	6	9
Re-RX	13	7	7		41	—	—

Next, for the German Credit data, we were able to obtain the highest level of recognition accuracy with E-Re-RX. In particular, we exceeded the Re-RX algorithm by 2%, although it has a high recognition accuracy, and reduced the number of rules by a significant 40%. Here again, we attribute the difference to working with a partial learning data set. Using fewer instances, as in LD', made it possible to classify those instances with fewer rules. Likewise, including a fewer instances in LDf resulted in fewer extracted rules. Accordingly, it can be seen that even after rule integration, our method resulted in fewer rules extracted than did the Re-RX algorithm.

For the Thyroid data set, we achieved results better than the existing methods: 5% better than Neural Network Bagging, and 3% better than Neural Network Adaboosting. We attribute this to the fact that we extracted Class 2 and Class 3 rules in the primary rule set, and Class 1 and Class 3 rules in the secondary rule set. The Thyroid data set consists almost entirely of instances that are Class 3, so in an ordinary fitting, a bias will exist toward fitting to Class 3, and so it is assumed to sometimes be impossible to fit to Class 1 and Class 2 correctly. Akhand et al. [10] reported a maximum value of 94.81%, but found that in the absence of a bias toward Class 3, changes in accuracy improvements were dictated by the extent to which Class 1 and Class 2 were fitted accurately. In our research, we were able to extract Class 1 and Class 3 rules from the partial data, and the instances that did not satisfy these rules were Class 2 in many cases. We were able to fit to Class 2 efficiently in this way and to extract rules with high recognition accuracy, even in a multiclass problem. As a result, the accuracy was much higher than that of previous methods.

Finally, for the Pageblock data set, our results were worse than those by Neural Network Adaboosting, but 3% better than those by Neural Network Bagging. Here, for reasons that are the same as in the Thyroid data set, dealing with a partial data set allowed us to extract Class 1 and Class 2 rules in the primary rule set for instances that did not satisfy the primary rules of Class 3, Class 4, or Class 5. In the secondary rule set, we were able to extract Class 4 and Class 5 rules, which can be seen to have high recognition accuracy. However, we were unable to extract Class 3 rules in this experiment. This can be attributed to the fact that Class 3 instances made up no more than 0.5% of the total data set. In other words, because Class 3 exerted little influence on the weight correction, it was not possible to classify by Class 3. It is thought this can be improved by preparing a data set consisting of instances that do not satisfy the primary or secondary rule sets and performing fitting and rule extraction to extract rules related to Class 3. This suggests that an effective approach to multiclass problems would be an iterative method in which instances that do not satisfy the rules are gathered into a new data set, on which fitting and rule extraction are performed iteratively until rules that identify all of the classes have been extracted. This implies a more intensive use of computing resources, but because it avoids the problem of setting up an unknown number of neural networks, we still consider it to be an effective method.

7   Conclusion

We first surveyed the various theoretical and historical backgrounds for neural data analysis to investigate the approaches for ensemble neural network rule extraction. Next, we set out to address three problems in ensemble neural networks: to increase recognition rates, to extract rules from ensemble neural networks, and to minimize the use of computing resources. We proposed a minimal ensemble neural network consisting of two standard MLPs, which enabled high recognition accuracy and the extraction of comprehensible rules. Furthermore, this enabled rule extraction that resulted in fewer rules than those in previously proposed methods. The results make it possible for the output from an ensemble neural network to be in the form of rules, thus breaking open the "black box" of ensemble neural networks. Ensemble neural networks promise a new approach to data mining, and we are confident that our results will help make data mining more useful and increase the opportunities to use data mining with high recognition accuracy.

Finally, as future work, we provide the following three open questions on the E-Re-RX algorithm:

1) The first is "Can the proposed E-Re-RX algorithm be extended to an ensemble neural network consisting of three or more MLPs and extract comprehensible rules?"

2) The second is "Can the proposed E-Re-RX algorithm find various optimal parameter values so that we can get comprehensible rules with higher recognition accuracy?"

3) The third is "Can the proposed E-Re-RX algorithm be extended to the use of neural network structures other than a standard MLP?"

References

1. Breiman, L.: Bagging predictors. Mach. Learn. 24, 123–140 (1996)
2. Freund, Y., Schapire, R.: Experiments with a new boosting algorithm. In: Proc. of the Thirteenth International Conference on Machine Learning, Bari, Italy, pp. 148–156 (1996)

3. Zhang, G.P.: Neural networks for classification: A Survey. IEEE Trans. Systems, Man and Cybernetics–Part C: Applications and Reviews 30(4), 451–462 (2000)
4. Rokach, L.: Ensemble-based classifiers. Artificial Intelligence Review 33, 1–39 (2010)
5. Yao, X., Islam, M.: Evolving artificial neural network ensembles. IEEE Computational Intelligence Magazine 3(1), 31–42 (2008)
6. Cybenko, G.: Approximation by superpositions of a sigmoidal function. Mathematics of Control, Signals, and Systems 2, 303–314 (1989)
7. Setiono, R.: A penalty-function approach for pruning feedforward neural networks. Neural Comp. 9(1), 185–204 (1997)
8. Bishop, C.: Neural Networks for Pattern Recognition. Oxford University Press (1995)
9. Setiono, R., Baesens, B., Mues, C.: Recursive neural network rule extraction for data with mixed attributes. IEEE Trans. Neural Netw. 19, 299–307 (2008)
10. Akhand, M.A.H., Murase, K.: Neural Network Ensembles. Lambert Academic Publishing (LAP) (2010)
11. Alpaydin, E.: Multiple Neural Networks and Weighted Voting. IEEE Trans. on Pattern Recognition 2, 29–32 (1992)
12. University of California, Irvine Machine Learning Repository, http://archive.ics.uci.edu/ml/
13. Hara, A., Hayashi, Y.: Ensemble neural network rule extraction using Re-RX algorithm. In: Proc. of WCCI (IJCNN) 2012, Brisbane, Australia, June 10-15, pp. 604–609 (2012)
14. Mitra, S., Hayashi, Y.: Neuro-Fuzzy Rule Generation: Survey in Soft Computing Framework. IEEE Trans. Neural Netw. 11(3), 748–768 (2000)
15. Gallant, S.I.: Connectionist expert systems. Commun. ACM 31, 152–169 (1988)
16. Saito, K., Nakano, R.: Medical diagnosis expert systems based on PDP model. In: Proc. IEEE Int. Conf. Neural Netw, San Diego, CA, pp. I.255–I.262 (1988)
17. Hayashi, Y.: Neural expert system using teaching fuzzy input and its application to medical diagnosis. Inform. Sci.: Applicat. 1, 47–58 (1994)
18. Hayashi, Y.: A neural expert system with automated extraction of fuzzy if-then rules and its application to medical diagnosis. In: Lippmann, R.P., Moody, J.E., Touretzky, D.S. (eds.) Advances in Neural Information Processing Systems, pp. 578–584. Morgan Kaufmann, Los Altos (1991)
19. Hudson, D.L., Cohen, M.E., Anderson, M.F.: Use of neural network techniques in a medical expert system. Int. J. Intell. Syst. 6, 213–223 (1991)
20. Takagi, H.: Fusion technology of fuzzy theory and neural network—Survey and future directions. In: Proc. Int. Conf. Fuzzy Logic and Neural Networks, Iizuka, Japan, pp. 13–26 (1990)
21. Buckley, J.J., Hayashi, Y., Czogala, E.: On the equivalence of neural nets and fuzzy expert systems. Fuzzy Sets Syst. 53(2), 129–134 (1993)
22. Hayashi, Y., Buckley, J.J.: Approximation between fuzzy expert systems and neural networks. Int. J. Approx. Res. 10, 63–73 (1994)
23. Buckley, J.J., Hayashi, Y.: Numerical relationship between neural networks, continuous function and fuzzy systems. Fuzzy Sets Syst. 60(1), 1–8 (1993)
24. Buckley, J.J., Hayashi, Y.: Hybrid neural nets can be fuzzy controllers and fuzzy expert systems. Fuzzy Sets and Syst. 60, 135–142 (1993)
25. Golea, M.: On the complexity of rule extraction from neural networks and network querying. In: Proc. the AIBS 1996 Workshop on the Rule Extraction from Trained Neural Networks, Brighton, UK, pp. 51–59 (1996)

26. Roy, A.: On connectionism, rule extraction, and brain-like learning. IEEE Trans. Fuzzy Systems 8(2), 222–227 (2000)
27. Zhou, Z.-H.: Rule Extraction: Using Neural Networks or for Neural Networks? J. Comput. Sci. & Technol. 19(2), 249–253 (2004)
28. Buckley, J.J., Hayashi, Y.: Fuzzy neural networks: A survey. Fuzzy Sets Syst. 66, 1–13 (1994)
29. Hayashi, Y., Buckley, J.J., Czogala, E.: Fuzzy neural network with fuzzy signals and weights. Int. J. Intell. Syst. 8(4), 527–573 (1993)
30. Ishibuchi, H., Kwon, K., Tanaka, H.: A learning algorithm of fuzzy neural networks with triangular fuzzy weights. Fuzzy Sets Syst. 71, 277–293 (1995)
31. Feuring, T., Buckley, J.J., Hayashi, Y.: A gradient descent learning algorithm for fuzzy neural networks. In: Proc. IEEE Int. Conf. Fuzzy Syst. FUZZ-IEEE 1998, Anchorage, AK, pp. 1136–1141 (1998)
32. Bologna, G.: Is it worth generating rules from neural network ensembles? J. of Applied Logic 2, 325–348 (2004)
33. Bologna, G.: A study on rule extraction from several combined neural networks. Int. J. Neural Syst. 11(3), 247–255 (2001)
34. Bologna, G.: A model for single and multiple knowledge based networks. Artificial Intelligence in Medicine 28, 141–163 (2003)
35. Zhou, Z.-H.: Extracting symbolic rules from trained neural network ensembles. AI Communications 16, 3–15 (2003)
36. Zhou, Z.-H.: Ensemble neural networks: Many could be better than all. Artificial Intelligence 137, 239–263 (2002)
37. Hara, A., Hayashi, Y.: A new neural data analysis approach using ensemble neural network rule extraction. In: Villa, A.E.P., Duch, W., Érdi, P., Masulli, F., Palm, G. (eds.) ICANN 2012, Part I. LNCS, vol. 7552, pp. 515–522. Springer, Heidelberg (2012)
38. Hansen, L.K., Salamon, P.: Neural network ensembles. IEEE Trans. Pattern Analysis and Machine Intelligence 12, 993–1001 (1990)
39. Adeodato, P.J.L., et al.: MLP ensembles improve long term prediction accuracy over single networks. Int. J. Forecasting 27, 661–671 (2011)
40. Hornik, K., et al.: Multilayer feedforward networks are universal approximators. Neural Netw. 2(5), 359–366 (1989)
41. Chorowski, J., Zurada, J.M.: Extracting Rules from Neural Networks as Decision Diagrams. IEEE Trans. Neural Netw. 22(12), 2435–2446 (2011)
42. Augasta, M.G., Kathirvalavakumar, T.: Reverse engineering the neural networks for rule extraction in classification problems. Neural Processing Letters 35, 131–150 (2012)
43. Barakat, N., Bradley, A.P.: Rule extraction from support vector machines: A review. Neurocomputing 74, 178–190 (2010)
44. Liu, S., et al.: Combined rule extraction and feature elimination in supervised classification. IEEE Trans. Nanobioscience 11(3), 228–236 (2012)
45. Zhou, Z.H.: Medical diagnosis with C4.5 rule preceded by artificial neural network ensemble. IEEE Trans. Information Technology in Biomedicine 7(1), 37–42 (2003)
46. Zhou, Z.H., et al.: A statistics based approach for extracting priority rules from trained neural networks. In: Proc. IEEE-INNS-ENNS Int. Conf. Neural Netw., Como, Italy, vol. 3, pp. 401–406 (2000)
47. We, X., et al.: Top 10 algorithms in data mining. Knowledge and Information Systems 14, 1–17 (2008)

48. Robert, B., et al.: Boosting of the margin: A new explanation for the effectiveness of voting methods. The Annals of Statistics 26(5), 1651–1686 (1998)
49. Duch, W., Setiono, R., Zurada, J.M.: Computational intelligence methods for rule-based data understanding. Proceedings of the IEEE 92(5), 771–805 (2004)
50. Tickle, A.B., et al.: The truth will come to light: Directions and challenges in extracting the knowledge embedded within trained artificial neural networks. IEEE Trans. Neural Netw. 9, 1057–1068 (1998)
51. Lin, C.T., Lee, C.S.G.: Neural fuzzy systems—A neuro–fuzzy synergism to intelligent systems. Prentice-Hall, Englewood Cliff (1996)
52. Khosravi, A., et al.: Comprehensive review of neural network-based prediction intervals and new advances. IEEE Trans. Neural Netw. 22(9), 1341–1356 (2011)

A New Method of Centers Location in Gaussian RBF Interpolation Networks

Marek Bazan and Ewa Skubalska-Rafajłowicz

Institute of Computer Engineering, Automatics and Robotics,
Department of Electronics, Wrocław University of Technology, Poland
{marek.bazan,ewa.rafajlowicz}@pwr.wroc.pl

Abstract. In this paper we present a new method of obtaining near-optimal points sets for interpolation by Gaussian radial basis functions networks. The method is based on minimizing the maximal value of the power function. The power function provides an upper bound on the local RBF interpolation error. We use Latin hypercube designs and a space-filling curve based space-filling designs as starting points for the optimization procedure. We restrict our attention to 1-D and 2-D interpolation problems. Finally, we provide results of several numerical experiments. We compare the performance of this new method with the method of [6].

Keywords: radial bases function network, interpolation, error bound, power function, computer experiment design.

1 Introduction

Radial bases functions (RBF) were introduced in the solution of the multivariate interpolation problem (see [26] and references cited therein). Radial basis function networks are two-layer feed-forward networks with RBFs as activation functions in the hidden units, and linear activation functions in the output units [22], [4], [25]. It is well known that Gaussian RBF networks can approximate any continuous mapping on a compact domain [23]. RBF networks have been extensively applied to pattern recognition [3], function approximation [23], [18], probability density function estimation [3], [37], [38], regression function estimation [25], [14], [19], approximating the boundary of an object in a binary image [29], to speed up deterministic search algorithms used for the local optimization [1], [2], to global optimization in connection with local deterministic procedures [15], [30] and creating surfaces using radial basis functions from scattered data [8], [20], among many others.

The purpose of interpolating RBF networks is to approximate functions $f : \mathcal{R}^d \to \mathcal{R}$ that are given as data $\{f(x_i)\}_{i=1:N}$ on a finite set $\mathbf{X} = \{\mathbf{x}_1, \ldots, \mathbf{x}_N\} \subset \Omega \subset \mathcal{R}^d$ of distinct points (centers, nodes, knots) by expression

$$s(\mathbf{x}) = \sum_{i=1}^{N} w_i \varphi_\beta(||\mathbf{x} - \mathbf{x}_i||), \tag{1}$$

L. Rutkowski et al. (Eds.): ICAISC 2013, Part I, LNAI 7894, pp. 20–31, 2013.
© Springer-Verlag Berlin Heidelberg 2013

where $||.||$ denotes the Euclidean distance between two points in $\mathcal{R}$ and $\varphi_\beta(r) =$ $\exp(-\beta r^2)$ is a one dimensional Gaussian function defined for a shape parameter $\beta = \frac{1}{2\sigma^2} > 0$. In the interpolant (1) we simply compute the coefficients w_i as the solution of the linear system

$$A_{\mathbf{X}}\mathbf{w} = \mathbf{f} \tag{2}$$

where $A_{\mathbf{X}} = (\varphi_\beta(||\mathbf{x}_i - \mathbf{x}_j||))_{i,j=1}^N$ is the information matrix for the set of nodes $\mathbf{X}$, $\mathbf{w} = (w_1, \ldots, w_N)^T$ and $\mathbf{f} = (f_1, \ldots, f_N)^T$.

Gaussian radial bases functions are infinitely smooth (C^∞) and analytic functions. Moreover the Gaussian interpolation matrix $A_{\mathbf{X}}$ is positive definite (thus it is invertible) if the centers are distinct [21]. If $A_{\mathbf{X}}$ is positive definite for any $\mathbf{X} \subset \Omega$ (consisting of distinct points), then φ_β is said to be positive definite.

Franke [10] found that it is very sensitive to the choice of parameter β. It is known that the Gaussian radial functions are susceptible to Runge's phenomenon, however there exist interpolation node distributions that prevent such oscillatory behavior of the solution and allow stable interpolation [24]. Usually interpolation matrix $A_{\mathbf{X}}$ is very ill-conditioned, and the weights obtained by solving (2) yield an interpolation mapping $s(x)$ that exhibits oscillatory behavior in between data points. Furthermore, the conditioning of the interpolation matrix grows with the problem size N, since the condition number of interpolation matrix $A_{\mathbf{X}}$, defined as $||A_{\mathbf{X}}||_2||A_{\mathbf{X}}^{-1}||_2$ (where $||.||_2$ is a spectral metric), depends mostly on $min_{x_i,x_j \in \mathbf{X}}||x_i - x_j||$. If we fix the number of nodes N the only factor which is important in the balance between the accuracy of interpolation and the conditioning of numerical computations is the shape parameter β. The dependence of the condition number on β parameter is less crucial, however too small values of β (too large values of σ) may result in instability of interpolation due to a bad conditioning. Moreover, it is possible to use the preconditioning methods which allows for the stable computation of Gaussian radial basis function interpolants (see for example [12], [9]).

It is known that, in general, the attainable error and the condition of the interpolation matrices cannot both be kept small [34]. However, this property is based on upper bounds of both factors only.

In the interpolation problems a proper choice of interpolation nodes, i.e., the proper experiment design, is essential for good approximations. It is advisable to keep the number of interpolation nodes at a reasonable level (N should be not too large), because it allows the controlling of the condition number of the interpolation matrix. Nevertheless, in many cases, the more important factor is the cost of the function evaluation. For example, in deterministic computer simulations, which are becoming widely used in science and engineering, the simulation model is often replaced by an approximating model, based on simulations in some points. Thus, the problem of node placement design for RBF interpolation should be considered also in the general context of experiment and computer experiment design methods. It is known that such type designs should at least be space-filling in some sense. With no additional assumptions, it is important to obtain information from the entire design space. Therefore, design points should be 'evenly spread' over the entire region. Several space-filling criteria are discussed in the literature [33], [17]. The design is often restricted to a d-dimensional grid of n levels in every dimension, i.e., such that for each dimension j all nodes coordinate x_{ij} are distinct. Such a design is called a Latin hypercube design (LHD) [33], [30]. The generation of so called low discrepancy sequences is also often used for space-filling points generation. Faure, Halton and Sobol sequences, are increasingly popular in computer experiments [33], [27], [39]. A maximin space-filling design is a set of points such that the separation distance (i.e. the minimal distance among pairs of points) is maximal. Notice, that the maximization of the separation distance influences positively the condition number of the design based RBF interpolation.

In this paper we propose a new method of obtaining near-optimal points sets for interpolation by Gaussian radial basis functions networks. Motivated by methods of selecting RBF centers based on placing prototypes of the centers initially at equidistributed (EQD) points generated along Sierpiński and Hilbert space-filling curves [28], [19], [39], [36], we propose a minmax optimization procedure which uses these space-filling curve based space-filling designs as starting points for minimizing the maximal value of the power function introduced by Schaback [41], [34], [6], [7].

We restrict our attention to the interpolation problems on a cube in $\mathcal{R}^d$, i.e., we assume that $\Omega = [-1, 1]^d$.

The paper is organized as follows. Section 2 provides known local error estimates for interpolation by radial basis functions. Section 3 formulates the minmax optimization problem leading to optimal center location. In section 4 we present algorithms used for the construction of near-optimal set of interpolation centers. Section 5 is devoted to numerical tests. Seven out of eight designs obtained using the proposed new method give upper bound values lower than that generated using the greedy algorithm presented in [6].

2   Interpolation Error Bounds

A general error bound for the interpolation of function $f : \mathbb{R}^d \to \mathbb{R}$ with (1) is derived (c.f. [41], [34], [40], page 176) using the Lagrange (cardinal) basis for the interpolation function, i.e.:

$$s(\mathbf{x}) = \sum_{i=1}^{N} u_i(\mathbf{x}) f_i,$$

where u_i is a certain continuous function $u_i : \Omega \to \mathcal{R}$, $i = 1, \ldots, N$ such that:

$$u_i(\mathbf{x}_j) = \delta_{ji}, \quad \text{i.e.} \quad u_i(\mathbf{x}) = \begin{cases} 1 \text{ for } \mathbf{x} = \mathbf{x}_i \\ 0 \text{ for } \mathbf{x} = \mathbf{x}_j \end{cases} \text{ and } \quad j = 1 \ldots N \quad \text{and} \quad j \neq i. \tag{3}$$

The existence of a vector $\mathbf{u}(x) = (u_1(\mathbf{x}), \ldots, u_N(\mathbf{x}))^T$ for a given $\mathbf{x}$ was shown in [41]. Notice that u depends on φ_β. Let

$$R(\mathbf{x}) := (\varphi_\beta(||\mathbf{x} - \mathbf{x}_1||), \varphi_\beta(||\mathbf{x} - \mathbf{x}_2||), \ldots, \varphi_\beta(||\mathbf{x} - \mathbf{x}_N||))^T.$$

Then the vector $\mathbf{u}(\mathbf{x})$ is a solution of the system of equations

$$A_{\mathbf{X}}\mathbf{u}(\mathbf{x}) = R(\mathbf{x}). \tag{4}$$

The interpolation error $|f(x) - s(x)|$ can be bounded by

$$|f(x) - s(x)| \leq P_{\varphi_\beta,\mathbf{X}}(x)|f|_{\mathcal{N}_{\varphi_\beta}(\Omega)},$$

where $P_{\varphi_\beta,\mathbf{X}}$ is a power function defined as

$$P_{\varphi_\beta,\mathbf{X}}(\mathbf{x})^2 := \varphi_\beta(0) - 2\sum_{j=1}^{N} u_j(\mathbf{x})\varphi_\beta(\|\mathbf{x} - \mathbf{x}_j\|) + \sum_{i,j=1}^{N} u_i(\mathbf{x})u_j(\mathbf{x})\varphi_\beta(\|\mathbf{x}_i - \mathbf{x}_j\|)$$

$$\tag{5}$$

and $|\cdot|_{\mathcal{N}_{\varphi_\beta}(\Omega)}$ is a norm in the native space generated by the radial basis function φ_β (reproducing kernel Hilbert space with φ_β as its reproducing kernel) [35]. Notice, that one can calculate a value of the power function (5) for any point of the domain Ω using (4). For a given radial basis function the power function (5) depends only on a location of data points from $\mathbf{X}$ within the domain Ω.

The interpolation matrix $A_{\mathbf{X}}$ is ill-conditioned and therefore to solve the system (4) we use the singular value decomposition of the matrix $A_{\mathbf{X}}$ (c.f. [13]). Solving (4) for any $\mathbf{x} \in \Omega$ one can calculate a value of the power function (5) for any point of the domain Ω. Checking whether the obtained $\mathbf{u}(\mathbf{x})$ has the property (3) enables us to choose the shape parameter β for the radial function φ_β. Appropriate choice of the value of the shape parameter is a different method of improving the conditioning of the matrix $A_{\mathbf{X}}$ than proposed in [9].

3 A Min-max Problem Formulation

From (2) one can conclude that $\max_{x\in\Omega} P_{\varphi_\beta,\mathbf{X}}(\mathbf{x})$ (Ω is a compact set) is the most important factor in the upperbounding of the interpolation error in the supremum norm.

Let

$$\underline{\mathbf{X}} = \left(x_1^{(1)}, x_1^{(2)}, \ldots, x_1^{(d)}, \ldots, x_N^{(1)}, x_N^{(2)}, \ldots, x_N^{(d)}\right) \in \Omega^N \subset \mathcal{R}^{N \cdot d}$$

represents an interpolation design $\mathbf{X} = \{\mathbf{x}_i\}_{i=1}^{N}$ where $\mathbf{x}_i = (x_i^{(1)}, x_i^{(2)}, \ldots, x_i^{(d)})$ ($i = 1, \ldots, N$). Notice, that in fact, $\underline{\mathbf{X}}$ is a concatenated vector of all design points contained in the set $\mathbf{X}$.

Let us define function $G : \mathbb{R}^{N \cdot d} \times \mathbb{R}^d \to \mathbb{R}$ as

$$G(\underline{\mathbf{X}}; \mathbf{x}) = P_{\varphi_\beta,\mathbf{X}}(\mathbf{x})^2. \tag{6}$$

An optimal design (location of centers) for the radial basis interpolation network with the radial basis function φ_β in the domain Ω can be defined as a global minimum with respect to $\max_{\mathbf{x}\in\Omega} P_{\varphi_\beta,\mathbf{X}}(\mathbf{x})^2$. Let us denote $F(\underline{\mathbf{X}}) = \|G(\underline{\mathbf{X}}; \cdot)\|_{sup}$. Then the minimization problem to find an optimal design reads:

$$\min_{\underline{\mathbf{X}} \in \Omega^N} F(\underline{\mathbf{X}}) = \min_{\underline{\mathbf{X}} \in \Omega^N} \|G(\underline{\mathbf{X}}; \cdot)\|_{sup} = \min_{\underline{\mathbf{X}} \in \Omega^N} [\max_{\mathbf{x} \in \Omega} G(\underline{\mathbf{X}}; \mathbf{x})]. \qquad (7)$$

4 Algorithms to Solve the Max and the Min Problems

Solving (7) consists of two optimization algorithms. An inner algorithm is used to find the maximum value of the squared power function $P_{\varphi_\beta, \mathbf{x}}(\mathbf{x})^2$ (6) on Ω for a given design $\mathbf{X}$. An outer algorithm is used to find a concatenated vector representing a design $\mathbf{X}$ which minimizes $F(\underline{\mathbf{X}})$ on the domain Ω^N, i.e., it produces an optimal (or at least near-optimal) interpolation design consisting of exactly N centers.

The outer optimization problem is a constrained minimization problem. The values of $\max_{\mathbf{x} \in \Omega} G(\underline{\mathbf{X}}_k; \mathbf{x})$ are obtained as a result of a simple scan of the domain Ω. Following the approach presented in [6], we maximize over some very large discrete set $Y \subset \Omega$ instead of maximizing on Ω.

To minimize $\min_{\underline{\mathbf{X}} \in \Omega^N} F(\underline{\mathbf{X}})$ we have used a non-gradient algorithm, as not much is known about properties of F.

4.1 A Constrained Non-linear Programming Algorithm

Every configuration $\underline{\mathbf{X}}$ in which at least one design point $\mathbf{x}_i$ ($i = 1, \ldots, N$) lies on the boundary $\delta\Omega$ of the domain Ω is on the constraint boundary of the minimization problem (7). The most common approach to deal with constraint violation is to add a penalty term that depends on how much the constraint is violated. If a current design contains points that are outside the domain Ω we have to project these points onto the boundary $\delta\Omega$.

In numerical experiments presented in this paper $\Omega = [-1, 1] \times [-1, 1]$. We do not use the most common projection method which is the orthogonal projection defined as $\underline{\mathbf{X}}^{(proj)} = \arg\min_{\underline{\mathbf{Y}} \in \delta\Omega} \|\underline{\mathbf{X}} - \underline{\mathbf{Y}}\|$. Such a projection transforms points from $\underline{\mathbf{X}}$ that lie outside Ω for which two constraints are violated into the closest corner of the domain. Such a situation automatically generates a singular design matrix if there are at least two points that are transformed into the same corner. It is not a rare situation. The projection for which the overlapping of transformed centers is less probable is to choose a point on the boundary which lies on the interval between the point $\mathbf{x}_i$ to be transformed and the center of the domain Ω.

Now, we can calculate (6) for $\underline{\mathbf{X}}^{(proj)}$ and add to $F(\underline{\mathbf{X}}^{(proj)})$ the penalty proportional to $\|\underline{\mathbf{X}}^{(proj)} - \underline{\mathbf{X}}\|$. Nevertheless, for the sake of simplicity, we omit a penalty term using only projection. This is motivated by the fact that adding a penalty term creates an artificial piece of information which is useless from the optimization point of view. The power function defined outside the domain Ω provides upperbounds for an interpolation problem defined on other domains than Ω.

In numerical experiments we have achieved the best values of the objective function F using the Rosenbrock algorithm initially described in [31] and modified by Jacob [16].

4.2 A Stable Calculation of the Objective Function in the Inner Algorithm

The calculation of (6) which is the objective function for the inner algorithm requires a stable calculation of the Lagrange representation $u(x)$ for any $x \in \Omega$ by solving (4). For $N > 40$ and for small values of shape parameter β (too large values of σ, i.e., close to a diameter of the domain space Ω) in Gaussian basis it may happen that a calculated solution $u(x)$ is not a cardinal solution (see property (3)).

Problems with a stable solution of (4) for the Gaussian with small values of a shape parameter were reported in e.g. [9]. Here we propose to choose the largest possible value of parameter δ that enables us to find a solution $u(x)$ which guaranties that the property (3) is maintained at the level of the absolute error of 10^{-7}. In the example presented in the next section (for $N = 54$) σ value set to the quarter of the diameter of $\underline{X}_k$ is sufficient.

4.3 Initial Designs

As mentioned in the previous paragraph we limit our numerical experiments to $\Omega = [-1, 1]^2$. To generate $\underline{X}_0$ we use four different methods:

1. Space-filling latin hypercube sampling method [33], [30].
2. A uniform design based on the Sierpiński space-filling curve [36].
3. A uniform design based on the Hilbert space-filling curve [36].
4. Quasi-optimal design obtained by the greedy algorithm due to De Marchi, Schaback and Wendland (DMSW) [6].

The advantage of initial configurations generated with the first three methods is that they are the initial configuration of N points in $\Omega \subset \mathbb{R}^d$ and N does not need to be a d-th power of a natural number. The fourth initial distribution is used in this paper not only as a starting point for the optimization but also as a reference for comparisons. Up to our knowledge the designs $\underline{X}_0$ generated with the algorithm DMSW produce the lowest values of $\|P_{\varphi_\beta, \mathbf{X}}(\mathbf{x})^2\|_{sup}$ over Ω among results published in the literature so far for the methods based on minimizing the power function (5).

5 Numerical Results

5.1 One Dimensional Example

In order to show that the proposed optimization algorithm produces designs that give a lower interpolation error we interpolate function $y = (1 + (5x)^2)^{-1}$ using a

Gaussian RBF network with 9 centers on the interval $[-1, 1]$. Radius parameter σ of Gaussians was set to 1. Figure 1 shows the interpolation curves obtained for three configurations of centers:

1. obtained by DMSW method [6],
2. centers are scaled zeros of the 9-th Tshebyshev polynomial of the first kind,
3. obtained by our optimization algorithm.

The smallest maximal error is equal to 0.16098 and is obtained by using the method proposed in the paper. The resulting error is slightly smaller than the maximal error for the Tshebyshev centers which is equal to 0.16489. The results obtained by DMSW algorithm [6] are worse with the error supremum equals to 0.21884. The new configuration decreases the Runge phenomenon compared to the configuration obtained by DMSW algorithm [6].

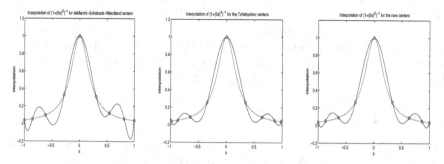

Fig. 1. Interpolation of the function $y = (1 + (5x)^2)^{-1}$ with the Gaussain radial basis function with a shape parameter equals to 1 on 9 nodes from the interval $[-1, 1]$ on three different node configurations a) obtained by DMSW algorithm [6] b) Tchebyshev knots c) obtained by our optimization algorithm

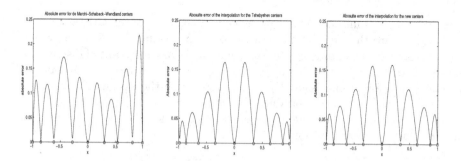

Fig. 2. Interpolation error for the interpolation of the function $y = (1 + (5x)^2)^{-1}$ with the Gaussain radial basis function with a shape parameter equals to 1 on 9 nodes from the interval $[-1, 1]$ on three different node configurations a) obtained by DMSW algorithm [6] b) Tchebyshev knots c) obtained by our optimization algorithm

5.2   Two Dimensional Example

In this section we present the performance of the proposed design optimization algorithm launched from 5 randomly generated points forming a Latin hypercube [33], one optimization started from a Sierpiński filling curve configuration of centers [36], another one started from a Hilbert filling curve configuration of centers [36] and one optimization started from the quasi-optimal configuration of centers generated by DMSW algorithm [6].

To guarantee that the objective function F is not too small and the non-linear optimisation algorithm runs properly we use a scaling factor of 10^7 in the function calculations, i.e., instead of minimizing F we minimize $10^7 F$.

Table 1 shows the results obtained for eight different starting configurations: five initial designs were generated using the Latin hypercube method, one initial design was a uniform design along the Sierpiński space-filling curve [36], the next initiali design was s uniform design along the Hilbert filling space curve [36] and the last one was generated by DMSW quasi-optimal method [6]. As one can see from this table in four out five different Latin hypercube starting configurations the proposed scheme was able to decrease the objective function value below the value calculated for the configuration at the starting configuration generated using the quasi-optimal method. Also starting from the Sierpiński and the Hilbert configuration the result was better although it was not better than for the successful Latin hypercube configurations.

Table 1. Results of numerical experiments for 54 knots placed in $\Omega = [-1, 1] \times [-1, 1]$. The first five rows were obtained using the proposed algorithm started from configurations generated using the Latin hypercube method [33]. The sixth row presents results for the Sierpiński space-filling curve based starting configuration [36]. The seventh row presents results for the Hilbert space-filling curve based starting configuration [36]. In the eighth row the optimization was started from the quasi-optimal configuration generated by DMSW method [6]. The first column describes the way the starting configuration was generated, the second one shows the objective function value F at the starting configuration and the third one shows the number of the objective function calculations to achieve the value that is shown in the fourth column.

starting configuration generation method	starting configuration objective f. val.	num. of obj. f. calculations	final configuration objective f. val.
Latin hypercube 1	8693.840221	23778	8.713339
Latin hypercube 2	24004.490524	63693	9.163693
Latin hypercube 3	21275.298287	34164	7.821087
Latin hypercube 4	63583.290885	37070	9.446265
Latin hypercube 5	22191.814212	37195	23.794642
Sierpiński filling curve	15117.265424	42476	13.522486
Hilbert filling curve	24429.318636	36652	12.395903
quasi-optimal	20.815944	36679	10.736679

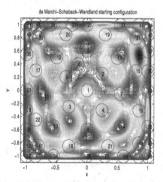 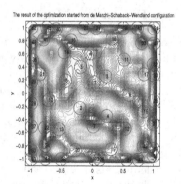

Fig. 3. Left) The quasi optimal configuration of 54 centers generated using DMSW method [6]. Right) The configuration obtained by our algorithm started from the quasi optimal configuration. Both configurations are plotted together with isolines of the squared power function.

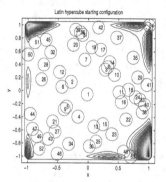 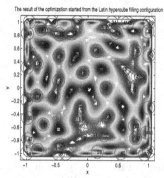

Fig. 4. Left) An example of latin hypercube configuration of 54 nodes generated using the algorithm from [33]. Right) The configuration obtained using by our optimization algorithm started from the the latin hypercube based configuration. Both configurations are plotted together with isolines of the squared power function.

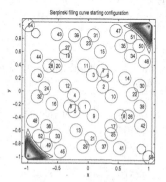 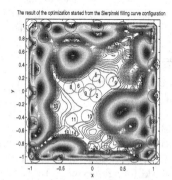

Fig. 5. Left) An example of a Sierpinski filling curve configuration of 54 nodes (c.f. [36]). Right) The design obtained by our optimization algorithm started from the Sierpiński space-filling curve based configuration. Both designs are plotted together with isolines of the squared power function.

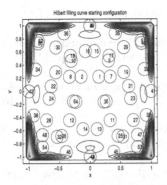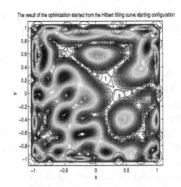

Fig. 6. Left) An example of a Hilbert filling curve configuration of 54 nodes (c.f. [36]). Right) The design obtained by our optimization algorithm started from the Hilbert space-filling curve based configuration. Both designs are plotted together with isolines of the squared power function.

6   Conclusions

We have presented a scheme of using constrained non-linear programming to calculate the optimal configurations of centers for a radial basis interpolation process. From eight designs obtained by the proposed optimization algorithm seven configurations give objective function values lower than that generated as an initial configuration by DMSW algorithm [6].

The work in this paper focused on the Gaussian kernel. There are many other positive definite kernels: inverse multiquadric [21], Wendland function [40], Sobolev splines [34] and others that can be constructed using a method described in [35]. It should be mentioned that the method proposed in this paper can be applied to other strictly positive definite radial bases function systems. Furthermore, the proposed method can be used also when we have to extend the near-optimal design by a new additional point.

Acknowledgment. Calculations have been carried out in the Wrocław Centre for Networking and Supercomputing (http://www.wcss.wroc.pl) grant No 205, using MATLAB 2012.

References

1. Bazan, M., Russenschuck, S.: Using neural networks to speed up optimization algorithms. Eur. Phys. J., AP 12, 109–115 (2000)
2. Bazan, M., Aleksa, M., Russenschuck, S.: An improved method using radial basis function neural networks to speed up optimization algorithms. IEEE Trans. on Magnetics 38, 1081–1084 (2002)
3. Bishop, C.M.: Pattern Recognition and Machine Learning. Springer Science+Business Media, New York (2006)
4. Broomhead, D.S., Lowe, D.: Multivariable Functional Interpolation and Adaptive Networks. Complex Systems 2, 321–355 (1988)

5. van Dam, E.: Two-dimensional minimax Latin hypercube designs. Discrete Applied Math. 156(18), 3483–3493 (2007)

6. De Marchi, S., Schaback, R., Wendland, H.: Near-optimal data-independent points locations for radial basis function interpolation. Adv. in Comp. Math. 23(3), 317–330 (2003)

7. De Marchi, S.: On optimal center locations for radial basis function interpolation: computational aspects. Rend. Sem. Mat. Univ. Pol. Torino, Splines and Radial Functions 61(3), 343–358 (2003)

8. Dyn, N., Levin, D., Rippa, S.: Numerical Procedures for Surface Fitting of Scattered Data by Radial Basis Functions. SIAM Journal of Scientific and Statistical Computing 7(2), 639–659 (1986)

9. Fasshauer, G.E., Zhang, J.G.: Preconditioning of Radial basis function interpolation systems via accelerated iterated approximate moving least squares approximation. In: Ferreira, A.J.M., et al. (eds.) Progress in Meshless Methods. Springer (2009)

10. Franke, R.: Scattered Data Interpolation, Test of Some Methods. Mathematics of Computation 38, 181–200 (1982)

11. Fornberg, B., Wright, G., Larsson, E.: Some observations regarding interpolants in the limit of flat radial basis functions. Computers Math. Applic. 47(1), 37–55 (2004)

12. Fornberg, B., Larsson, E., Flyer, N.: Stable computations with Gaussian radial basis functions. SIAM J. Sci. Comput. 33(2), 869–892 (2011)

13. Hansen, P.C.: Rank-deficient and discrete ill-posed problems. SIAM, Philadelphia (1998)

14. Girosi, F., Jones, M., Poggio, T.: Regularization theory and neural networks architectures. Neural Computation 7(2), 219–269 (1995)

15. Ishikawa, T.T., Matsunami, M.: A combined method for global optimization using radial basis function and deterministic approach. IEEE Trans. Magn. 35, 1730–1733 (1999)

16. Jacob, H.G.: Rechnergestützte Optimierung statischer und dynamischer Systeme. Springer (1982)

17. Kleijnen, J.P.C.: Design and Analysis of Simulation Experiments. Springer (2009)

18. Kainen, P.C., Kurková, V., Sanguineti, M.: Complexity of Gaussian-radial-basis networks approximating smooth functions. Journal of Complexity 25(1), 63–74 (2009)

19. Krzyżak, A., Skubalska-Rafajłowicz, E.: Combining space-filling curves and radial basis function networks. In: Rutkowski, L., Siekmann, J.H., Tadeusiewicz, R., Zadeh, L.A. (eds.) ICAISC 2004. LNCS (LNAI), vol. 3070, pp. 229–234. Springer, Heidelberg (2004)

20. Lin, G.F., Chen, L.H.: A spatial interpolation method based on radial basis function networks incorporating a semivariogram model. Journal of Hydrology 288, 288–298 (2004)

21. Micchelli, C.A.: Interpolation of Scattered Data: Distance Matrices and Conditionally Positive Definite Functions. Constructive Approximation 2, 11–22 (1986)

22. Moody, J., Darken, J.: Fast learning in networks of locally-tuned processing units. Neural Computation 1, 281–294 (1989)

23. Park, J., Sandberg, I.W.: Approximation and radial-basis-function networks. Neural Computation 5(2), 305–316 (1993)

24. Platte, R.B., Driscoll, T.A.: Polynomials and potential theory for Gaussian radial basis function interpolation. SIAM J. Numer. Anal. 43(2), 750–766 (2005)

25. Poggio, T., Girosi, F.: A Theory of Networks for Approximation and Learning, AI Lab, MIT, AI Memo 1140 (1989)
26. Powell, M.J.D.: Radial basis functions for multivariable interpolation: a review. In: Algorithms for Approximation. Claredon Press, Oxford (1987)
27. Rafajłowicz, E., Schwabe, R.: Halton and Hammersley sequences in multivariate nonparametric regression. Statistics and Probability Letters 76, 803–812 (2006)
28. Rafajłowicz, E., Skubalska-Rafajłowicz, E.: RBF nets based on equidistributed points. In: Proc. of 9th IEEE International Conf. Methods and Models in Automation and Robotics MMAR 2003, vol. 2, pp. 921–926 (2003)
29. Rafajłowicz, E., Skubalska-Rafajłowicz, E.: RBF nets for approximating an object's boundary by image random sampling. Nonlinear Analysis: Theory, Methods and Applications 71(12), 1247–1254 (2009)
30. Regis, R.G., Shoemaker, C.A.: Improved Strategies for Radial basis Function Methods for Global Optimization. J. of Global Optimization 37(1), 113–135 (2007)
31. Rosenbrock, H.H.: An automatic method for finding the greatest or least value of function. The Computer Journal 3(3), 175–184 (1960)
32. Sacks, J., Welch, W.J., Mitchell, T.J., Wynn, H.P.: Design and Analysis of Computer Experiments. Statistical Science 4(4), 409–435 (1989)
33. Santner, T.J., Williams, B.J., Notz, W.I.: The Design and Analysis of Computer Experiments. Springer Series in Stastistics (2003)
34. Schaback, R.: Error estimates and condition numbers for radial basis function interpolation. Advances in Computational Mathematics 3, 251–264 (1995)
35. Schaback, R.: Native Hilbert spaces for radial basis functions I. In: Müller, M.W., et al. (eds.) New Developments in Approximation Theory, 2nd Int. Dortmund Meeting (IDoMAT) 1998. Int. Ser. Numer. Math., vol. 132, pp. 255–282. Birkhäuser Verlag, Basel (1999)
36. Skubalska-Rafajłowicz, E.: Space-filling Curves in Multivariate Decision Problems. Wrocław University of Technology Press, Wrocław (2001) (in Polish)
37. Skubalska-Rafajłowicz, E.: RBF Neural Network for Probability Density Function Estimation and Detecting Changes in Multivariate Processes. In: Rutkowski, L., Tadeusiewicz, R., Zadeh, L.A., Żurada, J.M. (eds.) ICAISC 2006. LNCS (LNAI), vol. 4029, pp. 133–141. Springer, Heidelberg (2006)
38. Skubalska-Rafajłowicz, E.: Random Projection RBF Nets for Multidimensional Density Estimation. Int. J. Appl. Math. Comput. Sci. 18(4), 455–464 (2008)
39. Skubalska-Rafajłowicz, E., Rafajłowicz, E.: Sampling multidimensional signals by a new class of quasi-random sequences. Multidimensional System and Signal Processing 23, 237–253 (2012)
40. Wendland, H.: Scattered Data Approximation. Cambridge University Press (2005)
41. Wu, Z., Schaback, R.: Local error estimates for radial basis function interpolation of scattered data. IMA J. Numer. Anal. 13, 13–27 (1993)

Parallel Approach to Learning of the Recurrent Jordan Neural Network

Jarosław Bilski and Jacek Smolag

Częstochowa University of Technology,
Częstochowa, Poland
{Jaroslaw.Bilski,Jacek.Smolag}@iisi.pcz.pl

Abstract. This paper presents the parallel architecture of the Jordan network learning algorithm. The proposed solution is based on the high parallel three dimensional structures to speed up learning performance. Detailed parallel neural network structures are explicitly shown.

1 Introduction

The Jordan network is an example of dynamical neural networks. Dynamical neural networks have been investigated by many scientists in the last decade [6], [7]. To train the dynamical networks the gradient method was used, see e.g. [15]. In the classical case the neural networks learning algorithms are implemented on serial computer. Unfortunatelly, this method is slow because the learning algorithm requires high computational load. Therefore, high performance dedicated parallel structure is a suitable solution, see eg. [2] - [5], [13], [14]. This paper presents a new concept of the parallel realisation of the Jordan learning algorithm. A single iteration of the parallel architecture requires much less computation cycles than a serial implementation. The efficiency of this new architecture is very satisfying and is explained in the last part of this paper. The structure of the Jordan network is shown in Fig. 1.

The Jordan network has K neurons in the hidden layer and M neurons in the network output. The input vector contains N input signals and M previous outputs. Note that previous signals from output are obtained through unit time delay z^{-1}. Therefore, the network input vector

$$\left[1, x_1^{(1)}(t), ..., x_N^{(1)}(t), x_{N+1}^{(1)}(t), ..., x_{N+M}^{(1)}(t)\right]^T \tag{1}$$

in the Jordan network takes the form

$$\left[1, x_1^{(1)}(t), ..., x_N^{(1)}(t), y_1^{(2)}(t-1), ..., y_M^{(2)}(t-1)\right]^T \tag{2}$$

L. Rutkowski et al. (Eds.): ICAISC 2013, Part I, LNAI 7894, pp. 32–40, 2013.

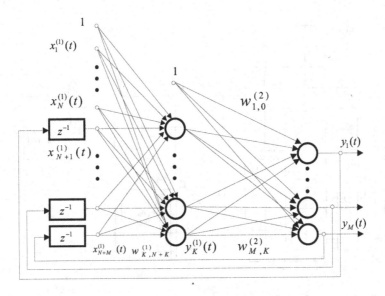

Fig. 1. Structure of the Jordan network

In the recall phase the network is described by

$$s_i^{(1)} = \sum_{k=0}^{N+M} w_{ik}^{(1)} x_k^{(1)}$$
$$y_k^{(1)}(t) = f(s_k^{(1)}(t))$$
$$s_j^{(2)} = \sum_{k=0}^{K} w_{jk}^{(2)} x_k^{(2)} \tag{3}$$
$$y_j^{(2)}(t) = f(s_j^{(2)}(t))$$

The parallel realisation of the recall phase algorithm uses architecture which requires many simple processing elements. The parallel realisation of the Jordan network in recal phase is depicted in Fig. 2a and its processing elements in Fig. 2b. Four kinds of functional processing elements are used in the proposed solution. The aim of the processing elements (PE) A is to delay outputs signals, so that values of signals appear on inputs of the network from previous instances. Processing elements of type B create matrix which includes values of weights of the first layer. The input signals are entered for rows elements parallelly, multiplied by weights and received results are summed in columns. The activation function for each neuron in the first layer is calculated after determination of product $\mathbf{w}_i^{(1)}\mathbf{x}^{(1)}$ in processing element of type D. The outputs of neurons in the first layer are inputs to the second layer simultaneously. The product $\mathbf{w}^{(2)}\mathbf{x}^{(2)}$ for the second layer is obtained in processing elements of type C similarly.

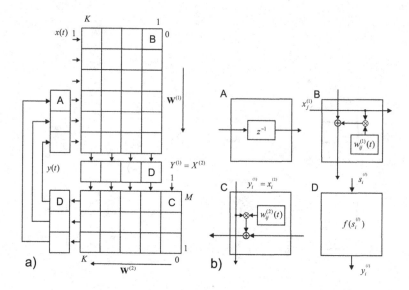

Fig. 2. Recal phase of the Jordan network and the structures of processing elements

The gradient method [15] is used to train the Jordan network. We minimise the following goal criterion

$$J(t) = \frac{1}{2}\sum_{j=1}^{M} \varepsilon_j^{(2)^2}(t) = \frac{1}{2}\sum_{j=1}^{M}\left(y_j^{(2)}(t) - d_j^{(2)}(t)\right)^2 \tag{4}$$

were $\varepsilon_j^{(2)}$ is defined as

$$\varepsilon_j^{(2)}(t) = y_j^{(2)}(t) - d_j^{(2)}(t) \tag{5}$$

For this purpose it is nesessary to calculate derivative of the goal funcion with respect to each weight. For weights in the second layer we obtain the following gradient

$$\nabla_{\alpha\beta}^{(2)} J(t) = \frac{\partial J(t)}{\partial w_{\alpha\beta}^{(2)}} = \sum_{j=1}^{M} \varepsilon_j^{(2)}(t)\frac{dy_j^{(2)}(t)}{dw_{\alpha\beta}^{(2)}} \tag{6}$$

and after some calculations we obtain derivative

$$\frac{dy_j^{(2)}(t)}{dw_{\alpha\beta}^{(2)}} =$$
$$\delta_{j\alpha}\frac{dy_\alpha^{(2)}(t)}{ds_\alpha^{(2)}}y_\beta^{(1)}(t) + \frac{dy_j^{(2)}(t)}{ds_j^{(2)}}\sum_{i=1}^{K} w_{ji}^{(2)}\frac{dy_i^{(1)}(t)}{ds_i^{(1)}}\sum_{k=1}^{M} w_{i,k+N}^{(1)}\frac{dy_k^{(2)}(t-1)}{dw_{\alpha\beta}^{(2)}} \tag{7}$$

Weights are updated according to the steepest descent algorithm as follows

$$w_{\alpha\beta}^{(2)}(t) = w_{\alpha\beta}^{(2)}(t-1) - \eta\nabla_{\alpha\beta}^{(2)} J(t) \tag{8}$$

For the first layer we have

$$\delta_j^{(2)}(t) = \varepsilon_j^{(2)}(t) \frac{dy_j^{(2)}(t)}{ds_j^{(2)}} \tag{9}$$

$$\varepsilon_i^{(1)}(t) = \sum_{j=1}^{M} \delta_j^{(2)}(t) w_{ji}^{(2)} \tag{10}$$

and we obtain the gradient

$$\nabla_{\alpha\beta}^{(1)} J(t) =$$
$$\frac{\partial J(t)}{\partial w_{\alpha\beta}^{(1)}} = \sum_{j=1}^{M} \varepsilon_j^{(2)}(t) \frac{dy_j^{(2)}(t)}{ds_j^{(2)}} \sum_{i=1}^{K} \left[\frac{dy_i^{(1)}(t)}{dw_{\alpha\beta}^{(1)}} w_{ji}^{(2)} \right] = \sum_{i=1}^{K} \frac{dy_i^{(1)}(t)}{dw_{\alpha\beta}^{(1)}} \varepsilon_i^{(1)}(t) \tag{11}$$

After a few calculations we get

$$\frac{dy_i^{(1)}(t)}{dw_{\alpha\beta}^{(1)}} =$$
$$\delta_{i\alpha} \frac{dy_\alpha^{(1)}(t)}{ds_\alpha^{(1)}} x_\beta^{(1)}(t) + \frac{dy_i^{(1)}(t)}{ds_i^{(1)}} \sum_{k=1}^{M} w_{i,k+N}^{(1)} \frac{dy_k^{(2)}(t-1)}{ds_k^{(2)}} \sum_{l=1}^{K} w_{kl}^{(2)} \frac{dy_l^{(1)}(t-1)}{dw_{\alpha\beta}^{(1)}} \tag{12}$$

and the weights can be updated by

$$w_{\alpha\beta}^{(1)}(t) = w_{\alpha\beta}^{(1)}(t-1) - \eta \nabla_{\alpha\beta}^{(1)} J(t) \tag{13}$$

The task of suggested parallel structure will be realisation of all calculations described by equations (6) - (8) and (11) - (13).

2   Parallel Realisation

In order to determine the derivative in the second layer it is required to know its previous values. Derivative values will be stored in E PE Fig. 4a. These elements will create 3D matrix of the dimension $M \times M \times (K+1)$, see Fig. 3. They will be useful for realizing inner sum in equation (7). Presented E PE multiply the respondent elements of derivative matrix $\frac{dy_j^{(2)}}{dw_{\alpha\beta}}$ by corresponding to them weights of the first layer, see Fig. 3. Then, received produtcts in the entire column are added to each other. The weights are delivered by columns. The first column is moved to the extreme right position (as a result of the rotation to the left) $W^{(1)}$ matrix. After a rotation of columns the previous actions are repeated. These operations are repeated K times until the first column of the matrix will revert to the original place. At the same time, the obtained results are sent to the upper 3D matrix of (F) PE (see Fig. 3 and Fig. 4b), multiplied by $w_{ji}^{(2)} \frac{dy_i^{(1)}}{ds_i^{(1)}}$ and $\frac{dy_j^{(2)}}{ds_j^{(2)}}$ and accumulated. The obtained results - calculation of equation (7) - are sent back to the lower 3D matrix. In the next step it is necessary to calculate

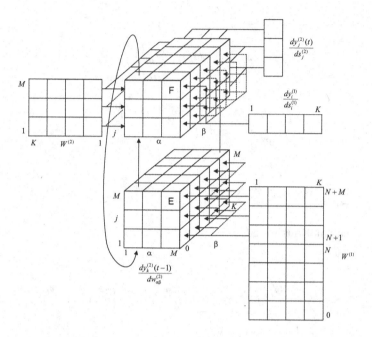

Fig. 3. Idea of learning the second layer

gradients eq.(6). This is depicted in Fig. 5. The element for weights updating in eq.(8) is shown in Fig. 6.

Suggested solution leads to acceleration of calculations, but it is not optimal solution yet. It results from the fact that after multiplication of lower 3D matrix and the weights matrix, serial summation follows. In this case multiplication and addition is realized in $M \times K$ steps. It is easily seen that changing manner

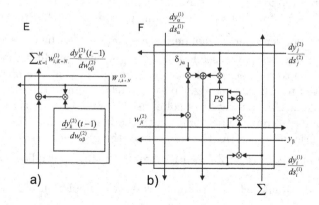

Fig. 4. The structure of the processing elements for learning the second layer

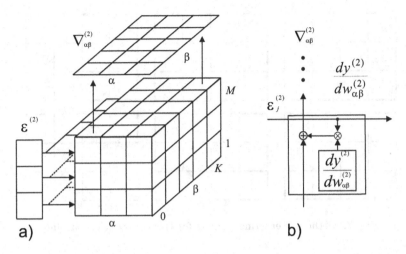

Fig. 5. Architecture for calculating of the gradient $\nabla^{(2)}_{\alpha\beta}$ for second layer learning and the structure of the processing element

of entering of values from weights matrix to derivatives matrix we can reduce the amount of steps required for execution of the multiplication and addition operations to $M + K - 1$. The manner of these weights entering is presented in Fig. 7. The multiplication is realised only for elements from the first column depicted by the thick line. In the first step only one element from the last row is taken into account. In the next cycles the number of rows is incremented, and the rows that have participated in multiplication are subject to rotation. Rotation is done from step one to the left until all rows reach the starting position. The rows are no longer included in the multiplication. As a result, the proposed modifications in subsequent steps, making the multiplication and summation, as described in the previous scenario. In this case we will receive the sum of the new inner product without waiting the M steps. For the first layer we need to calculate the derivatives (12). Note that equations (12) and (7) have identical structures. Therefore parallel realisation of the first layer learning is analogous to the second layer learning. The architecture of the first layer learning is shown in Fig. 8. Of course in this case the dimensions of the structure and processed data

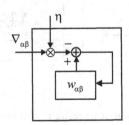

Fig. 6. The weights updating element

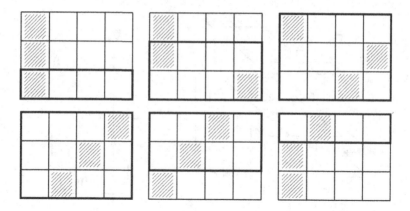

Fig. 7. Method of entering weights for the second layer learning

correspond to equation (12). After obtaining the derivatives, the value of $\epsilon_i^{(1)}(t)$ is calculated, see eq. (9) and (10). The structure for this operation is presented in Fig. 9. The gradient in eq. (11) is obtained from the analogous structure like in the second layer (see Fig. 5). All weights are updated in the same time by elements depicted in Fig. 6.

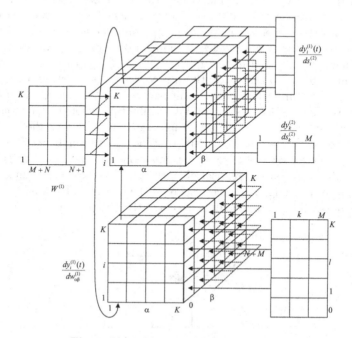

Fig. 8. Idea of learning of the first layer

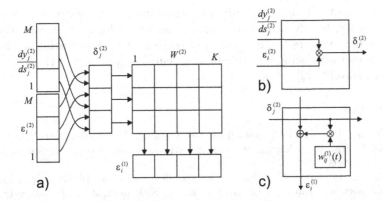

Fig. 9. Structure for calculating $\epsilon_i^{(1)}(t)$ in the first layer (a) and the processing elements (b) and (c)

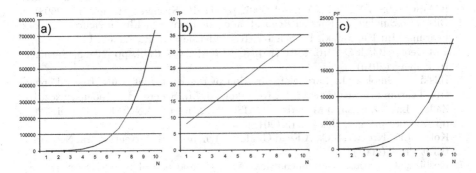

Fig. 10. Number of times cycles in a) classical (serial), b) parallel implementation and c) performance factor

3   Conclusion

In this paper the parallel realisation of the Jordan neural network was proposed. We assume that all multiplications and additions operations take the same time unit. For simplicity of the result presentation we assume that K=M=N in the network. We can compare computational performance of the Jordan parallel implementation with sequential architectures up to N=M=10 for inputs and outputs and up to 10 neurons (K) in the hidden layer of neural network. Computational complexity of the Jordan learning is of order $\mathcal{O}(K^5)$ and equals $TS = 2K^3M^2 + 2K^3MN + 2K^2M^3 + 2K^3M + 4K^2M^2 + 3K^2MN + 2KM^3 + 7K^2M + 4K^2N + 8KM^2 + KMN + 4K^2 + 6M^2$. In the presented parallel architecture each iteration requires only $TP = K + M + \max(K, M) + 5$ time units (see Fig. 10). Performance factor $(PF = TS/TP)$ of parallel realisation of the Jordan algorithm achieves nearly 21000 for N=10 inputs, K=10 neurons in the hidden layer and M=10 of neurons in the output layer and it grows very fast when these numbers grow, see Fig. 10. We observed that the performance of the proposed solution is promising. Analogous parallel aproach can be used for the advanced learning algorithm of feedforward neural networks, see eg. [1]. In the future research we plan to design parallel realisation of learning of other structures including probabilistic neural networks [9]-[11] and various fuzzy structures[8],[12].

References

1. Bilski, J.: The UD RLS Algorithm for Training the Feedforward Neural Networks. International Journal of Applied Mathematics and Computer Science 15(1), 101–109 (2005)
2. Bilski, J., Litwiński, S., Smoląg, J.: Parallel realisation of QR algorithm for neural networks learning. In: Rutkowski, L., Siekmann, J.H., Tadeusiewicz, R., Zadeh, L.A. (eds.) ICAISC 2004. LNCS (LNAI), vol. 3070, pp. 158–165. Springer, Heidelberg (2004)
3. Bilski, J., Smoląg, J.: Parallel realisation of the recurrent RTRN neural network learning. In: Rutkowski, L., Tadeusiewicz, R., Zadeh, L.A., Zurada, J.M. (eds.) ICAISC 2008. LNCS (LNAI), vol. 5097, pp. 11–16. Springer, Heidelberg (2008)
4. Bilski, J., Smoląg, J.: Parallel Realisation of the Recurrent Elman Neural Network Learning. In: Rutkowski, L., Scherer, R., Tadeusiewicz, R., Zadeh, L.A., Zurada, J.M. (eds.) ICAISC 2010, Part II. LNCS(LNAI), vol. 6114, pp. 19–25. Springer, Heidelberg (2010)
5. Bilski, J., Smoląg, J.: Parallel Realisation of the Recurrent Multi Layer Perceptron Learning. In: Rutkowski, L., Korytkowski, M., Scherer, R., Tadeusiewicz, R., Zadeh, L.A., Zurada, J.M. (eds.) ICAISC 2012, Part I. LNCS(LNAI), vol. 7267, pp. 12–20. Springer, Heidelberg (2012)
6. Kolen, J.F., Kremer, S.C.: A Field Guide to Dynamical Recurrent Neural Networks. IEEE Press (2001)
7. Korbicz, J., Patan, K., Obuchowicz, A.: Dynamic neural networks for process modelling in fault detection and isolation. Int. J. Appl. Math. Comput. Sci. 9(3), 519–546 (1999)
8. Li, X., Er, M.J., Lim, B.S., et al.: Fuzzy Regression Modeling for Tool Performance Prediction and Degradation Detection. International Journal of Neural Systems 20(5), 405–419 (2010)
9. Rutkowski, L.: Multiple Fourier series procedures for extraction of nonlinear regressions from noisy data. IEEE Transactions on Signal Processing 41(10), 3062–3065 (1993)
10. Rutkowski, L.: Non-parametric learning algorithms in the time-varying environments. Signal Processing 18(2), 129–137 (1989)
11. Rutkowski, L.: Generalized regression neural networks in time-varying environment. IEEE Trans. Neural Networks 15, 576–596 (2004)
12. Rutkowski, L., Przybył, A., Cpałka, K.: Novel Online Speed Profile Generation for Industrial Machine Tool Based on Flexible Neuro-Fuzzy Approximation. IEEE Transactions on Industrial Electronics 59(2), 1238–1247 (2012)
13. Smoląg, J., Bilski, J.: A systolic array for fast learning of neural networks. In: Proc. of V Conf. Neural Networks and Soft Computing, Zakopane, pp. 754–758 (2000)
14. Smoląg, J., Rutkowski, L., Bilski, J.: Systolic array for neural networks. In: Proc. of IV Conf. Neural Networks and Their Applications, Zakopane, pp. 487–497 (1999)
15. Williams, R., Zipser, D.: A learning algorithm for continually running fully recurrent neural networks. Neural Computation, 270–280 (1989)

Agent-Based Population Learning Algorithm for RBF Network Tuning

Ireneusz Czarnowski and Piotr Jędrzejowicz

Department of Information Systems, Gdynia Maritime University
Morska 83, 81-225 Gdynia, Poland
{irek,pj}@am.gdynia.pl

Abstract. Radial Basis Function Neural Networks (RBFNs) are quite popular due to their ability to discover and approximate complex non-linear dependencies within the data under analysis. The performance of the RBF network depends on numerous factors. One of them is a value of the RBF shape parameter. This parameter has a direct impact on performance of the transfer function of each hidden unit. Values of the transfer function parameters, including the value of its shape, are set during the RBFN tuning phase. Setting values of the transfer function parameters, including its shape can be viewed as the optimization problem in which the performance of the considered RBFN is maximized. In the paper the agent-based population learning algorithm finding the optimal or near optimal value of the RBF shape parameter is proposed and evaluated.

1 Introduction

Artificial Neural Networks are used to solve many different kind of problems such as classification, signal processing, pattern recognition, prediction, time series analysis, image preprocessing, speaker identification, etc. The RBF networks are considered as an universal approximation tool similarly to the multilayer perceptrons (MLPs). However, radial basis function networks usually achieve faster convergence since only one layer of weights is required [10].

A RBF network is constructed from a three-layer architecture with a feedback. The input layer consisting of a set of source units connects the network to the environment. The hidden layer consists of hidden neurons with radial basis functions [10]. RBFNs use different functions at each hidden unit. Nevertheless, RBFN design is not straightforward. One of the main problems with neural networks is the lack of consensus on how to best implement them [18].

RBFNs are generally non-linear and belong to a special class of tools which performance depends on the distance between an input vector and a center vector, called centroid, prototype or kernel of the basis function. RBFNs ability is to approximate complex non-linear mapping directly from the input-output data [13]. The performance of the RBF network depends on numerous factors. The basic problem with the RBFNs is to set an appropriate number of radial basis function, i.e. a number of hidden units. Deciding on this number results in fixing the number of clusters and their centroids. Another factor, called a shape

L. Rutkowski et al. (Eds.): ICAISC 2013, Part I, LNAI 7894, pp. 41–51, 2013.

parameter of radial basis function, plays also an important role from the point of view of accuracy and stability of the RBF-based approximations. In numerous reported applications RBFs contain free shape parameters, which can be tuned by users. In [9] it is viewed as a disadvantage and somewhat ironic since the user is forced to make a decision on the choice of the shape parameter. Such an approach can also decrease chances to finding the optimal network structure [9].

In [11] it was suggested that the shape of radial basis functions should be changed depending on the data distribution. Such a flexibility should result in assuring better approximation effect in comparison with other approaches, where, for example, radial basis function parameters are set by some *ad hoc* criterion. A discussion of several approaches to setting shape parameter values can be found in [11].

In RBFNs the transfer function is represented by the radial basis function in each hidden unit. The transfer function is a composition of the activation function and the output function. A large number of different transfer functions have been proposed in the literature. Universal transfer functions have been proposed by Hoffmann [12]. Their feature is an ability to change shape smoothly from one function form to another. A taxonomy of different transfer functions used for neural network design can be found in [8]. Several possibilities of using transfer functions (i.e. activation and output functions) of different types in neural network models, including regularization of networks with heterogeneous nodes, are discussed in [8].

The paper deals with the problem of deciding on the RBF shape parameter values with a view to optimize transfer function design. It is shown how the agent-based population learning algorithm can be used for the RBF shape parameter setting through selection of transfer functions and their parameters. In [5] the agent-based population learning algorithm was used to locate only prototypes within the produced clusters. In the proposed extended version of the algorithm, firstly clusters are produced. Next, the prototypes are determined. In the second step the parameters of the output function for each hidden unit are also determined including the type of the transfer function with its shape.

The goal of the paper is to show through computational experiment that the agent-based population learning algorithm used to locate prototypes and to set values of parameters of the radial basis functions can be competitive in comparison with its earlier version presented in [5], as well as with other RBFN training algorithms. To validate the approach, an extensive computational experiment has been carried-out. Performance of the proposed algorithm has been evaluated using several benchmark datasets from the UCI repository [1].

The paper is organized as follows. Section 2 gives a basic account of the RBF networks. Idea of the agent-based population learning algorithm is presented in Section 3. Section 4 explains main features of the proposed implementation of the agent-based population learning algorithm. Section 5 provides details on the computational experiment setup and discusses its results. Finally, the last section contains conclusions and suggestions for future research.

2   RBF Neural Network Background

The output of the RBF network is a linear combination of the outputs of the hidden units, i.e. a linear combination of the nonlinear radial basis function generating approximation of the unknown function. In case of the classification problems the output value is produced using the sigmoid function with a linear combination of the outputs of the hidden units as an argument. In general, the RBFN output function has the following form:

$$f(x, w, p) = \sum_{i=1}^{M} w_i G_i(r_i, p_i),$$ (1)

where M defines the number of hidden neurons, G_i is a radial basis function associated with i−th hidden neuron, p_i is a vector of parameters, which can include the location of centroids, dispersion or other parameters describing the radial function.

One of the most popular output functions of the RBF hidden units is the Gaussian function [3], which has been chosen to best fit data from each cluster. In such a case the output function takes the following form:

$$G(r, b) = e^{-\left(\frac{r}{b}\right)^2},$$ (2)

where r is a norm function denoted as $r = \|x - c\|$, where x is an input instance, c represents a centroid and b is a value of dispersion (or "width") of the radial function. The output function of the RBF hidden unit most frequently is calculated using the Euclidean distance although other measures of distance can be also used. Thus, in general case, r refers to the Euclidean norm [9].

The Gaussian function is an example of function where the input instances are analyzed with respect to the one particular point (centroid) in the data space. The Gaussian function is also an example of a simple local function. In [8] it has been concluded that such local functions are useful to produce circular neurons and a solution especially for classification problems. In [8] it is also shown, that RBFN constructed using local functions can be very sensitive when the data are incomplete

Alternatively to the Gaussian function bicentral functions are considered to be a more promising option. The bicentral functions are formed from N pair of sigmoids and are defined with respect to two centers $c_i - e^{b_i}$ and $c_i + e^{b_i}$. The bicentral functions are window type localized functions and are separable. A feature of the bicentral transfer functions is their flexibility in representing various probability densities. They can also produce decision region with convex shapes. These properties result from possibilities of moving the location of two centers, changing the function dispersion and setting a slope of the function [8]. The bicentral output function has the following form:

$$G(x, c, b, s) = \prod_{i}^{N} \sigma(e^{s_i}(x_i - c_i + e^{b_i}))(1 - \sigma(e^{s_i'}(x_i - c_i - e^{b_i}))),$$ (3)

where c represents a centroid, b is a corresponding width of the radial function, N is the dimension of the instance (i.e. the number of attributes), s and s' represent a slope of the function for the left and the right side in any dimension of the centroid, σ is a sigmoid function with argument z defined as follows: $\sigma(z) = \frac{1}{1+e^{-\beta z}}$, where β determines the slope of the function and is equal to s or s' respectively.

The RBF network initialization is a process, where the set of parameters of the radial basis functions, including the number of the radial basis functions, their shapes and the number of centroids with their locations, needs to be calculated or drawn. It is performed during the RBFN tuning. On the other hand, RBFNs involve finding a set of weights of links between neurons such that the network generates a desired output signals. The weights are determined in the RBF network training process. Both processes can be also viewed as solving the optimization task, where the optimization objective is to minimize the value of the target function by finding the optimal values of vector weights and vector of RBF parameters.

Since the RBF neural network initialization and training belong to the class of computationally difficult combinatorial optimization problems [10], it is reasonable to apply to solve this task one of the known metaheuristics. In this paper the agent-based population learning, proposed originally in [2], is applied as a collaborative approach to neural network tuning (see, for example [15]). In the paper the agent-based population learning algorithm is proposed for the purpose of the RBFN initialization including prototype selection and choice of shape parameters. In next sections details of the proposed approach are included.

3   Agent-Based Population Learning Algorithm

In [2] it has been shown that agent-based population learning search can be used as a robust and powerful optimizing technique. In the agent-based population learning implementation both - optimization and improvement procedures are executed by a set of agents cooperating and exchanging information within an asynchronous team of agents (A-Team). The A-Team concept was originally introduced in [15].

The concept of the A-Team was motivated by several approaches like blackboard systems and evolutionary algorithms, which have proven to be able to successfully solve some difficult combinatorial optimization problems. Within an A-Team agents achieve an implicit cooperation by sharing a population of solutions, to the problem to be solved.

An A-Team can be also defined as a set of agents and a set of memories, forming a network in which every agent remains in a closed loop. Each agent possesses some problem-solving skills and each memory contains a population of temporary solutions to the problem at hand. It also means that such an architecture can deal with several searches conducted in parallel. In each iteration of the process of searching for the best solution agents cooperate to construct, find and improve solutions which are read from the shared, common memory. All agents can work asynchronously and in parallel.

Main functionality of the agent-based population learning approach includes organizing and conducting the process of search for the best solution. It involves a sequence of the following steps:

- Generation of the initial population of solutions to be stored in the common memory.
- Activation of optimizing agents which execute some solution improvement algorithms applied to solutions drawn from the common memory and, subsequently, store them back after the attempted improvement in accordance with a user defined replacement strategy.
- Continuation of the reading-improving-replacing cycle until a stopping criterion is met. Such a criterion can be defined either or both as a predefined number of iterations or a limiting time period during which optimizing agents do not manage to improve the current best solution. After computation has been stopped the best solution achieved so far is accepted as the final one.

More information on the population learning algorithm with optimization procedures implemented as agents within an asynchronous team of agents (A-Team) can be found in [2]. In [2] also several A-Team implementations are described.

4 An Approach to the RBF Network Tuning

The paper deals with the problem of RBFN initialization through applying the agent-based population learning algorithm. The main goal is to find the optimal set of RBF network parameters with respect to:

- Producing clusters and determining their centroids.
- Determining the kind of transfer function for each hidden units and other parameters of the transfer function.

4.1 Producing Clusters and Determining Their Centroids

Under the proposed approach clusters are produced at the first stage of the initialization process. They are generated using the procedure based on the similarity coefficient calculated as proposed in [6]. Clusters contain instances with identical similarity coefficient and the number of clusters is determined by the value of the similarity coefficient. Thus the clusters are initialized automatically, which also means that the number of radial basis function is initialized automatically (for details see, for example, [6]).

Next from thus obtained clusters of instances centroids are selected. An agent-based algorithm with a dedicated set of agents is used to locate centroids within clusters. In the proposed approach, it is assumed that maximum two centroids can be selected from each cluster. Obviously, from clusters containing exactly one instance, only one centroid can be selected.

4.2   Determining the Kind of Transfer Function

Under the proposed approach the number of cluster centroids determines the kind of transfer function associated with a given hidden unit. When only one centroid is selected, the output of the RBF hidden unit is calculated using the Gaussian function (see equation no. 2). By introducing this condition it is assumed that such hidden have a circular shape of the transfer function.

When the number of selected centroids is greater than one the output of the RBF hidden unit is calculated using the bicentral function (see equation no. 3). In this case the algorithm uses a dedicated set of agents responsible for finding optimal values for the left and the right slope of the transfer function.

The proposed approach may result in producing a heterogenous function network.

4.3   Agent-Based Population Learning Algorithm Implementation

The main feature of the proposed agent-based population learning algorithm is its ability to select centroids and transfer function parameters in cooperation between agents. Most important assumptions behind the approach, can be summarized as follows:

- Shared memory of the A-Team is used to store a population of solutions to the RBFN initialization problem.
- A solution is represented by a string consisting of two parts. The first contains integers representing numbers of instances selected as centroids. The length of the first part of the string is equal to, at least, the number of clusters (i.e. the number of hidden units) and can be greater than the number of hidden units when one of the clusters is associated with two centroids. The detailed conditions on the centroid number have been introduced in subsection 4.2. The second part consists of real numbers for representing left and right slope of the transfer functions. This part contains $2N$ parameters per one hidden unit.
- The initial population is generated randomly.
- Initially, potential solutions are generated through randomly selecting one or two centroids from each of the considered clusters.
- Initially, the real numbers representing slopes are generated randomly.
- Each solution from the population is evaluated and the value of its fitness is calculated. The evaluation is carried out by estimating classification accuracy or error approximation of the RBFN, which is initialized using centroids, set of transfer function parameter indicated by the solution and trained using backpropagation algorithm.

The RBFN initialization problem is solved using two groups of optimizing agents. The first group includes agents executing procedures for centroid selection. These procedures are a local search with the tabu for prototype selection and a simple local search. The both procedures modify a solution by replacing a randomly selected instance with some other randomly chosen instance thus far not included within the improved solution, or by modification through adding or removing an instance from the improved solution. The only difference between them is that in the first procedure the replacing takes place only for instances which are not on the tabu list. After the replacement, the move is placed on the tabu list and remains there for a given number of iterations. Replacement and modification are performed randomly with the same probability equal to 0.5.

The second group of optimizing agents includes procedures for estimation of the slope parameters. One of them is the standard mutation which modifies the second part of a solution by generating new values of element in the string. The modification is carried out with a mutation rate of p_m. If the fitness function value has improved then the change is accepted. The second procedure is an application of the non-uniform mutation. The non-uniform mutation acts through modifying a solution by repeatedly adjusting value of the randomly selected element in the string until the fitness function value has improved or until k consecutive improvements have been attempted unsuccessfully. The value of the adjustment is calculated as:

$$\triangle(t', y) = y(1 - q^{(1 - \frac{t'}{2N'})q}),\tag{4}$$

where q is the uniformly distributed real number from $(0, 1]$, N' is equal to the length of the current string with values representing the slop of the transfer function and t' is a current number of adjustment. The mutation is performed with probability p_{mu}. Both mutation procedures have been successfully applied in [4].

5   Computational Experiment

This section contains the results of several computational experiments carried out with a view to evaluate the performance of the proposed approach. In particular, the reported experiments aimed at evaluating quality of the RBF-based classifiers constructed using the proposed approach. Experiments aimed at answering the question whether the proposed agent-based approach to RBF network tuning ($ABRBF\_Tuning$) performs better than classical methods of RBFN initialization? The proposed approach has been also compared with the earlier version of the approach called $ABRBFN\ 1$ introduced in [5], where the agent-based population learning algorithm has been used only to perform search for a location of centroids within each of the Gaussian kernel-based clusters.

In the reported experiments the following RBFN initialization approaches have been also compared:

- The k-*means* clustering with the agent-based population learning algorithm used to locate prototypes (in this case at the first stage the k-*means* clustering has been implemented and next, from thus obtained clusters, the prototypes have been selected using the agent-based population learning algorithm) - denoted as k-*meansABRBFN*.

- The k-*means* algorithm used to locate centroids for each of the Gaussian kernels (in this case at the first stage the k-*means* clustering has been implemented and the cluster centers have been used as prototypes) - denoted as k-*meansRBFN*.
- The random search for kernel selection - denoted as *randomRBFN*.

Evaluation of the proposed approaches and performance comparisons are based on the classification and the regression problems. For both cases the proposed algorithms have been applied to solve respective problems using several benchmark datasets obtained from the UCI Machine Learning Repository [1]. Basic characteristics of these datasets are shown in Table 1.

Each benchmark problem has been solved 50 times, and the experiment plan involved 10 repetitions of the 10-cross-validation scheme. The reported values of the quality measure have been averaged over all runs. The quality measure in case of the classification problems was the correct classification ratio - accuracy (*Acc*). The overall performance for regression problems has been computed by the mean squared error (*MSE*) calculated as the approximation error over the test set.

Parameter settings for computations involving *ABRBF_Tuning* are shown in Table 2. Values of the some parameters have been set arbitrarily in the trials and errors procedure.

Table 1. Datasets used in the reported experiment

Dataset	Type of problem	Number of instances	Number of attributes	Number of classes	Best reported results
Forest Fires	Regression	517	12	-	-
Housing	Regression	506	14	-	-
WBC	Classification	699	9	2	97.5% [1] (Acc.)
Credit	Classification	690	15	2	86.9% [1] (Acc.)
Sonar	Classification	208	60	2	97.1% [1] (Acc.)
Satellite	Classification	6435	36	6	-

Table 2. Parameter settings for *ABRBF_Tuning* in the reported experiment

Parameter	
Max number of iteration during the search	500
Max number of epoch reached in RBF network training	1000
Population size	60
Probability of mutation for the standard and non-uniform mutation (p_m, p_{mu})	20%
Range values for left and right slope of the transfer function	[-1,1]

The dispersion of the Radial function has been determined as suggested in [15]: $b_i = \min_{k,i=1,...,m;k\neq i} \{\|c_k - c_i\|\}$, where c_k and c_i are centers of clusters.

Table 3 depicts the performance comparison involving $ABRBF\_Tuning$, its earlier version ($ABRBFN\ 1$) and some other approaches to RBF initialization including the k-*means* clustering with the agent-based population learning algorithm. From the results it can be observed that the proposed algorithm assures competitive results in comparison to other approaches. The proposed approach to the RBF network tuning proves to be quite competitive in case of the regression problems. In case of the classification problem the $ABRBF\_Tuning$ has improved accuracy only for one dataset. In three cases the $ABRBF\_Tuning$ algorithm is not better than $ABRBFN\ 1$. The experiment results show that $ABRBF\_Tuning$ applied to the RBF initialization performs better than k-*meansABRBFN*, k-*meansRBFN* and *randomRBFN*. Only for one dataset the k-*meansABRBFN* produced better results.

The results in Table 3 further demonstrate that the $ABRBF\_Tuning$ can be superior to the other methods including MLP, Multiple linear regression, SVM and C4.5. This statement is supported by the fact that in seven cases the proposed algorithm has been capable to improve the generalization ability.

Table 3. Results obtained for different variants of the proposed algorithm applied to the task of the RBNF's training and their comparison with performance of several different competitive approaches

Problem:	Forest fires	Housing	WBC	Credit	Sonar	Satellite
Algorithm:	MSE			Acc. (%)		
$ABRBF\_Tuning$	**2.07**	**34.92**	94.24	84.05	**83.34**	83.32
$ABRBFN\ 1$ [5]	2.15	35.24	94.56	**84.56**	82.09	**85.05***
k-*meansABRBFN* [5]	2.29	35.87	**95.83**	84.16	81.15	83.57*
k-*meansRBFN* [5]	2.21	36.4	93.9	82.03	78.62	81.4*
randomRBFN [5]	3.41	47.84	84.92	77.5	72.79	74.84*
Neural network - MLP	2.11 [19]	40.62 [19]	96.7 [7]	84.6 [7]	**84.5** [7]	83.75 [14]
Multiple linear regression	2.38 [19]	36.26 [19]	-	-	-	-
SVR/SVM	**1.97** [19]	44.91 [19]	**96.9** [7]	84.8 [7]	76.9 [7]	85.0 [17]
C 4.5	-	-	94.7 [7]	**85.5** [7]	76.9 [7]	-

* Not present in [5].

6   Conclusions

In this paper the agent-based population learning algorithm for RBF neural network tuning is proposed. The task of the algorithm is to find optimal parameters of the transfer function including the type of the function and its shape, and the appropriate centroids within initialized clusters for each hidden units of the RBF network.

Important feature of the approach is that the number of clusters, location of centroids and the transfer function parameters are determined in parallel using a set of dedicated agents. In the reported computational experiment the proposed algorithm has proved to be not worse from the earlier its version and in some cases outperforms other techniques for RBF initialization.

Future research will focus on finding more effective configurations of the RBF networks by extending the approach adding ability to estimate output weights of the RBFN. A new set of optimizing agents is planned to be implemented. It is also planned to carry-out more refined statistical analysis of the results to obtain a better insight into properties of the proposed approach.

In the future it also is planned to implement the proposed agent-based population learning algorithm for construction of the cascade correlation neural network. It is believed that that selection of the most promising transfer function for each candidate unit from a pool of candidates by the agent-based population learning algorithm can bring benefits in term of the classification accuracy or the approximation error.

Acknowledgement. This research has been supported by the Polish Ministry of Science and Higher Education with grant no. N N519 576438 for years 2010-2013.

References

1. Asuncion, A., Newman, D.J.: UCI Machine Learning Repository. University of California, School of Information and Computer Science, Irvine, CA (2007), http://www.ics.uci.edu/~mlearn/MLRepository.html
2. Barbucha, D., Czarnowski, I., Jędrzejowicz, P., Ratajczak-Ropel, E., Wierzbowska, I.: e-JABAT - An Implementation of the Web-Based A-Team. In: Nguyen, N.T., Jain, I.C. (eds.) Intel. Agents in the Evol. of Web and Appl. SCI, vol. 167, pp. 57–86. Springer, Heidelberg (2009)
3. Broomhead, D.S., Lowe, D.: Multivariable Functional Interpolation and Adaptive Networks. Complex Systems 2, 321–355 (1988)
4. Czarnowski, I., Jędrzejowicz, P.: An agent-based approach to ANN training. Knowledge-Based Systems 19, 304–308 (2006)
5. Czarnowski, I., Jędrzejowicz, P.: An Approach to Cluster Initialization for RBF Networks. In: Graña, M., Toro., C., Posada, J., Howlett, R., Jain, L.C. (eds.) Advances in Knowledge-Based and Intelligent Information and Engineering Systems. Frontiers in Artificial Intelligence and Applications, vol. 243, pp. 1151–1160. IOS Press (2012)
6. Czarnowski, I.: Cluster-based Instance Selection for Machine Classification. Knowledge and Information Systems 30(1), 113–133 (2012)
7. Datasets used for classification: comparison of results. In. directory of data sets, http://www.is.umk.pl/projects/datasets.html (accessed September 1, 2009)
8. Duch, W., Jankowski, N.: Transfer Functions: Hidden Possibilities for Better Neural Networks. In: Proceedings of the 9th European Symposium on Artificial Neural Networks (ESANN), Brugge, pp. 81–94 (2001)
9. Fasshauer, G.E., Zhang, J.G.: On Choosing "Optimal" Shape Parameters for RBF Approximation. Numerical Algorithms 45(1-4), 345–368 (2007)

10. Gao, H., Feng, B., Hou, Y., Zhu, L.: Training RBF Neural Network with Hybrid Particle Swarm Optimization. In: Wang, J., Yi, Z., Żurada, J.M., Lu, B.-L., Yin, H. (eds.) ISNN 2006. LNCS, vol. 3971, pp. 577–583. Springer, Heidelberg (2006)
11. Hanrahan, G.: Artificial Neural Networks in Biological and Envoronmental Analysis. Analytical Chemistry Series. CRC Press, Taylor & Francis Group (2011)
12. Hoffmann, G.A.: Adaptive Transfer Functions in Radial Basis Function (RBF) Networks. In: Bubak, M., van Albada, G.D., Sloot, P.M.A., Dongarra, J. (eds.) ICCS 2004. LNCS, vol. 3037, pp. 682–686. Springer, Heidelberg (2004)
13. Huang, G.-B., Saratchandra, P., Sundararajan, N.: A Generalized Growing and Pruning RBF(GGAP-RBF) Neural Network for Function Approximation. IEEE Transactions on Neural Networks 16(1), 57–67 (2005)
14. Liang, N.-Y., Huang, G.-B., Saratchandran, P., Sundararajan, N.: A Fast and Accurate Online Sequential Learning Algorithm for Feedforward Networks. IEEE Transactions on Neural Networks 17(6), 1411–1423 (2006)
15. Sánchez, A.V.D.: Searching for a solution to the automatic RBF network design problem. Neurocomputing 42(1-4), 147–170
16. Talukdar, S., Baerentzen, L., Gove, A., de Souza, P.: Asynchronous Teams: Cooperation Schemes for Autonomous, Computer-Based Agents. Technical Report EDRC 18-59-96, Carnegie Mellon University, Pittsburgh (1996)
17. Wang, L., Yang, B., Chen, Y., Abraham, A., Sun, H., Chen, Z., Wang, H.: Improvement of Neural Network Classifier Using Floating Centroids. Knowledge Information Systems 31, 433–454 (2012)
18. Yonaba, H., Anctil, F., Fortin, V.: Comparing Sigmoid Transfer Functions for Neural Network Multistep Ahead Streamflow Forecasting. Journal of Hydrologic Engineering 15(4), 275–283 (2010)
19. Zhang, D., Tian, Y., Zhang, P.: Kernel-based Nonparametric Regression Method. In: Proceedings of the IEEE/WIC/ACM International Conference on Web Intelligence and Intelligent Agent Technology, pp. 410–413 (2008)

Forecasting Time Series with Multiple Seasonal Cycles Using Neural Networks with Local Learning

Grzegorz Dudek

Department of Electrical Engineering, Czestochowa University of Technology,
Al. Armii Krajowej 17, 42-200 Czestochowa, Poland
dudek@el.pcz.czest.pl

Abstract. In the article a simple neural model with local learning for forecasting time series with multiple seasonal cycles is presented. This model uses patterns of the time series seasonal cycles: input ones representing cycles preceding the forecast moment and forecast ones representing the forecasted cycles. Patterns simplify the forecasting problem especially when a time series exhibits nonstationarity, heteroscedasticity, trend and many seasonal cycles. The artificial neural network learns using the training sample selected from the neighborhood of the query pattern. As a result the target function is approximated locally which leads to a reduction in problem complexity and enables the use of simpler models. The effectiveness of the proposed approach is illustrated through applications to electrical load forecasting and compared with ARIMA and exponential smoothing approaches. In a day ahead load forecasting simulations indicate the best results for the one-neuron network.

Keywords: seasonal time series forecasting, short-term load forecasting, local learning, neural networks.

1 Introduction

Time series may contain four different components: trend, seasonal variations, cyclical variations, and irregular component. Seasonality is defined to be the tendency of time series data to exhibit some pattern that repeats periodically with variation. Sometimes a time series contains multiple seasonal cycles of different lengths. Fig. 1 shows such a time series, where we can observe annual, weekly and daily variations. This series represents hourly electrical load of the Polish power system. From this figure it can be seen that the daily and weekly profiles change during the year. In summer they are more flat than in winter. The daily profile depends on the day of the week as well. The profiles of the weekdays are similar to each other in the same period of the year. To the characteristic features of this time series its nonstationarity and heteroscedasticity should be included as well. These all features have to be captured by the flexible forecasting model.

The most commonly employed methods to modeling seasonal time series include [1]: seasonal autoregressive integrated moving average model (ARIMA), exponential

L. Rutkowski et al. (Eds.): ICAISC 2013, Part I, LNAI 7894, pp. 52–63, 2013.

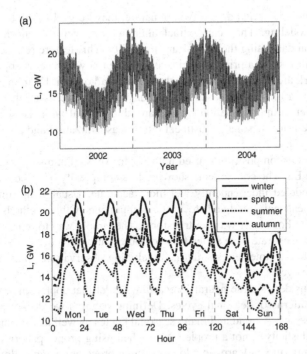

Fig. 1. The load time series of the Polish power system in three-year (a) and one-week (b) intervals

smoothing (ES), artificial neural networks (ANNs), dynamic harmonic regression, vector autoregression, random effect models, and many others.

The base ARIMA model with just one seasonal pattern can be extended for the case of multiple seasonalities. An example of such an extension was presented in [2]. A combinatorial problem of selecting appropriate model orders is an inconvenience in the time series modeling using multiple seasonal ARIMA. Another disadvantage is the linear character of the ARIMA model.

Another popular model – the Holt-Winters exponential smoothing was adapted by Taylor so that it can accommodate two and more seasonalities [2]. An advantage of the ES models is that they can be nonlinear. On the other hand it can be viewed as being of high dimension, as it involves initialization and updating of a large number of terms (level, periods of the intraday and intraweek cycles). In [1] more parsimonious formulation of ES is proposed. New exponentially weighted methods for forecasting time series that consist of both intraweek and intraday seasonal cycles can be found in [3].

Gould et al. [4] introduced the innovation state space models that underlie ES methods for both additive and multiplicative seasonality. This procedure provides a theoretical foundation for ES methods and improves on the current approaches by providing a common sense structure to the models, flexibility in modeling seasonal patterns, a potential reduction in the number of parameters to be estimated, and model based prediction intervals.

ANNs being nonlinear and data-driven in nature, may be well suited to the seasonal time series modeling. They can extract unknown and general information from multi-dimensional data using their self-learning ability. This feature releases a designer from a difficult task of a priori model selection. But new problems appear: the selection of network architecture as well as the learning algorithm. From many types of ANN most often in forecasting tasks the multilayer perceptron is used, which has a property of universal approximation. ANNs are able to deal with the seasonal time series without the prior seasonal adjustment but deseasonalization and also detrending is recommended [5].

The time series decomposition is used not only in ANNs, but also in other models, e.g. ARIMA and ES. The components showing less complexity than the original time series can be modeled independently and more accurate. Usually the time series is decomposed on seasonal, trend and stochastic components. Other methods of decompositions apply the Fourier or wavelet transform. The simple way to remove seasonality is to define the separate time series for each observation in a cycle, i.e. in the case of cycle of length n, n time series is defined including observations in the same position in successive cycles.

This paper considers simple neural forecasting model that approximates the target function using patterns of seasonal cycles. Defining patterns we do not need to decompose a time series. A trend and many seasonal cycles as well as the nonstationarity and heteroscedasticity is not a problem here when using proper pattern definitions. The proposed neural model learns in a local learning procedure which allows to model the target function in the neighborhood of the query pattern. As a result we get a local model which is better fitted in this neighborhood.

2   Patterns of the Time Series Seasonal Cycles

Our goal is to forecast the time series elements in a period of one seasonal cycle of the shortest length. In the case of the time series shown in Fig. 1 this is a daily cycle containing $n = 24$ elements (hourly loads). The time series is divided into sequences containing one seasonal cycle of length n. In order to eliminate trend and seasonal variations of periods longer than n (weekly and annual variations in our example), the sequence elements are preprocessed to obtain their patterns. The pattern is a vector with components that are functions of actual time series elements. The input and output (forecast) patterns are defined: $\mathbf{x} = [x_1 \; x_2 \; ... \; x_n]^T$ and $\mathbf{y} = [y_1 \; y_2 \; ... \; y_n]^T$, respectively. The patterns are paired ($\mathbf{x}_i$, $\mathbf{y}_i$), where $\mathbf{y}_i$ is a pattern of the time series sequence succeeding the sequence represented by $\mathbf{x}_i$. The interval between these sequences is equal to the forecast horizon τ.

The way of how the $\mathbf{x}$ and $\mathbf{y}$ patterns are defined depends on the time series nature (seasonal variations, trend), the forecast period and the forecast horizon. Functions transforming series elements into patterns should be defined so that patterns carry most information about the process. Moreover, functions transforming forecast sequences into patterns $\mathbf{y}$ should ensure the opposite transformation: from the forecasted pattern $\mathbf{y}$ to the forecasted time series sequence.

The forecast pattern $\mathbf{y}_i = [y_{i,1} \; y_{i,2} \; ... \; y_{i,n}]$ encodes the successive actual time series elements z in the forecast period $i+\tau$. $\mathbf{z}_{i+\tau} = [z_{i+\tau 1} \; z_{i+\tau 2} \; ... \; z_{i+\tau n}]$, and the corresponding input pattern $\mathbf{x}_i = [x_{i,1} \; x_{i,2} \; ... \; x_{i,n}]$ maps the time series elements in the period i preceding the forecast period: $\mathbf{z}_i = [z_{i,1} \; z_{i,2} \; ... \; z_{i,n}]$. Vectors $\mathbf{y}$ are encoded using current process parameters from the nearest past, which allows to take into consideration current variability of the process and ensures possibility of decoding. Some definitions of the functions mapping the original space Z into the pattern spaces X and Y, i.e. $f_x : Z \rightarrow X$ and $f_y : Z \rightarrow Y$ are presented in [6]. The most popular definitions are of the form:

$$f_x(z_{i,t}) = \frac{z_{i,t} - \overline{z}_i}{\sqrt{\sum_{l=1}^{n}(z_{i,l} - \overline{z}_i)^2}}, \qquad f_y(z_{i,t}) = \frac{z_{i+\tau,t} - \overline{z}_i}{\sqrt{\sum_{l=1}^{n}(z_{i,l} - \overline{z}_i)^2}}, \qquad (1)$$

where: $i = 1, 2, ..., N$ – the period number, $t = 1, 2, ..., n$ – the time series element number in the period i, τ – the forecast horizon, $z_{i,t}$ – the tth time series element in the period i, $\overline{z}_i$ – the mean value of elements in period i.

The function f_x defined using (1) expresses normalization of the vectors $\mathbf{z}_i$. After normalization these vectors have the unity length, zero mean and the same variance. When we use the standard deviation of the vector $\mathbf{z}_i$ components in the denominator of equation (1), we receive vector $\mathbf{x}_i$ with the unity variance and zero mean. Note that the nonstationary and heteroscedastic time series is represented by patterns having the same mean and variance.

Forecast pattern $\mathbf{y}_i$ is defined using analogous functions to input pattern function f_x, but it is encoded using the time series characteristic ($\overline{z}_i$) determined from the process history, what enables decoding of the forecasted vector $\mathbf{z}_{i+\tau}$ after the forecast of pattern $\mathbf{y}$ is determined. To calculate the forecasted time series element values on the basis of their patterns we use the inverse function $f_y^{-1}(y_{i,t})$.

3   Local Learning

The training data can have different properties in different regions of the input and output spaces thus it is reasonable to model this data locally. The local learning [7] concerns the optimization of the learning system on a subset of the training sample, which contains points from the neighborhood around the current query point $\mathbf{x}^*$. By the neighborhood of $\mathbf{x}^*$ in the simplest case we mean the set of its k nearest neighbors. A result of the local learning is that the model accurately adjusts to the target function in the neighborhood of $\mathbf{x}^*$ but shows weaker fitting outside this neighborhood. Thus we get model which is locally competent but its global generalization property is weak. Modeling the target function in different regions of the space requires re-learning of the model or even to construct different model, e.g. we can use a linear model for linear fragments of the target function while for the nonlinear fragments we can use a nonlinear model. The generalization can be achieved by using a set of local models that are competent for different regions of the input space. Usually these models are learned when a new query points are presented.

The error criterion minimized in local learning algorithm can be defined as follows:

$$E(\mathbf{x}^*) = \sum_{i=1}^{N} K(d(\mathbf{x}_i, \mathbf{x}^*), h) \delta(\mathbf{y}_i, f(\mathbf{x}_i)), \qquad (2)$$

where: N – number of training patterns, $K(d(\mathbf{x}_i, \mathbf{x}^*), h)$ – kernel function with bandwidth h, $d(\mathbf{x}_i, \mathbf{x}^*)$ – distance between the query pattern $\mathbf{x}^*$ and training pattern $\mathbf{x}_i$, $\delta(\mathbf{y}_i, f(\mathbf{x}_i))$ – error between the model response $f(\mathbf{x}_i)$ and the target response $\mathbf{y}_i$ when input pattern $\mathbf{x}_i$ is presented (this response can be a scalar value).

Various kernel functions might be used, including uniform kernels and Gaussian kernels which are ones of the most popular. The kernel is centered on the query point $\mathbf{x}^*$ and the bandwidth h determines the weight of the ith training pattern error in (2). When we use uniform kernel the training patterns for which $d(\mathbf{x}_i, \mathbf{x}^*) \leq h = d(\mathbf{x}_k, \mathbf{x}^*)$, where $\mathbf{x}_k$ is the kth nearest neighbor of $\mathbf{x}^*$, have unity weights. More distant patterns have zero weights, and therefore there is no need to use these points in the learning process. For Gaussian kernels all training points have nonzero weights calculated from the formula $\exp(-d^2(\mathbf{x}_i, \mathbf{x}^*)/(2h^2))$, which means that their weights decrease monotonically with the distance from $\mathbf{x}^*$ and with the speed dependent on h. In order to reduce the computational cost of determination of errors and weights for all training points we can combine both kernels and calculate weights according to the Gaussian kernel for only k nearest neighbors of $\mathbf{x}^*$. The computational cost is now independent of the total number of training patterns, but only on the number of considered neighbors k.

In the experimental part of this paper we use local learning procedure with uniform kernel.

4   Experimental Results

As an illustrative example of forecasting time series with multiple seasonal cycles using neural networks with local learning we study the short-term electrical load forecasting problem. Short-term load forecasting plays a key role in control and scheduling of power systems and is extremely important for energy suppliers, system operators, financial institutions, and other participants in electric energy generation, transmission, distribution, and markets.

In the first experiments we use the time series of the hourly electrical load of the Polish power system from the period 2002–2004. This series is shown in Fig. 1. The time series were divided into training and test parts. The test set contained 31 pairs of patterns from July 2004. The training part Ψ contained patterns from the period from 1 January 2002 to the day preceding the day of forecast.

We define the forecasting tasks as forecasting the power system load at hour $t = 1$, 2, ..., 24 of the day $j = 1, 2, ..., 31$, where j is the day number in the test set. So we get 744 forecasting tasks. In local learning approach for each task the separate ANNs were created and learned. The training set for each forecasting task is prepared as follows:

- first we prepare the set $\Omega = \{(\mathbf{x}_i, y_{i,t})\}$, where i indicates pairs of patterns from Ψ representing days of the same type (Monday, ..., Sunday) as days represented by a query pair $(\mathbf{x}^*, y_t^*)$,
- then based on the Euclidean distances $d(\mathbf{x}_i, \mathbf{x}^*)$ we select from Ω k nearest neighbors of the query pair getting the training set $\Phi = \{(\mathbf{x}_i, y_{i,t})\} \subset \Omega \subset \Psi$.

For example when the forecasting task is to forecast the system load at hour t on Sunday, model learns on k nearest neighbors of the query pattern which are selected from x-patterns representing the Saturday patterns and tth components of y-patterns representing the Sunday patterns.

ANN (the multilayer perceptron) learns the mapping of the input patterns to the components of output patterns: $f_t : X \rightarrow Y_t$. Number of ANN inputs is equal to the x-pattern components. To prevent overfitting ANN is learned using Levenberg-Marquardt algorithm with Bayesian regularization [8], which minimizes a combination of squared errors and net weights. The resulting network has good generalization qualities.

In the first experiment we assume $k = 12$. Since the target function f_t is modeled locally, using a small number of learning points, rather a simple form of this function should be expected, which implies small number of neurons. We tested the networks:

- composed of only one neuron with linear or bipolar sigmoidal activation function,
- with one hidden layer consisting of $m = 2, ..., 8$ neurons with sigmoidal activation functions and one output neuron with linear activation function. Such a network architecture can be seen as a universal approximator .

APE and MAPE (absolute percentage error and mean APE) is adopted here to assess the performance of the forecasting models. The results (MAPE for the training and test samples and the interquartile range (IQR) of $MAPE_{tst}$) of the 9 variants of ANNs are presented in tab. 1. Test errors for these variants are statistically indistinguishable (to check this we use the Wilcoxon rank sum test for equality of APE medians; $\alpha = 0.05$). It is observed that for the two-layered networks in many cases   most weights tends to zero (weights decay is a result of regularization,   thus some neurons can be eliminated. As an optimal ANN architecture that one with one neuron with sigmoidal activation function is chosen. This one-neuron ANN is used in the next experiments.

In the second experiment we examine the network performance depending on the number of the nearest neighbors k, i.e. the size of the training set Φ. We change k from 2 to 50. The results are shown in Fig. 2, where MAPE for the cases when the ANN is trained using all training points representing days of the same type as days represented by query pair, i.e. points from the set Ω, is also shown. As we can see from this figure the test error remains around 1 when $k \in [6, 50]$. For these cases $MAPE_{tst}$ are statistically indistinguishable when using Wilcoxon test. When we train ANN using patterns from the set Ω $MAPE_{tst}$ is statistically distinguishable greater than for $k \in [6, 50]$.

Table 1. Results of 9 variants of ANNs

	Number of neurons								
	1 lin	1 sig	2+1	3+1	4+1	5+1	6+1	7+1	8+1
$MAPE_{trn}$	0.80	0.88	1.12	1.11	1.09	1.09	1.08	1.09	1.10
$MAPE_{tst}$	1.03	0.98	0.98	0.98	1.00	1.00	1.02	1.02	1.01
IQR_{tst}	1.09	1.03	1.02	1.03	1.06	1.02	1.05	0.99	1.04

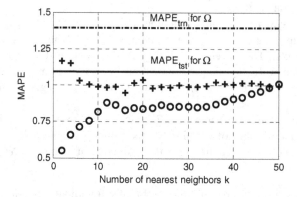

Fig. 2. MAPE for the training sets (rings) and test set (crosses) depending on k

In the local learning approach the thorny issue is the ratio of the training points number to the number of free parameters of the network. This ratio for our example even for one-neuron ANN is too small (12/25), which means that the model is oversized (it has too many degrees of freedom in relation to the problem complexity expressed by only a few training points). The regularization which has a form of a penalty for complexity is a good idea to solve this problem. Another idea is the feature selection or feature extraction as a form of dimensionality reduction. The most popular method of feature extraction is the principal component analysis (PCA). This procedure uses an orthogonal transformation to convert a set of multidimensional vectors of possibly correlated components into a set of vectors of linearly uncorrelated components called principal components. The number of principal components is less than or equal to the dimension of original vectors. In the next experiment we transform the 24-dimensional x-patterns into patterns with a smaller number of uncorrelated components using PCA. Fig. 3 shows relationship between MAPE and the number of principal components. From this figure it can be seen that the levels of errors are very similar. $MAPE_{tst}$ are statistically indistinguishable for different number of principal components. Using only first principal component we can built good neural forecasting model for our data. Such a model has only two parameters. The percent variance explained by the corresponding principal components are shown in Fig. 4. The first principal component explains 30% of the total variance.

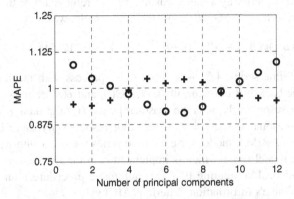

Fig. 3. MAPE for the training sets (rings) and test set (crosses) depending on the number of principal components

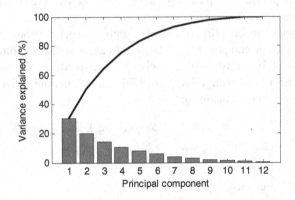

Fig. 4. The percent variance explained by the corresponding principal components

Now we compare the proposed one-neuron ANN with other popular models of the seasonal time series forecasting: ARIMA and ES. These models were tested in the next day electrical load curve forecasting problem on three time series of electrical load:

- PL: time series of the hourly load of the Polish power system from the period 2002–2004 (this time series was used in the experiments described above). The test sample includes data from 2004 with the exception of 13 untypical days (e.g. holidays),

- FR: time series of the half-hourly load of the French power system from the period 2007–2009. The test sample includes data from 2009 except for 21 untypical days,
- GB: time series of the half-hourly load of the British power system from the period 2007–2009. The test sample includes data from 2009 except for 18 untypical days.

In ARIMA the time series were decomposed into n series, i.e. for each t a separate series was created. In this way a daily seasonality was removed. For the independent modeling of these series ARIMA$(p, d, q) \times (P, D, Q)_m$ model was used:

$$\Phi(B^m)\phi(B)(1-B^m)^D(1-B)^d\, z_t = c + \Theta(B^m)\theta(B)\xi_t, \qquad (3)$$

where $\{z_t\}$ is the time series, $\{\xi_t\}$ is a white noise process with mean zero and variance σ^2, B is the backshift operator, $\Phi(.)$, $\phi(.)$, $\Theta(.)$, and $\theta(.)$ are polynomials of order P, p, Q and q, respectively, m is the seasonal period (for our data $m = 7$), d and D are orders of nonseasonal and seasonal differencing, respectivelly, and c is a constant.

To find the best ARIMA model for each time series we use a step-wise procedure for traversing the model space which is implemented in the **forecast** package for the **R** system for statistical computing [9]. This automatic procedure returns the model with the lowest Akaike's Information Criterion (AIC) value.

ARIMA model parameters, as well as the parameters of the ES model described below, were estimated using 12-week time series fragments immediately preceding the forecasted daily period. Untypical days in these fragments were replaced with the days from the previous weeks.

The ES state space models [10] are classified into 30 types depending on how the seasonal, trend and error components are taken into account. These components can be expressed additively or multiplicatively, and the trend can be damped or not. For example, the ES model with a dumped additive trend, multiplicative seasonality and multiplicative errors is of the form:

$$
\begin{aligned}
\text{Level}: & \quad l_t = (l_{t-1} + \phi b_{t-1})(1 + \alpha \xi_t), \\
\text{Growth}: & \quad b_t = \phi b_{t-1} + \beta(l_{t-1} + \phi b_{t-1})\xi_t, \\
\text{Seasonal}: & \quad s_t = s_{t-m}(1 + \gamma \xi_t), \\
\text{Forecast}: & \quad \mu_t = (l_{t-1} + \phi b_{t-1})s_{t-m},
\end{aligned}
\qquad (4)
$$

where l_t represents the level of the series at time t, b_t denotes the growth (or slope) at time t, s_t is the seasonal component of the series at time t, μ_t is the expected value of the forecast at time t, $\alpha, \beta, \gamma \in (0, 1)$ are the smoothing parameters, and $\phi \in (0, 1)$ denotes a damping parameter.

In model (4) there is only one seasonal component. For this reason, as in the case of the ARIMA model, time series is decomposed into n series, each of which represents the load at the same time t of a day. These series were modeled independently using an automated procedure implemented in the **forecast** package for the **R** system [9]. In this procedure the initial states of the level, growth and seasonal components are estimated as well as the smoothing and damping parameters. AIC was used for selecting the best model for a given time series.

In Table 2 results of PL, FR and GB time series forecasts are presented. In this table the results of forecast determined by the naïve method are also shown. The forecast rule in this case is as follows: the forecasted daily cycle is the same as seven days ago. The Wilcoxon test indicates statistically significant differences between $MAPE_{tst}$ for each pair of models and each time series, so we can indicate the one-neuron ANN as the best model for this data and ES as the second best model.

Table 2. Results of forecasting

Model	PL		FR		GB	
	$MAPE_{tst}$	IQR	$MAPE_{tst}$	IQR	$MAPE_{tst}$	IQR
ANN	1.44	1.41	1.64	1.70	1.65	1.70
ARIMA	1.82	1.71	2.32	2.53	2.02	2.07
ES	1.66	1.57	2.10	2.29	1.85	1.84
Naïve	3.43	3.42	5.05	5.96	3.52	3.82

The last experiment concerns time series forecasting up to seven daily periods ahead. In such tasks the y-patterns are defined using $\tau = 1, 2, ..., 7$. For each horizon τ the one-neuron ANN is trained using the same local learning scheme as for $\tau = 1$ described above. The forecast errors for PL, FR and GB time series in Fig. 5 are presented. For FR and GB data ANN gave the lowest errors. For PL data and $\tau > 2$ ES model is better, and for $\tau > 3$ also ARIMA model is better. The actual and forecasted fragments of the time series are shown in Fig. 6.

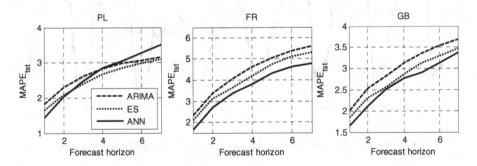

Fig. 5. The forecast errors for different horizons

Note that in the case of ARIMA and ES the model parameters are estimated on the basis of the time series fragment (12 weeks in our example) directly preceding the forecasted fragment. ANN learns on the training set composed of patterns represented daily periods from longer history. In local learning case the training patterns are selected using criterion based on the similarity to the current input pattern.

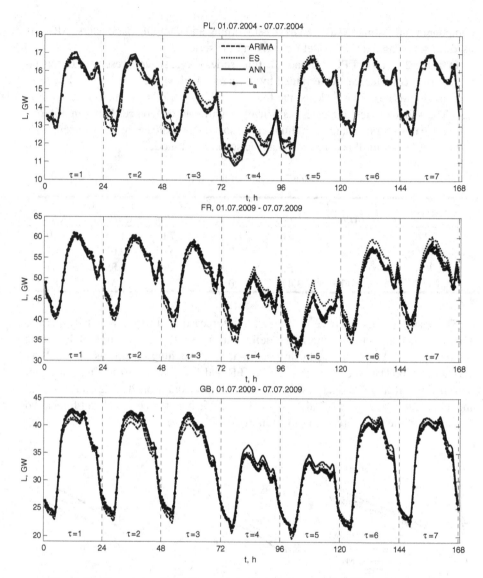

Fig. 6. The fragments of load time series and their forecasts for different horizons

5   Conclusions

In this article we examine a simple neural model with local learning for forecasting seasonal time series. At the initial stage of the forecasting procedure data are preprocessed to get patterns of the time series seasonal periods. An approach based on the patterns of the seasonal cycles simplify the problem of forecasting of the nonstationary and heteroscedastic time series with trend and many seasonal variations. After simplification the problem can be modeled using simpler tools. The existence of many seasonal cycles is not a problem when we use forecasting model based on patterns. We resign from the global modeling, which does not necessarily brings good results for the current query point. Instead, we approximate the target function locally in the neighborhood of the query point. The disadvantage of the local learning is the need to learn the model for each query point. But since the local complexity is lower than the global one, we can use a simple model that is quickly learned.

This approach is acceptable when we have enough time (some seconds) to learn model and prepare forecast. The learning speed is penalized by the selection of the nearest neighbors. As shown by simulation studies to model the local relationship between input and output patterns the one-neuron model is sufficient. This model turned out to be better than the conventional models (ARIMA and exponential smoothing) in one-day ahead forecasting of the electrical load time series and competitive in forecasting over longer time horizons.

Acknowledgments. The author would like to thank Professor James W. Taylor from the Saïd Business School, University of Oxford for providing French and British load data. The study was supported by the Research Project N N516 415338 financed by the Polish Ministry of Science and Higher Education.

References

1. Taylor, J.W., Snyder, R.D.: Forecasting Intraday Time Series with Multiple Seasonal Cycles Using Parsimonious Seasonal Exponential Smoothing. Department of Econometrics and Business Statistics Working Paper 9/09, Monash University (2009)
2. Taylor, J.W.: Short-Term Electricity Demand Forecasting Using Double Seasonal Exponential Smoothing. Journal of the Operational Research Society 54, 799–805 (2003)
3. Taylor, J.W.: Exponentially Weighted Methods for Forecasting Intraday Time Series with Multiple Seasonal Cycles. International Journal of Forecasting 26(4), 627–646 (2010)
4. Gould, P.G., Koehler, A.B., Ord, J.K., Snyder, R.D., Hyndman, R.J., Vahid-Araghi, F.: Forecasting Time-Series with Multiple Seasonal Patterns. European Journal of Operational Research 191, 207–222 (2008)
5. Zhang, G.P., Qi, M.: Neural Network Forecasting for Seasonal and Trend Time Series. European Journal of Operational Research 160, 501–514 (2005)
6. Dudek, G.: Similarity-based Approaches to Short-Term Load Forecasting. In: Zhu, J.J., Fung, G.P.C. (eds.) Forecasting Models: Methods and Applications, pp. 161–178. iConcept Press (2010), http://www.iconceptpress.com/www/site/download.paper.php?paperID=100917020141
7. Bottou, L., Vapnik, V.: Local learning algorithms. Neural Computation 4, 888–900 (1992)
8. Taylor, J.W., Snyder, R.D.: Forecasting Intraday Time Series with Multiple Seasonal Cycles Using Parsimonious Seasonal Exponential Smoothing. Department of Econometrics and Business Statistics Working Paper 9/09, Monash University (2009)
9. Hyndman, R.J., Khandakar, Y.: Automatic Time Series Forecasting: The Forecast Package for R. Journal of Statistical Software 27(3), 1–22 (2008)
10. Hyndman, R.J., Koehler, A.B., Ord, J.K., Snyder, R.D.: Forecasting with Exponential Smoothing: The State Space Approach. Springer (2008)

Reinforcement Learning in Discrete Neural Control of the Underactuated System

Zenon Hendzel, Andrzej Burghardt, and Marcin Szuster

Rzeszow University of Technology
Department of Applied Mechanics and Robotics
8 Powstancow Warszawy St., 35-959 Rzeszow, Poland
{zenhen,andrzejb,mszuster}@prz.edu.pl

Abstract. The article presents a new approach to the problem of a discrete neural control of an underactuated system, using reinforcement learning method to an on-line adaptation of a neural network. The controlled system is of the ball and beam type, which is the nonlinear dynamical object with the number of control signals smaller than the number of degrees of freedom. The main part of the neural control system is the actor-critic structure, that comes under the Neural Dynamic Programming algorithms family, realised in the form of Dual Heuristic Dynamic Programming structure. The control system includes moreover the PD controller and the supervisory therm, derived from the Lyapunov stability theorem, that ensures stability. The proposed neural control system works on-line and does not require a preliminary learning. Computer simulations have been conducted to illustrate the performance of the control system.

Keywords: Ball and Beam System, Dual Heuristic Dynamic Programming, Neural Dynamic Programming, Neural Network, Underactuated System Control, Reinforcement Learning.

1 Introduction

Underactuated systems (US) are included to a group of nonlinear mechanical systems, that have the number of the independent control signals smaller than the number of degrees of freedom. That results in difficulties in formulation of the stable control laws for real systems, where the mathematical object of the controlled system is highly nonlinear or partially unknown. The examples of the US are the ball and beam system [4, 3, 5], a ball on plane system, an inverted pendulum, a cart-pole system [1], a manipulator with elastic joints [12], a overhead trolley crane and a rotary crane [2], a submarine, a surface ship, a helicopter or an aircraft. US are often analysed in the literature, because that type of objects is widely meet in technical solutions of e.g. transportation, and there is no developed an universal control method of them.

The determination of control strategy that forces the US to complete the partly specified motion, is a challenging task, that requires to use of methods based on

L. Rutkowski et al. (Eds.): ICAISC 2013, Part I, LNAI 7894, pp. 64–75, 2013.

system's model knowledge or complex computational algorithms using e.g. artificial intelligence methods like neural networks (NN). The ball and beam system is willingly use to test performance of various control strategies. It consists of a boll rolling on the top of a long beam, that is fixed in a one side, and the second one can be moved using various technical solutions, what changes the angle of the beam rotation and results in motion of the ball. The ball and beam system has one crucial property, unstable open loop. For the fixed input signal (the beam angle) the output of the system (ball position), increases without limits. The problem is to generate the control signal for the actuator causing the beam rotation, that stabilise the ball in the desired position of the beam. There are few methods of control studied in the literature, that solve this problem by linearisation of the controlled system model and applying linear control methods like Proportional Derivative Integral (PID) control strategy as an example of non-model based control strategy or Linear Quadratic Regulator as an example of model based optimal control strategy [8]. Other studies base on the nonlinear model of the ball and beam and apply PD control strategies with compensation of model nonlinearities realised in the form of analytical calculations [14]. Another approaches uses PD controller coupled with algorithms that approximate the object nonlinearities, like model based adaptation algorithm [4] or NN [5], using some simplifications by replacing the classical problem of ball's position regulation, by the tracking control problem of the desired beam's angle computed analytically, that leads to the ball's stabilisation in the desired position. There were also, among other things, successful trails of implementation of Reinforcement Learning (RL) algorithms into US control problems [1, 3], but the learning process of actor-critic structure's NNs was of trial and error type or consists in alternate periodical off-line learning of actor and critic NNs. The presented innovative approach to the beam and ball stabilisation problem uses discrete Neural Dynamic Programming [1, 3, 9–11] method realised in a form of actor-critic structure in Dual Heuristic Dynamic Programming (DHP) configuration, which comes under RL algorithms. The actor's NN weights are adapted on-line, using signals generated by two critic's NNs, on the basis of the assumed value function. The actor generates the suboptimal control law, supported by the control signal of PD controller and the control signal generated by the supervisory term, derived from the Lyapunov stability theorem, that ensures a stability of the closed system loop. The main advantages of the proposed control system are successful stabilisation of the ball on the basis of only known desired position (regulator problem), on-line adaptation of the NNs' weights and lack of the trial and error learning or initial leaning process necessity. Actor and critic structures were realised in the form of the Random Vector Functional Link (RVFL) NNs with random fixed input weights and sigmoidal bipolar activation functions. The research project presented in the article continues authors' earlier works, related to the control of nonlinear systems, using NDP methods in DHP configuration [6, 7] and control of the ball end beam system using model based adaptive algorithm [4] or NN [5]. The article is organised as follows: the first section includes a short introduction to the USs control problems, the second section presents the ball and beam system and formulates its discrete dynamics model.

The third section includes description of the DHP structure and used NNs, the following section presents the control system and stability analysis. The next section shows results of the numerical test, the last section summarises the research project.

2   The Dynamics of the Ball and Beam System

The dynamics of the ball and beam system, schematically shown in Fig. 1, is modelled using Appell's transformation [4, 5] and can be written in the form

$$M(a, q)\ddot{q} + C(a, q, \dot{q})\dot{q} + G(q) + \tau_d(t) = u, \qquad (1)$$

where $q = [d_A\ \varphi]^T$, d_A – the distance between the A point of the ball and the end of the beam, φ – the angle of the beam rotation, $M(a, q)$, $C(a, q, \dot{q})$, $G(q)$ – matrices and vector, that derive from the dynamics of the ball and beam system, $\tau_d(t)$ – the vector of bounded disturbances, u – the control vector, $u = [0\ u_{[2]}]^T$.

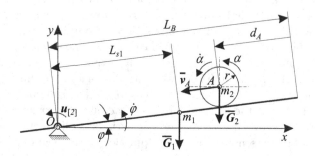

Fig. 1. Scheme of the ball and beam system

Using Euler's derivative approximation and a state vector in a form $z_{\{k\}} = \left[z_{1\{k\}}^T, z_{2\{k\}}^T\right]^T$, where $z_{1\{k\}}$ denotes to continuous vector q, a discrete notation of the ball and beam system's dynamics was obtained in a form

$$
\begin{aligned}
z_{1\{k+1\}} &= z_{1\{k\}} + z_{2\{k\}}h, \\
z_{2\{k+1\}} &= -M^{-1}(a, z_{1\{k\}})\left[C(a, z_{1\{k\}}, z_{2\{k\}})z_{2\{k\}} + G(a, z_{1\{k\}}) + \right. \\
&\quad \left. +\tau_{d\{k\}} - u_{\{k\}}\right]h + z_{2\{k\}},
\end{aligned}
\qquad (2)
$$

where h – a time discretization parameter, k – an index of iteration steps. The control problem of the ball and beam system is defined as searching for the control law, that minimises errors $e_{\{k\}}$ defined in the form

$$e_{1\{k\}} = z_{1\{k\}} - z_{d1\{k\}}, \qquad (3)$$

$$e_{2\{k\}} = z_{2\{k\}} - z_{d2\{k\}}, \qquad (4)$$

where the desire state is equal $z_d = \left[z_1^T, z_{d2}^T\right]^T$ ($z_{\{k\}} \to z_d, k \to \infty$), and the control algorithm remains stable. As long as in the synthesis of the control system is considered problem of the regulator, the desired state is equal $z_d = \left[d_{Ad\{k\}}, 0, 0, 0\right]^T$, where $d_{Ad\{k\}}$ is fixed in desired intervals. The filtered tracking error $s_{\{k\}}$ is defined on the basis of eq. (3) and (4) in the form

$$s_{\{k\}} = e_{2\{k\}} + \Lambda e_{1\{k\}} , \tag{5}$$

where Λ – constant, positive defined diagonal matrix.
On the basis of the ball and beam discrete dynamics model (2) and eq. (3) – (4), the filtered tracking error in step $k + 1$ is defined

$$s_{\{k+1\}} = -Y_f\left(a, z_{\{k\}}\right) + Y_d\left(z_{\{k\}}, z_{d\{k+1\}}\right) - Y_{\tau\{k\}} + M^{-1}\left(a, z_{1\{k\}}\right) h u_{\{k\}} , \tag{6}$$

where

$$
\begin{aligned}
Y_f\left(a, z_{\{k\}}\right) &= M^{-1}\left(a, z_{1\{k\}}\right) h \left[C\left(a, z_{\{k\}}\right) z_{2\{k\}} + G\left(a, z_{1\{k\}}\right)\right] , \\
Y_{\tau\{k\}} &= M^{-1}\left(a, z_{1\{k\}}\right) h \tau_{d\{k\}} , \\
Y_d\left(z_{\{k\}}, z_{d\{k+1\}}\right) &= z_{2\{k\}} - z_{d2\{k+1\}} + \Lambda\left[z_{1\{k\}} + z_{2\{k\}} h - z_{d1\{k+1\}}\right] = \\
z_{2\{k\}} &- z_{d2\{k\}} - z_{d3\{k\}} h + \Lambda\left[z_{1\{k\}} - z_{d1\{k\}} + z_{2\{k\}} h - z_{d2\{k\}} h\right] = \\
s_{\{k\}} &+ Y_e\left(z_{\{k\}}, z_{d\{k\}}, z_{d3\{k\}}\right) , \\
Y_e\left(z_{\{k\}}, z_{d\{k\}}, z_{d3\{k\}}\right) &= \Lambda e_{2\{k\}} h - z_{d3\{k\}} h ,
\end{aligned}
\tag{7}
$$

where $z_{d3\{k\}}$ is the vector of the second difference of $z_{d1\{k\}}$, that derives from the discrete form of the vector $z_{d2\{k+1\}}$. The vector $Y_f\left(a, z_{\{k\}}\right)$ contains all nonlinearities of the ball and beam system.

3 Neural Dynamic Programming Algorithm

NDP algorithms are a group of Forward Dynamic Programming (FDP) methods [9–11], which derives from the Bellman DP idea. It was possible to develop NDP algorithms family, thanks to appearance and rapid expansion in the control theory of NNs, which are able to approximate any nonlinear function with given accuracy. Then, in the early eighties [1], appeared an idea to use NNs to approximate forward the value function from the classical DP, instead of calculating it off-line, before the generated control law was applied to the controlled object. The group of structures derived using this approach was named NDP algorithms, and came under group of RL methods. The NDP algorithms family includes six algorithms [11] of which we had selected one and implemented it into the demanding ball and beam control task. The method of NNs weights adaptation using so called "learning with a critic", or RL, is very effective and gives positive results in complex control tasks, where other methods are not applicable.

The objective of the applied DHP algorithm in the proposed control system is to determine the sub-optimal control law, that minimises the value function

$V\left(s_{\{k\}}, u_{\{k\}}\right)$ [9–11], which is the function of the state $s_{\{k\}}$ and the control $u_{\{k\}}$ in a general case

$$V_{\{k\}}\left(s_{\{k\}}, u_{\{k\}}\right) = \sum_{k=0}^{N} \gamma^{k} L_{C\{k\}}\left(s_{\{k\}}, u_{\{k\}}\right), \qquad (8)$$

where N – the last step of the finite discrete process, γ – a discount factor $(0 \le \gamma \le 1)$, $L_{C}\left(s_{\{k\}}, u_{\{k\}}\right)$ – the local cost function in the step k.
The local cost function was assumed in the form

$$L_{C\{k\}}\left(s_{\{k\}}, u_{\{k\}}\right) = \tfrac{1}{2} s_{\{k\}}^{T} R s_{\{k\}} + \tfrac{1}{2} u_{\{k\}}^{T} Q u_{\{k\}}, \qquad (9)$$

where R, Q – the positive defined diagonal matrices.

The NDP algorithm in DHP configuration is schematically shown in Fig. 2.

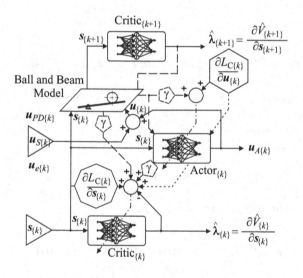

Fig. 2. Scheme of the DHP structure

It consists of the predictive model of the plant and two parametric structures realised in the form of NNs:

- critic – in the DHP algorithm estimates the derivative of the value function eq. (8) in respect to the state vector. The value function depends on the two elementary state vector $s_{\{k\}}$, so its derivative according to the state takes the form

$$\lambda_{\{k\}} = \begin{bmatrix} \dfrac{\partial V_{\{k\}}}{\partial s_{[1]\{k\}}} \\ \dfrac{\partial V_{\{k\}}}{\partial s_{[2]\{k\}}} \end{bmatrix}, \qquad (10)$$

what results in realisation of the critic in the form of two RVFL NNs

$$\hat{\lambda}_{[j]\{k,l\}}\left(\boldsymbol{x}_{Cj\{k\}},\boldsymbol{W}_{Cj\{k,l\}}\right)=\boldsymbol{W}_{Cj\{k,l\}}^{T}\boldsymbol{S}\left(\boldsymbol{D}_{C}^{T}\boldsymbol{x}_{Cj\{k\}}\right),\qquad(11)$$

where $j=1,2$, l – an index of the internal loop iteration, $\boldsymbol{W}_{Cj\{k,l\}}$ – the vector of output weights of j-th critic's NN, $\boldsymbol{x}_{Cj\{k\}}=\boldsymbol{\kappa}_{C}\left[1,s_{[j]\{k\}}\right]^{T}$ – the input vector of the j-th critic's NN, $\boldsymbol{\kappa}_{C}$ – constant diagonal matrix of positive input scaling coefficients, $\boldsymbol{S}\left(\boldsymbol{D}_{C}^{T}\boldsymbol{x}_{Cj\{k\}}\right)$ – the vector of sigmoidal bipolar neurons activation functions, $\boldsymbol{D}_{C}$ – the matrix of fixed input weights selected randomly in the NN initialization process. Critics' weights are adapted by the gradient method of the quality ratings built on the basis of the Temporal Difference errors, defined in the form

$$e_{C\{k,l\}}=\frac{\partial L_{C\{k\}}\left(s_{\{k\}}\right)}{\partial s_{\{k\}}}+\frac{\partial u_{\{k\}}}{\partial s_{\{k\}}}\frac{\partial L_{C\{k\}}\left(s_{\{k\}}\right)}{\partial u_{\{k\}}}+\qquad(12)$$
$$+\gamma\left[\frac{\partial s_{\{k+1\}}}{\partial s_{\{k\}}}+\frac{\partial u_{\{k\}}}{\partial s_{\{k\}}}\frac{\partial s_{\{k+1\}}}{\partial u_{\{k\}}}\right]\hat{\lambda}_{\{k+1\}}\left(\boldsymbol{x}_{Cj\{k+1\}},\boldsymbol{W}_{Cj\{k,l\}}\right)+$$
$$-\hat{\lambda}_{Cj\{k\}}\left(\boldsymbol{x}_{Cj\{k\}},\boldsymbol{W}_{Cj\{k,l\}}\right),$$

where $s_{\{k+1\}}$ derives from the predictive model of the ball and beam

$$s_{\{k+1\}}=-\boldsymbol{Y}_{f}\left(\boldsymbol{a},\boldsymbol{z}_{\{k\}}\right)+\boldsymbol{Y}_{d}\left(\boldsymbol{z}_{\{k\}},\boldsymbol{z}_{d\{k\}},\boldsymbol{z}_{3d\{k\}}\right)+\boldsymbol{M}^{-1}\left(\boldsymbol{a},\boldsymbol{z}_{1\{k\}}\right)h u_{\{k\}}.\qquad(13)$$

Critic's weights are adapted according to equation

$$\boldsymbol{W}_{Cj\{k,l+1\}}=\boldsymbol{W}_{Cj\{k,l\}}-\boldsymbol{\Gamma}_{A}e_{C[j]\{k\}}\boldsymbol{S}\left(\boldsymbol{D}_{C}^{T}\boldsymbol{x}_{Cj\{k\}}\right),\qquad(14)$$

where $\boldsymbol{\Gamma}_{C}$ – a positive defined diagonal matrix of NNs' adaptation rates.
– actor – generates the sub-optimal control law for the ball and beam system. The control object is an underactuated system, and there is only one control signal accessible, because of that the actor is realised in the form of one RVFL NN

$$u_{A\{k,l\}}\left(\boldsymbol{x}_{A\{k\}},\boldsymbol{W}_{A\{k,l\}}\right)=\boldsymbol{W}_{A\{k,l\}}^{T}\boldsymbol{S}\left(\boldsymbol{D}_{A}^{T}\boldsymbol{x}_{A\{k\}}\right),\qquad(15)$$

where $\boldsymbol{W}_{A\{k,l\}}$ – the vector of output weights of the actor's NN, $\boldsymbol{x}_{A\{k\}}$ – the input vector to the actor's NN, that consists of scaled values as the state of the closed system loop $s_{\{k\}}$, errors $e_{\{k\}}$, desired $z_{d\{k\}}$ and realised $z_{\{k\}}$ state values, $\boldsymbol{D}_{A}$ – the matrix of fixed input weights selected randomly in the NN initialization process. Scheme of the actor RVFL NN is shown in Fig. 3. Actor's weights are adapted using gradient method of the quality rating defined in the form

$$e_{A\{k,l\}}=\frac{\partial L_{C\{k\}}\left(s_{\{k\}}\right)}{\partial u_{\{k\}}}+\gamma\frac{\partial s_{\{k+1\}}}{\partial u_{\{k\}}}\hat{\lambda}_{\{k+1,l\}}\left(\boldsymbol{x}_{C\{k+1\}},\boldsymbol{W}_{C\{k,l\}}\right),\qquad(16)$$

according to equation similar to eq. (14).

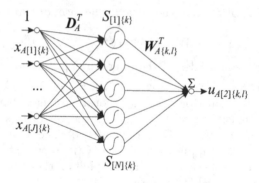

Fig. 3. Scheme of the RVFL NN

Interesting future of the NDP algorithms is adaptation process of NNs' weights. It is realised in a form of internal loop with iteration index l. In every k-th step of the discrete control process, there are executed calculation connected to actor's and critic's weights adaptation, according to conception shown in Fig. 4.

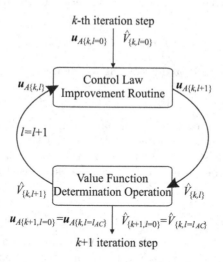

Fig. 4. Conception of the NDP structure adaptation process

At the beginning of the k-th iteration step $l = 0$. On the basis of available information, actor NN's weights are adapted according to assumed adaptation law by minimisation of the error rate (16). This part of the algorithm is called "Control Law Improvement Routine" [11], it leads to enumerate values of the actor NN ($W_{A\{k,l+1\}}$). The next step is called "Value Function Determination Operation", it consist in adaptation of critic's weights, according to assumed adaptation law, by minimisation of the error rate (12) based on the Temporal

Difference errors. It leads to calculation of $\boldsymbol{W}_{Cj\{k,l+1\}}$. Then internal loop iteration index l is increased and next cycle of the NDP structure internal loop adaptation starts. The internal loop is break, when quality rating $e_{A\{k,l\}}$ (16) is smaller than assumed boundary ($e_{A\{k,l\}} < \boldsymbol{E}_A$, $\boldsymbol{E}_A$ – a positive constant), or $l \geq l_{AC}$, where l_{AC} - is assumed maximal number of internal loop iteration cycles. After matching one of this conditions, $\boldsymbol{W}_{A\{k,l+1\}}$ becomes $\boldsymbol{W}_{A\{k+1,l\}}$, $\boldsymbol{W}_{Cj\{k,l+1\}}$ becomes $\boldsymbol{W}_{Cj\{k+1,l\}}$. After that index k is increased, actor generates control signal and receives information about a new state.

4 Stability Analysis

The presented control system consists of actor-critic structure, that generates the control signal $\boldsymbol{u}_{A\{k\}}$, the PD controller with control signal $\boldsymbol{u}_{PD\{k\}}$, the supervisory term, derived using Lyapunov stability theorem ($\boldsymbol{u}_{S\{k\}}$), and the additional control signal $\boldsymbol{u}_{e\{k\}}$, that derives from the discretization of the ball and beam model process. The scheme of the proposed control system with DHP actor–critic structure is shown in Fig. 5. The overall control signal is assumed in the form

$$\boldsymbol{u}_{\{k\}} = \frac{1}{h}\boldsymbol{M}\left(\boldsymbol{a}, \boldsymbol{z}_{1\{k\}}\right)\left\{-\boldsymbol{u}_{A\{k\}} + \boldsymbol{I}^*\boldsymbol{u}_{S\{k\}} - \boldsymbol{u}_{PD\{k\}} - \boldsymbol{u}_e\left(\boldsymbol{z}_{\{k\}}, \boldsymbol{z}_{d\{k\}}, \boldsymbol{z}_{d3\{k\}}\right)\right\},$$
(17)

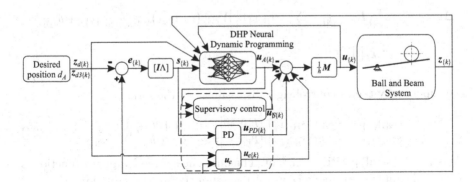

Fig. 5. Scheme of the neural control system with DHP structure

where particular control signals and matrices take the form

$$\boldsymbol{u}_{PD\{k\}} = \boldsymbol{K}_D\,\boldsymbol{s}_{\{k\}}\,,$$
$$\boldsymbol{K}_D = \begin{bmatrix} 0 & 0 \\ K_{D[2,1]} & K_{D[2,2]} \end{bmatrix},$$
$$\boldsymbol{I}_S^* = \begin{bmatrix} 0 & 0 \\ I_{S[2,1]}^* & I_{S[2,2]}^* \end{bmatrix},$$
$$\boldsymbol{u}_{e\{k\}} = \left[\boldsymbol{\Lambda}\boldsymbol{e}_{2\{k\}}h - z_{d3\{k\}}h\right]^T [0\ 1]^T\,,$$
(18)

and $\boldsymbol{u}_{S\{k\}} = \left[u_{S[1]\{k\}} \ u_{S[2]\{k\}}\right]^T$, $\boldsymbol{u}_{e\{k\}} = \left[0 \ u_{e[2]\{k\}}\right]^T$, $\boldsymbol{K}_D$ – the fixed matrix of the PD controller gains, $\boldsymbol{I}_S^*$ – the matrix of the supervisory control term, $I_{S[2,j]}^* = 1$ for $\left|s_{[j]\{k\}}\right| \geq \phi_{[j]}$ and $I_{S[2,j]}^* = 0$ when $\left|s_{[j]\{k\}}\right| < \phi_{[j]}$, $\phi_{[j]}$ – a constant, $j = 1, 2$. For $I_{S[2,j]}^* = 1$, and (17) inserted into (6), we obtain

$$\boldsymbol{s}_{\{k+1\}} = \boldsymbol{s}_{\{k\}} - \boldsymbol{Y}_f\left(\boldsymbol{a}, \boldsymbol{z}_{\{k\}}\right) - \boldsymbol{Y}_{\tau\{k\}} - \boldsymbol{u}_{A\{k\}} + \boldsymbol{I}_S^*\boldsymbol{u}_{S\{k\}} - \boldsymbol{u}_{PD\{k\}} \ . \quad (19)$$

Let us assume the positive definite Lyapunov candidate function

$$L = \frac{1}{2}\boldsymbol{s}^T \boldsymbol{s} \ , \quad (20)$$

its derivative can by discretised and assume in the form

$$\Delta L_{\{k\}} = \boldsymbol{s}_{\{k\}}^T \left[\boldsymbol{s}_{\{k+1\}} - \boldsymbol{s}_{\{k\}}\right] \ . \quad (21)$$

Substituting (19) into (21) we obtain

$$\Delta L_{\{k\}} = \boldsymbol{s}_{\{k\}}^T \left[-\boldsymbol{Y}_f\left(\boldsymbol{a}, \boldsymbol{z}_{\{k\}}\right) + \left[Y_{e[1]\{k\}} \ 0\right]^T - \boldsymbol{Y}_{\tau\{k\}}+ \right.$$
$$\left. -\boldsymbol{u}_{A\{k\}} + \boldsymbol{I}_S^*\boldsymbol{u}_{S\{k\}} - \boldsymbol{u}_{PD\{k\}}\right] \ . \quad (22)$$

For the vector of disturbances bounded to $\boldsymbol{Y}_{\tau\{k\}} < b_{d[j]}$, where $b_{d[j]}$ – positive constant, the difference of the Lyapunov candidate takes the form

$$\Delta L_{\{k\}} \leq -\boldsymbol{s}_{\{k\}}^T \boldsymbol{K}_D \boldsymbol{s}_{\{k\}} + \sum_{j=1}^{2} \left|s_{[j]\{k\}}\right| \left[\left|Y_{f[j]}\left(\boldsymbol{a}, \boldsymbol{z}_{\{k\}}\right)\right| + \left|u_{A[j]\{k\}}\right| + b_{d[j]}\right]$$
$$+ \left|s_{[1]\{k\}}\right| \left|Y_{e[1]\{k\}}\right| + \sum_{j=1}^{2} s_{[j]\{k\}} u_{S[j]\{k\}} \ . $$
$$(23)$$

The supervisory therm control signal is assumed in the form

$$u_{S[1]\{k\}} = -\text{sgn}\left(s_{[1]\{k\}}\right) \left[F_{[1]} + \left|Y_{e[1]\{k\}}\right| + b_{d[1]} + \eta_{[1]}\right] \ ,$$
$$u_{S[2]\{k\}} = -\text{sgn}\left(s_{[2]\{k\}}\right) \left[F_{[2]} + \left|u_{A[2]\{k\}}\right| + b_{d[2]}\right] + \eta_{[2]} \ , \quad (24)$$

where $\eta_{[j]}$ – a small positive constant. The difference of the Lyapunov function is negative definite. The designed control algorithm guarantees reduction of $\left|s_{[j]\{k\}}\right|$ for $\left|s_{[j]\{k\}}\right| \geq \phi_{[j]}$. For initial condition $\left|s_{[j]\{k=0\}}\right| < \phi_{[j]}$ we get $\left|s_{[j]\{k\}}\right| < \phi_{[j]}$ for $\forall k \geq 0$, $j = 1, 2$.

5   Results of the Numerical Test

The numerical test of the proposed neural control system was performed using Matlab/Simulink software simulation environment. In this section, for the sake of simplicity, index k is omitted and the time discretisation parameter $h=0.01$ [s]. The objective of the control system was to stabilise the ball in the require position, where the vector of the desired state of the ball and beam system was $z_d = [d_{Ad}, 0, 0, 0]^T$, and the ball's desired position $d_{Ad} = 0.0$ [m] for $t \in <0, 20)$ [s], $d_{Ad} = 0.7$ [m] for $t \in <20, 40)$ [s], $d_{Ad} = 0.5$ [m] for $t \in <40, 60)$ [s], $d_{Ad} = 0.15$ [m] for $t \in <60, 80)$ [s], $d_{Ad} = 0.4$ [m] for $t \in <80, 100)$ [s]. The initial position of the ball was equal $d_A = 0.1$ [m], and the initial angle of the beam rotation $\varphi = 0$ [rad], for $t = 0$ [s].

According to the assumed control law (17), the overall control signal $u_{[2]}$, shown in Fig. 8.a), consists of the actor's NN control signal $u_{A[2]}$, Fig. 8.b), the PD control signal, Fig. 8.c), the supervisory term's control signal and the control signal $u_{e[2]}$, both in Fig. 8.d). The actor's NN weights are adapted fast, because of its method of RL in the inner loop of the algorithm, what cause, that the actor's NN control signal takes the dominant part in the overall control signal. The values of the PD control signal and other additional control signals are small in the comparison to the actor's control signal. Its values increase temporarily only when the disturbances occur (the change of the desired ball's position). Peak values of signals presented in figures are caused by a discrete changes of the $z_{d1[1]}$, what tends to high values of its derivative, it could be easily eliminated by a fluent change of this value, but it would change the problem's conditions.

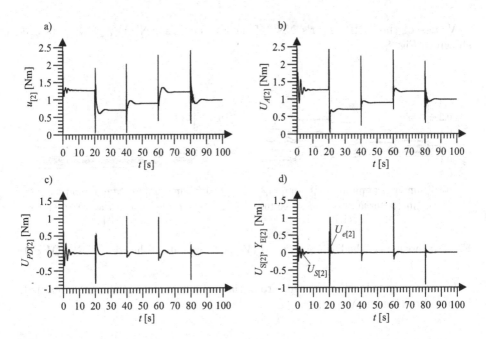

Fig. 6. a) The overall control signal $u_{[2]}$, b) the actor's NN control signal $U_{A[2]}$, $U_A = -\frac{1}{h}M^{-1}u_A$, b) the PD control signal $U_{PD[2]}$, $U_{PD} = -\frac{1}{h}M^{-1}K_D s$, d) the supervisory term's control signal $U_{S[2]}$, $U_S = -\frac{1}{h}M^{-1}I_S^* u_S$ and the control signal $U_{e[2]}$, $U_e = -\frac{1}{h}M^{-1}u_e$

The desired $(z_{d1[1]})$ and realised $(z_{1[1]})$ positions of the ball are shown in Fig. 7.a), the desired $(z_{d1[2]} = 0)$ and realised $(z_{1[2]})$ angles of the beam's turn are shown in Fig. 7.b). The ball's position, after some stabilisation time, pursues its desired value.

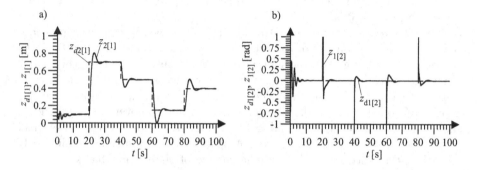

Fig. 7. a) Desired $(z_{d1[1]}$ - dashed line) and realised $(z_{1[1]}$ - continuous line) position of the ball, b) desired $(z_{d1[2]} = 0$ - dashed line) and realised $(z_{1[2]}$ - continuous line) angle of the beam rotation.

Values of the DHP actor's NN $(\boldsymbol{W}_A)$ and critic's NN $(\boldsymbol{W}_{C2})$ weights are shown in Fig. 8.

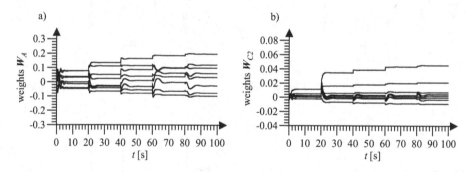

Fig. 8. a) weights of the DHP actor's NN $(\boldsymbol{W}_A)$, b) weights of the critic's 2 NN $(\boldsymbol{W}_{C2})$

In the numerical test were used zero initial weights. Values of weights remained bounded during the test.

6   Conclusion

We proposed the discrete neural control system for the ball stabilisation with NDP structure in DHP configuration. The presented control algorithm consists of the actor-critic structure, realised in form of RVFL NNs, the PD controller and the supervisory term, which ensures stability of the control process.

The proposed control system presents new approach to the ball and beam stabilisation problem, where NNs' weights learning process uses idea of RL, it proceeds on-line, and thanks to a method of weights adaptation in the internal loop, it boosts learning process, prevents to time consuming trial end error learning and exclude necessity of the preliminary learning. The numerical test pointed out performance of the proposed solution, even with the worst case of learning process with zero initial output-layer weights of NNs, what is especially important taking into account specific of the controlled US. The proposed control system with NDP algorithm is stable, values of errors and weights of NNs are bounded.

References

1. Barto, A.G., Sutton, R.S., Anderson, C.W.: Neuronlike Adaptive Elements that Can Solve Difficult Learning Control Problems. IEEE Transactions on Systems, Man and Cybernetics 13, 834–846 (1983)
2. Blajer, W., Kolodziejczyk, K.: Contol of Underactuated Mechanical Systems with Servo-Constraints. Nonlinear Dynamics 50, 781–791 (2007)
3. Eaton, P.H., Prokhorov, D.V., Wunsch, D.C.: Neurocontroller Alternatives for Fuzzy Ball-and-Beam Systems With Nonuniform Nonlinear Friction. IEEE Transactions on Neural Networks and Learning Systems 11, 423–435 (2000)
4. Burghardt, A., Giergiel, J.: Modelling and Control of an Underactuated Sphere and Beam System. Communications in Nonlinear Science and Numerical Simulation 16, 2350–2354 (2011)
5. Hendzel, Z., Burghardt, A.: Adaptive Neural Network Control of Underactuated System. In: 4th International Conference on Neural Computation Theory and Applications, pp. 505–509. SciTePress, Barcelona (2012)
6. Hendzel, Z., Szuster, M.: Discrete Model-Based Dual Heuristic Programming in Wheeled Mobile Robot Control. In: 10th International Conference on Dynamical Systems - Theory and Applications, Lodz, pp. 745–752 (2009)
7. Hendzel, Z., Szuster, M.: Discrete Model-Based Adaptive Critic Designs in Wheeled Mobile Robot Control. In: Rutkowski, L., Scherer, R., Tadeusiewicz, R., Zadeh, L.A., Zurada, J.M. (eds.) ICAISC 2010, Part II. LNCS (LNAI), vol. 6114, pp. 264–271. Springer, Heidelberg (2010)
8. Keshmiri, M., Jahromi, A.F., Mohebbi, A., Amoozgar, M.H., Xie, W.F.: Modeling and Control of Ball and Beam System Using Model Based and Non-model Based Control Approaches. International Journal on Smart Sensing and Intelligent Systems 5, 14–35 (2012)
9. Powell, W.B.: Approximate Dynamic Programming: Solving the Curses of Dimensionality. Wiley Interscience, Princeton (2007)
10. Prokhorov, D., Wunch, D.: Adaptive Critic Designs. IEEE Transactions on Neural Networks 8, 997–1007 (1997)
11. Si, J., Barto, A.G., Powell, W.B., Wunsch, D.: Handbook of Learning and Approximate Dynamic Programming. IEEE Press, Wiley-Interscience (2004)
12. Spong, M.W.: Modeling and control of elastic joint robot. Journal of Dynamic Systems, Measurement, and Control 109, 310–319 (1987)
13. Spong, M.W.: Underactuated Mechanical Systems. In: Siciliano, B., Valavanis, K.P. (eds.) Control Problems in Robotics and Automation. LNCIS, vol. 230, pp. 135–150. Springer, Heidelberg (1998)
14. Wen, Y.: Nonlinear PD Regulation for Ball and Beam System. International Journal of Electrical Engineering Education 46, 59–73 (2009)

Associative Text Representation and Correction

Adrian Horzyk and Marcin Gadamer

AGH University of Science and Technology, Automatics and Biomedicine Engineering
Department, 30-059 Cracow, Mickiewicza Av. 30, Poland
{horzyk,gadamer}@agh.edu.pl

Abstract. Linguistic communication takes a major role in human communication and information exchange. Information is usually transferred in a text form - sentences. Text descriptions allow us define new terms, gather knowledge and learn more quickly thanks to the associative mechanisms that work in our brains. Automatic and intelligent text processing and compression are very important nowadays. This paper introduces a novelty associative way of storing, compressing and processing sentences. This paper describes an associative linguistic habit neural graphs (AL-HNG) that are able to store and activate various important associative relations between letters and words simultaneously in many sentences. These graphs enable us to semi-automatically define various terms and contextually process text corrections after the knowledge collected from previously read texts. The ALHNG construction has a linear computational complexity. The association and triggering interconnected elements in any given context have a constant computational complexity. It also compresses sentences in a very effective way.

Keywords: linguistic habit graphs, associative linguistic habit neural graphs, associative neurocomputation, text compression, associative artificial intelligence AAI, bio-inspired techniques for text mining.

1 Introduction

Information is crucial for the World today, due to the fact that it enables interconnection and development. Various relations of objects and actions can be better used thanks to the flow of information. Information exchange let us to join and cooperate more effectively. Knowledge of individuals also rapidly increases as a result of a faster information exchange [11]. Information can be transferred by various media and in various forms: texts, pictures, images, movies, sounds, voice, music, touches, smells, tastes etc. Not all media can transmit information quickly or to a long distance. Not all information are precise and unambiguous. Information reception and interpretation strongly depend on the recipient's reception abilities and his actual knowledge [5]. Knowledge is a product of association and memorizing abilities of biological brains. Information is triggered off by other previously incoming information and its context. The context can be divided into external (coming from actions in space and time in the immediate past and present) and internal (coming from individual association and

L. Rutkowski et al. (Eds.): ICAISC 2013, Part I, LNAI 7894, pp. 76–87, 2013.

knowledge). Every individual builds up his own knowledge and contexts for the next associations during his lifetime. The actual knowledge of each individual strongly determines how new incoming data will be associated and interpreted. Many misunderstandings comes from a different knowledge (learned facts and relations or memorized experiences) and variously formed associations in brains of various individuals [6].

The human brain is an unbelievably effective computational mechanism. Its neurons fire up at the most several dozen times a second solving uneasy computational tasks. There is no time and no place for nested loops and other time consuming classic algorithms and computational techniques known from today computer science. Nowadays algorithms spend a vast amount of time on searching through various data collections. Data in these collections are poorly interconnected with each other and cannot actively interact, therefore it is necessary to use various searching algorithms and data transformations to obtain some pieces of information from such collections. The strategy of the biological brains differs considerably in the mechanism of data connection, storing and searching techniques. There is approximately a few thousand connections for each neuron on average. As a matter of fact, sagacious or talented people in general have even more connections in some parts of their brains. It means that the connections play a major role in thinking, intelligence and also in data processing. These connections are not accidental but they reflect important relations between neurons and these what they represent. The richness of connections within the brain is able to interconnect many related data and their combinations. Precious time is not lost for searching and looping. Thanks to this rich interconnection network, the brain can be very effective in computation and unbelievably fast in solving intricate tasks that are computationally or numerically unsolvable or hardly solvable using classical computational techniques because of the high computational complexity of searching algorithms and techniques that secondary try to find data relations instead of activation of previously memorized relations and their strength. The brains not only memorize these relations but also allow the data to automatically and autonomously activate them in given external and knowledge based internal contexts.

This paper focuses on a specialized graph constructions that is able to reflect, memorize and weigh natural relations between letters and words in human languages. The natural letter and word order is used to construct a neural graph that is able to associate and memorize the natural human linguistic habits. They can learn from texts written by people and transform the information of orders, frequencies and contexts into the graph structure and its labels and weights. Moreover, each vertex in this graph is active as well as each neuron in a biological brain. The active graph vertexes - called here neurons - and edges - called here connections - are used to represent and then to recall the order and contextual dependencies between letters and words in corrected texts. There is used a biological technique for text mining, defining of various terms and for text corrections.

This paper introduces a novelty Associative Linguistic Habit Neural Graphs (ALHNG) that are able to gather linguistic habits of many individuals and use them to define terms of a language, interconnect them in a way people do, show and trigger off the most probable following words in a given context and help to semi-automatically correct mistakes in texts. This neural graph represents many active connections between letters and words of a given language that can be automatically triggered off as a result of activation of any combination of other neurons representing a given phrase of the internal context. The ALHNG graph obtains information from texts that have been written by people and learns. There is a possibility to build up the graph also for an individual person and use it to recognize if a given text has been written by a person. Nevertheless, the main goal of this paper is to demonstrate the use of this graph for a semi-automatic text correction.

Currently, there are used various dictionaries, Levenstein metric and some grammatical rules for text correction by most of the word processors [8] [12]. There are many approaches and mechanisms in order to collect and store this information. Language models based on n-grams of words (also enriched with POS tags) are well known for more than 20 years and used for speech recognition, machine translation and automatic text tagging [1], [4], [9]. There are many other approaches how to construct models to the analysis of the text, such as: mentioned before n-grams, formal and transaction grammar, rule-based systems [10], corpus-driven methods [7] etc.

Today, the text analysis is not deep as well as advanced to detect many linguistic mistakes and misused words. Nowadays, text processors and even search engines that try to correct a text which is filled with mistakes, are only able to suggest separated words or phrases. They are usually unable to suggest the word order, more likely or used words or phrases in a given context of other words. Moreover, if the analysed word is found in the dictionary a correction is usually not suggested at all even if the analysed word is completely mistaken in a given context. To find out better solution to the text correction problem there have to be used a kind of knowledge that would be able to determine and suggest what words or phrases should probably be written in a given context. There are too many combinations of word orders and many contexts in order to store and analyse them when using classical text algorithms and databases. It would take too much time, memory space and other computational resources to be attractive to mass users.

Our research is focused on an attempt to use the existing texts in order to build algorithms which will be able to find out and process as many relations between words as possible using specialized associative graphs. Furthermore, important relations between words in any sentence can be quickly checked in the known context as well as being used for correcting inappropriate word uses. That can be used for a correction of inappropriate word uses. A construction of the maximum extended and general Associative Linguistic Habit Neural Graph (ALHNG) for English and Polish language has been undertaken to realize this goal. The ALHNG is built on the basis of many text corpora from various sources.

The intelligent semi-automatic text correction is one of the common, important and practical problem that can be satisfactorily solved by the ALHNG graphs. This graph is rather insufficient, however, it can aid the writer to find out various mistakes in the text. It can also suggest various options of correction in the context of other words in the sentence he wrote. Moreover, the various suggested options are weighted by the frequency of their uses by other people in the past and by a given context of the other words in the analysed sentences. Thanks to the associative connections in this graph, the checking process and determining the subgraph of the most probable corrections are always available in the constant computational complexity. Therefore it is possible to use this solution even on powerless computers and mobile phones if this graph only fits in the RAM memory.

2   Text Storing, Representation and Compression

Nowadays, many methods and algorithms for text processing and compression are known. Texts can be stored in arrays, lists, streams, files and as a part of some objects and classes. A huge amount of texts and other data are stored usually in databases. Databases relations and scripting languages make it possible to emphasize, select or mark some parts of texts and combine them. Some selected parts of texts can be also related to each other or hyper-textually connected. The number of related parts of texts are far less than the average number of connections between biological neurons.

Various parts of texts represent objects, properties, actions etc. They are connected by its neighbourhood and proximity in texts. Reading texts can influence the context of our thinking, therefore modifying it and triggering off associated and memorized data that can usually form some parts of information. The main goal of texts is triggering off associations in our brains. It lets the brain change its context of thinking, learn or notice something new or important. Some parts of texts can be more significant than the others. A stream of text can be also produced during associative processes that take place in our brains. They reflect the most significant associations in a given context of thinking. The brains do not make all pieces of information available at any time. The information can be retrieved only by triggering it by a suitable context in associative processes. Texts can be produced as a dynamic product of associative processes that have been triggered in the brain in a given context. Brains have no stocks of memory, no table nor list structures where texts can be stored in a way they are stored in computer RAM or other memory or storage media. Today computer memories are passive, i.e. data are only stored but they are autonomously unable to actively influence other data. This strategy is fundamentally justified by nowadays computational methodologies and computer constructions where only algorithms in a form of computer programs can read, evaluate, modify data, write and store results of computations in various kinds of such passive memories. Data could influence each other and modify themselves aside from a program processing in the today computational methodologies. Otherwise, the programs could not by able to find appropriate data and their algorithmically determinate logic and routines could be confused, destroyed and unable to further run. All data are fully under the control of programs and algorithms in classical computer science.

Brains have no such computational strategies, no fixed programs of solving tasks, no permanently stored data and their relations. They let data and their discriminative combinations to interconnect and actively influence. The strength of such connections can be dynamically modified by incoming data all the time. Synaptic biochemical mechanisms make it possible to quickly and temporarily change the influence of connected neurons in order to quickly and temporarily store some new relations. Neurons can trigger genetic programs and activate various plasticity processes that lead to change or create new connections, change the discrimination threshold or input combinations they are sensitive to. Each neuron represents and discriminates some combinations of inputs but this definition can change in time. Together with changes in neurons, associations and computational results of the whole network change as well. We can state that the whole brain program still dynamically slightly changes during all thinking processes and after the influence of incoming data combinations. There is no certainty for associative programs or memorized data combination permanence or stability. Thanks this active associative mechanism our brains are flexible about learning, tuning and adapting to changing situation however at the cost of limited memorizing and recalling abilities. The major goal of thinking is to find out valuable associated information for a given task and context on a basis of the individual knowledge that has been formed after incoming data and information in the past.

The introduced ALHNG graph does not reflect all biological features so it is able to be stable and permanent development which increases its associative abilities suitable to the amount of read texts and their transformation into its inner structure and parameters. This graph is an aggregated representation of read sentences. The graph contains information about the frequencies and authenticity of word orders in the read texts. The connections between neurons represent various level of the backward contexts for all represented words. The neurons of this graph can be externally activated in various combinations and time sequence triggering off other connected neurons with various intensity suggesting the next possibly words for the given context of externally activated neurons. Each inflectionally different word is represented exactly as the ones in this graph. Moreover, each word is represented as a letter sequence and these sequences are partially shared by various similar words. The relations and order of words are represented by various levels of weighted connections. The representation cost is low and the compression rate is high. Furthermore, such representation lets us to get all possible word successors in a constant computational complexity. Finally, we can quickly get information about all similar and related words and use them to semi-automatically define any word or word sequence represented in this graph after all read texts.

3   ALHNG Neural Network Construction

The ALHNG is a kind of neural network that has a graph structure. It consists of neurons (graph vertixes) that represent letters, apostrophes and some special neurons that lead to the first letters of words (word start neuron) and to the first words of sentences (sentence start neuron). The graph structure of this neural network is constructed a few times during the readings of the text corpora. All read words are segmented into separate letters and transformed into letter neurons that are interconnected in the way that reflects the sequence of letters in these words (Fig. 1). The same letter can be represented by a few letter neurons but in various context of various words. The letter neurons are not duplicated in the same contexts of the same previous sequences of letter neurons. In this case, only the weight of existing connections are incremented by one. Each word consisting of letters and sometimes an apostrophe is represented by an interconnected sequence of letter neurons. The letter neuron representing the last letter in the given word is also called the word neuron. The word neurons are secondary interconnected in many ways to reflect word orders and previous word contexts in read sentences. Each word is represented exactly by a single word neuron in this graph. Various inflectional forms are treated as various words and are represented by various word neurons. The representation of any word in this graph is never duplicated. The word neurons are marked grey in Fig. 1 and 2. The letter tree is a very thrifty way for representing many words and their same initial letters. The thrift of such representation grows with a number of represented words. The similar words are closely related by the same initial letters. Each word neuron can be reached in a constant computational complexity. Usually all inflectional forms can be simple and quickly retrieved.

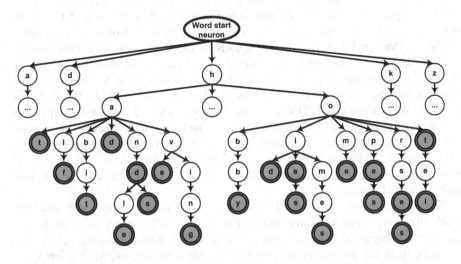

Fig. 1. The very small piece of the ALHNG neural network structure showing the letter neuron tree with connections reflecting letter sequences in the selected words

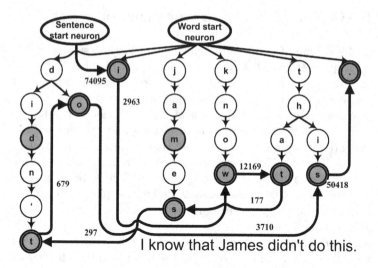

Fig. 2. The small piece of the ALHNG neural network structure with interconnections between the following words in the presented sentence

The main strength of ALHNG is at the connections between the word neurons. The word neurons are interconnected by ASEQ and ACON connections, where ASEQ means an associative sequence and ACON means an associative context. First of all, the word neurons are naturally ASEQ connected after the sequences words from read sentences of the text corpora (Fig. 2). All connections (edges of the graph) are direct and weighted by the frequency of these word sequences. To unambiguously read sentences using this graph, it is necessary to add some extra context connections (ACON) interconnecting previous words with the next word to explicitly point out the next word in the read sequence and the given word order. The associative context connections are added only if the context of the previous word neuron is ambiguous to determine which neuron should be activated next in the context of the previously activated word neurons after the read text corpora. Figure 2 shows the ASEQ connections between the word neurons for the sample sentence: "I know that James didn't do this." Extra contextual connections (ACON) of various levels depend on other word sequences in the other sentences of given text corpora. The bigger text corpora is the more contextual connections are necessary. The thrift of such representation also grows with a number of represented sentences. Figure 3 shows how the number of contextual connections changes in the reference to the number or words and sentences in the text corpora.

Figure 4 shows up six selected steps of ALHNG network construction where gradually new connections are added. First, the ASEQ connections are added for each word sequence after the read sentences. These connections join together words in their natural sequence in which they are in sequences. After a few steps some word sequences become ambiguous in this graph topology, therefore the next contextual connections should be added. If an ambiguous process occurs,

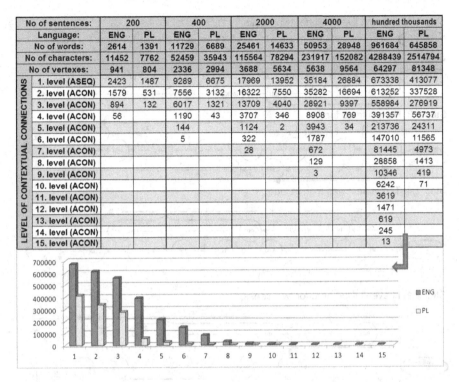

No of sentences:	200		400		2000		4000		hundred thousands	
Language:	ENG	PL	ENG	PL	ENG	PL	ENG	PL	ENG	PL
No of words:	2614	1391	11729	6689	25461	14633	50953	28948	961684	645858
No of characters:	11452	7762	52459	35943	115564	78294	231917	152082	4288439	2514794
No of vertexes:	941	804	2336	2994	3688	5634	5638	9564	64297	81348
1. level (ASEQ)	2423	1487	9289	6675	17969	13952	35184	26884	673338	413077
2. level (ACON)	1579	531	7556	3132	16322	7550	35282	16694	613252	337528
3. level (ACON)	894	132	6017	1321	13709	4040	28921	9397	558984	276919
4. level (ACON)	56		1190	43	3707	346	8908	769	391357	56737
5. level (ACON)			144		1124	2	3943	34	213736	24311
6. level (ACON)			5		322		1787		147010	11565
7. level (ACON)					28		672		81445	4973
8. level (ACON)							129		28858	1413
9. level (ACON)							3		10346	419
10. level (ACON)									6242	71
11. level (ACON)									3619	
12. level (ACON)									1471	
13. level (ACON)									619	
14. level (ACON)									245	
15. level (ACON)									13	

(Left axis: LEVEL OF CONTEXTUAL CONNECTIONS)

Fig. 3. The comparison of context connection levels and number of such interconnections for various text corpora

then some ACON context connections are added between previous and the next word neurons in order to support the next neurons to be activated first and make the activation sequence unambiguous and correct reflecting the read sentences from the text corpora. The context connections (ACON) can be of different levels. The context connections are added as long as the actual read word sequence is ambiguous and there are still some previous word neurons that can be used as context for next ambiguous activation of word neurons. Usually, a few previous words are enough to make the word sequence unambiguous even for the huge text corpora as is shown in Fig. 3. The level of contextual connection (ACON) is defined as the number of the word neurons in the actually read sentence they are between contextually connected word neurons. In step 1.2 in Fig. 4 there is added the contextual connection between the word neurons "so" and "went". There is only the single word neuron "i" between them in this sequence so the level of the contextual connection between these two words is equal one.

The ALHNG neural network shown in Fig. 4 is constructed for the following sentences: "I haven't lived here for two weeks. So I went back. He would go for it. Tom said it was a good idea." The connection labels show the type of connection: the direct ASEQ connections "1" and contextual ACON connections "2" in Fig. 4.

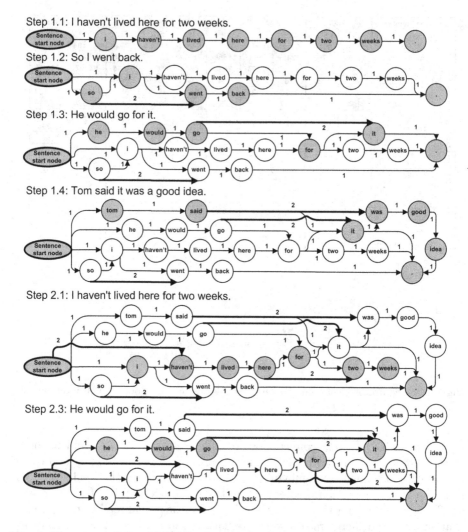

Fig. 4. The steps of the ALHNG neural network construction during the first and second read of the text consisting of four sentences where some ASEQ and ACON connections are added

4   Semi-automatic Associative Text Correction

The process of semi-automatic associative text correction starts always from activation of "Sentence start neuron" (Fig. 5). Next, the following neurons of corrected sentence are activated. The context of previously activated word neurons displays the next alternative word neurons that usually appear in this context (Fig. 5) by using ASEQ and ACON context connections. The connections are strengthen by the frequencies of them, which are computed after the text

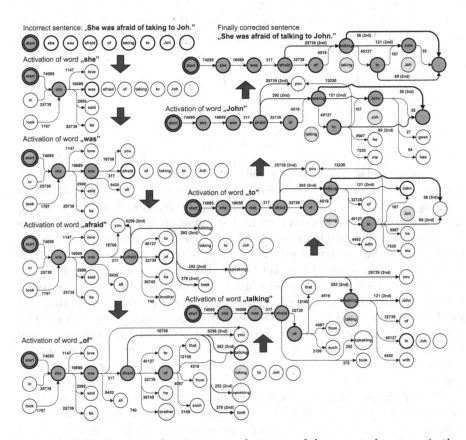

Fig. 5. The following steps of activating word neurons of the corrected sentence in the context of the previously activated word neurons

CORRECTION TOOL	Mistake found in word "taking"	Suggestions for correction of "taking"	Mistake found in word "Joh"	Suggestions for correction of "Joh"	Incorrrect sentence: She was afraid of *taking* to *Joh.*
					Corrected sentence:
Word 2007	NO	NO	YES	"John"	She was afraid of *taking* to John.
Libre Office Writer	NO	NO	YES	"Jo"	She was afraid of *taking* to Jo.
Google (google.com)	NO	NO	YES	"John"	She was afraid of *taking* to John.
ALHNG neural network	YES	"talking"	YES	"John"	She was afraid of **talking** to **John.**

Fig. 6. The comparison of the correction results obtained for two word processors, one leading search engine and the described neural network ALHNG

corpora during the construction of ALHNG neural network. The activated neurons stimulate the next connected neurons taking into account the weights computed after frequencies of such word sequences (2). The stimulation of the neuron (1) is defined using external stimulation (extIn), internal stimulation (inIn) and his previous state in the time step $t-1$. The weight (2) is defined by the frequency of this connection (f_i) between word neurons and is normalized by the sum of frequencies of all other input connections of a given neuron.

$$x(t) = \frac{x(t-1)}{2} + extIn(t) + \sum_{j=1}^{J} w_j * intIn_j(t) \tag{1}$$

$$w_i = \frac{f_i}{\sum_{j=1}^{J} f_j} \tag{2}$$

As a matter of fact, both ASEQ and ACON connections are activated from neurons every time. It was assumed that the neuronal excitation of the word neurons is reduced by half of the previous excitation in each step (1). In this way the contextual connections have far less influence on the next word neurons activation with the growing level of this contextual connection. The closer the context is, the bigger impact on excitation level of the next word neurons will occur. If the activation of the word neuron does not suit the possible word neurons, the correction to the most similar or frequent word will be suggested. If the suggested word neurons are followed by the word neurons representing next words in the corrected sentence, the suggestion is strengthen even more. This algorithm of semi-automatic correction works well under the assumption that the ALHNG neural network has been constructed after a possibly huge amount of text corpora. The results of correction of the incorrect sentence are shown in Fig. 5.

The experiments show that many nowadays correction tools do not notice mistaken words that are in their dictionaries even if the mistaken words have no meaning in a given context. The corrections made by ALHNG neural network have been compared to corrections obtained by well-known computer application like: MS Word, Libre Office Writer and search engine Google (Fig. 6).

5   Summary and Conclusion

In this paper the novelty ALHNG neural network and their use for semi-automatic correction have been described. The new correction abilities have been achieved thanks to the use of the described active associative mechanism implemented in the graph structure of the presented neural network. These investigations have shown that direct connections between related objects like letters and words have great significance and should be used to construct even more effective algorithms. This strategy also is probably used in natural neural networks in our brains and let us to associate data so fast. The experiments have shown that the correction can be better if the context of previous words is used. The context can be learned using ALHNG neural network and a huge amount of text corpora. The obtained results are usually much better than corrections obtained by nowadays leading applications and search engines that have implemented some algorithms for text corrections.

References

[1] Abney, S.: Part-of-Speech Tagging and Partial Parsing. Corpusbased Methods in Language and Speech Processing 2, 1–23 (1996)

[2] Back, R.J.R.: Refinement calculus, Parallel and reactive programs. In: de Bakker, J.W., de Roever, W.-P., Rozenberg, G. (eds.) REX 1989. LNCS, vol. 430, pp. 42–66. Springer, Heidelberg (1990)

[3] Gadamer, M., Horzyk, A.: Text analysis and correction using specialized linguistic habit graphs LHG. Automation (2012)

[4] Ganapathiraju, M., Manoharan, V., Klein-Seetharaman, J.: Statistical Analysis of the Indus Script Using n-Grams. PLOS ONE 5, 16 (2010)

[5] Horzyk, A., Tadeusiewicz, R.: A Psycholinguistic Model of Man-Machine Interactions Based on Needs of Human Personality. In: Cyran, K.A., Kozielski, S., Peters, J.F., Stańczyk, U., Wakulicz-Deja, A. (eds.) Man-Machine Interactions. AISC, vol. 59, pp. 55–67. Springer, Heidelberg (2009)

[6] Horzyk, A.: Information Freedom and Associative Artificial Intelligence. In: Rutkowski, L., Korytkowski, M., Scherer, R., Tadeusiewicz, R., Zadeh, L.A., Zurada, J.M. (eds.) ICAISC 2012, Part I. LNCS, vol. 7267, pp. 81–89. Springer, Heidelberg (2012)

[7] Hunston, S., Francis, G.: Pattern Grammar: A Corpus-Driven Approach to the Lexical Grammar of English. Computational Linguistics 27, 318–320 (2000)

[8] Konstantinidis, S.: Computing the Levenshtein distance of a regular language. In: IEEE Information Theory Workshop 2005 (2005)

[9] Robertson, A.M., Willett, P.: Applications of n-grams in textual information systems. Journal of Documentation 54, 48–69 (1998)

[10] Suchanek, F.M., Ifrim, G., Weikum, G.: Combining linguistic and statistical analysis to extract relations from web documents. In: Proceedings of the 12th ACM SIGKDD International Conference on Knowledge Discovery and Data Mining, KDD 2006, p. 712 (2006)

[11] Tadeusiewicz, R., Rowinski, T.: Computer science and psychology in information society. AGH (2011)

[12] Yujian, L., Bo, L.: A Normalized Levenshtein Distance Metric. IEEE Transactions on Pattern Analysis and Machine Intelligence 29, 1091–1095 (2007)

Some Aspects of Neural Network State Variable Estimator Improvement in Induction Motor Drive

Jerzy Jelonkiewicz and Łukasz Laskowski

Czestochowa University of Technology, Dabrowskiego 69, 42-201 Poland
{jerzy.jelonkiewicz,lukasz.laskowski}@iisi.pcz.pl

Abstract. Some aspects of state variable estimator improvement is proposed in the paper. The estimator approximates stator current components in the rotor flux reference frame with the help of neural networks. Some modification of the training procedure is considered that leads to the estimator accuracy improvement. Provided tests confirmed this feature but further steps are necessary to increase state variables estimation in the low supplying frequency range.

1 Introduction

In many vector controlled induction motor drives applications rotor speed measurement or estimation is not necessary for adjustment of its operating point effectively. Such a case relates to traction drives where torque value is rather used than a vehicle speed. Moreover the absence of the rotor speed measurement increases robustness and reliability of the drive. Therefore control strategies that use other than rotor speed state variables are especially welcome. For the vector control strategy, the most needed state variable of the motor is the rotor flux in terms of its phase angle and amplitude as it allows any of advanced control schemes to be implemented.

Among various techniques to estimate rotor flux, the Model Reference Adaptive System approach looks to be the most promising as it offers higher accuracy due to closed-loop operation [4]. However considered scheme suffers from variety of drawbacks like: integration drift, sensibility to noise present in the measured signals or parameters variation of the motor. On the other hand, in a control circuit, much useful are stator current components in the rotor flux reference frame which can be easily calculated knowing rotor flux position and amplitude. Such a scheme, presented in [5], simplifies and improves estimation part of the control circuit, but requires rotor flux position detection which involves all the above mentioned drawbacks related to this task. Although there are other effective methods applicable in this case using fuzzy modeling [1][2][3], proposed NN estimator of stator current components in the rotor flux reference frame seems to be an interesting solution as it employs completely different approach to the problem. The intention of the paper is to find out how artificial intelligence tools are useful in the stator current components estimation in the rotor reference frame and how accurate is the estimator in the whole frequency and load range

L. Rutkowski et al. (Eds.): ICAISC 2013, Part I, LNAI 7894, pp. 88–95, 2013.

and feasible in the vector control strategy. The idea of such an estimator although mentioned in [7] has not been investigated widely. Only in [7][8][9] some results of the neural network estimator were presented but its accuracy has not been evaluated enough to confirm its usefulness in the vector control scheme. It looks like there is no possibility to find a compromise in network weights adjustment, when implemented in the straightforward way, to fulfill high accuracy estimation of the required state variables in the whole input frequency range. Therefore the paper investigates some possibility to improve the accuracy of the estimator particularly in the low frequency range. Firstly some knowledge extraction from available input signals is presented which improves the accuracy of the estimator. Unfortunately, this modification of the input vector selection is not sufficient in the low input frequency range. Then another idea is proposed which assumes some division of the input frequency into subranges with independent, separately trained NN higher accuracy estimators. Finally, the latter idea has been aggregated to create one neural network estimator with hidden layer weights defined by a polynomial function. Due to estimated stator current components the vector controlled induction motor drive is considerably simplified, while offering sensor less operation.

2   MRAS-Based Induction Motor State Variables Estimator

Considered MRAS (Model Reference Adaptive System) estimator uses reference model based on the following equations of the rotor flux components in the stationary reference frame:

$$\Psi_{rd} = \frac{L_r}{L_m} \left[\int (u_{sD} - R_s i_{sD})\, dt - L'_s i_{sD} \right] \tag{1}$$

$$\Psi_{rq} = \frac{L_r}{L_m} \left[\int (u_{sQ} - R_s i_{sQ})\, dt - L'_s i_{sQ} \right] \tag{2}$$

where L_m, L_r, L_s are: magnetizing inductance, rotor self inductance and stator transient inductance. However adaptive model is defined as:

$$\hat{\Psi}_{rd} = \frac{1}{T_r} \int \left(L_m i_{sD} - \hat{\Psi}_{rd} - \omega_r T_r \hat{\Psi}_{rq} \right) dt \tag{3}$$

$$\hat{\Psi}_{rq} = \frac{1}{T_r} \int \left(L_m i_{sQ} - \hat{\Psi}_{rq} - \omega_r T_r \hat{\Psi}_{rd} \right) dt \tag{4}$$

where T_r is rotor time constant.

When both models are connected in well known closed loop system, they estimate rotor flux and motor speed. Unfortunately, due to pure integrators that exist in both models, the system fails to work properly for the sake of offsets and measurement inaccuracies in the sampled voltages and currents. This problem can be corrected with the help of a low pass filter to approximate the integrator but it fails at low speed range due to unavoidable phase shift at these frequencies. Other solution, proposed in [6] is based on drift and dc-offset compensator using feedback integrator. This idea, although effective, cures not origin of the problem but final effect of the estimator performance.

Solution proposed in [5] is based on the above mentioned MRAS estimator with slight modification. As opposed from the classical way of obtaining tuning signal where both: amplitude and phase of rotor flux components are compared, in the modified estimator only the phase angle is used to produce stator current components in the rotor flux reference frame (i_{xy}). These components then form a tuning signal which PI controller converts to the rotor speed. It is expected that proposed estimator should have better features than the classical one as used phase angle of the rotor flux is less susceptible to the integration drift. The idea of the estimator shows Fig. 1.

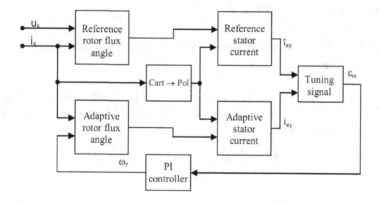

Fig. 1. Stator current components MRAS estimator

Expected features of the modified estimator have been partly confirmed. The estimator presents fine accuracy in the whole input frequency range but some sensitivity to rotor flux angle calculation error due to the integration drift is still on [5]. Encountered problems with classical MRAS-type estimator turned authors attention to a promising estimation technique using neural networks structures.

3   Neural Network Estimator Based on Stator Voltage and Current Components

As some authors reported an excellent performance of the NN estimators [8][9], first and straightforward approach to the problem was to consider only various combinations of stator voltage and current components and their delayed values as input vector. For this rather complex problem relatively big neural network was proposed with two hidden layers, 10 neurons each. For the tests the induction motor with the following parameters was considered:

$P_n = 1100W, U_n = 380V, R_s = 6.88\Omega, R_r = 6.35\Omega, L_{ls} = 34 \times 10^{-3}H, L_{lr} = 34 \times 10^{-3}H, L_m = 450 \times 10^{-3}H$, rated torque $T_n = 7.6Nm$

Data set for training and tests purposes covered frequency range 5-50 Hz and there were 360 samples in each operating point, being a combination of the frequencies: 5, 10, 20, 30, 40, 50 Hz and three load torque levels of the motor (no load, half load and full load). Obtained results show table 1.

Table 1. Results of the training of the stator current components in the rotor flux reference frame estimator

Input vector	Output vector	Network structure	MSE
$i_{sd}, i_{sq}, u_{sd}, u_{sq}$	i_{sx}, i_{sy}	4-10-10-2	2.34×10^{-4}
$i_{sd}, i_{sq}, u_{sd}, u_{sq}, i_{sd}^{-1}, i_{sq}^{-1}$	i_{sx}, i_{sy}	6-10-10-2	1.41×10^{-4}
$i_{sd}, i_{sq}, u_{sd}, u_{sq}, u_{sd}^{-1}, u_{sq}^{-1}$	i_{sx}, i_{sy}	4-10-10-2	1.38×10^{-4}
$i_{sd}, i_{sq}, u_{sd}, u_{sq}, i_{sd}^{-1}, i_{sq}^{-1}, u_{sd}^{-1}, u_{sq}^{-1}$	i_{sx}, i_{sy}	4-10-10-2	2.34×10^{-4}

These rather poor results in training were also confirmed in the simulation tests in Matlab-Simulink environment. The training error is practically independent of the input vector selection and is mostly generated in the low excitation frequency range of the motor (below 10 Hz). It appears that considered neural structures due to strong non-linear nature of induction motor are unable to assure high enough accuracy of the approximated state variables.

The next step in the estimator design is to compare results obtained from the network for the different frequencies of the current and voltage, applied to the input of the neural network. The second parameter changed in the tests was the load level of the motor. Selected values were 0, 4 and 8 Nm. Obtained results show table 2.

Table 2. Accuracy of the neural network in selected points of frequency and load

f[Hz]	M[Nm]	$I_{sx}\epsilon_{\%max}$	$I_{sx}\epsilon_{\%avg}$	$I_{sx}\epsilon_{\%min}$	$I_{sy}\epsilon_{\%max}$	$I_{sy}\epsilon_{\%avg}$	$I_{sy}\epsilon_{\%min}$
50	0	1.13	0.12	-0.72	19.66	-5.69	-37.76
50	4	6.15	2.47	-0.66	7.06	-1.70	-4.14
50	8	15.00	4.22	-3.85	15.61	6.06	-1.85
25	0	0.00	-1.19	-1.74	11.27	-11.29	-30.85
25	4	10.71	4.53	-3.70	21.84	8.38	1.60
25	8	30.59	10.56	-16.97	61.66	28.24	11.06
10	0	27.82	19.99	9.22	155.42	-204.80	-458.86
10	4	42.72	27.47	9.61	81.47	28.45	-4.97
10	8	168.45	11.66	-161.07	130.08	67.01	14.62

As seen in it, the neural network shows the highest accuracy at the nominal frequency of the motor, so the error in this range is the smallest. When going down with the frequency, the estimation error are becoming higher. For the frequency f=10 Hz they are not acceptable. So, some procedure to solve the problem needs to be applied.

As previously presented, the neural network exhibits low relative errors for frequencies near nominal one and the whole load range. We can even accept errors down to 25 Hz. But with the frequency going further down, the relative error is increasing, reaching average level around 204,8% for the frequency 10 Hz and no load conditions. It seems, that such a neural network has application limited to near nominal frequency range and no one advanced control scheme can be considered. Such a conclusion is an effect of strong non-linearity of the induction motor model, especially in the low frequency range. This feature of the induction motor transfers to the behaviour of the presented neural network. Extended tests of different neural networks configuration (not presented in the paper) proved that there is no single network that may follow the estimation task in the whole frequency range. Therefore the idea of several neural networks that may be trained and operate in subranges of the required frequency appeared. To proceed this idea different neural networks were trained and tested to see their behaviour and accuracy in the low frequency range. Fortunately, they were accurate enough in their subranges. Moreover, initial configuration of the neural network (4-10-10-2), proved to be accurate enough in tested frequency subranges. In case of covering the whole frequency by a few neural networks, responsible for their sub-ranges, the complete state variables estimator needs to consider switching between networks when crossing subranges. The big question is how smooth these switching can be and would it influence the stability of the control system? Another idea how to cope with problem is to describe the values of the weights for subranged neural networks with a help of approximation functions. This solution should assure smoothness of the transfer between the networks. Unfortunately, it appeared not to be so straight forward. Firstly, obtained diagram of the input weight changes along the operating frequency looks quite complicated (Fig. 2) and difficult to approximate with any polynomial function.

The diagrams were gained for random selected initial weight values. To solve this problem some changes in the training procedure of the subranged networks were introduced. It was noticed that the training procedure for the subranged networks goes better when it is started from the highest frequency (50 Hz) and proceeds gradually down to the lowest (e.g. 5 Hz) and initial values for the subsequent networks are obtained from the higher frequency trained neighbour. As seen in Fig. 3 obtained diagrams reached some regularity and are promising in terms of tuning approximating functions.

Considering features of the diagrams we can take that the neurons input weights are constant at frequency range 30-50 Hz and the bias weights are the same for the 20-50 Hz range. As a consequence of this assumption, the approximation function for the input weights and biases can be selected for the frequency range 0-30 Hz and 0-20 Hz respectively.

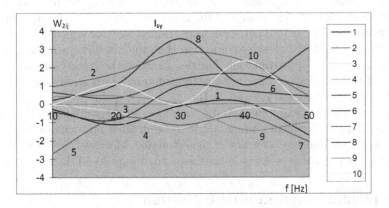

Fig. 2. Diagram of input weights changes for random selected initial values

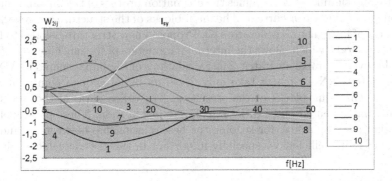

Fig. 3. Diagram of input weights changes for extended low frequency range

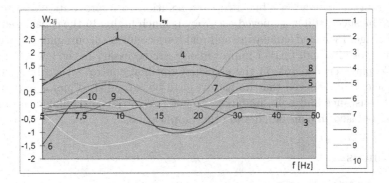

Fig. 4. Diagram of input weights changes for modified training procedure

The last sentence can conclude the whole approach to the problem if not considering suspicious wide change of the input weights in the 0-30 Hz range. In the previous tests the neural networks were trained only for selected frequencies (5, 10, 20 and 30 Hz) with the assumption that the networks work fine within the ranges and the approximation functions reflect the nature of the weight changes. To prove that another tests were attempted with additional networks for in-between frequencies: 7.5 and 15 Hz.

As seen in Fig. 4, weight changes diagram looks slightly different which indicates that 0-30 Hz frequency range needs to be divided into smaller that 5 Hz subranges to reach higher accuracy of the estimator. Moreover, previous conclusion concerning constant weights in the frequency range 30-50 Hz is maintained.

4   Implementation in a DSP System

Proposed NN estimator of the stator current components in the rotor reference frame was the basis of the control scheme. It plays crucial role in the control structure and significantly simplifies the estimation process of the flux and torque components of the stator current. The main blocks of the structure are generated with a help of fuzzy neural generators [7]. Proposed new structure belongs to field oriented methods, which allows the internal parameters of the machine to be fully controlled even in transient states. The calculations of the implemented in ADDU 21161L system NN estimator take only 21.36 μs living enough computational power for remaining blocks of the structure. The other parts of the structure are being implemented and will be intensively tested soon. These parts include blocks that are responsible for keeping the best relationship between i_{sx} and i_{sy} in terms of motor efficiency, especially important in the electric vehicle drive.

5   Conclusions

The paper considers NN estimator of the flux and torque components of stator current. When applied in the straightforward way its accuracy in the low frequency range is not acceptable. Proposed solution to improve its performance seems to be successful as achieved accuracy is much higher in the considered frequency range. Provided simulation and real tests confirm encouraging features of the estimator although further improvements are necessary in the low frequency range. It plays crucial role in the efficiency optimal control structure for electric vehicle. It is believed that its features can be extended to motor parameter changes resistance and noise immunity to get real robust and reliable estimator that can be used in considered and other applications.

References

1. Li, X., Er, M.J., Lim, B.S., et al.: Fuzzy Regression Modeling for Tool Performance Prediction and Degradation Detection. International Journal of Neural Systems 20(5), 405–419 (2010)

2. Rutkowski, L., Przybyl, A., Cpalka, K.: Novel Online Speed Profile Generation for Industrial Machine Tool Based on Flexible Neuro-Fuzzy Approximation. IEEE Transactions on Industrial Electronics 59(2), 1238–1247 (2012)
3. Rutkowski, L., Cpalka, K.: Flexible neuro-fuzzy systems. IEEE Transactions on Neural Networks 14, 554–574 (2003)
4. Ohyama, K., Asher, G.M., Sumner, M.: Comparison of the practical performance and operating limits of sensorless induction motor drive using a closed loop flux observer and a full order flux observer. In: Proc. EPE 1999, Lausanne, on CD (1999)
5. Jelonkiewicz, J.: Modified MRAS estimator in sensorless vector control of induction motor. In: XII Symposium PPEE 2007, Wisla, pp. 305–308 (2007)
6. Sumner, M., Spiteri Staines, C., Gao, Q., Asher, G.: Sensorless Speed Operation of Cage Induction Motor using Zero Drift Feedback Integration with MRAS Observer. In: Proc. EPE 2005, Dresden, on CD (2005)
7. Vas, P.: Artificial Intelligence-Based Electrical Machines and Drives. Monographs in Electrical and Electronic Engineering, vol. 45. Oxford University Press, Oxford (1999)
8. Kuchar, M., Branstetter, P., Kaduch, M.: ANN-based speed estimator for induction motor. In: Proc. EPE-PEMC 2004, Riga, on CD (2004)
9. Grzesiak, L., Ufnalski, B.: DTC drive with ANN-based stator flux estimator. In: Proc. EPE, Dresden, on CD (2005)
10. Jelonkiewicz, J., Przybyl, A.: Knowledge extraction from data for neural network state variables estimators in induction motor. In: SENE 2005, Lodz, pp. 211–216 (2005)

The Echo State Network on the Graphics Processing Unit

Tūreiti Keith and Stephen J. Weddell

Dept. of Electrical & Computer Engineering, University of Canterbury, New Zealand
tureiti.keith@gmail.com, steve.weddell@canterbury.ac.nz

Abstract. Extending on previous work, the Echo State Network (ESN) and Tikhonov Regularisation (TR) training algorithms were implemented for both the CPU, an Intel i7-980; and the GPU, an Nvidia GTX480. The implementation used all 4 cores of the CPU, and all 480 cores of the GPU. The execution times of these implementations were measured and compared. In the ESN case, speed-ups were observed at reservoir sizes greater than 1,024. The first significant speed-ups of 6 and and 5 were observed at a reservoir size of 2,048 in double and single precision respectively. In the case of Tikhonov Regularisation, no significant speed-ups were observed.

Keywords: echo state network, GPU, Tikhonov regularisation.

1 Introduction

The Echo State Network (ESN) was introduced by Jaeger in 2001 [1]. In 2002, Maass conceived of the Liquid State Machine (LSM) [2]. These efforts mark the beginning of what is now referred to as Reservoir Computing [3]. At the core of a Reservoir Computer (RC) is a randomly generated dynamical system – a *reservoir* of dynamics. The output of an RC is a linear combination of signals tapped from this reservoir. An RC may also (but not necessarily) accept inputs which perturb the reservoir. [1, 2, 3]

This work extends on previous work to implement the Echo State Network on the Graphics Processing Unit (GPU) [4]. The following sections detail the implementation of the ESN and an offline training algorithm based on Tikhonov Regularisation. Section 2 presents the Echo State Network, the Tikhonov Regularisation algorithm, and the GPU. Details of the GPU implementation are given in Sect. 3, and the method for testing the behaviour of this implementation in Sect. 4. The results of these experiments are given in Sect. 5.

2 Background

2.1 The Echo State Network

The Echo State Network (ESN) is a form of Recurrent Neural Network (RNN) topology that lends itself to offline training via linear regression. At the core of an

L. Rutkowski et al. (Eds.): ICAISC 2013, Part I, LNAI 7894, pp. 96–107, 2013.

ESN is a sparse, randomly connected RNN comprising sigmoidal neurons. This is referred to as the "reservoir". The output of the ESN is composed of linear neurons that tap signals from the RNN. It is the linear output that facilitates ESN training via linear regression. [1, 3]

Equations (1) & (2) define the behaviour of the network. Equation (1),

$$\mathbf{x}(n) = f\left(\mathbf{W}_{\text{in}}\mathbf{u}(n) + \mathbf{W}\mathbf{x}(n-1) + \mathbf{W}_{\text{ofb}}\mathbf{y}(n-1)\right), \tag{1}$$

describes the state of the neurons in the reservoir $\mathbf{x}$ at time n after receiving an input $\mathbf{u}(n-1)$. Here $\mathbf{W}_{\text{in}}$ represents the input weights, $\mathbf{W}$ the reservoir weights, $\mathbf{W}_{\text{ofb}}$ the optional output feedback, and $f(\ldots)$ a sigmoidal activation function. The state of the reservoir is then used in (2),

$$\mathbf{y}(n) = f_{\text{out}}\left(\mathbf{W}_{\text{out}} \begin{bmatrix} \mathbf{u}(n) \\ \mathbf{x}(n) \end{bmatrix}\right), \tag{2}$$

to calculate the ESN output $\mathbf{y}(n)$. Here $\mathbf{W}_{\text{out}}$ are the output weights and $f_{\text{out}}(\ldots)$ is the linear activation function. [1]

At the core of the Echo state Network is its reservoir, represented by the weight matrix $\mathbf{W}$ given in (1). This is a sparse and randomly generated matrix. [1]. Equation (3),

$$\rho = \max\left(|\lambda(\mathbf{W})|\right), \tag{3}$$

gives the spectral radius of $\mathbf{W}$. This is the largest absolute eigenvalue of $\mathbf{W}$, and is typically scaled to a value less than, but close to one. Equation (4),

$$\mathbf{W} = \frac{\rho\mathbf{W}_{\text{rand}}}{\max\left(|\lambda(\mathbf{W}_{\text{rand}})|\right)}, \tag{4}$$

can be used to scale a random matrix, $\mathbf{W}_{\text{rand}}$, to a desired spectral radius, ρ. [1, 5]

Linear regression can be used to train an Echo State Network offline. Only the output matrix, $\mathbf{W}_{\text{out}}$, is trained. One approach to obtain the output matrix $\mathbf{W}_{\text{out}}$ is a form of linear regression known as Tikhonov Regularisation (TR) or Ridge Regression. Equation (5),

$$\mathbf{W}_{\text{out}} = \mathbf{Y}_{\text{target}}\mathbf{X}^T \left(\mathbf{X}\mathbf{X}^T + \alpha^2\mathbf{I}\right)^{-1}, \tag{5}$$

describes TR used to calculate $\mathbf{W}_{\text{out}}$. Here $\mathbf{Y}_{\text{target}}$ is the training target, α is a regularisation constant and $\mathbf{X}$,

$$\mathbf{X} = \begin{bmatrix} \mathbf{u}(1) \ldots \mathbf{u}(n) \ldots \mathbf{u}(N) \\ \mathbf{x}(1) \ldots \mathbf{x}(n) \ldots \mathbf{x}(N) \end{bmatrix}, \tag{6}$$

is a history of the state vector and input vector for N time steps collected while processing training input data with (1). [1, 3, 5, 6]

Equation (5) requires a square matrix inversion. The matrix may not be invertible, however, singular value decomposition can be used to find a pseudo-inverse. [7, 8]

2.2 The General Purpose Graphics Processing Unit

The General Purpose Graphics Processing Unit (GPGPU, or just GPU) is a highly parallel computing platform available to desktop and laptop users. Toolkits for working with GPUs include the open and cross-platform OpenCL; Nvidia's Cuda [9]; and AMD's Heterogeneous Computing Platform, the GPU component is based on OpenCL. Due to the availability of an Nvidia platform with Cuda-based Blas and Sparse mathematics libraries, Nvidia hardware and tools were used in this work. The Nvidia GPU and the Cuda programming model are briefly described in this section.

The Nvidia Cuda Programming Model. Nvidia refers to their GPGPUs as single instruction multiple thread devices (SIMT). The same instruction is executed in parallel on different pieces of data, as per Flynn's single instruction multiple device (SIMD) architecture. However, the SIMT model also allows for conditional branching[1]. On an Nvidia Cuda device, a programmer writes a *kernel* of code that defines these instructions. [10, 11]

On execution, a kernel is run in multiple SIMT threads. Each thread has access to private local memory, shared memory visible to a group of threads (called a *thread block*), and global memory. At run time, a kernel has access to the thread's *thread index*. This can be used to determine which addresses of memory to access. The thread index is a vector of up to three dimensions, and is unique for each thread within the thread block. The dimensionality of the thread index and, therefore, the thread block, allows the programmer to model vector, 1D; matrix, 2D; or volume, 3D calculations.

3 Implementation Details

3.1 The Toolchain

Two Echo State Network and Tikhonov Regularisation implementations were built, one targeting the CPU, the other the GPU. Table 1 summarises the tools used for each implementation. The remainder of this section details a selection of these tools.

Cuda C++. This is a programming language designed for use with the Nvidia Cuda toolchain. It is an extension of a subset of the existing C++ ISO/IEC 14882:2003 standard. The primary goal of this language is to facilitate the programming of Single Instruction Multiple Thread (SIMT) code. Using Cuda C++, a developer can compose *kernels*. These kernels are executed on the GPU with instruction-level parallelism across multiple threads (See Sect. 2.2).

---

[1] Such branching typically impacts negatively on the efficiency of the GPU. [10]

Table 1. ESN and GPU implementation tools

| | GPU | | CPU | |
	ESN	TR	ESN	TR
Language	C++, Cuda C++ r4.2		GNU Octave	
Compiler	gcc 4.6.2, nvcc r4.2		Interpreted	
Libraries	Cuda, Cublas, Cusparse, Curand			
	Magma 1.2			
			Atlas 3.8.4	
			Blas 3.3.1, Lapack 3.3.1	

The Cuda Libraries. These are distributed gratis with the Nvidia drivers. The libraries used for this project include release 4.2 of the Cuda, Cublas, Cusparse, and Curand libraries. The Cuda library coupled with the Nvidia Cuda Compiler facilitate the use of C++ language level extensions for kernel development. The Cublas library provides GPU implementations of the well known Blas level 1, 2, and 3 routines. The Cusparse library provides GPU implementations of some sparse matrix storage formats and operations. The Curand library provides pseudo-random number generation routines.

The Nvidia Cuda Compiler. Also known as nvcc, the Nvidia Cuda Compiler is used to compile Cuda C++ code. It is capable of producing both architecture specific, and compute-capability dependent code. In the latter case, the compiler generates a first-pass compilation, preparing a distributable for Just-In-Time (JIT) compilation. JIT compilation occurs on first execution of the code on the target GPU. With the correct settings on the target PC, the resulting JIT compiled binaries are cached for later use, and are updated with a change to the Nvidia drivers.

The Atlas Library. This is also known as the Automatically Tuned Linear Algebra Software library. It is a free software project to provide tuned Blas and Lapack routines. In this instance, the Atlas library interfaces with the reference Fortran77 implementation of Blas, and its accompanying Lapack implementation.

The Magma Library. Magma is a free software project to migrate Lapack routines to the GPU. Magma currently implements hybrid CPU/GPU versions of Lapack routines calling, in this instance, a mixture of Cublas, Magma Lapack, and the Fortran77 reference Lapack routines.

GNU Octave. Octave is a high-level interpreted programming language for linear algebra. The GNU Octave environment/interpreter is free software. In this instance Octave interfaces with the Atlas library to perform linear algebraic operations.

3.2   Implementing the ESN and TR Algorithms

The Echo State Network and Tikhonov Regularisation algorithms were implemented for the GPU and CPU using the toolchain described in Sect. 3.1. Blas, Sparse, Lapack, and Pseudo Random Number libraries, along with bespoke kernels were used to implement (1), (2), (3), (4),(5), and (6). The details of the GPU implementation follow, and are summarised in Table 2.

Table 2. ESN and GPU implementation details

Operation		Implementation
Reservoir generation, (3) & (4)	$\mathbf{W}_{\text{rand}}$	Curand pseudo-random number generator
	$\lambda\left(\mathbf{W}_{\text{rand}}\right)$	Magma eigenvalue extraction
	$\underline{\rho\mathbf{W}_{\text{rand}}}$	Cublas scalar-vector multiplication
ESN state calculation, (1)	$\mathbf{W}_{\text{in}}\mathbf{u}\left(n\right)$, $\mathbf{W}_{\text{ofb}}\mathbf{y}\left(n-1\right)$	Cublas matrix-vector multiplication
	$\mathbf{W}\mathbf{x}\left(n-1\right)$	Cusparse matrix-vector multiplication (with $\mathbf{W}$ stored in compressed sparse row, CSR, format [12, 13])
	$f\left(\ldots+\ldots+\ldots\right)$	Single bespoke kernel
ESN output calculation, (2)	$\begin{bmatrix}\mathbf{u}\left(n\right)\\\mathbf{x}\left(n\right)\end{bmatrix}$	Cuda memory copy
	$f_{\text{out}}\left(\mathbf{W}_{\text{out}}\left[\ldots\right]\right)$	Cublas matrix-vector multiplication (f_{out} is linear)
Tikhonov Regularisation, (5)	$\mathbf{X}\mathbf{X}^T+\alpha^2\mathbf{I}$	Cublas matrix-matrix & scalar-vector multiplication, vector addition
	$\left(\ldots\right)^{-1}$	Magma SVD, Cublas matrix-matrix multiplication, bespoke diagonal matrix inversion kernel
	$\mathbf{Y}_{\text{target}}\mathbf{X}^T\left(\ldots\right)$	Cublas matrix-matrix multiplication

Calculating the ESN Reservoir State. Described in (1), this implementation uses Cublas matrix-vector multiplication to perform $\mathbf{W}_{\text{in}}\mathbf{u}\left(n\right)$ and $\mathbf{W}_{\text{ofb}}\mathbf{y}(n-1)$. As $\mathbf{W}$ is sparse (see Sect. 2.1), $\mathbf{W}\mathbf{x}\left(n-1\right)$ is performed using Cusparse matrix-vector multiplication. $\mathbf{W}$ is stored in compressed sparse row (CSR) format [12, 13]. A single bespoke kernel executes the activation function $f\left(\ldots\right)$, and the addition of factors $\mathbf{W}_{\text{in}}\mathbf{u}\left(n\right)$, $\mathbf{W}\mathbf{x}\left(n-1\right)$, and $\mathbf{W}_{\text{ofb}}\mathbf{y}\left(n-1\right)$. Here, $f\left(\ldots\right)$ is a hyperbolic tangent. When a user initiates an ESN reservoir state calculation, they can choose to provide multiple time-steps of input data, e.g. training data, and collect the input and reservoir state vectors in host memory as per (6). This state history can be later used to train the ESN as per (5).

There is a limit to the amount of input data that may be used, this is dependent on the size of the ESN, and the memory available on the GPU. Similarly, if the reservoir state vector history is to be used for training, then the size of the history will be limited by the size of the GPU memory, and the accompanying matrices described in (5). The implementation does not currently warn of memory limitations.

Calculating the ESN Output. The ESN output, (2), is calculated using Cublas and Cuda memory copy operations. A Cuda device-side memory copy is used to stack the vectors $\mathbf{u}(n)$ and $\mathbf{x}(n)$. A Cublas matrix-vector multiplication is used to perform

$$\mathbf{W}_{\text{out}} \begin{bmatrix} \mathbf{u}(n) \\ \mathbf{x}(n) \end{bmatrix}.$$

The Tikhonov Regularisation Algorithm. Described in (5), this was implemented using Cublas and Magma libraries. Blas matrix-matrix and scalar-vector multiplications were used to obtain $\left(\mathbf{X}\mathbf{X}^T + \alpha^2\mathbf{I}\right)$. To invert this result, singular value decomposition is used [8, 7]. This was implemented using Magma provided SVD, Cublas matrix-matrix multiplication, and a bespoke diagonal-matrix pseudo-inverse kernel.

Reservoir Generation. To generate a reservoir of a given spectral radius and connectivity, (3) & (4) were implemented. This required the pseudo-random number generating library, Curand, to create $\mathbf{W}_{\text{rand}}$ with the desired connectivity, and a Magma routine to extract its eigen-values. Cublas scalar-vector multiplication was used to scale $\mathbf{W}_{\text{rand}}$ as per (4).

4   Experimental Configuration

The goal of these experiments is to gather information that will help users decide when best to perform Echo State Network and Tikhonov Regularisation algorithms on a GPU, and when best to use a CPU. Four experiments have been devised, two of which have been executed. Two further experiments are described in Sect. 7. The two executed experiments examine the relative speed performance of CPU and GPU based ESN and TR algorithms in both double and single precision. The methods and equipment used to perform this evaluation follow.

4.1   Hardware

To perform this comparison, a multi-core Intel Core i7-920 was used as the CPU, and an Nvidia GTX480 as the GPU. Both are representative of high-end commodity hardware in their respective domains. Comparative information on these processors is presented in Table 3.

Table 3. Selected CPU and GPU parameters

	Intel Core i7-920	Nvidia GTX480
Core count	4	480
Thread count	8	23,040
Core clock speed	2.67 GHz	1.401 GHz
Warp size	–	32
Concurrent kernels	–	1
Memory[2]	6 GiB	1.5 GiB
Memory clock speed	1.066 GHz	1.848 GHz
Shared memory per block	–	48 KiB
PCI bus speed[3]	–	2.5 GiT/s

4.2   Measurement Variables

Selected variables were isolated to measure the Echo State Network and Tikhonov Regularisation speed performance. To measure ESN speed performance, three independent variables were isolated – reservoir size, calculation precision and hardware type. The same independent variables were isolated for TR speed performance measurements, with an additional fourth variable, the number of execution time-steps. This is the number of columns, N, in (6). The remaining variables were controlled. A summary of the values used in the experiment is given in Table 4, where irrelevant variables are indicated with a "–".

Table 4. ESN and TR speed comparison variables

Variable	ESN Values	TR Values
Hardware	{Intel i7-980, Nvidia GTX-480}	
Calculation precision	{double, single}	
ESN reservoir size	$\{2^4, 2^5, \ldots, 2^{11}\}$	
ESN execution time steps	2^{10}	$\{2^4, 2^5, \ldots, 2^{16}\}$
ESN input size	2^4	
ESN output size	2^4	
ESN output feedback	present	–
ESN reservoir connectivity	10 %	–
ESN reservoir spectral radius (ρ)	0.9	–
Tikhonov regularisation factor (α)	–	0.1

4.3   Measurement Method

To ensure statistically valid measurements, each timing measurement was repeated 20 times. The first 10 timing measurements were discarded to reduce

---

[2] Host-side random access memory compared with GPU-side global memory.

[3] GiT/s (gibitransfers per second) is equivalent to gibibytes per second and includes PCI protocol overheads.

the impact of any just-in-time compiled elements. For each point in independent variable space, a mean and standard deviation execution time was recorded.

5   Results

The execution times of the Echo State Network are given in Fig. 1. Tikhonov Regularisation executions times are given in Figs. 2 & 3. From these measurements, ESN and TR mean speed-up times are presented in Tables 5 & 6 respectively.

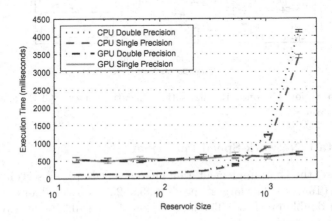

Fig. 1. Mean Echo State Network execution times – CPU versus GPU

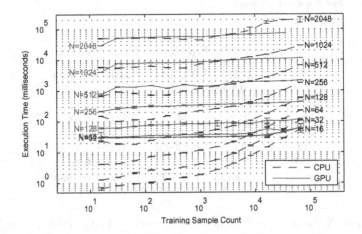

Fig. 2. Double precision Tikhonov Regularisation execution times – CPU versus GPU for varying reservoir sizes (r)

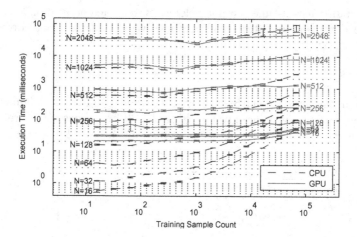

Fig. 3. Single precision Tikhonov Regularisation execution times – CPU versus GPU for varying reservoir sizes (r)

5.1   Echo State Network Speed Performance

In the ESN case, the GPU implementation gives a speed-up at reservoir sizes of 1024 and 2048 (Table 5). The largest speed-up, 5.9923, is observed for a reservoir size of 2048 in double precision. The largest slow-down is 0.2107 at a reservoir size of 16 in single precision.

Table 5. Echo State Network execution: Observed GPU speed-up. The largest and smallest speed-ups are given in bold.

Reservoir Size	ESN Execution: ESN Speed-up	
	Double Precision	Single Precision
16	**0.2130 ± 0.1314**	**0.2107 ± 0.1048**
32	0.2368 ± 0.1483	0.2486 ± 0.1076
64	0.2602 ± 0.0600	0.2227 ± 0.1153
128	0.2944 ± 0.0416	0.2944 ± 0.0392
256	0.3499 ± 0.1034	0.3590 ± 0.0891
512	0.6151 ± 0.1308	0.5498 ± 0.1500
1024	2.0243 ± 0.0314	1.4407 ± 0.1164
2048	**5.9923 ± 0.0563**	**4.9652 ± 0.0893**

For small ESNs, it is likely that host-GPU memory transfers dominate ESN calculation time. Also, it is probable that the GPU is not fully occupied, and therefore not performing at full capacity or efficiency. The slower clock speed of the GPU will also contribute to a slower than CPU execution time. As the ESNs become larger, it is likely that the occupancy of the GPU improves, and the dominance of host-GPU memory transfers decreases. The CPU, running 4 cores and 8 threads, reaches its computational capacity earlier than the GPU, which has 480 cores and 23,040 threads. GPU thread occupancy and the impact of memory transfers is yet to be measured.

5.2 Tikhonov Regularisation Speed Performance

In the TR case, the speed-up of the extreme reservoir sizes was calculated. The speed-ups for $r = 16$ and $r = 2048$ are given in Table 6.

Table 6. Tikhonov Regularisation execution: Observed GPU speed-up. The largest and smallest speed-ups are given in bold.

History Size	TR Execution: GPU Speed-up			
	$r = 2048$		$r = 16$	
	Double Precision	Single Precision	Double Precision	Single Precision
16	1.6961 ± 0.0156	$\mathbf{1.0357 \pm 0.0107}$	$\mathbf{0.0197 \pm 0.3367}$	0.0266 ± 0.1029
32	1.0022 ± 0.0187	1.0675 ± 0.0062	0.0273 ± 0.0158	0.0306 ± 0.0270
64	0.9499 ± 0.0067	1.1372 ± 0.0079	0.0305 ± 0.0364	0.0329 ± 0.0423
128	0.9498 ± 0.0045	1.1199 ± 0.0048	0.0340 ± 0.0456	0.0397 ± 0.0566
256	0.8814 ± 0.0066	1.0737 ± 0.0054	0.0435 ± 0.0342	0.0467 ± 0.0458
512	0.8012 ± 0.0076	1.0735 ± 0.0077	0.0495 ± 0.0303	0.0498 ± 0.1220
1024	$\mathbf{0.7910 \pm 0.0076}$	1.1291 ± 0.0067	0.0608 ± 0.0196	0.0693 ± 0.0406
2048	0.9824 ± 0.0091	1.1499 ± 0.0059	0.0879 ± 0.0095	0.1059 ± 0.0201
4096	1.0605 ± 0.0075	1.1310 ± 0.0061	0.1398 ± 0.0149	0.1690 ± 0.0277
8192	1.3258 ± 0.2617	1.1621 ± 0.0158	0.2366 ± 0.0024	0.2950 ± 0.0040
16384	2.3569 ± 0.0929	1.3997 ± 0.2584	0.4067 ± 0.0031	0.5010 ± 0.0325
32768	$\mathbf{2.6813 \pm 0.0118}$	1.4287 ± 0.1147	0.6557 ± 0.0307	0.8196 ± 0.0361
65536	$-$	$\mathbf{1.6864 \pm 0.2362}$	0.8561 ± 0.2424	$\mathbf{1.2571 \pm 0.0289}$

In the $r = 16$ case one speed-up of 1.2571 occurred at a history size of 65,536 in single precision, all other measures gave a slow-down. The largest slow-down, 0.0197, was observed for a history size of 16 in double precision. It should be noted that several of the calculated speed-ups in this set have accumulated standard deviations that are larger than the mean, implying that the variability of measurements at these points is too high to give an accurate measure.

In the $r = 2048$ case speed-ups were observed at most measurement points, excluding from a history size of 64 to 2,048 in the double precision case. The greatest speed-up, 2.6813, was observed at a history size of 32,768 in double precision. The largest single precision speed-up, 1.6864 was observed at a history size of 65,536. The greatest slow-down 0.7910 was observed at a history size of 1024 in the double precision case. It should be noted that in the $r = 2048$, double precision case, the measurement at history size 65,536 could not be taken as the GPU had reached its global memory limits.

The slow-down observed may be partly attributed to host-GPU memory transfers that take place. The current implementation uses Magma's SVD implementation. The Magma SVD requires inputs from, and returns outputs to host memory; whereas the TR implementation generates SVD inputs and processes SVD outputs on the GPU. This necessitates additional host-GPU memory transfers. While it is likely that these transfers impact the GPU TR execution time, the actual impact of these transfers is yet to be assessed.

6　Conclusion

The Echo State Network and Tikhonov Regularisation training algorithms were implemented for both the CPU, an Intel i7-980; and the GPU, an Nvidia GTX480. The execution times of these implementations were measured and compared.

In the ESN case, speed-ups were observed at reservoir sizes greater than 1,024. The first significant speed-ups of 5.9923 and 4.9652 were observed at a reservoir size of 2,048 in double and single precision respectively.

In the case of Tikhonov Regularisation, no significant speed-ups were observed, and memory limitations were seen for large reservoir state history sizes. This may be due to host-GPU memory transfers required to perform singular value decomposition.

7　Future Work

Experimental refinement, two further experiments, and profiling work is planned. Large variations are observed at some measurement points (See Sect. 5.2), which warrants further investigation. This may be an indication that the measurement "warm-up" time was insufficient. Two further experiments will be conducted. These aim to compare the execution times of the CPU and GPU implementations as reservoir connectivity changes, and when performing a full train-test cycle on chaotic time-series data. Finally, the GPU implementation will be profiled. This may yield information on inefficiencies in the design of the program, and therefore guide us to points of optimisation.

References

[1] Jaeger, H.: The 'echo state' approach to analysing and training recurrent neural networks. GMD - German National Research Institute for Computer Science, GMD Report 148 (December 2001)

[2] Maass, W., Natschlager, T., Markram, H.: Real-time computing without stable states: a new framework for neural computation based on perturbations. Neural Comput 14(11), 2531–2560 (2002)

[3] Lukoševičius, M., Jaeger, H.: Reservoir computing approaches to recurrent neural network training. Computer Science Review 3(3), 127–149 (2009)

[4] Keith, T., Weddell, S., Van Cutsem, T.: Gpu implementation of an echo state network for optical wavefront prediction. In: Grosspietsch, E., Klöckner, K. (eds.) Proceedings of the Work in Progress Session, 20th Euromicro Intl. Conf. on Parallel, Distributed & Network-based Processing, Garching, Germany. SEA-Publications, Johannes Kepler University, Austria (2012)

[5] Jaeger, H.: Tutorial on training recurrent neural networks, covering BPTT, RTRL, EKF and the "echo state network" approach. German National Research Center for Information Technology. Technical Report 159 (October 2002)

[6] Tikhonov, A.N.: Solution of incorrectly formulated problems and the regularization method. Soviet Math. Dokl. 4, 1035–1038 (1963)

[7] Golub, G., Kahan, W.: Calculating the singular values and pseudo-inverse of a matrix. Journal of the Society for Industrial and Applied Mathematics: Series B, Numerical Analysis 2(2), 205–224 (1965)

[8] Press, W.H., Teukolsky, S.A., Vetterling, W.T., Flannery, B.P.: Numerical Recipes 3rd Edition: The Art of Scientific Computing, 3rd edn. Cambridge University Press, New York (2007)

[9] Nvidia Corporation. Nvidia cuda. Nvidia Corporation (October 2012), http://www.nvidia.com/object/cuda_home_new.html

[10] NVIDIA Corporation, NVIDIA CUDA C Programming Guide, version 4.2. NVIDIA Corporation, Santa Clara (April 2012)

[11] Flynn, M.: Some Computer Organizations and Their Effectiveness. IEEE Trans. Comput. C-21, 948+ (1972)

[12] NVIDIA Corporation, CUDA Toolkit 4.2 CURAND Library, version 4.2. NVIDIA Corporation, Santa Clara (March 2012)

[13] Eaton, J.W., Bateman, D., Hauberg, S.: GNU Octave: A high-level interactive language for numerical computations, version 3.6.1, 3rd edn. Free Software Foundation, Inc., Boston (2011)

Solution of Inverse Kinematics by PSO Based on Split and Merge of Particles

Koji Kinoshita, Kenji Murakami, and Masaharu Isshiki

Ehime University, 3 Bunkyo-cho, Matsuyama, Ehime, Japan
kinoshita@cs.ehime-u.ac.jp
http://ipr20.cs.ehime-u.ac.jp/

Abstract. This paper investigates the use of particle swarm optimization (PSO) with repeating splits and merges at predetermined intervals. After a split, there is no exchange of information between the particles, which belong to different swarms. Hence, even though one particle may be trapped in a local minimum, the others are not affected. If the other particles find a better solution, the trapped particle can escape the local minimum when the particles are merged. In order to verify the efficacy of the proposed method, we applied it to the learning of a neural network for solving the inverse kinematics problem of a manipulator with uncertain parameters. The back-propagation rule requires the Jacobian of the forward kinematics, but this cannot be calculated due to uncertainties. Because PSO does not require the derivative of the objective function, it is suitable for this problem. A simulation result shows that the proposed method can obtain more accurate inverse kinematics than either global best (gbest) PSO or local best (lbest) PSO.

Keywords: particle swarm optimization, split and merge, neural network, inverse kinematics.

1 Introduction

Inverse kinematics comprises the computations needed to find the joint angles for a given Cartesian position and orientation of an end-effector. The solution can be used to determine joint motions that will correct measured errors in the position of an end-effector, and thus to effectively control the manipulator. However, this computation is difficult because the relationship between the joint angles and the position of the end-effector is nonlinear. Closed-form solutions are known for only a few simple manipulators. Hence, the gradient method is used to obtain a numerical solution [1]. However, if there is uncertainty in the parameters of the kinematics, neither analytical nor numerical solutions can be computed. Multilayer neural networks can approximate any continuous nonlinear mapping [2], and so neural network methods have been studied for obtaining a model of inverse kinematics [3, 4]. When we apply the back-propagation rule, which is commonly used for updating the coupling weights, the Jacobian of the forward kinematics is required [5]. If the manipulator has uncertain parameters, however, we cannot calculate the Jacobian.

L. Rutkowski et al. (Eds.): ICAISC 2013, Part I, LNAI 7894, pp. 108–117, 2013.

Particle swarm optimization (PSO), which was inspired by the social behavior of flocking birds and schooling fish, was proposed by Kennedy and Eberhart [6]. The particles, which are candidates for the solution, move about in the solution space, seeking to find a global solution by following a simple law of exchanging information with each other. PSO does not require the derivative of the objective function. Several researchers have proposed solving inverse kinematics problems by using a neural network based on PSO [7–9]. However, Kennedy has pointed out that although global best (gbest) PSO converges quickly, it may become trapped in a local minimum [10].

In order to prevent the swarm being trapped in a local minimum, we introduce splitting and merging of the particles at predetermined intervals. After a split, there is no exchange of information between the separated particles. Hence, even though one particle may be trapped in a local minimum, the others are not affected. If another particle finds a better solution, the trapped particles can escape the local minimum after merge.

This paper is structured as follows. Section 2 provides a brief introduction to PSO and then describes in detail the proposed splitting and merging of the particles. In Section 3, we explain the inverse kinematics problem and solve it by using a neural network based on PSO. In Section 4, we perform a simulation for a three-link manipulator. Finally, we present our conclusions in section 5.

2   PSO with Induced Splitting and Merging

In this section, we summarize PSO, which was originally introduced by Kennedy and Eberhart [6]. It is known that the particles tend to converge quickly and the swarm loses its diversity. This hinders the search for a global solution. In order to maintain the diversity of the swarm, we induce splitting and merging of the particles.

2.1   Overview of Particle Swarm Optimization

PSO was inspired by the social behavior of flocking birds and schooling fish. A group of P agents, called *particles*, search through the domain $\mathbf{D} \subseteq R^n$. The position of each particle is denoted by $x_p \in \mathbf{D}$, $(p = 1, \cdots, P)$, and the set of particles is referred to as the *swarm* $\mathbf{S} = \{x_1, \cdots, x_P\}$. Each particle in the swarm moves through the domain $\mathbf{D}$ in search of the global minimum x_0 of the objective function $F(x) \in R$. The searching trajectory for each particle is determined by a simple law that incorporates its momentum, its memory, and the information shared between the particles in its neighborhood. Different types of neighborhoods have been explored [10, 12], but the standard neighborhood is global, i.e., all particles share the best position that is found by any particle in the swarm.

In each iteration, the next position of each particle is determined by its current position $x_p(t)$ and velocity $v_p(t+1)$, as shown in (1):

$$x_p(t+1) = x_p(t) + v_p(t+1) \ , \tag{1}$$

where t denotes the iteration. The next velocity of each particle is determined by its current velocity $\boldsymbol{v}_p(t)$ (momentum), the best position ever found by that particle $\text{pbest}_p(t)$ (memory), and best position ever found by the swarm $\text{gbest}(t)$ (shared information), as shown in (2):

$$\boldsymbol{v}_p(t+1) = \gamma\boldsymbol{v}_p(t) + C_1\text{rand}_1\left(\text{pbest}_p(t) - \boldsymbol{x}_p(t)\right)$$
$$+ C_2\text{rand}_2(\text{gbest}(t) - \boldsymbol{x}_p(t)) , \tag{2}$$

where γ, C_1, and C_2 are positive constants and rand_1 and rand_2 are random numbers from a uniform distribution in the range $[0, 1]$. In order to prevent the velocity from becoming very large, upper and lower limits can be set. Hence, the velocity update rule is given by

$$v_{pi}(t+1) = \begin{cases} v_{\min}, & v_{pi}(t+1) < v_{\min} \\ v_{pi}(t+1), & v_{\min} < v_{pi}(t+1) < v_{\max} \\ v_{\max}, & v_{pi}(t+1) > v_{\max}, \end{cases} \tag{3}$$

where v_{pi} is the i-th component of $\boldsymbol{v}_p$ and $v_{\max}$ and $v_{\min}$ are the upper and lower limits, respectively.

A schematic of a search conducted with PSO is illustrated in Fig. 1.

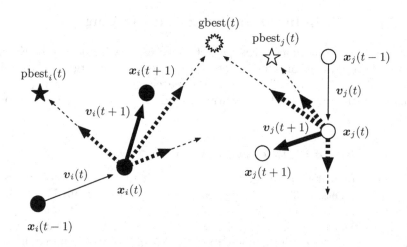

Fig. 1. Illustration of PSO

The PSO algorithm is as follows:

1) Randomly generate the initial position $\boldsymbol{x}_p(0)$ and velocity $\boldsymbol{v}_p(0)$ for each of the particles.
2) Evaluate the objective function for each particle, and set the initial personal best (pbest) and global best as follows: $\text{pbest}_p(0) = \boldsymbol{x}_p(0)$ and $\text{gbest}(0) = \arg\max_{\boldsymbol{x}_p} F(\boldsymbol{x}_p(0))$.

3) Update the velocity and position by using (2) and (1).
4) Evaluate the objective function at the new position.
5) Update the personal best, if $F(\boldsymbol{x}_p(t+1)) < E(\text{pbest}_p(t))$.
6) Update the global best, if $\min_p F(\boldsymbol{x}_p(t+1)) < F(\text{gbest}(t))$.
7) Go to 3) until the maximum iteration is satisfied.

We call this algorithm gbest PSO.

2.2   Splitting and Merging of the Swarm

Kennedy has pointed out that gbest PSO converges quickly, but it may become trapped in a local minimum [10]. This happens because the swarm loses diversity since the search is always performed as a single swarm. In order to prevent the swarm being trapped in a local minimum, we introduce splitting and merging of the particles at predetermined intervals. After a split, there is no exchange of information between the separated particles. Hence, even though one particle may be trapped, the others are not affected. If another particle finds a better solution, the trapped particles can escape from local minimum after merging the particles.

There are various methods, such as k-means clustering, for splitting particles. It is expected that clustering does not preserve the diversity of the swarm, but is similar to the situation of searching with only a few particles. This is because clustering organizes the particles into groups whose members are similar in some way. We propose a method that divides the particles based on their Euclidean distance from gbest (Fig. 2). The particles in the swarm that are farthest from gbest are regarded as heterogeneous ones. When the particles are split, the best solution in each swarm becomes the gbest of it. When the particles are merged, the best gbest of each swarm becomes the gbest of whole swarm.

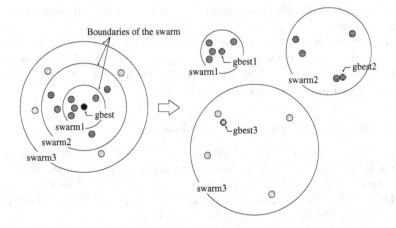

Fig. 2. Split of the particles

To apply our method, it is necessary to determine the swarm's boundaries, which are determined by the states of the particles. In practice, we calculate the Euclidean distance of each from gbest, $D_p = \|x_p - \text{gbest}\|$, and sort the particles in ascending order according to D_p. After sorting, we denote the particle index as $\tau(p)$, where $\tau(\cdot)$ is the permutation of the index. The boundaries are set by the largest distance $\Delta D_{\tau(p)} = D_{\tau(p)+1} - D_{\tau(p)}$. Fig. 3 illustrates a split.

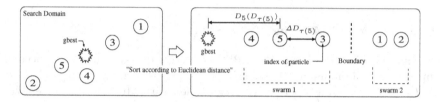

Fig. 3. Boundaries based on the Euclidean distance

In the example shown in the figure, there are five particles that are split into two swarms. In k-means clustering, the two swarms would be $\{x_1, x_3\}$ and $\{x_2, x_4, x_5\}$. In our method, however, the two swarms are $\{x_3, x_4, x_5\}$ and $\{x_1, x_2\}$.

3   Solving Inverse Kinematics of Manipulator by NN-PSO

Inverse kinematics comprises the computations necessary for finding the joint angles for a given Cartesian position and orientation of an end-effector. This computation is difficult because the relation between the joint angles and the position of the end-effector is nonlinear. The gradient method is used to find a numerical solution [1]. However, if there is uncertainty in the parameters for the kinematics, we cannot compute the analytically or numerical solutions. Hence, the computation of inverse kinematics based on the learning of neural networks has been proposed.

In this section, we describe the inverse kinematics problem and how it can be solved by using a neural network. The difficulty in applying the back-propagation rule for inverse kinematics is discussed. The advantages of applying PSO for the learning of a neural network are explained.

3.1   Inverse Kinematics of a Manipulator

For a given manipulator with K degree of freedom, a joint configuration establishes the unique position and orientation in Cartesian space of the end-effector. We denote the joint variables by $q = [q_1, \cdots, q_K]^{\mathrm{T}}$. Also, we define the position variables that describe the manipulator tasks by $r = [r_1, \cdots, r_L]^{\mathrm{T}}$, where r and q are related by the forward kinematics equation

$$r = f(q). \tag{4}$$

The inverse kinematics problem is to find the inverse mapping of (4):

$$q = f^{-1}(r) \ .$$ (5)

Due to the nonlinearity of $f(\cdot)$, obtaining a closed-form solution is impossible for most manipulators. Moreover, if there is uncertainty in any of the parameters of the manipulator, then we cannot obtain the inverse kinematics by a direct numerical approach.

3.2 Neural Network for Solving Inverse Kinematics

A multi-layer neural network can approximate any continuous nonlinear mapping [2]. Hence, the inverse kinematics can be obtained by using a neural network.

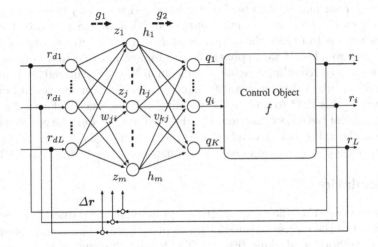

Fig. 4. Network structure and control object

Fig. 4 shows the neural network and control object for solving the inverse kinematics problem. A desired trajectory $r_d(t) = (r_{d1}(t), \cdots, r_{dL}(t))^{\mathrm{T}}$, where $t = 1, \cdots, T$ represents the data number, is given as input to a multi-layered neural network. We delete the data number in order to simplify the notation in the following statement. Let the input signal to the hidden layer be $z = (z_1, \cdots, z_m)^{\mathrm{T}}$ and the coupling weight from the input layer to the hidden layer be w_{ji}. The mapping g_1 from r_d to z is expressed as

$$z = \begin{pmatrix} \sum_{i=1}^{L+1} w_{1i} r_{di} \\ \vdots \\ \sum_{i=1}^{L+1} w_{mi} r_{di} \end{pmatrix} = g_1(r_d) \ ,$$ (6)

where $r_{d,L+1} = 1$ is the bias input and $w_{j,L+1}$ is the threshold. Let the output of the hidden layer be $h = (h_1, \cdots, h_m)^{\mathrm{T}}$ and the transformation from the input to the output in the hidden layer be the sigmoid function $\sigma(\cdot)$. The output of the hidden layer is expressed as

$$h_j = \frac{1}{1 + \exp(-z_j)} = \sigma(z_j). \tag{7}$$

The output of the neural network and the coupling weight from the hidden layer to the output layer are represented as $q = (q_1, \cdots, q_K)^{\mathrm{T}}$ and v_{kj}, respectively. The mapping g_2 from z to q is expressed as

$$q = \begin{pmatrix} \sum_{j=1}^{m+1} v_{1j} h_j \\ \vdots \\ \sum_{j=1}^{m+1} v_{Kj} h_j \end{pmatrix} = \begin{pmatrix} \sum_{j=1}^{m} v_{1j} \sigma(z_j) + v_{1,m+1} \\ \vdots \\ \sum_{j=1}^{m} v_{Kj} \sigma(z_j) + v_{K,m+1} \end{pmatrix} = g_2(z) , \tag{8}$$

where $h_{m+1} = 1$ is the bias input and $v_{j,m+1}$ is the threshold.

Let the forward kinematics be f and the realized trajectory be $r = f(q)$. The inverse model f^{-1} is obtained on the neural network if $\Delta r = r_d - r = 0$. The goal of this scheme is to reduce the output error $E(w, v) = \|\Delta r(w, v)\|$ by updating the coupling weights. If we apply the back-propagation rule that is commonly used to update the coupling weights, the Jacobian $\partial f / \partial q$ is required [5]. However, we cannot calculate the Jacobian if there is uncertainty in the control object. Therefore, we use PSO to update the coupling weights, since it does not require the derivative of the object function, i.e., the Jacobian $\partial f / \partial q$. The position of the particle is the collection of weights, $x = (w_{11}, \cdots, w_{m,L+1}, v_{11}, \cdots, v_{K,m+1})^{\mathrm{T}}$. The dimension of the solution domain becomes $m \times (L + 1) + K \times (m + 1)$.

4   Simulation

In order to verify the efficacy of splitting and merging the particles, we applied this method to the inverse kinematics problem for a three-link manipulator that moves in the horizontal plane (Fig. 5). The forward kinematics is expressed as follows:

$$r_1 = l_1 \cos q_1 + l_2 \cos(q_1 + q_2) + l_3 \cos(q_1 + q_2 + q_3) \tag{9}$$
$$r_2 = l_1 \sin q_1 + l_2 \sin(q_1 + q_2) + l_3 \sin(q_1 + q_2 + q_3) , \tag{10}$$

where (r_1, r_2) and (q_1, q_2, q_3) represent the end-effector position and the joint angles, respectively. In addition, l_1, l_2, and l_3 are the lengths of each of the links.

A three-layered neural network was prepared. The input and output layers were composed of two and three neurons, respectively. We evaluated for desired trajectories $r_d(t)$ (linear, rectangular, or figure-eight form), as shown in Fig. 6, and uniformly distributed random points $r_{d1} \in [0.1, 0.6]$, and $r_{d2} \in [0.2, 0.3]$. The objective function is the root-mean-square (RMS) error between the desired trajectory and the position of the end-effector,

$$\mathrm{RMS} = \sqrt{\frac{1}{T} \sum_{t=1}^{T} \{(r_{d1}(t) - r_1(t))^2 + (r_{d2}(t) - r_2(t))^2\}} . \tag{11}$$

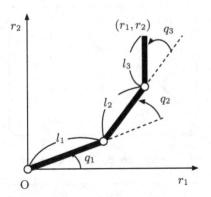

Fig. 5. Three-link manipulator

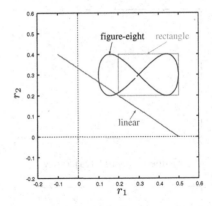

Fig. 6. Desired trajectory

The parameters of the simulation are listed in Table 1. In this simulation, the inertia weight γ and the acceleration constants C_1, C_2 were set by the construction factor method (CFM), which was presented by Clerc and Kennedy [11]. We set the interval for splitting and merging based on experiment.

Table 1. Simulation parameters

length of link 1	$l_1 = 0.3[m]$
length of link 2	$l_2 = 0.35[m]$
length of link 3	$l_3 = 0.4[m]$
amount of data	$T = 100$
number of neurons in the hidden layer	$m = 6$
range of initial weight	uniform random number in $[-10, 10]$
maximum iterations	5000
splitting and merging interval	100
number of particles	$P = 21$
number of clusters	$C = 3$
inertia weight	$\gamma = 0.729$
acceleration constant	$C_1, C_2 = 1.4955$
limitation on velocity	$V_{min} = -0.1, V_{max} = 0.1$

We measured the RMS error after updating was terminated for 1,000 sets of initial weights that had different values. We compared gbest PSO, local best (lbest) PSO with ring topology, and our split-and-merge PSO. In split-and-merge PSO, the particles were split by k-means clustering and the proposed method.

Fig. 7 shows the accumulated histogram of the RMS error for each method. The horizontal axis represents the RMS error when the iteration terminated. The vertical axis represents the cumulative relative frequency. For all the desired trajectories, the proposed method provides the accurate inverse kinematics.

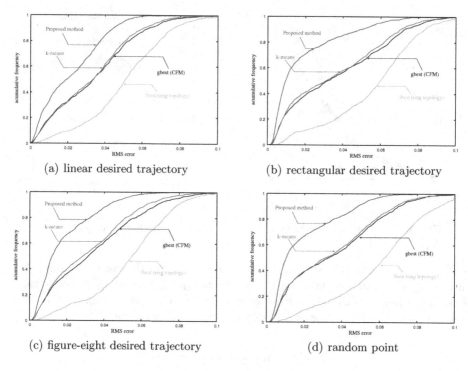

(a) linear desired trajectory

(b) rectangular desired trajectory

(c) figure-eight desired trajectory

(d) random point

Fig. 7. Accumulated histogram of the RMS error

As mentioned in the above section, splitting and merging by using k-means clustering did not obtain a better performance, although we performed simulations with several different sets of intervals. Since ring topology provides a mechanism for slowing down information propagation in the particle population, it cannot obtain a better performance in this experiment. Many iterations would be required if we wanted to obtain a more accurate inverse model by using lbest PSO.

5   Conclusion

In this paper, we proposed splitting and merging particles in a swarm. After a split, the particles do not exchange information, and so a particle that may be trapped in a local minimum is able to escape from local minimum after merging. Simulation results showed that the proposed method performs much better than conventional PSO.

We experimented with different values before setting the constant interval for splitting and merging. Further work is needed to determine how to adjust the interval depending on the state of the particles. In addition, we will compare the performance of our algorithm with other method based on multiple swarms [15].

References

1. Wampler, C.W.: Manipulator Inverse Kinematic Solutions Based on Vector Formulations and Damped Least-Squares Methods. IEEE Trans. Systems, Man and Cybernetics 16(1), 93–101 (1986)
2. Funahashi, K.: On the Approximate Realization of Continuous Mappings by Neural Networks. Neural Networks 2(3), 183–192 (1989)
3. Guez, A., Ahmad, Z.: Solution to the Inverse Kinematics Problem in Robotics by Neural Networks. In: Proc. IEEE Int. Conf. Neural Networks, pp. 617–621 (1988)
4. Mao, Z., Hsia, T.C.: Obstacle Avoidance Inverse Kinematics Solution of Redundant Robots by Neural Networks. Robotica 15, 3–10 (1997)
5. Jordan, M.I., Rumelhart, D.E.: Forward Models: Supervised Learning with a Distal Teacher. Cognitive Science 16, 307–354 (1992)
6. Kennedy, J., Eberhart, R.: Particle Swarm Optimization. In: Proc. Int. Conf. on Neural Networks, pp. 1942–1948 (1995)
7. Wen, X., Sheng, D., Huang, J.: A Hybrid Particle Swarm Optimization for Manipulator Inverse Kinematics Control. In: Huang, D.-S., Wunsch II, D.C., Levine, D.S., Jo, K.-H. (eds.) ICIC 2008. LNCS, vol. 5226, pp. 784–791. Springer, Heidelberg (2008)
8. Wen, X., Sheng, D., Guo, J.: Manipulator Inverse Kinematics Control Based on Particle Swarm Optimization Neural Network. In: Proc. SPIE 7129 - The Int. Society for Opt. Eng., art. no. 712911 (2008)
9. Li, Z.M., Li, C.G., Lv, S.J.: A Method for Solving Inverse Kinematics of PUMA560 Manipulator Based on PSO-RBF Network. In: Proc. of Int. Conf. on Natural Comput., pp. 298–301 (2012)
10. Kennedy, J.: Small Worlds and Mega-minds: Effects of Neighborhood Topology on Particle Swarm Performance. In: Proc. IEEE Congr. Evol. Comput., pp. 1931–1938 (1999)
11. Clerc, M., Kennedy, J.: The Particle Swarm - Explosion, Stability, and Convergence in a Multidimensional Complex Space. IEEE Trans. on Evol. Comput. 6, 58–73 (2002)
12. Kennedy, J., Mendes, R.: Population Structure and Particle Swarm Performance. In: Proc. IEEE Congr. Evol. Comput., pp. 1671–1675 (2002)
13. del Valle, Y., et al.: Particle Swarm Optimization: Basic Concepts, Variants and Applications in Power Systems. IEEE Trans. EC 12(2), 171–195 (2008)
14. Kameyama, K.: Particle Swarm Optimization: A Survey. IEICE Transactions on Information and Systems E92-D(7), 1354–1361 (2009)
15. Yen, G.G., Daneshyari, M.: Diversity-based Information Exchange among Multiple Swarms in Particle Swarm Optimization. In: Proc. IEEE Congr. Evol. Comput., pp. 1686–1693 (2006)

Probabilistic Neural Network Structure Reduction for Medical Data Classification

Maciej Kusy and Jacek Kluska

Faculty of Electrical and Computer Engineering, Rzeszow University of Technology,
35-959 Rzeszow, W. Pola 2, Poland
{mkusy,jacklu}@prz.edu.pl

Abstract. Probabilistic neural network (PNN) consists of the number of pattern neurons that equals the cardinality of the data set. The model design is therefore complex for large database classification problems. In this article, two effective PNN reduction procedures are introduced. In the first approach, the PNN's pattern layer neurons are reduced by means of a k-means clustering procedure. The second method uses a support vector machines algorithm to select pattern layer nodes. Modified PNN networks are compared with the original model in medical data classification problems. The prediction ability expressed in terms of the 20% test set error for the networks is assessed. By means of the experiments, it is shown that the appropriate pruning of the pattern layer neurons in the PNN enhances the performance of the classifier.

Keywords: probabilistic neural network, k-means clustering, support vector machines, classification, prediction ability.

1 Introduction

The probabilistic neural network (PNN), proposed by Specht [1] is a direct implementation of the Bayes classifier. It can quickly learn from input data but requires one neuron in the pattern layer for each training example [2]. PNNs have found their implementation in variety of classification fields. It was presented in image classification and recognition [3], [4], earthquake magnitude prediction [5] or medical diagnosis and prediction [6]–[9]. The important contribution was provided in [10] where PNN was applied to pattern classification in time-varying environment.

Since PNN consists of a single node for each data, various modifications of the network have been proposed. For example, in [11], by estimating probability density functions as a mixture of the Gaussian densities with varying covariance matrices it was possible to design PNN so that it used fewer nodes than training patterns. The work in [12] presented learning vector quantization technique for finding representative patterns to be used as neurons in PNN. In [13], the authors presented a Generalized Fisher algorithm for PNN and showed that it required significantly fewer nodes and interconnection weights than original model. The reference in [3] presented the reduction of the size of the training data for PNN

L. Rutkowski et al. (Eds.): ICAISC 2013, Part I, LNAI 7894, pp. 118–129, 2013.

by hierarchical clustering. Here, the reciprocal neighbors technique was applied which allowed to gather the examples which were closest to each other. In [14], the quantization method for PNN structure was proposed. The input space was divided into a fixed-size hyper-grid and within each hyper-cube a representative cluster centres were computed. Therefore, the number of training vectors in each hyper-cube was reduced to one. The research in [15] presented the automatic construction of PNN by the use of a dynamic decay adjustment algorithm. The model was dynamically built during training which automatically optimized the number of hidden neurons. The work reported in [4] proposed PNN with no distance matrix needed for storing the pairwise distances between input examples and the vector to be classified. It was achieved by maintaining the nearest neighbor table of indices of the nearest cluster for each cluster. In [16], a supervised PNN structure determination algorithm was introduced. The procedure employed genetic algorithm for pattern layer neuron selection.

It is necessary to note that the PNN model is equipped with the intrinsic smoothing parameter of the pattern layer neurons activated by Gaussian function. It must be estimated on the basis of a classification performance. Three approaches are usually regarded: single parameter for whole PNN, separate parameter for each variable (dimension) or single parameter for each class. In the research, a diverse procedures have been developed to solve the problem [2], [6], [16], [17].

In this article, two alternative approaches of the structure minimization of the probabilistic neural network are introduced. The first method is based on the application of k-means clustering algorithm to input data in order to determine the optimal number of centroids as the representation of the pattern layer neurons. In the second solution, the support vector machine procedure is applied which, out of the entire training database, provides the set of support vectors. The support vectors form then the layer of pattern nodes of PNN. Both techniques are tested on the medical data sets.

This paper is composed of the following sections. Section 2 discusses probabilistic neural network highlighting its basics, a structure and a principle of operations. In Section 3, the reduction of PNN structure by means of a k-means clustering and support vector machines algorithm is proposed. Section 4 briefly describes the input data used in the research. Additionally, the performance of the standard and the modified PNN models is here verified. Finally, in Section 5, the conclusions are presented.

2   Probabilistic Neural Network

Assume, we are given an input vector $\mathbf{x} \in \mathbb{R}^n$ which belongs to one of the predefined classes $g = 1, 2, \ldots, G$. Let the probability of the vector $\mathbf{x}$ belonging to the class g equals p_g, the cost associated with classifying the vector into class g is c_g and that the probability density functions: $y_1(\mathbf{x}), y_2(\mathbf{x}), \ldots, y_G(\mathbf{x})$ for all classes are known. Then, according to the Bayes theorem, when $g \neq h$, the vector $\mathbf{x}$ is classified to the class g, if $p_g c_g y_g(\mathbf{x}) > p_h c_h y_h(\mathbf{x})$. Usually $p_g = p_h$ and $c_g = c_h$, thus one can infer that if $y_g(\mathbf{x}) > y_h(\mathbf{x})$, then the vector $\mathbf{x}$ belongs to the class g.

In real data classification problems, data set distribution is usually unknown and an approximation of the probability density function $y_g(\mathbf{x})$ has to be determined. This can be achieved using the Parzen method [18] where the probability density function for multiple variables can be expressed as follows

$$y(\mathbf{x}) = \frac{1}{l} \sum_{i=1}^{l} W_i(\mathbf{x}, \mathbf{x}_i), \qquad (1)$$

where $W_i(\mathbf{x}, \mathbf{x}_i) = \sigma_1^{-1} \ldots \sigma_n^{-1} F\left(\sigma_1^{-1}(x_{i1} - x_1), \ldots, \sigma_n^{-1}(x_{in} - x_n)\right)$, $F(\cdot)$ is the weighting function which has to be appropriately selected [19], l is the number of input patterns, and $\sigma_1, \ldots, \sigma_n$ denote standard deviations computed relative to the mean of n variables $x_1, \ldots, x_n$. Usually, the Gaussian function is a common choice for weighting in (1).

The formula in (1) defines the structure and the operation of PNN. If we consider a Gaussian function as the activation for the probability density function and assume that this function is computed for the examples of class g then Parzen's definition takes the following form

$$y_g(\mathbf{x}) = \frac{1}{l_g (2\pi)^{n/2} (\det \Sigma_g)^{1/2}} \sum_{i=1}^{l_g} \exp\left(-\frac{1}{2} (\mathbf{x}_{g,i} - \mathbf{x})^T \Sigma_g^{-1} (\mathbf{x}_{g,i} - \mathbf{x})\right), \quad (2)$$

where $\Sigma_g = \mathrm{diag}\left(\sigma_{g,1}^2, \ldots, \sigma_{g,n}^2\right)$ is the covariance matrix, l_g is the number of the examples of class g, $\sigma_{g,j}$ denotes the smoothing parameter associated with j-th variable and the g-th class, and $\mathbf{x}_{g,i}$ is the i-th training vector $(i = 1, \ldots, l_g)$ from the class g. The formula presented in (2) provides one of $g = 1, \ldots, G$ summation neurons of PNN structure. The elements of the preceding layer, the pattern neurons, feed the component to the sum which is measured over each of the examples of g-th class. Therefore, l_g hidden neurons constitute the input for g-th summation neuron. Finally, the output layer determines the output for the vector $\mathbf{x}$ in accordance with the Bayes's decision rule based on the outputs of all the summation layer neurons

$$G^*(\mathbf{x}) = \arg\max_g \{y_g(\mathbf{x})\}, \qquad (3)$$

where $G^*(\mathbf{x})$ denotes the predicted class for the pattern $\mathbf{x}$. Thus, the pattern layer requires $l = l_1 + \ldots + l_G$ nodes.

In this paper, single smoothing parameter for each attribute and class is applied. The choice of this variant of σ selection imposes, in accordance with formula (2), the inevitability of storing a $G \times n$ matrix of σ's. Hence, the g-th summation neuron yields to the decision layer the output signal (2) but with $\sigma_{g,j}$ as the intrinsic parameter. Therefore, the smoothing parameter is computed for the j-th variable of each class g. Such an approach gives the possibility of emphasizing the similarity of the vectors belonging to the same class. The values of σ's are determined using the conjugate gradient method.

3   PNN Reduction Methods

In this section, two approaches of PNN structure simplification are presented. Both solutions consist in decreasing the number of pattern neurons of the network. The first method is based upon k-means procedure. The second idea utilizes the support vectors for PNN training.

3.1   The Use of k-Means Clustering for PNN Structure Reduction

The k-means algorithm is a data clustering method [20] which is considered to be one of the top ten algorithms in data mining [21]. The procedure finds k clusters, such that all the records within each cluster are similar to each other and distinct from records in other clusters. The grouping process relies on the iterative minimization of the sum of squared distances computed between input vectors and the cluster center. An initial set of clusters is defined, and the cluster centres are repeatedly updated until no modification of their coordinate values takes place.

The first approach in PNN structure reduction uses k-means algorithm in a simple iterative way. The number of clusters of class g in s-th iteration is determined according to the formula

$$i_{s,g} = \text{round}\left(\frac{s}{N}\eta l_g\right), \quad s = 1, \ldots, N-1, \tag{4}$$

where η is a fraction of training data ($1 - \eta$ is the part for testing) and round (x) is the function that rounds the real positive number x to the nearest integer. In this paper, we assume $\eta = 0.8$, and $N = 10$. It is important to notice, that only $i_{s,g}$ pattern layer neurons of class g are involved in computation of the signal for the summation layer neuron. The **Algorithm 1** summarizes the proposed method.

Algorithm 1. PNN architecture optimization based on k-means clustering.

Randomly determine training and test sets
for $s = 1$ to $N - 1$ **do**
  for $g = 1$ to G **do**
    | Compute $i_{s,g}$ cluster centres for training set
  end
  Train PNN on $c_s = \sum_{g=1}^{G} i_{s,g}$ cluster centres
  Read $\sigma_1^{(1)}, \ldots, \sigma_n^{(G)}$ which minimize PNN training error
  Calculate test error E_{test} for PNN on test set
end

Now, if we define the reduction ratio R as a quotient of the number of pattern neurons by the size of the training data set for the PNN

$$R(s) = \frac{\sum_{g=1}^{G} i_{s,g}}{\eta l} \cong \frac{s}{N}, \quad s = 1, \ldots, N-1,$$ (5)

then the optimal ratio in the sense of the stated problem is $R(s^*)$ for

$$s^* = \arg \min_{1 \leqslant s \leqslant N-1} E_{test}(s),$$ (6)

where $E_{test}(s)$ is the test error obtained by the s-th cluster's variant and s^* is computed numerically.

3.2   The Use of Support Vector Machines for PNN Structure Reduction

Support vector machine (SVM) [22] is one of the most accurate methods among all well-known classification algorithms [21]. It constructs an optimal classifier for the input vector $\mathbf{x}_i$ ($i = 1, \ldots, l$) from the class labelled $y_i = \pm 1$. Two types of SVM algorithms are usually applied in data mining problems: C-SVM model and ν-SVM model [23]. In this research, C-based SVM is used. The C-SVM training amounts to the solution of the following quadratic programming optimization (QP) problem

$$\begin{cases} \max_{\boldsymbol{\alpha}} W(\boldsymbol{\alpha}) = -\dfrac{1}{2} \langle \boldsymbol{\alpha}, \mathbf{H}\boldsymbol{\alpha} \rangle + \langle \boldsymbol{\alpha}, \mathbf{1} \rangle \\[2mm] 0 \leqslant \boldsymbol{\alpha} \leqslant C \cdot \mathbf{1}, \quad \langle \boldsymbol{\alpha}, \mathbf{y} \rangle = 0, \end{cases}$$ (7)

where $\langle \cdot, \cdot \rangle$ denotes the scalar product, $\boldsymbol{\alpha} = [\alpha_1, \ldots, \alpha_l]^T$ is the vector of Lagrange multipliers, $\mathbf{H} = \{y_i y_j K(\mathbf{x}_i, \mathbf{x}_j)\}$ is $l \times l$ matrix, $K(\cdot, \cdot)$ is the kernel function, $\mathbf{y} = [y_1, \ldots, y_l]^T$ is the vector of class labels, $\mathbf{0} = [0, \ldots, 0]^T$ and $\mathbf{1} = [1, \ldots, 1]^T$. Once the solution of (7) is obtained in terms of $\boldsymbol{\alpha}$ vector, the optimal classifier is formulated

$$\text{class}(\mathbf{x}) = \text{sign} \left(\sum_{i=1}^{l} \alpha_i y_i K(\mathbf{x}_i, \mathbf{x}) + b \right).$$ (8)

The input vectors $\mathbf{x}_i$ having $\alpha_i > 0$ are called support vectors (SVs). They constitute a sufficient sub-set out of given input data for a sample prediction. As it can be observed, the solution of the QP problem in (7) involves the constraint for α_i which requires the choice of unknown C parameter. The value of C coefficient introduces additional capacity control for the classifier. The adjustment of C provides greater or smaller number of support vectors what, in turn, influences the classification accuracy. In this research, by setting different values of C constraint, we are capable of obtaining different sets of support vectors. Depending on the considered data set and the value of C, the number of pattern neurons of PNN changes.

The final classification outcome also depends on the kernel function $K(\cdot, \cdot)$ applied in (8). Much study in recent years has been devoted to adopting different kernels for SVM [24]–[26]. In this contribution, the Gaussian kernel function is applied with the spread constant (sc) as the parameter:

$$K(\mathbf{x}, \mathbf{y}) = \exp\left(-\frac{\|\mathbf{x} - \mathbf{y}\|^2}{2(sc)^2}\right). \tag{9}$$

An appropriate range of the spread constant has to be estimated which is realized numerically with the assumption of achieving the highest generalization ability of the classifier.

For C and sc parameters, the final sets of values A_C and A_{sc} are assumed, respectively. The SVM based PNN reduction methodology is summarized in form of **Algorithm 2**.

Algorithm 2. PNN architecture optimization based on SVM

Randomly determine training and test sets
for $C \in A_C$ **and** $sc \in A_{sc}$ **do**
    Perform SVM classification on training set
    Select support vectors SVs
    Train PNN on SVs
    Read $\sigma_1^{(1)}, \ldots, \sigma_n^{(G)}$ which minimize PNN training error
    Calculate test error E_{test} for PNN on test set
end

The particular values for both, A_C and A_{sc} are provided in Section 4.2.

4 Results

In the simulations, seven UCI machine learning repository medical data sets are used [27]: Wisconsin breast cancer (WBC): 683 instances with 9 attributes (binary classification), Pima Indians diabetes (PID): 768 cases having 8 features (binary classification), Haberman's survival (HS): 306 patients and 3 measured variables (binary classification), Cardiotocography (CTG): 2126 measurements on 23 attributes (three state classification), Thyroid (T): 7200 instances with 21 attributes (three state classification), Dermatology (D): 358 cases each of 34 features (six data sets classification) and diagnostic Wisconsin breast cancer (DWBC): 569 instances having 30 variables (binary classification). Additionally, authors' real ovarian cancer (OC) data set is used in the simulations: it represents 199 women after ovarian cancer treatment with 17 parameters registered for each case. The data is obtained from the Clinical Department of Obstetrics and Gynecology of Rzeszow State Hospital in Poland. The analysis of treatment of ovarian cancer and its hormonal and genetic aspects are studied in [28].

In all cases, no data preprocessing (normalization, feature extraction) is performed. After random selection of 20% of the input data for testing purposes, training and test sets are preserved for all the data and each method what makes both approaches comparable.

The following sections present the comparison of the prediction ability measured for the standard PNN model and the networks for which the number of pattern neurons is reduced by means of two proposed approaches: the application of k-means method to cluster the data, and the use of the support vectors as the new database. The prediction ability of the examined classifiers is determined on the basis of the test error (E_{test}) computed on the 20% of input examples randomly extracted from each of given data sets. The number of the test vectors for WBC, PID, HS, CTG, T, D, DWBC and OC data sets is equal 137, 154, 61, 425, 1440, 72, 456 and 40, respectively. The bottom rows of Tables 1–4 present the test error for original PNN.

4.1   Experimental Results after the Use of Algorithm 1

Tables 1–4 illustrate the test error computed after data clustering according to **Algorithm 1** for all considered data sets. The sum $\sum_{g=1}^{G} i_{s,g}$ defines the total number of pattern layer neurons. It can be observed that in each data classification case, by reducing the number of pattern neurons of PNN, it is possible to find the smaller test error than the one computed with the use of all pattern neurons of the model. It is also worth to note that, in all data classification cases, the decrease of the test error takes place more than once.

The most gainful reduction ratio R can be read from the Tables 1–4, e.g. for WBC data set it takes the value $R = 55/(0.8 * 683) \cong 0.1$. Therefore, instead of 683 cases of original data we can use their substitutes but about 10 times smaller in number.

Table 1. The number of cluster centres used in determining PNN structure and the test error for WBC data set (left table) and PID data set (right table)

s	$i_{s,1}$	$i_{s,2}$	Pattern neurons	E_{test} [%]	s	$i_{s,1}$	$i_{s,2}$	Pattern neurons	E_{test} [%]
1	36	19	55	6.569	1	40	21	61	62.337
2	71	38	109	8.029	2	80	43	123	29.220
3	107	57	164	10.949	3	120	64	184	29.220
4	142	76	218	15.328	4	160	86	246	38.311
5	178	96	274	14.599	5	200	107	307	31.168
6	213	115	328	10.219	6	240	128	368	28.571
7	248	134	384	9.489	7	280	150	430	29.220
8	284	153	437	11.679	8	320	171	491	33.766
9	320	172	492	7.299	9	360	193	553	32.467
All	355	191	546	9.489	All	400	214	614	31.818

Table 2. The number of cluster centres used in determining PNN structure and the test error for HS data set (left table) and CTG data set (right table)

s	$i_{s,1}$	$i_{s,2}$	Pattern neurons	E_{test} [%]
1	18	7	25	24.590
2	36	13	49	24.590
3	54	20	74	26.229
4	72	26	98	27.868
5	90	33	123	26.229
6	108	39	147	26.229
7	126	46	172	26.229
8	144	52	196	27.868
9	162	59	221	57.377
All	180	65	245	31.147

s	$i_{s,1}$	$i_{s,2}$	$i_{s,3}$	Pattern neurons	E_{test} [%]
1	132	24	14	170	19.058
2	265	47	28	340	21.411
3	397	71	42	510	28.470
4	530	94	56	680	36.941
5	662	118	71	851	35.294
6	794	142	85	1021	11.529
7	927	165	99	1191	15.529
8	1059	189	113	1361	12.470
9	1191	212	127	1530	16.941
All	1324	236	141	1701	15.529

Table 3. The number of cluster centres used in determining PNN structure and the test error for T data set (left table) and D data set (right table)

s	$i_{s,1}$	$i_{s,2}$	$i_{s,3}$	Pattern neurons	E_{test} [%]
1	13	29	533	575	60.625
2	27	59	1067	1153	43.402
3	40	88	1600	1728	89.166
4	53	118	2133	2304	7.222
5	67	147	2667	2881	6.458
6	80	176	3200	3456	7.638
7	93	206	3733	4032	80.833
8	106	235	4266	4607	6.597
9	120	265	4800	5185	94.5141
All	133	294	5333	5760	11.181

s	$i_{s,1}$	$i_{s,2}$	$i_{s,3}$	$i_{s,4}$	$i_{s,5}$	$i_{s,6}$	Pattern neurons	E_{test} [%]
1	9	6	5	4	4	2	30	26.388
2	18	11	10	8	8	3	58	15.277
3	27	17	14	11	11	5	87	18.055
4	36	23	19	15	15	6	114	11.111
5	45	29	24	19	19	8	142	12.500
6	53	34	29	23	23	10	172	11.111
7	62	40	34	27	27	11	201	8.333
8	71	46	38	30	30	13	229	13.888
9	80	51	43	34	34	14	258	18.055
All	89	57	48	38	38	16	286	13.888

Table 4. The number of cluster centres used in determining PNN structure and the test error for DWBC data set (left table) and OC data set (right table)

s	$i_{s,1}$	$i_{s,2}$	Pattern neurons	E_{test} [%]
1	17	29	46	23.009
2	34	57	91	25.664
3	51	86	137	9.735
4	68	114	182	43.363
5	85	143	228	30.973
6	102	172	274	50.442
7	119	200	319	35.398
8	136	229	365	49.558
9	153	257	410	21.239
All	170	286	456	32.743

s	$i_{s,1}$	$i_{s,2}$	Pattern neurons	E_{test} [%]
1	11	5	16	60.000
2	21	11	32	25.000
3	32	16	48	32.500
4	42	22	64	17.500
5	53	27	80	7.500
6	63	32	95	30.000
7	74	38	112	20.000
8	84	43	127	12.500
9	95	49	144	20.000
All	105	54	159	15.000

4.2 Experimental Results after the Use of Algorithm 2

The second approach of PNN reduction consists in extracting the set of support vectors (SVs) out of the entire original data set and setting SVs as the network's pattern neurons. The process of SVs selection is performed according to **Algorithm 2**. The verification of C and sc settings requires a vast number of experiments.

The grid search for both C constraint and sc spread constant is performed: $A_C = \{10^{-1}, 10^0, 10^1, 10^2, 10^3, 10^4, 10^5, 10^6\}$ and $A_{sc} = \{0.08, 0.2, 0.3, 0.5, 0.8, 1.2, 1.5, 2, 5, 10, 50, 80, 100, 200, 500\}$. The optimal values of (C^*, sc^*) are computed as follows:

$$(C^*, sc^*) = \arg \min_{(C, sc) \in A_C \times A_{sc}} \{E_{test}(C, sc)\} \qquad (10)$$

where E_{test} is the test error and C^*, sc^* are computed numerically.

The results are shown in Tables 5–6. From these tables one can read the number of support vectors used to construct the PNN's pattern layer and the lowest test errors calculated by the modified network. Two bottom rows indicate the test error for the original PNN and best results obtained by means of **Algorithm 1**.

One can observe that the use of the support vectors as the pattern neurons provides the decrease in the test error of PNN in all data classification cases.

Table 5. The number of support vectors used in determining PNN structure and the test error for WBC, PID, HS and CTG data sets

sc	WBC $C^* = 10^4$		PID $C^* = 10^2$		HS $C^* = 10^0$		CTG $C^* = 10^3$	
	SVs	E_{test} [%]	SVs	E_{test} [%]	SVs	E_{test} [%]	SVs	E_{test} [%]
0.08	43	13.138	319	64.935	135	26.229	162	86.117
0.2	48	15.328	314	64.935	134	26.229	144	48.705
0.3	47	14.598	310	64.935	136	26.229	142	26.588
0.5	47	10.218	304	64.935	133	26.229	152	11.294
0.8	48	18.978	300	64.935	137	26.229	172	25.176
1.2	49	13.868	303	64.935	138	26.229	207	32.705
1.5	54	10.948	305	64.935	134	26.229	240	18.823
2	71	14.598	302	44.155	135	26.229	288	7.058
5	182	9.489	300	48.051	139	26.229	557	24.47
10	244	8.029	333	36.363	142	26.229	909	22.352
50	329	10.218	551	31.168	171	27.868	1601	14.823
80	357	10.218	593	31.818	181	36.065	1662	15.058
100	361	9.489	607	31.818	183	32.786	1673	17.176
200	368	9.489	614	31.818	200	31.147	1682	17.176
500	368	9.489	614	31.818	220	32.786	1690	15.529
All	546	9.489	614	31.818	245	31.147	1701	15.529
Best k-means	55	6.569	368	28.571	25	24.590	1021	11.529

Table 6. The number of support vectors used in determining PNN structure and the test error for T, D, DWBC and OC data sets

sc	T $C^* = 10^1$ SVs	E_{test} [%]	D $C^* = 10^3$ SVs	E_{test} [%]	DWBC $C^* = 10^6$ SVs	E_{test} [%]	OC $C^* = 10^{-1}$ SVs	E_{test} [%]
0.08	785	40.138	86	34.722	31	21.239	112	15.000
0.2	764	15.208	110	11.111	36	62.832	113	15.000
0.3	765	11.458	133	12.500	36	7.965	117	12.500
0.5	755	16.388	158	8.333	39	27.434	119	17.500
0.8	754	8.958	186	6.944	47	19.469	121	15.000
1.2	790	8.125	214	8.333	54	10.619	130	17.500
1.5	815	9.167	239	8.333	65	23.894	137	20.000
2	874	7.500	262	9.722	78	57.522	139	17.500
5	1014	14.931	285	13.888	174	55.752	148	15.000
10	1103	6.875	286	13.888	276	49.558	153	15.000
50	1701	68.125	286	13.888	456	32.743	157	15.000
80	2045	40.763	286	13.888	456	32.743	158	15.000
100	2242	23.958	286	13.888	456	32.743	158	15.000
200	2954	71.458	286	13.888	456	32.743	158	15.000
500	4209	7.916	286	13.888	456	32.743	158	15.000
All	5760	11.181	286	13.888	456	32.743	159	15.000
Best k-means	2881	6.458	201	8.333	137	9.735	80	7.500

5   Conclusions

In this article, we considered the problem of the minimization of the number of PNN pattern layer neurons. This problem was solved along with the maximization of the generalization ability of the network. For this purpose we proposed two heuristic algorithms. The first solution relied on k-means input data clustering and the use of the cluster centres as the pattern layer neurons. In the second method, by performing SVM data classification, we determined the set of support vectors and we merely allowed the support vectors to represent the nodes in the pattern layer.

The reduced PNN models were compared with standard PNN in the classification problem of seven commonly available medical databases and one authors' own data set. In each case, the networks prediction ability was verified by computing the test error on 20% of the samples randomly separated from entire data set. The results presented in this contribution confirmed the validity of PNN structure reduction of both proposed methods. It was shown that in all data classification tasks, the reduction of the number of pattern layer neurons improved the prediction ability of the network.

It is highly probable to obtain better results, i.e.: both, smaller number of pattern neurons and the lower generalization error, after shrinking the grid search.

Because of the limited space of the article, the results are only shown for E_{test}. Similar study was performed for additional performance measures: the sensitivity, the specificity and the area under the receiver operating characteristic. The values of these measures were also better for reduced PNN.

Acknowledgements. This work was supported in part by the National Science Centre (Poland) under Grant No. NN 514 705540.

References

1. Specht, D.F.: Probabilistic Neural Networks. Neural Networks 3, 109–118 (1990)
2. Specht, D.F.: Enhancements to the probabilistic neural networks. In: IEEE International Joint Conference on Neural Networks, pp. 761–768. IEEE Press, Baltimore (1992)
3. Chtioui, Y., Bertrand, D., Barba, D.: Reduction of the size of the learning data in a probabilistic neural network by hierarchical clustering. Application to the discrimination of seeds by artificial vision. Chemometrics and Intelligent Laboratory Systems 35, 175–186 (1996)
4. Franti, P., Kaukoranta, T., Shen, D.-F., Chang, K.-S.: Fast and Memory Efficient Implementation of the Exact PNN. IEEE Trans. Image Processing 9, 773–777 (2000)
5. Adeli, H., Panakkat, A.: A probabilistic neural network for earthquake magnitude prediction. Neural Networks 22, 1018–1024 (2009)
6. Gorunescu, F., Gorunescu, M., El-Darzi, E., Gorunescu, S.: An evolutionary computational approach to probabilistic neural network with application to hepatic cancer diagnosis. In: IEEE Symposium on Computer-Based Medical Systems, pp. 461–466. IEEE Press, Dublin (2005)
7. Shan, Y., Zhao, R., Xu, G., Liebich, H.M., Zhang, Y.: Application of probabilistic neural network in the clinical diagnosis of cancers based on clinical chemistry data. Analytica Chimica Acta 471, 77–86 (2002)
8. Huang, C.-J., Liao, W.-C.: A Comparative Study of Feature Selection Methods for Probabilistic Neural Networks in Cancer Classification. In: IEEE International Conference on Tools with Artificial Intelligence, pp. 451–458. IEEE Press, Sacramento (2003)
9. Mantzaris, D., Anastassopoulos, G., Adamopoulos, A.: Genetic algorithm pruning of probabilistic neural networks in medical disease estimation. Neural Networks 24, 831–835 (2011)
10. Rutkowski, L.: Adaptive Probabilistic Neural Networks for Pattern Classification in Time-Varying Environment. IEEE Trans. Neural Networks 15, 811–827 (2004)
11. Traven, H.G.C.: A Neural Network Approach to Statistical Pattern Classification by 'Semiparametic' Estimation of Probability Density Functions. IEEE Trans. Neural Networks 2, 366–377 (1991)
12. Burrascano, P.: Learning Vector Quantization for the Probabilistic Neural Network. IEEE Trans. Neural Networks 2, 458–461 (1991)
13. Streit, R.L., Luginbuhl, T.E.: Maximum Likelihood Training of Probabilistic Neural Networks. IEEE Trans. Neural Networks 5, 764–783 (1994)
14. Zaknich, A.: A vector quantisation reduction method for the probabilistic neural network. In: IEEE International Conference on Neural Networks, pp. 1117–1120. IEEE Press, Huston (1997)

15. Berthold, M.R., Diamond, J.: Constructive training of probabilistic neural networks. Neurocomputing 19, 167–183 (1998)
16. Mao, K.Z., Tan, K.-C., Ser, W.: Probabilistic Neural-Network Structure Determination for Pattern Classification. IEEE Trans. Neural Networks 11, 1009–1016 (2000)
17. Specht, D.F., Romsdahl, H.: Experience with adaptive probabilistic neural networks and adaptive general regression neural networks. In: IEEE World Congress on Computational Intelligence 2, pp. 1203–1208. IEEE Press, Orlando (1994)
18. Parzen, E.: On estimation of a probability density function and mode. Annals of Mathematical Statistics 36, 1065–1076 (1962)
19. Masters, T.: Practical Neural Networks Recipes in C++. Academic Press, San Diego (1993)
20. Hartigan, J.A., Wong, M.A.: A k-means clustering algorithm. J. Royal Stat. Soci.- Ser. C (Applied Statistics) 1, 100–108 (1979)
21. Wu, X., Kumar, V., Quinlan, J.R., Ghosh, J., Yang, Q., Motoda, H., McLachlan, G.J., Ng, A., Liu, B., Yu, P.S., Zhou, Z.-H., Steinbach, M., Hand, D.J., Steinberg, D.: Top 10 algorithms in data mining. Knowledge Information Systems 14, 1–37 (2008)
22. Vapnik, V.: The Nature of Statistical Learning Theory. Springer, New York (1995)
23. Schölkopf, B., Smola, A.J., Williamson, R.C., Bartlett, P.L.: New support vector algorithms. Neural Computation 12, 1207–1245 (2000)
24. Gunn, S.R.: Support Vector Machines for Classification and Regression. Technical Report, University of Southampton (1998)
25. Schölkopf, B., Burges, C.J.C., Smola, A.J.: Advances in Kernel Methods – Support Vector Learning. MIT Press, Cambridge (1999)
26. Schölköpf, B., Smola, A.J.: Learning with Kernels: Support Vector Machines, Regularization, Optimization, and Beyond. MIT Press, Cambridge (2002)
27. UCI Machine Learning Repository, archive.ics.uci.edu/ml/datasets.html
28. Skret, A., Lozinski, T., Chrusciel, A.: Epidemiology of ovarian cancer: Hormonal and genetic aspects. In: Congress of the European Society for Gynecologic and Obstetric Investigation, pp. 189–205. CIC Edizioni Internazionali, Rome (2001)

Development of Explicit Neural Predictive Control Algorithm Using Particle Swarm Optimisation

Maciej Ławryńczuk

Institute of Control and Computation Engineering, Warsaw University of Technology
ul. Nowowiejska 15/19, 00-665 Warsaw, Poland
M.Lawrynczuk@ia.pw.edu.pl

Abstract. This paper describes development of a nonlinear Model Predictive Control (MPC) algorithm. The algorithm is very computationally efficient because for control signal calculation an explicit control law is used, no on-line optimisation is necessary. The control law is implemented by a neural network which is trained off-line by means of a particle swarm optimisation algorithm. Inefficiency of a classical gradient-based training algorithm is demonstrated for the polymerisation reactor. Moreover, the discussed MPC algorithm is compared in terms of accuracy and computational complexity with two suboptimal MPC algorithms with model linearisation and MPC with full nonlinear optimisation.

Keywords: Process control, Model Predictive Control, neural networks, optimisation, particle swarm optimisation, soft computing.

1 Introduction

Model Predictive Control (MPC) is a computer control strategy in which the control action is optimised over some future time horizon [8,15]. Thanks to the fact that a dynamic model is used for prediction of the future behaviour of the process, MPC algorithms, unlike any other control technique, can easily take into account constraints imposed on process inputs (manipulated variables) and outputs (controlled variables), which usually decide on quality, economic efficiency and safety. Secondly, MPC can be efficiently used for multivariable processes, with many inputs and outputs. As a result, MPC algorithms have been successfully used for years in many areas [14].

Because behaviour of numerous processes is typically nonlinear, nonlinear models, rather than simple linear ones, are used for prediction in MPC [3,10,15]. Although different types of nonlinear models can be used in MPC, neural models are particularly interesting. In order to reduce complexity of on-line calculations, suboptimal MPC algorithms are more and more popular in which the neural model is successively linearised on-line and the obtained linear approximation is used for prediction. Thanks to linearisation, the control signal can be calculated on-line from an easy to solve quadratic programming task [5,7,11,15]. To further

L. Rutkowski et al. (Eds.): ICAISC 2013, Part I, LNAI 7894, pp. 130–139, 2013.

reduce computational burden an explicit variant of the suboptimal MPC algorithm can be used in which constraints are treated somehow heuristically, but it makes it possible to replace quadratic programming with an explicit control law. The coefficients of this law are calculated on-line from a simple matrix decomposition task and a solution of a set of linear equations [6]. The necessity of model linearisation and matrix inversion can be also eliminated as shown in [4], in such a case the explicit control law is implemented by a neural network trained off-line. Data sets necessary for training and validation of such a neural network are generated by the classical explicit MPC algorithm. Unfortunately, development of the classical algorithm is an essential part of the design procedure, which may be a disadvantage.

In this paper alternative development of the explicit neural MPC algorithm is discussed. Unlike the algorithm presented in [4], the neural network is not trained to approximate behaviour of the classical explicit MPC algorithm, but the network used for control law calculation is trained directly off-line. Because such an optimisation problem may be difficult, non-convex and multimodal, a particle swarm optimisation algorithm is used. Efficiency of the discussed approach is demonstrated for the polymerisation process. Particle swarm optimisation approaches have been extensively used for global optimisation [1]. In control system engineering they have been used for off-line tuning parameters of the PID controller [12] and for on-line nonlinear optimisation in MPC algorithms [13,16].

2   Model Predictive Control Algorithms

In MPC algorithms [8,15] at each consecutive sampling instant k, $k = 0, 1, 2, \ldots$, a set of future control increments is calculated

$$\triangle \boldsymbol{u}(k) = [\triangle u(k|k) \, \triangle u(k+1|k) \ldots \triangle u(k+N_{\mathrm{u}}-1|k)]^{\mathrm{T}} \tag{1}$$

It is assumed that $\triangle u(k+p|k) = 0$ for $p \geq N_{\mathrm{u}}$, where N_{u} is the control horizon. The objective of the algorithm is to minimise differences between the reference trajectory $y^{\mathrm{ref}}(k+p|k)$ and predictions $\hat{y}(k+p|k)$ over the prediction horizon $N \geq N_{\mathrm{u}}$, i.e. for $p = 1, \ldots, N$. Assuming that constraints are imposed on the value and the rate of change of the input variable, future control increments (1) are determined from the following MPC optimisation task

$$\min_{\triangle \boldsymbol{u}(k)} \left\{ \sum_{p=1}^{N} (y^{\mathrm{ref}}(k+p|k) - \hat{y}(k+p|k))^2 + \lambda \sum_{p=0}^{N_{\mathrm{u}}-1} (\triangle u(k+p|k))^2 \right\}$$

subject to $\tag{2}$

$$u^{\min} \leq u(k+p|k) \leq u^{\max}, \ p = 0, \ldots, N_{\mathrm{u}} - 1$$
$$- \triangle u^{\max} \leq \triangle u(k+p|k) \leq \triangle u^{\max}, \ p = 0, \ldots, N_{\mathrm{u}} - 1$$

where $\lambda > 0$ is a weighting coefficient. Only the first element of the determined sequence (1) is applied to the process, i.e. $u(k) = \triangle u(k|k) + u(k-1)$. At the next sampling instant, $k+1$, the prediction is shifted one step forward and the whole procedure is repeated.

3   Explicit Neural MPC Algorithm Using Particle Swarm Optimisation

Let the dynamic neural model of the process be described by

$$y(k) = f(\boldsymbol{x}(k)) = f(u(k - \tau), \dots, u(k - n_{\mathrm{B}}), y(k - 1), \dots, y(k - n_{\mathrm{A}})) \quad (3)$$

where integers n_{A}, n_{B}, τ define the order of dynamics, $\tau \le n_{\mathrm{B}}$. In such a case predictions $\hat{y}(k + p|k)$ are nonlinear functions of the calculated policy (1) and the whole optimisation problem (2) is nonlinear, frequently non-convex. That is why suboptimal MPC algorithms are frequently used in which at each sampling instant on-line a linear approximation of the model (3) is calculated. Thanks to linearisation, the MPC optimisation task (2) becomes a quadratic programming problem.

3.1   The Explicit Control Law

If the constraints are removed from the MPC optimisation task (2), one has

$$\min_{\triangle\boldsymbol{u}(k)} \left\{ J(k) = \left\| \boldsymbol{y}^{\mathrm{ref}}(k) - \hat{\boldsymbol{y}}(k) \right\|^2 + \| \triangle \boldsymbol{u}(k) \|_{\boldsymbol{\Lambda}}^2 \right\} \quad (4)$$

where

$$\boldsymbol{y}^{\mathrm{ref}}(k) = \left[y^{\mathrm{ref}}(k + 1|k) \dots y^{\mathrm{ref}}(k + N|k) \right]^{\mathrm{T}}$$
$$\hat{\boldsymbol{y}}(k) = \left[\hat{y}(k + 1|k) \dots \hat{y}(k + N|k) \right]^{\mathrm{T}}$$

are vectors of length N, $\boldsymbol{\Lambda} = \mathrm{diag}(\lambda, \dots, \lambda)$ is a matrix of dimensionality $N_{\mathrm{u}} \times N_{\mathrm{u}}$. It can be shown [5] that if the linear approximation of the neural model is used for prediction, the output predictions are linear functions of the future control sequence $\triangle \boldsymbol{u}(k)$

$$\hat{\boldsymbol{y}}(k) = \boldsymbol{G}(k) \triangle \boldsymbol{u}(k) + \boldsymbol{y}^0(k) \quad (5)$$

where the matrix $\boldsymbol{G}(k)$ of dimensionality $N \times N_{\mathrm{u}}$ contains step-response coefficients of the linearised model, the vector $\boldsymbol{y}^0(k) = \left[y^0(k + 1|k) \dots y^0(k + N|k) \right]^{\mathrm{T}}$ is the free trajectory which depends only on the past. Using the prediction equation (5), the optimisation problem of the explicit MPC algorithm (4) becomes

$$\min_{\triangle\boldsymbol{u}(k)} \left\{ J(k) = \left\| \boldsymbol{y}^{\mathrm{ref}}(k) - \boldsymbol{G}(k) \triangle \boldsymbol{u}(k) - \boldsymbol{y}^0(k) \right\|^2 + \| \triangle \boldsymbol{u}(k) \|_{\boldsymbol{\Lambda}}^2 \right\}$$

Due to the fact that the minimised cost function $J(k)$ is quadratic, optimal control moves can be calculated analytically, without any optimisation. One obtains the explicit control law

$$\triangle \boldsymbol{u}(k) = \boldsymbol{K}(k)(\boldsymbol{y}^{\mathrm{ref}}(k) - \boldsymbol{y}^0(k)) \quad (6)$$

where

$$\boldsymbol{K}(k) = (\boldsymbol{G}^{\mathrm{T}}(k)\boldsymbol{G}(k) + \boldsymbol{\Lambda})^{-1}\boldsymbol{G}^{\mathrm{T}}(k) \quad (7)$$

is a matrix of dimensionality $N_{\mathrm{u}} \times N$.

At each sampling instant k of the classical explicit MPC algorithm the following steps are repeated on-line:

1. The linear approximation of the neural model for the current operating point is found [5].
2. Step response coefficients which comprise the matrix $G(k)$ are calculated [5].
3. The nonlinear free trajectory $y^0(k)$ is calculated using a neural model of the process [5].
4. The matrix $K(k)$ is calculated from Eq. (7).
5. The future control increments $\triangle u(k)$ are found from Eq. (6).
6. The first element of the obtained vector $\triangle u(k)$ is applied to the process.
7. Iteration number is increased ($k := k + 1$), the algorithm goes to step 1.

The same neural model is used for linearisation and the free trajectory calculation. Matrix inversion in Eq. (7) is calculated in a numerical efficient way using the LU (Low-Upper) matrix decomposition with partial pivoting [6].

3.2   The Algorithm with Direct Calculation of the Matrix $K_1(k)$

The explicit MPC algorithm discussed in the following part of the paper is much simpler than the rudimentary explicit algorithm described in the previous subsection. First, the first element of the vector $\triangle u(k)$ (i.e. the quantity $\triangle u(k|k)$) is only calculated. In place of the control law (6) the formula

$$\triangle u(k|k) = K_1(k)(y^{\mathrm{ref}}(k) - y^0(k)) \qquad (8)$$

is used where $K_1(k)$ is the first row of the matrix $K(k)$. Secondly, the non-linear model is not linearised on-line, step-response coefficients of the linearised model and the dynamic matrix $G(k)$ are not calculated on-line, the inverse matrix $(G^{\mathrm{T}}(k)G(k) + \Lambda)^{-1}$ is not calculated on-line. The vector $K_1(k) = [k_{1,1}(k) \ldots k_{1,N}(k)]^{\mathrm{T}}$ for the current operating point is directly calculated by a neural network which is called a neural approximator. The algorithm uses two neural networks: NN_1 is a dynamic model of the process, NN_2 is a neural approximator. At each sampling instant k of the algorithm the following steps are repeated on-line:

1. The nonlinear free trajectory $y^0(k)$ is calculated using a neural model of the process (the network NN_1).
2. The vector $K_1(k)$ is calculated using the neural approximator (the network NN_2).
3. The current control increment $\triangle u(k|k)$ is found from Eq. (8).
4. The obtained solution is projected onto the admissible set of constraints.
5. The obtained solution is applied to the process.
6. Iteration number is increased ($k := k + 1$), the algorithm goes to step 1.

Although the control laws (6) and (8) can be easily derived forgetting the constraints imposed on the manipulated variable in the general MPC optimisation task (2), the obtained value of the control signal may not satisfy real limitations of the actuator. That is why the following constraints imposed on the currently calculated control signal are taken into account

$$u^{\min} \leq u(k|k) \leq u^{\max}, \quad -\triangle u^{\max} \leq \triangle u(k|k) \leq \triangle u^{\max}$$

The control increment $\triangle u(k|k)$ calculated from Eq. (8) is hence projected onto the admissible set of constraints

$$
\begin{aligned}
&\text{if } \triangle u(k|k) < -\triangle u^{\max} \ \triangle u(k|k) = -\triangle u^{\max} \\
&\text{if } \triangle u(k|k) > \triangle u^{\max} \ \triangle u(k|k) = \triangle u^{\max} \\
&u(k|k) = \triangle u(k|k) + u(k-1) \\
&\text{if } u(k|k) < u^{\min} \ u(k|k) = u^{\min} \\
&\text{if } u(k|k) > u^{\max} \ u(k|k) = u^{\max} \\
&u(k) = u(k|k)
\end{aligned}
\tag{9}
$$

3.3   Training the Network NN$_2$ Using Particle Swarm Optimisation

Elements of the vector $\boldsymbol{K}_1(k)$, i.e. scalars $k_{1,p}(k)$ for $p = 1, \ldots, N$, are calculated on-line by the neural approximator–the network NN$_2$ for the current operating point of the process. The operating point is defined by control signals applied to the process at some previous sampling instants and measurements of the output signal for the current and some previous instants. The quantities $k_{1,p}$ are hence functions of the following arguments

$$k_{1,p} = g_p(u(k-1), \ldots, u(k-\tilde{n}_{\mathrm{B}}), y(k), \ldots, y(k-\tilde{n}_{\mathrm{A}}))$$

where integers $\tilde{n}_{\mathrm{A}}$ and $\tilde{n}_{\mathrm{B}}$ define the current operating point. In this study the MultiLayer Perceptron (MLP) network with one hidden layer and linear outputs [2] is used as the NN$_2$ network. It has $\tilde{n}_{\mathrm{A}} + \tilde{n}_{\mathrm{B}} + 1$ inputs. Outputs of the network are described by the following equation

$$
k_{1,p}(k) = w_{p,0}^2 + \sum_{i=1}^{K} w_{p,i}^2 \varphi \left(w_{i,0}^1 + \sum_{j=1}^{\tilde{n}_{\mathrm{B}}} w_{i,j}^1 u(k-j) \right.
$$

$$
\left. + \sum_{j=0}^{\tilde{n}_{\mathrm{A}}} w_{i,\tilde{n}_{\mathrm{B}}+j+1}^1 y(k-j) \right)
\tag{10}
$$

where K is the number of hidden nodes, φ denotes the transfer function of the hidden units (e.g. $\varphi = \tanh$), weights of the first layer are denoted by $w_{i,j}^1$ for $i = 1, \ldots, K$, $j = 1, \ldots, \tilde{n}_{\mathrm{A}} + \tilde{n}_{\mathrm{B}} + 1$, biases of the first layer are denoted by $w_{i,0}^1$ for $i = 1, \ldots, K$, weights of the second layer are denoted by $w_{p,i}^2$ for $p = 1, \ldots, N$, $i = 1, \ldots, K$, biases of the second layer are denoted by $w_{p,0}^2$ for $p = 1, \ldots, N$.

The training procedure for the network NN_2 is as follows. First, a series of random changes of the reference trajectory is assumed. These changes comprise the training data set, the number of the training patterns is S. Similarly, the validation data set is generated. Next, parameters of the network, i.e. weights, are optimised through simulations of the explicit MPC algorithm for the assumed training changes of the reference trajectory. The optimisation problem is defined for S training patterns

$$\min_{w_{i,j}^1, \ w_{p,i}^2} \left\{ SSE = \sum_{k=1}^{S} \left[(y^{ref}(k) - y(k))^2 + \lambda(\triangle u(k|k))^2 \right] \right\}$$

subject to   (11)

$$\triangle u(k|k) = \boldsymbol{K}_1(k)(\boldsymbol{y}^{ref}(k) - \boldsymbol{y}^0(k))$$

$$u^{min} \le u(k|k) \le u^{max}$$

$$-\triangle u^{max} \le \triangle u(k|k) \le \triangle u^{max}$$

where $y(k)$ denotes the output of the simulated process for consecutive sampling instants $k = 1, \ldots, S$, elements of the vector $\boldsymbol{K}_1(k)$ are calculated form Eq. (10). Satisfaction of inequality constraints is enforced by the projection procedure (9). The optimisation task (11) is nonlinear, it may be non-convex and multimodal. That is why classical, gradient-based optimisation algorithms are likely to terminate at local minima. A straightforward choice is to use global optimisation methods. In this study the particle swarm optimisation algorithm is used.

4   Simulation Results

The considered example process is a polymerisation reaction taking place in a jacketed continuous stirred tank reactor [9]. The reaction is the free-radical polymerisation of methyl methacrylate with azo-bis-isobutyronitrile as initiator and toluene as solvent. The output NAMW (Number Average Molecular Weight) is controlled by manipulating the inlet initiator flow rate F_I. The reactor exhibits significantly nonlinear behaviour. It cannot be controlled efficiently by classical MPC schemes based on constant linear models [5,7,9,15].

The fundamental model (a set of ordinary differential equations solved using the Runge-Kutta RK45 method) is used as the real process during simulations. At first, the dynamic neural model NN_1 of the MLP type is developed. It has the general structure

$$y(k) = f(u(k-2), y(k-1), y(k-2))$$

As input and output variables have different orders of magnitude, they are scaled as $u = 100(F_I - F_{I0})$, $y = 0.0001(NAMW - NAMW_0)$ where $F_{I0} = 0.028328$, $NAMW_0 = 20000$ correspond to the initial operating point. The sampling time is 1.8 min. The network has 6 hidden nodes with the $\varphi = \tanh$ transfer function. For training the BFGS (Broyden-Fletcher-Goldfarb-Shanno) optimisation algorithm is used. Model development is thoroughly discussed in [5].

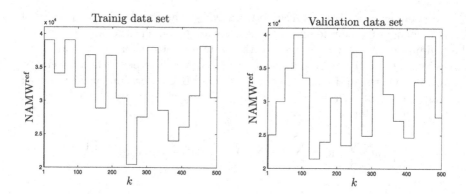

Fig. 1. The first 500 samples of the training data set (*left*) and the first 500 samples of the validation data set (*right*), the complete sets have 2000 samples

Table 1. Accuracy of the neural approximator NN$_2$ for gradient-based and particle swarm optimisation algorithms

Optimisation algorithm	SSE$_{\text{training}}$	SSE$_{\text{validation}}$
Gradient-based optimisation	5.273419×10^{11}	4.179207×10^{11}
Particle swarm optimisation	2.515997×10^{10}	3.319000×10^{10}

In order to train the neural approximator (the network NN$_2$), a series of random changes of the reference trajectory is generated. Both training and validation data sets have 2000 samples, the first quarters of them (for good presentation) are shown in Fig. 1. The prediction horizon is $N = 10$. The network has 2 inputs ($u(k-1)$ and $y(k)$), 3 hidden nodes with the $\varphi = \tanh$ transfer function and 9 outputs, due to process delay the quantity $k_{1,1}(k)$ is always 0. The optimisation problem (11) is solved by means of the gradient-based algorithm (the BFGS algorithm with shifted penalty function) and the particle swarm optimisation algorithm (the population size is 25, the maximum number of epochs is 2000). Numerical values of the obtained SSE (the Sum of Squared Errors) objective function are given in Table 1. The trajectories obtained as a result of optimisation in two compared algorithms much better demonstrate inefficiency of the classical approach and efficiency of the particle swarm optimisation algorithm. Fig. 2 shows the first quarters of input and output trajectories obtained in the gradient-based and particle swarm optimisation algorithms. In the first case the optimisation routine finds the solution which is a shallow local minima. Unfortunately, the explicit MPC does not follow the assumed reference trajectory. Conversely, the particle swarm optimisation algorithm finds parameters of the neural approximator NN$_2$ which gives good closed loop trajectories.

Next, the following four nonlinear MPC algorithms are compared:

a) the discussed explicit MPC algorithm with neural approximation and particle swarm optimisation used for off-line training of the network NN$_2$,

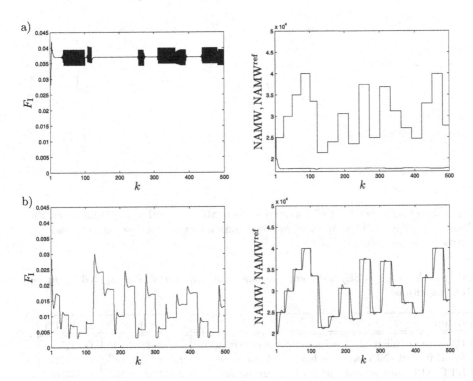

Fig. 2. The first 500 samples of input (F_I) and output (NAMW) trajectories for the validation data set trajectory NAMW^{ref} obtained in the explicit MPC algorithm: a) for optimisation of the neural approximator NN$_2$ the gradient algorithm is used, b) for optimisation the PSO algorithm is used

   b) the classical explicit MPC algorithm with Nonlinear Prediction and Linearisation (MPC-NPL), with on-line successive linearisation of the neural dynamic model (the NN$_1$ network) and LU matrix decomposition [6],

   c) the MPC-NPL algorithm with on-line successive linearisation of the neural dynamic model (the NN$_1$ network) and quadratic programming [5,7,15],

   c) the MPC-NO algorithm with on-line nonlinear optimisation in which the neural dynamic model (the NN$_1$ network) is used for prediction without any simplifications [7,15].

Parameters of all MPC algorithms are the same $N = 10$, $\lambda = 0.2$, in the last three approaches $N_u = 3$. The manipulated variable is constrained: $F_I^{\min} = 0.003$, $F_I^{\max} = 0.06$, $\triangle F_I^{\max} = 0.005$. Fig. 3 shows trajectories obtained in the discussed explicit MPC algorithm and in the classical explicit MPC-NPL algorithm with on-line successive linearisation and LU matrix decomposition repeated at each sampling instant. Table 2 shows accuracy of all compared algorithms in terms of the SSE index and their computational complexity (in Millions of FLoating OperationS) for the whole simulation scenario (100 iterations). For the polymerisation process the all three suboptimal algorithms give control accuracy very close

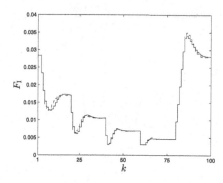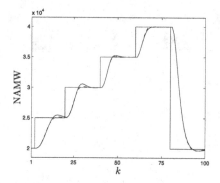

Fig. 3. Simulation results: the discussed explicit MPC algorithm (*solid line*) and the classical explicit MPC-NPL algorithm with on-line successive linearisation and LU matrix decomposition (*dashed line*)

Table 2. Accuracy (SSE) and computational load (MFLOPS) of compared nonlinear MPC algorithms

Algorithm	SSE	MFLOPS
Discussed explicit MPC with neural approximation	2.218638×10^9	0.164554
Explicit MPC-NPL with on-line LU decomposition	2.211703×10^9	0.217110
MPC-NPL with on-line quadratic programming	2.211703×10^9	0.404686
MPC-NO with on-line nonlinear optimisation	2.210627×10^9	4.109900

to that of the "ideal" computationally demanding MPC-NO approach. Moreover, the discussed explicit MPC algorithm works very similarly as the classical explicit MPC-NPL algorithm with on-line successive linearisation of the neural dynamic model and LU matrix decomposition. At the same time it is very computationally efficient: it is 25% more efficient when compared with the classical explicit algorithm and as much as 60% more efficient in comparison with the MPC-NPL algorithm with on-line quadratic programming.

5   Conclusions

The explicit MPC algorithm discussed in this paper is very computationally efficient because, unlike the classical explicit approach [6], successive on-line model linearisation and matrix calculations are not necessary. The current value of the control signal is calculated using a simple explicit formula and the neural approximator. Such a network can be trained off-line to mimic behaviour of the classical explicit MPC algorithm [4]. In this work an alternative development of the explicit neural MPC algorithm is discussed. The neural approximator is trained directly off-line, without the necessity of designing the classical explicit algorithm. As the resulting optimisation problem may be difficult, non-convex and multimodal, the particle swarm optimisation algorithm is used.

Acknowledgement. The work presented in this paper was supported by Polish national budget funds for science.

References

1. Eberhart, R.C., Shi, Y., Kennedy, J.: Swarm Intelligence. Morgan Kaufmann (2001)
2. Haykin, S.: Neural networks–a comprehensive foundation. Prentice Hall, Englewood Cliffs (1999)
3. Henson, M.A.: Nonlinear model predictive control: current status and future directions. Computers and Chemical Engineering 23, 187–202 (1998)
4. Ławryńczuk, M.: Explicit neural network-based nonlinear predictive control with low computational complexity. In: Szczuka, M., Kryszkiewicz, M., Ramanna, S., Jensen, R., Hu, Q. (eds.) RSCTC 2010. LNCS (LNAI), vol. 6086, pp. 649–658. Springer, Heidelberg (2010)
5. Ławryńczuk, M.: Neural networks in model predictive control. In: Nguyen, N.T., Szczerbicki, E. (eds.) Intelligent Systems for Knowledge Management. SCI, vol. 252, pp. 31–63. Springer, Heidelberg (2009)
6. Ławryńczuk, M.: Explicit nonlinear predictive control of a distillation column based on neural models. Chemical Engineering and Technology 32, 1578–1587 (2009)
7. Ławryńczuk, M.: A family of model predictive control algorithms with artificial neural networks. International Journal of Applied Mathematics and Computer Science 17, 217–232 (2007)
8. Maciejowski, J.M.: Predictive control with constraints. Prentice Hall, Harlow (2002)
9. Maner, B.R., Doyle, F.J., Ogunnaike, B.A., Pearson, R.K.: Nonlinear model predictive control of a simulated multivariable polymerization reactor using second-order Volterra models. Automatica 32, 1285–1301 (1996)
10. Morari, M., Lee, J.H.: Model predictive control: past, present and future. Computers and Chemical Engineering 23, 667–682 (1999)
11. Nørgaard, M., Ravn, O., Poulsen, N.K., Hansen, L.K.: Neural networks for modelling and control of dynamic systems. Springer, London (2000)
12. Pillay, N., Govender, P.: Particle swarm optimization of PID tuning paremeters: optimal tuning of single-input-single-output control loops. LAP Lambert Academic Publishing (2010)
13. Pourjafari, E., Mojallali: Predictive control for voltage collapse avoidance using a modified discrete multi-valued PSO algorithm. ISA Transactions 50, 195–200 (2011)
14. Qin, S.J., Badgwell, T.A.: A survey of industrial model predictive control technology. Control Engineering Practice 11, 733–764 (2003)
15. Tatjewski, P.: Advanced control of industrial processes, Structures and algorithms. Springer, London (2007)
16. Yousuf, M.S.: Nonlinear predictive control using particle swarm optimization: application to power systems. VDM Verlag (2010)

Designing of State-Space Neural Model and Its Application to Robust Fault Detection

Marcin Mrugalski

Institute of Control and Computation Engineering,
University of Zielona Góra,
ul. Podgórna 50, 65–246 Zielona Góra, Poland
M.Mrugalski@issi.uz.zgora.pl

Abstract. This paper presents a new methodology of designing of non-linear dynamic neural model in the state-space representation. Furthermore, an application of the Unscented Kalman Filter to the training of the designed neural model is also shown. The final part of this work provides an illustrative example of the application of the proposed methodology to the identification and robust fault detection of the tunnel furnace.

Keywords: Dynamic GMDH neural network, state-space representation, non-linear dynamic system identification, Unscented Kalman Filter, robust fault detection.

1 Introduction

The effectiveness of the *Fault Detection and Isolation* (FDI) systems [1–3] and *Fault Tolerant Control* schemes (FTC) [4–6] mostly depends on the quality of the models obtained in the process of the system identification. The *Artificial Neural Networks* (ANNs) are often applied in the process of the dynamic non-linear system identification [2, 7–9].

Unfortunately, ANNs have some disadvantages, which limit the effectiveness of the developed FDI and FTC systems. The most important disadvantage is inefficient quality of the neural model following from the inappropriate selection of the network architecture and the errors following from inaccurate estimation of the neurons parameters. The high quality of the neural model is crucial because it is used in the FDI systems to generate the residuals which should be close to zero in the fault-free case, and it should be distinguishably different from zero in the faulty case. Under such an assumption, the faults are detected by the application of a fixed threshold on the residual signal. Unfortunately, appearing of the neural model uncertainty or measurements noise can lead to false alarms or undetected faults. Among other disadvantages, only rare approaches ensure the stability of the neural models during the process of the dynamic system identification and usually not available description of a neural model in the state-space representation. Moreover, there is a limited number of approaches that allow mathematically to describe the neural model uncertainty [10, 11] and

L. Rutkowski et al. (Eds.): ICAISC 2013, Part I, LNAI 7894, pp. 140–149, 2013.
© Springer-Verlag Berlin Heidelberg 2013

this factor has the main impact on effectiveness of the contemporary FDI and FTC systems.

To tackle this problem the *Group Method of Data Handling* (GMDH) approach can be employed [11–14]. The concept of this approach relies on replacing the complex neural model by the set of the hierarchically connected partial models (neurons). In this paper a new structure of the multi-input and multi-output dynamic neuron in the state-space representation is proposed. This description enables to obtain constrains of the parameter estimates which warranty the stability of dynamic GMDH neural model. In order to obtain the constrained parameter estimates and the neural model uncertainty the *Unscented Kalman Filter* (UKF) [15] was applied. This knowledge enable to calculate the adaptive threshold which should contain the real system response in the fault-free mode. An occurrence of the fault is signaled when system output crosses the adaptive threshold.

2   The Synthesis of GMDH Neural Models

Let us assume that in the general case each neuron in the GMDH network has the following form:

$$\hat{s}_{i,j,k}^{(l)} = \mathcal{F}\left(r_{i,k}^{(l)}, p_{i,j}^{(l)}\right),\tag{1}$$

where: $r_{i,k}^{(l)} \in \mathbb{R}^{n_r}$ for $i = 1, ..., n_R$ are the neuron input vectors formed as the combinations of the neural model inputs $r_{i,k}^{(l)} = [u_{i,k}^{(l)}, ..., u_{j,k}^{(l)}]^T$, $\hat{s}_{i,j,k}^{(l)} \in \mathbb{R}^{n_s}$ for $j = 1, ..., n_N$ are the neurons outputs vectors formed as the combinations of the network outputs $[\hat{y}_{i,k}^{(l)}, ..., \hat{y}_{j,k}^{(l)}]^T$, $p_{i,j}^{(l)} \in \mathbb{R}^{n_r \times n_s}$ denotes the parameter estimate matrix, $\mathcal{F}(\cdot)$ is an activation function, and l is the number of layer the GMDH network.

The process of the synthesis of the first layer of the GMDH neural network begins from the creation of a set of n_R vectors of neuron inputs $r_{i,k}^{(l)}$ based on the combinations of the model inputs $u_k \in \mathbb{R}^{n_u}$ belonging to the training data set $\mathcal{T}$. The number of the vectors $r_{i,k}^{(l)}$ depends on the number of model inputs n_u and the number of the neuron inputs n_r. Each i-th vector $r_{i,k}^{(l)}$ constitutes the neurons stimulation which results in the formation of j-th neurons and their outputs $\hat{s}_{i,j,k}^{(l)}$, which are the estimates of the modeled system outputs. The number n_N of these neurons, for the each subsequent i-th vector $r_{i,k}^{(l)}$, depends on the number of modeled output signals n_y and an assumed number of the neurons inputs n_r.

In the case of the GMDH neural network the behaviour of each partial model should reflect the behaviour of the system being identified. It follows from the rule of the GMDH algorithm that the parameters of each partial model are estimated in such a way that its output is the best approximation of the real system output. In this situation, the partial model should have the ability to represent the dynamics. To tackle this problem, in this paper a dynamic neuron in the state-space representation is defined. The proposed dynamic neuron consists of two submodules: the linear state-space module and the activation module.

The behavior of the linear state-space part of a dynamic neuron is described by the following equation:

$$z_{k+1} = Az_k + Br_{i,k}, \tag{2}$$

$$\tilde{s}_{i,j,k} = Cz_k + Dr_{i,k}, \tag{3}$$

where $r_{i,k} \in \mathbb{R}^{n_r}$ and $\tilde{s}_{i,j,k} \in \mathbb{R}^{n_s}$ are the inputs and outputs of the linear state-space submodule of the dynamic neuron. $A \in \mathbb{R}^{n_z \times n_z}$, $B \in \mathbb{R}^{n_z \times n_r}$, $C \in \mathbb{R}^{n_s \times n_z}$, $D \in \mathbb{R}^{n_s \times n_r}$, $z_k \in \mathbb{R}^{n_z}$, where n_z represents the order of the dynamics. Additionally, the matrix A has an upper-triangular form, i.e.

$$A = \begin{bmatrix} a_{11} & a_{12} & \cdots & a_{1,n_z} \\ 0 & a_{22} & \cdots & a_{2,n_z} \\ \vdots & & \ddots & \vdots \\ 0 & 0 & \cdots & a_{n_z,n_z} \end{bmatrix}. \tag{4}$$

This mean that the dynamic neuron is asymptotically stable iff:

$$| a_{i,i} | < 1, \quad i = 1, ..., n_z. \tag{5}$$

Moreover:

$$C = \mathrm{diag}(c_1, ..., c_{n_s}, \underbrace{0, ..., 0}_{n_z - n_s}). \tag{6}$$

The linear state-space submodule output is used as the input for the activation module:

$$\hat{s}_{i,j,k} = \mathcal{F}(\tilde{s}_{i,j,k}). \tag{7}$$

with $\mathcal{F}(\cdot) = [f_1(\cdot), ..., f_{n_s}(\cdot)]^T$ where $f_i(\cdot)$ denotes a non-linear activation function (e.g., a hyperbolic tangent).

In order to estimate the unknown parameters of the dynamic neurons the *Unscented Kalman Filter* (UKF) [15] can be applied. In the subsequent part of the paper, it will be shown that, the UKF-based constrained parameter estimation warranties the asymptotically stable neurons of the GMDH model. Moreover, an application of this algorithm to the parameter estimation process enables to obtain the uncertainty of the partial models, simultaneously. After the estimation, the parameters of the neurons are not modified during the further network synthesis. The obtained parameter estimates and their uncertainty enable calculation of the neuron responses and the adaptive threshold, which can be applied in the robust fault detection scheme.

At the next stage of GMDH network synthesis, a validation data set $\mathcal{V}$ is used to calculate the processing error $Q(\hat{s}_{i,j}^{(l)})$ of each partial model in the current l-th network layer.

$$Q = \begin{bmatrix} Q(\hat{s}_{1,1,k}^{(l)}) & \cdots & Q(\hat{s}_{1,j,k}^{(l)}) & \cdots & Q(\hat{s}_{1,n_N,k}^{(l)}) \\ \cdots & \cdots & \cdots & \cdots & \cdots \\ Q(\hat{s}_{i,1,k}^{(l)}) & \cdots & Q(\hat{s}_{i,j,k}^{(l)}) & \cdots & Q(\hat{s}_{i,n_N,k}^{(l)}) \\ \cdots & \cdots & \cdots & \cdots & \cdots \\ Q(\hat{s}_{n_R,1,k}^{(l)}) & \cdots & Q(\hat{s}_{n_R,j,k}^{(l)}) & \cdots & Q(\hat{s}_{n_R,n_N,k}^{(l)}) \end{bmatrix} \tag{8}$$

Based on the chosen evaluation criterion [16], it is possible to select the best-fitted neurons in the layer. Selection methods in the GMDH neural networks play the role of a mechanism of structural optimization at the stage of constructing a new layer of neurons. According to the chosen selection method, elements that introduce too big processing error are removed. In order to achieve this goal the following method based on the soft selection can be applied:

Input : Q – the matrix of the quality indexes of all dynamic neurons in the l-th layer, n_o – the number of opponent neurons, n_w – the number of winnings required for i-th neuron selection.
Output : The set of neurons after selection.

(1) Select $j = 1$ column of matrix Q representing the quality indexes of all n_R neurons modeling j-th vector of system outputs $s_{i,j,k}$ created on the basis of all $i = 1, \ldots, n_R$ vectors of system inputs $r_{i,k}$.
(2) Conduct series of n_y competitions between each i-th neuron in the j-th column and n_o randomly selected neurons (the so-called *opponent*) from the same column. The i-th neuron is the so-called *winner* neuron when:

$$Q(\hat{s}_{i,1,k}^{(l)}) \leq Q_o(\hat{s}_{i,1,k}^{(l)}), \tag{9}$$

where $o = 1, \ldots, n_o$ and Q_o denotes a quality index of the opponent neuron;
(3) Select the neurons for the $(l+1)$-th layer with the number of winnings bigger than n_w (the remaining neurons are removed);
(4) Repeat the steps (1)–(3) for $j = 2, \ldots, n_N$ column of matrix Q representing the quality indexes of all neurons modeling the remaining $j = 2, \ldots, n_N$ vectors of system outputs $\hat{s}_{i,1,k}^{(l)}$.

After the selection procedure, the outputs of the selected neurons become the inputs to the neurons in the subsequent layer. During the synthesis of the GMDH neural network, the number of layers suitably increases (Fig. 1).

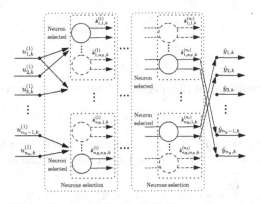

Fig. 1. Synthesis of the GMDH neural network

In the next stage of GMDH network synthesis the termination condition testing is performed. For this reason the quality indexes $Q(\hat{s}_{i,j}^{(l)})$ for all neurons included in the l layer are calculated. The quality index $Q_{j,min}^{(l)}$ represents the processing error for the best neuron in this layer which approximates the j-th vector of system outputs:

$$Q_{j,min}^{(l)} = \min_{i=1,\dots,n_R} Q(\hat{s}_{i,j}^{(l)}) \quad \text{for} \quad j = 1,\dots,n_N. \tag{10}$$

The values $Q(\hat{s}_{i,j}^{(l)})$ can be determined with the application of the defined evaluation criterion, which was used in the selection process. The synthesis of the network is completed when each of the calculated quality indexes reaches the minimum:

$$Q_{j,min}^{(l_{opt})} = \min_{l=1,\dots,n_l} Q_{j,min}^{(l)} \quad \text{for} \quad j = 1,\dots,n_N. \tag{11}$$

The termination of the synthesis appears independently for each vector of system outputs $\hat{s}_{i,j}^{(l)}$ and as a result a set of quality indexes, corresponding to each vector of system outputs is obtained $Q_1, Q_2, \dots, Q_{n_N}$.

3   Parameters Estimation of Dynamic Neurons

Let us define a state vector (in order to simplify the notation, the indexes $_i^{(l)}$ in the $r_{i,k}^{(l)}$ and $_{i,j}^{(l)}$ in $\hat{s}_{i,j,k}^{(l)}$ are omitted):

$$x_k = \begin{bmatrix} p_k \\ z_k \end{bmatrix}, \tag{12}$$

which is composed of the parameter vector of the neuron p_k as well as of the state of the neuron, which is described in a form:

$$z_{k+1} = A(p_k)z_k + B(p_k)r_k, \tag{13}$$

$$\tilde{s}_k = C(p_k)z_k + D(p_k)r_k, \tag{14}$$

$$\hat{s}_k = \mathcal{F}(\tilde{s}_k). \tag{15}$$

The vector p_k is composed of the diagonal elements of the matrix A, i.e.

$$p_k = [a_{11}, \dots, a_{n,n}, \dots]^T, \tag{16}$$

while the remaining elements of p_k are composed of the remaining parameters of A, as well as all elements of B, C and D. Thus, the dimension of p_k is:

$$n_p = \frac{(n_z \times n_z) + n_z}{2} + n_z \times n_r + n_s + n_s \times n_r. \tag{17}$$

It should be also pointed out that instead of $\boldsymbol{A}$ $(\boldsymbol{B}, \boldsymbol{C}, \boldsymbol{D})$ the notation $\boldsymbol{A}(\boldsymbol{p}_k)$ $(\boldsymbol{B}(\boldsymbol{p}_k), \boldsymbol{C}(\boldsymbol{p}_k), \boldsymbol{D}(\boldsymbol{p}_k))$ is introduce which clearly denotes the dependence on $\boldsymbol{p}_k$.

Finally, the state-space model is:

$$\boldsymbol{x}_{k+1} = \begin{bmatrix} \boldsymbol{p}_k \\ \boldsymbol{A}(\boldsymbol{p}_k)\boldsymbol{z}_k + \boldsymbol{B}(\boldsymbol{p}_k)\boldsymbol{r}_k \end{bmatrix} + \boldsymbol{\varpi}_k = \tag{18}$$
$$\mathcal{G}(\boldsymbol{x}_k, \boldsymbol{r}_k) + \boldsymbol{\varpi}_k,$$

$$\boldsymbol{s}_k = \mathcal{F}(\boldsymbol{C}(\boldsymbol{p}_k)\boldsymbol{z}_k + \boldsymbol{D}(\boldsymbol{p}_k)\boldsymbol{r}_k) + \boldsymbol{v}_k = \tag{19}$$
$$\mathcal{H}(\boldsymbol{x}_k, \boldsymbol{r}_k) + \boldsymbol{v}_k.$$

where $\mathcal{G} : \mathbb{R}^n \times \mathbb{R}^{n_r} \to \mathbb{R}^n$ and $\mathcal{H} : \mathbb{R}^n \times \mathbb{R}^{n_r} \to \mathbb{R}^{n_s}$ are the process and observation models, respectively. $\boldsymbol{r}_k \in \mathbb{R}^{n_r}$ and $\boldsymbol{s}_k \in \mathbb{R}^{n_s}$ are the inputs and outputs data, $\rho(\boldsymbol{x}_0), \rho(\boldsymbol{\varpi}_{k-1}), \rho(\boldsymbol{v}_k)$ are the *Probability Density Function* (PDF), where $\boldsymbol{x}_0 \in \mathbb{R}^n$ is the initial state vector, $\boldsymbol{\varpi}_{k-1} \in \mathbb{R}^n$ is the process noise, and $\boldsymbol{v}_0 \in \mathbb{R}^n$ is the measurement noise. It is assumed that the process noise and the measurement noise are uncorrelated. Moreover, mean and covariance of $\rho(\boldsymbol{\varpi}_{k-1})$ and $\rho(\boldsymbol{v}_k)$ are known and equal to zero and $\boldsymbol{Q}, \boldsymbol{R}$.

The profit function which is the value of the conditional PDF of the state vector $\boldsymbol{x}_k \in \mathbb{R}^n$ given the past and present measured data $\boldsymbol{s}_1, \ldots, \boldsymbol{s}_k$ is defined as follows:

$$J(\boldsymbol{x}_k) \triangleq \rho(\boldsymbol{x}_k | (\boldsymbol{s}_1, \ldots, \boldsymbol{s}_k)). \tag{20}$$

The parameter and state estimation problem can be defined as the maximization of (20). In order to solve the following problem the UKF can be applied [17]. UKF employs the unscented transform, which approximates the mean $\hat{\boldsymbol{s}}_k \in \mathbb{R}^{n_s}$ and covariance $\boldsymbol{P}_k^{ss} \in \mathbb{R}^{n_s \times n_s}$ of the random vector $\boldsymbol{s}_k$ obtained from the non-linear transformation $\boldsymbol{s}_k = \mathcal{H}(\boldsymbol{x}_k)$, where $\boldsymbol{x}_k$ is a random vector, which mean $\hat{\boldsymbol{x}}_k \in \mathbb{R}^n$ and covariance $\boldsymbol{P}_k^{xx} \in \mathbb{R}^{n \times n}$ are assumed to be known.

The task of training of dynamic neuron relies on the estimation of parameters vector $\boldsymbol{x}_k$ which satisfies the following interval constraint:

$$-1 + \delta \leq \boldsymbol{e}_i^T \boldsymbol{x}_k \leq 1 - \delta, \quad i = 1, \ldots, n \tag{21}$$

where: $\boldsymbol{e}_i \in \mathbb{R}^{n_p + n}$ whereas $\boldsymbol{e}_1 = [1, 0, \ldots, 0]^T$, $\boldsymbol{e}_2 = [0, 1, \ldots, 0]^T$, ..., $\boldsymbol{e}_{n_p + n} = [0, 0, \ldots, 1]^T$, and δ is a small positive value. These constrains follow directly from the asymptotic stability condition (5). While δ is introduced in order to make the above mentioned problem tractable.

The neural model has a cascade structure what follows from the fact that the neuron outputs constitute the neuron inputs in the subsequent layers. The neural model which is the result of the cascade connection of dynamic neurons is asymptotically stable, when each of neurons is asymptotically stable [18]. So, a fulfilment of (5) (being a result of (21)) for each neuron allows obtaining an asymptotically stable dynamic GMDH model. Thus, the objective of the interval-constrained parameter-estimation problem is to maximize (20) subject to (21).

In order to perform the neuron training process it is necessary to truncate the probability density function at the n constraint edges given by the rows of the state interval constraint (21) such that the pseudomean $\hat{x}_{k,k}^t$ of the truncated PDF is an interval-constrained state estimate with the truncated error covariance $P_{k,k}^{xx}$. The probability density function truncation procedure allows avoiding the explicit on-line solution of a constrained optimization problem at each time step. Moreover, it assimilates the interval-constraint information in the state estimate $\hat{x}_{k|k}^t$ and the error covariance $P_{k|k}^{xxt}$. The details of the of PDF truncation procedure in the paper [15] can be found.

The application of the UKF allows obtaining the state estimates as well as the uncertainty of the GMDH model in the form of a matrix P^{xxt} which can then be applied to the calculation of the adaptive threshold and to perform a robust fault detection:

$$\hat{y}_{i,k}^m = \mathcal{F}_i \left(c_i \hat{x}_k - t_{n_t-n_p}^{\alpha/2} \hat{\sigma}_i \sqrt{c_i P^{xxt} c_i^T} \right), \tag{22}$$

$$\hat{y}_{i,k}^M = \mathcal{F}_i \left(c_i \hat{x}_k + t_{n_t-n_p}^{\alpha/2} \hat{\sigma}_i \sqrt{c_i P^{xxt} c_i^T} \right), \tag{23}$$

where c_i stands for the i-th row ($i = 1, ..., n_s$) of the matrix C of the output neuron, $\hat{\sigma}_i$ is the standard deviation of the i-th fault-free residual and $t_{n_t-n_p}^{\alpha/2}$ is the t-Student distribution quantile.

4   Experimental Results

The objective of this section is to design a GMDH model according to the approaches described in the previous sections and its application to the robust fault detection of the tunnel furnace. The considered tunnel furnace is designed to mimic, in the laboratory conditions, the real industrial tunnel furnaces, which can be applied in the food industry or production of ceramics among others. The furnace is equipped with three electric heaters and four temperature sensors, so it can be considered as a three-input and four-output system $(t_1, t_2, t_3, t_4) = f(u_1, u_2, u_3)$, where the $t_1, \ldots, t_4$ represent measurements of the temperatures from sensors and values $u_1, \ldots, u_3$ denote the input voltages allowing to control the heaters. The data set used for the identification consists of 2600 samples and was filtered with the Matlab Signal Processing Toolbox. The output signals were scaled linearly taking into consideration the response range of the output neurons (e.g. for the hyperbolic tangent neurons this range is $[-1, 1]$.

The parameters of the dynamic neurons in the state-space representation were estimated with the application of the UKF training algorithm presented in the section 3. The selection of best performing neurons in terms of their processing accuracy was realized with the application of the soft selection method based on the following evaluation criterion:

$$Q_V = \sum_{k=1}^{n_V} (s_k - \hat{s}_{n,k}^{(l)})^2 / \sum_{k=1}^{n_V} s_k^2. \tag{24}$$

Table 1. Values of $Q_V(\hat{t}_1) - Q_V(\hat{t}_4)$ for the best neurons in the subsequent layers for the validation data

Layer	$Q_V(\hat{t}_1)$	$Q_V(\hat{t}_2)$	$Q_V(\hat{t}_3)$	$Q_V(\hat{t}_4)$
1	0.1000	0.0880	0.0798	0.0902
2	0.0322	0.0510	0.0498	0.0602
3	0.0302	0.0317	0.0266	0.0334
4	0.0261	0.0212	0.0199	0.0224
5	0.0283	0.0244	0.0229	0.0256

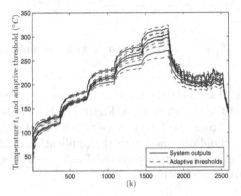

Fig. 2. Temperatures $t_1 - t_4$ of the tunnel furnace and the corresponding adaptive thresholds obtained with the dynamic GMDH model

Table 2. Values of $Q_V(\hat{t}_1) - Q_V(\hat{t}_4)$ for the non-linear dynamic GMDH obtained with the application of the UKF and ARS

Algorithm	$Q_V(\hat{t}_1)$	$Q_V(\hat{t}_2)$	$Q_V(\hat{t}_3)$	$Q_V(\hat{t}_4)$
UKF	0.0261	0.0212	0.0199	0.0224
ARS	0.1540	0.0934	0.2834	0.1398

Table 2 presents the values of the evolution criterion for the subsequent layers, i.e. these values are obtained for the best performing neurons in a particular layer of the GMDH neural network. The results show that the gradual decrease of the value of the evaluation criterion Q_V occurs when a new layer of the GMDH network is introduced. It follows from the increase of the model complexity as well as its modelling abilities. However, when the model is too complex (5-th layer of the network), the Q_V increases. Additionally, for the sake of comparison, in the table the results obtained with the application of the Adaptive Random Search (ARS) algorithm with the orthogonal projection, introduced in order to keep the neurons stable [19] are also presented. Moreover, figure 2 show the temperatures $t_1 - t_4$ of the tunnel furnace and the adaptive thresholds obtained with the application (22-23) for the validation data (no fault case).

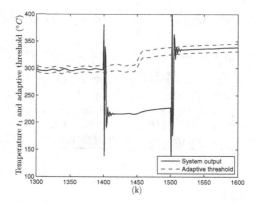

Fig. 3. Detection of the faulty temperature sensor with the application of the adaptive threshold

After the synthesis of the GMDH model, it is possible to employ it for the robust fault detection of the tunnel furnace. Figure (3) presents the measurements of the temperature t_1 from the faulty sensor (simulated during 120 seconds) and the adaptive threshold obtained with the application of the GMDH neural network. As it can be seen fault is detected for $k = 1400$ when value of the temperature t_1 crosses the adaptive threshold.

5   Conclusions

The objective of this paper was concerned with designing the robust fault detection system based on the dynamic GMDH neural network. The state-space representation of the neurons and application of the UKF to parameters estimation allows to obtain the stable non-linear dynamic GMDH neural model. Moreover, the application of the UKF enables to calculate the adaptive threshold of the GMDH model and apply it to the robust fault detection of the dynamic systems. In the experimental part of the paper the results of application of the proposed approach to the identification and robust fault detection of the tunnel furnace are presented. Moreover, the comparison of the identification results shows ascendancy of the UKF over the ARS algorithm. Finally, the resulting robust fault detection scheme is successively applied to detection of faulty temperature sensor in the tunnel furnace.

Acknowledgments. The work was supported by the National Science Centre of Poland under grant: 2011-2014

References

1. Ding, S.: Model-based Fault Diagnosis Techniques: Design Schemes, Algorithms, and Tools. Springer, Heidelberg (2008)
2. Korbicz, J., Kościelny, J.: Modeling, Diagnostics and Process Control: Implementation in the DiaSter System. Springer, Berlin (2010)

3. Mrugalski, M., Witczak, M.: State-space gmdh neural networks for actuator robust fault diagnosis. Advances in Electrical and Computer Engineering 12(3), 65–72 (2012)
4. Niemann, H.: A model-based approach to fault-tolerant control. International Journal of Applied Mathematics and Computer Science 22(1), 67–86 (2012)
5. Noura, H., Theilliol, D., Ponsart, J.C., Chamseddine, A.: Fault-tolerant Control Systems: Design and Practical Applications. Springer, London (2009)
6. Pedro, J., Dahunsi, O.: Neural network based feedback linearization control of a servo-hydraulic vehicle suspension system. International Journal of Applied Mathematics and Computer Science 21, 137–147 (2011)
7. Mrugalski, M., Witczak, M., Korbicz, J.: Confidence estimation of the multi-layer perceptron and its application in fault detection systems. Engineering Applications of Artificial Intelligence 21(6), 895–906 (2008)
8. Mrugalski, M.: An unscented kalman filter in designing dynamic gmdh neural networks for robust fault detection. International Journal of Applied Mathematics and Computer Science 23(1), 157–169 (2013)
9. Witczak, M., Korbicz, J., Mrugalski, M., Patton, R.J.: A gmdh neural network based approach to robust fault detection and its application to solve the damadics benchmark problem. Control Engineering Practice 14(6), 671–683 (2006)
10. Patan, K., Witczak, M., Korbicz, J.: Towards robustness in neural network based fault diagnosis. International Journal of Applied Mathematics and Computer Science 18(4), 443–454 (2008)
11. Korbicz, J., Mrugalski, M.: Confidence estimation of gmdh neural networks and its application in fault detection system. International Journal of System Science 39(8), 783–800 (2008)
12. Ivakhnenko, A.G., Mueller, J.A.: Self-organization of nets of active neurons. System Analysis Modelling Simulation 20, 93–106 (1995)
13. Mrugalski, M., Arinton, E., Korbicz, J.: Dynamic gmdh type neural networks. In: Neural Networks and Soft Computing: Proceedings of the Sixth International Conference. Advances in Soft Computing, pp. 698–703. Springer-Verlag Company, New York (2003) ISBN: 3-7908-0005-8
14. Mrugalski, M., Korbicz, J.: Least mean square vs. Outer bounding ellipsoid algorithm in confidence estimation of the GMDH neural networks. In: Beliczynski, B., Dzielinski, A., Iwanowski, M., Ribeiro, B. (eds.) ICANNGA 2007, Part II. LNCS, vol. 4432, pp. 19–26. Springer, Heidelberg (2007)
15. Teixeira, B., Torres, L., Aguirre, L., Bernstein, D.: On unscented kalman filtering with state interval constraints. Journal of Process Control 20(1), 45–57 (2010)
16. Mueller, J., Lemke, F.: Self-organising Data Mining. Libri, Hamburg (2000)
17. Julier, S., Uhlmann, J.: Unscented filtering and nonlinear estimation. Proceedings of the IEEE 92(3), 401–422 (2004)
18. Lee, T., Jiang, Z.: On uniform global asymptotic stability of nonlinear discrete-time systems with applications. IEEE Trans. Automatic Control 51(10), 1644–1660 (2006)
19. Walter, E., Pronzato, L.: Identification of Parametric Models from Experimental Data. Springer, Berlin (1997)

Employing Self-Organizing Map
for Fraud Detection

Dominik Olszewski[1], Janusz Kacprzyk[2], and Sławomir Zadrożny[2]

[1] Faculty of Electrical Engineering,
Warsaw University of Technology, Poland
olszewsd@ee.pw.edu.pl
[2] Systems Research Institute,
Polish Academy of Sciences, Poland
{janusz.kacprzyk,slawomir.zadrozny}@ibspan.waw.pl

Abstract. We propose a fraud detection method based on the user accounts visualization and threshold-type detection. The visualization technique employed in our approach is the Self-Organizing Map (SOM). Since the SOM technique in its original form visualizes only the vectors, and the user accounts are represented in our work as the matrices storing a collection of records reflecting the user sequential activities, we propose a method of the matrices visualization on the SOM grid, which constitutes the main contribution of this paper. Furthermore, we propose a method of the detection threshold setting on the basis of the SOM U-matrix. The results of the conducted experimental study on real data in the field of telecommunications fraud detection confirm the advantages and effectiveness of the proposed approach.

Keywords: fraud detection, Self-Organizing Map, threshold classification, visualization, telecommunications data visualization.

1 Introduction

The Self-Organizing Map (SOM) is an example of the artificial neural network architecture. It was by introduced by T. Kohonen in [1] as a generalization and extension of the concepts proposed in [2]. This algorithm can be also interpreted as a visualization technique, since the algorithm performs a projection from multidimensional space to 2-dimensional space, this way creating a map structure. The location of points in 2-dimensional grid aims to reflect the similarities between the corresponding objects in multidimensional space. Therefore, the SOM algorithm allows for visualization of relationships between objects in multidimensional space. An exhaustive and detailed description of the SOM method can be found in [3].

We employ the SOM method in the fraud detection framework. Fraud detection using a visualization technique is a particularly profitable approach, since it assures the two significant advantages. First of all, a graphical representation of an analyzed dataset is eligible for convenient and fast analysis and interpretation,

L. Rutkowski et al. (Eds.): ICAISC 2013, Part I, LNAI 7894, pp. 150–161, 2013.
© Springer-Verlag Berlin Heidelberg 2013

even by a non-expert, who can formulate some conclusions or at least suspicions due to the analyzed data (for example, the person may notice certain fraudulent activity). Second of all, the efficient and effective visualization technique (like, for example, the SOM) combined with a chosen classification algorithm (performing the actual detection) leads to satisfactory detection results.

1.1 Related Work

There is a number of fraud detection problems, including financial frauds [4–6], Internet frauds [7–9], and telecommunications frauds [10–13], to name but a few. A common major difficulty associated with all those fraud detection fields is that there is a large amount of data that needs to be analyzed, and simultaneously, there is only a small number of fraudulent samples, which could be used as the training data for the supervised methods. Consequently, this problem essentially inhibits and limits an application of the supervised techniques. The SOM approach proposed for fraud detection in this work is an unsupervised method, therefore, it is robust to the mentioned before difficulty, and consequently, it is especially useful in the fraud detection framework.

The general problem of fraud detection has been reviewed in [14, 15].

The visualization approach to fraud detection appears relatively rarely in the literature, and the problem apparently has not yet gained the deserved attention. In the paper [7], a neural visualization of network traffic data for computer intrusion detection is proposed. The system introduced in [7] applies neural projection architectures to detect anomalous situations taking place in a computer network. By its advanced visualization facilities, the proposal of [7] provides an overview of the network traffic, as well as identification of anomalous situations tackled by computer networks. The authors of [6] consider six classes of data mining techniques, i.e., classification, regression, clustering, prediction, outlier detection, and visualization, in context of the fraud detection issue. According to one of the conclusions of [6], data visualization provides an easily understandable presentation of data and converts complicated data characteristics into clear patterns, which allow users to view the complex patterns or relationships uncovered in the data mining process.

However, both of the mentioned works ([7] and [6]) refer to a specific fraud detection field – computer intrusion detection in [7] and financial fraud detection in [6]. Furthermore, both these papers deal with the detection of single fraudulent user activities. Nevertheless important is the problem of detection of the entire fraudulent user accounts resulting from a sequential repeatedly committed user fraudulent behavior, which is the issue considered in our paper (the term "user account" is explained in Section 3).

1.2 Our Proposal

In this paper, we propose a fraud detection based on the SOM visualization and classification. Consequently, the proposed approach consists of the two main steps:

Step 1. SOM visualization of the multidimensional data of the user accounts.
Step 2. The actual fraud detection on the basis of the threshold-type binary classification algorithm.

In Step 1, the entire user accounts are visualized in 2-dimensional space of the SOM grid. The user accounts are numerically represented as data matrices storing a collection of records reflecting the user activities. In other words, the accounts are the data objects characterized by features possessing their own inner-dimensionality (consequently, creating the matrices). Since the standard SOM technique visualizes only single vectors, it is necessary to formulate a method of the user accounts visualization on the SOM grid, which is the main proposal of this paper (described in details in Section 4).

In Step 2, the threshold-type binary classification algorithm performs the final detection of fraudulent accounts. In our paper, we propose also a method of the classification threshold setting on the basis of the SOM U-matrix.

The advantage of the introduced method is that it is a general fraud detection approach, i.e., it is not oriented to certain particular field or application, and it can be easily adopted in every information system collecting the data deriving from users sequential activity. Furthermore, our approach is an unsupervised technique, thus, avoiding the problems associated with insufficient training data, which essentially affect the final detection results of supervised data mining methods (mentioned in Section 1.1).

The experimental study conducted on real data in the field of fraud detection in telecommunications verifies and confirms the usefulness and effectiveness of the proposed approach, and it demonstrates the benefits associated with the preliminary data visualization, which transforms the input high-dimensional information into a 2-dimensional image – easy and convenient for analysis and interpretation, even by non-experts. Although our experiments have been carried out on the specific telecommunications dataset, the proposed approach itself is more general, and it can be easily applied in case of different datasets containing the data reflecting the users repeatedly evinced behavior.

1.3   The Remainder of This Paper

The rest of this paper is organized as follows: in Section 2, the SOM algorithm is described; in Section 3, the representation of the user data is described and explained; in Section 4, the main proposal of our paper, i.e., a method of the user accounts visualization on the SOM, is presented; in Section 5, the actual fraud detection is described; in Section 6, the experimental results are reported; while Section 7 summarizes the whole paper, and points out certain directions of the future research.

2   Self-Organizing Map

The SOM algorithm provides a non-linear mapping between a high-dimensional original data space and a 2-dimensional map of neurons. The neurons are arranged according to a regular grid, in such a way that the similar vectors in input space are represented by the neurons close in the grid. Therefore, the SOM technique visualize the data associations in the input high-dimensional space.

It was shown in [16] that the results obtained by the SOM method are equivalent to the results obtained by optimizing the following error function:

$$e\left(\mathcal{W}\right) = \sum_{r} \sum_{x_\mu \in V_r} \sum_{s} h_{rs} D\left(x_\mu,\, w_s\right) \tag{1}$$

$$\approx \sum_{r} \sum_{x_\mu \in V_r} D\left(x_\mu,\, w_r\right) + K \sum_{r} \sum_{s \neq r} h_{rs} D\left(w_r,\, w_s\right), \tag{2}$$

where x_μ are the objects in high-dimensional space, w_r and w_s are the prototypes of objects on the grid, h_{rs} is a neighborhood function (for example, the Gaussian kernel) that transforms non-linearly the neuron distances (see [3] for other choices of neighborhood functions), $D\left(\cdot,\, \cdot\right)$ is the squared Euclidean distance, and V_r is the Voronoi region corresponding to prototype w_r. The number of prototypes is sufficiently large so that $D\left(x_\mu,\, w_s\right) \approx D\left(x_\mu,\, w_r\right) + D\left(w_r,\, w_s\right)$.

According to equation (2), the SOM error function can be decomposed as the sum of the quantization error and the topological error. The first one minimizes the loss of information, when the input patterns are represented by a set of prototypes. By minimizing the second one, we assure the maximal correlation between the prototype dissimilarities and the corresponding neuron distances, this way assuring the visualization of the data relationships in the input space.

The SOM error function can be optimized by an iterative algorithm consisting of two steps (discussed in [16]). First, a quantization algorithm is executed. This algorithm represents each input pattern by the nearest neighbor prototype. This operation minimizes the first component in equation (2). Next, the prototypes are arranged along the grid of neurons by minimizing the second component in the error function. This optimization problem can be solved explicitly using the following adaptation rule for each prototype [3]:

$$w_s = \frac{\sum_{r=1}^{M} \sum_{x_\mu \in V_r} h_{rs} x_\mu}{\sum_{r=1}^{M} \sum_{x_\mu \in V_r} h_{rs}}, \tag{3}$$

where M is the number of neurons, and h_{rs} is a neighborhood function (for example, the Gaussian kernel of width $\sigma\left(t\right)$). The width of the kernel is adapted in each iteration of the algorithm using the rule proposed by [17], i.e., $\sigma\left(t\right) = \sigma_i \left(\sigma_f / \sigma_i\right)^{t/N_{iter}}$, where $\sigma_i \approx M/2$ is typically assumed in the literature (for example, in [3]), and σ_f is the parameter that determines the smoothing degree of the principal curve generated by the SOM algorithm [17].

3   User Account Representation

The term "user account", in our work, denotes a set of data records assigned to a one particular individual user. A record stores the information describing certain single operation or activity of the individual. In other words, a user account reflects certain sequential activity of a single user. Depending on the information system considered the records and the sets of records may somewhat vary. For example, in case of the telecommunications information system, the record will store the data characterizing a single call. This kind of call description is often referred to as the Call Data Record (CDR) – storing the basic information, or Call Detailed Record (the same CDR abbreviation) – storing the precise detailed information. And consequently, a telecommunication account will assemble a set of the CDRs.

Each record consists of some number of fields, which are a unit inseparable portion of information. For example, in case of the telecommunications system, the basic CDR may consist of: start-time, destination, and duration.

A set of records creates a data matrix representing a user account. Taking into consideration the standard data mining terminology, and casting the user account onto such framework, we can interpret the account as an object (pattern, observation) consisting of multidimensional features. In other words, one can say that the features have their own inner-dimensionality. And, in Section 4, we will demonstrate, how to visualize the user accounts on the SOM grid.

4   SOM Visualization of the User Accounts

The user accounts are represented by data matrices assembling a sequence of records. Typically, the number of records is a lot larger than the number of fields in a single record. Hence, a data matrix representing a single user account has the following form:

$$
\begin{pmatrix} f_{11} & \cdots & f_{1m} \\ & \vdots & \\ f_{n1} & \cdots & f_{nm} \end{pmatrix}, \tag{4}
$$

where n is the number of records (the number of inner-dimensions of features), m is the number of features (fields) in a single record, and $n \gg m$.

A single user account can be visualized on the SOM by executing the following two steps:

Step 1. SOM visualization of all features of the account.
Step 2. Computing the centroid of the features on the SOM grid, and as a result, obtaining a one 2-dimensional point visualizing the entire account.

In Step 1, we visualize all features of a single user account, i.e., we project the columns of the matrix given in (4) onto the SOM grid.

In Step 2, we visualize the entire account as the geometrical center (centroid) of all account features projected on the SOM.

Regarding the relation $n \gg m$ in (4), it is much more beneficial to reduce the inner-dimensionality of features (fields of the records) by projecting them onto the SOM grid as the first operation, and next, to compute the centroids of the visualized 2-dimensional features in order to obtain the account visualization.

The process of the user account visualization using the SOM technique is presented in Fig. 1, where f_1, f_2, and f_3 denote the three example features, which are also the vertices of a triangle. The centroid of the triangle (laying on the intersection of its geometrical medians) is the desired target visualization of the entire account.

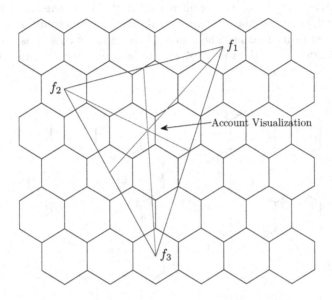

Fig. 1. Visualization of an example user account

As it is shown in Fig. 1, the final account visualization does not necessarily need to correspond to a particular neuron on the SOM grid. The account is simply represented by a pair of coordinates, and on the basis of these coordinates, it is recognized by the employed classification algorithm (described in Section 5) as non-fraudulent or fraudulent.

5   Fraud Detection

After the user accounts in an analyzed dataset are visualized on the SOM grid, one needs to detect the fraudulent ones among them. This can be accomplished using a chosen binary classification algorithm. The fraudulent accounts visualized on the SOM are treated in our study as outliers. Therefore, the fraud detection in our work comes down to the outlier detection problem. A useful tool in the outlier detection is the simple threshold-type binary classification technique. In our study, we propose to apply that algorithm, because it is an effective approach, when operating on the SOM grid (2-dimensional space), and also, its computational simplicity makes it an efficient method. We do not focus on the classification problem itself, however of course, one may consider employing the different classification algorithms, also, the mathematically more advanced ones.

The classification method utilized in this paper is presented graphically in 2-dimensional space (like in case of the SOM visualization space) in Fig. 2. An example SOM grid is depicted as the background. The method detects the fraudulent accounts visualized beforehand on the SOM grid. The accounts localized inside the circle illustrating the classification threshold are considered to be non-fraudulent, while the accounts laying outside the circle (account 5 and account 9) are detected as fraudulent. The center of the circle is chosen as the centroid of the SOM grid, while the radius of the circle is set according to the method described in Section 5.1.

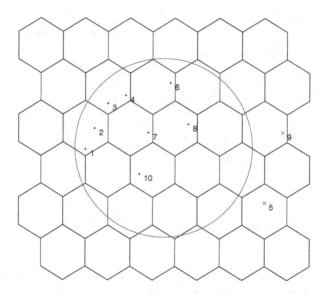

Fig. 2. Graphical illustration of the threshold-type binary classification method

5.1   Classification Threshold Setting

We propose to set the classification threshold to the value of the dissimilarity between the SOM grid centroid and the SOM neuron corresponding to the maximal value in the U-matrix corresponding to that SOM. The U-matrix is a graphical presentation of SOM. Each entry of the U-matrix corresponds to a neuron on the SOM grid, while value of that entry is the average dissimilarity between the neuron and its neighbors. Therefore, the series of high values in the U-matrix (so called "ridges" of the U-matrix) represent the borderlines separating the data clusters on the SOM grid.

In our study, one needs to separate the non-fraudulent and fraudulent user accounts. Therefore, we expect to have only one ridge in the U-matrix of our SOM, and the classification threshold should possibly most accurately reflect that ridge.

Naturally, one may wonder about using some clustering technique in order to detect fraudulent accounts. It is, of course, possible, however, in our work, we decided to use the described threshold-type binary classification algorithm, because of its computational simplicity, efficiency, and empirically confirmed efficacy. Moreover, in our experimental research, it was convenient to obtain the Receiver Operating Characteristics (ROC) curves evaluating the investigated approaches, by simply shifting the threshold value (see Section 6.3).

6   Experiments

In our experimental study, we have evaluated the proposed fraud detection method on the basis of the comparison with the classical Gaussian-Mixture-Model-based (GMM-based) fraud detection technique. The experiments have been conducted on the telecommunications dataset, i.e., the telecommunications frauds have been being detected.

6.1   Dataset Description

We have used the dataset consisting of 100 accounts of selected telecommunication users in the city of Warsaw in Poland. The data was collected in the time interval between 1.03.2008 and 1.04.2008. A single call has been represented by the call data record (CDR). Each CDR contains the information about a specific call, made by a specific user. Hence, CDR consists of certain fields, such as: destination, start-time, or duration. Notice that the abbreviation CDR refers to the "call data record," and not to the "call detail record" – the output log of the Private Branch Exchange (PBX) that holds all the detailed data of each phone call made. This is because we have utilized in our experimental study only the three mentioned basic features of a phone call, i.e., the destination, the start-time, and the duration of a call. Among the all 100 investigated telecommunication accounts 10 were fraudulent.

6.2   GMM-Based Fraud Detection Method

As the reference method, we have used the traditional GMM-based fraud detection approach [18]. According to the principles of the method, for each user account, the GMM model is built, and the fraudulent accounts are chosen as the ones significantly deviated from the reference user account, which reflects the most typical user traits and behaviors. The degree of deviation from the reference account is determined using an arbitrary set threshold. In case of the analyzed telecommunications dataset, each GMM model consisted of three Gaussian probability distributions corresponding to three CDR fields. The prior probabilities of each GMM model were equal, i.e., they were set to the value $\frac{1}{3}$.

6.3   Evaluation Criterion

As the evaluation criterion, we have used the Receiver Operating Characteristics (ROC) curves. This is a traditional way to investigate the performance of the fraud detection methods [19]. The ROC curves show the fraud detection probability (true positive rate) versus the false alarm probability (false positive rate). The perfect point on the ROC graph is the (0, 1) point, which corresponds to detection of all frauds with simultaneous zero false alarms rate. Therefore, the perfect ROC is the curve containing that point. The closer to that result is the ROC curve, the better is the assessed detection method. On the other hand, the point (1, 0) reflects the lowest detection performance. In order to evaluate a specific curve, the Area Under ROC (AUROC) metric is used. It simply measures the area under the curve, and the perfect value of AUROC is 1. Also an important value in assessment of the ROC curve is the highest fraud detection rate corresponding to the zero false alarms rate (HDZF), and, the lowest false alarms rate corresponding to the maximal (i.e., 1) fraud detection rate (LFMD). The perfect value of HDZF is 1, and the perfect value of LFMD is 0.

In order to obtain the ROC curves evaluating the two examined methods, the threshold value of the classification algorithm (in case of our method) and the threshold measuring the deviation from the reference user account (in case of the GMM-based method) have been uniformly decreased.

6.4   Experimental Results

The results of our experiments are shown in Figs. 3, 4(a), and 4(b). Figure 3 presents the U-matrix of the SOM visualizing the investigated telecommunications dataset. The marking letters 'N' denote the non-fraudulent accounts, while the marking letters 'F' denote the fraudulent accounts. Figures 4(a) and 4(b) show the ROC curves corresponding to the GMM-based method (Fig. 4(a)) and to the proposed method (Fig. 4(b)).

After setting the classification threshold of our method to the constant value chosen according to the method described in Section 5.1, the fraud detection rate was 0.9, while the false alarms rate was 0.1.

As it is easily noticeable in Fig.3, the proposed SOM visualization of the user accounts can clearly point out the large majority of the fraudulent accounts. Our visualization maps the input complicated high-dimensional data onto a regular 2-dimensional SOM grid. Therefore, the information provided be our method can be easily and intuitively analyzed and interpreted, even by a non-expert, who will be strongly suggested to properly mark the fraudulent accounts in the dataset.

Furthermore, our experimental research confirmed the superiority of the proposed approach over the standard GMM-based fraud detection method. The superiority was ascertained on the basis of the generated ROC curves and computed AUROC values (0.844 vs. 0.936).

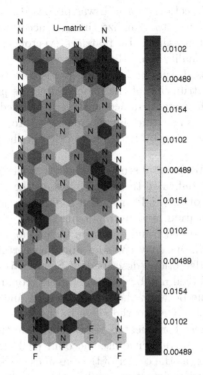

Fig. 3. U-matrix of the SOM visualizing the investigated telecommunications dataset

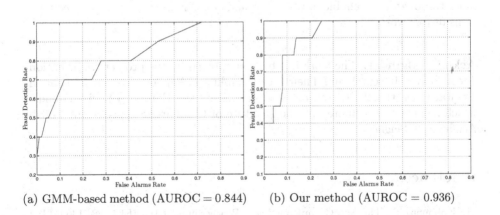

(a) GMM-based method (AUROC = 0.844)   (b) Our method (AUROC = 0.936)

Fig. 4. ROC curves of the two examined fraud detection methods

7 Summary and Future Research

In this paper, a fraud detection approach was proposed. The approach employs the SOM technique in order to visualize the user accounts. Since the user account are numerically represented by matrices (vectors of features possessing their own inner-dimensionality), and the standard SOM approach visualizes only single vectors, we proposed a method of matrices visualization on the SOM grid, which was the main contribution of the paper. After the projection of the user accounts on the SOM, the fraudulent accounts were detected using the threshold-type binary classification algorithm. Furthermore, we proposed a method of the classification threshold setting by finding the ridge in the U-matrix of a given SOM.

The results of our experimental study conducted in the field of telecommunications fraud detection confirmed the effectiveness of the proposed approach by showing the advantages of fast and convenient fraud detection on the basis of the graphical data representation, and by reporting the superiority of our method over the classical GMM-based fraud detection technique.

In the future research, one may consider applying certain different methods performing the actual detection (described in Section 5). For example, SOM clustering (with the enforced number of two clusters) could be performed. Also, the separation borderline between the non-fraudulent and fraudulent accounts could be more accurately fitted to the ridge in the U-matrix of a given SOM – it could be certain more complicated geometrical line than the circle chord. Moreover, one can utilize a reference user account (reflecting the most typical user traits and behaviors) as the center of the classification circle threshold. This could provide more accurate detection results.

Finally, the experiments on other datasets (for example, financial frauds or Internet frauds) would make the experimental evaluation of the proposed method more thorough and reliable, and they would confirm the assertions and conclusions of this work.

Acknowledgment. The work has been supported by the project "Information Technologies: Research and Their Interdisciplinary Applications" of the Human Capital Operational Programme (co-financed by the European Social Found), which has been coordinated by the Institute of Computer Science of the Polish Academy of Sciences.

References

1. Kohonen, T.: The Self-Organizing Map. Proceedings of the IEEE 28, 1464–1480 (1990)
2. Kohonen, T.: Self-Organized Formation of Topologically Correct Feature Maps. Biological Cybernetics 43(1), 59–69 (1982)
3. Kohonen, T.: Self-Organizing Maps, 3rd edn. Springer (2001)

4. Jha, S., Guillen, M., Westland, J.C.: Employing Transaction Aggregation Strategy to Detect Credit Card Fraud. Expert Systems with Applications 39, 12650–12657 (2012)
5. Bhattacharyya, S., Jha, S., Tharakunnel, K., Westland, J.C.: Data Mining for Credit Card Fraud: A Comparative Study. Decision Support Systems 50, 602–613 (2011)
6. Ngai, E.W.T., Hu, Y., Wong, Y.H., Chen, Y., Sun, X.: The Application of Data Mining Techniques in Financial Fraud Detection: A Classification Framework and an Academic Review of Literature. Decision Support Systems 50, 559–569 (2011)
7. Corchado, E., Herrero, A.: Neural Visualization of Network Traffic Data for Intrusion Detection. Applied Soft Computing 11, 2042–2056 (2011)
8. Kim, Y., Lee, S.J., Lim, J.I.: Fraud Detection for Information Reliability from the Internet in Forensic Accounting. Journal of Internet Technology 11(3), 323–331 (2010)
9. Ku, Y., Chen, Y., Chiu, C.: A Proposed Data Mining Approach for Internet Auction Fraud Detection. In: Yang, C.C., et al. (eds.) PAISI 2007. LNCS, vol. 4430, pp. 238–243. Springer, Heidelberg (2007)
10. Olszewski, D.: A Probabilistic Approach to Fraud Detection in Telecommunications. Knowledge-Based Systems 26, 246–258 (2012)
11. Farvaresh, H., Sepehri, M.M.: A Data Mining Framework for Detecting Subscription Fraud in Telecommunication. Engineering Applications of Artificial Intelligence 24(1), 182–194 (2011)
12. Olszewski, D.: Fraud Detection in Telecommunications Using Kullback-Leibler Divergence and Latent Dirichlet Allocation. In: Dobnikar, A., Lotrič, U., Šter, B. (eds.) ICANNGA 2011, Part II. LNCS, vol. 6594, pp. 71–80. Springer, Heidelberg (2011)
13. Hilas, C.S., Mastorocostas, P.A.: An Application of Supervised and Unsupervised Learning Approaches to Telecommunications Fraud Detection. Knowledge-Based Systems 21, 721–726 (2008)
14. Bolton, R.J., Hand, D.J.: Statistical Fraud Detection: A Review. Statistical Science 17(3), 235–255 (2002)
15. Kou, Y., Lu, C.T., Sinvongwattana, S., Huang, Y.P.: Survey of Fraud Detection Techniques. In: Proceedings of the 2004 IEEE International Conference on Networking, Sensing & Control (March 2004)
16. Heskes, T.: Self-Organizing Maps, Vector Quantization, and Mixture Modeling. IEEE Transactions on Neural Networks 12(6), 1299–1305 (2001)
17. Mulier, F., Cherkassky, V.: Self-Organization as an Iterative Kernel Smoothing Process. Neural Computation 7(6), 1165–1177 (1995)
18. Taniguchi, M., Haft, M., Hollmen, J., Tresp, V.: Fraud Detection in Communications Networks Using Neural and Probabilistic Methods. In: IEEE International Conference on Acoustics Speech and Signal Processing, ICASSP 1998, vol. 2, pp. 1241–1244. IEEE (1998)
19. Fawcett, T.: ROC Graphs: Notes and Practical Considerations for Data Mining Researchers. Technical Report Technical Report HPL-2003-4, HP Labs (2003)

A Study on the Scalability of Artificial Neural Networks Training Algorithms Using Multiple-Criteria Decision-Making Methods

Diego Peteiro-Barral* and Bertha Guijarro-Berdiñas

Dept. of Computer Science, University of A Coruña,
Campus de Elviña s/n, 15071, A Coruña, Spain
{dpeteiro,cibertha}@udc.es
http://www.lidiagroup.org/

Abstract. In recent years, the unrestrainable growth of the volume of data has raised new challenges in machine learning regarding scalability. Scalability comprises not simply accuracy but several other measures regarding computational resources. In order to compare the scalability of algorithms it is necessary to establish a method allowing integrating all these measures into a single rank. These methods should be able to i) merge results of algorithms to be compared from different benchmark data sets, ii) quantitatively measure the difference between algorithms, and iii) weight some measures against others if necessary. In order to manage these issues, in this research we propose the use of TOPSIS as multiple-criteria decision-making method to rank algorithms. The use of this method will be illustrated to obtain a study on the scalability of five of the most well-known training algorithms for artificial neural networks (ANNs).

Keywords: Machine learning, scalability, artificial neural networks, multiple-criteria decision-making methods.

1 Introduction

In machine learning, scalability is defined by the effect that an increase in the size of the training set has on the computational performance of an algorithm (accuracy, training time and allocated memory). So the challenge is to find a tradeoff among them or, in other words, getting "good enough" solutions as "fast" as possible and as "efficiently" as possible. This issue becomes critical in situations in which there exist temporal or spatial constraints like: real-time applications dealing with large data sets, unapproachable computational problems requiring learning, or initial prototyping requiring quickly-implemented solutions.

* This work was supported by Secretaría de Estado de Investigación of the Spanish Government under projects TIN 2009-02402 and TIN2012-37954, and by the Xunta de Galicia through projects CN2011/007 and CN2012/211, all partially supported by the European Union ERDF. Diego Peteiro-Barral acknowledges the support of Xunta de Galicia under *Plan I2C* Grant Program.

L. Rutkowski et al. (Eds.): ICAISC 2013, Part I, LNAI 7894, pp. 162–173, 2013.

A sample of the interest generated by large-scale learning was revealed with the organization of the workshop PASCAL Large Scale Learning Challenge [1] at the 25th International Conference on Machine learning (ICML'08). It was concerned with the scalability and efficiency of machine learning algorithms with respect to computational, memory and communication resources. In order to deal with large data sets, it is essential to minimize training time and allocated memory while maintaining accuracy. However, up to now, most machine learning algorithms do not provide an appropriate balance among them. Most algorithms tend to look with favor on one of these variables against others. A more recent sample of the relevance of scalability in learning, also known as "big learning", was disclosed with the conference of the Neural Information Processing Systems Foundation (NIPS'2011), aiming to provide a forum for exchanging solutions that address big learning problems. The relevance of these conferences for researchers and practitioners is meaningful.

In recent years, several researchers have addressed the issue of scalability of machine learning algorithms [2–4]. Scalability is wider than simple evaluations of accuracy. Scalability involves many aspects such as error, training time and memory requirements that should be merged into a single evaluation framework in order to rank algorithms. Such framework should be able to handle three different aspects: i) merging results of algorithms to be compared from different benchmark data sets, ii) being able to quantitatively measure the difference between algorithms, and iii) being able to weight some measures against others if necessary. In order to manage these issues, we propose to use a multiple-criteria decision-making method to rank algorithms. In this research, this framework will be applied to experimentally assess the scalability of five of the most popular training algorithms for ANN: gradient descent, gradient descent with momentum and adaptive learning rate, scaled conjugate gradient, Levenberg-Marquardt and stochastic gradient descent. To the best knowledge of the authors, this is a novel research that will shed light on the scalability of ANN training algorithms.

The remainder of this paper is structured as follows: section 2 describes the training algorithms, section 3 presents the measures of scalability used in this research, section 4 describes the MCDM method used, section 5 presents the experimental procedure followed, and section 6 shows the results obtained, and section 7 shows the conclusions and future lines of research.

2   Training Algorithms for ANN

This section gives a brief overview of the five training algorithms for ANNs considered in this research: gradient descent, gradient descent with momentum and adaptive learning rate, scaled conjugate gradient, Levenberg-Marquardt and stochastic gradient descent.

2.1   Gradient Descent

Gradient descent is one of the simplest training algorithms for ANNs. In the batch version, the algorithm starts with a random weight vector denoted by $w^{(0)}$.

Then, it iteratively updates the weight vector such that, at step τ, it moves a short distance in the direction of the greatest rate of decrease of the error, that is in the direction of the negative gradient, evaluated at $w^{(\tau)}$ [5]:

$$\Delta w^{(\tau)} = -\eta \nabla E_{w^{(\tau)}}$$

where the parameter ∇ is the learning rate and E is the error function evaluated at $w^{(\tau)}$. Note that the gradient is re-evaluated at each step. It is expected that the value of E will decrease at each step.

2.2   Gradient Descent with Momentum and Adaptive Learning Rate

The performance of the gradient descent algorithm is very sensitive to the proper setting of the learning rate η. If the learning rate is set too high, the algorithm can oscillate and become unstable. If the learning rate is too small, the algorithm takes too long to converge. Note that it is not practical to determine the optimal setting for the learning rate before training. With standard gradient descent, the learning rate is held constant throughout training. However, the performance of the gradient descent algorithm can be improved if it allows the learning rate to change during the training process. An adaptive learning rate attempts to keep the learning step size as large as possible while keeping learning stable.

Another very simple technique for improving the performance of the gradient descent algorithm is to add a momentum term [6]. The modified gradient descent formula is given by:

$$\Delta w^{(\tau)} = -\eta \nabla E_{w^{(\tau)}} + \mu \Delta w^{(\tau-1)}$$

This term adds inertia to the motion through weight space smoothing out the oscillations of the algorithm whilst speeding up the convergence. Moreover, the momentum term can be helpful in reducing the likelihood of finding a local minima.

2.3   Scaled Conjugate Gradient

With simple gradient descent, the direction of each step is given by the local negative gradient of the error function, and the step size is determined by an arbitrary learning rate parameter. A better procedure would be to consider some search direction in weight space, and then find the minimum of the error function along that direction. The minimum along the search direction $d^{(\tau)}$ then gives the next value for the weight vector:

$$w^{(\tau+1)} = w^{(\tau)} + \delta^{(\tau)} d^{(\tau)}$$

where the parameter $\lambda^{((\tau))}$ is chosen to minimize:

$$E(\lambda) = E(w^{(\tau)} + \lambda d^{(\tau)})$$

This gives an automatic procedure for setting the step length [7].

2.4   Levenberg-Marquardt

The Levenberg-Marquardt [8, 9] algorithm was designed specifically for minimizing a sum-of-squares error $(E = \frac{1}{2} \sum_n \epsilon_n^2 = \frac{1}{2} \|\epsilon\|^2)$. Suppose we are currently at point w_{old} in weight space and we move to a point w_{new}. If the displacement $w_{new} w_{old}$ is small then the error vector ϵ can be expanded to first order in Taylor series:

$$\epsilon(w_{new}) = \epsilon(w_{old}) + Z(w_{new} - w_{old})$$

where the matrix Z is defined with elements

$$(Z)_{ni} = \frac{\partial \epsilon^n}{\partial w_i}$$

If the error is minimized with respect to the new weights w_{new} then:

$$w_{new} = w_{old} - (Z^T Z)^{-1} Z^T \epsilon(w_{old})$$

where the Hessian can be written in the form $H = Z^T Z$. Since there is no guarantee that the Hessian H is positive definite, a correction term can be introduced to cover this problem by

$$H = H + \delta I$$

where I is the identity matrix and δ is a parameter which value changes during training to guarantee the positive definiteness of the Hessian matrix.

The weight update formula could be applied iteratively in order to try to minimize the error function. The problem is that the update term could turn out to be relatively large. This problem is addressed by seeking to minimize the error function whilst at the same time trying to keep the step size small so as to ensure that the linear approximation remains valid.

2.5   Stochastic Gradient Descent

In the stochastic version of gradient descent, the error function is evaluated for just one sample at a time. The weights update rule is:

$$\Delta w^{(\tau)} = -\eta \nabla E^n_{w^{(\tau)}}$$

where the different samples n in the training set are selected at random order. It is expected a steady reduction in error since the average direction of motion in weight space should approximate the negative of the local gradient [5]. An important advantage of the stochastic approach over batch methods arises if there is a high degree of redundant information in the data set. Another potential advantage of the stochastic approach is that it has the possibility of escape from local minima.

3 Scalability Measures

Performance measures such as mean squared error or class accuracy are inadequate to evaluate the performance of learning algorithms in large data sets since they do not take into account all aspects involved in scalability.

Scalability measures must take into consideration error, time and memory constraints. Thus, the goal is to find a learning algorithm that obtains the lowest error in the shortest time using the smaller number of samples. However, there are no standard measures of scalability. In order to overcome this issue, those measures defined in the PASCAL large scale learning challenge [1] will be used in this research. In this challenge, six scalar measures were defined based on three figures (see Figure 1).

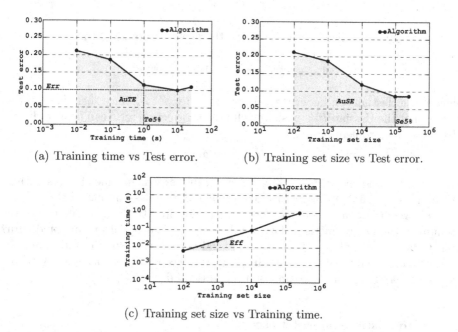

(a) Training time vs Test error.   (b) Training set size vs Test error.

(c) Training set size vs Training time.

Fig. 1. Performance measures in terms of scalability, where the six scalar measures are marked in italic on the three figures.

- Figure 1(a) shows *Training time* vs *Test error*. It is obtained by displaying the evolution of the test error along certain time budgets and employing the *largest dataset* the algorithm can deal with. We compute the following scalar measures based on this figure:
  - *Err*: minimum test error (standard class error [10] for classification and MSE [10] for regression tasks).
  - *AuTE*: area under Training time vs Test error curve.
  - *Te5%*: the time t for which the test error e falls below a threshold $\frac{e - Err}{e} < 0.05$.

- Figure 1(b) shows *Training set size* vs *Test error*. It is obtained by displaying the different training set sizes, $10^{[2,3,4...]}$, and the corresponding test errors achieved. Based on this curve, we compute:
  - *AuSE*: area under Training set size vs Test error curve.
  - *Se5%*: the size s for which the test error e falls below a threshold $\frac{e-Err}{e} < 0.05$
- Figure 1(c) shows *Training set size* vs *Training time*. It is obtained by displaying the different training set sizes and the corresponding training time needed by the algorithm. We compute the following scalar measure based on this curve:
  - *Eff*: slope b of the curve by using a least squares fit to ax^b.

Following PASCAL, algorithms should be ranked for each of these six measures and compute the score of each algorithm as its average position with regard to the six rankings. For example, an algorithm that ranks first in three measures and second in the remaining three will obtain a final score of $\frac{1+1+1+2+2+2}{6} = 1.5$. Note, however, that this procedure do not take into consideration the magnitude of the measures but simply the ranking. This may lead to unfair results, mostly if some algorithms perform notably good or bad. In order to overcome this issue, the use of a multiple-criteria decision-making method is proposed.

4   Multiple-Criteria Decision-Making

Classification algorithms are normally evaluated in terms of multiple criteria. But how can multiple criteria be handle into a single evaluation model? Multiple-criteria decision-making [11] (MCDM) is focused on addressing the aforementioned issue. MCDM methods evaluate classifiers from different aspects and produce rankings of classifiers [12]. A multi-criteria problem is formulated using a set of alternatives $\{a_1, a_2, \ldots, a_m\}$ and criteria $\{k_1, k_2, \ldots, k_n\}$. The decision matrix is formulated as

$$
\begin{pmatrix}
x_{11} & x_{12} & \cdots & x_{1n} \\
x_{21} & x_{22} & \cdots & x_{2n} \\
\vdots & \vdots & \ddots & \vdots \\
x_{m1} & x_{m2} & \cdots & x_{mn}
\end{pmatrix}
$$

where x_{ij} represents the performance measure of the ith alternative in the jth criterion.

Among many MCDM methods that have been developed up to now, Technique for Order of Preference by Similarity to Ideal Solution (TOPSIS) [13] is a well-known method that will be used in this research. TOPSIS finds the best algorithms by minimizing the distance to the ideal solution whilst maximizing the distance to the anti-ideal one. The extension of TOPSIS proposed by Opricovic and Tzeng [14] and Olson [15] is used in this research. The steps of the method are described as follows:

1. Compute the decision matrix consisting of m alternatives and n criteria. For alternative A_i, $i = 1, \ldots, m$, the performance measure of the jth criterion C_j, $j = 1, \ldots, n$, is represented by x_{ij}.
2. Compute the normalized decision matrix. The normalized value r_{ij} is calculated as

$$r_{ij} = \frac{x_{ij}}{\sqrt{\sum_{i=1}^{m} x_{ij}^2}}$$

3. Establish a set of weights w, where w_j is the weight of the jth criterion and $\sum_{j=1}^{n} w_j = 1$, and compute the weighted normalized decision matrix. The weighted normalized value v_{ij} is computed as

$$v_{ij} = r_{ij} w_j$$

4. Find the ideal alternative solution S^+ and the anti-ideal alternative solution S^-, which are computed as,

$$S^+ = \{v_1^+, \ldots, v_n^+\} =$$
$$= \left\{ \left(\max_i v_{ij} | i \in I' \right), \left(\min_i v_{ij} | i \in I'' \right) \right\}$$

and

$$S^- = \{v_1^-, \ldots, v_n^-\} =$$
$$= \left\{ \left(\min_i v_{ij} | i \in I' \right), \left(\max_i v_{ij} | i \in I'' \right) \right\}$$

respectively, where I' is associated with benefit criteria and I'' is associated with cost criteria.
5. Compute the distance of each alternative from the ideal solution and from the anti-ideal solution, using the Euclidean distance,

$$D_i^+ = \sqrt{\sum_{j=1}^{n} (v_{ij} - v_j^+)^2}$$

and

$$D_i^- = \sqrt{\sum_{j=1}^{n} (v_{ij} - v_j^-)^2}$$

respectively
6. Compute the ratio R_i^+ equal to the relative closeness to the ideal solution,

$$R_i^+ = \frac{D_i^-}{D_i^+ + D_i^-}$$

7. Rank alternatives by maximizing the ratio R_i^+

4.1   Combining Divergent Rankings

While the rankings of alternatives on several data sets may agree, it is common the case in which they disagree. Thus, the problem of handling multiple criteria is translated into a problem of handling multiple rankings.

In this research, we propose to rank the alternatives in a secondary ranking that combines divergent rankings by re-applying the MCDM method using as inputs the values of the MCDM on the primary rankings. In this manner, the MCDM method is arranged in a two-step pipeline in which the output values of the primary rankings are used as inputs in the secondary ranking (see Figure 2).

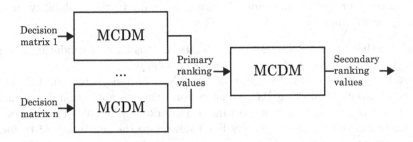

Fig. 2. Combination of divergent rankings obtained on different data sets

5   Experimental Study

The aim of this research is to experimentally evaluate the scalability of five of the most popular training algorithms for ANNs using a MCDM method.

5.1   Data Sets

Training algorithms were applied to two common tasks in machine learning: classification and regression. Table 1 shows the data sets used in this research with a brief description of their features: number of inputs, classes, training samples and test samples, and learning task.

Table 1. Characteristics of each dataset

Dataset	Inputs	Classes	Training	Test	Task
Connect-4	42	3	60,000	7,557	Classification
Covertype	54	2	100,000	50,620	Classification
KDDCup99	42	2	494,021	311,029	Classification
Friedman	10	1	1,000,000	100,000	Regression
Lorenz	8	1	1,000,000	100,000	Regression

Connect-4, Covertype and KDD Cup 99 data set are available at the UCI Machine Learning Repository [16]. On the other hand, Friedman and Lorenz are artificial datasets. The former is defined by the equation $y = 10sin(\pi x_1 x_2) + 20(x_3 - 0.5)^2 + 10x_4 + 5x_5 + \sigma(0,1)$ where the input attributes $x_1, \ldots, x_{10}$ are generated independently from a uniform distribution on the interval $[0, 1]$. On the other hand, Lorenz is defined by the simultaneous solution of three equations $\frac{dX}{dt} = \delta Y - \delta X$, $\frac{dY}{dt} = -XZ + rX - Y$, $\frac{dZ}{dt} = XY - bZ$, where the systems exhibits chaotic behavior for $\delta = 10$, $r = 28$ and $b = \frac{8}{3}$.

5.2   Experimental Procedure

The following procedure was done in order to evaluate the scalability of the training algorithms:

- Divide the data set using holdout validation. This kind of validation is suitable because the size of the data sets is very large.
- Set the number of hidden units of the ANNs to twice plus one the number of inputs. Following [17], going beyond this number should not make any difference. Also, it is important to remark that the aim here is not to investigate the optimal topology but to evaluate the scalability of training algorithms and thus, it is interesting to use networks as large as possible. Set the parameters of the ANNs to default values (learning rate 0.001, goal accuracy 0.01, maximum number of epochs 1000, etc.).
- For each data set, train the ANNs and compute the six scalar measures of scalability defined in Section 3: Err, AuTE, Te5%, AuSE, Se5% and Eff.
- Rank the algorithms using TOPSIS method. The values of the weights corresponding with each criterion are assigned equally. Note also that all measures are cost criteria, i.e. the smaller the better.
- Combine the primary ranking results of the different data sets (see Table 1) in a secondary, final ranking using TOPSIS.

6   Results and Discussion

Table 2 shows the results of the five training algorithms on the five data sets using the six scalar measures of scalability. Based on these six measures, TOPSIS obtains a ranking value also shown in Table 2 (the larger the value the better).

The results showed in this table demonstrate the change in approach when the learning algorithms are evaluated in terms of scalability. Notice that in many cases algorithms with lower test error rank worse than others. For example, Table 2(a) shows that LM obtains a much lower error than GD (-15%) and GDX (-8%). However, LM ranks worse than GD and GDX. In spite of its good accuracy, the long training time of LM makes this algorithm worse in terms of scalability.

Table 3 summarizes the TOPSIS values of each algorithm on each data set. As can be seen, there is no agreement on the ranking among the different data sets. In order to provide a single answer a secondary ranking is applied using as inputs the TOPSIS values of the five algorithms on the five data sets.

Table 2. Performance results of Connect-4, Covertype, KDD Cup 99, Frieadman and Lorenz data sets and primary TOPSIS values

(a) Connect-4 data set.

Name	TOPSIS	Err	AuTE	Te5%	AuSE	Se5%	Eff
GD	0.9057	0.38	5.16e1	1.08e2	0.97	1.00e2	0.43
GDX	0.7189	0.31	3.71e1	7.98e1	0.92	6.00e4	0.40
LM	0.2110	0.23	3.79e2	7.80e2	0.77	1.00e4	0.77
SCG	0.9389	0.21	7.01e1	2.62e2	0.77	1.00e4	0.50
SGD	0.7099	0.16	5.32e1	2.36e2	0.54	6.00e4	0.54

(b) Covertype data set.

Name	TOPSIS	Err	AuTE	Te5%	AuSE	Se5%	Eff
GD	0.8765	0.38	1.24e2	2.78e2	1.20	1.00e3	0.49
GDX	0.8674	0.42	4.74e1	1.01e2	1.32	1.00e4	0.41
LM	0.2431	0.24	6.41e2	1.74e3	0.94	1.00e4	0.84
SCG	0.6308	0.20	1.64e2	5.80e2	0.81	1.00e5	0.55
SGD	0.6426	0.13	1.21e2	7.83e2	0.62	1.00e5	0.58

(c) KDDCup99 data set.

Name	TOPSIS	Err	AuTE	Te5%	AuSE	Se5%	Eff
GD	0.8341	0.13	4.29e1	5.53e1	0.43	1.00e2	0.50
GDX	0.8130	0.15	2.55e1	5.93e1	0.46	1.00e3	0.44
LM	0.3923	0.11	2.21e2	1.24e3	0.46	1.00e4	0.80
SCG	0.6808	0.14	1.10e2	3.54e2	0.51	1.00e4	0.55
SGD	0.4603	0.00	8.85e0	1.35e3	0.07	4.94e5	0.59

(d) Friedman data set.

Name	TOPSIS	Err	AuTE	Te5%	AuSE	Se5%	Eff
GD	0.6424	8.33	2.19e3	7.51e1	36.77	1.00e3	0.37
GDX	0.7805	4.41	1.83e3	7.20e1	24.57	1.00e5	0.37
LM	0.9079	0.11	1.11e3	8.74e2	8.57	1.00e5	0.59
SCG	0.9150	0.79	1.67e3	1.71e2	10.33	1.00e5	0.44
SGD	0.3442	0.21	2.24e4	1.12e4	6.88	1.00e5	0.68

(e) Lorenz data set.

Name	TOPSIS	Err	AuTE	Te5%	AuSE	Se5%	Eff
GD	0.9676	0.74	4.82e2	6.17e1	2.98	1.00e2	0.36
GDX	0.6022	2.66	2.45e2	2.04e1	13.63	1.00e4	0.26
LM	0.9380	0.00	3.26e3	5.19e2	0.00	1.00e5	0.54
SCG	0.9939	0.01	5.61e2	1.38e2	0.05	1.00e4	0.43
SGD	0.3828	0.01	6.54e3	9.96e3	0.69	1.00e6	0.67

Table 3. Summary of the primary TOPSIS rankings

Name	Connect-4		Covertype		KDDCup99		Friedman		Lorenz	
	Value	Rank	Value	Rank	Value	Rank	Value	Rank	Value	Rank
GD	0.9057	2	0.8765	1	0.8341	1	0.6424	4	0.9676	2
GDX	0.7189	3	0.8674	2	0.8130	2	0.7805	3	0.6022	4
LM	0.2110	5	0.2431	5	0.3923	5	0.9079	2	0.9380	3
SCG	0.9389	1	0.6308	4	0.6808	3	0.9150	1	0.9939	1
SGD	0.7099	4	0.6426	3	0.4603	4	0.3442	5	0.3828	5

Table 4. Secondary TOPSIS ranking

Name	Rank	TOPSIS	Connect-4	Covertype	KDDCup99	Friedman	Lorenz
GD	1	0.9543	0.9057	0.8765	0.8341	0.6424	0.9676
GDX	3	0.8562	0.7189	0.8674	0.8130	0.7805	0.6022
LM	5	0.3147	0.2110	0.2431	0.3923	0.9079	0.9380
SCG	2	0.9354	0.9389	0.6308	0.6808	0.9150	0.9939
SGD	4	0.3218	0.7099	0.6426	0.4603	0.3442	0.3828

Table 4 shows the results of the secondary ranking. Note that this method not only provides a ranking but it give information about how close are algorithms one each other. As can be seen, GD is ranked first but TOPSIS also indicates that it is *closely* followed by SCG. These two algorithms show a good tradeoff between accuracy and training time. On the other hand, SGD and LM are ranked fourth and fifth, respectively. Despite usually obtaining the best accuracy in classification and regression tasks, their long training time has a negative impact on their performance. Halfway, GDX is ranked third. It usually obtains a worse performance than SGD and LM but in a much shorter lapse of time.

Finally, we established in TOPSIS the set of weights equally, i.e. the importance of every criterion is considered to be the same. Note that this procedure can be easily adapted to other sort of problems in which one or several criteria may be more relevant than others. This is also true in the second step of the methodology in which the rankings obtained on each data set are merged in a single ranking. In this case, for example, we may be interested in promote classification problems rather than regression problems.

7 Conclusions

Most published researches concerning learning algorithms simply assess their performance in terms of accuracy. In this paper, the scalability of five of the most popular training algorithms for ANNs has been evaluated: GD, GDX, LM, SGD and SCG. Since there are no standard measures of scalability, those defined in the PASCAL Large Scale Learning Challenge were used. These measures assess the scalability of algorithms in terms of error, computational effort, allocated memory and training time.

The evaluation of the algorithms in terms of multiple criteria led us to apply a MCDM method. In particular, TOPSIS was used in this research. Moreover, we proposed a two-step approach to combine divergent rankings coming from the evaluation of the training algorithms on different data sets. Moreover, the use of a MCDM method allows to measure the distance among algorithms whilst easily use the weights to enhance some criteria against the others.

For future work, we plan to extend this research to different MCDM methods. In this case, we would have to face the combination of different rankings obtained by different methods on different data sets.

References

1. Sonnenburg, S., Franc, V., Yom-Tov, E., Sebag, M.: PASCAL Large Scale Learning Challenge. Journal of Machine Learning Research (2009)
2. Strigl, D., Kofler, K., Podlipnig, S.: Performance and scalability of gpu-based convolutional neural networks. In: 18th Parallel, Distributed and Network-Based Processing (PDP), pp. 317–324. IEEE (2010)
3. Casey, K., Garrett, A., Gay, J., Montgomery, L., Dozier, G.: An evolutionary approach for achieving scalability with general regression neural networks. Natural Computing 8(1), 133–148 (2009)
4. Peteiro-Barral, D., Bolón-Canedo, V., Alonso-Betanzos, A., Guijarro-Berdiñas, B., Sánchez-Maroño, N.: Toward the scalability of neural networks through feature selection. Expert Systems with Applications 40(8), 2807–2816 (2013)
5. Bishop, C.M.: Neural networks for pattern recognition (1995)
6. Plaut, D.C., Nowlan, S.J., Hinton, G.E.: Experiments on learning by back propagation (1986)
7. Møller, M.F.: A scaled conjugate gradient algorithm for fast supervised learning. Neural Networks 6(4), 525–533 (1993)
8. Levenberg, K.: A method for the solution of certain non-linear problems in least squares. Quarterly Journal of Applied Mathmatics 2(2), 164–168 (1944)
9. Marquardt, D.W.: An algorithm for least-squares estimation of nonlinear parameters. Society for Industrial & Applied Mathematics 11(2), 431–441 (1963)
10. Weiss, S.M., Kulikowski, C.A.: Computer systems that learn: classification and prediction methods from statistics, neural nets, machine learning, and expert systems. Morgan Kaufmann, San Francisco (1991)
11. Zeleny, M.: Multiple criteria decision making, vol. 25. McGraw-Hill, NY (1982)
12. Gang, K., Lu, Y., Peng, Y., Yong, S.: Evaluation of classification algorithms using mcdm and rank correlation. International Journal of Information Technology & Decision Making 11(01), 197–225 (2012)
13. Hwang, C.L., Yoon, K.: Multiple attribute decision making: methods and applications: a state-of-the-art survey, vol. 13. Springer, New York (1981)
14. Opricovic, S., Tzeng, G.H.: Compromise solution by MCDM methods: A comparative analysis of VIKOR and TOPSIS. European Journal of Operational Research 156(2), 445–455 (2004)
15. Olson, D.L.: Comparison of weights in TOPSIS models. Mathematical and Computer Modelling 40(7-8), 721–727 (2004)
16. Frank, A., Asuncion, A.: UCI machine learning repository (2010)
17. Hecht-Nielsen, R.: Neurocomputing. Addison-Wesley (1990)

Testing the Generalization of Feedforward Neural Networks with Median Neuron Input Function

Andrzej Rusiecki

Wroclaw University of Technology, Wroclaw, Poland
andrzej.rusiecki@pwr.wroc.pl

Abstract. In this paper, we present a preliminary experimental study of the generalization abilities of feedforward neural networks with median neuron input function (MIF). In these networks, proposed in our previous work, the signals fed to a neuron are not summed but a median of input signals is calculated. The MIF networks were designed to be fault tolerant but we expect them to have also improved generalization ability. Results of first experimental simulations are presented and described in this article. Potentially improved performance of the MIF networks is demonstrated.

1 Introduction

Artificial neural networks have been applied in many different fields, including pattern recognition, function approximation, signal or image processing, etc., because their ability to model complex input-output relationships. However, it is widely known that their generalization abilities strongly depend on many factors, such as network size and architecture, number of training samples, training algorithm and its parameters. It is also commonly believed that nets with too much capacity (having too many parameters and larger VC-dimension) overfit the training data [3]. In fact, this dependence is not so simple [2,5], and there exist many algorithms improving generalization abilities of neural networks [17]. Standard and commonly used techniques are Bayessian regularization [9,11] and early stopping based on cross-validation [1,12]. We do not intend to present here a novel approach outperforming existing solution. The main goal of this article is to investigate generalization ability, considered as additional advantage of using new feedforward networks with median input functions.

In our previous work, we proposed novel feedforward neural network architecture with median neuron input function (MIF) [16]. In such networks the summation of input signals is replaced with median, which could possibly make the network more tolerant to node faults. Experimental studies revealed that MIF networks are indeed fault tolerant. Though designed to tolerate links (weights) or nodes (neurons) failures, the MIF networks can be expected to present more advantageous features. In this article, we want to investigate their generalization ability, assuming that replacing summation with the median may potentially improved network performance.

L. Rutkowski et al. (Eds.): ICAISC 2013, Part I, LNAI 7894, pp. 174–182, 2013.

2   Median Neuron Input Function

In the classic neuron model, weighted inputs are fed to the summing junction. Then the weighted sum, is transmitted to the transfer function block, which produces the neuron output. It is clear then, that every change of individual input elements can have an obvious impact on the effect of neuron computation. However, for a neuron where the summation is replaced with more robust operation, this is not necessarily true. In other words: the neuron output, if generated with median neuron input, can be less sensitive to the changes in the inputs, than in the case of simple sum.

The MIF neuron output is defined as [16]:

$$y_{out} = f(\text{med}\{w_i x_i\}_{i=1}^{N}),\tag{1}$$

where $f(\cdot)$ denotes neuron transfer function (e.g sigmoid or linear), x_j are neuron inputs, w_i is the ith input weight and N denotes input size. The main disadvantage of the MIF neuron is that calculating its output is computationally more expensive (median vs. sum). Another problem may appear when such networks are to be trained with gradient-based learning algorithms. The median input function is not differentiable in all its domain, so the gradient cannot be easily estimated. This is why, we proposed to use an approximation based on the gradient for a simple sum. As our previous efforts demonstrated, such approach seems to be very effective not only for median neuron input functions, but also for error performance criterions based on the median of residuals.

The idea is then as follows: whenever a gradient of median function is needed, we assume that the derivative depends on each neuron input. It results in a training step, where the entire vector of input weights is modified, including those directly influencing the median value. Additional advantage (save its computational simplicity) is that in practice, the training progress converges faster, avoiding, to certain degree, flat regions of the gradient.

Let us consider, for simplicity, a simple feedforward neural network with one hidden layer. We assume that a training set consists of n pairs: $\{(\boldsymbol{x}_1, \boldsymbol{t}_1), (\boldsymbol{x}_2, \boldsymbol{t}_2), \ldots, (\boldsymbol{x}_n, \boldsymbol{t}_n)\}$, where $\boldsymbol{x}_i \in R^N$ and $\boldsymbol{t}_i \in R^M$. For the given input vector $\boldsymbol{x}_i = (x_{i1}, x_{i2}, \ldots, x_{iN})^T$, the output of the jth neuron of the hidden layer may be written as:

$$z_{ij} = f_1(\text{med}\{w_{jk} x_{ik} - b_j\}_{k=1}^{N}) = f_1(u_{ij}), \quad \text{for } j = 1, 2, \ldots, L,\tag{2}$$

where $f_1(\cdot)$ is the activation function of the hidden layer, w_{jk} is the weight between the kth net input and jth neuron, and b_j is the bias of the jth neuron (hidden layer consists of L neurons). Network output vector $\boldsymbol{y}_i = (y_{i1}, y_{i2}, \ldots, y_{iM})^T$ is then given as:

$$y_{iv} = f_2(\text{med}\{w_{vj}^{(2)} z_{ij} - b_v^{(2)}\}_{j=1}^{L}) = f_2(u_{iv}), \quad \text{for } v = 1, 2, \ldots, M.\tag{3}$$

Here $w_{vj}^{(2)}$ is the weight between the vth neuron of the output layer and the jth neuron of the hidden layer, $b_v^{(2)}$ is the bias of the vth neuron of the output layer, and $f_2(\cdot)$ denotes the activation function. We want to minimize simple MSE (mean squared error) criterion::

$$E_{MSE} = \frac{1}{n}\sum_{i=1}^{n}(r)_i^2,\qquad(4)$$

where r_i^2 are squared residuals:

$$r_i^2 = \sum_{v=1}^{M}(y_{iv} - t_{iv})^2.\qquad(5)$$

We assume, to illustrate the basis of training the MIF network, that all the network weights are updated according to the gradient-descent learning algorithm. Such assumption can be made without loss of generality, because this approach may be easily extended to any other gradient-based learning method, using backpropagation strategy to calculate the gradient of the error, regarding the network's weights. For the considered network with one hidden layer, the weights are updated iteratively, taking steps proportional to the negative of the gradient, written as follows:

$$\Delta w_{jk} = -\alpha\frac{\partial E_{MSE}}{\partial w_{jk}} = -\alpha\frac{\partial E_{MSE}}{\partial r_i}\frac{\partial r_i}{\partial w_{jk}},\qquad(6)$$

$$\Delta w_{vj}^{(2)} = -\alpha\frac{\partial E_{MSE}}{\partial w_{vj}^{(2)}} = -\alpha\frac{\partial E_{MSE}}{\partial r_i}\frac{\partial r_i}{\partial w_{vj}^{(2)}},\qquad(7)$$

where the term α denotes a learning coefficient. When calculating the gradients one should remember that u_{ij} and u_{iv} consists also of median operation. For the case of gradient calculation, the median is replaced with simple sum, so the derivatives of the residua are assumed to be given as:

$$\frac{\partial r_i}{\partial w_{jk}} = f_2'(u_{iv})w_{vj}^{(2)}f_1'(u_{ij})x_{ik},\qquad(8)$$

and

$$\frac{\partial r_i}{\partial w_{vj}^{(2)}} = f_2'(u_{iv})z_{ij},\qquad(9)$$

where $f_1'(\cdot)$ and $f_2'(\cdot)$ denote the derivatives of the activation functions in hidden and output layer, respectively. Such simplification, as it was experimentally demonstrated, makes the training process effective [16].

Why is the MIF network more tolerant to node faults of stuck-at-0 type than the network with summation? The explanation of this phenomenon seems to be rather simple. We assume, that during the training process, the information is distributed more uniformly between the network weights. This is why one may expect that such network should be potentially also more robust to overfitting.

3 Experimental Results

To test the resistance to overfitting of the MIF networks (and to compare it to other network types), we decided to examine the structures on three training tasks, namely: function approximation, time series prediction and pattern recognition. Such tasks should not be too complex, in order to allow networks of larger size to overfit training data.

3.1 Testing Methodology

To fully reveal the overfitting phenomenon, we decided to corrupt the data for function approximation and time series prediction with small Gaussian noise of the form $N(0.0, 0.2)$. For the classification problem such addition was unnecessary because of the overlapping classes borders.

For each task, we tested several network architectures with different number of hidden neurons (as described in the Tables). For the function approximation task network performances for two numbers of training patterns were also examined. To test generalization abilities of the MIF networks, we decided to compare five different approaches to network training. The first one was an ordinary feedforward network without validation (FFN), the second one was the MIF network (also without validation). The networks with early stopping, based on validation incorporated into the training process, were also examined as traditional validation network (VFFN), and MIF network with validation (VMIF). For the network with validation, 30% of the training data constituted validating set, on which the network performance was tested during training process.

Another tested method was the robust LMLS (Least Mean Log Squares) algorithm [8,15]. Robust learning methods [14] are considered to be less sensitive to outlying data points and different kinds of noise. These methods do not fit the training patterns as close, as possible, so one may expect that they could be also less sensitive to overfitting in the presence of noise.

All the tested networks were trained with the same resilient backpropagation algorithm [13] (similar results we obtained also for the conjugated gradient learning method [6]). It is worth to notice, that applying the well-known and popular Levenberg-Marquardt algorithm [7] would not be a proper choice, because its fast convergence may cause problems when training with validation [5]. Moreover, it can be used only with squared error criterion, so it cannot be combined with the LMLS method. To make the comparison reliable, all the training parameters were the same for each tested network. Simulation results measured by a mean squared error (MSE), calculated on testing data sets, were averaged over 20 runs and gathered in Tables 1–4 and presented in the Figures 1–4.

3.2 Function Approximation

The first testing task was to approximate one-dimensional sine function given as:

$$y = \sin(\pi x). \tag{10}$$

Table 1. The averaged MSE for the networks trained to approximate sine function (step size 0.05)

Hidden neurons	5		10		15		20		25	
Algorithm	Mean	S.D.	Mean	S.D.	Mean	S.D.	Mean	S.D.	Mean	S.D.
FFN	0.0240	0.0114	0.0435	0.0171	0.1007	0.0634	0.3002	0.1843	0.3527	0.3406
MIF	0.0250	0.0212	0.0388	0.0102	0.0825	0.0412	0.0750	0.0208	0.1087	0.0734
VFFN	0.0977	0.1185	0.1301	0.1530	0.2715	0.1668	0.4931	0.2112	0.3625	0.1964
VMIF	0.1512	0.1554	0.0286	0.0292	0.0866	0.1525	0.0592	0.0369	0.0998	0.0609
LMLS	0.0338	0.0245	0.0464	0.0179	0.0904	0.0448	0.2599	0.1726	0.2990	0.1685

Table 2. The averaged MSE for the networks trained to approximate sine function (step size 0.01)

Hidden neurons	5		10		15		20		25	
Algorithm	Mean	S.D.	Mean	S.D.	Mean	S.D.	Mean	S.D.	Mean	S.D.
FFN	0.0032	0.0014	0.0069	0.0019	0.0097	0.0049	0.0160	0.0061	0.0204	0.0154
MIF	0.0063	0.0113	0.0046	0.0013	0.0060	0.0022	0.0110	0.0033	0.0112	0.0063
VFFN	0.0181	0.0160	0.0166	0.0055	0.0242	0.0164	0.0362	0.0201	0.0596	0.0681
VMIF	0.0159	0.0137	0.0058	0.0019	0.0091	0.0056	0.0135	0.0068	0.0118	0.0056
LMLS	0.0070	0.0113	0.0110	0.0138	0.0094	0.0031	0.0161	0.0071	0.0187	0.0120

To prepare the data, the independent variable was sampled in the range $[-1, 1]$ with a step 0.05 or 0.01 and dependent variable was calculated based on equation (10).

Looking at the Tables 1 (case 1, less training patterns) and 2 (case 2, more training patterns), one may notice very similar results. First of all, the regular network with validation presents the worst performance in both cases. The MIF network with validation acts well when the network size is large but is much less efficient for the smallest (minimal) network. Regular networks without validation and network trained with the LMLS algorithm perform relatively well for smaller network sizes but their performance dramatically drops for larger networks, especially in the case when the number of training examples is smaller. What is interesting, the performance of the MIF network seems to be, on average, the best. Its performance for the minimal size is slightly worse than for the regular network (but much better than for the MIF with validation) and it outperforms all the other approaches (save the MIF with validation) for larger sizes.

3.3   Time Series Prediction

As a time series prediction task, we decided to use well-known chaotic Mackey-Glass flow series [10,17], defined by differential equation:

$$\frac{dx}{dt} = 0.2\frac{x_\tau}{1 + x_\tau^{10}} - 0.1x, \tag{11}$$

where x_τ is the value of variable x at time $t - \tau$. Setting $x(0) = 1.2$ and $\tau = 17$ we obtained non-periodic and non-convergent time series. We used 4 previous observations to predict the next series value.

The averaged results for the prediction task were gather in the Table 3. Similarly to the approximation task, the classic approach with validation presents the worst performance. Once again, the MIF network with validation provides poor

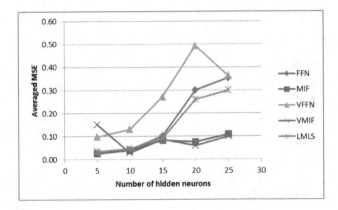

Fig. 1. The averaged MSE for the networks trained to approximate sine function (step size 0.05)

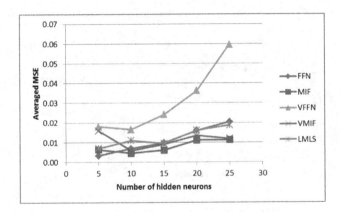

Fig. 2. The averaged MSE for the networks trained to approximate sine function (step size 0.01)

performance for smaller and relatively good performance for larger networks. Differences between regular network without validation and network trained with the LMLS algorithm are almost imperceptible. The best performance is obtained, in almost each case, for the MIF network (outperformed only for the largest size by the MIF with validation).

Table 3. The averaged MSE for the networks trained on time series prediction

Hidden neurons	2		5		10		20	
Algorithm	Mean	S.D.	Mean	S.D.	Mean	S.D.	Mean	S.D.
FFN	0.0532	0.0392	0.0732	0.0344	0.0901	0.0201	0.1147	0.0383
MIF	0.0442	0.0336	0.0655	0.0326	0.0700	0.0284	0.1002	0.0524
VFFN	0.3942	0.4409	0.1071	0.0815	0.2383	0.1264	0.3500	0.2515
VMIF	0.1686	0.1302	0.1011	0.0694	0.0864	0.0491	0.0975	0.0312
LMLS	0.0517	0.0349	0.0741	0.0298	0.0868	0.0191	0.1194	0.0470

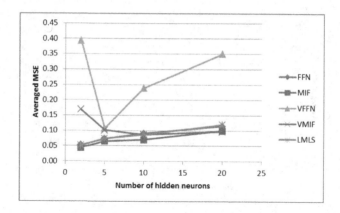

Fig. 3. The averaged MSE for the networks trained on time series prediction

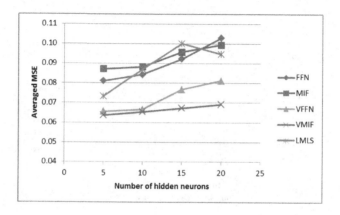

Fig. 4. The averaged MSE for the networks trained trained on the classification problem

3.4   Classification Problem

The task was defined as a classification problem with two classes, where data points were generated from two-dimensional normal distributions with identical standard deviations. The means of these distributions were in the distance of 2 standard deviations, so the classes were in practice, partially overlapping. We do not present here classification rates, because testing data were also randomly generated. The performance of training approaches is based again on the averaged MSE (Table 4).

As it was expected, the situation for the classification is different than in the previous cases. Now, the validation-based early stopping could reveal its advantages [17]. Three approaches without validation present much worse performance than those with validation included in the training process. However, it is worth to notice, that the MIF networks with validation outperforms classic networks with validation for each network size.

Table 4. The averaged MSE for the networks trained on the classification problem

Hidden neurons	5		10		15		20	
Algorithm	Mean	S.D.	Mean	S.D.	Mean	S.D.	Mean	S.D.
FFN	0.0810	0.0071	0.0844	0.0078	0.0923	0.0105	0.1029	0.0166
MIF	0.0872	0.0309	0.0883	0.0188	0.0958	0.0238	0.0993	0.0221
VFFN	0.0656	0.0019	0.0665	0.0034	0.0767	0.0105	0.0812	0.0123
VMIF	0.0637	0.0020	0.0654	0.0031	0.0673	0.0035	0.0692	0.0038
LMLS	0.0733	0.0039	0.0870	0.0151	0.1000	0.0304	0.0947	0.0165

4   Summary and Conclusion

This paper presented a preliminary study of the generalization abilities of feedforward network with median neuron input functions. As our experiments demonstrated, the MIF networks can have, in certain conditions, better performance than traditional approaches. Moreover, designed to be tolerant to neuron faults, they can be also considered as a simple tool to increase network generalization ability, especially when the network size is larger than the minimal size sufficient for a given problem. Our future efforts should be focused on more extensive experimental study on the MIF network generalization, as well as theoretical investigation, aiming at explaining the phenomenon of their improved performance.

References

1. Amari, S., Murata, N., Muller, K.-R., Finke, M., Yang, H.H.: Asymptotic statistical theory of overtraining and cross-validation. IEEE Transactions on Neural Networks 8(5), 985–996 (1997)
2. Bartlett, P.: For valid generalization the size of the weights is more important than the size of the network. In: Advances in Neural Information Processing Systems, vol. 9, p. 134. The MIT Press (1997)
3. Baum, E.B., Haussler, D.: What size net gives valid generalization? Neural Computation 1, 151–160 (1989)
4. Bishop, C.M.: Neural Networks for Pattern Recognition. Oxford University Press (1995)
5. Caruana, R., Lawrence, S., Lee Giles, C.: Overfitting in Neural Nets: Backpropagation, Conjugate Gradient, and Early Stopping. In: Proc. Neural Information Processing Systems Conference, pp. 402–408 (2000)
6. Hagan, M.T., Demuth, H.B., Beale, M.H.: Neural Network Design. PWS Publishing, Boston (1996)
7. Hagan, M.T., Menhaj, M.B.: Training Feedforward Networks with the Marquardt Algorithm. IEEE Trans. on Neural Networks 5(6), 989–993 (1994)
8. Liano, K.: Robust error measure for supervised neural network learning with outliers. IEEE Transactions on Neural Networks 7, 246–250 (1996)
9. MacKay, D.: A Practical Bayesian Framework for Backprop Networks. Neural Computation 4(3), 448–472 (1992)
10. Mackey, M.C., Glass, L.: Oscillations and chaos in physiological control systems. Science 197, 287–289 (1977)

11. Neal, R.M.: Bayesian Learning for Neural Networks. Springer, New York (1996)
12. Prechelt, L.: Early stopping - But when? In: Orr, G.B., Müller, K.-R. (eds.) Neural Networks: Tricks of the Trade. LNCS, vol. 1524, pp. 55–69. Springer, Heidelberg (1998)
13. Riedmiller, M., Braun, H.: A direct adaptive method for faster backpropagation learning: The RPROP algorithm. In: Proceedings of the IEEE International Conference on Neural Networks (ICNN), San Francisco, pp. 586–591 (1993)
14. Rusiecki, A.: Robust MCD-based backpropagation learning algorithm. In: Rutkowski, L., Tadeusiewicz, R., Zadeh, L.A., Zurada, J.M. (eds.) ICAISC 2008. LNCS (LNAI), vol. 5097, pp. 154–163. Springer, Heidelberg (2008)
15. Rusiecki, A.: Fast Robust Learning Algorithm Dedicated to LMLS Criterion. In: Rutkowski, L., Scherer, R., Tadeusiewicz, R., Zadeh, L.A., Zurada, J.M. (eds.) ICAISC 2010, Part II. LNCS (LNAI), vol. 6114, pp. 96–103. Springer, Heidelberg (2010)
16. Rusiecki, A.L.: Fault tolerant feedforward neural network with median neuron input function. Electronics Letters 41(10), 603–605 (2005)
17. Wang, W., Van Gelder, P.H.A.J.M., Vrijling, J.K.: Some issues about the generalization of neural networks for time series prediction. In: Duch, W., Kacprzyk, J., Oja, E., Zadrożny, S. (eds.) ICANN 2005, Part II. LNCS, vol. 3697, pp. 559–564. Springer, Heidelberg (2005)

Biological Plausibility in an Artificial Neural Network Applied to Real Predictive Tasks

Alberione Braz da Silva and João Luís Garcia Rosa

Laboratório de Computação Bio-inspirada (BioCom), Departamento de Ciências da Computação, Instituto de Ciências Matemáticas e de Computação – ICMC, Universidade de São Paulo - Campus de São Carlos, Caixa Postal 668 13560-970 – São Carlos-SP, Brazil
{abraz,joaoluis}@icmc.usp.br

Abstract. Biologically plausible artificial neural networks represent a promising novel approach in bio-inspired computational systems. In these systems, the models are based on existing knowledge of neurophysiological processing principles. Research in this field has increased in the last few years and has generated new viewpoints, propositions and models that are closer to the known features of the human brain. Some researchers have recently focused their studies on this innovative field in order to establish a consensus on what an artificial neural network is in the domain of biological realism. Domain specific synthetic data sets are generally used in the evaluation of those artificial neural networks because they simulate predictive tasks and potential problems caused by human intervention. This paper deals with the analysis of influence of the anomalies generated by human intervention in credit approval process. Such anomalies modify real classification, performance and accuracy. In this analysis, we evaluated a real data set that represents human actions over personal credit approval and fraud identification by using a biologically more plausible artificial neural network proposal.

Keywords: spike response model, point neuron activation function, spiking neuron model, spike-timing-dependent plasticity.

1 Introduction

Research in biologically plausible artificial neural networks concerns itself with the theoretical analysis and computational modeling of characteristics of the cerebral cortex. It considers recent knowledge about the brain and needs a comprehension with clarity of the brain functionalities. The importance of this type of research is an attempt to create artificial models that are closer to the human brain so as to better understand the workings of natural biological neural networks.

The biological characteristics implementation in artificial neural network models sometime needs assumptions, simplifications and constraints to ensure good computational performance and better problem resolution. Thereby, several artificial neural network models implementations do not consider some of the natural

L. Rutkowski et al. (Eds.): ICAISC 2013, Part I, LNAI 7894, pp. 183–192, 2013.

neural network aspects, but instead specifically meet computational criteria and lead to reduce the natural biological inspiration of artificial models. Furthermore, in bio-inspired systems analyses are applied to datasets that represent non-real human decision-making tasks or simulated tasks. In other words, they are synthetic or built datasets that do not represent real situation of a human intervention, because they are controlled situations.

Recently, Silva and Rosa [18] proposed unifying the views of Maass [10], O'Reilly [13], Rosa [15] and Silva and Rosa [17] on biological plausibility for artificial neural networks, which were based on the principles of Ramón y Cajal and Hebb (see table 1). In addition, consideration was taken of Knudsen and O'Reilly's position on the lack of biological realism in supervised learning [2] (see table 1). In order to consolidate their proposition, Silva and Rosa [18] developed a network model that covers all principles previously discussed therefore could be considered more biologically plausible.

This paper aims to present an evaluation of the computational performance of the more biologically realistic artificial neural model by using a database that represents real predictive tasks and comparing the behavior of the real task with that generated by the model. We also present an analysis of computational influences on training and pattern recognition of the more realistic biological mechanisms implemented in the model. Furthermore, we show how assumptions, constraints and simplifications may lead to weak biological representation.

2   The Alleged Biologically Plausible Artificial Neural Network Model

In this evaluation, we used *Topological Transition Spiking Logistic and Response Model* (TTSLRM) that it based on model proposed by Silva and Rosa [18] in the unification of the views of Maass [10], O'Reilly [13], Rosa [15] and Silva and Rosa [17] on biological plausibility. Considered biologically more plausible, the model is characterized by: being a finite directed graph where the vertices represent the neurons and the edges represent the synapses [1]; having a response function based on *Spiking Response Neuron Model* [10]; employing the supervised learning algorithms GeneRec (*Generic Recirculation*) and unsupervised learning STDP (*Spike-Timing-Dependent Plasticity*) [4] [16] [19] proposed by O'Reilly [14] and Gerstner and Kistler [4], respectively; and having a control function that represents the elements that act on the binding affinities between transmitters and receptors of pre- and postsynaptic neurons [15] (see table 2).

The main modification in Silva and Rosa [18] model was the replacement of the *point neuron activation function* [14] in supervised learning algorithm by a new logistic sigmoid function variation. This new variation replaced the membrane potential parameter (V_m) in point neuron activation function (see equation 1) by Spiking Response Neuron Model response function or kernel potential function [10] (see equation 3). This modification was possible due to subtraction of the activation states in plus and minus phase, made by the generalized

Table 1. Main principles and hypothesis that support biological plausibility in artificial neural networks

Principles and Hypothesis	Author	Description
Dynamic Polarization	Ramón y Cajal	"Electric signals inside a nervous cell flow only in a direction: from neuron reception (often the dendrites and cell body) to the axon trigger zone" [8]
Connectional Specificity	Ramón y Cajal	"Nerve cells do not communicate indiscriminately with one another or form random networks" [7]
Brain plasticity	Donald O. Hebb	"When an axon of cell A is near enough to excite a cell B and repeatedly or persistently takes part in firing it, some growth process or metabolic change takes place in one or both cells such that A's efficiency, as one of the cells firing B, is increased." [5]
Supervised Learning	Eric I. Knudsen	"One way that experience shapes constituent networks of the brain is through supervised learning" [9]
Supervised Learning	Randall C. O'Reilly	Bi-directional activation propagation can operate essentially as an Error-driven Learning, using some of signals required for teaching that are available [13]

Table 2. Control function variables definition by Rosa [15]

Elements	Symbol	Description
gene expression	γ_v	the new controller of gene expression (at target cell)
binding affinity degree	φ_v	the new binding affinity degree of receptor (at target cell)
amount of substrate	ψ_u	the increasing of the amount of substrate (at origin cell)
type of post-synaptic potential	$\rho_{u,v}$	the type of post-synaptic potential (excitatory or inhibitory) in relation to the type of transmitter and receptor, by means of direct action

Legend: Subscripts u and v represent pre and post-synaptic neuron, respectively.

recirculation algorithm (GeneRec), which implicitly calculates the derivative of the activation function [14]. A similar strategy has been used in Backpropagation algorithm, but the derivative of the activation function is calculated in explicit form where its use is necessary, differently from GeneRec. In this way, it is possible to use any arbitrary activation function without having to use its derivative [14]. Based on previous proposal and in the equations (1) or its simplified form (2) and (3)), we have:

$$y_j(t) = \frac{\gamma[V_m(t) - \Theta]}{\gamma[V_m(t) - \Theta] + 1} \tag{1}$$

$$y_j(t) = \frac{1}{\left(1 + \frac{1}{\gamma[V_m(t) - \Theta]}\right)} \tag{2}$$

where V_m represents membrane potential; γ represents gain or learning rate; and Θ represents activation threshold.

$$\xi_{u,v}(t) = \frac{(e^{(-\frac{t-\delta}{\tau_m})} - e^{(-\frac{t-\delta}{\tau_s})})}{1 - (\frac{\tau_s}{\tau_m})} \tag{3}$$

In equation 3, called Spiking Response Model response function or kernel potential function [10], u and v represent pre and post-synaptic neuron, respectively; τ_s represents the synapse time constant; τ_m represents the membrane time constant; t represents the current time; δ represents the time delay constant in axonal transmission; and Θ represents activation threshold.

According to O'Reilly [14], the rate code output (eq. 1) simulates the average output of a spiking neurons population. Therefore, we can do $V_m(t) \approx \xi_{u,v}(t)$ and replace term $V_m(t)$ in equation (2) by $\xi_{u,v}(t)$ equation.

$$y_j(t) = \frac{1}{(1 + \dfrac{1}{\gamma[\frac{(e^{(-\frac{t-\delta}{\tau_m})} - e^{(-\frac{t-\delta}{\tau_s})})}{1 - (\frac{\tau_s}{\tau_m})} - \Theta]})} \tag{4}$$

$$y_j(t) = \frac{\frac{\gamma}{(1-(\frac{\tau_s}{\tau_m}))}[e^{(-\frac{t-\delta}{\tau_m})} - e^{(-\frac{t-\delta}{\tau_s})} - (1 - (\frac{\tau_s}{\tau_m}))\Theta]}{\frac{\gamma}{(1-(\frac{\tau_s}{\tau_m}))}[e^{(-\frac{t-\delta}{\tau_m})} - e^{(-\frac{t-\delta}{\tau_s})} - (1 - (\frac{\tau_s}{\tau_m}))\Theta] + 1} \tag{5}$$

Hence it implies that eq. (1) is specific case of eq. (5) when we replace $\tau_s = 0$ that leads $(-\frac{t-\delta}{\tau_s}) \to -\infty$ and $e^{(-\frac{t-\delta}{\tau_s})} \to 0$. According to these considerations we can then write

$$y_j(t) = \frac{\frac{\gamma}{(1-(0))}[e^{(-\frac{t-\delta}{\tau_m})} - 0 - (1 - (0))\Theta]}{\frac{\gamma}{(1-(0))}[e^{(-\frac{t-\delta}{\tau_m})} - 0 - (1 - (0))\Theta] + 1} \tag{6}$$

$$y_j(t) = \frac{\gamma[e^{(-\frac{t-\delta}{\tau_m})} - \Theta]}{\gamma[e^{(-\frac{t-\delta}{\tau_m})} - \Theta] + 1} \tag{7}$$

Comparing equations (1) and (7), we have that both equations are similar, $V_m(t) \approx e^{(-\frac{t-\delta}{\tau_m})}$ – in this specific case – and it does not consider synapse time term ($\tau_s = 0$) in eq. (1) or eq. (2). Therefore, this simplification, as equation (2) shows, may be considered less biologically plausible since synapse time does exist in natural processes [8]. To sum up, we showed mathematically that certain model simplification may reduce biological plausibility.

3   Evaluation

The evaluation of real predictive tasks was conducted using two real bases for personal credit approval. These bases represent real predictive tasks as they contain results of human intervention in some attributes and classes. These human interventions may alter the quality of the base or generate noise and/or outliers, but the outliers may also represent fraudulent behavior on the part of the applicant or commercial establishment in question.

The personal credit base (PC) is composed of 22 attributes and 5 classes[1] (see table 3). Among the attributes there is one called "in review" representing whether there is human action (personal credit specialists) involved in approving or refusing the credit application, and if there is, the reason for this intervention. This attribute was not used in training and was removed from patterns presented in recognition as it may have led to misleading results. This data set also has a class called "in review", but its aim is to represent the need for specialist intervention in the final decision – approved or refused or bureau –, or in other words, a human action after classification by the credit approval procedural system.

The Fraud bases – *Fraud (FD)* and *Fraud Outliers (FO)* –, similar to the PC base, are composed of 22 attributes, but 6 classes[2] (see table 3). The additional class, called "fraud", represents effective fraud behavior through a priori knowledge.

The bases that reflect real predictive tasks have a high degree of complexity due to different mental behavior among those people involved (applicant, attendant, specialist or groups of specialists in the business). Besides this, there are visual indicators of the applicant's behavior or generalizations based on previous behavioral situations (feeling) that lead the specialists to alter their more likely responses and that are not explicit in the database. In addition, there is a behavior created to take advantage of established rules or avoid negative behavioral situations.

Table 3. Dataset Description That Represents the Real Predictive Tasks

Dataset	Patterns	Input Attributes	Patterns by Classes				
PC			approved	refused	analysis	bureau	
	2017	22 + 4 Classes	138	731	1106	42	
FD			approved	refused	analysis	bureau	fraud
	2017	22 + 5 Classes	138	692	980	42	165
FO			approved	refused	analysis	bureau	fraud
	2008	22 + 5 Classes	133	691	980	41	163

Legend: *PC* = Personal Credit database focusing in Credit Approval; *FD* = Personal Credit database focusing in Fraud Objects Classification; e *FO* = Personal Credit database focusing in Fraud Outliers Classification.

---

[1] Personal Credit (PC) database classes descriptions: *approved* – automatic approval or by an expert action; *refused* – automatic refusal or by an expert action; *bureau* – refusal by an outside contractor expert action; and *inreview* – redirect to expert group for analysis.

[2] Fraud (FD) and Fraud Outliers (FO) database classes descriptions: *approved* – automatic approval without fraud behavior or by an expert action; *refused* – automatic refusal or by an expert action; *bureau* – refusal by an outside contractor expert action; *inreview* – redirect to expert group for analysis; and *fraud* – refusal by fraud behavior.

In the pre-evaluation of the *Topological Transition Spiking Logistic and Response Model* (TTSLRM) use was made of the binary matrix dataset *Optical Recognition of Handwritten Digits* (see table 4) of the *University of California - Irvine* (UCI) [11] in order to establish a reference for computational performance indicators for the TTSLRM network. The UCI base was chosen for its complexity and because there was no need for previous knowledge of the attributes or rule definitions. This could have generated a specific behavior or inconsistent and incomprehensible results in the analysis of the base to establish this reference.

Table 4. Dataset Description used in the initial validation

Dataset	Patterns	Input Attributes	Patterns by Classes
HD			000 001 002 003 004 005 006 007 008 009
	1934	32x32	189 198 195 199 186 187 195 201 180 204

Legend: *HD* = Optical Recognition of Handwritten Digits of UCI dataset [11].
Observation: UCI's dataset was chosen because it is complex and does not require a priori knowledge of the attributes or rules definition.

In both evaluations we used the strategy of ten-fold cross validation associated with the Stratified Folds technique in order to assure proportionality of the patterns in each pair of files training-recognition generated from the original dataset [3] [6]. In this way we eliminated distortions caused by a higher incidence of a certain type of class in the samples. However, in the *Fraud Outliers* base, the strategy was applying a test dataset with 9 objects (tuples) considered anomalies (outliers or noises). In the evaluation of computational performance results of the model in these bases we used recall, precision, F-measure and accuracy indicators.

Other data used here are the parameters necessary for configuration of the TTSLRM and its two learning algorithms – GeneRec [12,14] and STDP [4]. These parameters are described in table 5.

Once the reference indexes were established for the computational efficiency of the model (see table 6) by means of the UCI base, we went on to evaluate the personal credit base with a focus on the authorization of credit approval supported in the following classes: Approved, Refused, Bureau and Analysis. The result of this analysis showed both high accuracy and performance of the TTSLRM in the classification of objects of this type (see table 6), in spite of the high complexity of bases representing real predictive tasks.

The evaluation of the dataset aimed at the identification of fraudulent behavior showed a slight drop in performance, coverage and accuracy, but also showed a slight increase in precision, maintaining a good computational performance (see table 6). These variations can be explained by the fact that an object that has a fraudulent behavior may be refused by the human action of a specialist even before it is identified as fraud.

Table 5. Parameters employed in learning and recognition steps [17]

Parameter	Symbol	Value or Interval
generec learning rate	η	0.28
STDP learning rate	A	0.011 to 0.99
balancing factor between two learning type	K_{bl}	0.6
error rate	-	3×10^{-4}
weights	w	0.0 to 1.0
membrane time constant	τ_m	40 to 2000 ms
synapse time constant	τ_s	20 to 1000 ms
pulse firing threshold	Θ	0.1 to 0.8 mV
time constant used to calculate the neural refractoriness	τ	2000 to 8000 ms
time delay constant in axonal transmission	δ	20 to 200 ms
gene expression	γ_v	0 to 1
amount of substrate	ψ_u	1 to n normalized
affinity degree of receptor	φ_v	0 to 1
type of transmitter and receptor	$\rho_{u,v}$	3 or 5

Legend: u = pre-synaptic neuron; v = post-synaptic neuron.

Human actions on a base with real predictive tasks are highly visible when trying to classify outliers generated by the intervention of a specialist (in our case). This behavior may be observed in the results obtained from the analysis of the *Fraud Outliers* base, which was trained with the *Fraud* base with the removal of 9 objects considered outliers (generating *Fraud Outliers* base) – 5 approved, 1 refused, 1 Bureau and 2 frauds – and was applied to recognition the dataset composed of the 9 objects removed from the *Fraud* base. The low accuracy and performance (see table 6) were caused by the 5 approved objects as their approval was due to the human intervention of a specialist with external contractual knowledge outside the criteria for authorization. However, if it is considered that the class attributed by the classifier was the analysis class and the attribute "in review" showed that the approval was through the action of a specialist, the accuracy of the base rises significantly and the performance of the model returns to the level of the results obtained in the *Fraud* base as shown in the results of the base *Fraud Outliers Adjusted* (*FA*) (see in table 6). This shows that the TTSLRM displays high computational performance, even in complex bases that deal with real predictive tasks, often presenting anomalies, noises and outliers.

To sum up, the more biologically plausible artificial neural network model TTSLRM displays excellent computational performance in analyses of synthetic or real datasets that represent real predictive tasks or not, as shown in the table 6. As well as this, it confirms the need to apply models of biologically more plausible artificial neural networks to datasets resulting from real predictive tasks. This is because the influence of biological aspects, ever closer to the characteristics of the cerebral cortex in the learning activities of the models, provides fine tuning in the representation of knowledge, enabling models to achieve high computational performance.

Table 6. Outcomes from the application of the 10-fold cross validation technique show that TTSLRM network display better performance and accuracy in Personal Credit (PC) and Fraud bases (FD) than Handwritten Digits (HD)

dataset	recall	precision	F-measure	accuracy
HD	0,9700±0,0136	0,9674±0,0211	0,9686±0,0131	0,9449±0,0244
PC	0,9819±0,0112	0,9869±0,0078	0,9844±0,0051	0,9692±0,0099
FD	0,9658±0,0250	0,9872±0,0096	0,9761±0,0122	0,9536±0,0230
FO	0,4444	1	0,6154	0,4444
FA	0,8889	1	0,9412	0,8889

Legend: *Data sets*: HD = UCI Optical Recognition of Handwritten Digits; PC = Original Personal Credit database; FD = Fraud in Personal Credit database; FO = Fraud in Personal Credit database for Outliers Analysis; and FA = Fraud in Personal Credit database for Outliers Analysis by classes adjusted in recognition samples. *indexes*: Efficiency = recall; effectiveness = precision; performance = F-measure; and efficacy = accuracy.

4   Concluding Remarks

The computation influence of the biologically plausible elements implemented in the model TTSLRM modified the network's behavior in solving the problem of real predictive tasks. We may cite the behavior generated by more realistic bio-inspired learning, which is a combination of error-based learning and Hebbian learning. This combination greatly influenced the learning process of the artificial neural network because the supervised learning acted by adjusting the weight in such a way as to resolve the task, while the Hebbian learning functioned as an optimizer by increasing the contrast of the representations by means of a positive contribution for the more active units and a negative contribution for the less active units, aligned with Hebb's postulate (see table 1). In this case, the behavior generated by learning resulted in a positive contribution and increased the quality of the computational performance indexes – accuracy and F-measure.

Other biologically plausible elements implemented that influenced the TTSLRM computationally were the variables γ_v, φ_v and ψ_u of the control function (see table 2) because they alter the weights through their internal products. This leads the network to increase computational complexity as the weights had to take on very small or very large values to compensate for the values of the variables in weight adjustment in the network training processes.

The comparison between equations (1) and (7) showed that the simplification was not included a complete representation of spike rate process, i.e., it was not considering both synapse and membrane time terms because of equation (1) assumption.

The high level of complexity of the Personal Credit, Fraud and Fraud Outliers bases, representative of real predictive tasks, enabled a more refined qualitative evaluation of the TTSLRM. Analysis of the Personal Credit base showed high potential in the task of pattern recognition in any type of task, real or synthetic (see fig. 1). Analysis of the Fraud base demonstrated the ability of the model to identify abnormal behavior generated by human intervention with a priori

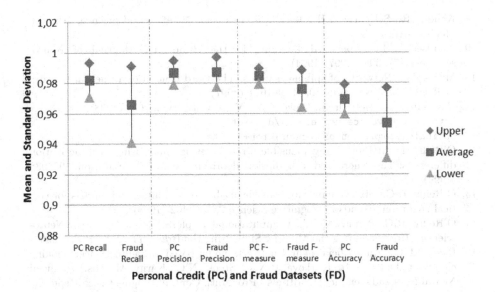

Fig. 1. Ten Fold Cross-Validation results. Detail of the result in Personal Credit and Fraud bases for the recognizing pattern process.

knowledge (see fig. 1). Also, the analysis of the Fraud Outliers base showed the influence of a priori, contractual and external knowledge on electronic authorization criteria.

Finally, the analyses conducted with the TTLSRM in real predictive task bases for personal credit approval, with a focus on authorization and fraud, showed improvement in performance and accuracy of the network, enabling a deeper analysis of human behavior on a base for personal credit approval, leading to a better understanding of business behavior. In addition, the ability of the TTLSRM was shown in analysis of datasets that represent real predictive tasks.

References

1. Barabási, A.L., Albert, R.: Emergence of scaling in random networks. Science 286, 509–512 (1999)
2. Crick, F.: The Recent Excitement about Neural Networks. Nature 337, 129–132 (1989)
3. Faceli, K., Lorena, A.C., Gama, J., Carvalho, A.C.P.L.F.: Artificial Intelligence - A machine learning approach. LTC Press (2011) (in Portuguese)
4. Gerstner, W., Kistler, W.: Spiking Neuron Models: Single Neurons, Populations, Plasticity. Cambridge University Press (2002)
5. Hebb, D.: The Organization of Behavior. Cambridge-Wiley (1949)
6. Japkowicz, N., Shah, M.: Evaluating Learning Algorithms: A Classification Perspective. Cambridge University Press (2011)
7. Kandel, R., Schwartz, J.H., Jessell, T.M.: Essentials of Neural Science and Behavior. Appleton and Lange, Stamford, Connecticut (1995)

8. Kandel, R., Schwartz, J.H., Jessell, T.M.: Principles of Neural Science, 4th edn. McGraw-Hill (2000)
9. Knudsen, E.I.: Supervised Learning in the Brain. The Journal of Neuroscience 14(7), 3985–3997 (1994)
10. Maass, W.: Networks of spiking neurons: The third generation of neural network models. Neural Networks 10, 1659–1671 (1997)
11. Newman, D.J., Hettich, S., Blake, C.L., Merz, C.J.: Irvine, CA (1998), http://archive.ics.uci.edu/ml/datasets/ Optical+Recognition+of+Handwritten+Digits
12. O'Reilly, R.C.: Biologically plausible error-driven learning using local activation differences: The generalized recirculation algorithm. Neural Computation, 895–938 (1996)
13. O'Reilly, R.C.: Six principles for biologically-based computational models for cortical cognition. Trends in Cognitive Science 2, 455–462 (1998)
14. O'Reilly, R.C., Munakata, Y.: Computational Explorations in Cognitive Neuroscience - Understanding the Mind by Simulating the Brain. The MIT Press (2000)
15. Rosa, J.L.G.: An artificial neural network model based on neuroscience: Looking closely at the brain. In: Kurková, R.N.V., Steele, N.C., Kárný, M. (eds.) Artificial Neural Nets and Genetic Algorithms - Proc. Intl. Conf. in Prague, Czech Republic, pp. 138–141. Springer (2001)
16. Ruf, B., Schmitt, M.: Self-Organization of Spiking Neurons Using Action Potential Timing. IEEE Transactions on Neural Network 9(3) (1998)
17. Silva, A.B., Rosa, J.L.G.: Biological Plausibility in Artificial Neural Networks: An Improvement on Earlier Models. In: Proc. The 7th. International Conference on Machine Learning and Applications, ICMLA 2008, San Diego, California, USA, December 11-13, IEEE Computer Society Press (2008)
18. Silva, A.B., Rosa, J.L.G.: Advances on Criteria for Biological Plausibility in Artificial Neural Networks: Think of Learning Processes. In: Proc. The 2011 International Joint Conference on Neural Networks, IJCNN 2011, San Jose, California, USA, July 31-August 5, pp. 1394–1401. IEEE Computer Society Press (2011) ISBN: 978-1-4244-9636-5
19. Song, S., Miller, K.D., Abbott, L.F.: Competitive hebbian learning through spike-timing-dependent synaptic plasticity. Nature Neuroscience 3(9), 919–926 (2000)

Random Sieve Based on Projections for RBF Neural Net Structure Selection

Ewa Skubalska-Rafajłowicz and Ewaryst Rafajłowicz

Institute of Computer Engineering control and Robotics,
Wrocław University of Technology, Wrocław , Poland
`ewa.rafajlowicz@pwr.wroc.pl`

Abstract. Our aim is to propose a method for selecting a radial basis functions terms to be included into a neural net model. As it is frequently met in practice, we consider the case of a deficit in the admissible number of observations (learning sequence) in comparison with a much larger number of candidate terms. The proposed approach is based on a random sieve that aims at selecting only necessary RBF's by a hierarchy of a large number of random mixing of candidate RBF's and testing their significance. The results of simulations are also reported.

Keywords: random projections, RBF, neural nets, model selection.

1 Introduction

RBF neural nets have been the subject of intensive research for many years. We refer the reader to a selected collection of more recent papers and monographs [8], [5], [12], [15], [4], [10] [6], [7], [20], [21], [22], [32], where references to earlier works can be found.

In opposite to the present paper, most of the proposed methods require more observations than candidate terms. Here, we admit a much larger initial size of an RBF net than the length of a learning sequence. One can wonder how it can be possible to select terms in such cases. The idea is based on random projections of a part of the RBF's and considering them as one term with randomly selected parameters (or a random mixture of RBF's). Then, we repeatedly test the validity of such a mixture of terms, repeating also their random projections.

There are some relationships of our approach with group testing [13] for selecting a regression function terms (see [14] for a survey of group testing approaches). Notice, however, that in [13] the grouping is done according to values of terms, while here we propose grouping by their random mixing.

Methods that are based on penalizing too many terms, such as AIC, BIC, C_p, GIC as well as cross-validation or bootstrap (see [9] for these and other criteria) either require candidate nets to be nested or lead to the need of comparing all the subsets of candidate terms. With the exception of so called forward term selection (as done in regression function estimation) they are not applicable in our case of a larger initial net structure than the length of a learning sequence.

L. Rutkowski et al. (Eds.): ICAISC 2013, Part I, LNAI 7894, pp. 193–204, 2013.

An aspect – rarely considered in the literature – is a choice of inputs in a learning sequence for a net structure selection. The exceptions in this respect include: [1], [17] and the bibliography cited there in.

Random projections have proved their usefulness in solving many highly dimensional problems (see [27], [28], [29], where also the references to the probabilistic background of random projections can be found).

Simultaneously with this paper in [26] we have proposed a method for selecting an optimum experiment design when a random projections method is used for selecting terms in a regression function estimation. A method sketched briefly in [26] differs from the one presented here in several respects:

1. the algorithm presented here is dedicated for RBF nets,
2. it is improved in comparison to the one in [26] by adding preliminary reduction of the net structure, which leads to more efficient use of a learning sequence,
3. it can be used not only for selecting proper RBF's to be introduced to a net, but also for the choice of independent variables.

2   Problem Statement

For simplicity of the exposition we consider the following version of a RBF net:

$$y(\mathbf{x}) = \sum_{j=1}^{r} a_j \, Ker(||\mathbf{x} - \mathbf{C}_j||/h_1) + \sum_{k=1}^{\widetilde{K}} b_k \, Ker(||\mathbf{x} - \mathbf{c}_k||/h_2), \qquad (1)$$

where $\mathbf{x} \in \mathbf{R}^d$ is a vector of the net inputs, $y(\mathbf{x})$ is its output (univariate for simplicity of the exposition), while $Ker : \mathbf{R}^1 \to \mathbf{R}^1$ is a nonnegative kernel function such that $\int_{-\infty}^{\infty} Ker(t)\,dt = 1$, $\int_{-\infty}^{\infty} t\,Ker(t)\,dt = 0$, $\int_{-\infty}^{\infty} t^2\,Ker(t)\,dt < \infty$, the Gaussian kernel being the most popular. In (1) the RBF net is split into two parts. The first one has centers at points $\mathbf{C}_j \in \mathbf{R}^d$, weights $\mathbf{C}_j$, $j = 1, 2, \ldots, r$ and smoothing parameter $h_1 > 0$. This part plays a special role, because we consider it as a part of an RBF net that is expected to be present in the final RBF net structure. In applications this part may represent a general trend, while the second summand in (1) is intended to model more subtle details. For this reason, we usually select the number of neurons in this part $\widetilde{K}$ much larger than r, which is the number of terms in the first part. Consequently, RBF centers $\mathbf{c}_k \in \mathbf{R}^d$, $k = 1, 2, \ldots, \widetilde{K}$ are placed more densely than centers $\mathbf{C}_j$'s, while the smoothing parameter h_2 should be smaller than $h - 1$ in order to better approximate fine details.

We assume that we have a learning sequence $(\mathbf{x}_i, y_i)$, $i = 1, 2, \ldots, n$ at our disposal, where $\mathbf{x}_i \in \mathbf{R}^d$'s are input vectors, while y_i's are observed outputs of a certain surface or a system that our RBF net is expected to approximate. In order to tune (1) to approximate y_i's by $y(\mathbf{x}_i)$'s we have to choose weights a_i's. We also have to select proper terms in the second part of (1) and tune the corresponding weights. In more detail, our aim is to find

$$\sum_{m=1}^{K} b_{k(m)} \, Ker(||\mathbf{x} - \mathbf{c}_{k(m)}||/h_2), \tag{2}$$

where K is much smaller than $\widetilde{K}$ and a sequence of indexes $k(m)$, $m=1, 2, \ldots, K$, which a subsequence of all indexes $k = 1, 2, \ldots, \widetilde{K}$. In other words, our aim is to select a sub-net of (1) of the form:

$$y(\mathbf{x}) = \sum_{j=1}^{r} a_j \, Ker(||\mathbf{x} - \mathbf{C}_j||/h_1) + \sum_{m=1}^{K} b_{k(m)} \, Ker(||\mathbf{x} - \mathbf{c}_{k(m)}||/h_2) \tag{3}$$

and to tune its parameters in such a way that $\sum_{i=1}^{n}(y_i - y(\mathbf{x}_i))^2$ is minimized.

In our problem statement $0 \leq K < \widetilde{K}$ is also a decision variable. In order to ensure the possibility of estimating a_j, $j = 1, 2, \ldots, r$ and $b_{k(m)}$, $m = 1, 2, \ldots, K$ we have to confine to K such that $r + K \leq n$.

Our task is difficult, because of our assumption that the length n of the learning sequence is much smaller than $\widetilde{K}$. This assumption implies that we must admit errors in selecting a structure of our RBF net.

We leave outside the scope of this paper the problems of proper selection of smoothing parameters $0 < h_2 \leq h_1$ assuming that they are reasonably chosen. We refer the reader to [8], [32], and the bibliography cited therein for methods of selecting smoothing parameters. Concerning the choice of centers $\mathbf{c}_k$'s, $\mathbf{C}_j$'s positions notice that the approach proposed here contains implicitly a way of selecting centers positions $\mathbf{c}_{k(m)}$, $m = 1, 2, \ldots, K$ from a much larger collection $\mathbf{c}_k$, $k = 1, 2, \ldots, \widetilde{K}$. After selecting them, one can adjust their positions as well as positions of $\mathbf{C}_j$'s using more traditional methods that are well suited for a fine positions adjustment of a relatively small number of RBF centers.

It is convenient to introduce a shorthand notations:

N1) for the first sub-net $\mathbf{v}(\mathbf{x}) = [v_1(\mathbf{x}), v_2(\mathbf{x}), \ldots, v_r(\mathbf{x})]^T$, where T denotes the transposition, $v_j(\mathbf{x}) \stackrel{def}{=} Ker(||\mathbf{x} - \mathbf{C}_j||/h_1)$, $j = 1, 2, \ldots, r$ and $\mathbf{a} = [a_1, a_2, \ldots, a_r]^T$,

N2) for the second sub-net $\mathbf{w}(\mathbf{x}) = [w_1(\mathbf{x}), w_2(\mathbf{x}), \ldots, w_{\widetilde{K}}(\mathbf{x})]^T$, $w_k(\mathbf{x}) \stackrel{def}{=} Ker(||\mathbf{x} - \mathbf{c}_k||/h_2)$, $k = 1, 2, \ldots, \widetilde{K}$.

Note that $\mathbf{v} : \mathbf{R}^d \to \mathbf{R}^r$ and $\mathbf{w} : \mathbf{R}^d \to \mathbf{R}^{\widetilde{K}}$.

Using this notation our RBF net can be rewritten as follows:

$$y(\mathbf{x}) = \mathbf{a}^T \, \mathbf{v}(\mathbf{x}) + \mathbf{b}^T \, \mathbf{w}(\mathbf{x}), \tag{4}$$

where $\mathbf{b} \stackrel{def}{=} [b_1, b_2, \ldots, b_{\widetilde{K}}]^T$. In our approach to selecting RBF net structure we shall use the so called t-Student statistical test. Its proper usage requires the assumption that our initial RBF net has a sufficiently rich structure that allows for generating our learning sequence as follows:

$$y_i = (\mathbf{a}^0)^T \mathbf{v}(\mathbf{x}_i) + \sum_{m=1}^{K} b^0_{k(m)}\, w_{k(m)}(\mathbf{x}_i) + \varepsilon_i \quad i = 1, 2, \ldots, n, \qquad (5)$$

where $\mathbf{a}^0 \in \mathbf{R}^r$ and $b^0_{k(m)}$, $m = 1, 2, \ldots, K$ are unknown parameters, while output observations y_i contain additive i.i.d. random errors ε_i, $i = 1, 2, \ldots, n$. We assume that $\varepsilon_i \sim \mathcal{N}(0, \sigma_\varepsilon^2)$ for formal derivations, although one can use our algorithm on heuristic grounds, even if these assumptions are violated.

3   Random Projections of Model Terms and Outline of Their Selection

Details of the proposed method are presented in the next section, while here we present a general idea.

Our starting point is the following model

$$\bar{y}(\mathbf{x}, \mathbf{a}, \beta, \mathbf{s}) = \mathbf{a}^T \mathbf{v}(\mathbf{x}) + \beta\, \mathbf{s}^T \mathbf{w}(\mathbf{x}), \qquad (6)$$

where $\mathbf{a} \in \mathbf{R}^r$ are unknown weights of our preliminary RBF net, $\beta \in \mathbf{R}$ is an unknown weight of randomly mixed RBF's $\mathbf{w}(\mathbf{x})$. Random mixing of these terms is done by multiplying them by random vector $\mathbf{s} \in \mathbf{R}^{\tilde{K}}$ which is drawn at random by the experimenter from the multivariate Gaussian distribution: $\mathcal{N}(\mathbf{0}, \sigma_s^2 \mathbf{I}_{\tilde{K}})$, $\sigma_s > 0$, where $\mathbf{I}_{\tilde{K}}$ is $\tilde{K} \times \tilde{K}$ identity matrix. Later on, we shall write $\mathbf{s} \sim \mathcal{N}(\mathbf{0}, \sigma_s^2 \mathbf{I}_{\tilde{K}})$.

Remark 1. *Model (6) resembles a model that was proposed in [2] for selecting terms in a regression function (see also [31] page 131) as well as models used in the dimensionality reduction (see [24] and the bibliography cited therein). However, the fundamental difference is in that here $\mathbf{s}$ is selected at random and only β is estimated, while in [2] both β and $\mathbf{s}$ are estimated, which confines the possibility of applying the latter approach when $\tilde{K} + r \ll n$, as assumed here. In [24] parameters of several deterministic projections of $\mathbf{x}$ itself are estimated.*

Before starting our random sieve of RBF's in $\mathbf{w}(\mathbf{x})$ it is expedient to test whether our preliminary net, spanned by RBF's contained in $\mathbf{v}(\mathbf{x})$ is properly selected. Notice that we can use classical tools of regression analysis (see, e.g., [31]), because the number of terms in $\mathbf{v}(\mathbf{x})$ is smaller than the length of a learning sequence. In particular, one can estimate $\mathbf{a}$ by minimizing $\sum_{i=1}^{n}(y_i - \mathbf{a}^T \mathbf{v}(\mathbf{x}_i))^2$ and then test the hypothesis that particular components of $\mathbf{a}$ are zero. After reducing those RBF's that correspond to nonessential parameters, we can start our random sieve.

For fixed $\mathbf{s}$, estimates $\hat{\mathbf{a}}$, $\hat{\beta}$ of parameters $\mathbf{a}$ and β are obtained by ordinary least squares (OLS), i.e., minimizing

$$\min_{\mathbf{a},\beta} \sum_{i=1}^{n} [y_i - \bar{y}(\mathbf{x}_i, \mathbf{a}, \beta, \mathbf{s})]^2, \qquad (7)$$

Then, we state the null hypothesis: $H_0 : \beta = 0$. Under assumptions: (5) and $\varepsilon_i \sim \mathcal{N}(0, \sigma_\varepsilon^2)$ we can test it by the well known t-test for regression parameters (see, e.g., [23]). The rejection of H_0 means that our observations contradict the hypothesis that $\beta = 0$. This is an indicator that the mixture $\mathbf{s}^T \mathbf{w}(\mathbf{x})$ may contain terms that are useful in modeling the learning sequence by our RBF net. To convince ourselves, new $\mathbf{s}$ is drawn $\mathcal{N}(\mathbf{0}, \sigma_s^2 \mathbf{I}_{\widetilde{K}})$ and the estimation (7) and the test are repeated rep times, say.

If H_0 was rejected a sufficient number of times ($0.2\,rep$, say), we conclude that $\mathbf{w}(\mathbf{x})$ may contain terms that are worth introducing into the model. Otherwise, we stop the algorithm, concluding that only $\mathbf{a}^T \mathbf{v}(\mathbf{x})$ are essential and we have to re-estimate $\mathbf{a}$ by OLS.

If H_0 was rejected sufficiently many times, we have to identify which terms are important. To this end vector $\mathbf{w}(\mathbf{x})$ will be repeatedly divided (roughly) in half in further derivations. To define subdivisions it is convenient to introduce an overloaded notation defined as follows $\widetilde{K}//2$ is : if $\widetilde{K}$ is even, then $\widetilde{K}//2 = \widetilde{K}/2$, otherwise, $\widetilde{K}//2$ is understood as the largest integer less than $\widetilde{K}/2$ for $\mathbf{w}_L(\mathbf{x})$ vectors and as the smallest integer larger than $\widetilde{K}/2$ for $\mathbf{w}_R(\mathbf{x})$ vectors. The same convention is used for further subdivisions $\mathbf{w}_{LL}(\mathbf{x})$, $\mathbf{w}_{LR}(\mathbf{x})$ etc. and for random vectors $\mathbf{s}_L, \mathbf{s}_R \sim \mathcal{N}(\mathbf{0}, \sigma_s^2 \mathbf{I}_{\widetilde{K}//2})$, assuming that they have the same dimensions as the corresponding $\mathbf{w}_L(\mathbf{x})$, $\mathbf{w}_R(\mathbf{x})$, $\mathbf{w}_{LL}(\mathbf{x})$, $\mathbf{w}_{LR}(\mathbf{x})$ vectors. Furthermore, we assume that random vectors $\mathbf{s}_L, \mathbf{s}_R, \mathbf{s}_{LL}, \mathbf{s}_{LR}$ etc. are mutually independent.

The corresponding left and right parts of $\mathbf{w}(\mathbf{x})$ will be denoted by $\mathbf{w}_L(\mathbf{x})$, $\mathbf{w}_R(\mathbf{x})$, $\mathbf{w}_{LL}(\mathbf{x})$, $\mathbf{w}_{LR}(\mathbf{x})$, $\mathbf{w}_{RL}(\mathbf{x})$, $\mathbf{w}_{RR}(\mathbf{x})$ etc. In subsequent steps the following RBF nets will be used:

$$\bar{y}(\mathbf{x}, \mathbf{a}, \beta_L, \beta_R, \mathbf{S}) = \mathbf{a}^T \mathbf{v}(\mathbf{x}) + \beta_L \mathbf{s}_L^T \mathbf{w}_L(\mathbf{x}) + \beta_R \mathbf{s}_R^T \mathbf{w}_R(\mathbf{x}), \qquad (8)$$

where $\mathbf{a} \in \mathbf{R}^r$, $\beta_L, \beta_R \in \mathbf{R}$, $\mathbf{s}_L, \mathbf{s}_R \in \mathbf{R}^{\widetilde{K}//2}$, $\mathbf{S} \stackrel{def}{=} [\mathbf{s}_L, \mathbf{s}_R]$, $\mathbf{w}_1(\mathbf{x}), \mathbf{w}_2(\mathbf{x}) \in \mathbf{R}^{\widetilde{K}//2}$

We state the hypothesis that in (8) $H_{0L} : \beta_L = 0$ and analogously $H_{0R} : \beta_R = 0$. We draw $\mathbf{s}_L$ and $\mathbf{s}_R$ at random and we find the estimate $\hat{\mathbf{a}}$, $\hat{\beta}_L$ and $\hat{\beta}_R$ by

$$\min_{\mathbf{a}, \beta_I, \beta_R} \sum_{i=1}^{n} [y_i - \bar{y}(\mathbf{x}_i, \mathbf{a}, \beta_L, \beta_R, \mathbf{S})]^2. \qquad (9)$$

and t test is applied for $\hat{\beta}_L$ and $\hat{\beta}_R$. Then we store the results of testing and $\mathbf{s}_L$ and $\mathbf{s}_R$ are again drawn at random and (9) and t tests are repeated rep times, say. Simultaneously, we increment counters, denoted as c_L, and c_R, each time when $H_{0L} : \beta_L = 0$, respectively $H_{0R} : \beta_R = 0$, is rejected. If, for preselected threshold $0 < \theta < 1$, we have $c_L < \theta\,rep$ and $c_R < \theta\,rep$, then STOP – there are no additional RBF's that are essential for our net.. Otherwise, if $c_L \geq \theta\,rep$ and $c_L > c_R$ we split $\mathbf{w}_L(\mathbf{x})$ in half and we repeat the above steps for model

$$\bar{\bar{y}}(\mathbf{x}, \mathbf{a}, \beta_{LL}, \beta_{LR}, \ldots) = \mathbf{a}^T \mathbf{v}(\mathbf{x}) + \beta_{LL} \mathbf{s}_{LL}^T \mathbf{w}_{LL}(\mathbf{x}) + \beta_{LR} \mathbf{s}_{LR}^T \mathbf{w}_{LR}(\mathbf{x}), \qquad (10)$$

(or for its 'right' counterpart). Simultaneously, if also $c_R \geq \theta\,rep$, we keep $\mathbf{w}_R(\mathbf{x})$ terms for further considerations as prospective, otherwise we skip $\mathbf{w}_R(\mathbf{x})$ in further steps. If our algorithm attains the stage that $\mathbf{w}_{LR...RL}(\mathbf{x})$ contains only one element we add it, after t test, to the list of candidates to be introduced to our RBF net. If the list of prospective terms is not empty, we enter it as a new $\mathbf{w}(\mathbf{x})$ list and repeat the entire procedure. Finally, we have a list of candidates that is used as the extension of $\mathbf{v}(\mathbf{x})$, the parameters of the extended RBF net are re-calculated and undergo t tests. A more detailed description of the above approach is given in the next section.

4 Detailed Description of the Algorithm.

Below, we present a detailed description of the random sieve algorithm. The notations are the same as in the previous section. In parenthesis we provide suggested values of parameters that were verified in simulations as useful.

Preparations:
- Collect observations $(\mathbf{x}_i, y_i)$, i=1,2,..., n.
- Select RBF centers $\mathbf{C}_j$, $j = 1, 2, ..., r$ and $\mathbf{c}_k$, $k = 1, 2, ..., \widetilde{K}$.
- Select kernel Ker (Gaussian) and smoothing parameters $0 < h_1 < h_2$ (h_1 and h_2 should be selected taking the number of observations into account and a fine tuning based on cross-validation should be performed).
- Form vectors $\mathbf{v}(\mathbf{x})$ and $\mathbf{w}(\mathbf{x})$ according to N1) and N2).
- Select parameters: $\sigma_s > 0$ ($\sigma_s = 3$) for generating random vectors $\mathbf{s}$ etc.
- Choose working significance level $0 < \alpha < 1$ ($\alpha = 0.1$) that is used in t-test for random sieve and final check significance level $0 < \alpha_f < \alpha < 1$ ($\alpha_f = 0.05$).
- Choose the number of random projections $rep \geq 1$ ($rep = 200$), i.e., the number of repetitions of random projections and t-test before deciding whether a group of RBF's is prospective or not.
- Select the threshold $0 < \theta < 1$ ($\theta = 0.2$) as the fraction of positive trials required to consider a group of RBF's as perspective (see [3] for the explanations on critism when multiple testing is used).

Initialization:
- Set counter $c_0 = 0$. It counts how many times H_0 was rejected for a group of RBF's under consideration.
- Prepare three empty lists: *candidates* (of RBF's to be added to a net), *prospective* (RBF's worth to be considered as the most perspective) and *waiting* (the list of RBF's to be considered later).
- Check whether $\mathbf{v}(\mathbf{x})$ does not contain unnecessary RBF's. To this end, solve the following OLS problem: $\min_{\mathbf{a}} \sum_{i=1}^{n}(y_i - \mathbf{a}^T \mathbf{v}(\mathbf{x}_i))^2$ and test the sequence of hypothesis $H_0 : \mathbf{a}^{(j)} = 0$, $j = 1, 2, ..., r$. This is realizable due to our assumption that $r < n$. Remove from $\mathbf{v}(\mathbf{x})$ those $v_j(\mathbf{x})$ for which $H_0 : \mathbf{a}^{(j)} = 0$ was not rejected[1]. Rename the obtained vector as $\mathbf{v}(\mathbf{x})$ again and again denote its length by r.

---

[1] If the resulting list of preliminary RBF's is empty, select at least one additional candidate RBF and add it to this list.

Step 1. Draw at random $\mathbf{s} \in \mathbf{R}^{\tilde{K}}$, $\mathbf{s} \sim \mathcal{N}(\mathbf{0}, \sigma_s^2 \mathbf{I}_{\tilde{K}})$. Form RBF net (6) and calculate $\hat{\mathbf{a}}(\mathbf{s})$ and $\hat{\beta}(\mathbf{s})$ by OLS. Test the hypothesis: $\hat{\beta}(\mathbf{s}) = 0$ at the level α. If the hypothesis is rejected, the set $c_0 = c_0 + 1$.

Step 2. Repeat Step 1 *rep* times. If $c_0 < \theta \, rep$, STOP with the message: *probably there are no RBF's from the list* $\mathbf{w}(\mathbf{x})$ *to be added*, otherwise, go to Step 3.

Step 3. Enter all the terms from $\mathbf{w}(\mathbf{x})$ to the *prospective* list.

Step 4. Split the *prospective* list in half. Replace $\mathbf{w}_L(\mathbf{x})$ in (8) by the left part of this list and $\mathbf{w}_R(\mathbf{x})$ by the right half. Set counters $c_L = 0$, $c_R = 0$.

Step 5. Generate random Gaussian vectors $\mathbf{s}_L$ and $\mathbf{s}_R$ of the same lengths as the current $\mathbf{w}_L(\mathbf{x})$ and $\mathbf{w}_R(\mathbf{x})$ and calculate $\hat{\mathbf{a}}(\mathbf{S})$, $\hat{\beta}_L(\mathbf{s}_L)$ and $\hat{\beta}_R(\mathbf{s}_R)$ by minimizing (9). Test the hypothesis: $\hat{\beta}_L(\mathbf{s}_L) = 0$ (respectively, $\hat{\beta}_R(\mathbf{s}_R) = 0$) and set $c_L = c_L + 1$ (respectively, set $c_L = c_L + 1$), if it is rejected.

Step 5. Repeat Step 5 *rep* times. If $c_L < \theta \, rep$ AND $c_R < \theta \, rep$, go to Step 6. Otherwise, if $c_L \geq c_R$ and

> **Step 5a.** if current $\mathbf{w}_L(\mathbf{x})$ contains more than one term, then replace all the content of *prospective* list by $\mathbf{w}_L(\mathbf{x})$ and add $\mathbf{w}_R(\mathbf{x})$ to the *waiting* list, but only if $c_R \geq \theta \, rep$, otherwise, reject $\mathbf{w}_R(\mathbf{x})$ from considerations and go to Step 4,

> **Step 5b.** if current $\mathbf{w}_L(\mathbf{x})$ contains exactly one term, than add it to the *candidate* list and add $\mathbf{w}_R(\mathbf{x})$ to the *waiting* list, but only if $c_R \geq \theta \, rep$, otherwise, reject $\mathbf{w}_R(\mathbf{x})$ from further considerations. Then replace the content of the *prospective* list by all the *waiting* list, set the *waiting* list to be empty and go to Step 4.

If $c_L < c_R$, perform Steps 5a) and 5b), replacing the roles $\mathbf{w}_L(\mathbf{x})$ and $\mathbf{w}_R(\mathbf{x})$.

Step 6. Final decisions:

- If list *candidates* is empty, STOP with the message: *probably there are no RBF's from* $\mathbf{w}(\mathbf{x})$ *to be added*.
- If the length of the *candidates* list is larger than 0 but not larger than $(n-r)$, then add this list to $\mathbf{v}(\mathbf{x})$, estimate the parameters of the extended RBF net and test their significance at the level α_f. Reject nonsignificant RBF's, re-calculate parameters $\mathbf{a}$ and selected b_k's and STOP, providing the final list of RBF's.
- If the length of the *candidates* list is larger than $(n-r)$, then the candidate list is still too long in comparison to available data. It is desirable to enlarge the learning sequence, replace $\mathbf{w}(\mathbf{x})$ by the list of candidates and go to Step 3. If we cannot get additional learning examples, we can still replace $\mathbf{w}(\mathbf{x})$ by the list of candidates and go to Step 3, but this time it is more probable than certain essential RBF's will be left outside the final net structure.

Remark 2. *The above algorithm can also be used for simultaneous selection of RBF's and input variables. To this end, it suffices to replace* $\mathbf{v}_j(\mathbf{x})$*'s by* $Ker(\|Sel_D[\mathbf{x} - \mathbf{C}_j]\|/h_1)$ *and* $w_k(\mathbf{x})$ *by* $Ker(\|Sel_D[\mathbf{x} - \mathbf{c}_k]\|/h_2)$*, where the selector function* $Sel_D[.]$ *is defined as follows.* D *is a subset of those indexes* $\{1, 2, \ldots, d\}$ *of input variables that are not set to zero by function Sel. For example, if* $d = 4$ *and* $D = 1, 4$*, then* $Sel_D[[x^{(1)}, x^{(2)}, x^{(3)}, x^{(4)}]] = [x^{(1)}, 0, 0, x^{(4)}]$*.*

5 Simulations

The aim of our simulations was to verify performance of the algorithm using an example of moderate size. For clarity of the interpretation we have simulated a simple RBF net with input variables on the unit square. Preliminary positions of Gaussian RBF's, i.e., those included in $\mathbf{v}(\mathbf{x})$ were in the nodes of the following grid: $(i\,0.2,\ j\,0.2)$, $i,\ j = 0, 1, \ldots, 5$. Thus, $\mathbf{v}(\mathbf{x})$ contained $r = 36$ elements, but

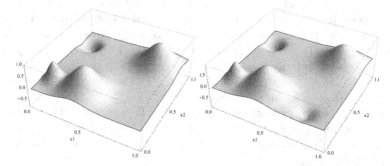

Fig. 1. "True" surface (left panel) and its reconstruction by one of the randomly sieved BRF net (right panel)

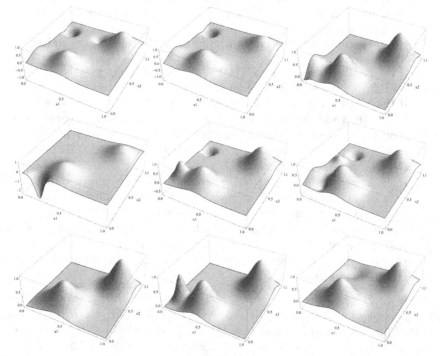

Fig. 2. A collection of randomly sieved RBF nets for approximating the surface shown in Fig. 1 (left panel)

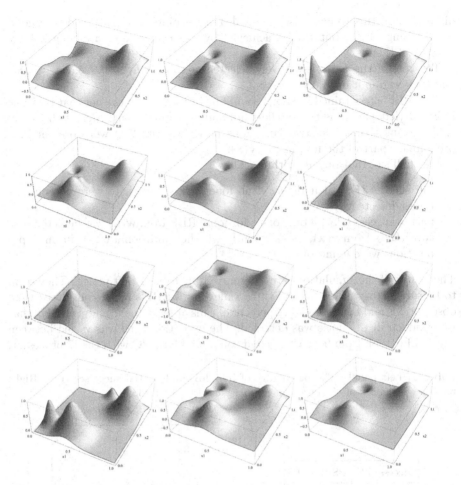

Fig. 3. The second collection of randomly sieved RBF nets for approximating the surface shown in Fig. 1 (left panel)

only two of them (higher hills in Fig. 1) had weights 2.5 in our simulations, the rest of the weights were set to zero. As candidates $\mathbf{w}(\mathbf{x})$ to be entered to the net we take RBF's with centers at the grid: $(i\,0.1,\ j\,0.1)$, $i, j = 0, 1, \ldots, 10$. Thus, $\widetilde{K} = 121$ and we have $r + \widetilde{K} = 157$ RBF's to be selected. To this end only $n = 50$ observations $(\mathbf{x}_i,\ y_i)$'s were generated, where $\mathbf{x}_i$'s are generated as the Hammersley sequence (see Tablet1). The reason for selecting a quasi-random sequence of the Halton and Hammersley type is that it has proved to be useful in other tasks such as regression estimation (see [19], [30]). Their usefulness results from a better conditioning of the matrix $M \overset{def}{=} \sum_{i=1}^{r} \mathbf{v}(\mathbf{x}_i)\,\mathbf{v}^T(\mathbf{x}_i)$, which has $\kappa(M) \overset{def}{=} \frac{\lambda_{max}(M)}{\lambda_{min}(M)} = 9622$ and we can avoid using a regularization. For comparison, when $\mathbf{x}_i$'s are generated as uniform random variables, then $\kappa(M)$ is of the order 10^6 and a kind of regularization is necessary (see, e.g., [15] for a discussion on this topic). Also classical design points (see [16]) lead to a good conditioning of M, but this is achieved by the necessity of applying a large number of them.

The rest of the parameters were selected as follows $h_1 = 0.025$, $h_2 = 0.005$ and they were not optimized, $\sigma_s = 3$, $\sigma_\epsilon = 0.1$.

Two RBF's (contained in $\mathbf{w}(\mathbf{x})$) should be introduced to the net that is visible in Fig. 1 (left panel) as the smallest hill and as the hole, with weights 0.75 and -0.75, respectively. The two large hills (with weights 2.5) were present in a preliminary part of the net, i.e., in $\mathbf{v}(\mathbf{x})$.

We shall say that our algorithm achieved:

- full success (FS), if it detected all four RBF's and there were no spurious terms detected,
- partial success (PS), if only one additional RBF from $\mathbf{w}(\mathbf{x})$ was detected plus two RBF's from $\mathbf{v}(\mathbf{x})$, independently whether additional terms in improper positions were found or not.

The results of the simulations are summarized in Table 1 (left panel). They seem to be satisfactory, since we had three times more RBF's to be considered than observations and in about eighty percent of runs at least one from two RBF's that were hidden in the noise was detected. The execution time was varied between runs and it took from 9 to 122 seconds on a standard PC with the i7 processor.

Table 1. Left panel – the percentage of full (FS) and partial successes (PS). Right panel – a sequence of 50 Hammersley points used in simulations.

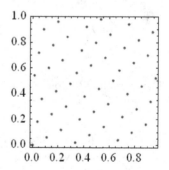

Success	FS	PS	FS+PS
%	18.2	63.6	81.8

6   Concluding Remarks

An important feature of the proposed approach is the dimensionality reduction that comes from random projections of candidate RBF's. The idea of using random projections for this purpose was introduced by the first author in [25] in the context of usually even larger models arising in the identification of nonlinear time series. This aspect of the present paper as well as bounds on the probabilities of properly selecting all necessary RBF's, while avoiding introducing spurious ones are outside the scope of this paper.

One can consider other strategies of running calculations of divided and randomly projected sub-nets that are more suitable for parallel computers. The proposed approach can also be useful in signal restoration (see, e.g., [11]) for selecting sin terms that are used for a signal approximation.

References

1. Bazan, M., Skubalska-Rafajłowicz, E.: A new method of centers location in Gaussian RBF interpolation networks. In: Rutkowski, L., et al. (eds.) ICAISC 2013, Part I. LNCS (LNAI), vol. 7894, pp. 20–31. Springer, Heidelberg (2013)
2. Cook, R.D., Weisberg, S.: Partial one-dimensional regression models. Amer. Stat. 58, 110–116 (2004)
3. Donoho, D., Jin, J.: Higher criticism for detecting sparse heterogeneous mixtures. The Annals of Statistics 32, 962–994 (2004)
4. Fornberg, B., Larsson, E., Flyer, N.: Stable computations with Gaussian radial basis functions. SIAM J. Sci. Comput. 33(2), 869–892 (2011)
5. Fu, X., Wang, L.: Data dimensionality reduction with application to simplifying RBF network structure and improving classification performance. IEEE Transactions on Systems, Man, and Cybernetics – Part B: Cybernetics 33(3), 399–409 (2003)
6. Hansen, P.C.: Rank-deficient and discrete ill-posed problems. SIAM, Philadelphia (1998)
7. Girosi, F., Jones, M., Poggio, T.: Regularization theory and neural networks architectures. Neural Computation 7(2), 219–269 (1995)
8. Gyorfi, L., Kohler, M., Krzyżak, A., Walk, H.: A Distribution-free Theory of Nonparametric Regression, ch. 21. Springer, Berlin (2000)
9. Konishi, S., Kitagawa, G.: Information Criteria and Statistical Modeling, Springer (2008)
10. Krzyżak, A., Linder, T.: Radial Basis Function Networks and Complexity Regularization in Function Learning. IEEE Trans. Neural Networks 9, 247–256 (1998)
11. Krzyżak, A., Rafajłowicz, E., Pawlak, M.: Moving average restoration of bandlimited signals from noisy observations. IEEE Transactions on Signal Processing 45, 2967–2976 (1997)
12. Leonardisa, A., Bischof, H.: An efficient MDL-based construction of RBF networks. Neural Networks 11, 963–973 (1998)
13. Lewis, S.M., Dean, A.M.: Detection of interactions in experiments on large numbers of factors (with discussion). Journal of the Royal Statistical Society, Series B 63, 633–672 (2001)
14. Morris, M.D.: An Overview of Group Factor Screening. In: Dean, A.M., Lewis, S.M. (eds.) Screening Methods for Experimentation in Industry, Drug Discovery, and Genetics, ch. 9, pp. 191–207. Springer, New York (2006)
15. Orr, M.J.: Regularization in the selection of basis function centers. Neural Computation 7(3), 606–623 (1995)
16. Rafajłowicz, E., Myszka, W.: Optimum experimental design for a regression on a hypercube-generalization of Hoel's result. Annals of the Institute of Statistical Mathematics 40, 821–827 (1988)
17. Rafajłowicz, E., Pawlak, M.: Optimization of centers' positions for RBF nets with generalized kernels. In: Rutkowski, L., Siekmann, J.H., Tadeusiewicz, R., Zadeh, L.A. (eds.) ICAISC 2004. LNCS (LNAI), vol. 3070, pp. 253–259. Springer, Heidelberg (2004)

18. Rafajłowicz, E., Skubalska-Rafajłowicz, E.: RBF nets based on equidistributed points. In: Proceedings of 9th IEEE Int. Conf.: Methods and Models in Automation and Robotics MMAR, pp. 921–926 (2003)
19. Rafajłowicz, E., Schwabe, R.: Halton and Hammersley sequences in multivariate nonparametric regression. Statistics and Probability Letters 76, 803–812 (2006)
20. Rutkowski, L.: Adaptive Probabilistic Neural Networks for Pattern Classification in Time-Varying Environment. IEEE Trans. Neural Networks 15(4), 811–827 (2004)
21. Rutkowski, L.: Generalized Regression Neural Networks in Time-Varying Environment. IEEE Trans. Neural Networks 15(3), 576–596 (2004)
22. Rutkowski, L.: New Soft Computing Techniques for System Modeling. Pattern Classification and Image Processing. Springer, Heidelberg (2004)
23. Seber, G.A.F.: Linear regression Analysis. Wiley, New York (1977)
24. Shaker, A.J., Prendergast, L.A.: Iterative application of dimension reduction methods. Electronic Journal of Statistics 5, 1471–1494 (2011)
25. Skubalska-Rafajłowicz, E.: Experiments with neural network for modeling of nonlinear dynamical systems: Design problems. Lecture presented at The Newton's Mathematical Institute, Cambridge, DAE seminar led by D. Uciński (2011), www.newton.ac.uk/programmes/DAE/seminars/072010301.html
26. Skubalska-Rafajłowicz, E., Rafajłowicz, E.: Random projections in regression model selection and corresponding experiment design problems. To be presented at Model Oriented Data Analysis Conference, Lagów, Poland (June 2013)
27. Skubalska-Rafajłowicz, E.: Random projection RBF nets for multidimensional density estimation. International Journal of Applied Mathematics and Computer Science 18(4), 455–466 (2008)
28. Skubalska-Rafajłowicz, E.: Detection and estimation translations of large images using random projections. In: 7th International Workshop Multidimensional (nD) Systems (nDs), September 5-7 (2011)
29. Skubalska-Rafajłowicz, E.: Neural networks with sigmoidal activation functions–dimension reduction using normal random projection. Nonlinear Anal.: Theory, Methods & Appl. 71, e1255–e1263 (2009)
30. Skublska-Rafajłowicz, E., Rafajłowicz, E.: Sampling multidimensional signals by a new class of quasi-random sequences. Multidimensional System and Signal Processing 23, 237–253 (2012)
31. Weisberg S.: Applied Linear Regression. Wiley & Sons, Inc., Hoboken (2005)
32. Xu, L., Krzyżak, A., Yuille, A.: On radial basis function nets and kernel regression: statistical consistency, convergence, rates and receptive field size. Neural Networks 4, 609–628 (1994)

Eigenvalue Spectra of Functional Networks in fMRI Data and Artificial Models

Katarzyna Zając and Jarosław Piersa

Faculty of Mathematics and Computer Science,
Nicolaus Copernicus University, Poland
{zajac,piersaj}@mat.umk.pl

Abstract. In this work we provide a spectral comparison of functional networks in fMRI data of brain activity and artificial energy-based neural model. The spectra (set of eigenvalues of the graph adjacency matrix) of both networks turn out to obey similar decay rate and characteristic power-law scaling in their middle parts. This extends the set of statistics, which are already confirmed to be similar for both neural models and medical data, by the graph spectrum.

Keywords: fMRI, functional networks, neural networks, graph spectrum.

1 Motivation

Recent focus on graph-theoretical description of large-scale real networks caused an avalanche of reports concerning real brain structures and artificial neural networks in this context. Among frequently analysed statistics, degree distribution, transport efficiency, clustering, fault tolerance [3] seem to be most frequently regarded. This seems hardly surprising as they are fairly simple to compute and provide clear conceptual meaning.

In this work we go slightly beyond this classical set of features and focus on the set of eigenvalues of the analysed network (graph spectrum). Such analyses are far less common in theoretical researches concerning ANN[1] and next to absent in experimental neuroscience, though they can still provide a wide qualitative description of the graph, for instance bi-partioning [6]. We provide numerical results concerning spectra of functional graphs from open-accessed fMRI data from BIRN[2] as well as simplified activation-flow of recurrent network. We note a striking similarity between the decay of eigenvalues in functional networks from both sources.

The outline of the paper: in Sec. 2 we describe the methodology and results obtained from fMRI functional graphs. In Sec. 3 we briefly reiterate an

---

[1] Abbreviations used throughout the paper: ANN — Artificial Neural Network, fMRI — functional Magneric Resonance Imagining, AF — Activation Flow (model), ER — Erdős-Rényi (graph), WS — Watts-Strogatz (graph), AB — Albert-Barabasi (graph).

[2] http://www.birncommunity.org/resources/data/

L. Rutkowski et al. (Eds.): ICAISC 2013, Part I, LNAI 7894, pp. 205–214, 2013.

activation-flow model of ANN [13] and recall its spectral properties [14]. The results are compared and discussed in Sec. 4. Sec. 5 concludes the paper and points out potential future research.

2   Spectra of fMRI Functional Brain Graphs

For the study of functional brain graphs, we used fMRI data provided by Biomedical Informatics Research Network (BIRN): we downloaded the data from the open-accessed Function BIRN Data Repository (for more information see the website http://www.birncommunity.org/resources/data/). The data contain a raw stream of output of the medical devices, which measured blood-oxygen level in the cells of brain during execution of simple tasks. The fMRI data studied in this paper come from the two-folded run of sensorimotor task, performed by a right handed, non-smoking, healthy women. In Fig. 1 we present the images, which are fragments of obtained scans.

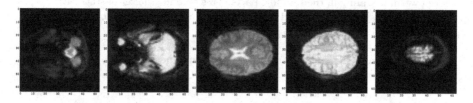

Fig. 1. Representative fMRI scans from the first sensorimotor task at the time $t = 4$ out of 85 timesteps

The raw data are presented as a set of voxels. Each voxel v, for a given time $t \in \{1, \ldots, n_t\}$, is described by three coordinates $x \in \{1, \ldots, n_x\}$, $y \in \{1, \ldots, n_y\}$, $z \in \{1, \ldots, n_z\}$. By v^t_{xyz} we denote a value of a voxel v with coordinates x, y, z, at a time t. In our analysis we use two datasets. Each dataset consists of 85 three-dimensional data, that represent human brain activity; each volume for a given timestep $t = 1, \ldots, 85$. For a further analysis we use representative fragments of the size $34 \times 40 \times 20$ of volumes imaging human brain, for $t = 1, \ldots, 85$, each frame taken every 3 seconds, so the whole measurement lasted 4:15 minutes.

Based on the fMRI data $D = \{v^t_{xyz} \mid x = 1, \ldots, n_x; \ y = 1, \ldots, n_y; \ z = 1, \ldots, n_z; \ t = 1, \ldots, n_t\} \subset \mathbb{Z}^{n_x} \times \mathbb{Z}^{n_y} \times \mathbb{Z}^{n_z} \times \mathbb{Z}^{n_t}$, we define a *functional activity multigraph* $G = (V, E)$ as follows. For each voxel v, with its coordinates (x, y, z), the *average activity matrix* $A = [a_i] \in \mathbb{M}_{n \times 1}(\mathbb{R})$, where $n = n_x \cdot n_y \cdot n_z$, is defined as

$$A(i := z \cdot n_x \cdot n_y + y \cdot n_x + x) = a_i = \frac{1}{n_t} \sum_{t=0}^{n_t} v^t_{xyz} \ .$$

Using this matrix we define the adjacency matrix of the functional network $Adj = [adj_{ij}] \in \mathbb{M}_{n \times n}(\mathbb{R}_{\geq 0})$, $n = n_x \cdot n_y \cdot n_z$ as

$$Adj(i, j) = ad_{ij} = \begin{cases} |\rho(i, j)| \cdot \sqrt{A(i) \cdot A(j)} & \text{if } |\rho(i, j)| \geq \Theta \\ 0 & \text{otherwise} \end{cases}, \quad (1)$$

where i and j are the voxel indicates, ρ stands for Pearson correlation coefficient of the activity of the voxels, and Θ is a threshold parameter picked between 0.1 and 1. Fig. 2 depicts fragments of the correlation matrices before thresholding.

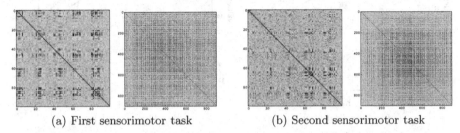

(a) First sensorimotor task   (b) Second sensorimotor task

Fig. 2. The fragments of the correlation matrices for the sensorimotor tasks

We can now proceed to the definition of the functional activity multigraph $G = (V, E)$. The number of the vertices is equal to the number of voxels in D, and each vertex is labelled with coordinates of the corresponding voxel. Between vertices labelled as a and b, there is an edge with a weight equal to $Adj(a, b)$, iff $Adj(a, b) > 0$. Note, that for some thresholds Θ, the obtained graph may not be connected. In that case, as a resulting graph G we assign its maximal connected component, so $|V| \leq n$; see the first two columns of the Table 1 for examples.

The vertex degree distributions of the functional graphs, obtained from described data for thresholds $\Theta = 0.7$ and $\Theta = 0.9$ are given in Fig. 3. We note that they obey a power law formula, which is in agreement with results of Eguiluz et al., see [7], although the threshold values are slightly higher in our case.

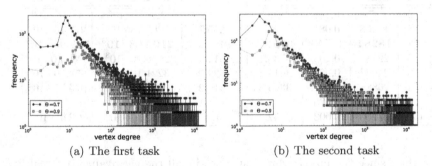

(a) The first task   (b) The second task

Fig. 3. Vertex degree distribution of the functional brain network during the sensorimotor tasks for the two thresholds $\Theta = 0.7$, and $\Theta = 0.9$

We are interested in computing the *spectrum* spec(Adj), that is the set of all eigenvalues of the adjacency matrix:

$$\text{spec}\,(Adj) = \{\lambda \in \mathbb{C} : \exists_x \in \mathbb{C}^n, \quad \text{such that } Adj \cdot x = \lambda \cdot x\}. \tag{2}$$

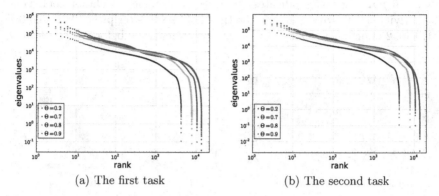

(a) The first task   (b) The second task

Fig. 4. Spectra of the functional brain networks during the sensorimotor tasks for various thresholds Θ

Table 1. Statistics of the positive values of the spectra of the two fMRI datasets (the first and second sensorimotor task, respectively), for varying threshold. Columns from the leftmost denote: threshold, size of the network, minimum eigenvalue, average, median, maximum eigenvalue, variance

Θ	Size	min	mean	median	max	variance
0.9	3544	0.882	1029.1	533.5	$62.87 \cdot 10^3$	$4.74 \cdot 10^6$
0.8	10545	0.150	1739.5	717.8	$327.43 \cdot 10^3$	$32.30 \cdot 10^6$
0.7	**16435**	**0.199**	**2375.4**	**949.4**	**$682.98 \cdot 10^3$**	**$85.87 \cdot 10^6$**
0.6	21084	0.029	2879.5	1210.9	$1052.26 \cdot 10^3$	$160.05 \cdot 10^6$
0.5	24541	0.051	3248.5	1489.4	$1413.60 \cdot 10^3$	$250.33 \cdot 10^6$
0.4	26919	0.085	3426.2	1705.5	$1758.03 \cdot 10^3$	$351.79 \cdot 10^6$
0.3	27200	0.000	3580.5	1952.9	$2082.54. \cdot 10^3$	$490.56 \cdot 10^6$
0.2	27200	0.034	3176.1	1577.9	$2372.76 \cdot 10^3$	$599.33 \cdot 10^6$
0.9	6770	0.111	2118.8	779.4	$329.58 \cdot 10^3$	$48.37 \cdot 10^6$
0.8	13268	0.081	3420.0	1255.7	$1268.18 \cdot 10^3$	$272.40 \cdot 10^6$
0.7	**18284**	**0.099**	**3751.7**	**1466.1**	**$2107.08 \cdot 10^3$**	**$509.93 \cdot 10^6$**
0.6	22184	0.105	3739.1	1512.3	$2746.26 \cdot 10^3$	$698.150 \cdot 10^6$
0.5	24967	0.080	3614.3	1522.9	$3221.10 \cdot 10^3$	$853.56 \cdot 10^6$
0.4	26888	0.011	3343.6	1416.2	$3563.98 \cdot 10^3$	$976.57 \cdot 10^6$
0.3	27200	0.025	3098.1	1337.1	$3799.74 \cdot 10^3$	$1.138 \cdot 10^9$
0.2	27200	0.003	2552.4	907.1	$3950.20 \cdot 10^3$	$1.240 \cdot 10^9$

Note that, since the matrix *Adj* is symmetric, all the eigenvalues are real, i. e. spec $(Adj) \subset \mathbb{R}$, see [6]. The resulting positive eigenvalues were sorted decreasingly and showed in the loglog plots, see Fig. 4. The plots of the spectra for the thresholds $\Theta = 0.3, 0.4, 0.5, 0.6$ are almost overlapping with the results for threshold $\Theta = 0.7$, therefore they are omitted.

The statistics for positive eigenvalues of the resulting graphs are summarized in the Table 1. Interestingly, for larger threshold values the plots exhibit small fluctuation toward developing a power law dependency in the middle part, and than truncate exponentially. The segment of this behaviour is quite small but noticeable, especially for $\Theta = 0.7$.

The exact threshold value Θ needs to be adjusted 'manually'. Threshold values selected too strictly may cause removal of vital edges, too generously may preserve unused resources and, in the end, yield a structural, rather than functional graph. In both of the cases the resulting functional network tend to lose its critical properties. Similar loss of criticality outside fixed control parameter was observed in [9], but also fMRI-based researches focus solely on the values, that yield critical state, see for an instance [7].

3   Spectra of Activation-Flow-Based Model

The prohibitive complexity of the brain dynamics drew us to design a simplified model, which is able to mimic at least some of its characteristic features in the graph-theoretical terms. The activation-flow model, discussed in [13], already turned out to develop a scale-free degree dependency (*ibidem.*) as well as some features, which are typical for the small-world graphs, see [12].

In a nutshell, the model consists of a number of *abstract neurons* $v \in \mathcal{V}$ described by their spatial locations and accumulated *activity* $\sigma_v \in \mathbb{N}_{\geq 0}$. The neurons are connected with symmetric *synapses* with the probability proportional to $|v_1, v_2|^{-\alpha}$, where v_1, v_2 are neurons to be connected, $|-,-|$ is Euclidean distance, and α is a *decay exponent*. We denote the set of synapses by $\mathcal{E}$. Each connection has its gaussian-drawn *weight* $w_{uv} \in \mathbb{R}$, which indicates its excitatory ($w_{uv} > 0$) or inhibitory ($w_{uv} < 0$) nature. The activity is allowed to be moved between the neurons within following constraints: it cannot be negative ($\forall_{v \in \mathcal{V}} \ \sigma_v \geq 0$) and its total sum is constant $\sum_{v \in \mathcal{V}} \ \sigma_v = Const$. The constant total activity mimics the critical state of the network, so that it neither vanishes nor explodes, see [4]. As a result we can describe the state of the network by its *activity configuration* $\bar{\sigma} = [\sigma_v]_{v \in \mathcal{V}}$. We define an *energy function* $E : \mathbb{Z}^{|\mathcal{V}|} \to \mathbb{R}$ on this configuration space as follows

$$E(\bar{\sigma}) = \sum_{\{v_1, v_2\} \in \mathcal{E}} w_{v_1 v_2} |\sigma_{v_1} - \sigma_{v_2}|. \tag{3}$$

If the energy is to be minimized, we can see that two neurons connected with positive weight (excitatory) synapse shall tend to share similar levels of activity, while those connected with inhibitory one ($w_{v_1 v_2} < 0$) will prefer high differences in accumulated σ-s (high activity in v_1 silences v_2).

The activity is allowed to flow around the network through synapses according to a stochastic, energy-driven dynamics. At each timestep of the evolution, a single unit of activity is transferred between a pair of neurons, which can be read as a change form configuration $\bar{\sigma}$ to $\bar{\sigma}'$. If such transfer reduces the energy, than it is unconditionally accepted. Otherwise (when $E(\bar{\sigma}') - E(\bar{\sigma}) > 0$) it is accepted with probability exponentially decaying with the growth of the energy. The evolution is run until the network reaches a stable state of the activity configuration, or for

a predefined number of time steps. It is not difficult to see relations to the Boltzmann machines dynamics [1], except for adjustments to account for multi-state
(rather than binary) neurons. The time-scale of the simulation can be roughly
estimated as 10^9 iterations/$(10^4$neurons $\cdot 10^3 \frac{1}{s}$(spiking frequency)) $\simeq 10^2 s$. The
estimation is rather crude, but puts the model somewhere nearby the time of
fMRI scans, see Sec 2.

Let d_{uv} denote the total number of accepted transfers of activity from u to v,
which occurred during the dynamics. Define a *spike-flow* or *functional activity-
flow graph* of the system as a subgraph of $(\mathcal{V}, \mathcal{G})$ with multiple edges induced by
these synapses of $\mathcal{E}$, which had a vital number of transferred units of activity,
that is $\mathcal{G}_1 := (\mathcal{V}, \mathcal{E}_1)$, where $\mathcal{E}_1 = \{e = \{u, v\} \in \mathcal{E} : d_{uv} + d_{vu} \geq \theta\}$, with
θ standing for a threshold parameter. Note that, the thresholding parameter
θ (lower-case), while has a similar meaning of removal unused resources as in
section 2, denoted by capital Θ, but not necessarily the same value and they
should not be confused. The edge multiplicities in the functional graphs are
equal to the the total activity with flew through the synapse, in other words for
$e = \{uv\}$ we have

$$M(e) := \begin{cases} d_{uv} + d_{vu} & \text{if } e \in \mathcal{E}_1 \\ 0 & \text{otherwise.} \end{cases} \tag{4}$$

Recall that the theoretical analyses of spectra for alike model with deterministic
winner-take-all dynamics and in full graphs were studied by Schreiber [15], who
predicted what i-th principal eigenvalue of the graph should behave as $\frac{c}{i^2}$. Numerical results concerning of activation flow model were studied in [14] and to
some extend confirmed this power law-scaling though with an exponential cut-off
of the eigenvalue tail. Interestingly, spectra of recurrent networks with fully connected graph (unlike geometrically-dependent, as in this work) also confirmed
similar scaling, but among small number of principal eigenvalues only, see [11].

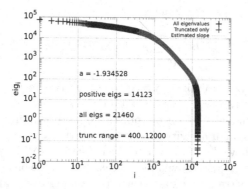

Fig. 5. Log-log plot of the spectrum of the functional graph in activation-flow model,
i-th eigenvalue vs i. Eigenvalues are sorted decreasingly. The highlighted middle part of
the plot indicates a power scaling ($eig_i \propto i^{-2}$). The network consists of approx. $2 \cdot 10^4$
neurons.

Table 2. Simple statistics of the spectrum of the AF model for varying sample sizes. Columns from the leftmost denote: size of the network (number of neurons), minimum positive eigenvalue, mean, median, maximum eigenvalue, variance.

Size	min	mean	median	max	variance
3048	.133	815.3	256.4	11694.2	$1.7 \cdot 10^6$
3754	.074	960.5	267.3	18015.7	$2.8 \cdot 10^6$
4557	.006	953.2	264.8	13209.6	$2.8 \cdot 10^6$
12530	.040	1962.2	301.6	54041.2	$1.9 \cdot 10^7$
21460	.026	2298.1	287.7	74826.1	$3.3 \cdot 10^7$

The plot of i-th eigenvalue vs. i is depicted in Fig 5. In addition Tab. 2 summarizes the basic statistics of the spectra for various data, though we note, that such statistics can be highly misleading when compared directly. Indeed, entries in adjacency matrix depend of threshold θ and number of transfers d_e, and one might expect that the latter is proportional to the total number of activity in the network (the more total activity is, the more transfers can occur). It is not difficult to see, that if the total sum of σ-s is increased c times than we have: $(Ac) \cdot x = (Ax) \cdot c = (\lambda x) \cdot c = (\lambda c) \cdot x$. So when the initial activity is multiplied by constant c, than the eigenvalues are also multiplied by c. As a result we conclude that the simple numerical statistics, however interesting, might be deceiving and one should look at the whole shape of the spectrum. In particular, since the power-law-formula distribution X^p, does not have a finite second moment for $p \geq -3$ and even first moment for $p \geq -2$, both mean and variance can be highly misleading statistics.

4   Discussion

Before proceeding to direct comparison we first briefly provide the spectral properties of the best-known graph models, adapted in large scale networks.

First we would like to recall Erdős-Rényi graph model [8], which for a given set of vertices and the probability $p \in (0..1)$ randomly and independently includes each of possible $\binom{n}{2}$ edges into the final graph with probability p: $\mathbb{P}(\{u, v\} \in \mathcal{E}) = p$.

Next random graph to be discussed is a Watts-Strogatz model [16]. Starting from n vertices organized into a ring, each connected with k nearest neighbours, every edge is randomly rewired with probability $p \in [0..1]$. Clearly for $p = 0$ the resulting graph is an unaltered initial periodic lattice, while for $p = 1$ one obtains random ER-graph.

Last of the graph models, to be discussed, was designed by Albert and Barabasi [2]. The construction procedure begins with small clique and iteratively adds new vertices (v_i in i-th step) into the graph, each connected to m existing nodes picked selectively: $\mathbb{P}(\{v_i, u\} \in \mathcal{E}) = \frac{deg(u)}{\sum_{w \in \mathcal{V}} deg(w)}$. The growth is terminated upon reaching desired network size.

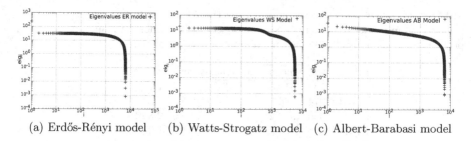

(a) Erdős-Rényi model   (b) Watts-Strogatz model   (c) Albert-Barabasi model

Fig. 6. Reference spectra of ER, WS and AB random graphs

Spectra of above reference models are presented in Fig. 6. One should note here, that all the reference models are unweighted single-edge graphs, while the discussed activation-flow model is clearly a multigraph. However, there is a shortage of random graph models, which would account for edge multiplicity.

Nonetheless, the shapes of the spectra clearly distinct from obtained functional graph in activation flow model as well as fMRI-obtained network. It seems to be a foregone conclusion in the case of Erdős-Rényi and Watts-Strogatz models, as the obey binomial degree distribution sequences, while the AF model and fMRI turned out to obey a power low decay [13]. The shapes are also different for Albert-Barabasi model, despite the fact that this one is known to reproduce graphs with power law-degree sequences [2]. Interestingly, the fMRI results seem to be able to partially replicate some fluctuations in shape of the Watts-Strogatz spectrum. WS graphs for the probability parameter $10^{-3} < p < 10^{-1}$ are known to be *small-world graphs* (see [16]), but their degree distribution is approximately binomial. We conclude that the obtained spectra are unlike any of the described random graph models, though perhaps random multigraph models would turn out more accurate in predicting.

Instead, as discussed in Section 2, for the threshold value $\Theta = 0.7$ the obtained fMRI functional graphs exhibit a developed power law decay of eigenvalues again in their middle part and than a clear exponential truncation of the eigenvalues. Interestingly, this feature is strikingly similar to one returned by functional graphs of the activation flow model. Somehow unsettling, the segment of validity of such scaling is significantly smaller for fMRI graphs, for the model from Sec. 3 this value was numerically estimated at the 60%, see [14].

Additionally, recall that both functional networks obey a power-law degree distribution, and they share roughly similar way of extraction of the functional network. The statistics, as shortlisted in Tables 1 and 2 follow generally the same tendency, although vary between exact values by even an order of magnitude. However we note that, the power-law distributions may not have finite second or even first moments (see Fig. 7), so one must be careful when inferring just by these values.

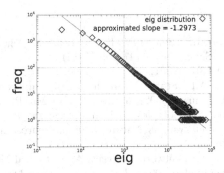

Fig. 7. Empirical distribution of the positive eigenvalues of the model discussed in Sec. 3. Bean lengths are approximately 75 units wide and the plot consists of 1000 beans. Each bean is marked with rhombus, rather than a bar due to log-plot issues. Approximated slope, was fit with least-squares.

5   Conclusion

To conclude, we compared fMRI imagings with artificial model of neural activity in the terms of shape of the eigenvalues of the functional network. We clearly ruled out random graphs of type Erdős and Rényi, Watts-Strogatz or preferential attachment as equivalent model. Instead, the complex dynamics and resource thresholding turn out to be able to reproduce similar results. We still miss an answer whether the power-law scaling should be truncated at some point as the results seem to suggest, or it is just an artefact stemming from small sample size.

In this paper we extend the functional brain network analysis with the spectral properties. Moreover, we compare the spectral properties of functional brain network obtained from freely accessed fMRI data, with artificial models, including activation-flow model, developed in [13]. In the further work it would be interesting to compare the fMRI graph and the functional activity-flow graph in the terms of graph spectral distance (see [10]). Moreover, one can describe the differences between these graphs, using spectral reconstruction techniques, see [5]. This approach can enhance the structure of the functional activity-flow graph to better simulate the behaviour of human brain.

Acknowledgment. The work has been supported by Ministry of Science and Higher Education research grant DEC-2011/01/N/ST6/01931.

Data used for this study were downloaded from the Function BIRN Data Repository   (`http://fbirnbdr.nbirn.net:8080/BDR/`),   supported   by grants to the Function BIRN (U24-RR021992) Testbed funded by the National Centre for Research Resources at the National Institutes of Health, U.S.A.

References

1. Ackley, D.H., Hinton, G.E., Sejnowski, T.J.: A Learning Algorithm for Boltzmann Machines. Cognitive Science 9(1), 147–169 (1985), doi:10.1016/S0364-0213(85)80012-4
2. Albert, R., Barabasi, A.L.: Statistical mechanics of complex networks. Reviews of Modern Physics 74 (January 2002), doi:10.1103/RevModPhys.74.47
3. Bullmore, E., Sporns, O.: Complex brain networks: graph theoretical analysis of structural and functional systems. Nature Reviews, Neuroscience 10 (March 2009), doi:10.1038/nrn2575
4. Chialvo, D.: Critical brain networks. Physica A: Statistical Mechanics and its Applications 340(4) (September 2004), doi:10.1016/j.physa.2004.05.064
5. Comellas, F., Diaz-Lopez, J.: Spectral reconstruction of complex networks. Physica A: Statistical Mechanics and its Applications 387(25), 6436–6442 (2008), doi:10.1016/j.physa.2008.07.032
6. Cvetković, D., Rowlingson, P., Simić, S.: Eigenspaces of graphs. Cambridge University Press (1997)
7. Eguiluz, V., Chialvo, D., Cecchi, G., Baliki, M., Apkarian, V.: Scale-free brain functional networks. Physical Review Letters PRL 94, 018102 (2005), doi:10.1103/PhysRevLett.94.018102
8. Erdős, P., Rényi, A.: On random graphs I. Publ. Math. Debrecen 6, 290–297 (1959)
9. Fraiman, D., Balenzuela, P., Foss, J., Chialvo, D.R.: Ising-like dynamics in large-scale functional brain networks. Physical Review E 79(6) (June 2009), doi:10.1103/PhysRevE.79.061922
10. Jovanović, I., Stanić, A.: Spectral distances of graphs. Linear Algebra and its Applications 436(5), 1425–1435 (2012), doi:10.1016/j.laa.2011.08.019
11. Piekniewski, F.: Spectra of the Spike Flow Graphs of Recurrent Neural Networks. In: Alippi, C., Polycarpou, M., Panayiotou, C., Ellinas, G. (eds.) ICANN 2009, Part II. LNCS, vol. 5769, pp. 603–612. Springer, Heidelberg (2009)
12. Piersa, J.: Diameter of the spike-flow graphs of geometrical neural networks. In: Wyrzykowski, R., Dongarra, J., Karczewski, K., Waśniewski, J. (eds.) PPAM 2011, Part I. LNCS, vol. 7203, pp. 511–520. Springer, Heidelberg (2012)
13. Piersa, J., Piekniewski, F., Schreiber, T.: Theoretical model for mesoscopic-level scale-free self-organization of functional brain networks. IEEE Transactions on Neural Networks 21(11) (2010), doi:10.1109/TNN.2010.2066989
14. Piersa, J., Schreiber, T.: Spectra of the Spike-Flow Graphs in Geometrically Embedded Neural Networks. In: Rutkowski, L., Korytkowski, M., Scherer, R., Tadeusiewicz, R., Zadeh, L.A., Zurada, J.M. (eds.) ICAISC 2012, Part I. LNCS, vol. 7267, pp. 143–151. Springer, Heidelberg (2012)
15. Schreiber, T.: Spectra of winner-take-all stochastic neural networks, arXiv (2010), http://arxiv.org/abs/0810.3193v2
16. Watts, D., Strogatz, S.: Collective dynamics of 'small-world' networks. Nature 393, 440–442 (1998), doi:10.1038/30918

A Multi-objective Subtractive FCM Based TSK Fuzzy System with Input Selection, and Its Application to Dynamic Inverse Modelling of MR Dampers

Mohsen Askari, Jianchan Li, and Bijan Samali

Center for Built Infrastructure Research,
University of Technology Sydney, Australia
{mohsen.askari,jianchun.li,bijan.samali}@uts.edu.au

Abstract. A new encoding scheme is presented for a fuzzy-based nonlinear system identification methodology, using the subtractive Fuzzy C-Mean clustering and a modified version of non-dominated sorting genetic algorithm. This method is able to automatically select the best inputs as well as the structure of the fuzzy model such as rules and membership functions. Moreover, three objective functions are considered to satisfy both accuracy and compactness of the model. The proposed method is then employed to identify the inverse model of a highly nonlinear structural control device, namely Magnetorheological (MR) damper. It is shown that the developed evolving Takagi–Sugeno-Kang (TSK) fuzzy model can identify and grasp the nonlinear dynamics of inverse systems very well, while a small number of inputs and fuzzy rules are required for this purpose.

Keywords: TSK fuzzy system, inverse modelling, MR damper, Subtractive clustering, Fuzzy C-Mean Clustering.

1 Introduction

Structural control shows great potential for reducing vibrations in various civil structures under dynamic loading. Magneto-Rheological (MR) dampers are one of the most promising new devices that are widely used as semi-active control devises. Therefore, and for the purpose of modelling and simulation, a forward model of MR damper is needed. Recently, inverse model of MR damper is also used in conjunction with classical controller to convert the desired force to a proper voltage to be sent to MR damper [1]. However, the hysteretic behaviour of nonlinear dynamical friction mechanism of the MR fluid, makes the identification of both forward and inverse model of this semi-active device significantly difficult.

The Takagi–Sugeno-Kang (TSK) fuzzy model uses IF–THEN rules to approximate a wide class of nonlinear systems by fuzzy blending of local linear approximations. This method employs linear models in the consequent part of the Fuzzy System (FS). The schematic structure of a T–S fuzzy model is shown in Figure 1.

L. Rutkowski et al. (Eds.): ICAISC 2013, Part I, LNAI 7894, pp. 215–226, 2013.

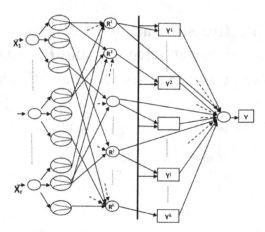

Fig. 1. Structure of a TSK Fuzzy Model (**r:** number of inputs; **k:** number of rules)

Various methods, such as clustering algorithms, linear least squares and nonlinear optimisation methods are used for tuning of antecedent and consequent parameters of the FS [2, 3]. To accommodate new input data, adaptive online learning of TSK fuzzy models has been developed in [4]. From another point of view, the design of a fuzzy model can be formulated as a search problem in an appropriate multidimensional space, where every point represents a possible fuzzy model. Due to the capability of search within irregular and multidimensional spaces, evolutionary algorithms (EAs), such as GA and evolutionary strategies have been extensively used.

In conventional EA-based fuzzy modelling methods, the structure of the FS, e.g., the suitable inputs, are prescribed and parameters of the rules and MFs are optimized. [5]. However, selecting the most relevant inputs, among numerous possible options, is an important and challenging problem for construction of an FS. Therefore, some studies on finding the best possible combination of relevant inputs are reported [2, 6]. However such encoding scheme, deals with a large number of to-be-tuned parameters, causing a huge computational burden and hence making the optimization process very time consuming. Furthermore, application of such method requires a good knowledge on the expected bounds of every parameter at the outset of the design, which may not be available. On the other hand, the excessive number of inputs and rules, not only affects the compactness and transparency of the underlying model, but also increases the complexity of the computations necessary for real-time implementation of the resulting model.

In order to develop an accurate, yet compact FS, in this paper, an evolving TSK fuzzy model is introduced. The proposed method is based on subtractive clustering technique combined with fuzzy c-mean clustering method (FCM) and a new modified version of non-dominated sorting genetic algorithm (MNSGAII). For this purpose, an encoding scheme, using a bi-section chromosome is introduced. The first section of the chromosome encodes the selected inputs and the second one encodes the rules and the MFs parameters. The best chromosome is searched and evolved through the MNSGAII with three objective functions, i.e., number of inputs, number of rules and RMS error between the target and predicted outputs.

2   Preliminaries

2.1   TSK Fuzzy Structure

Most neural fuzzy systems employ the inference method proposed by Mamdani in which the consequent parts are defined by fuzzy sets. A Mamdani-type fuzzy rule has the form:

$$If\ x_1\ is\ A_{1j}(m_{1j}, \sigma_{1j})\ and\ x_2\ is\ A_{2j}(m_{2j}, \sigma_{2j}) \dots and\ x_n\ is\ A_{nj}(m_{nj}, \sigma_{nj})$$
$$THEN\ y\ is\ B_j(m_j, \sigma_j).$$

where m_{ij} and σ_{ij} represent a Gaussian membership function with mean and deviation, respectively, of the ith dimension and the jth rule node. The consequent B_j of the jth rule is aggregated into one fuzzy set for the output variable y. In addition, Takagi, Sugeno and Kang introduced a modified inference scheme which in the first two parts of the fuzzy inference process, fuzzifying the inputs and applying the fuzzy operator, are exactly same as Mamdani model [7]. However, instead of fuzzy sets being used, the conclusion part of a rule in TSK fuzzy model, is a linear combination of the crisp inputs, as follows:

$$If\ x_1\ is\ A_{1j}(m_{1j}, \sigma_{1j})\ and\ x_2\ is\ A_{2j}(m_{2j}, \sigma_{2j}) \dots and\ x_n\ is\ A_{nj}(m_{nj}, \sigma_{nj})$$
$$THEN\ y = w_{0j} + w_{1j}x_1 + \dots + w_{nj}x_n$$

where m_{ij} and σ_{ij} represent a Gaussian membership function with mean and deviation, respectively, of the ith dimension and the jth rule node. Since the consequent of a rule is crisp, the defuzzification step becomes obsolete in the TSK inference scheme. Instead, the model output is computed as the weighted average of the crisp rule outputs. This computation is less expensive than calculating the center of gravity.

2.2   Subtractive Clustering

The subtractive clustering algorithm considers each of the available data points as a possible candidate for the centres of the data clusters. For this purpose, a matrix consisting of n sets of m-dimensional input–output data, $\{x_1, .., x_n\}$, normalized within the hypercube of dimension M is considered.

The density measure for every data point, xi, is defined as

$$D_i = \sum_{j=1}^{n} \exp\left(-\frac{\|x_i - x_j\|^2}{(r_a/2)^2}\right), \tag{1}$$

where, $\| \ \|$ denotes the Euclidean distance and r_a is the prescribed radius of the hyperspheres, within which the neighbouring points are considered to be more important than the others. Hence, a data point will have a high density value if it has many neighboring data points. The data point, x_{C_1}, with the highest density, D_{C_1}, is then selected as the first cluster centre.

In order to select the next cluster centre, the data points near the first cluster centre, x_{C_1}, should be forced to be less important. For this purpose, the modified densities are defined as:

$$D_{mi} = D_i - D_{C_1} \exp\left(-\frac{\|x_i - x_{C_1}\|^2}{(r_b/2)^2}\right). \tag{2}$$

The constant r_b specifies a neighbourhood of x_{C_1} where the modified density must become smaller. Generally, r_b should be selected larger than r_a, e.g. $1.5r_a$ (Chiu 1994). Now, the next data point, x_{C_2}, with the largest modified density is selected as the next cluster centre, and so on.

2.3   FCM Based TSK Model Identification

Fuzzy C-Mean is one of the strongest clustering algorithms that can be used to identify the clusters. The objective function of the FCM is defined by:

$$J_b(U, Z) = \sum_{i=1}^{c} \sum_{k=1}^{N} (\mu_{ik})^m \|x_k - z_i\|^2, \tag{3}$$

where x_k denotes the point in data space, $k = 1, 2,..., N$; N denotes the number of data points; Z_i stands for the final cluster center, $i = 1, 2,..., c$; c corresponds to the number of fuzzy rules; $\mu_{ik} \in [0,1]$ is the fuzzy membership degree of the kth data pair pertaining to the ith fuzzy subset.

It is assumed that μ_{ik} is constrained with following equation:

$$\sum_{i=1}^{c} \mu_{ik} = 1, \ k = 1, 2, ..., N. \tag{4}$$

The C-means algorithm for clustering in n dimensions produces C-means vectors that present c classes of data. The problem of finding the fuzzy clusters in the data set is now solved as a constrained optimization problem using FCM algorithm, considering the minimization of the function in Eq.(3) over the domain data set and taking into account the constrains in Eq.(4). The results of FCM imply the clustering centers together with the corresponding membership degrees. The main steps for identifying the TSK fuzzy model based on FCM are given as follows:

Step 1:   Given c, m, and the initial clustering centers for all $k = 1, 2,..., N$ and $i = 1, 2,..., c$. Set an initial fuzzy c-partition matrix $U = [\mu_{ik}]$ to indicate the membership value for the ith cluster representatives.

Step 2: Calculate the following equation:

$$z_i = \frac{\sum_{k=1}^{N} z_k (\mu_{ik})^m}{\sum_{k=1}^{N} (\mu_{ik})^m}, \ i = 1, 2, ..., c \tag{5}$$

Step 3 Update U to adjust

$$\mu_{ik} = \left[\sum_{j=1}^{c} \left(\frac{x_k - Z_i}{x_k - Z_j}\right)^{\frac{2}{m-1}}\right]^{-1} \tag{6}$$

Step 4 Check for termination. If

$$\|U_k - U_{k-1}\| < \varepsilon \tag{7}$$

stop; otherwise, let $k = k + 1$ and return to step 2.

Step 5: Identify the consequent parameters using orthogonal leas squares (OLS) method. We have:

$$y = \emptyset\theta \tag{8}$$

where $\emptyset = [\beta_1, ..., \beta_n, \beta_1 x_1, ..., \beta_n x_1, ..., \beta_1 x_m, ..., \beta_n x_m$,and $\theta = [p_0^1, ..., p_m^1, p_0^2, ..., p_m^2, p_0^n, ..., p_m^n]^T$ signifies the consequent parameters.

In regard to the least squares solutions,

$$\theta = (\emptyset^T \emptyset)^{-1} \emptyset^T y. \tag{9}$$

Here we convert $[\emptyset^T \emptyset]$ into an orthogonal matrix $[W^T W]$. By implementing iteration and conversion algorithms, the $(m + 1) \times n$ coupled equations become mutually independent, thereby calculating the consequent parameters θ.

2.4   Modified Non-dominated Sorting Genetic Algorithm II for Optimization of Integer-Real Parameters Handling

Genetic algorithms (GAs) are general purpose population based stochastic search techniques which mimic the principles of natural selection and genetics laid down by Charles Darwin. The way the variables are coded is clearly essential for GAs' efficiency. Real coded genetic algorithms (RCGAs), which use real numbers for encoding, have fast convergence towards optimal than binary and grey coded GAs. Also, RCGAs overcomes the difficulty of ''Hamming Cliff'' as in binary coded GAs.

In the case when, the adjustable parameters are integer, many applications of GAs are available in the literature, some of them use binary coded GA while some others use real coded representation. Recently, a robust GA namely MI-LXPM, for solving integer and mixed integer nonlinear programming problems is introduced by Kusum Deep et.al [8]. The proposed algorithm however uses a single objective function. In this paper, the main features of MI-LXPM, including Laplace Crossover, Power Mutation together with the truncation procedure for handling the integer parameters have been adopted into one of the most common multi objective GA, Non-Dominated Sorting Genetic Algorithm type II (NSGAII) to find a non-dominated sorting Pareto front for designing an accurate and compact TSK fuzzy inverse model of MR damper.

3   Proposed Hybrid Learning Algorithm

As outlined before, subtractive clustering can be used for initial estimation of the number of clusters as well as the centers. In order to find the efficient clusters for each dimension, m, in the input space, the only variable parameter that must be chosen appropriately is the neighbourhood radius r_{am}. Furthermore, to design an accurate yet compact model, a minimal number of inputs which are the most relevant ones to the model should be selected carefully. To this end, the aforementioned genetic algorithm is used to intelligently select the required inputs as well as the initial clusters to be modified by FCM to obtain an accurate and concise TSK fuzzy model.

3.1   Genetic Encoding Scheme

All the inputs in m dimensions are considered to be involved into the fuzzy model for which the corresponding r_as are incorporated into a single chromosome, as shown in Figure 2. The length of the chromosome, representing the fuzzy model, would then be equal to 2n+1, where n is the number of candidate inputs.

The first part of chromosome indicates the selected inputs, where the value 1 in each gene shows that the corresponding input is used in the fuzzy model and then the corresponding r_a in the second part of chromosome is searched for. If the value of 0 is assigned to the gene m in the first part, it means that the proposed input would not be selected and hence the gene n+ m in the next part is irrelevant.

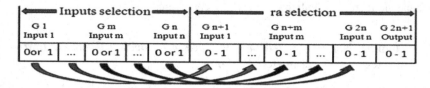

Fig. 2. Encoding scheme for individual chromosomes

Based on the encoding scheme proposed above, the proposed TSK fuzzy learning algorithm is developed as follows:

Step 1: Encode all the parameters into one chromosome using the proposed encoding scheme.

Step 2: Generate the initial population of the chromosomes.

Step 3: Find the initial clusters from the collected data using subtractive clustering method and based on the selected inputs and their corresponding neighbourhood radius values of each chromosome.

Step 4: Update the clusters by FCM for each chromosome (Use the number and the initial cluster's centers achieved in step 3).

Step 5: Derive a TSK fuzzy model out of each chromosome, using the proposed obtained clusters in step 4 and least squares estimator.

Step 6: Based on the resulting rules, fuzzy input structure and the MF parameters, for every chromosome, evaluate three objective functions, namely, *the number of inputs, the number of rules* and *the modelling RMSE*. In fact, considering the first two factors as objective functions leads us to have a concise model while the last objective function is the representative of accuracy and can be computed from the following equation, where L is the number of data points, $\hat{Y}$ is the predicted output and Y is the target output:

$$J_{RMSE} = \sqrt{\frac{1}{L} \sum_{i=1}^{n} (Y_i - \hat{Y}_i)^2} \tag{10}$$

Step 7: Rank all the chromosomes based on the objective function values.

Step 8: Choose parents using tournament selection method, to be used in the next step for crossover and mutation.

Step 9: Perform Laplace crossover and mutation operators to the parents to generate new set of individuals called off-springs.

Step 10: Evaluate the objective function of the new individuals and rank them. Steps 3-8 will be repeated for a fixed number of generations. The final answer is the chromosome whose objective function is smaller in the last generation.

4   Inverse Model of MR Damper Using the Proposed Learning Algorithm

In this section, the proposed evolving TSK fuzzy modelling approach is applied to develop a model of inverse behaviour of MR damper. This is a challenging problem due to the inherent hysteretic and highly nonlinear dynamics of the MR damper.

Forward dynamics of MR damper, provides the force exerted on the two sides of the MR damper, under a given displacement and subject to a known command voltage. Conversely, the inverse dynamics, useful for semi-active vibration control, provides the required voltage input for generating a specific control force, under a specified displacement scenario. Numerical inverse solution of the complicated non-linear equations of an MR damper is difficult and time consuming, and hence, unsuitable for the purpose of control design. Therefore, it is important to establish a fast, fuzzy inverse model, which can directly predict the required input voltage. In this paper the data for training the proposed fuzzy model are collected from the simulation of the mathematical model for the MR damper proposed by Spencer et al.

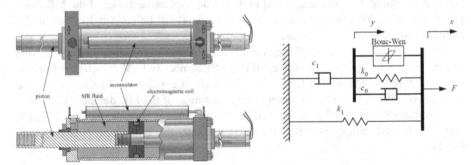

Fig. 3. A typical MR Damper (left), Proposed Mechanical Model of the MR Damper used in data collection (right)

4.1   Data Collection

In order to obtain a high quality trained fuzzy model, high quality training and testing data must be collected first. To make the identified model fully represent the underlying system, the training samples should cover all possible combinations and ranges of input variation in which the MR damper will operate. This is to ensure that the TSK model trained by these samples can accurately represent the behaviour of the MR damper.

Spencer et al. (1997) proposed a new phenomenological model based on a Bouce–Wen hysteresis model for a prototype MR damper developed by the Lord Corporation. The simple mechanical model of the MR damper is shown in Figure 3 and is governed by the following complex equations:

$$F = c_1 \dot{y} + k_1 (x - x_0) \tag{11}$$

$$\dot{y} = \frac{1}{c_0 + c_1} [\alpha z + c_0 \dot{x} + k_0 (x - y)] \tag{12}$$

$$\dot{z} = -\gamma |\dot{x} - \dot{y}| z |z|^{n-1} - \beta (\dot{x} - \dot{y}) |z|^n + A(\dot{x} - \dot{y}) \tag{13}$$

$$\alpha = \alpha_a + \alpha_b u \tag{14}$$

$$c_1 = c_{1_a} + c_{1_b} u \tag{15}$$

$$c_0 = c_{1_a} + c_{1_b} u \tag{16}$$

$$\dot{u} = -\eta(u - v) \tag{17}$$

According to the model shown in Figure 3, the force, f, of the damper is obtained if the patterns of displacement x and voltage v are prescribed. However, most of the time, it is hard to have access to a clean displacement signal. On the other hand, installing the accelerometers into the structure is easy and therefore the acceleration signal is available. For this reason and to derive an applicable model of the MR damper, the acceleration data as well as the voltage data will be collected in this study, from the aforementioned mathematical model.

A set of typical parameters of the 1000kN MR damper is presented in Table 1. Note that the maximum operational voltage of this MR damper is 10 V, which is defined as the saturation voltage of the damper and is obtained experimentally. Moreover, the situation of 0 V will also be common during operation of the MR damper. Therefore, range of the voltage signal is set as 0–10 V, in this paper. Likewise, the displacement range of the MR damper is ±20 cm while its frequency ranges from approximately 0–5 Hz.

Table 1. Typical Parameters of a 1000kN MR Damper

Parameter	Values	Parameters	Values
c_{0_a} (N s/cm)	110.0	α_a (N/cm)	46.2
c_{0_b} (N s/cm V)	114.3	α_b (N/cm V)	41.2
k_0 (N/cm)	0.002	γ (cm^{-2})	164.0
c_{1_a} (N s/cm)	8359.2	β (cm^{-2})	164.0
c_{1_b} (N s/cm)	7482.9	A	1107.2
k_1 (N/cm)	0.0097	n	2
x_0 (cm)	0	η (s^{-1})	100

Signals of generated accelaration and voltage for training the fuzzy model are shown in Figure 4. A time step of 0.005 second is used to produce a total of 10,000 data set through 50s simulation.

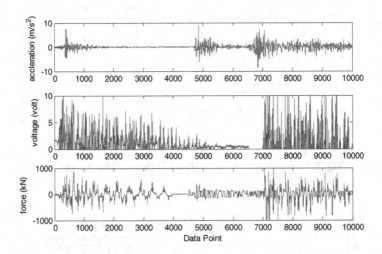

Fig. 4. Collected Data

4.2   Inverse Model of MR Damper

In this section, a TSK inverse model of MR damper has been obtained using the proposed method in pervious section.

For the current study, it is assumed that the input vector for the TSK fuzzy model consists of 16 input variables. The 16 candidates to the model include the past and current accelerations $acc(t - 13), acc(t - 12), acc(t - 11), ..., acc(t - 1), acc(t)$, as well as forces $f(t-1)$ and $f(t)$ where t denotes the time step. The output is the predicted voltage v(t). Figure 5 shows the final obtained Pareto front. As can be seen, there is a trade-off between model complexity and accuracy. It must be mentioned that, if the complexity is not very important for the designer, the point with the minimum RMS error can be selected as the final solution or the optimization can be run with the only objective of error minimisation. Here however, the red point is chosen as the compromised solution to consider both accuracy and compactness of the model. This solution results in a simple fuzzy model with only seven inputs, eighteen rules and an acceptable RMS error of 0.44. This error is calculated using predicted and real voltages. The predicted voltage of the designed model should be then sent to the forward model to generate the applied force. Figure 6, is the comparison between the target force and the generated one where the good tracking of the original signal using the new approach is depicted. The RMS error between the target and the predicted force is about 37.87 kN which compared to the maximum capacity of the proposed MR damper (1000kN) is acceptable (less than 4%).

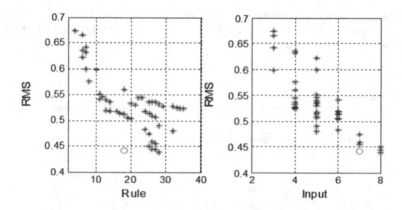

Fig. 5. Pareto Front for Fuzzy Model of Inverse MR Damper

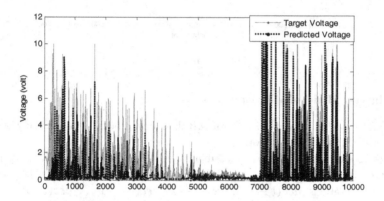

Fig. 6. The comparison between the target and generated voltage

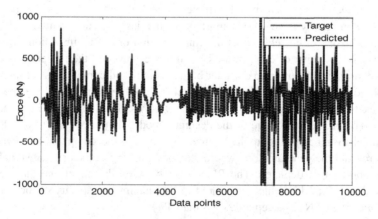

Fig. 7. The comparison between the target and generated force

4.3 Model Validation

To validate the accuracy of the developed TSK fuzzy model, in identifying the inverse dynamic behaviour of an MR damper, a set of validation data is generated from the mathematical model of a 10000kN MR damper (Formulas 11-17). Therefore 10000 data points are collected over 10s simulation with time increment of 0.001. Figure 8 shows the histories of validation data for acceleration, voltage and force.

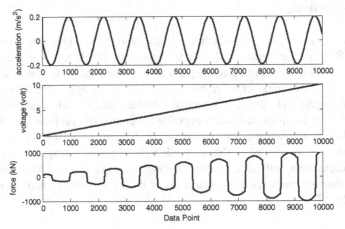

Fig. 8. Validation data

Using the proper validation set of data, including acceleration and voltages, the predicted forces are as shown in Figure 9, which almost follows the target force generated by the mathematical model. The maximum error here is 75N which is 7.5% of the maximum target force.

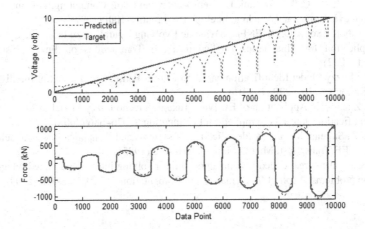

Fig. 9. Comparison between the predicted and target voltages and forces (Validation data)

It should be mentioned that, based on the dynamics of MR damper, when the displacement is zero, the generated force, regardless of the voltage, will be zero as well. Therefore, when the generated force is zero, the voltage could be anything and that is why the predicted voltage in some points are very different to the target although the generated force derived from the predicted voltage, is very close to the target one.

5   Conclusion

A new TSK fuzzy modelling approach, using the evolving combination of subtractive clustering, FCM and modified NSGA-II is presented. The latter, is a great help to handle the mixed-integer optimisation problems as we deal with both integer, and non-integer adjustable parameters in this study. Using this approach, the most suitable minimal inputs and rules are searched simultaneously, such that the resulting fuzzy model is of compact size and acceptable accuracy. The proposed methodology is then applied to emulate the inverse dynamic behaviour of a 1000kN MR damper. Results show that the model is able to predict the required voltage of MR damper using the acceleration and force history, making the application of MR dampers for control engineering purposes more practical, as the linear control theory can be applied directly.

References

1. Askari, M., Li, J., Samali, B.: Semi-Active LQG Control of Seismically Excited Nonlinear Buildings using Optimal Takagi-Sugeno Inverse Model of MR Dampers. Procedia Engineering 14, 2765–2772 (2011)
2. Yager, R., Filev, D.: Generation of Fuzzy Rules by Mountain Clus ering. Journal of Intelligent and Fuzzy Systems 2, 209–219 (1994)
3. Jang, J.S.R., Sun, C.T., Mizutani, E.: Neuro-Fuzzy and Soft Computing. A Computational Approach to Learning and Machine Intelligence. Prentice-Hall (1997)
4. Kasabov, N.K., Song, Q.: 'DENFIS: Dynamic Evolving Neural-fuzzy Inference System and its Application for Time-series Prediction. IEEE Transactions on Fuzzy Systems 10, 144–154 (2002)
5. Chiu, S.: Fuzzy Model Identification based on Cluster Estimation. Journal of Intelligent and Fuzzy Systems 2, 267–278 (1994)
6. Du, H., Zhang, N.: Application of Evolving Takagi–Sugeno Fuzzy Model to Nonlinear System Identification. Journal of Applied Soft Computing 8, 676–686 (2008)
7. Takagi, T., Sugeno, M.: Fuzzy identification of systems and its application to modeling and control. IEEE Trans. Syst. Man Cybern 15, 116–132 (1985)
8. Deep, K., et al.: A real coded genetic algorithm for solving integer and mixed integer optimization problems. Applied Mathematics and Computation 212(2), 505–518 (2009)

Hybrid State Variables - Fuzzy Logic Modelling of Nonlinear Objects

Łukasz Bartczuk, Andrzej Przybył, and Piotr Dziwiński

Institute of Computational Intelligence
Częstochowa University of Technology, Poland
{lukasz.bartczuk,andrzej.przybyl,piotr.dziwinski}@iisi.pcz.pl

Abstract. In this paper a new hybrid method for modelling of non-linear dynamic systems is proposed. It uses fuzzy logic system together with state variables technique to obtain the local linear approximation performed continuously for successive operating points. This approach provides good accuracy and allows the use of very convenient and well-known method from linear control theory to analyse the obtained model.

1 Introduction

Models of various physical phenomena are often used in practice. This is because the possession of the real object model allows to build precise control system, failure prediction and knowledge extraction from the modelled object [17]. Unfortunately, often only simplified models of the analysed objects are available which have too low precision and therefore they are not very useful in practice. The simplified models are often linear and they usually do not include all the phenomena. As a result, these models are accurate enough in certain (i.e. linear) operating points only. However, they are very useful, considering the fact of the possibility of use the well-known methods of the control theory, which refer to the linear models.

While the objects in the real world are usually nonlinear it would be very useful to have an improved (i.e. more precise) linear model which will be able to model accurately enough the nonlinear phenomenon. In the literature this issue is widely investigated. For example in [3, 12, 13] there is proposed method for modelling of dynamic systems using the theory of the state variables with use the method of sector-nonlinearity. The modelling is based on identification of the sectors which are the basis for the local linear approximation of a nonlinear object. Other authors ([21]) propose the use of models of the plants which have a known structure and parameters of the linear part of the plant and a static nonlinearity that is not known. The proposed isolated nonlinearities allows to obtain the accurate model of the plant, based on the initially known simplified linear model. However this method transforms the linear model into the nonlinear one and lost the advantage of the linear modelling.

In this paper we propose a new method of the nonlinear modelling in which the linear model is improved by the way which allows to increase their accuracy

L. Rutkowski et al. (Eds.): ICAISC 2013, Part I, LNAI 7894, pp. 227–234, 2013.

and maintaining the advantage of the linear model. In contrast to the sector nonlinearities method [3, 12, 13] our method uses fuzzy rules to modelling variability of individual (selected) coefficients of the matrix (from the used algebraic equations and a state variables theory) instead of using them to modelling of nonlinearity of object sectors as a whole. Thus, the output of fuzzy rules used in the model will be referenced more to the variability of some model parameters than to indicate the sectors of its nonlinearity. This implies undeniably benefit which includes possibility of interpretation of dependence between values of defined coefficients (which are functions of the model parameter/s) and points of work.

This paper is organized into six sections. In the next section an idea of the proposed modelling method is presented. In Section 3 we describe intelligent system for nonlinear modelling. Section 4 shows the evolutionary generation of the models of nonlinear dynamic systems and Section 5 presents experimental results. Conclusions are drawn in Section 6.

2   Idea of the Proposed Method

Let's consider the nonlinear dynamic system described by the linear algebraic equation and based on the the the state variables technique ([15]), i.e.

$$\mathbf{x}(k+1) = (\mathbf{I} + \mathbf{A} \cdot T) \cdot \mathbf{x}(k) + \mathbf{B} \cdot T \cdot \mathbf{u}(k), \tag{1}$$

$$\mathbf{y} = \mathbf{C} \cdot \mathbf{x}, \tag{2}$$

where $\mathbf{A}, \mathbf{B}$ and $\mathbf{C}$ are system input and output matrices, $\mathbf{I}$ is the identity matrix with appropriate size, $\mathbf{x}, \mathbf{u}, \mathbf{y}$ are vectors of state variables, input and output signals respectively. This model presents a local linear approximation of the nonlinear object in an arbitrary chosen operating point. It refers to continuous objects noted in discrete form with time step T, connected with the current time t by the dependency $t = kT$, where $k = 1, 2, \ldots$. Modelling with use of the dynamic phenomena description as state variables and fuzzy rules is based on the observable canonical form of the state equations [15].

The significant improvement (in the sense of increasing the accuracy) of such model is possible when the local linear approximation will be performed continuously for each current operating point ([17]). More precisely, the system matrix in linear model will be corrected by adding a correction matrix $\mathbf{P_A}$ in such a way to increase the model accuracy, i.e.:

$$\mathbf{x}(k+1) = (\mathbf{I} + (\mathbf{A} + \mathbf{P_A}(k)) \cdot T) \cdot \mathbf{x}(k) + \mathbf{B} \cdot T \cdot \mathbf{u}(k), \tag{3}$$

where $\mathbf{P_A}(k)$ is the corrections matrix for system matrix $\mathbf{A}$. Despite the fact that operating point changes over time during the process, a local re-determination of coefficients matrix in any new point is possible. For the discretization with the suitable short time step T that solution is enough accurate, even if the first order approximation is used.

3 Intelligent System for Nonlinear Modelling

In proposed method the coefficients of the correction matrix $\mathbf{P_A}(k)$ are generated by multi-input, single-output fuzzy system [1, 2, 5–11, 14, 18–20, 22]. This idea is graphically depicted on fig. 1.

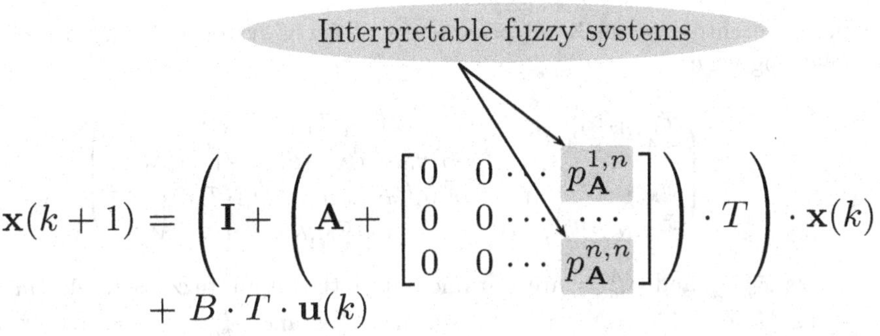

$$\mathbf{x}(k+1) = \left(\mathbf{I} + \left(\mathbf{A} + \begin{bmatrix} 0 & 0 & \cdots & p_{\mathbf{A}}^{1,n} \\ 0 & 0 & \cdots & \cdots \\ 0 & 0 & \cdots & p_{\mathbf{A}}^{n,n} \end{bmatrix} \right) \cdot T \right) \cdot \mathbf{x}(k)$$
$$+ B \cdot T \cdot \mathbf{u}(k)$$

Fig. 1. The idea of the hybrid modelling method based on fuzzy logic system and modelling technique with the use of state variables

Each of the systems has a collection of N fuzzy IF $-$ THEN rules in the form:

$$\mathcal{R}^r : \text{IF } x_1 \text{ is } A_1^r \text{ AND } \ldots \text{ AND } x_n \text{ is } A_n^r \text{ THEN } y \text{ is } B^r, \tag{4}$$

where $\mathbf{x} = [x_1, \ldots, x_n] \in \mathbf{X} \subset \mathbf{R}^n$ is a vector of input signals, $y \in \mathbf{Y} \subset \mathbf{R}$ is an output value, $A_1^r, A_2^r, \ldots, A_n^r$ and $B^r(y), r = 1, \ldots, N$ are fuzzy sets characterized by membership functions $\mu_{A_i^r}(x_i)$ and $\mu_{B^r}, i = 1, \ldots, n, r = 1, \ldots, N$.

Each fuzzy rule (4) determines fuzzy set $\overline{B}^r \subset R$ whose membership function is given by following formula

$$\mu_{\overline{B}^r}(y) = \mu_{\mathbf{A}^r \to B^r}(\overline{\mathbf{x}}, y) = T \left\{ \mathop{T^*}_{i=1}^{n} \left(\mu_{A_i^r}(x_i) \right), \mu_B^r(y) \right\}, \tag{5}$$

where T and T^* are t-norms operators (not necessarily the same) [19]. As a result of aggregation of the fuzzy sets $\overline{B}^r$ we obtain the fuzzy set B' with membership function given by

$$\mu_{B'}(y) = \mathop{S}_{r=1}^{N} \left\{ \mu_{\overline{B}^r}(y) \right\}, \tag{6}$$

where S denotes t-conorm operator [19]. The defuzzification can be realized by the center of area method defined in the discrete form by following formula

$$\overline{y} = \frac{\sum\limits_{r=1}^{N} \overline{y}_B^r \cdot \mu_{B'}(\overline{y}_B^r)}{\sum\limits_{r=1}^{N} \mu_{B'}(\overline{y}_B^r)}, \tag{7}$$

where $\overline{y}_B^r$ are centers of the membership functions $\mu_{B^r}(y), r = 1, \ldots, N$.

4   Evolutionary Construct of the Matrix of the Corrections

In order to create interpretable model of the dynamic processes we use the evolutionary strategy (μ, λ) (see e.g. [4, 10]). The purpose of this is to obtain the parameters of systems described in the previous sections. In the process of evolution we assumed, that:

- In single chromosome **X** all parameters of fuzzy systems (7) are coded in following way:

$$
\mathbf{X} = \begin{pmatrix}
\overline{x}^A_{1,1,1}, \sigma^A_{1,1,1}, \cdots, \overline{x}^A_{1,1,n}, \sigma^A_{1,1,n}, \overline{y}^B_{1,1}, \sigma^B_{1,1}, \cdots, \\
\overline{x}^A_{1,N,1}, \sigma^A_{1,N,1}, \cdots, \overline{x}^A_{1,N,n}, \sigma^A_{1,N,n}, \overline{y}^B_{1,N}, \sigma^B_{1,N}, \cdots, \\
\overline{x}^A_{M,1,1}, \sigma^A_{M,1,1}, \cdots, \overline{x}^A_{M,1,n}, \sigma^A_{M,1,n}, \overline{y}^B_{M,1}, \sigma^B_{M,1}, \cdots, \\
\overline{x}^A_{M,N,1}, \sigma^A_{M,N,1}, \cdots, \overline{x}^A_{M,N,n}, \sigma^A_{M,N,n}, \overline{y}^B_{M,N}, \sigma^B_{M,N}
\end{pmatrix}, \tag{8}
$$

where $\overline{x}^A_{m,r,i}$ and $\sigma^A_{m,r,i}$ are parameters of the input fuzzy sets A^r_i, $m = 1, \ldots, M$; $r = 1, \ldots, N$; $i = 1, \ldots, n$, and $\overline{x}^B_{m,r}$ and $\sigma^B_{m,r}$ are parameters of the output fuzzy sets B^r for m-th fuzzy system; M - number of nonzero elements of correction matrix $\mathbf{P_A}$.
- Fitness function is based on difference between output signals $\hat{x}_1$, $\hat{x}_2$ generated by the created model at step $k + 1$ and corresponding reference x_1, x_2 values:

$$
fitness(\mathbf{X}) = \sqrt{\frac{1}{2 \cdot K} \sum_{k=1}^{K} \left(\begin{array}{c} (x_1(k+1) - \hat{x}_1(k+1))^2 + \\ (x_2(k+1) - \hat{x}_2(k+1))^2 \end{array} \right)}, \tag{9}
$$

where K is a number of reference values. Starting values for the model are reference values at step 1. In practical implementation, the actual reference values will be obtained by the non-invasive observation, for example by processing a data packets, which are sent in the real-time in the Ethernet network (see e.g. [16]).
- Genes in chromosomes **X** were initialized according with method described in [10].

Detailed description of the evolutionary strategy $(\mu + \lambda)$, used to train neuro-fuzzy systems, can be found in [4, 10].

5   Experimental Results

In our paper we considered the well-known harmonic oscillator as an example to demonstrate the usefulness of the proposed modelling method:

$$
\frac{d^2 x}{dt^2} + 2\zeta\omega \frac{dx}{dt} + \omega^2 x = 0, \tag{10}
$$

where ζ, ω are oscillator parameters, and $x(t)$ is a reference value of the modelled process as function of time. The main parameter of the oscillator ω (angular

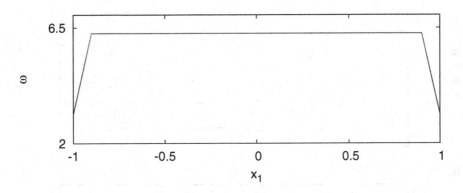

Fig. 2. The value of ω parameter as the function of state variable x_1

frequency) is intentionally modified in some operating points in simulation to make the object nonlinear, as depicted in Fig. 2. In our simulations ζ is the constant value $\zeta = 0$.

We used the following state variables: $x_1(t) = dx(t)/dt$ and $x_2(t) = x(t)$. In such case the system matrix $\mathbf{A}$ is described as follows:

$$\mathbf{A} = \begin{bmatrix} 0 & -\omega^2 \\ 1 & 0 \end{bmatrix}, \tag{11}$$

and matrix of the corrections $\mathbf{P_A}$ is in the form:

$$\mathbf{P_A} = \begin{bmatrix} 0 & p_{12}(\mathbf{x}) \\ 0 & p_{22}(\mathbf{x}) \end{bmatrix}. \tag{12}$$

In our method we assume that the system matrix A is known, so the goal of the modelling was to recreate the unknown parameters of correction matrix $p_{12}(\mathbf{x})$ and $p_{22}(\mathbf{x})$ in such a way that the model reproduces the reference data as accurately as possible. Because in general case the analytical dependences used to generate the reference data are not known in order to recreate unknown parameters we used multi-input, single-output fuzzy systems. As the input of each system the measurable output signals of modelled process $\hat{x}_1(k)$ and $\hat{x}_2(k)$ were used. The outputs of fuzzy systems were used as the values of correction matrix parameters $p_{12}(\mathbf{x})$ and $p_{22}(\mathbf{x})$. The accuracy of the model was determined by comparing values of its output signals $\hat{x}_1(k)$ and $\hat{x}_2(k)$ with reference values $x_1(k)$ and $x_2(k)$. The error was computed according to formula (9).

In our simulations the neuro-fuzzy systems (7) with Gaussian membership functions and algebraic t-norm were used. In order to determine membership functions parameters (mean value and standard deviation) we used evolutionary strategy (μ, λ) which is characterized by the following parameters: $\mu = 50, \lambda = 300, p_m = 0.077$ and $p_c = 0.7$ and the number of generations $= 2000$.

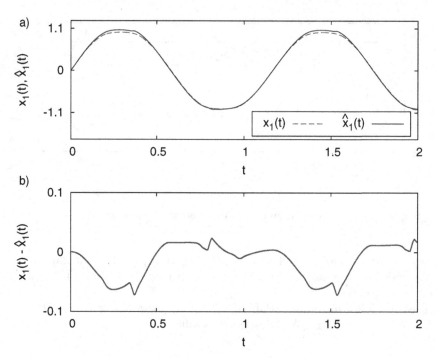

Fig. 3. Comparison between the reference and estimated data

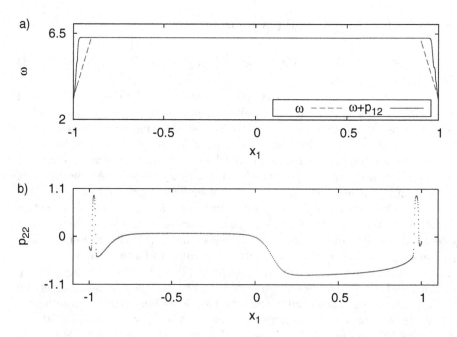

Fig. 4. Comparison between the actual and modelled by fuzzy system values of matrix coefficients

The neuro-fuzzy systems (7) obtained as results of evolutionary process are characterized by 5 rules, 2 inputs ($\hat{x}_1(k)$ and $\hat{x}_2(k)$) and single output. The experimental results are depicted in Fig. 4-6. The accuracy of nonlinear modelling obtained in out simulations (the average RMSE) was lower than 0.002.

It should be noted that difference between the reference and estimated data are negligible (Fig. 3). In addition, differences between actual and modelled by the fuzzy system (7) values of matrix $\mathbf{P_A}$ coefficients are also acceptable.

6 Conclusion

In this paper a new method for modelling of nonlinear dynamic systems was proposed. This method is based on the local linear approximation performed continuously for successive operating points. It allows to use the very convenient and well-known method from linear control theory to analyse the obtained model.

Moreover, the proposed hybrid modelling method, based on fuzzy logic system and state variables technique, gives the potential possibility to the interpretation of accumulated knowledge.

The simulation shows the fully usefulness of the proposed method.

Acknowledgment. The project was financed by the National Science Center on the basis of the decision number DEC-2012/05/B/ST7/02138.

References

1. Bartczuk, Ł., Rutkowska, D.: Type-2 Fuzzy Decision Trees. In: Rutkowski, L., Tadeusiewicz, R., Zadeh, L.A., Zurada, J.M. (eds.) ICAISC 2008. LNCS (LNAI), vol. 5097, pp. 197–206. Springer, Heidelberg (2008)
2. Bartczuk, Ł., Rutkowska, D.: Medical Diagnosis with Type-2 Fuzzy Decision Trees. In: Kącki, E., Rudnicki, M., Stempczyńska, J. (eds.) Computers in Medical Activity. AISC, vol. 65, pp. 11–21. Springer, Heidelberg (2009)
3. Chang, W.J., Chang, W., Liu, H.-H.: Model-based fuzzy modeling and control for autonomous underwater vehicles in the horizontal plane. Journal of Marine Science and Technology 11(3), 155–163 (2003)
4. Cordon, O., Herrera, F., Hoffmann, F., Magdalena, L.: Genetic Fuzzy Systems: Evolutionary tuning and learning of fuzzy knowledge bases. World Scientific (2001)
5. Cpałka, K., Rutkowski, L.: Compromise approach to neuro-fuzzy systems. In: Sincak, P., Vascak, J., Kvasnicka, V., Pospichal, J. (eds.) Intelligent Technologies - Theory and Applications, vol. 76, pp. 85–90. IOS Press (2002)
6. Cpałka, K., Rutkowski, L.: Flexible Takagi Sugeno fuzzy systems. In: Proceedings of the International Joint Conference on Neural Networks, IJCNN 2005, Montreal, pp. 1764–1769 (2005)
7. Cpałka, K., Rutkowski, L.: Flexible Takagi-Sugeno Neuro-Fuzzy Structures for Nonlinear Approximation. WSEAS Transactions on Systems 4(9), 1450–1458 (2005)
8. Cpałka, K.: A method for designing flexible neuro-fuzzy systems. In: Rutkowski, L., Tadeusiewicz, R., Zadeh, L.A., Żurada, J.M. (eds.) ICAISC 2006. LNCS (LNAI), vol. 4029, pp. 212–219. Springer, Heidelberg (2006)

9. Cpałka, K., Rutkowski, L.: A new method for designing and reduction of neuro-fuzzy systems. In: 2006 IEEE International Conference on Fuzzy Systems, pp. 1851–1857 (2006)
10. Cpałka, K.: On evolutionary designing and learning of flexible neuro-fuzzy structures for nonlinear classification. In: Nonlinear Analysis Series A: Theory, Methods and Applications, vol. 71, Elsevier (2009)
11. Cpałka, K.: A New Method for Design and Reduction of Neuro-Fuzzy Classification Systems. IEEE Transactions on Neural Networks 20(4), 701–714 (2009)
12. Johansen, T.A., Shorten, R., Murray-Smith, R.: On the Interpretation and Identification of Dynamic Takagi-Sugeno Fuzzy Models. IEEE Transactions on Fuzzy Systems 8(3) (2000)
13. Kamyar, M.: Takagi-Sugeno Fuzzy Modeling for Process Control Industrial Automation. Robotics and Artificial Intelligence (EEE8005), School of Electrical, Electronic and Computer Engineering (2008)
14. Li, X., Er, M.J., Lim, B.S., et al.: Fuzzy Regression Modeling for Tool Performance Prediction and Degradation Detection. International Journal of Neural Systems 20(5), 405–419 (2010)
15. Ogata, K.: Modern Control Engineering. Prentice Hall (2001)
16. Przybył, A., Smoląg, J., Kimla, P.: Real-time Ethernet based, distributed control system for the CNC machine. Electrical Review 2010-2 (2010) (in Polish)
17. Przybył, A., Cpałka, K.: A new method to construct of interpretable models of dynamic systems. In: Rutkowski, L., Korytkowski, M., Scherer, R., Tadeusiewicz, R., Zadeh, L.A., Zurada, J.M. (eds.) ICAISC 2012, Part II. LNCS, vol. 7268, pp. 697–705. Springer, Heidelberg (2012)
18. Rutkowski, L., Cpałka, K.: Flexible neuro-fuzzy systems. IEEE Trans. Neural Networks 14(3), 554–574 (2003)
19. Rutkowski, L.: Computational Intelligence: Methods and Techniques. Springer (2008)
20. Rutkowski, L., Przybył, A., Cpałka, K.: Novel Online Speed Profile Generation for Industrial Machine Tool Based on Flexible Neuro-Fuzzy Approximation. IEEE Transactions on Industrial Electronics 59(2), 1238–1247 (2012)
21. Schroder, D.: Intelligent Observer and Control Design for Nonlinear Systems. Springer, Heidelberg (2000)
22. Zalasiński, M., Cpałka, K.: Novel algorithm for the on-line signature verification. In: Rutkowski, L., Korytkowski, M., Scherer, R., Tadeusiewicz, R., Zadeh, L.A., Zurada, J.M. (eds.) ICAISC 2012, Part II. LNCS, vol. 7268, pp. 362–367. Springer, Heidelberg (2012)

Properties of Plausibility Conflict
of Belief Functions

Milan Daniel

Institute of Computer Science, Academy of Sciences of the Czech Republic
Pod Vodárenskou věží 2, CZ – 182 07 Prague 8, Czech Republic
milan.daniel@cs.cas.cz

Abstract. This theoretical contribution studies mathematical properties of plausibility conflict of belief functions. The analysis is performed
for belief functions defined on 2-element frames, then the results are
generalized to general finite frames. After that, an analogous analysis
of Liu's degree of conflict is presented, to enable its comparison to the
plausibility conflict. To be more efficient, a simplification of formula and
computation of Liu's degree of conflict is suggested.
A series of examples and graphical demonstrations are included.

Keywords: belief functions, Dempster-Shafer theory, internal conflict,
conflict between belief functions, plausibility conflict, degree of conflict,
uncertainty.

1   Introduction

Belief functions are one of the widely used formalisms for uncertainty representation and processing that enable representation of incomplete and uncertain
knowledge, belief updating, and combination of evidence. They present a principal notion of the Dempster-Shafer Theory or the Theory of Evidence [16].

When combining belief functions (BFs) by the conjunctive rules of combination, conflicts often appear which are assigned to $\emptyset$ by non-normalized conjunctive rule $\odot$ or normalized by Dempster's rule of combination $\oplus$. Combination
of conflicting BFs and interpretation of conflicts is often questionable in real
applications, thus a series of alternative combination rules was suggested and a
series of papers on conflicting belief functions was published, e.g. [2,5,15,18].

In [9], new ideas concerning interpretation, definition, and measurement of
conflicts of BFs were introduced. We presented three new approaches to interpretation and computation of conflicts: combinational conflict, plausibility conflict, and comparative conflict. Differences were made between conflicts between
BFs and internal conflicts of single BF; a conflict between BFs was distinguished
from the difference between BFs.

The presented contribution studies mathematical properties of the plausibility
conflict of BFs introduced in [9]. Properties of both internal conflicts and conflicts
between BFs are analyzed. To complete the topic, an analogical analysis of Liu's
degree of conflict is performed and comparison of the degree of conflict with the
plausibility conflict is presented.

L. Rutkowski et al. (Eds.): ICAISC 2013, Part I, LNAI 7894, pp. 235–246, 2013.

2　State of the Art

2.1　General Primer on Belief Functions

We assume classic definitions of basic notions from theory of *belief functions* [16] on finite frames of discernment $\Omega_n = \{\omega_1, \omega_2, ..., \omega_n\}$, see also [4–9]; for illustration or simplicity, we often use 2- or 3-element frames Ω_2 and Ω_3.

A *basic belief assignment (bba)* is a mapping $m : \mathcal{P}(\Omega) \longrightarrow [0,1]$ such that $\sum_{A \subseteq \Omega} m(A) = 1$; the values of the bba are called *basic belief masses (bbm)*. $m(\emptyset) = 0$ is usually assumed. A *belief function (BF)* is a mapping $Bel : \mathcal{P}(\Omega) \longrightarrow [0,1]$, $Bel(A) = \sum_{\emptyset \neq X \subseteq A} m(X)$. A *plausibility function* $Pl(A) = \sum_{\emptyset \neq A \cap X} m(X)$. There is a unique correspondence among m and corresponding Bel and Pl thus we often speak about m as of belief function.

A *focal element* is a subset X of the frame of discernment, such that $m(X) > 0$. If all the focal elements are *singletons* (i.e. one-element subsets of Ω), then we speak about a *Bayesian belief function* (BBF); in fact, it is a probability distribution on Ω. If all the focal elements are either singletons or whole Ω (i.e. $|X| = 1$ or $|X| = |\Omega|$), then we speak about a *quasi-Bayesian belief function* (qBBF), that is something like 'un-normalized probability distribution', but with a different interpretation. If there is the only focal element $A \subset \Omega$, i.e. $m(A) = 1$, we speak about *categorical belief function*; in the case of $m(\Omega) = 1$ we speak about *vacuous belief function* (VBF); in the case of $m(A) > 0$ and $m(\Omega) = 1 - m(A)$ we speak about *simple support belief function*. If all focal elements are nested, we speak about *consonant belief function*; if all focal elements have a non-empty intersection, we speak about *consistent belief function*[1].

Dempster's (conjunctive) rule of combination $\oplus$ is given as $(m_1 \oplus m_2)(A) = \sum_{X \cap Y = A} K m_1(X) m_2(Y)$ for $A \neq \emptyset$, where $K = \frac{1}{1-\kappa}$, $\kappa = \sum_{X \cap Y = \emptyset} m_1(X) m_2(Y)$, and $(m_1 \oplus m_2)(\emptyset) = 0$, see [16]; putting $K = 1$ and $(m_1 \oplus m_2)(\emptyset) = \kappa$ we obtain the *non-normalized conjunctive rule of combination* $\odot$, see e. g. [17].

Let us recall U_n the *uniform Bayesian belief function*[2] [9], i.e., the uniform probability distribution on Ω_n, and *normalized plausibility of singletons*[3] of Bel: the BBF $Pl\_P(Bel)$ such, that $(Pl\_P(Bel))(\omega_i) = \frac{Pl(\{\omega_i\})}{\sum_{\omega \in \Omega} Pl(\{\omega\})}$ [3,7]. Smets' pignistic probability is given by $BetP(\omega) = \sum_{\omega \in X \subseteq \Omega} \frac{1}{|X|} \frac{m(X)}{1 - m(\emptyset)}$ [17].

An *indecisive BF* (or nondiscriminative BF) is a BF, which does not prefer any $\omega_i \in \Omega_n$, i.e., BF which gives no decisional support for any ω_i, i.e., BF such that $h(Bel) = Bel \oplus U_n = U_n$, i.e., $Pl(\{\omega_i\}) = const.$, i.e., $(Pl\_P(Bel))(\{\omega_i\}) = \frac{1}{n}$, [11].

---

[1]　Note that any categorical BF is simple support BF, that any simple support BF is consonant, and that any consonant BF is consistent. Note, further, that the reverse implications do not hold true.

[2]　U_n which is idempotent w.r.t. Dempster's rule $\oplus$, and moreover neutral on the set of all BBFs, is denoted as $_nD0'$ in [7], $0'$ comes from studies by Hájek & Valdés.

[3]　Plausibility of singletons is called *contour function* by Shafer in [16], thus $Pl\_P(Bel)$ is a normalization of contour function in fact.

2.2 Belief Functions on 2-Element Frame of Discernment

Our analysis of conflicts is motivated by Hájek-Valdés algebraic analysis of BFs on 2-element frame $\Omega_2 = \{\omega_1, \omega_2\}$ [13,14], further elaborated by the author of this study, e.g. in [4,6]. Thus we present some of related notions which are used here.

There are only three possible focal elements $\{\omega_1\}, \{\omega_2\}, \{\omega_1, \omega_2\}$ and any nor-malized *basic belief assignment (bba)* m is defined by a pair $(a, b) = (m(\{\omega_1\}), m(\{\omega_2\}))$ as $m(\{\omega_1, \omega_2\}) = 1 - a - b$; this is called *Dempster's pair* or simply *d-pair* in [4,6,13,14] (it is a pair of reals such that $0 \le a, b \le 1, a + b \le 1$)[4].

Extremal d-pairs are the pairs corresponding to BFs for which either $m(\{\omega_1\}) = 1$ or $m(\{\omega_2\}) = 1$, i.e., $(1, 0)$ and $(0, 1)$. The set of all non-extremal d-pairs is denoted as D_0; the set of all non-extremal *Bayesian d-pairs* (i.e. d-pairs corre-sponding to Bayesian BFs, where $a + b = 1$) is denoted as G; the set of d-pairs such that $a = b$ is denoted as S, the set where $b = 0$ as S_1, analogically the set where $a = 0$ as S_2 (simple support BFs). Vacuous BF is denoted as $0 = (0, 0)$ and there is a special BF (d-pair) $0' = (\frac{1}{2}, \frac{1}{2}) = U_2$, see Figure 1. (VBF 0 is neutral w.r.t. Dempster's rule, i.e. for any BF Bel it holds that $Bel \oplus 0 = Bel = 0 \oplus Bel$; similarly $0'$ is neutral in G, i.e., $(a, 1 - a) \oplus 0' = (a, 1 - a) = 0' \oplus (a, 1 - a)$, and generally $Bel \oplus U_n = Bel = U_n \oplus Bel$ for any BBF Bel on Ω_n).

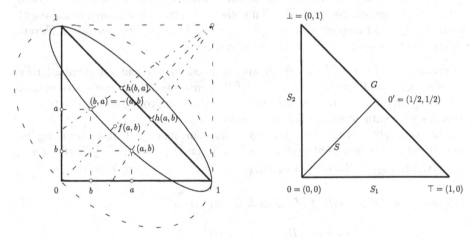

Fig. 1. Dempster's semigroup D_0. Homomorphism h is in this representation a pro-jection to group G along the straight lines running through the point $(1, 1)$.

In D_0, we need further: $h(a, b) = (a, b) \oplus 0' = (\frac{1-b}{2-a-b}, \frac{1-a}{2-a-b})$, in general $h(Bel) = Bel \oplus U_n = Pl\_P(Bel)$.

Let us denote $D_0^{\ge 0'} = \{(a, b) \in D_0 \mid (a, b) \ge 0', \text{ i.e.,} a \ge b\}$ and analogically $D_0^{\le 0'} = \{(a, b) \in D_0 \mid (a, b) \le 0', \text{ i.e., } a \le b\}$. And analogically subsets of G:

---

[4] Analogically, we can represent any BF on Ω_n as a 2^{n-2}-tuple $(a_1, a_2, ..., a_{2^n-2})$, or as a 2^{n-1}-tuple $(a_1, a_2, ..., a_{2^n-2}; a_{2^n-1})$ if we want to underline value $m(\Omega) = a_{2^n-1}$. For non-normalized BFs we can use $(a_1, a_2, ..., a_{2^n-2}; a_{2^n-1} \mid e)$, where $e = m(\emptyset)$.

$G^{\leq 0'}$ and $G^{\geq 0'}$; $G^{\leq 0'} = \{(a, 1-a) \in D_0 \mid (a, 1-a) \leq 0', \text{ i.e., } a \leq 0.5\}$, $G^{\geq 0'} = \{(a, 1-a) \in D_0 \mid (a, 1-a) \geq 0', \text{ i.e., } a \geq 0.5\}$.

For more details and algebraic results see [4,6,13,14]. For the first results of generalization to Ω_3 see [11]. The situation is much more complicated there, as instead of 2-dimensional triangle for Ω_2 there is 6-dimensional simplex for Ω_3, there are two kind of dimensions, and adequately more complicated structures.

2.3   Conflict of Belief Functions

When combining two BFs Bel_1, Bel_2 given by m_1 and m_2 conflicting belief masses $m_1(X) > 0$, $m_2(Y) > 0$, where $X \cap Y = \emptyset$, often appear. The sum of products of such conflicting masses corresponds to $m(\emptyset)$ when non-normalized conjunctive rule of combination $\odot$ is applied and $m = m_1 \odot m_2$. This sum is called *weight of conflict between belief functions Bel_1 and Bel_2* in [16], and it is commonly used when dealing with conflicting belief functions. Unfortunately, the name and interpretation of this notion does not correctly correspond to reality. We often obtain positive sum of conflicting belief masses even if two numerically same belief functions[5] are combined, see e.g. examples discussed by Almond [1] already in 1995 and by Liu [15], for another examples see [9].

Liu further demonstrates [15] that neither distance nor difference are adequate measures of conflicts between BFs. Thus she uses a two-dimensional (composed) measure *degree of conflict* $cf(m_1, m_2) = (m_{\ominus}, difBet^{m_2}_{m_1})$, see Section 4. Nevertheless the nature of conflict is not captured there.

Internal conflicts. $IntC(m_i)$ which are included in particular individual BFs are distinguished from *conflict between BFs* $C(m_1, m_2)$ in [9]; the entire sum of conflicting masses is called *total conflict*; and three approaches to conflicts were introduced: combinational, plausibility and comparative.

Unfortunately there are not yet any precise formulas, but only bounding inequalities for *combinational conflicts*: $\frac{1}{2}TotC(m, m)) \leq IntC(m) \leq TotC(m, m)$,
$$TotC(m_1, m_2) - (IntC(m_1) + IntC(m_2)) \leq C(m_1, m_2) \leq TotC(m_1, m_2).$$

Internal plausibility conflict of BF Bel. is defined as

$$Pl\text{-}IntC(Bel) = 1 - max_{\omega \in \Omega} Pl(\{\omega\}),$$

where Pl is the plausibility equivalent to Bel.

Let us denote by $\Omega_{PlC}(Bel_1, Bel_2)$ the set of *elements* $\omega \in \Omega_n$ with conflicting Pl_P masses $\Omega_{PlC}(Bel_1, Bel_2) = \{\omega \in \Omega_n \mid (Pl\_P(Bel_1)(\omega) - \frac{1}{n})(Pl\_P(Bel_2)(\omega) - \frac{1}{n}) < 0\}$ [9]. *Plausibility conflict between BFs Bel_1 and Bel_2* is then defined by the formula

$$Pl\text{-}C(Bel_1, Bel_2) = min(Pl\text{-}C_0(Bel_1, Bel_2), (m_1 \odot m_2)(\emptyset)),$$

---

[5] All BFs combined by $\oplus$ and $\odot$ are assumed to be mutually independent, even if they are numerically same.

where

$$Pl\text{-}C_0(Bel_1, Bel_2) = \sum_{\omega \in \Omega_{PlC}(Bel_1, Bel_2)} \frac{1}{2} |Pl\_P(Bel_1)(\omega) - Pl\_P(Bel_2)(\omega)|.$$

If $(Pl\_P(Bel_1)(\omega_i) - \frac{1}{n})(Pl\_P(Bel_2)(\omega_i) - \frac{1}{n}) \geq 0$ for all $\omega_i \in \Omega_n$ then BFs Bel_1 and Bel_2 on Ω_n are mutually non-conflicting (there is no conflict between them). The reverse statement does not hold true, see e.g. Example 1. (Example 5 in [9], Example 8 in [8]). BFs (a, b) and (c, d) on Ω_2 are mutually non-conflicting iff $(a - b)(c - d) \geq 0$.

Example 1. Let us suppose Ω_6, now; and two intuitively non-conflicting BFs m_1 and m_2.

X :	$\{\omega_1\}$ $\{\omega_2\}$ $\{\omega_3\}$ $\{\omega_4\}$ $\{\omega_5\}$ $\{\omega_6\}$ $\{\omega_1, \omega_2, \omega_3, \omega_4\}$
$m_1(X)$:	1.00
$m_2(X)$:	1.00

$Pl\_P(m_1) = (1.00, 0.00, 0.00, 0.00, 0.00, 0.00)$,
$Pl\_P(m_2) = (0.25, 0.25, 0.25, 0.25, 0.00, 0.00)$, $\Omega_{PlC}(m_i, m_j) = \{\omega_2, \omega_3, \omega_4\}$, as
$Pl\_P(m_2)(\omega_i) = \frac{1}{4} > \frac{1}{6}$ for $i = 2, 3, 4$, whereas $Pl\_P(m_1)(\omega_i) = 0 < \frac{1}{6}$ for
$i = 2, 3, 4$, (the other elements are non-conflicting: $Pl\_P(m_1)(\omega_1) = 1 > \frac{1}{6}$,
$Pl\_P(m_2)(\omega_1) = \frac{1}{4} > \frac{1}{6}$, $Pl\_P(m_1)(\omega_i) = 0 = Pl\_P(m_2)(\omega_i)$ for $i = 5, 6$;
$Pl\text{-}C(m_1, m_2) = min(0.375, 0.00) = 0.00$.

The idea of comparative conflictness / non-conflictness is based on a specification of bbms to smaller focal elements such that fit to focal elements of the other BF as much as possible. *The comparative conflict between BFs Bel_1 and Bel_2 is defined as the least difference of such more specified bbms derived from the input m_1 and m_2.*

2.4   Couples of Totally Non-conflicting Belief Functions

From [9] we know, that if two BFs have non-empty intersection $\bigcap_{m_1(X)>0} X \cap \bigcap_{m_2(X)>0} X \neq \emptyset$ of all their focal elements (specially if all their focal elements are nested), then they are both internally and mutually non-conflicting. A non-conflicting character of consonant BFs (nested focal elements) is mentioned already in [16]. On Ω_2 the following special case holds true for all three types of conflicts (combinational, plausibility and comparative conflicts).

Fact 1. *Any couple of BFs $(a, 0), (c, 0) \in S_1$ or $(0, b), (0, d) \in S_2$ is a totally non-conflicting couple of BFs. (There is neither internal conflict nor conflict between BFs.) There are no other totally non-conflicting pairs of BFs on Ω_2.*

3   Properties of Plausibility Conflict

3.1   Internal Plausibility Conflict

Let us start with BFs without internal plausibility conflict. There is no plausibility internal conflict in BF (a, b) on Ω_2 iff $(Pl\_P(a, b))(\omega_i) = 1$ iff $a = 0$ or $b = 0$.

Proposition 1. *(i) Belief functions without internal conflict defined on Ω_2 are just BFs from S_1 and S_2.*
(ii) Belief functions without internal conflict defined on Ω_n are just BFs such that $\bigcap_{m(X)>0} X \neq \emptyset$, i.e., iff there exists $\omega_i \in \Omega_n$, such that $Pl(\{\omega_i\}) = 1$, it holds true that $\omega_i \in \bigcap_{m(X)>0} X$, i.e. for consistent BFs.

Proposition 2. *(i) Plausibility internal conflict Pl-IntC linearly[6] increases from 0 to 1/2 for BFs from semigroup S (from 0 to $0'$), $G^{\leq 0'}$ (from $(0,1)$ to $0'$) and $G^{\geq 0}$ ($0'$ in upper index) (from $(1,0)$ to $0'$).*
(ii) Plausibility internal conflict increases from 0 to $min_i(h(a,b))(\omega_i)$ for BFs from h-line containing (a,b) (from the h-line's intersection with S_i to its intersection with G).
(iii) Plausibility internal conflict is constant on vertical lines for BFs from $D_0^{\leq 0}$ ($0'$ in upper index) (i.e. $(a,b$, such that $a \leq b$), whereas it is constant on horizontal lines on $D_0^{\geq 0}$, see dashed lines in Figure 2.
(iv) In general, plausibility internal conflict Pl-IntC increases from 0 to $(n-1)/n$ for BFs from 0 to U_n, and for BFs from categorical BFs to U_n; Pl-IntC increases from 0 to $1-max_{\omega \in \Omega_n}(h(Bel)(\{\omega\}))$ for all BFs with the same $h(Bel)$.

Situation of plausibility internal conflict of BFs on Ω_2 is graphically presented in Figure 2. The directions of the arrows show the directions in which internal conflict decreases. A lines without arrows along S_1 and S_2 represent constant (zero) internal conflict of BFs from these subsemigroups, dashed lines represent positive constant internal conflict.

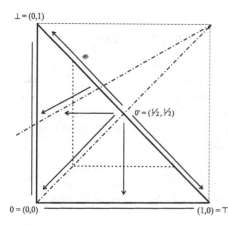

Fig. 2. Plausibility internal conflict

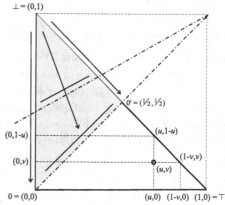

Fig. 3. Plausibility conflict between fixed BF (u,v) and general BF (a,b) on Ω_2

---

[6] k multiplication of internal conflict follows k multiplication of a in $(a,a) \in S$ and $(a, 1-a) \in G^{\leq 0'}$ and of b in $(1-b, b) \in G^{\geq 0}$.

3.2 Plausibility Conflict between Belief Functions

Let us start our presentation of plausibility conflict between BFs Pl-C on Ω_2 as it it is easily imaginable and nicely presentable on a figure.

Let us assume combination of any BF on Ω_2 with fixed BF (u, v) now. Three situations were studied in [10]: $(u, v) = 0'$, $(u, v) \in G$ and a general (u, v) $0 < u + v < 1$. Let us present only the general case here, see Figure 3.

There is no plausibility conflict between (u, v) and any BF (a, b) such that $(u - v)(a - b) \geq 0$, i.e., when (a, b) is in the same subsemigroup $D_0^{\geq 0}$ or $D_0^{\leq 0'}$ as (u, v) is, (see the white area on Figure 3). On the other hand, there is positive plausibility conflict between (u, v) and any BF (a, b) such that $(u - v)(a - c) < 0$ (see the grey area). $Pl\_P(u, v) = h(u, v) = (\frac{1-v}{2-u-v}, \frac{1-u}{2-u-v})$, similarly for (a, b), BFs are plausibility non-conflicting if and only if $(\frac{1}{2} - h_1(u, v))(\frac{1}{2} - h_1(a, b)) \geq 0$, thus iff $(u - v)(a - b) \geq 0$.

Plausibility conflict between (u, v) and (a, b) increases from $|\frac{1}{2} - \frac{1-u}{2-u-v}|$ to $|\frac{1}{2} - \frac{1-u}{2-u-v}| + \frac{1}{2}$ for any BFs from G, S_i; in detail from ϵ surrounding of $0'$ to the corresponding conflicting extremal BF in G, respectively from ϵ surrounding of 0 to the corresponding conflicting extremal BFs in $S_i's$. Similarly, Pl-$C((u, v), (a, b))$ increases for BFs on h-lines closer to the corresponding conflicting extremal element, while conflict between (u, v) and (a, b) is same for all BFs laying on the same h-line, see Figure 3, arrows represent decreasing of conflicts between (a, b) and (u, v), in the grey area $(D_0^{\leq 0})$ which contains BFs conflicting with given (u, v), for detail see [10].

Plausibility conflict between general BFs Bel and a given Bel_{UV} on Ω_n increases from Pl-$C(Bel_{UV}, U_n)$ to Pl-$C(Bel_{UV}, U_n) + \frac{n-1}{n}$ for any BFs from ϵ surroundings of 0, U_n and indecisive BFs to the corresponding conflicting categorical BF. Pl-$C(Bel, Bel_{UV})$ is constant for all BFs with the same $h(Bel)$.

4 Liu's Degree of Conflict

4.1 Definition and Properties of Liu's Degree of Conflict

To complete the topic we have to include also a comparison of the presented approach with Liu's "degree of conflict among belief functions" [15]. Similarly to comparative conflict, Liu does not consider an internal conflict in her approach. As we have analysed only conflict between two belief functions till now, we will do the same also with Liu's degree of conflict.

Let us recall degree of conflict cf which is defined as $cf(m_i, m_j) = (m_\oplus(\emptyset),$ $difBetP_{m_i}^{m_j})$ in [15], where $m_\oplus(\emptyset)$ should be rather $m_\ominus(\emptyset)$ (more precisely $(m_i \ominus m_j)(\emptyset))$ in fact, and the second component $difBetP_{m_i}^{m_j}$ is defined as $difBetP_{m_i}^{m_j} = max_{A \subseteq \Omega}(|BetP_{m_i}(A) - BetP_{m_j}(A)|)$. We can simplify this using the following lemma.

Lemma 1. *For any belief functions Bel_i, Bel_j given by bbas m_i, m_j the following holds true:*

$$difBetP_{m_i}^{m_j} = Diff(BetP_{m_i}, BetP_{m_j}) = \frac{1}{2} \sum_{\omega \in \Omega} |BetP_{m_i}(\{\omega\}) - BetP_{m_j}(\{\omega\})|.$$

Specially, it holds that $difBetP_{(c,d)}^{(a,b)} = Diff((\frac{1+a-b}{2}, \frac{1+b-a}{2}), (\frac{1+c-d}{2}, \frac{1+d-c}{2})) = \frac{1}{2}(|a-b-c+d|)$ *on* Ω_2.

Proof. $difBetP_{m_i}^{m_j} = max_{A \subseteq \Omega}(|BetP_{m_i}(A) - BetP_{m_j}(A)|)$. Let us suppose that max to be effected for $A_M \subset \Omega$. Let $BetP_{m_i}(A_M) \geq BetP_{m_j}(A_M)$; it is possible to show that $A_M \subseteq \{\omega \,|\, BetP_{m_i}(\{\omega\}) \geq BetP_{m_j}(\{\omega\})\}$ and $\{\omega \,|\, BetP_{m_i}(\{\omega\}) \leq BetP_{m_j}(\{\omega\})\} \subseteq \overline{A}_M$.

$BetP_{m_i}(A_M) - BetP_{m_j}(A_M) = \sum_{\omega \in A_M}(BetP_{m_i}(\{\omega\}) - BetP_{m_j}(\{\omega\}))$,

$BetP_{m_i}(\overline{A}_M) - BetP_{m_j}(\overline{A}_M) = \sum_{\omega \in \overline{A}_M}(BetP_{m_i}(\{\omega\}) - BetP_{m_j}(\{\omega\}))$,

$BetP_{m_i}(\overline{A}_M) - BetP_{m_j}(\overline{A}_M) = 1 - BetP_{m_i}(A_M) - (1 - BetP_{m_j}(A_M)) = -\sum_{\omega \in A_M}(BetP_{m_i}(\{\omega\}) - BetP_{m_j}(\{\omega\}))$,

$|BetP_{m_i}(\overline{A}_M) - BetP_{m_j}(\overline{A}_M)| = |\sum_{\omega \in A_M}(BetP_{m_i}(\{\omega\}) - BetP_{m_j}(\{\omega\}))|$. Due to $BetP_{m_i}(\{\omega\}) \geq BetP_{m_j}(\{\omega\})$ for all $\omega \in A_M$ and $BetP_{m_i}(\{\omega\}) \leq BetP_{m_j}(\{\omega\})$ for all $\omega \in \overline{A}_M$, we have:

$|BetP_{m_i}(\overline{A}_M) - BetP_{m_j}(\overline{A}_M)| = \sum_{\omega \in \overline{A}_M}|BetP_{m_i}(\{\omega\}) - BetP_{m_j}(\{\omega\})|$

$|BetP_{m_i}(\overline{A}_M) - BetP_{m_j}(\overline{A}_M)| = \sum_{\omega \in A_M}|BetP_{m_i}(\{\omega\}) - BetP_{m_j}(\{\omega\})|$. Thus $\sum_{\omega \in \Omega}|BetP_{m_i}(\{\omega\}) - BetP_{m_j}(\{\omega\})| = \sum_{\omega \in A_M}|BetP_{m_i}(\{\omega\}) - BetP_{m_j}(\{\omega\})| + \sum_{\omega \in \overline{A}_M}|BetP_{m_i}(\{\omega\}) - BetP_{m_j}(\{\omega\})| = 2 \cdot \sum_{\omega \in A_M}|BetP_{m_i}(\{\omega\}) - BetP_{m_j}(\{\omega\})|$.

Analogously for $BetP_{m_i}(A_M) \leq BetP_{m_j}(A_M)$. $\square$

As a side effect, we have a simplification of computational complexity of cf: instead of computing 2^n differences of pignistic probabilities of general subsets of Ω using $difBetP_{m_i}^{m_j}$, it is enough to compute n differences of singletons using $Diff(BetP_{m_i}, BetP_{m_j})$, moreover pignistic probabilities of all singletons we need for obtaining of $BetP(A)$ for computation of pignistic probabilities of general subsets of the frame in the original case.

Corollary 1. *Having already computed pignistic probabilities $BetP_i$ and $BetP_j$ of belief functions Bel_i and Bel_j defined by bbas m_i, m_j, computational complexity of the first component of degree of conflict cf was reduced to $O(n)$.*

Back to conflicts again: What may be a non-conflicting pair of BFs here? It seems that such a pair, where degree of conflict is zero, i.e. where there is no conflict. As there are two components of cf, no conflict would appear only when both of them are zero, thus 0 would not be non-conflicting even with consonant BFs. Hence we will consider $min(m_{\odot}(\emptyset), difBetP_{m_i}^{m_j}) = min((m_{\odot}(\emptyset), Diff(BetP_{m_i}, BetP_{m_j}))$. Thus 0 is non-conflicting with any BF, and there is no problem with full conflicts as $min(1,1) = 1$ (minimum does not decrease full conflicts).

For behaviour of cf, resp. of its components ($m_{\odot}(\emptyset)$ and $Diff(BetP_{m_i}, BetP_{m_j})$) on Ω_2, see Figures 4 and 5 where combination of a fixed (u,v) with any BF from Ω_2 is presented. The only non-conflicting BFs are 0 and those with $BetP(a,b) = BetP(u,v)$, thus (taking $v = 1 - u$) cf ignores neutrality – non-conflictness of $0'$ resp. U_n on BBFs. Hence it, consequently, cannot consider non-conflictness of different BFs which prefer/oppose same element(s) of Ω. Disjunctive non-conflicting areas: stand alone 0 and $\{(a,b) | BetP(a,b) = (u, 1-u)\}$ do not seem to be intuitive, or reasonably interpretable.

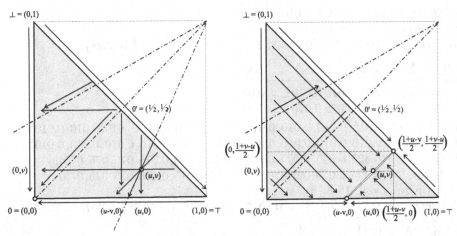

Fig. 4. $m_\ominus(\emptyset)$ for $m_\ominus = (a,b)\ominus(u,v)$, where (a,b) is a general BF and (u,v) is a fixed general BF, both on Ω_2

Fig. 5. $DifBetP_{(u,v)}^{(a,b)}$ of general BF (a,b) and fixed general BF (u,v) on Ω_2

4.2   Comparison of Plausibility Conflict with Degree of Conflict cf

As we can see from Figures 3, 4, and 5 main difference is in non-conflicting BFs, see the following examples.

Example 2 (Difference of plausibility conflict from cf on Ω_2).

$m_3 = (0.50, 0.46)$, $Pl\_P(m_3) = (0.519231, 0.480769)$, $BetP(m_3) = (0.52, 0.48)$,
$m_4 = (0.95, 0.01)$, $Pl\_P(m_4) = (0.951923, 0.048077)$, $BetP(m_4) = (0.97, 0.03)$,
$\Omega_{PlC}(m_3, m_4) = \emptyset$, $Pl\text{-}C(m_3, m_4) = 0$,
$difBetP_{m_4}^{m_3} = 0.45$, $m_\ominus(\emptyset) = 0.442$;

$m_5 = (0.50, 0.50)$, $Pl\_P(m_5) = (0.50, 0.50)$, $BetP(m_5) = (0.50, 0.50)$,
$m_6 = (1.00, 0.00)$, $Pl\_P(m_6) = (1.00, 0.00)$, $BetP(m_6) = (1.00, 0.00)$,
$\Omega_{PlC}(m_5, m_6) = \emptyset$, $Pl\text{-}C(m_5, m_6) = 0$,
$difBetP_{m_6}^{m_5} = 0.50$, $m_\ominus(\emptyset) = 0.50$.

We can see big and maximal $difBetP$ and $m_\ominus(\emptyset)$ at BF, which have 0 mutual plausibility conflict, as maximal $difBetP$ of non-conflicting BFs is 0.5 on Ω_2, and $\frac{n-1}{n}$ on Ω_n, in general. For higher absolute values of $difBetP$ of non-conflicting BFs we need larger frames of discernment, see the next example.

Example 3 (Difference of plausibility conflict from cf on $\Omega_5, \Omega_{10}, \Omega_{100}$).

$\Omega_5:$	X :	$\{\omega_1\}$	$\{\omega_2\}$	$\{\omega_3\}$	$\{\omega_4\}$	$\{\omega_5\}$	$\{\omega_1, \omega_2\}$	$\{\omega_3, \omega_4, \omega_5\}$	Ω_5
$m_i(X):$		0.70	0.04	0.01	0.01	0.01	0.10	0.03	0.10
$m_j(X):$		0.20	0.13	0.14	0.14	0.14	0.04	0.06	0.15

$Pl\_P(m_i) = (0.576923, 0.153846, 0.089744, 089744, 089744)$,
$BetP(m_i) = (0.77, 0.11, 0.04, 0.04, 0.04)$,
$Pl\_P(m_j) = (0.221590, 0.181818, 0.198864, 0.198864, 0.198864)$,

$BetP(m_j) = (0.25, 0.18, 0.19, 0.19, 0.19)$,
$\Omega_{PlC}(m_i, m_j) = \emptyset$, $Pl\text{-}C(m_i, m_j) = 0$,
$difBetP_{m_j}^{m_i} = 0.52$, $m_\ominus(\emptyset) = 0.5328$, $cf(m_i, m_j) = (0.52, 0.5328)$

$\Omega_{10}:$	X :	$\{\omega_1\}$	$\{\omega_2\}$	$\{\omega_3\}$	...	$\{\omega_{10}\}$
	$m_i(X):$	0.910	0.010	0.010	...	0.010
	$m_j(X):$	0.325	0.075	0.075	...	0.075

$Pl\_P(m_i) = (0.910, 0.010, 0.010, 0.010, 0.010, 0.010, 0.010, 0.010, 0.010, 0.010)$,
$BetP(m_i) = (0.910, 0.010, 0.010, 0.010, 0.010, 0.010, 0.010, 0.010, 0.010, 0.010)$,
$Pl\_P(m_j) = (0.325, 0.075, 0.075, 0.075, 0.075, 0.075, 0.075, 075, 075, 075)$,
$BetP(m_j) = (0.325, 0.075, 0.075, 0.075, 0.075, 0.075, 0.075, 075, 075, 075)$,
$\Omega_{PlC}(m_i, m_j) = \emptyset$, $Pl\text{-}C(m_i, m_j) = 0$,
$difBetP_{m_j}^{m_i} = 0.585$, $m_\ominus(\emptyset) = 0.6975$, $cf(m_i, m_j) = (0.585, 0.6975)$.

$\Omega_{100}:$	X :	$\{\omega_1\}$	$\{\omega_2\}$	$\{\omega_3\}$	...	$\{\omega_{100}\}$
	$m_i(X):$	0.9010	0.0010	0.0010	...	0.0010
	$m_j(X):$	0.0199	0.0099	0.0099	...	0.0099

x_y
$Pl\_P(m_i) = (0.901, 0.001, 0.001, ..., 0.001)$, $BetP(m_i) = (0.901, 0.001, 0.001, ...,$
$0.001)$, $Pl\_P(m_j) = (0.0199, 0.0099, 0.0099, ..., 0.0099)$, $BetP(m_j) = (0.0199,$
$0.0099, 0.0099, ..., 0.0099)$, $\Omega_{PlC}(m_i, m_j) = \emptyset$, $Pl\text{-}C(m_i, m_j) = 0$,
$difBetP_{m_j}^{m_i} = 0.8811$, $m_\ominus(\emptyset) = 0.98119$, $cf(m_i, m_j) = (0.8811, 0.98119)$.

On the other hand we should show an examples, with significantly less both $difBetP_{m_j}^{m_i}$ and $m_\ominus(\emptyset)$ than in the previous examples, but with BFs having positive plausibility conflict, comparable with $cf(m_i, m_j)$:

Example 4 (Accordance of plausibility conflict and cf on Ω_2 and Ω_5).

$m_7 = (0.30, 0.20)$, $Pl\_P(m_7) = (0.535353, 0.464646)$, $BetP(m_7) = (0.55, 0.45)$,
$m_8 = (0.25, 0.35)$, $Pl\_P(m_8) = (0.464286, 0.535714)$, $BetP(m_8) = (0.45, 0.55)$,
$\Omega_{PlC}(m_7, m_8) = \{\omega_1, \omega_2\} = \Omega_2$, $Pl\text{-}C(m_7, m_8) = min(0.069, 0.11) = 0.069$,
$difBetP_{m_8}^{m_7} = 0.1$, $m_\ominus(\emptyset) = 0.11$;

$\Omega_5:$	X :	$\{\omega_1\}$	$\{\omega_3\}$	$\{\omega_4\}$	$\{\omega_1,\omega_2\}$	$\{\omega_3,\omega_4\}$	$\{\omega_1,\omega_2,\omega_3\}$	$\{\omega_1,\omega_5\}$	$\{\omega_2,\omega_5\}$	$\{\omega_3,\omega_5\}$	$\{\omega_4,\omega_5\}$	Ω_5
	$m_i(X):$	0.15	0.15	0.05	0.40	0.10	0.05					0.15
	$m_j(X):$							0.15	0.15	0.15	0.40	0.15

$Pl\_P(m_i) = (0.350, 0.275, 0.200, 0.125, 0.050)$,
$BetP(m_i) = (0.38\bar{6}, 0.23\bar{6}, 0.23\bar{6}, 0.120, 0.020)$,
$Pl\_P(m_j) = (0.122449, 0.122449, 0.122449, 0.224490, 0.408163)$,
$BetP(m_j) = (0.105, 0.105, 0.105, 0.230, 0.455)$,
$\Omega_{PlC}(m_i, m_j) = \{\omega_1, \omega_2\,\omega_4\,\omega_5\}$, $Pl\text{-}C(m_i, m_j) = min(0.418878, 0.525) = 0.418878$,
$difBetP_{m_j}^{m_i} = 0.545$, $m_\ominus(\emptyset) = 0.525$, $cf(m_i, m_j) = (0.545, 0.525)$.

Example 5 (Accordance of plausibility conflict and cf of highly conflicting BFs on Ω_2).

$m_{15} = (0.98, 0.01)$, $Pl_-P(m_{15}) = (0.980198, 0.019802)$, $BetP(m_{15}) = (0.985, 0.015)$,
$m_{16} = (0.01, 0.98)$, $Pl_-P(m_{16}) = (0.019802, 0.980198)$, $BetP(m_{16}) = (0.015, 0.985)$,
$\Omega_{PlC}(m_{15}, m_{16}) = \{\omega_1, \omega_2\} = \Omega_2$, $Pl\text{-}C(m_{15}, m_{16}) = min(0.960396, 0.9605) = 0.960396$, $dif BetP^{m_{15}}_{m_{16}} = 0.97$, $m_\ominus(\emptyset) = 0.9605$.

4.3 Summary of Analysed Approaches

The plausibility conflict seems to be better of the presented approaches. It distinguishes internal conflicts of BFs from the conflict between them. It respects neutrality of 0 and of U_n on Bayesian BFs, conflict neutrality of indecisive BFs, and also mutual non-conflictness of BFs which prefer/oppose same elements of frame of discernment. This approach has applicable formulas for computation of size of conflict.

The only disadvantage of the plausibility conflict is its simple utilization of $Diff$ for computation of values of conflicts. E.g. difference of $(a_1, b_1) = (0.48, 0.52)$ and $(c_1, d_1) = (0.98, 0.02)$ is the same as that of $(a_2, b_2) = (0.26, 0.74)$ and $(c_2, d_2) = (0.76, 0.24)$, whereas the first conflict should be less as (a_1, b_1) is close to neutral $0'$, thus only 'a part' of the difference should be really conflicting, whereas both $(a_2, b_2), (c_2, d_2)$ have almost the same difference from $0'$ thus their almost entire mutual difference should really be conflicting.

Similarly to plausibility approach, Liu's degree of conflict also has applicable formulas, but her approach does not distinguish internal conflict of BFs, it does not respect neutrality of U_n for BBFs, and poses hard interpretable disjunctive areas of BFs non-conflicting with a given one. A difference is also used there.

5   Conclusion

Mathematical properties of the plausibility conflict of belief functions (BFs) are analyzed in this study. Both internal plausibility conflict $Pl\text{-}IntC$ inside BFs and plausibility conflict between BFs $Pl\text{-}C$ are studied. Analysis and comparison to Liu's degree of conflict cf [15] is included. As a side effect of this study, computational complexity of degree of conflict cf was reduced.

Liu's degree of conflict distinguishes conflict between BFs from $m_\ominus(\emptyset)$ and from distance/difference of BFs. Plausibility conflict goes further to the nature of conflict; it captures mutual non-conflictness of BFs which prefer/oppose same elements of the frame of discernment. Further it also distinguishes internal conflict of single belief functions from conflict between them.

Nevertheless, the presented representation of conflict between BFs is still not fully corresponding to the complete nature of conflict as some kind of a difference is partially included in the definition of both of degree of conflict and in plausibility conflict.

All of the theoretical results can be used as a basis for better understanding of conflicts of BFs in general and for further study of conflict to improve the presented approaches or to create a new approach capturing the nature of conflict of belief functions as much as possible.

Acknowledgments. This research is supported by the grant P202/10/1826 of the Grant Agency of the Czech Republic. The partial institutional support RVO: 67985807 is also acknowledged. The author is grateful to Eva Pospíšilová for creation of the useful and illuminative figures.

References

1. Almond, R.G.: Graphical Belief Modeling. Chapman & Hall, London (1995)
2. Ayoun, A., Smets, P.: Data association in multi-target detection using the transferable belief model. Int. Journal of Intelligent Systems 16(10), 1167–1182 (2001)
3. Cobb, B.R., Shenoy, P.P.: A Comparison of Methods for Transforming Belief Functions Models to Probability Models. In: Nielsen, T.D., Zhang, N.L. (eds.) ECSQARU 2003. LNCS (LNAI), vol. 2711, pp. 255–266. Springer, Heidelberg (2003)
4. Daniel, M.: Algebraic structures related to Dempster-Shafer theory. In: Bouchon-Meunier, B., Yager, R.R., Zadeh, L.A. (eds.) IPMU 1994. LNCS, vol. 945, pp. 51–61. Springer, Heidelberg (1995)
5. Daniel, M.: Distribution of Contradictive Belief Masses in Combination of Belief Functions. In: Bouchon-Meunier, B., Yager, R.R., Zadeh, L.A. (eds.) Information, Uncertainty and Fusion, pp. 431–446. Kluwer Academic Publishers, Boston (2000)
6. Daniel, M.: Algebraic Structures Related to the Combination of Belief Functions. Scientiae Mathematicae Japonicae 60(2), 245–255 (2004); Sci. Math. Jap. Online 10, 501–511 (2004)
7. Daniel, M.: Probabilistic Transformations of Belief Functions. In: Godo, L. (ed.) ECSQARU 2005. LNCS (LNAI), vol. 3571, pp. 539–551. Springer, Heidelberg (2005)
8. Daniel, M.: New Approach to Conflicts within and between Belief Functions. Technical report V-1062, ICS AS CR, Prague (2009)
9. Daniel, M.: Conflicts within and between Belief Functions. In: Hüllermeier, E., Kruse, R., Hoffmann, F. (eds.) IPMU 2010. LNCS (LNAI), vol. 6178, pp. 696–705. Springer, Heidelberg (2010)
10. Daniel, M.: Conflicts of Belief Functions. Technical report V-1108, ICS AS CR, Prague (2011)
11. Daniel, M.: Introduction to an Algebra of Belief Functions on Three-element Frame of Discernment — A Quasi Bayesian Case. In: Greco, S., Bouchon-Meunier, B., Coletti, G., Fedrizzi, M., Matarazzo, B., Yager, R.R. (eds.) IPMU 2012, Part III. CCIS, vol. 299, pp. 532–542. Springer, Heidelberg (2012)
12. Haenni, R.: Aggregating Referee Scores: an Algebraic Approach. In: 2nd International Workshop on Computational Social Choice, COMSOC 2008, Liverpool, UK (2008)
13. Hájek, P., Havránek, T., Jiroušek, R.: Uncertain Information Processing in Expert Systems. CRC Press, Boca Raton (1992)
14. Hájek, P., Valdés, J.J.: Generalized algebraic foundations of uncertainty processing in rule-based expert syst. (dempsteroids). Comp. and Artif. Intell. 10, 29–42 (1991)
15. Liu, W.: Analysing the degree of conflict among belief functions. Artificial Intelligence 170, 909–924 (2006)
16. Shafer, G.: A Mathematical Theory of Evidence. Princeton University Press, Princeton (1976)
17. Smets, P.: The combination of evidence in the transferable belief model. IEEE-Pattern Analysis and Machine Intelligence 12, 447–458 (1990)
18. Smets, P.: Analyzing the combination of conflicting belief functions. Information Fusion 8, 387–412 (2007)

The Use of Intuitionistic Fuzzy Values in Rule-Base Evidential Reasoning

Ludmila Dymova, Pavel Sevastjanov, and Kamil Tkacz

Institute of Comp.& Information Sci., Czestochowa University of Technology,
Dabrowskiego 73, 42-200 Czestochowa, Poland
sevast@icis.pcz.pl

Abstract. A new approach to the rule-base evidential reasoning based on the synthesis of fuzzy logic, Atannasov's intuitionistic fuzzy sets theory and the Dempster-Shafer theory of evidence is proposed. It is shown that the use of intuitionistic fuzzy values and the classical operations on them directly may provide counter-intuitive results. Therefore, an interpretation of intuitionistic fuzzy values in the framework of Dempster-Shafer theory is proposed and used in the evidential reasoning. Using the real-world example, it is shown that such an approach provides reasonable and intuitively obvious results when the classical method of rule-base evidential reasoning cannot produce any reasonable results.

Keywords: Rule-base evidential reasoning, Atannasov's intuitionistic fuzzy sets, Dempster-Shafer Theory.

1 Introduction

The methods of rule-base evidential reasoning are based on the synthesis of the tools of Fuzzy Sets theory (FST) and the Dempster-Shafer theory (DST). The integration of FST and DST within symbolic, rule-based models primarily was used for solving control and classification problems [4,5,15,22,26]. These approaches seem to be justified in the solution of control and classification problems when outputs can be presented by real values.

On the other hand, if we deal with decision support systems, system's outputs can be only the names or labels of corresponding actions or decisions, e.g., the names of medical diagnoses. It is clear that in such cases, the methods based on conventional fuzzy logic, developed for the controlling can not be used at least directly. A more suitable for the building decision support systems seems to be the so-called $RIMER$ approach proposed in [24,25] based on the Evidential Reasoning approach [23].

In the framework of $RIMER$ approach, the final outcome obtained as the aggregation of belief rules is presented as $O = \{(D_j, \beta_j)\}$, where β_j, $j = 1$ to N, is the aggregated degree of belief in the decision (hypothesis, action, diagnosis) D_j. Therefore, the decision characterised by the maximal aggregated degree of belief is the best choice. So the $RIMER$ approach can be used for building decision support systems. Nevertheless, there are two restrictions in the $RIMER$

L. Rutkowski et al. (Eds.): ICAISC 2013, Part I, LNAI 7894, pp. 247–258, 2013.

approach that reduce its ability to deal with uncertainties that decision makers often meet in practice.

The first restriction is that in the framework of $RIMER$ approach, a degree of belief can be assigned only to a particular hypothesis, not to a group of them, whereas the assignment of a belief mass to a group of events is a key principle of the DST.

The second restriction is concerned with the observation that in many real-world decision problems we deal with different sources of evidence and the combination of them is needed. The $RIMER$ approach does not provide a technique for the combination of evidence from different sources.

It is important that usually the advantages of the approaches based on the rule-base evidential reasoning were demonstrated using simple numerical examples and only a few examples of solving real-world problems using these approaches were found in the literature [5,21,19]. The methods used in these papers are charged with two above mentioned restrictions of $RIMER$ approach. The method used in [16] is free of the second restriction while the first one is retained.

In [11,13,17], a new approach free of both above mentioned restrictions was developed and used for the solution of real-world problems.

It is important that in all above mentioned approaches to the rule-base evidential reasoning, the conventional fuzzy logic was used. For example, the following rule may be used: $If\ x\ is\ Low\ Then\ D$, where Low is some fuzzy class defined by the corresponding membership function $\mu_{Low}(x)$, D is a name of decision. Nevertheless, in practice we often deal with the intersecting fuzzy classes, e.g., Low and $Middle$ and therefore we often have $\mu_{Low}(x) > 0$ and $\mu_{Middle}(x) > 0$. Then if $\mu_{Low}(x) > \mu_{Middle}(x)$ we state that $x\ is\ Low$ and information of nonzero $\mu_{Middle}(x)$ is lost, whereas the difference between $\mu_{Middle}(x)$ and $\mu_{Low}(x)$ may be very small.

In the current paper, we will show that such loss of information may lead to incorrect results in the rule-base evidential reasoning and a new method for the solution of these problems based in the synthesis of Atanassov's intuitionistic fuzzy sets (A-IFS) [1] and DST will be developed.

For these reasons, the rest of paper is set out as follows. Section 2 presents the basic definition of DST and A-IFS, the commonly used arithmetical operations on intuitionistic fuzzy values $IFVs$ and the representation of these operations in the framework of DST needed for the subsequent analysis. In Section 3, we present our new approach to the rule-base evidential reasoning based on the synthesis of A-IFS and DST and perform its advantages using examples obtained with the use of expert system for diagnostic of type 2 diabetes developed on the base of our approach. Finally, the concluding section summarises the paper.

2   Preliminaries

2.1   The Basic Definitions of DST

The origins of the Dempster-Shafer theory (DST) go back to the work by A.P. Dempster [8] who developed a system of upper and lower probabilities. Following this work his student G. Shafer [18] provided a more thorough explanation of belief functions.

Assume A are subsets of X. It is important to note that a subset A may be treated also as a question or proposition and X as a set of propositions or mutually exclusive hypotheses or answers. A DS belief structure has associated with it a mapping m, called basic probability assignment (bpa), from subsets of X into a unit interval, $m : 2^X \to [0,1]$ such that $m(\emptyset) = 0$, $\sum_{A \subseteq X} m(A) = 1$. The subsets of X for which the mapping does not assume a zero value are called focal elements.

Shafer [18] introduced a number of measures associated with DS belief structure.

The measure of belief is a mapping $Bel : 2^X \to [0,1]$ such that for any subset B of X it can be presented as $Bel(B) = \sum_{\emptyset \neq A \subseteq B} m(A)$.

A second measure introduced by Shafer [18] is a measure of plausibility. The measure of plausibility associated with m is a mapping $Pl : 2^X \to [0,1]$ such that for any subset B of X it can be presented as $Pl(B) = \sum_{A \cap B \neq \emptyset} m(A)$. It is easy to see that $Bel(B) \leq Pl(B)$. DS provides an explicit measure of ignorance about an event B and its complementary $\overline{B}$ as a length of an interval $[Bel(B), Pl(B)]$ called the belief interval (BI). It can also be interpreted as imprecision of the "true probability" of B [18].

The core of the evidence theory is the Dempsters rule of combination of evidence from different sources. The rule assumes that information sources are independent. With two belief structures m_1, m_2, the Dempster's rule of combination is defined as follows:

$$m_{12}(A) = \frac{\sum_{B \cap C = A} m_1(B) m_2(C)}{1 - K}, A \neq \emptyset, m_{12}(\emptyset) = 0, \qquad (1)$$

where $K = \sum_{B \cap C = \emptyset} m_1(B) m_2(C)$ is called the degree of conflict which measures the conflict between the pieces of evidence. Zadeh [27] underlined that this rule involves counter-intuitive behaviors in the case of considerable conflict.

It is important to note that the Dempster's rule is commutative and associative, but not idempotency operators. Nevertheless, in spite of the lack of idempotency, the Dempster's rule is successfully used in different real-world applications.

2.2   The Basics of A-IFS

The concept of A-IFS (the reasons for such notation are presented in [9]) is based on the simultaneous consideration of membership μ and non-membership ν of an element of a set to the set itself (see formal definition in [1]). It is postulated that $0 \leq \mu + \nu \leq 1$. Following to [1], we call $\pi_A(x) = 1 - \mu_A(x) - \nu_A(x)$ the hesitation degree of the element x in the set A. Hereinafter, we shall call an object $A = \langle \mu_A(x), \nu_A(x) \rangle$ intuitionistic fuzzy value (IFV).

The operations of addition $\oplus$ and multiplication $\otimes$ on $IFVs$ were defined by Atanassov [2] as follows. Let $A = \langle \mu_A, \nu_A \rangle$ and $B = \langle \mu_B, \nu_B \rangle$ be $IFVs$. Then

$$A \oplus B = \langle \mu_A + \mu_B - \mu_A \mu_B, \nu_A \nu_B \rangle, \tag{2}$$

$$A \otimes B = \langle \mu_A \mu_B, \nu_A + \nu_B - \nu_A \nu_B \rangle. \tag{3}$$

These operations were constructed in such a way that they produce $IFVs$. Using operations (2) and (3), in [7] the following expressions were obtained for any integer $n=1,2,..$:

$$nA = A \oplus ... \oplus A = \langle 1 - (1 - \mu_A)^n, \nu_A^n \rangle, \quad A^n = A \otimes ... \otimes A = \langle \mu_A^n, 1 - (1 - \nu_A)^n \rangle.$$

It was proved later that these operations produce $IFVs$ not only for integer n, but also for all real values $\lambda > 0$, i.e.

$$\lambda A = \langle 1 - (1 - \mu_A)^\lambda, \nu_A^\lambda \rangle, \tag{4}$$

$$A^\lambda = \langle \mu_A^\lambda, 1 - (1 - \nu_A)^\lambda \rangle. \tag{5}$$

The operations (2)-(5) have good algebraic properties [20]:

An important problem is the comparison of $IFVs$. Therefore, the specific methods which are rather of heuristic nature were developed to compare $IFVs$. For this purpose, Chen and Tan [6] proposed to use the so-called score function (or net membership) $S(x) = \mu(x) - \nu(x)$. Let A and B be $IFVs$. It is intuitively appealing that if $S(A) > S(B)$ then A should be greater (better) than B, but if $S(A) = S(B)$ this does not always mean that A is equal to B. Therefore, Hong and Choi [14] in addition to the above score function introduced the so-called accuracy function $H(x) = \mu(x) + \nu(x)$ and showed that the relation between functions S and H is similar to the relation between mean and variance in statistics. Xu [20] used the functions S and H to construct order relations between any pair of intuitionistic fuzzy values A and B as follows:

$$
\begin{aligned}
&If\,(S(A) > S(B)),\,then\,B\,is\,smaller\,than\,A;\\
&If\,(S(A) = S(B)),\,then\\
&(1)\,If\,(\,H(A)=H(B)),\,then\,A=B;\\
&(2)\,If\,(H(A) < H(B)),\,then\,A\,is\,smaller\,than\,B.
\end{aligned}
\tag{6}
$$

In [12], we have shown that operation (2)-(5) and (6) have some undesirable properties which may lead to the non-acceptable results in applications:

1. The addition (2) is not an addition invariant operation. Let A, B and C be $IFVs$. Then $A < B$ (in sense of (6)) does not always lead to $(A \oplus C) < (B \oplus C)$.
2. The operation (4) is not preserved under multiplication by a real-valued $\lambda > 0$, i.e., inequality $A < B$ (in sense of (6)) does not necessarily imply $\lambda A < \lambda B$.

2.3 Interpretation of *A-IFS* in the Framework of *DST*

It was shown in [10] that *DST* may serve as a good methodological base for interpretation of *A-IFS*. It was proved in [10] that IFV $A = \langle \mu_A(x), \nu_A(x) \rangle$ may be represented by the belief interval $BI_A(x) = [Bel_A(x), Pl_A(x)]$, where $Bel_A(x) = \mu_A(x)$ and $Pl_A(x) = 1 - \nu_A(x)$ (see [10] for formal definitions and more detail). This interpretation makes it possible to represent mathematical operations on $IFVs$ as operations on belief intervals. The use of the semantics of *DST* makes it possible to enhance the performance of *A-IFS* when dealing with the operations on $IFVs$. In [12], two sets of operations on $IFVs$ based on the interpretation of intuitionistic fuzzy sets in the framework of *DST* are proposed and analysed. The first set of operations is based on the treatment of belief interval as an interval enclosing a true probability. The second set of operations is based on the treatment of belief interval as an interval enclosing a true power of some statement (argument, hypothesis, *ets*). It was shown in [12] that the non-probabilistic treatment of belief intervals representing $IFVs$ performs better than the probabilistic one and operations based on the probabilistic and non-probabilistic treatments of belief intervals representing $IFVs$ perform better than operations on $IFVs$ defined in the framework of conventional *A-IFS*.

Therefore, here we shall use only the treatment of belief interval as an interval enclosing a true power of some statement.

Let $X = \{x_1, x_2, ..., x_n\}$ be a finite universal set. Assume A is a subset of X. It is important to note that in the framework of *DST* a subset A may be treated also as a question or proposition and X as a set of propositions or mutually exclusive hypotheses or answers. In such a context, a belief interval $BI(A) = [Bel(A), Pl(A)]$ may be treated as an interval enclosing a true power of statement (argument, proposition, hypothesis, *etc*) that $x_j \in X$ belongs to the subset $A \subseteq X$. Obviously, the value of such a power lies in interval [0,1].

Therefore, a belief interval $BI(A) = [Bel(A), Pl(A)]$ as a whole may be treated as an imprecise (interval-valued) statement (argument, proposition, hypothesis, *etc*) that $x_j \in X$ belongs to the set $A \subseteq X$.

Based on this reasoning, we can say that if we pronounce this statement, we can obtain some result, e.g., as a reaction on this statement or as an answer to some question, and if we repeat this statement twice, the result does not change.

Such a reasoning implies the following property of addition operator:
$BI(A) = BI(A) \oplus_B BI(A) \oplus_B ... \oplus_B BI(A)$.

This is possible only if we define the addition $\oplus_B$ of belief intervals as follows: $BI(A) \oplus_B BI(A) = \left[\frac{Bel(A)+Bel(A)}{2}, \frac{Pl(A)+Pl(A)}{2} \right]$. So the addition of belief intervals is represented by their averaging.

Therefore, if we have n different statements represented by belief intervals $BI(A_i)$ then their sum $\oplus_B$ can be defined as follows:

$$BI(A_1) \oplus_B BI(A_2) \oplus_B .... \oplus_B BI(A_n) = \left[\frac{1}{n} \sum_{i=1}^{n} Bel(A_i), \frac{1}{n} \sum_{i=1}^{n} Pl(A_i) \right]. \quad (7)$$

The other operation on belief intervals are presented in [12] as follows:

$$BI(A) \otimes_B BI(B) = [Bel(A)Bel(B), Pl(A)Pl(B)], \qquad (8)$$

$$\lambda BI(A) = [\lambda Bel(A), \lambda Pl(A)], \qquad (9)$$

where λ is a real value in the interval $[0,1]$ as for $\lambda > 1$ this operation does not always provide a true belief interval. This restriction is justified enough since we define operations on belief intervals to deal with decision making problems, where λ usually represents the weight of local criterion, which is lesser than 1.

$$BI(A)^{\lambda} = [Bel(A)^{\lambda}, Pl(A)^{\lambda}], \qquad (10)$$

$$BI(A)^{BI(B)} = [Bel(A)^{Pl(B)}, Pl(A)^{Bel(B)}]. \qquad (11)$$

It is justified in [12] that to compare belief intervals it is enough to compare their centres.

It is proved in [12] that introduced operations on belief intervals are free of undesirable properties (1),(2) of conventional operations on $IFVs$.

3   The Synthesis of Fuzzy Logic and $A - IFS$ in the Rule-Based Evidential Reasoning

To present our approach in a more transparent form, in this section we shall use a relatively simple example of building the expert system for diagnosing type 2 diabetes which makes it possible to show the features of the proposed approach and avoid here the use of complicated general expressions.

The following tests are recommended by the World Health Organization (WHO) for diagnosis of the type 2 diabetes:

Test 1. A fasting plasma glucose test measures blood glucose in a person who has not eaten anything for at least 8 hours.

Test 2. An oral glucose tolerance test measures blood glucose after a person fasts at least 8 hours and 2 hours after the person drinks a glucose- containing beverage.

These tests are used to detect diabetes and pre-diabetes. Although, WHO proposes crisp intervals for blood glucose which correspond to the health (H), Pre-diabetes (H,D) and diabetes (D), in practice doctors use for diagnostics, e.g., such fuzzy concepts as Low, Medium and Big blood glucose, which can be presented by corresponding membership functions as in Fig.1, where μ_L, μ_M, μ_B correspond to the $\mu_{Low}, \mu_{Medium}, \mu_{Big}$, respectively. Here we shall treat the diagnosis Pre-diabetes as an intermediate one when a doctor hesitates in choice between the Health and Diabetes diagnoses. Therefore, the diagnosis Pre-diabetes in the spirit of DST can be treated as the compound hypothesis (H,D). Based on the known approaches to the rule-base evidential reasoning [11,23] we get the

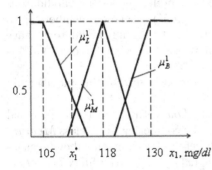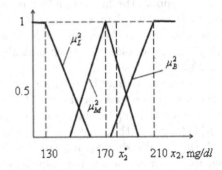

Fig. 1. Test 1 (blood glucose x_1) and Test 2 (blood glucose x_2)

following rules:

$$IF\, x_1\ is\ Low\ Then\ m_1^*(H) = \mu_L(x_1),$$
$$IF\, x_1\ is\ Medium\ Then\ m_1^*(H,D) = \mu_M(x_1);$$
$$IF\ x_1\ is\ Big\ Then\ m_1^*(D) = \mu_B(x_1),$$
$$IF\, x_2\ is\ Low\ Then\ m_2^*(H) = \mu_L(x_2),$$
$$IF\, x_2\ is\ Medium\ Then\ m_2^*(H,D) = \mu_M(x_2);$$
$$IF\ x_2\ is\ Big\ Then\ m_2^*(D) = \mu_B(x_2),$$

(12)

where *bpas* $m_1^*(H)$, $m_1^*(H,D)$, $m_1^*(D)$ and $m_2^*(H)$, $m_2^*(H,D)$, $m_2^*(D)$ should be additionally normalised. For $x_1 = x_1^*$ and $x_2 = x_2^*$ (see Fig.1) using the above rules (12) from the first test we get the diagnosis H (with $m_1^*(H) = \mu_L^1(x_1^*)$) and from the second one - (H,D) (with $m_2^*(H,D) = \mu_M^1(x_2^*)$).

Since these two tests are different sources of evidence, to obtain the final diagnosis they should be combined using an appropriate combination rule. Nevertheless, the above approach may lead to the controversial, counterintuitive results. That may be explained as follows. In the test 1, we take into account only diagnosis H, whereas the diagnosis (H,D) is possible as well with a non-zero value of membership function $\mu_M^1(x_1^*)$. Similarly, in the test 2 we are not taking into account the possible diagnosis D.

Summarizing , we can say that the known methods of rule-base evidential seasoning lead to the loss of important information which may affect the final results.

To avoid this problem, we propose to use the tools of intuitionistic fuzzy set theory. To clarify the basics of proposed approach, consider an example which can be treated as an extension of reasoning used by Atannasov [3] to explain the essence of $A - IFS$.

Let us consider a general presidential election where 30% of eligible population votes for the first candidate (X) and 50% - for the second one (Y). The rest of the votes, 20%, are for none or lost for some other reason. For the first candidate X one can state that the membership $\mu(X)$ of the eligible population to those who supports the first candidate is equal to 0.3; the membership $\mu(Y)$ to those who doesn't support the first candidate because they prefer the second candidate is equal to 0.5; Therefore, we can say that $\nu(X) = \mu(Y)$ is the non-membership to those who support the candidate X. Similarly, for the second candidate we have $\nu(Y) = \mu(X)$ and the uncertain part also known as hesitation degree $\pi(X, Y)$ is equal to 0.2.

This reasoning may be used for the presentation of intersecting membership functions. Let us consider the Fig. 1.

It is seen that x_1^* belongs to the fuzzy class Low with the membership equal to $\mu_L^1(x_1^*)$, but at the same time it belongs to the competing fuzzy class $Medium$ with the membership equal to $\mu_M^1(x_1^*)$. Therefore, based on the above reasoning, we can say that the non-membership $\nu_L^1(x_1^*)$ of x_1^* to the fuzzy class Low is equal to $\mu_M^1(x_1^*)$ as with this degree of membership it belongs to the competing class $Medium$. Using the same reasoning for the class $Medium$ we can present the final result by two $IFVs$: $\langle \mu_L^1(x_1^*), \nu_L^1(x_1^*) \rangle$, $\langle \mu_M^1(x_1^*), \nu_M^1(x_1^*) \rangle$, where $\mu_L^1(x_1^*) = \nu_M^1(x_1^*)$ and $\mu_M^1(x_1^*) = \nu_L^1(x_1^*)$. Similarly, for the test 2 (see Fig. 1) we get the following result: $\langle \mu_M^2(x_2^*), \nu_M^2(x_2^*) \rangle$, $\langle \mu_B^2(x_2^*), \nu_B^2(x_2^*) \rangle$, where $\mu_M^2(x_2^*) = \nu_B^2(x_2^*)$ and $\mu_B^2(x_2^*) = \nu_M^2(x_2^*)$.

It is easy to see that the examples presented in Fig. 1 are constructed in such a way that always $\mu_L^1(x_1) + \nu_L^1(x_1) \leq 1$, $\mu_M^1(x_1) + \nu_M^1(x_1) \leq 1$, $\mu_B^1(x_1) + \nu_B^1(x_1) \leq 1$ and $\mu_L^2(x_2) + \nu_L^2(x_2) \leq 1$, $\mu_M^2(x_2) + \nu_M^2(x_2) \leq 1$, $\mu_B^2(x_2) + \nu_B^2(x_2) \leq 1$. Therefore, in the framework of proposed approach, the hesitation degrees $\pi_L(x_1)$, $\pi_M(x_1)$, $\pi_B(x_1)$ and $\pi_L(x_2)$, $\pi_M(x_2)$, $\pi_B(x_2)$ can be analysed as well.

An important question arises: does the fundamental property of $A - IFS$ $(\mu(x) + \nu(x)) \leq 1$ hold for all cases when we deal with the intersecting fuzzy classes? Below we shall show that this property holds only if membership functions of competing fuzzy classes satisfy jointly some reasonable and justified conditions which are not so important in the framework of traditional approach. Let us consider some illustrative examples. In Fig. 1, we can see that competing membership functions intersect in the points where the values of membership functions are less or equal to 0.5, and therefore the fundamental property of $A - IFS$ $(\mu(x) + \nu(x)) \leq 1$ holds. In Fig. 2, we can see that if competing membership functions intersect in the points where the values of membership functions are equal to 0.5 we have $(\mu_L(x) + \nu_L(x)) = 1$, $(\mu_M(x) + \nu_M(x)) = 1$ and $(\mu_B(x) + \nu_B(x)) = 1$. Obviously there are no any hesitation degrees in this case.

On the other hand, if the membership functions intersect in the point where their values are greater than 0.5 (see Fig.2), the fundamental property of $A - IFS$ may be violated. It is easy to see that in the interval $[x_1, x_3]$ we have $(\mu_B(x) + \nu_B(x)) > 1$. In our opinion, this non-acceptable result is obtained as the membership functions $\mu_M(x)$ and $\mu_B(x)$ were built improperly. Really, all $x \in [x_1, x_2]$ belong completely to the fuzzy class $Medium$ and therefore they cannot belong to the another class, whereas we have $\mu_B(x) \geq 0$ in this interval. Maybe, this type of reasoning seems to be too restrictive ones, but it reflects well the specificity of the decision making based on the intersecting membership functions representing competing fuzzy classes, such as Low, $Medium$, Big, ets.

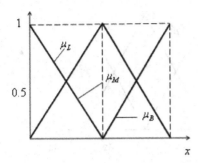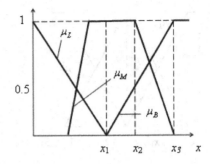

Fig. 2. The example of an inappropriate building of membership functions

To avoid the above-mentioned problem, the membership functions of competing fuzzy classes should be constructed in such a way that if one of them is equal to 1 then the other one should be equal to 0.

Using the notation of $A - IFS$ and DST (the basic probability assignment (bpa), m) we can represent the rules for the example presented in Fig. 1 as follows:

$$
\begin{aligned}
&IF(x_1 = x_1^*)\,Then\,m^1(H) = \left\langle \mu_L^1(x_1^*), \nu_L^1(x_1^*) \right\rangle, \\
&m^1(H, D) = \left\langle \mu_M^1(x_1^*), \nu_M^1(x_1^*) \right\rangle, m^1(D) = \left\langle \mu_B^1(x_1^*), \nu_B^1(x_1^*) \right\rangle, \\
&IF(x_2 = x_2^*)\,Then\,m^2(H) = \left\langle \mu_L^2(x_2^*), \nu_L^2(x_2^*) \right\rangle, \\
&m^2(H, D) = \left\langle \mu_M^2(x_2^*), \nu_M^2(x_2^*) \right\rangle, m^2(D) = \left\langle \mu_B^2(x_2^*), \nu_B^2(x_2^*) \right\rangle.
\end{aligned}
\tag{13}
$$

Of course, in this case we have: $m^1(D) = \left\langle \mu_B^1(x_1^*), \nu_B^1(x_1^*) \right\rangle = \langle 0, 1 \rangle$, $m^2(H) = \left\langle \mu_L^2(x_2^*), \nu_L^2(x_2^*) \right\rangle = \langle 0, 1 \rangle$.

The next step is the combination of obtained $bpas$. Taking into account that operations $\oplus$ and $\otimes$ on $IFVs$ provide $IFVs$ as well, there is no need, in our case, for the normalisation of Dempster's combination rule (1). Therefore, in our example, the combined $bpas$ may be presented as follows:

$$
\begin{aligned}
&m^{12}(H) = m^1(H) \otimes m^2(H) \oplus m^1(H) \otimes m^2(H, D) \oplus m^2(H) \otimes m^1(H, D), \\
&m^{12}(D) = m^1(D) \otimes m^2(D) \oplus m^1(D) \otimes m^2(H, D) \oplus m^2(D) \otimes m^1(H, D), \\
&m^{12}(H, D) = m^1(H, D) \otimes m^2(H, D).
\end{aligned}
\tag{14}
$$

Since the operation $\oplus_B$ and $\otimes_B$ on belief intervals provide belief intervals too, there in no need to normalise the Dempster's combination rule (1), when belief intervals are used for representation of $IFVs$. To obtain the corresponding combination rule it is enough to substitute operations $\oplus$ and $\otimes$ in (14) with $\oplus_B$ and $\otimes_B$ and replace intuitionistic fuzzy-valued $bpas$ by corresponding belief intervals.

To represent the advantages of proposed approaches, consider the critical example presented in Fig.3. Using conventional fuzzy logic, from (12) we get $bpas$ $m_1^*(H) = 0.55$, $m_1^*(H, D) = 0$, $m_1^*(D) = 0$ and $m_2^*(H) = 0$, $m_2^*(H, D) =$

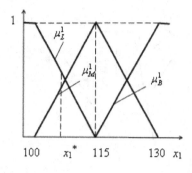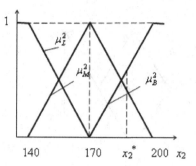

Fig. 3. Critical example

0, $m_2^*(D) = 0.6$. Since after normalisation we obtain $m_1(H) = 1$, $m_1(H, D) = 0$, $m_1(D) = 0$ and $m_2(H) = 0$, $m_2(H, D) = 0$, $m_2(D) = 1$, the degree of conflict K between the pieces of evidence is equal to 1 and therefore the classical Dempster's combination rule (1) cannot be used. Therefore, the use of conventional fuzzy logic in the rule-base evidential reasoning cannot provide any reasonable result in the considered real-world example.

On the other hand, according to the doctor's opinion, in our case the diagnosis Pre-diabetes seems to be more justified than Diabetes and Diabetes is more preferable than Health. The Pre-diabetes is intuitively obvious for the doctor in the considered example. Moreover, in his informal, but based on common sense analysis, the doctor considered the values $m^1(H) = 0.55$, $m^1(H, D) = 0.45$, $m^1(D) = 0$ and $m^2(H) = 0$, $m^2(H, D) = 0.4$, $m^2(D) = 0.6$ as the arguments in favour of corresponding diagnoses. It is easy to see that the sum of arguments in favour of Pre-diabetes $m^1(H, D) + m^2(H, D)$ is grater than the sum of arguments in favour of Diabetes $m^1(D) + m^2(D)$ which is greater than $m^1(H) + m^2(H)$.

Nevertheless, from (13) and (14) we obtain the following intuitionistic fuzzy-valued result:

$m^{12}(H) = \langle 0.22, 0.19 \rangle$, $m^{12}(H, D) = \langle 0.18, 0.82 \rangle$, $m^{12}(D) = \langle 0.27, 0.175 \rangle$.

To compare obtained $IFVs$, the rules (6) was used. The following values of score function have been obtained

$S(m^{12}(H)) = 0.027$, $S(m^{12}(H, D)) = -0.64$, $S(m^{12}(D)) = 0.095$.

Since $S(m^{12}(D)) > S(m^{12}(H)) > S(m^{12}(H, D))$ then (see (6)) we obtain the counter-intuitive diagnosis-Diabetes.

Then using in (13) and (14) the belief intervals representing corresponding $IFVs$ and operations $\oplus_B$ and $\otimes_B$ instead of $\oplus$ and $\otimes$ in (14) we get the following resulting belief intervals $m^{12}(H) = [0.073, 0.073]$, $m^{12}(H, D) = [0.18, 0.18]$, $m^{12}(D) = [0.09, 0.09]$ (factually, we have obtained real-valued results, but this a specificity of our example and usually we obtain interval-valued results).

Since in our case, $m^{12}(H, D) > m^{12}(D) > m^{12}(H)$ we obtain the intuitively obvious diagnosis - Pre-diabetes.

Summarising, we can say that the interpretation of $A - IFS$ in the framework of DST makes in possible to use more information in the evidential- reasoning, and as a consequence to obtain reasonable results when the synthesis of classical fuzzy logic and DST is failed. The counter-intuitive results obtained with the use of (13) and (14) when operations the $\oplus$ and $\otimes$ are used may be caused by bad properties of these operations (see subsection 2.2).

4   Conclusion

In this paper, a new method for the rule-base evidential reasoning based on the synthesis of $A - IFS$, fuzzy logic and the DST is proposed and analysed using the critical real-world example of type 2 diabetes diagnostics. It is shown that the direct use of intuitionistic fuzzy values and classical operations on them may lead to the counter-intuitive results. This may be a consequence of bad properties of classical operation on intuitionistic fuzzy values. It is shown that the interpretation of $A - IFS$ in the framework of DST makes in possible to use more information in the evidential reasoning and as a consequence to obtain reasonable results when the synthesis of classical fuzzy logic and DST is failed.

References

1. Atanassov, K.T.: Intuitionistic fuzzy sets. Fuzzy Sets and Systems 20, 87–96 (1986)
2. Atanassov, K.: New operations defined over the intuitionistic fuzzy sets. Fuzzy Sets and Systems 61, 137–142 (1994)
3. Atanassov, K.: Intuitionistic Fuzzy Sets. Springer Physica-Verlag, Berlin (1999)
4. Binaghi, E., Madella, P.: Fuzzy Dempster-Shafer reasoning for rule-based classifiers. Intelligent Syst. 14, 559–583 (1999)
5. Binaghi, E., Gallo, I., Madella, P.: A neural model for fuzzy Dempster-Shafer classifiers. International Journal of Approximate Reasoning 25, 89–121 (2000)
6. Chen, S.M., Tan, J.M.: Handling multicriteria fuzzy decision-making problems based on vague set theory. Fuzzy Sets and Systems 67, 163–172 (1994)
7. Dey, S.K., Biswas, R., Roy, A.R.: Some operations on intuitionistic fuzzy sets. Fuzzy Sets and Systems 114, 477–484 (2000)
8. Dempster, A.P.: Upper and lower probabilities induced by a muilti-valued mapping. Ann. Math. Stat. 38, 325–339 (1967)
9. Dubois, D., Gottwald, S., Hajek, P., Kacprzyk, J., Prade, H.: Terminological difficulties in fuzzy set theory-The case of "Intuitionistic Fuzzy Sets". Fuzzy Sets and Systems 156, 485–491 (2005)
10. Dymova, L., Sevastjanov, P.: An interpretation of intuitionistic fuzzy sets in terms of evidence theory: Decision making aspect. Knowledge-Based Systems 23, 772–782 (2010)
11. Dymova, L., Sevastianov, P., Bartosiewicz, P.: A new approach to the rule-base evidential reasoning: Stock trading expert system application. Expert Systems with Applications 37, 5564–5576 (2010)
12. Dymova, L., Sevastjanov, P.: The operations on intuitionistic fuzzy values in the framework of Dempster-Shafer theory. Knowledge-Based Systems 35, 132–143 (2012)

13. Dymova, L., Sevastianov, P., Kaczmarek, K.: A stock trading expert system based on the rule-base evidential reasoning using Level 2 Quotes. Expert Systems with Applications 39, 7150–7157 (2012)
14. Hong, D.H., Choi, C.-H.: Multicriteria fuzzy decision-making problems based on vague set theory. Fuzzy Sets and Systems 114, 103–113 (2000)
15. Ishizuka, M., Fu, K.S., Yao, J.T.P.: Inference procedure and uncertainty for the problem reduction method. Inform. Sci. 28, 179–206 (1982)
16. Khatibi, V., Montazer, G.A.: A fuzzy-evidential hybrid inference engine for coronary heart disease risk assessment. Expert Systems with Applications 37, 8536–8542 (2010)
17. Sevastianov, P., Dymova, L., Bartosiewicz, P.: A framework for rule-base evidential reasoning in the interval setting applied to diagnosing type 2 diabetes. Expert Systems with Applications 39, 4190–4200 (2012)
18. Shafer, G.: A mathematical theory of evidence. Princeton University Press, Princeton (1976)
19. Straszecka, E.: Combining uncertainty and imprecision in models of medical diagnosis. Information Sciences 176, 3026–3059 (2006)
20. Xu, Z.: Intuitionistic preference relations and their application in group decision making. Information Sciences 177, 2363–2379 (2007)
21. Xu, D.-L., Liu, J., Yang, J.-B., Liu, G.-P., Wang, J., Jenkinson, I., Ren, J.: Inference and learning methodology of belief-rule-based expert system for pipeline leak detection. Expert Systems with Applications 32, 103–113 (2007)
22. Yager, R.R.: Generalized probabilities of fuzzy events from belief structures. Information Sciences 28, 45–62 (1982)
23. Yang, J.B.: Rule and utility based evidential reasoning approach for multiattribute decision analysis under uncertainties. European Journal of Operational Research 131, 31–61 (2001)
24. Yang, J.B., Liu, J., Wang, J., Sii, H.S., Wang, H.: Belief rule-base inference methodology using the evidential reasoning approach - RIMER. IEEE Transactions on Systems Man and Cybernetics. Part A-Systems and Humans 36(2), 266–285 (2006)
25. Yang, J.B., Liu, J., Xu, D.L., Wang, J., Wang, H.: Optimization Models for Training Belief-Rule-Based Systems. IEEE Transactions on Systems Man and Cybernetics, Part A-Systems and Humans 37(4), 569–585 (2007)
26. Yen, J.: Generalizing the Dempster-Shafer theory to fuzzy sets. IEEE Transactions on Systems Man and Cybernetics 20, 559–570 (1990)
27. Zadeh, L.: A simple view of the Dempster-Shafer theory of evidence and its application for the rule of combination. AI Magazine 7, 85–90 (1986)

Financial Stock Data and Ordered Fuzzy Numbers

Dariusz Kacprzak[1], Witold Kosiński[2,3], and W. Konrad Kosiński[2]

[1] University of Technology, Wiejska 45, 15-351 Białystock, Poland
[2] Polish-Japanese Institute of Information Technology, Koszykowa 86, 02-008 Warsaw, Poland
[3] Kazimierz Wielki University of Bydgoszcz, Chodkiewicza 30, 85-064 Bydgoszcz, Poland
d.kacprzak@pb.edu.pl, wkos@pjwstk(ukw).edu.pl, wkosin@yahoo.com

Abstract. Financial stock time series are presented together with the so-called Japanese candlesticks. Model of Ordered Fuzzy Numbers is shortly presented and its use in presentation of Japanese candlesticks. Then the ogive, the graphical representation of the cumulative relative frequency of transactions is introduced, as the next characteristic of price time series. Linear operations on ogive curves are defined. It is shown that ogive is reflecting some properties of stock time series additional to the Japanese candlestick.

Keywords: time series, Ordered Fuzzy Number (OFN), Step Ordered Fuzzy Numbers (SOFN), Japanese candlestick, ogive.

1 Introduction

Economics is the social science that studies the production, distribution and consumption of goods and services. One of the basic tools used in economics are economic models. A model is a theoretical construction which represents economic processes with a set of variables and a set of logical and quantitative relationships between them. The application of these variables in models involves the knowledge of their numerical values. However, in reality many economic variables are difficult to be measured with precision. For example information appearing in the financial market is the most uncertain since what happens in the world has an effect on quotations of financial instruments. On the other hand, how the information influences the market is decided by investors by taking a long or short position in the market. In addition imprecise terms, such as high economic growth, high unemployment, low inflation are commonly used.

One method to model imprecise terms is application of fuzzy sets and numbers, in particular Ordered Fuzzy Numbers (OFN). In this paper we confine our interest to financial market and to attempt to model financial stock data represented by time series and some histograms. In our approach the Japanese Candlesticks will be modeled using OFN and some their generalized concepts, taking into account the histograms of transactions in particular price intervals (cf. Appendix for the short presentation of OFN). The use of OFN allows modeling uncertainty associated with financial data. Thanks to well-defined arithmetic of ordered fuzzy numbers, one can reach models of fuzzy time series. Our investigations are aimed at the construction of a decision support system in future. It will be the subject of further research.

L. Rutkowski et al. (Eds.): ICAISC 2013, Part I, LNAI 7894, pp. 259–270, 2013.

2 Model of Japanese Candlestick

On present financial market formal methods on which decision support systems (DSS) are based have their sources in 3 groups: technical analysis, fundamental analysis and portfolio one. In the present paper we focus our attention on the methods following the technical analysis. Most tools in this range follow historical data of prices (i.e. the quotations of financial instruments such as stock prices or currency pair) and their characteristic moments (points). It is commonly assumed that trends, or patterns, in historical data are rather regular and may repeat. Those facts may be regarded as a basis in designing a particular DSS for financial market.

On financial market one can observe two type of investors. In the first group the fundamental analysis is most often in use, while in the second group tools of the basis technical analysis play the main role. Participants of each group must make a subjective assessment either of macroeconomic factors or signals of technical analysis. For all of them the human factor is a cause of uncertainty as well.

On the stock market analyzing graphs that describe price and volume changes, one can try to identify configurations that change with time and on this basis to make a forecast about future trends. According to the literature, cf.[11], one distinguishes two formation types: formations that forecast change in the actual (present) trends and formations that forecast a continuation of the present trends.

Fig. 1. Japanese candlesticks of WIG20 index in the period September 29 - November 7, 2012

Making investment decisions based on observation of each single quotation is very difficult or even impossible, when price changes tens times a minute. The human mind does not handle large numbers or macro ideas well. The data required to produce a standard bar chart consists of the open, high, low, and close prices for the time period under study. A bar chart consists of vertical lines representing the high to low range in prices for that day. The high price refers to the highest price that the issue traded during that day. Likewise, the low price refers to the lowest price traded that day. For years, the only other price element used in bar charting was the close price. Most bar charts have been always displayed with a volume histogram at the bottom.

To illustrate movements in the price of a financial instrument over time and to make their decisions the investors of the second group very often uses price charts such as Japanese Candlestick Chart (cf. Fig.1). On Fig.1 we present Japanese candlestick chart of WIG20 on Warsaw Stock Exchange Market.

Japanese candlestick charts [7] do not require anything new or different as far as data are concerned. Open, high, low, and close are all that is needed to do candlestick charting. The Japanese Candlestick chart are four dimensional time series taken with given frequency, i.e. for one day, for one hour, for a quoter of an hour, for one minute, or so. Each entry in the series gives four prices: low, open, close and high, respectively. One should notice that using this type of price chart, a large part of the information about the temporal process is lost, since in a given time period (i.e. one hour or a quoter of an hour) the price must have changed hundreds of times. The open-high-low-close chart (also OHLC chart, or simply bar chart) and Japanese Candlestick are most often used in technical analysis. Both types of charts are presented in Fig. 2.

The box in Fig. 2 that makes up the difference between the open and close prices, is called the real body of the candlestick. The height of the body is the range between the day's open price and the day's close price. When this body is black, it means that the closing price was lower than the opening price. When the closing price is higher than the opening, the body is white.

When drawing candlestick charts by hand, the Japanese use red instead of white to represent the up days (close higher than open). With the use of a computer, this is not feasible because red would be printed as black on most printers and you could not tell the up days from the down days.

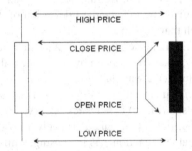

Fig. 2. Japanese candlesticks: Left - open, Right - black

In this work as a financial data we mean the quotations of financial instruments (e.g. stock prices or currency pair). In practice, quotations of financial instruments are represented using price charts [7,11].

3   Japanese Candlesticks and OFN

In the last paper [10] the authors proposed an original concept of financial fuzzy time series models, based on financial data in the form of Japanese Candlestick Charts. In their approach the Japanese candlesticks were modeled using Ordered Fuzzy Numbers. They called them Ordered Fuzzy Candlesticks (OFC). The use of Ordered Fuzzy Numbers has allowed the authors modeling uncertainty associated with financial data. They use two classes of possible shape functions: affine and Gauss-type, to model representative pair of OFN.

Let us consider a time series $\{X_t : t = 1, 2, .., n\}$ of a financial instrument representing price changes as a function of time steps. It is not important, at the moment, how long the time distance between subsequent time steps is: it could be a day, an hour or a minute. To designate the center of the Ordered Fuzzy Candlestick (OFC) the authors of [10] use classical average known in financial mathematics of time series X_t. They were

$$\text{Simple Average } SA = \frac{1}{n} \sum_{i=1}^{n} X_i ,$$

$$\text{Linear Weighted Average } LWA = \frac{1}{\sum_{j=1}^{n} j} \sum_{i=1}^{n} i X_i , \tag{1}$$

$$\text{Exponential Average } EA = \frac{1}{\sum_{j=1}^{n} (1-\alpha)^{n-j}} \sum_{i=1}^{n} (1-\alpha)^{n-i} X_i , \text{with } \alpha \in (0,1) .$$

Notice that two last averages have the fading memory property: the recent prices have a bigger impact on the average that the very first ones. In [10] they use two classes of possible shape functions: affine and Gauss-type, to model representative pair of OFN. However, to fix the critical points of those functions they introduce two pairs of additional parameters C_1, C_2, given by the standard deviation of X_t, and S_1, S_2 from the set $\{SA, LWA, AE\}$, such that $S_1 \leq S_2$.

Then, in the case of open candlestick (i.e. $X_1 \leq X_n$) the values $f(0) = high(X_t) - C_1$, $f(1) = S_1$, $g(1) = S_2$, and $g(0)$ is given by some integral constraint with two additional parameters A, B, in such a way that $S_1, S_2 \in [low(X_t), high(X_t)]$. They have assumed that the function g is increasing, while h decreasing, and both are continuous.

Then, in the case of closed (black) candlestick (i.e. $X_n \leq X_1$) the values $f(0) = high(X_t) + C_2$, $f(1) = S_2$, $g(1) = S_1$, and $g(0)$ is given by some integral constraint. They have also assumed that the function f is increasing, while g decreasing, and both are continuous. We can see that Ordered Fuzzy Candlestick corresponding to closed Japanese Candlestick has different orientation than that corresponding to open one.

The authors of [10] have made some experimental studies, constructing their OFC for selected time series of quotations of EUR/USD for 1-hour period from the January 2011. They have also shown that for two different time series X_t and Y_t having the same Japanese candlestick, because the main prices (i.e. OHLC) are the same, however the OFC are different. It shows that the model they accepted introduces additional information to Japanese candlestick.

Thanks to well-defined arithmetic of OFN the authors of [10] have constructed models of fuzzy time series, such as e.g. an autoregressive process , where all input values are OFC, while the coefficients and output values are arbitrary OFN, in the form of classical equations, without using rule-based systems. Finally, some applications of those models for modeling and forecasting selected financial time series were presented in [10].

In our approach we introduce different type of fuzzy candlesticks equipped with additional information based on the histogram corresponding to given time series of prices. Moreover, we claim that the characteristic points of OFN used by those authors have some drawbacks, since making operation of additions on OFC different main prices are summed up.

Now to our method we use Ordered Fuzzy Numbers to represent four prices [6]. Our method is based on trapezoidal type numbers (cf. Fig. 3), in which four characteristic values are written in the order of prices: low, open, close, high. If a pair of functions (f, g) has to represent Japanese Candlestick, then $f(0) = low(X_t)$, $f(1) = open(X_t)$, $g(1) = close(X_t)$, and $g(0) = high(X_t)$.

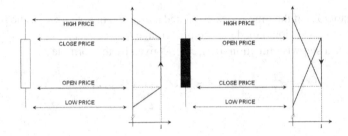

Fig. 3. Japanese candlesticks represented by OFN, Left - open(increasing), Right - black (decreasing)

To model the Japanese candlestick the support of OFN (f, g), i.e. $[f(0), g(0)]$ represents the maximal range of the prices between $low(X_t)$ and $high(X_t)$. The kernel of the OFN represents the range of prices between the open and closed, ones. We will show in the paper that the OFN can be successfully applied in the presentation of stock prices giving transparent image of the stock exchange. In addition, as in the case of Japanese candlestick, charts built on Ordered Fuzzy Numbers produce suitable information on which investors can make investment decisions. Such information, however, requires sometimes particular confirmation by means of other tools such as technical analysis indicators and related how the situation will develop in the stock exchange.

One of the most popular and frequently used by investors tools are moving averages, which can be related to the opening prices, closing, low or high, and calculated within a certain number of periods of the past. Average of the close price is the most popular, of course . When we use the description of stock prices by the Ordered Fuzzy Numbers then a simple moving average (SMA) can be defined by the formula:

$$SMA_n = \frac{1}{n}(P_0 + P_1 + \cdots + P_{m-1}),$$

where P_i, $i = 0, ..., m - 1$ are Ordered Fuzzy Numbers describing the earlier periods of stock prices, P_0 is OFN from the last period, m is the number of periods.

An additional advantage of presenting stock exchange data with Ordered Fuzzy Numbers is that when we want to analyze specific prices, such as closing price, it is enough to connect the appropriate points of the Ordered Fuzzy Numbers and get line charts. This can be also illustrated. At last, but not the least we have defuzzification functionals (cf. Appendix) for our disposal.

4   Cumulative Histogram and Its Ogive

Let us make the splitting of a fixed price range $\mathcal{P} = [P_0, P_F)$ into K subintervals

$$[P_0, P_F) = \bigcup_{i=0}^{K-1} [p_i, p_{i+1}), \text{where } P_0 = p_0 < p_1 < ... < p_K = P_F. \qquad (2)$$

Take the histogram of the time series presented above and denote by e_{i+1} the frequency of operations (transactions) made in the price range $[p_i, p_{i+1}), i = 0, 1, .., K - 1$. We will introduce a stepwise function $h(x), x \in \mathcal{P}$ given by the formula

$$h(x) = e_{i+1}^h , \text{ when } x \in [p_i, p_{i+1}), i = 0, 2, .., K - 1. \qquad (3)$$

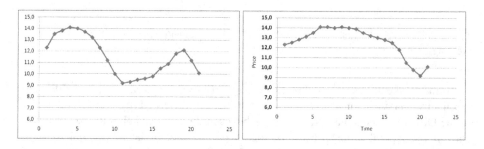

Fig. 4. Two price charts with the same OHLC and the same black candlestick on Fig. 5

If we sum up all transactions for this time series, i.e. $\sum_{i=0}^{K-1} e_{i+1}$ and call it S_h, we may introduce the second function h_R which measures the relative frequency of this time series given by the formula

$$h_R(x) = \frac{h(x)}{S_h} = \frac{e_{i+1}^h}{S_h} \text{ when } x \in [p_i, p_{i+1}), i = 0, 2, .., K - 1. \qquad (4)$$

In our situation we may wish to highlight the proportion of transactions that lie below each subinterval. In such case after [7]) (cf. p. 48) we introduce the so-called **ogive**, i.e. the cumulative relative frequency distribution which is defined identically to the probability distribution, i.e. for $x \in [p_i, p_{i+1})$ cumulative relative frequency is

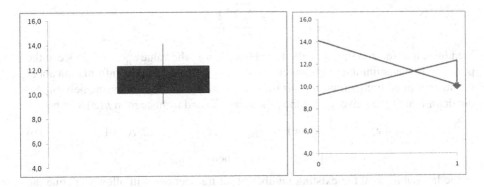

Fig. 5. Japanese and trapezoidal candlesticks for both price charts from Fig.4

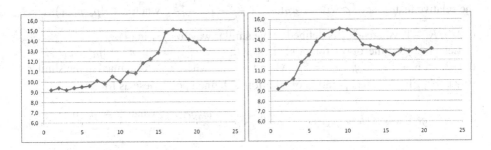

Fig. 6. Price charts with the same OHLC and the same open candlestick on Fig. 7

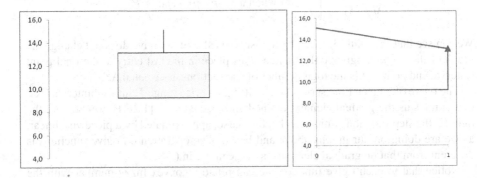

Fig. 7. Japanese and trapezoidal candlesticks for both price charts from Fig.6

$$c_{i+1}^h = \sum_{j=1}^{i+1} \frac{e_j^h}{S_h}.$$ (5)

We notice that for x in the last subinterval $[p_{K-1}, p_K)$ the value $c_K^h = 1$. Hence at the point p_K in the definition of the function ogive, in order to keep the information about the number of all transactions for this time series we put different value, namely S_h. So our definition of the ogive h_C for the time series X_t and its histogram $h(x)$ will be

$$h_C(x) = c_{i+1}^h \text{, when } x \in [p_i, p_{i+1}), i = 0, 1, 2, ..., K-1,$$ (6)

$$\text{and } h_C(x) = S_h \text{ , when } x = p_K.$$

In the last subinterval the existing number of all transactions will allow to define the operation of addition of two ogive functions and the multiplication by a positive scalar.

We introduce the operation of addition of two cumulative relative frequency distributions as follows. Let $Y_t, t = 1, 2, ..,$ be another time series with values in the price range $\mathcal{P}$, and $g(x)$ its histogram while S_g is the sum of all transactions, then, in view of (4), the relative histogram g_R will be $g_R(x) = \dfrac{g(x)}{S_g} = \dfrac{e_{i+1}^g}{S_g}$, when $x \in [p_i, p_{i+1}), i = 0, 2, .., K-1$, where e_{i+1}^g is defined in the similar way to e_{i+1}^h in (4).

Let $g_C(x)$ be the ogive for $g(x)$, i.e. $g_C(x) = c_{i+1}^g$ when $x \in [p_i, p_{i+1}), i = 0, 1, 2, ..., K-1$, and $g_C(x) = S_g$, when $x = p_K$, where c_{i+1}^g is defined in the similar way to c_{i+1}^h in (5). The operation of addition is defined pointwiese as follows

$$(h_C + g_C)(x) =: (h+g)_C(x) = \begin{cases} w_h h_c(x) + w_g g_C(x) \text{, when } x \in [p_0, p_K) \\ S_h + S_g, \qquad \text{when} \quad x = p_K \end{cases}$$ (7)

with $w_h + w_g = 1$, where $w_h = \dfrac{S_h}{S_h + S_g}$, $w_g = \dfrac{S_g}{S_h + S_g}$.

This definition may be used to define the scalar multiplication of any h_C by a positive constant $\lambda \in \mathbf{R}^+$, as

$$\lambda h_C(x) = \begin{cases} h_C(x) \text{ when } x \in [p_0, p_K), p_0 = P_0 \\ \lambda S_h \quad \text{when} \quad x = p_K, p_K = P_F \end{cases}.$$ (8)

We can see that the multiplication by a positive scalar of an ogive does not change the graph of the original ogive; only change takes place in the last entry at the final point (interval end point): it is the total number of transactions, here equal λS_h.

The ogive of a given time series with splitting its price range $\mathcal{P}$ into subintervals (cf. (2) reminds us the gradual element defined and discussed in [1,2]. However, here the ogive is the step function, which can be, of course, approximated by a piecewise linear, as we are doing on our graphs above and below. The operation on ogive functions is different from that on gradual elements, as we can see in (7-8).

Notice that to each ogive function we can relate a convex fuzzy number with the support contained in the right-open interval $[P_0, P_F)$, and apply all defuzzification functionals, those classical for CFN. It is rather obvious that the center of gravity defuzzification functional is more appropriate than any other functional. In the present examples

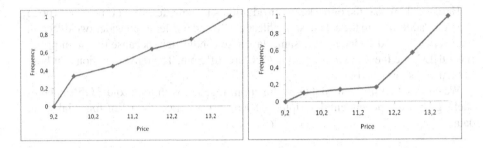

Fig. 8. Ogive functions corresponding to the price charts in Fig.4

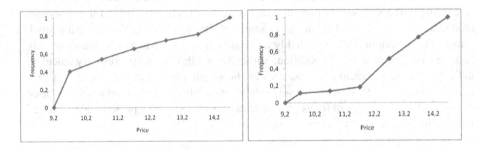

Fig. 9. Ogive functions corresponding to the price charts in Fig.6

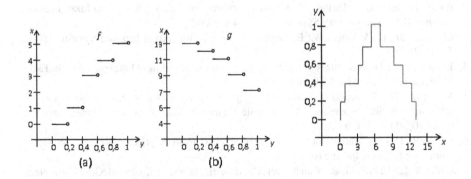

Fig. 10. Example of Step Ordered Fuzzy Number $A = (f, g)$: Left -(a) function f, (b) function g, Right - membership functions of A

all classical four defuzzification functionals: MOM, LOM, FOM and ROM will give for ogive function the same value.

Here we show that the ogive keeps an additional information about time series (price chart) X_t additional to the Japanese candlestick. To end this let us consider two different time series X_t and Y_t having the same Japanese candlestick, because the main prices (i.e. OHLC) are the same, however the OFC are different. The ogive functions for both of them are shown on Fig. 6.

We can see that in our model ogive functions together with trapezoidal OFN candlesticks give two independent descriptors of time series (price charts) of financial stock data.

5 Conclusions

The paper presents an application of a new model of fuzzy numbers called Ordered Fuzzy Numbers and ogive functions in characterization of stock-exchange problems. According to the authors, it opens up great opportunities to use OFN in the economic modelling. This is illustrated on the example of the using of OFN to describe stock prices. The description allows quickly and easily find price patterns in the same way like the candlestick charts. In addition, arithmetic in OFN model makes easy calculate indicators of the technical analysis, such as the simple moving average, which is presented in the work. Moreover, the ogive shows its applicability in characterizing price charts. Further research will focus on a combination of share price presented by Ordered Fuzzy Numbers and the volume of transactions.

References

1. Dubois, D., Prade, H.: Gradual elements in a fuzzy set. Soft. Comput. 12, 165–175 (2008), doi:10.1007/s00500-007-0187-6
2. Fortin, J., Dubois, D., Fargier, H.: Gradual numbers and their application to fuzzy interval analysis. IEEE Trans. Fuzzy Syst. 16(2), 388–402 (2008)
3. Goetschel Jr., R., Voxman, W.: Elementary fuzzy calculus. Fuzzy Sets and Systems 18(1), 31–43 (1986)
4. Kacprzak, D.: Ordered fuzzy numbers in economical modelling. Optimum - Studia Ekonomiczne (3), 263–281 (2010) (in Polish)
5. Kacprzak, D.: Przychód i koszt całkowity przedsiębiorstwa wyrażony przy użyciu skierowanych liczb rozmytych, Zarządzanie i Finanse. Journal of Management and Finance 10(2/1), 139–149 (2012)
6. Kacprzak, D.: Applications of ordered fuzzy numbers to stock prices representation. Optimum - Studia Ekonomiczne (6) (2012)
7. Keller, G.L., Litchfield, R.: Candlestick Charting Explained, 3rd edn. McGraw-Hill, New York (2006)
8. Kosiński, W., Prokopowicz, P., Ślęzak, D.: On algebraic operations on fuzzy reals. In: Rutkowski, L., Kasprzyk, J. (eds.) Proc. of the Sixth Int. Conference on Neutral Networks and Soft Computing, Zakopane. Advances in Soft Computing, Physica-Verlag, Heidelberg (2002)

9. Kosiński, W., Prokopowicz, P., Kacprzak, D.: Fuzziness – representation of dynamic changes by ordered fuzzy numbers. In: Seising, R. (ed.) Views on Fuzzy Sets and Systems. STUD-FUZZ, vol. 243, pp. 485–508. Springer, Heidelberg (2009)
10. Marszałek, A., Burczyński, T.: Financial fuzzy time series models based on ordered fuzzy numbers. In: Pedrycz, W., Chen, S.-M. (eds.) Time Series Analysis, Model. & Applications. ISRL, vol. 47, pp. 77–95. Springer, Heidelberg (2013)
11. Morris, G.L., Litchfield, R.: Candlestick Charting Explained. Timeless Techniques for Trading Stocks and Futures, 3rd edn. McGraw-Hill, New York (2006)
12. Kosiński, W.: On defuzzyfication of ordered fuzzy numbers. In: Rutkowski, L., Siekmann, J.H., Tadeusiewicz, R., Zadeh, L.A. (eds.) ICAISC 2004. LNCS (LNAI), vol. 3070, pp. 326–331. Springer, Heidelberg (2004)
13. Kosiński, W.: On fuzzy number calculus. Int. J. Appl. Math. Comput. Sci. 16(1), 51–57 (2006)
14. Kosiński, W., Prokopowicz, P., Ślęzak, D.: Ordered fuzzy numbers. Bulletin of the Polish Academy of Sciences, Sér. Sci. Math. 51(3), 327–338 (2003)
15. Kosiński, W., Prokopowicz, P.: Algebra of fuzzy numbers. Matematyka Stosowana. Matematyka dla Społeczeństwa 5(46), 37–63 (2004) (in Polish)
16. Kosiński, W., Piasecki, W., Wilczyńska-Sztyma, D.: On Fuzzy Rules and Defuzzification Functionals for Ordered Fuzzy Numbers. In: Burczyński, T., Cholewa, W., Moczulski, W. (eds.) Proc. of AI-Meth 2009 Conference, Gliwice. AI-METH Series, pp. 161–178 (Nowvember 2009)
17. Kosiński, W., Wilczyńska-Sztyma, D.: Defuzzification and implication within ordered fuzzy numbers. In: WCCI 2010 IEEE World Congress on Computational Intelligence, CCIB, Barcelona, Spain, July 18-23, pp. 1073–1079 (2010)
18. Nguyen, H.T.: A note on the extension principle for fuzzy sets. J. Math. Anal. Appl. 64, 369–380 (1978)

Appendix

Proposed recently by the second author and his two coworkers: P.Prokopowicz and D. Ślęzak [8,14,15] an extended model of convex fuzzy numbers [18] (CFN), called Ordered Fuzzy Numbers (OFN), does not require any existence of membership functions. In this model we can see an extension of CFN - model, when one takes a parametric representation of fuzzy numbers know since 1986, [3] of convex fuzzy numbers.

Definition 1. By an Ordered Fuzzy Number we understand a pair of functions(f, g) defined on the unit interval $[0, 1]$, which are functions of bounded variations.

Notice that if under particular assumptions concerning properties of f and g, namely
- $f \leq g$ are both invertible, i.e. inverse functions f^{-1} and g^{-1} exist,
- f is increasing, and g is decreasing, and such that $f \leq g$ (pointwise),
then we can construct a membership functions $\mu(x)$ of a convex fuzzy number with the help of the inverses of f and g.

On OFN, denoted by $\mathcal{R}_{BV}$, four algebraic operations have been proposed between fuzzy numbers and crisp (real) numbers, in which componentwise operations are present. In particular

$$f_C(y) = f_A(y) \star f_B(y), \qquad g_C(y) = g_A(y) \star g_B(y), \tag{9}$$

where "$\star$" works for "$+$", "$\cdot$", and "$\div$", respectively, and where $A \div B$ is defined, if the functions $|f_B|$ and $|g_B|$ are bounded from below. Notice that the subtraction of B is the same as the addition of the opposite of B, i.e. the number $(-1) \cdot B$, and consequently $B - B = 0$. From this follows that any fuzzy algebraic equation $A + X = C$ with given A and C as OFN possesses a solution, that is OFN, as well. Moreover, to any convex and continuous fuzzy number correspond two OFNs, they differ by the orientation: one has positive, say (f, g), another (g, f) has negative.

A relation of **partial ordering** in the space of all OFN, denoted by $\mathcal{R}$, can be introduced by defining the subset of 'positive' Ordered Fuzzy Numbers: a number $A = (f, g)$ is not less than zero, and by writing

$$A \geq 0 \quad \text{iff} \quad f \geq 0, \, g \geq 0. \tag{10}$$

In this way the set $\mathcal{R}_{BV}$ becomes a partially ordered ring.

In dealing with applications of fuzzy numbers we need set of functionals that map each fuzzy number into real, and in such a way that is consistent with operations on reals. Those operations are called defuzzifications. To be more strict we introduce

Definition 2. A map ϕ from the space $\mathcal{R}_{BV}$ of all OFN's to reals is called a **defuzzification functional** if is satisfies: 1) $\phi(c^{\ddagger}) = c$, 2) $\phi(A + c^{\ddagger}) = \phi(A) + c$, 3) $\phi(cA) = c\phi(A)$, for any $c \in \mathbf{R}$ and $A \in \mathcal{R}$. where $c^{\ddagger}(s) = (c, c)$, $s \in [0, 1]$, represents crisp number (a real) $c \in \mathbf{R}$.

From this follow that each defuzzification functional must be homogeneous of order one, restrictive additive, and some how normalized.

Step Ordered Fuzzy Numbers. It is worthwhile to point out that a class of ordered fuzzy numbers (OFNs) represents the whole class of convex fuzzy numbers.

Important consequence of this fact is the possibility of introducing a subspace of OFN composed of pairs of step functions. If we fix a natural number K and split $[0, 1)$ into $K - 1$ subintervals $[a_i, a_{i+1})$, i.e. $\bigcup_{i=1}^{K-1} [a_i, a_{i+1}) = [0, 1)$, where $0 = a_1 < a_2 <$ ... $< a_K = 1$, and define a **step function** f of resolution K by putting u_i on each subinterval $[a_i, a_{i+1})$, then each such function f is identified with a K-dimensional vector $f \sim \mathbf{u} = (u_1, u_2...u_K) \in \mathbf{R}^K$, the K-th value u_K corresponds to $s = 1$, i.e. $f(1) = u_K$. Taking a pair of such functions we have an Ordered Fuzzy Number from $\mathcal{R}_{BV}$. Now we introduce

Definition 3. By a Step Ordered Fuzzy Number A of resolution K we mean an ordered pair (f, g) of functions such that $f, g : [0, 1] \rightarrow \mathbf{R}$ are K-step functions.

We use $\mathcal{R}_K$ for denotation the set of elements satisfying Def. 3. The example of a Step Ordered Fuzzy Number and its membership function are shown in Fig. 10.

It is obvious that each element of the space $\mathcal{R}_K$ may be regarded as an approximation of elements from $\mathcal{R}_{BV}$, by increasing the number K of steps we are getting the better approximation. The norm of $\mathcal{R}_K$ is assumed to be the Euclidean one of $\mathbf{R}^{2K}$, then we have a inner-product structure for our disposal.

Diversity of Opinion Evaluated by Ordered Fuzzy Numbers

Magdalena Kacprzak[1], Witold Kosiński[1,2], and Katarzyna Węgrzyn-Wolska[3]

[1] Polish-Japanese Institute of Information Technology, Koszykowa 86, 02-008 Warsaw, Poland
[2] Kazimierz Wielki University of Bydgoszcz, Chodkiewicza 30, 85-064 Bydgoszcz, Poland
[3] ESIGETEL, 33, Victor Hugo, 94800 Villejuif, France
kacprzak@pjwstk.edu.pl, wkos@pjwstk(ukw).edu.pl,
katarzyna.wegrzyn@esigetel.fr

Abstract. Diversity of opinion is an empirical fact often appearing in social networks. In the paper known statistical methods of evaluation is substituted by fuzzy concepts, namely Step Ordered Fuzzy Numbers (SOFN). SOFN are extentions of Ordered Fuzzy Numbers (OFN) introduced by Kosiński, Prokopowicz and Ślęzak in 2002. In 2011 Kacprzak and Kosiński observed that SOFN may be equipped with a lattice structure. In consequence, Boolean operations like conjunction, disjunction and, what is more important, diverse types of implications can be defined on SOFN. In this paper we show how SOFN can be applied for modelling diversity of beliefs even in fuzzy expressions.

Keywords: diversity of opinion, Ordered Fuzzy Number (OFN), Step Ordered Fuzzy Numbers (SOFN), Opinion Mining (OM).

1 Introduction

Social networking websites such as Facebook, Twitter or LinkedIn have changed the Image of the Web over the last few years. Popular social networking sites have surpassed Search Engines (Google) for the most visited pages. The Web has become more a social media tool than a tool for information searching. At the same time the volume of content on the social media, blogs, etc. is growing at an exponential rate. With such an explosive growth of content, it is useful to feat this knowledge. The main goal is to retrieve the data from the social network contents and to put this knowledge to practical use in the form of prediction and prevention. That is why the Text Mining (TM) and Social Network Analysis (SNA) has become a necessity [3], [26], [27] for analysing not only information but also the connections across the information. The main objective of TM is to enable scientists to identify the necessary information as efficiently as possible, finding the relationships between available information by applying algorithmic, statistical, and data management methods to this knowledge.

The amount of information available in textual resources on the Web is huge and growing. For this reason, Information Extraction (IE) that aims at automatic or semi-automatic collection of structured data of specific type from textual corpora of given

L. Rutkowski et al. (Eds.): ICAISC 2013, Part I, LNAI 7894, pp. 271–281, 2013.

domain (such as medicine, economics, etc.) is in the mainstream of academic and industrial research.

However, information arriving via Web is different and different humans have different opinion about it. Hence the problem of diversity arises. Diversity of belief is an empirical fact. A large and growing body of work has used this diversity to explain various everyday life phenomena. Our paper deals with evaluating diversity of opinion of beliefs.

The first part of our paper introduces a short presentation of Ordered Fuzzy Numbers. The next part presents our approach to use Ordered Fuzzy Numbers to evaluate the level of truth or the human's belief, if the sentence is expressed by a human. If the sentence is expressed by an agent in a multi-agent system then we could try to evaluate the agent's belief about the agents' belief. The paper is the first step in the application of the fuzzy logic which stands behind the Step Ordered Fuzzy Numbers in modelling the Diversity of Humans' Belief. The conclusion summaries our study and introduces future challenges for our project.

2   Fuzzy Numbers

In real life we often use notions like bad weather, high temperature, small women, high humidity, obese man, or a firm which does well. Let us focus on these expressions. When we say that somebody is obese, when we talk about obesity? As a criterion we may consider body mass index (BMI) - a measurement which compares weight and height. However, in every day chatting, nobody calculates this index and then such an assessment deeply depends on a performer of the claim. For example, if a talker is from the United States of America then he surely does not say that obese is a person who weigh 80 kg and is 165 centimeters tall. Whereas a Frenchman will decidedly sticks that this person is at least overweight. Therefore the evaluation whether or not somebody is obese is very subjective and depends on diverse features of a performer of this action. Expressions which are not clear-cut and for which it is difficult to assign one from the values *true* or *false*, occur not only in human communication but also in software engineering, e.g., in rules exploited in fuzzy controllers. To capture diversity of approaches concerning expressions like "obesity", in literature are considered multi-valued logics [22, 23] or fuzzy logics [29]. The ways of modelling of uncertainty of software agents is broadly discussed in [12].

In this paper we propose new approach in which **ordered fuzzy numbers** (OFN) are applied. In our approach we use Ordered Fuzzy Numbers to evaluate the level of truth or the human's belief, if the sentence is expressed by a human in the natural language, i.e. in the fuzzy way.

The theory of fuzzy numbers [6] is that set up by Dubois and Prade [7], who proposed a restricted class of membership functions, called (L, R)–numbers with shape functions L and R. However, approximations of fuzzy functions and operations are needed if one wants to follow Zadeh's [29] extension principle. It leads to some drawbacks that concern properties of fuzzy algebraic operations, as well as to unexpected and uncontrollable results of repeatedly applied operations. These problems are resolved in

Ordered Fuzzy Numbers. OFN were invented by Kosiński, Prokopowicz and Ślęzak in the previous decade [16–20].

The definition of OFN uses the extension of the parametric representation of convex fuzzy numbers.

2.1   Ordered Fuzzy Numbers

Proposed by the second author and his two coworkers: P.Prokopowicz and D. Ślęzak [16–20] an extended model of convex fuzzy numbers [24] (CFN), called ordered fuzzy numbers (OFN), does not require any existence of membership functions. In this model we can see an extension of CFN - model, when one takes a parametric representation of fuzzy numbers know since 1986, [9] of convex fuzzy numbers.

Definition 1. By an Ordered Fuzzy Number we understand a pair of functions(f, g) defined on the unit interval $[0, 1]$, which are functions of bounded variations.

Notice that if

1. $f \leq g$ are both invertible, i.e. inverse functions f^{-1} and g^{-1} exist,
2. f is increasing, and g is decreasing, and such that
3. $f \leq g$ (pointwise),

then we can construct a membership functions $\mu(x)$ of a convex fuzzy number with the help of the inverses of f and g. In general, however, those conditions may not hold and membership function needs not to exist.

On OFN, denoted by $\mathcal{R}_{BV}$, four algebraic operations have been proposed between fuzzy numbers and crisp (real) numbers, in which componentwise operations are present. In particular if $A = (f_A, g_A), B = (f_B, g_B)$ and $C = (f_C, g_C)$ are mathematical objects called Ordered Fuzzy Numbers, then the sum $C = A + B$, product $C = A \cdot B$, division $C = A \div B$ and scalar multiplication by real $r \in \mathbf{R}$, are defined in natural way:

$$r \cdot A = (r f_A, r g_A),$$

and

$$f_C(y) = f_A(y) \star f_B(y), \qquad g_C(y) = g_A(y) \star g_B(y), \qquad (1)$$

where "$\star$" works for "+", "·", and "÷", respectively, and where $A \div B$ is defined, if the functions $|f_B|$ and $|g_B|$ are bounded from below. Notice that the subtraction of B is the same as the addition of the opposite of B, i.e. the number $(-1) \cdot B$, and consequently $B - B = 0$. From this follows that any fuzzy algebraic equation $A + X = C$ with given A and C as OFN possesses a solution, that is OFN, as well. Moreover, to any convex and continuous fuzzy number correspond two OFNs, they differ by the orientation: one has positive, say (f, g), another (g, f) has negative.

A relation of partial ordering in the space $\mathcal{R}_{BV}$ can be introduced by defining the subset of 'positive' Ordered Fuzzy Numbers: a number $A = (f, g)$ is not less than zero, and by writing

$$A \geq 0 \quad \text{iff } f \geq 0, \text{ and } g \geq 0. \qquad (2)$$

In this way the set $\mathcal{R}_{BV}$ becomes a partially ordered ring. Notice, that for each two fuzzy numbers $A = (f_A, g_A), B = (f_B, g_B)$ as above, we may define $A \wedge B =: F$ and $A \vee B =: G$, both from $\mathcal{R}$, by the relations $F = (f_F, g_F)$ and

$$\text{if } f_F(s) = \inf\{f_A(s), f_B(s)\}, g_F(s) = \inf\{g_A(s), g_B(s)\}, \text{for } \forall s \in [0, 1]. \tag{3}$$

Similarly, we define $G = A \vee B$.

In dealing with applications of fuzzy numbers we need set of functionals that map each fuzzy number into real, and in such a way that is consistent with operations on reals. Those operations are called defuzzifications. To be more strict we introduce

Definition 2. A map ϕ from the space $\mathcal{R}_{BV}$ of all OFN's to reals is called a **defuzzification functional** if is satisfies:

1. $\phi(c^{\ddagger}) = c$,
2. $\phi(A + c^{\ddagger}) = \phi(A) + c$,
3. $\phi(cA) = c\phi(A)$, for any $c \in \mathbf{R}$ and $A \in \mathcal{R}_{BV}$.

where $c^{\ddagger}(s) = (c, c), s \in [0, 1]$, represents crisp number (a real) $c \in \mathbf{R}$.

From this follow that each defuzzification functional must be homogeneous of order one, restrictive additive, and some how normalized.

2.2   Step Ordered Fuzzy Numbers

It is worthwhile to point out that a class of ordered fuzzy numbers (OFNs) represents the whole class of convex fuzzy numbers.

Important consequence of this fact is the possibility of introducing a subspace of OFN composed of pairs of step functions. If we fix a natural number K and split $[0, 1)$ into $K - 1$ subintervals $[a_i, a_{i+1})$, i.e. $\bigcup_{i=1}^{K-1} [a_i, a_{i+1}) = [0, 1)$, where $0 = a_1 < a_2 < ... < a_K = 1$, and define a **step function** f of resolution K by putting u_i on each subinterval $[a_i, a_{i+1})$, then each such function f is identified with a K-dimensional vector $f \sim u = (u_1, u_2...u_K) \in \mathbf{R}^K$, the K-th value u_K corresponds to $s = 1$, i.e. $f(1) = u_K$. Taking a pair of such functions we have an Ordered Fuzzy Number from $\mathcal{R}_{BV}$. Now we introduce

Definition 3. By a **Step Ordered Fuzzy Number** A of resolution K we mean an ordered pair (f, g) of functions such that $f, g : [0, 1] \to \mathbf{R}$ are K-step functions.

We use $\mathcal{R}_K$ for denotation the set of elements satisfying Def. 3. The example of a Step Ordered Fuzzy Number and its membership function are shown in Fig. 1 and Fig. 2 (where for the better image the vertical intervals connecting steps of the functions have been drawn). The set $\mathcal{R}_K \subset \mathcal{R}_{BV}$ has been extensively elaborated by our students in [10] and [21]. We can identify $\mathcal{R}_K$ with the Cartesian product of $\mathbf{R}^K \times \mathbf{R}^K$ since each K-step function is represented by its K values. It is obvious that each element of the space $\mathcal{R}_K$ may be regarded as an approximation of elements from $\mathcal{R}_{BV}$, by increasing the number K of steps we are getting the better approximation. The norm of $\mathcal{R}_K$ is

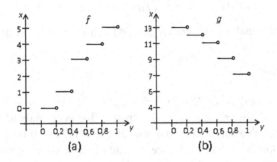

Fig. 1. Example of a step ordered fuzzy number $A = (f, g) \in \mathcal{R}_K$, (a) f, and (b) g

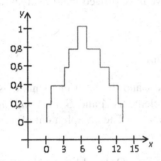

Fig. 2. Membership function of the above Step Ordered Fuzzy Number $A = (f, g) \in \mathcal{R}_K$

assumed to be the Euclidean one of $\mathbf{R}^{2K}$, then we have a inner-product structure for our disposal.

On the space $\mathcal{R}_K$ a representation formula for a general non-linear defuzzification functional $H : \mathbf{R}^K \times \mathbf{R}^K \to \mathbf{R}$ satisfying the conditions 1.– 3., can be given as a linear composition of arbitrary homogeneous of order one, continuous function G of $2K - 1$ variables, with the 1D identity function, i.e.

$$H(\underline{u}, \underline{v}) = u_j + \tag{4}$$
$$G(u_2 - u_j, ..., u_K - u_j, v_1 - u_j, ..., v_K - u_j),$$
$$\text{with } \underline{u} = (u_1, ..., u_K), \underline{v} = (v_1, ..., v_K),$$

and some $1 \leq j \leq K$. It is seen that G is given by F in which its j-th argument was put equal to zero. Of course v_j can substitute u_j in (4).

3   Lattice Structure on $\mathcal{R}_K$

Let us consider the set $\mathcal{R}_K$ of Step Ordered Fuzzy Numbers with operations $\vee$ and $\wedge$ such that for $A = (f_A, g_A)$ and $B = (f_B, g_B)$,

$$A \vee B = (sup\{f_A, f_B\}, sup\{g_A, g_B\}),$$

$$A \wedge B = (inf\{f_A, f_B\}, inf\{g_A, g_B\}).$$

In [13] we have shown that the algebra $(\mathcal{R}_K, \vee, \wedge)$ defines a lattice structure.

3.1   Binary SOFN

Let us introduce a subsets $\mathcal{N}$ of $\mathcal{R}_K$ such that each element of $\mathcal{N}$ is a binary vector. Then we have both a join and a meet in $\mathcal{N}$. In fact, for every pair of numbers from the set $\{0, 1\}$ we can determine *max* and *min* and it is always 0 or 1. Therefore $\mathcal{N}$ creates a *complete lattice*. In such a lattice we can distinguish the greatest element $\underline{1}$ represented by the vector $= (1, 1, ..., 1)$ and the least element $\underline{0}$ represented by the vector $(0, 0, ..., 0)$.

In our previous paper [13] we have proved that the algebra $(\mathcal{N}, \vee, \wedge)$ is a complete lattice.

3.2   Complement and Negation

In a lattice in which the greatest and the least elements exist it is possible to define complements. We say that two elements A and B are *complements* of each other if and only if $A \vee B = \underline{1}$ and $A \wedge B = \underline{0}$. The complement of a number A will be marked with $\neg A$ and is defined as follows:

Definition 4. Let $A \in \mathcal{N}$ be a Step Ordered Fuzzy Number represented by a binary vector $(a_1, a_2, \ldots, a_{2K})$. By the complement of A we understand

$$\neg A = (1 - a_1, 1 - a_2, \ldots, 1 - a_{2K}).$$

A bounded lattice for which every element has a complement is called a *complemented lattice*. Moreover, the structure of Step Ordered Fuzzy Numbers $\{\mathcal{N}, \vee, \wedge\}$ forms a complete and complemented lattice in which complements are unique. In fact it is a *Boolean algebra*. In the example with $K = 2$ a set of universe is created by binary vectors

$$\mathcal{N} = \{(a_1, a_2, a_3, a_4) \in \mathbf{R}^4 : a_i \in \{0, 1\}, \text{for } i = 1, 2, 3, 4\}.$$

The complements of elements are $\neg(0, 0, 0, 0) = (1, 1, 1, 1)$, $\neg(0, 1, 0, 0) = (1, 0, 1, 1)$, $\neg(1, 1, 0, 0) = (0, 0, 1, 1)$ etc.

Now we can rewrite the definition of the complement in terms of a new mapping.

Definition 5. For any $A \in \mathcal{N}$ we define its negation as

$$N(A) := (1 - a_1, 1 - a_2, \ldots, 1 - a_{2K}), \text{if } A = (a_1, a_2, \ldots, a_{2K}).$$

One can refer here to known facts from the theory of fuzzy implications (cf. [1, 2, 8]) and to write the strong negation N in terms of the standard strong negation N_I on the unit interval $I = [0, 1]$ defined by $N_I(x) = 1 - x$, $x \in I$, namely $N((a_1, a_2, \ldots, a_{2K})) = ((N_I(a_1), N_I(a_2), \ldots, N_I(a_{2K}))$.

3.3 Implications

In the classical Zadeh's fuzzy logic the definition of a fuzzy implication on an abstract lattice $\mathcal{L} = (L, \leq_L)$ is based on the notation from the fuzzy set theory introduced in [8].

Definition 6. Let $\mathcal{L} = (L, \leq_L, 0_L, 1_L)$ be a complete lattice. A mapping $\mathcal{I} : L^2 \to L$ is called a fuzzy implication on $\mathcal{L}$ if it is decreasing with respect to the first variable, increasing with respect to the second variable and fulfills the border conditions

$$\mathcal{I}(0_L, 0_L) = \mathcal{I}(1_L, 1_L) = 1_L, \mathcal{I}(1_L, 0_L) = 0_L. \tag{5}$$

Now, possessing the lattice structure of $\mathcal{R}_K$ (SOFN) and the Boolean structure of our lattice $\mathcal{N}$, we can repeat most of the definitions know in the Zadeh's fuzzy set theory. The first one is the Kleene–Dienes operation, called a binary implication, already introduced in our previous paper [13] as the new implication (cf. Definition 4 in [13])

$$\mathcal{I}_b(A, B) = N(A) \vee B, \text{ for any} A, B \in \mathcal{N}. \tag{6}$$

In other words, the result of the binary implication $\mathcal{I}_b(A, B)$, denoted in [13] by $A \to B$, is equal to the result of operation *sup* for the number B and the complement of A:

$$A \to B = sup\{\neg A, B\}.$$

Next we may introduce the Zadeh implication by

$$\mathcal{I}_Z(A, B) = (A \wedge B) \vee N(A), \text{ for any} A, B \in \mathcal{N}. \tag{7}$$

Since in our lattice $\mathcal{R}_K$ the arithmetic operations are well defined we may introduce the counterpart of the Lukasiewicz implication by

$$\mathcal{I}_L(A, B) = C, \text{ where } C = 1 \wedge (1 + B - A). \tag{8}$$

In the calculating the RHS of (8) we have to regard all numbers as elements of $\mathcal{R}_K$, since by adding the Ordered Fuzzy Number A from $\mathcal{N}$ to the crisp number 1 we may leave the subset $\mathcal{N} \subset \mathcal{R}_K$. However, the operation $\wedge$ will take us back to the lattice $\mathcal{N}$. It is obvious that in our notation $1_N = 1$. The explicit calculation will be: if $C = (c_1, c_2, \ldots, c_{2K}), A = (a_1, a_2, \ldots, a_{2K}), B = (b_1, b_2, \ldots, b_{2K})$, then $c_i = min\{1, 1 - a_i + b_i\}$, where $1 \leq i \leq 2K$.

It is obvious that all implications $\mathcal{I}_b, \mathcal{I}_Z$ and $\mathcal{I}_L$ satisfy the border conditions (5) as well as the 4th condition of the classical binary implication, namely $\mathcal{I}(0_N, 1_N) = 1_N$.

4 Modelling Diversity of Beliefs with SOFN

In this section we show how diversity of opinion (and belief) can be modelled by means of Step Ordered Fuzzy Numbers. Assume a given number of users of a social networks are expressing their opinion about some facts. Moreover, they are trying to formulate some sentences in the form of reasoning, called in computer science - associative rules.

Their statements are expressed in the natural language hence we should extend our model with a set L of **linguistic variables**. By linguistic variables we mean variables which values are from the set of words or sentences of a natural (or artificial) language. Formally it is a foursome

$$l = (Z, T, U, m)$$

where

- Z is a name of variable l,
- T is a set of fuzzy terms which can be assigned to l,
- U is a digital interval of values of l,
- m is a rule (function) which assigns Ordered Fuzzy Numbers to terms from the set T.

For example, let l describes *air temperature*, then fuzzy terms which can be assigned to l are *low, medium, high*, digital values for *air temperature* are assumed to be from the interval $[5, 30]$. Those fuzzy terms may be represented by Ordered Fuzzy Numbers. Hence each human in our group from the social network can attached his/her OFN's representation of the same linguistic variable via the rule m.

Since a current state of the weather changes and people react differently in the same weather conditions in various situations for various people different representations of m may be accepted for the same fuzzy term. In this way, for people from USA or France distinct criteria for obesity are possible for formal modelling.

Now, consider a system with three people A, B, C. They express their opinion about possible decision for jogging depending on the air temperature and the air humidity. The linguistic variable: air humidity, will have fuzzy values : *very low, acceptable, unacceptable,*

The tasks of humans A and B are to evaluate the air temperature and the humidity of the whether, exchange digital values for fuzzy expressions and then provide these data to make their decision. The decision operates on the third linguistic variable, i.e., *jogging speed*. Values of this variable are from the interval $[5,15]$ and are described by terms *slow, fast, very fast,*

Application of SOFN in modelling humans' opinion has great advantage since allows for manipulating fuzzy expressions rather then strict digital values. It makes possible to design an automatic system of evaluation of humans' opinion and to form a tool for diversity evaluation.

Let us assume that our SOFN are 6 dimensional. Each subsequent pair of its components describe the level of true, hence we have 4 value logic, if we have 3 linguistic variables . Let v_l be a valuation function which for every formula assigns an ordered fuzzy number and assume that (111111) means absolutely true and (000000) means absolutely false. Values between (111111) and (000000), like e.g. (10100) express different kinds of half-truth. We may assume that 11 corresponds to true value, 10 partially true (1/2 true), and 01– to partially not true (1/2 not true).

The most important problem when we consider fuzzy beliefs of humans is how to check properties of such defined situation. The question is about a language in which we can evaluate whether some property is true or not. Let us discus it now. Assume that in the above example the next human D appears. It tries to guess the decision of human C, i.e., human D needs to learn what action C decided to perform. D beliefs that if A says that the temperature is *low* and B says that the humidity is *very low* then C decides to run *very fast*. To create a formula describing this property use here a commonly accepted language of epistemic logic based on Kripke structure [11]. In this formalism we can write

$$B_D(A\_says\_low) \wedge B_D(B\_says\_verylow) \rightarrow B_D(C\_says\_veryfast)$$

where $B_D(T)$ informally means that human D beliefs that T holds. Our aim is to verify whether this formula is true in a model of the system from the example.

Furthermore, we know that human D is not sure about beliefs of humans A and B and assumes that terms *low* and *very low* are interpreted by OFN. Notice that D may depart from the truth but not so much. However, if we take into account classical two-valued logic then the formula $B_D(A\_says\_low) \wedge B_D(B\_says\_verylow)$ is not true. It stems from the fact that beliefs of D about beliefs of A and B are not true. For some digital values they agree but for another not. Although the OFN representations are not the same they are very similar. In two-valued logic we lose this important information. Therefore, we propose to use new, innovative approach in which Step Ordered Fuzzy Numbers are applied. In Section 3 we showed that SOFN creates a lattice with Boolean operations of conjunction, disjunction and implication. Therefore it is possible to employ these numbers as a logical values for OFN. Let v_l be a valuation function which for every formula assigns an Ordered Fuzzy Number and assume that (111111) means absolutely true and (000000) means absolutely false. Values between (111111) and (000000), like e.g. (10100) express different kinds of half-truth. Below is given a hypothetical assignment:

(a) $v_l(B_D(A\_says\_low)) = (101101)$
(b) $v_l(B_D(B\_says\_verylow)) = (100111)$
(c) $v_l(B_D(C\_says\_runfast)) = (000000)$

Analyze intuitions concerning these values. In (a) it is assumed that the human D does not know exactly for which digital values from [5,30] term *close* is ascribed since the assigned value does not equal to (11111). However, if the interval [5,30] is divided into 3 parts then in parts one and three the human D agrees (at least partially) with the human B. Similar interpretation is for value (100111) assigned to formula $B_D(B\_says\_slow)$. In (c) it is assumed that the human D has no idea what and when the human C says about jogging. Based on these values we can determine value of the whole formula by using each of our implications introduced earlier. In each case the final true value will be the same:

$$v_l(B_D(A\_says\_low) \wedge B_D(B\_says\_verylow) \rightarrow$$
$$B_D(C\_says\_veryfast)) = \neg(100101) \vee (000000) = (011010).$$

It means that the human D guesses faultlessly the kind of activity of the human C. Such information surely cannot be expressed by classical logical values *true* and *false*. Although multi-valued and fuzzy logics can deal with more than two values such a precise knowledge can be captured only by Ordered Fuzzy Numbers.

5 Conclusion

The paper lays the foundations of new logic based on Step Ordered Fuzzy Numbers which will be very helpful in capturing how humans can reason about fuzzy expressions. This is innovative approach to modelling human's beliefs and their uncertainty about beliefs of other humans. We show motivation for introducing such a new logic. The application of it we mainly find in analyzing humans' communication when knowledge base of humans is represented by a set of Ordered Fuzzy Numbers expressing diverse humans' attitudes. Furthermore, SOFN, when are applied as logical values for propositions and other formulas of the applied language, give much more information than that something is *true* or *false*. We hope that this innovative approach is very promising in specification and verification of diversity of opinion. It could be also very useful in reasoning about software agents which are decision support systems. For example, we can analyze activity of agents which assist clients with their decisions in e-shops, i.e., agents which support users of a system in making decisions and choosing a right product.

Acknowledgement. The work on the paper of the second author (W.K.) was partially support by the Project N N516 481940 from the Polish National Scientific Center.

References

1. Baczyński, M., Jayaram, B.: Fuzzy Implications. STUDFUZZ, vol. 231. Springer, Heidelberg (2008)
2. Baczyński, M.: S-implications in Atanassov's intuitionistic and interval-valued fuzzy set theory revisited. In: Developments in Fuzzy Sets, Intuitionistic Fuzzy Sets, Generalized Nets and Related Topicss, vol. 1, pp. 33–42. IBS PAN - SRI PAS, Warsaw (2009)
3. Bruijn, B., Martin, J.: Getting to the (c)ore of knowledge: mining biomedical literature. Int. Journal Medical Informatics 67, 7–18 (2002)
4. Budzynska, K., Kacprzak, M., Rembelski, P.: Perseus. Software for analyzing persuasion process. Fundamenta Informaticae 93(1-3), 65–79 (2009)
5. Guanrong, C., Pham, T.T.: Introduction to Fuzzy Sets, Fuzzy Logic and Fuzzy Control Systems. CRC Press LLC, New York (2001)
6. Czogała, E., Pedrycz, W.: Elements and Methods of Fuzzy Set Theory. PWN, Warsaw (1985) (in Polish)
7. Dubois, D., Prade, H.: Operations on fuzzy numbers. International Journal of Systems Science 9(6), 613–626 (1978)
8. Fodor, J.C., Roubens, M.: Fuzzy Preference Modelling and Multicriteria Decision Support. Kluwer Academic Publishers, Dordrecht (1994)
9. Goetschel Jr., R., Voxman, W.: Elementary fuzzy calculus. Fuzzy Sets and Systems 18(1), 31–43 (1986)
10. Gruszczyńska, A., Krajewska, I.: Fuzzy calculator on step ordered fuzzy numbers. UKW, Bydgoszcz (2008) (in Polish)
11. Fagin, R., Halpern, J.Y., Moses, Y., Vardi, M.Y.: Reasoning about Knowledge. MIT Press, Cambridge (1995)
12. Halpern, J.Y.: Reasoning about Uncertainty. MIT Press, Cambridge (2005)

13. Kacprzak, M., Kosiński, W.: On lattice structure and implications on ordered fuzzy numbers. In: Proc. of the 7th Conference of the European Society for Fuzzy Logic and Technology (EUSFLAT), pp. 267–274 (2011)
14. Klir, G.J.: Fuzzy arithmetic with requisite constraints. Fuzzy Sets and Systems 91, 165–175 (1997)
15. Kosiński, W.: On fuzzy number calculus. International Journal of Applied Mathematics and Computer Science 16(1), 51–57 (2006)
16. Kosiński, W., Prokopowicz, P., Ślęzak, D.: Fuzzy numbers with algebraic operations: algorithmic approach. In: Klopotek, M., Wierzchoń, S.T., Michalewicz, M. (eds.) Proc. Intelligent Information Systems, IIS 2002, Sopot, Poland, June 3-6, pp. 311–320. Physica Verlag, Heidelberg (2002)
17. Kosiński, W., Prokopowicz, P., Ślęzak, D.: Drawback of fuzzy arithmetics - new intutions and propositions. In: Burczyński, T., Cholewa, W., Moczulski, W. (eds.) Proc. Methods of Aritificial Intelligence, pp. 231–237. PACM, Gliwice (2002)
18. Kosiński, W., Prokopowicz, P., Ślęzak, D.: On algebraic operations on fuzzy numbers. In: Klopotek, M., Wierzchoń, S.T., Trojanowski, K. (eds.) Intelligent Information Processing and Web Mining, Proc. of the International IIS: IIPWM 2003 Conference held in Zakopane, Poland, June 2-5, pp. 353–362. Physica Verlag, Heidelberg (2003)
19. Kosiński, W., Prokopowicz, P., Ślęzak, D.: Ordered fuzzy numbers. Bulletin of the Polish Academy of Sciences, Sér. Sci. Math. 51(3), 327–338 (2003)
20. Kosiński, W., Prokopowicz, P.: Algebra of fuzzy numbers. Applied Mathematics. Mathematics for Society 5(46), 37–63 (2004) (in Polish)
21. Kościeński, K.: A module of step ordered fuzzy numbers in control movement material point. PJIIT, Warsaw (2010) (in Polish)
22. Lukasiewicz, J.: Elements of the Mathematical Logic. PWN, Warsaw (1958) (in Polish)
23. Malinowski, G.: Many-valued logics. In: Goble, L. (ed.) The Blackwell Guide to Philosophical Logic, pp. 309–335. Blackwell Publishers, Oxford (2001)
24. Nguyen, H.T.: A note on the extension principle for fuzzy sets. Journal of Math. Anal. Appl. 64, 369–380 (1978)
25. Prokopowicz, P.: Algorithmization of Operations on Fuzzy Numbers and its Applications. Ph. D. Thesis, IPPT PAN (2005) (in Polish)
26. Spasic, I., Ananiadu, S., McNaught, J., Kumar, A.: Text mining and ontologies in biomedicine: making sense of raw text. Brief Bioinform. 6(3), 239–251 (2005)
27. Swanson, D.R.: Medical literature as a potential source of new knowledge. Bull. Med. Libr. Assoc. 78(1), 29–37 (1990)
28. Starosta, B., Kosiński, W.: Meta sets – another approach to fuzziness. In: Seising, R. (ed.) Views on Fuzzy Sets and Systems. STUDFUZZ, vol. 243, pp. 509–532. Springer, Heidelberg (2009)
29. Zadeh, L.A.: The role of fuzzy logic in the management of uncertainty in expert systems. Fuzzy Sets and Systems 11(3), 199–227 (1983)

Hardware Implementation of P1-TS Fuzzy Rule-Based Systems on FPGA

Jacek Kluska and Zbigniew Hajduk

Faculty of Electrical and Computer Engineering, Rzeszow University of Technology,
35-959 Rzeszow, W. Pola 2, Poland
jacklu@prz.edu.pl,
zhajduk@kia.prz.edu.pl

Abstract. This paper presents an FPGA hardware implementation of a special case of the fuzzy rule-based system, called P1-TS. The novelty of this work is recursive hardware architecture. The recursive implementation of the rule-based system allows us to build a versatile digital circuit for which FPGA logic resources requirements are small and independent on the number of input variables. The number of inputs is only limited by the capacity of the memory that stores the consequents of the rules. In our implementation, increasing the number of variables by 1 approximately doubles calculation time of the hardware device. We use floating-point arithmetic which ensures a higher dynamic range and makes that there is no need to focus on normalizing variables values to fixed word length.

Keywords: polynomial fuzzy rule-based system, fuzzy hardware, FPGA, recursion.

1 Introduction

Fuzzy logic models are currently successfully used in many engineering applications including modeling, control and identification of dynamical systems, robotics, technical and medical diagnosis, expert systems and data mining. Diverse techniques can be applied to implement the models of fuzzy systems, depending on application demands, e.g. the desired response time. The simplest way of implementation is a program designed for general-purpose computer. However, the hardware implementations are best suited for high-speed demands [1], [2].

In the book [3], the analytical theory of the fuzzy rule-based systems was presented. It was proved that for some class of the Takagi-Sugeno-Kang models, in which the input variables are represented by linear and complementary membership functions of the fuzzy sets, the system of their "If-then" rules is equivalent to a multi-linear function, being a special case of the Kolmogorov-Gabor polynomial. It was shown that such class of systems, denoted by P1-TS, can be successfully applied in many fields, e.g. for PID-like optimal control of the nonlinear dynamical processes (cf. [4]), identification of some class of the nonlinear dynamical processes, navigation of the mobile robots, and so on.

L. Rutkowski et al. (Eds.): ICAISC 2013, Part I, LNAI 7894, pp. 282–293, 2013.
© Springer-Verlag Berlin Heidelberg 2013

It is well known that the fuzzy systems in general suffer from the "curse of dimensionality" problem [5]. In the multiple-input-single-output (MISO) P1-TS system, by adding an extra dimension to the input space, we observe a twofold increase in the number of fuzzy "If-then" rules. Different approaches have been proposed to solve the rule explosion problem in the fuzzy rule-based systems [6]. In [3] it was shown that in the polynomial fuzzy systems, the curse of dimensionality problem can be substantially alleviated by means of recursion and meta-rules.

While applying fuzzy logic techniques for real-time complex applications, we should use an effective and high-speed approach in the hardware design methodology (cf. [7], [8], [9]). Recently, the field-programmable gate-array (FPGA) has attracted more attention than before, providing a possible solution in this issue. The advantages of the FPGA include their programmable hard-wired feature, fast time-to-market, shorter design cycle, embedding processors, low power consumption, and higher density for the implementation of the digital system. FPGA provides a compromise between the special-purpose application-specified integrated-circuit hardware and general purpose processors.

It should be added that the traditional implementations of fuzzy systems using FPGA work well as long as there are only two or three inputs. If the number of inputs is increased by one, then Look-Up-Table (LUT) using traditional implementation methods becomes very difficult to handle. The size of the LUT grows exponentially as inputs are added [10] and this is the consequence of the curse of dimensionality problem.

To avoid the above problems, in this contribution we introduce a new method of FPGA implementation of the MISO P1-TS system. The paper is organized as follows. In Section 2, the basic notions concerning P1-TS system with many inputs and one output and two theorems are given. Section 3 describes the hardware recursive implementation of the system, including the basic floating-point components, hardware recursive architecture, communication module and FPGA prototype description. Section 4 concludes the paper.

2   P1-TS System

Let us consider a MISO rule-based system with input variables $z_1, ..., z_n$, and the output S. Every input is from the nondegenerete interval $z_k \in [-\alpha_k, \beta_k]$, $(\beta_k + \alpha_k > 0, k = 1, \ldots, n)$. The set $D^n = [-\alpha_1, \beta_1] \times \ldots \times [-\alpha_n, \beta_n]$ defines a hypercuboid. For any input z_k, we define two membership functions of fuzzy sets $N_k = N(z_k)$, and $P_k = P(z_k)$, where P is an algebraic complement to N:

$$N(z_k) = \frac{\beta_k - z_k}{\alpha_k + \beta_k}, \quad P(z_k) = 1 - N(z_k), \quad k = 1, \ldots, n. \tag{1}$$

This system is defined by 2^n rules in the form of implications

$$\text{If } z_1 \text{ is } A_{i_1} \text{ and ... and } z_n \text{ is } A_{i_n}, \text{ then } S = q_j, \tag{2}$$

where $(i_1, \ldots, i_n) \in \{0, 1\}^n$ and

$$A_{i_k} = \begin{cases} N_k, & \text{for } i_k = 0 \\ P_k, & \text{for } i_k = 1 \end{cases}, \quad k = 1, \ldots, n. \tag{3}$$

We assume that the consequents q_j of the rules in (2) are real numbers, i.e. a zero-order Takagi-Sugeno model is considered. The above rule-based system we will call P1-TS one.

Theorem 1. *Let us define the following multilinear function*

$$f_0(\mathbf{z}) = \sum_{(p_1, \ldots, p_n) \in \{0,1\}^n} \theta_{p_1, \ldots, p_n} z_1^{p_1} \cdots z_n^{p_n}, \tag{4}$$

where $\theta_{(.)} \in \mathbb{R}$. For every function of the type (4) there exists a MISO P1-TS system such that its output $S(\mathbf{z}) = f_0(\mathbf{z})$, $\forall \ \mathbf{z} \in D^n$ and (1) – the inputs of this system are components of $\mathbf{z}$, (2) – two linear membership functions defined by (1) are assigned to each component of the vector $\mathbf{z}$, and (3) – the system is defined by 2^n fuzzy rules in the form of (2) – (3). By solving 2^n linear equations one can find all consequents q_j of the rules. For a nonzero volume of the hypercuboid D^n, the unique solution always exists. (The proof is given in [3]).

Theorem 2. *For any natural $n \geq 2$, the crisp output of any P1-TS system with the inputs $z_1, \ldots, z_n$ can be computed recursively*

$$\begin{aligned} S_n = \ &N_n(z_n) S_{n-1}(z_1, \ldots, z_{n-1} \mid q_1, \ldots, q_{2^{n-1}}) \\ &+ P_n(z_n) S_{n-1}(z_1, \ldots, z_{n-1} \mid q_{2^{n-1}+1}, \ldots, q_{2^n}), \end{aligned} \tag{5}$$

where

- *$S_n = S_n(z_1, \ldots, z_n \mid q_1, \ldots, q_{2^n})$ is the crisp output of the P1-TS system with n input variables and the consequents of the rules constituting the vector $[q_1, \cdots, q_{2^n}]^T$, described by the following fuzzy rules*

$$\left. \begin{aligned} R_1: \quad &\text{If } \mathcal{P}_1 \text{ and } z_n \text{ is } N_n, \text{ then } S = q_1, \\ &\vdots \\ R_{2^{n-1}}: \quad &\text{If } \mathcal{P}_{2^{n-1}} \text{ and } z_n \text{ is } N_n, \text{ then } S = q_{2^{n-1}}, \\ R_{2^{n-1}+1}: \ &\text{If } \mathcal{P}_1 \text{ and } z_n \text{ is } P_n, \text{ then } S = q_{2^{n-1}+1}, \\ &\vdots \\ R_{2^n}: \quad &\text{If } \mathcal{P}_{2^{n-1}} \text{ and } z_n \text{ is } P_n, \text{ then } S = q_{2^n}, \end{aligned} \right\} \tag{6}$$

and $\mathcal{P}_1, \ldots, \mathcal{P}_{2^{n-1}}$ are antecedents of the rules in the P1-TS system with the inputs $z_1, \ldots, z_{n-1}$, i.e.

$$\left. \begin{aligned} \underbrace{\text{If } z_1 \text{ is } N_1 \text{ and } \ldots \text{ and } z_{n-1} \text{ is } N_{n-1}}_{\mathcal{P}_1}, \text{ then } S = q_1, \\ \vdots \\ \underbrace{\text{If } z_1 \text{ is } P_1 \text{ and } \ldots \text{ and } z_{n-1} \text{ is } P_{n-1}}_{\mathcal{P}_{2^{n-1}}}, \text{ then } S = q_{2^{n-1}}. \end{aligned} \right\} \tag{7}$$

- $N_n(z_n)$ and $P_n(z_n)$ are membership functions for the input variable $z_n \in [-\alpha_n, \beta_n]$ defined by (1),
- $S_{n-1}(z_1, \ldots, z_{n-1} \mid q_1, \ldots, q_{2^{n-1}})$ is the crisp output of the P1-TS system described by the fuzzy rules (7), with the inputs $(z_1, \ldots, z_{n-1}) \in D^{n-1}$ and the consequents of the rules constituting the vector $[q_1, \cdots, q_{2^{n-1}}]^T$,
- $S_{n-1}(z_1, \ldots, z_{n-1} \mid q_{2^{n-1}+1}, \ldots, q_{2^n})$ is the crisp output of the P1-TS system described by the fuzzy rules (7), with input variables $(z_1, \ldots, z_{n-1}) \in D^{n-1}$, where its consequents are replaced by $[q_{2^{n-1}+1}, \ldots, q_{2^n}]^T$. (The proof is given in [3]).

When the number of inputs is large, we can use the meta-rules, i.e. the rules which are equivalent to some subset of the single rules expressed in the form of (2) – (3). Sometimes we consider a special case of the rule-based system, in which $\alpha_k = 0$ and $\beta_k = 1$ for $k = 1, \ldots, n$, i.e. $D^n = [0, 1]^n$. In such a case the inputs take the values from the interval $[0, 1]$, therefore, we can call the rule-based system "logical" one, since the labels of fuzzy sets N_k are interpreted as *almost false*, and the labels of fuzzy sets P_k are interpreted as *almost true*. Such systems process the information expressed in continuous, multi-valued logic.

3   Hardware Implementation of P1-TS System

P1-TS system can be hardware implemented in a few different ways. One of them is based on direct-parallel realization of equation (4) for a specific number of input variables. The advantage of such implementation is high speed of data processing; many arithmetic operations, e.g. addition and multiplication, are done simultaneously. Nevertheless, the disadvantages of such implementation are great difficulties in the description of P1-TS system for higher number of inputs and high requirements of FPGA logic resources. Namely, increasing a number of input variables by one doubles required amount of the hardware resources.

In this paper we prefer the other way of hardware implementation of P1-TS system, which is based on recursive procedure, expressed by equation (5). Such implementation is relatively easy to describe using hardware description languages (HDLs), e.g. Verilog or VHDL. However, P1-TS implementation in this case is slower than direct one, because all arithmetic operations are done sequentially. Nevertheless, FPGA logic resource requirements are very low and independent on the number of input variables. Moreover, the number of input variables is only limited by the capacity of the memory that stores the consequents values of the rules. Taking into account advantages and disadvantages of possible P1-TS system hardware implementations, the "recursive" method has been chosen.

3.1   Basic Floating-Point Components

In our hardware implementation of P1-TS system, we propose to use single precision floating-point arithmetic (IEEE 754 standard [11]), instead of most common used – fixed point one. FPGA implementation of floating-point arithmetic

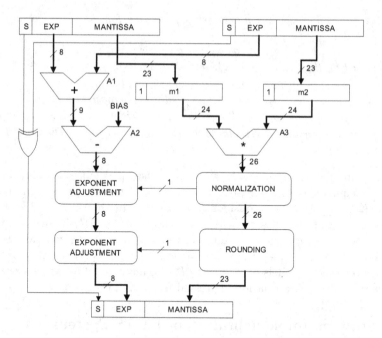

Fig. 1. Architecture of the floating point multiplier and divider

is more complicated and requires more logic resources [12], [13], but ensures higher dynamic range and makes that there is no need to focus on normalizing variables values to fixed word length. In order to realize P1-TS system based on recursion expressed by Theorem 2, four fundamental floating-point operations are required: addition, subtraction, multiplication and division. FPGA implementations of such operations are usually available as the IP cores (Intellectual Property cores), supplied by the FPGA vendors. However, in this case, the IP cores are vendor-dependent and cannot be used under different FPGA design software and implemented in different FPGA chips, e.g. Altera, Xilinx or Actel. To ensure maximum portability of HDL description of P1-TS system between different FPGAs we have developed our own Verilog HDL description of floating-point components, which realize basic arithmetic operations. Architecture of the components is discussed below.

Floating point multiplication is the simplest of four basic arithmetic operations. In general, the multiplication of two numbers is accomplished by multiplication of the mantissas and adding of the exponents. Simplified architecture of the floating-point multiplier is depicted in Fig. 1. The crucial block which architecture has an essential influence on the performance of the floating-point component, is the fixed-point multiplier A3. As this block, 3-stages pipelined multiplier, which consists of four 12-bit fast array multipliers and two adders, has been applied (general idea of fast array multiplier is described in [14]). Normalization block in Fig. 1 is a shift register, conditionally right-shifting the result of the mantissas multiplication. Final result of floating-point multiplication

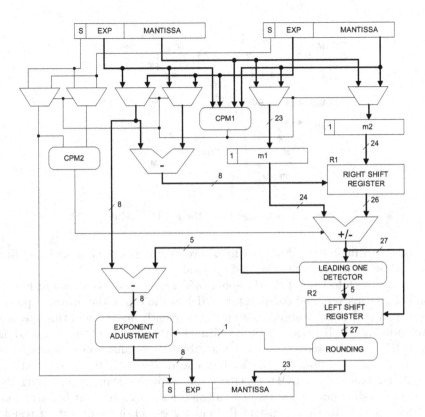

Fig. 2. Architecture of the floating point adder/subtractor

is rounded to nearest even mode [11]. Rounding requires 3 additional bits, computed in A3 block: guard bit, round bit and sticky bit. Executing of floating-point multiplication takes 5 clock cycles.

The structure of the floating-point divider is roughly the same as the multiplier, shown in Fig. 1. In general, the division of two numbers is accomplished by division of the mantissas and subtraction of the exponents. Therefore, in case of the divider, blocks A1 ... A3 perform different functions: A1 is a subtractor, A2 is an adder and A3 block accomplishes fixed point division. As a division method used in A3 block, the simple serial algorithm described in detail in [12] has been exploited. Normalization block performs conditionally left-shift operation. Round to the nearest even mode is implemented as well. Floating-point divider needs 26 clock cycles to establish division result.

Floating point addition is more complex than multiplication. Two numbers can only be added if the exponents are the same. Thus, pre-normalization process is required which aligns the mantissa of absolute smaller value of two operands. Next, aligned mantissas are added if two floating point operands have the same sign, otherwise subtracted. Finally, the new mantissa needs to be normalized and the new exponent has to be calculated and adjusted, according to the result

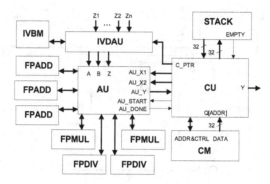

Fig. 3. Block diagram of the P1-TS module

of mantissa normalization. Subtracting of two operands can be done by adding them with inverted sign of the second operand.

Simplified architecture of floating-point adder/subtractor is shown in Fig. 2. Group of multiplexers and comparator CMP1 in the top of the drawing, points the operand with smaller absolute value. Subsequently, mantissa of this operand is pre-normalized in R1 block by right shifting for the number of times depending on the difference between the exponents values. Normalization of added/sub-tracted mantissas is done by the leading one detector (LOD) block and the left-shift R2 block. As a LOD, specific combinatorial circuit, determining the position of leading one in the result of aligned mantissas addition/subtraction, has been used. Both shift registers R1 and R2 establish its operation results within one clock cycle. Overall floating-point operation performed by the module from Fig. 2, takes only 5 clock cycles.

3.2 Recursive Implementation of P1-TS System

Simplified block diagram of the hardware recursive implementation of P1-TS system for n input variables is shown in Fig. 3. Bolded lines in the diagram represent multi-bit buses, whereas generic lines stand for the single-bit signals. P1-TS module consists of several function blocks, performing specific operations. The most important block, which accomplish recursive algorithm, is the control unit (CU) equipped with consequents memory (CM) and multi-level hardware stack. CM block stores consequents values of the rules. Control unit requires additional arithmetic unit (AU) block, which performs the following calculations

$$AU\_Y = \frac{B - Z}{A + B} \cdot AU\_X1 + \frac{A + Z}{A + B} \cdot AU\_X2. \tag{8}$$

Input variables A, B and Z of the AU block are provided by the block IVDAU (input values determining for arithmetic unit), connected with the block IVBM (input values boundaries memory). IVDAU block stores α_k and β_k values for the input variable z_k and assigns these values to the A, B and Z variables, depending

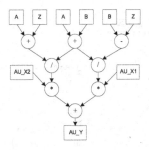

Fig. 4. Operation diagram of the arithmetic unit

on the index k. The index k is represented by the C_PTR pointer generated by the CU block, e.g. if C_PTR has the value of 0 then $(A, B, Z) = (\alpha_1, \beta_1, z_1)$, etc.

Arithmetic unit realizes equation (8) and exploits floating-point operations. All components described in Subsection 3.1 has been applied to perform this equation. FPADD in Fig. 4 stands for floating-point adder/subtractor, FPMUL is a floating-point multiplier and FPDIV denominates floating-point divider. In order to speed up the calculations, arithmetic unit uses three FPADD blocks, two FPMUL blocks and two FPDIV blocks. Operation diagram, which describes in detail how the calculation are performed by the AU block, is depicted in Fig. 4. Two addition $A + Z$ and $A + B$, and one subtraction $B - Z$ are executed simultaneously. Subsequently, two divisions and two multiplications are executed in parallel, as well. Such arrangement of operations shortens overall calculation time by almost 50%.

The control unit is described by the algorithmic state machine (ASM) chart presented in Fig. 5. After activating START signal which initializes computations, the number of currently used input variables (n) is rewritten to the index register IDX, consequents memory pointer Q_PTR is cleared and ASM goes form IDLE state (0) to the state 1. In this state, the value of IDX register is compared to 1 (the lowest level of recursion). If it is not equal to 1, ASM goes to the state 2 and subsequently 3, where - in sequence - value of the internal register TMP is pushed into the stack, IDX register is decremented and a concatenation of Q_PTR, IDX and a direct value is pushed into the stack, as well. The direct value contains the state number to which ASM will go after executing state 8. ASM returns to the state 1 after state 3. If the comparison in the state 1 gives positive result, ASM goes to states 4 ... 8, where arithmetic unit is engaged. After completion of arithmetic operation (AU_DONE = 1), data overrun of the stack is checked. If the stack is not empty, last pushed values are popped from the stack. After executing state 8 ASM goes to the state 9 or 10, depending on the value pushed into the stack in the state 3 or 11. If the next state is 9, then the arithmetic unit is also launched, but with different input values than in the states 4 and 5. In the states 10 and 11 the computation result of the arithmetic unit and a concatenation, similar to this one from the state 3, are pushed into the stack. New value is also assigned to the Q_PTR register.

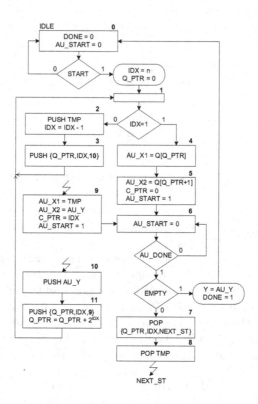

Fig. 5. Simplified ASM chart for the control unit

ASM ends up its operation if stack will be empty after executing states 4 ... 6. In this case the output Y of the control unit will contain the crisp output value of the P1-TS system. Let us note that Q_PTR pointer incremented by 1 acts like a bottom index of the consequents of the rule. Value of the particular consequent for Q_PTR index is read from consequents memory and, in the ASM chart, is denoted as Q[Q_PTR].

3.3 Communication Module

To facilitate practical use of the P1-TS module, additional communication module has been developed. The module provides data transfer between P1-TS module and PC computer. Its basic function is to load the values of the rules consequents to the consequents memory and store them in an external flash memory. Communication module also allows setting up a number of actually used input variables, and for debugging purposes – transferring values of input variables, initializing computations and reading back the result, as well.

Simplified block diagram of the communication module is depicted in Fig. 6. The main component of the module is the command realization block (CRB). Commands from PC computer, such as moving single consequent to the selected

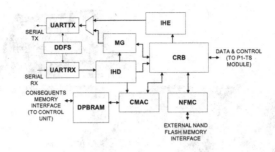

Fig. 6. Block diagram of the communication module

memory location or rewriting consequents memory content to non-volatile flash memory, etc., are transmitted via UART block, which consists of UART transmitter (UARTTX), receiver (UARTRX) and direct digital frequency synthesizer (DDFS). DDFS block provides clock frequency for UART transmitter/receiver and determines the data transfer rate. Currently, data are transferred with 115.2 kb/s. Communication between the module and PC is based on Intel HEX protocol [15]. Therefore, two important block of communication module are Intel HEX decoder (IHD) and encoder (IHE). To ensure reliable data transfer, each transmitted Intel HEX record, which also contain a checksum, has to be acknowledged by the receiver, i.e. the communication module or PC. Other components of the communication module are message generator (MG), consequents memory access controller (CMAC), NAND flash memory controller (NFMC) and dual-port block RAM memory (DPBRAM). The consequents of the P1-TS system are stored in an external NAND flash memory. On power up or in reply to PC command, content of the flash memory is copied to dual port block RAM, which has much shorter access time than the external NAND flash. Consequents memory is, in fact, located in the communication module and implemented as a dual port block RAM (dedicated memory block inside FPGA). First port of the block RAM is directly connected to the control unit of P1-TS module, while second port is driven to the CMAC block.

3.4   FPGA Prototype

P1-TS module along with the communication module have been implemented in a prototype board with Xilinx Spartan-6 FPGA (XC6SLX100-3FGG676), primary developed for FPGA-based programmable controller [16]. A photo of FPGA prototype board with simple panel board is presented in Fig. 7.

P1-TS and communication modules were created as a set of IP cores, described in Verilog HDL [17]. Their implementation in XC6SLX100 FPGA utilizes small amount of logic resources: 4671, 6-input, slice LUTs (7.4% of total available LUTs) and 2498 slice registers (1.9% of available registers). Implemented circuit can be clocked with maximum frequency of 97 MHz. Table 1 shows the real computation time required by the developed hardware implementation for 2 to 16 input variables.

Fig. 7. Photo of FPGA prototype board

Table 1. Computation time of the FPGA hardware implementation for different number of input variables of the P1-TS system. The module was tested with 90 MHz frequency.

# input variables	Clock cycles	Computation time [μs]
2	182	2.02
3	432	4.8
4	932	10.35
5	1932	21.46
6	3932	43.68
7	7932	88.13
8	15932	177.02

# input variables	Clock cycles	Computation time [μs]
9	31420	349.11
10	62906	698.95
11	125878	1398.64
12	251822	2798.02
13	503710	5596.77
14	1007486	11194.28
15	2018038	22422.64
16	4030142	44779.35

4   Conclusions

Recursive implementation of the P1-TS system allows us to build a versatile digital circuit for which FPGA logic resources requirements are small and independent on the number of input variables. The number of inputs is only limited by the capacity of the memory that stores the consequents of the rules. Currently implemented version of P1-TS module utilizes dual port RAM block of 64k 32-bit locations (256 KB). Therefore, maximum number of inputs is limited to 16. However, it is very easy to increase the capacity of RAM by combining together more memory blocks and in consequence, the number of available input variables can be higher with the same logic resources utilization.

The programmable logic controllers are much slower than our device. For example for the output generation of the P1-TS system with 4 inputs, GE Fanuc VersaMax controller needs 36.7 ms, Siemens S7-1200 – 2.4 ms and soft-PLC Beckhoff CP6607 – 139 μs, whereas our hardware device needs only 10.3 μs.

In our implementation, increasing the number of variables by 1 approximately doubles calculation time of P1-TS output.

The developed system can be used as a control device for real-time applications.

Acknowledgments. This work was supported in part by the National Science Centre (Poland) under Grant No. NN 514 705540.

References

1. Zavala, A.H., Nieto, O.C.: Fuzzy Hardware: A Retrospective and Analysis. IEEE Trans. Fuzzy Systems 20(4), 623–635 (2012)
2. Sulaiman, N., Obaid, Z.A., Marhaban, M.H., Hamidon, M.N.: FPGA-Based Fuzzy Logic: Design and Applications – a Review. Proc. Int. J. Eng. and Technol. (IACSIT) 1(5), 491–503 (2009)
3. Kluska, J.: Analytical Methods in Fuzzy Modeling and Control. STUDFUZZ, vol. 241. Springer, Heidelberg (2009) Kacprzyk, J. (ed.)
4. Piegat, A., Olchowy, M.: Does an Optimal Form of an Expert Fuzzy Model Exist? In: Rutkowski, L., Scherer, R., Tadeusiewicz, R., Zadeh, L.A., Zurada, J.M. (eds.) ICAISC 2010, Part I. LNCS (LNAI), vol. 6113, pp. 175–184. Springer, Heidelberg (2010)
5. Kosko, B.: Fuzzy Engineering. Prentice Hall (1997)
6. Güven, M.K., Passino, K.M.: Avoiding Exponential Parameter Growth in Fuzzy Systems. IEEE Trans. Fuzzy Systems 9(1), 194–199 (2001)
7. Gniewek, L., Kluska, J.: Family of fuzzy J-K flip-flops based on bounded product, bounded sum and complementation. IEEE Trans. Syst., Man, Cybern. B, Cybern. 28(6), 861–868 (1998)
8. Kluska, J., Hajduk, Z.: Digital implementation of fuzzy Petri net based on asynchronous fuzzy RS flip-flop. In: Rutkowski, L., Siekmann, J.H., Tadeusiewicz, R., Zadeh, L.A. (eds.) ICAISC 2004. LNCS (LNAI), vol. 3070, pp. 314–319. Springer, Heidelberg (2004)
9. Gniewek, L., Kluska, J.: Hardware implementation of fuzzy Petri net as a controller. IEEE Trans. Syst., Man, Cybern. B, Cybern. 34(3), 1315–1324 (2004)
10. McKenna, M., Wilamowski, B.M.: Implementing a Fuzzy System on a Field Programmable Gate Array. In: Int. Joint Conf. Neural Networks, IJCNN 2001, Washington, DC, July 15-19, pp. 189–194 (2001)
11. IEEE Standard Board and ANSI: IEEE Standard for Binary Floating-Point Arithmetic. IEEE Std 754-2008
12. Thakkar, A.J., Ejnioui, A.: Design and implementation of double precision floating point division and square root on FPGAs. In: IEEE Aerospace Conference Proceedings, March 5-11, p. 7 (2006)
13. Hajduk, Z.: A floating point unit for the hardware virtual machine. Measurement Automation and Monitoring (PAK) 57(1), 82–85 (2011) (in Polish)
14. Meyer-Baese, U.: Digital Signal Processing with Field Programmable Gate Arrays, 3rd edn. Springer, Heidelberg (2007)
15. Intel Corp.: Hexadecimal Object File Format Specification. Revision A (1988)
16. Hajduk, Z., Sadolewski, J., Trybus, B.: Multiple tasks in FPGA-based programmable controller. e-Informatica 5(1), 77–85 (2011)
17. Thomas, D.E., Moorby, P.R.: The Verilog Hardware Description Language, 5th edn. Kluwer Academic Publishers (2002)

Evolutionary Strategy for the Fuzzy Flip-Flop Neural Networks Supervised Learning Procedure

Piotr A. Kowalski[1,2]

[1] Systems Research Institute, Polish Academy of Sciences,
ul. Newelska 6, PL-01-447 Warsaw, Poland
`pakowal@ibspan.waw.pl`
[2] Cracow University of Technology,
Department of Automatic Control and Information Technology
ul. Warszawska 24, PL-31-155 Cracow, Poland
`pkowal@pk.edu.pl`

Abstract. The aim of this paper is present the usage of $(\mu + \lambda)$ Evolutionary Strategy to evolve the architecture, and primarily the connection weights, for Fuzzy Flip-Flop Neural Networks. Due to the specific transfer function of this fuzzy-based neural network and its numerical derivatives, Back Propagation algorithm can be used for the training process, but it has very week convergence rates. Therefore Evolutionary Strategy as a heuristic learning algorithm will be applied here. In the article some numerical properties of proposed approach will be exposed. They will concern on natural example such as function approximation and data classification. It exhibits better results in terms of faster convergence and least square-error. Finally some conclusions and ideas for future work will be under discussion.

Keywords: recurrent neural network, fuzzy flip-flop neural network, fuzzy neuron, evolutionary strategy, supervising learning procedure.

1 Introduction

This paper outlines the author's research related to the use of genetic algorithms [11, 28] , and in particular evolutionary algorithms [2] to optimize the parameters of the Fuzzy Flip-Flop Neural Network. This type of the network was introduced by Professor Hirota and his scientific team in 1980 [9, 10, 24]. Unfortunately, for nearly twenty years it was almost exclusively the subject of theoretical work [8]. The main reason for this was the lack of access to high-speed computing machines, and consequently absence of universal algorithms of supervised learning. In particular, it was difficult to consider the possibility of using a specialized algorithm for adaptation of parameters based on even the simplest heuristics.

This fuzzy network is a very special case of a recursive network [27], and its construction is based on a combination of the idea of the classical neural networks but with activation function based on the principle of a J-K flip-flop or D flip-flop [21], where the classical binary logic was replaced by fuzzy operators [6, 7]. With

L. Rutkowski et al. (Eds.): ICAISC 2013, Part I, LNAI 7894, pp. 294–305, 2013.

this modification, the fuzzy neural networks have much better properties related to pattern recognition and knowledge discovery. This network is characterized by more accurate approximation of processes and structures in the human brain such as neurons and memory.

Uniqueness and diversity of the activation functions conditioned lack of effective application of well-known classical learning methods, such as at least one of the most popular Back Propagation Learning procedure [27]. The main obstacle for using such a well-known method of supervised training for this neural networks is the absence of analytical derivative operator based on the information on the current value of the activation function - as it is the case with the use of functions like sigmoid, hyperbolic tangent or linear. In the literature there is only one known procedure of effective learning algorithm for the fuzzy neural network described above. It is the Bacterial Memetic Algorithm [5, 26] introduced by the group of Professor Laszlo T. Koczy [21]. Algorithm presented in this article will be second one, and obtained results can serve as a reference for future work in this area.

2   Fuzzy Flip-Flop Neuron

At the beginning short discussion of main methodology investigated here will be presented. First, let us consider typical - known from the digital technique - J-K Flip-Flop shown in Figure 1. It has two primary inputs J and K, the clock input, the outputs Q and negation of the output signal $\overline{Q}$. Output Q_{n+1} at state $n+1$ is calculated on the basis of the binary inputs J, K, and the previous output (state) Q_n, according to logical formula

$$Q_{n+1} = (J \vee \overline{K}) \wedge (J \vee Q_n) \wedge (\overline{K} \vee \overline{Q_n}). \tag{1}$$

Fig. 1. J-K Flip Flop

The over bar notation denotes negation in classical logic defined as $\overline{K} = 1 - K$. The feedback in this J-K flip-flop is realized by connecting the negation of output to the input K ($K_n = \overline{Q}_{n-1}$). Then, the output depends only on the inputs J and the previous state Q_{n-1}.

The above described Flip-Flop, based on digital signals 0 and 1 and the functions $\vee$ and $\wedge$ are well-known logical (binary) operators. For the generalization of the Flip-Flop to continuous signals, the fuzzy logic has been introduced.

The above operators were replaced by their equivalents used in the axioms of fuzzy logic set theory [13]. Therefore a binary operator *and* was replaced by a function of the fuzzy t-norms and the binary operator *or* appropriate - the previously accepted t-norm - co-norm. For simplicity this paper has adopted notation i for t-norms and u for the corresponding co-norms. This convention is common in the literature related to the Fuzzy Flip-Flop Neural Networks [16].

Thus the function performed by a fuzzy flip-flop takes the following formula:

$$Q_{n+1} = (J \, u \, Q_n) \, i \, (J \, u \, Q_n) \, i \, (Q_n \, u \, (1 - Q_n)) \tag{2}$$

The Fuzzy J-K Flip-Flop can be treated as an artificial recurrent neuron where signal J represents weighted inputs and Q can be treated as an output from neuron.

In the above formula the negation was used in accordance with the principle of this operation used in fuzzy logic ($\overline{K} = 1 - K$). The feedback connection ($K_{n+1} = 1 - \overline{Q_n}$) is a very important part of the fuzzy neuron. In this way the feedback is implemented within each of the considered neurons. It allows a network based on this solution much better resemble the natural process of information processing that is similar to the natural neural network implemented in the brain. Additional problem - for modelling such created a network - is to determine the fuzzy initial state of neurons associated with the idea of Flip-Flops as the activation function [22].

2.1   Trigonometric operators

In the present work the neurons with activation function based on the trigono-metric t-norm and co-norm were used:

$$i(x, y) = \frac{2}{\pi} \arcsin(\sin(x\frac{2}{\pi}) \sin(y\frac{2}{\pi}) \tag{3}$$

$$u(x, y) = \frac{2}{\pi} \arccos(\cos(x\frac{2}{\pi}) \cos(y\frac{2}{\pi}) \tag{4}$$

It is relatively simple function. Its important advantage is the absence of addi-tional parameters in formula, as it occurs e.g. in Yager operators. Formal proof showing that formulated trigonometric fuzzy functions fulfill the conditions of t-norms and s-norms can be found in [21]. Detailed studies related to the selection of such fuzzy functions can be found in [22]. In Figure 2 the graphs of described trigonometric relations $u(x, y)$ and $i(x, y)$ are presented.

For such a fuzzy neuron structures one should still examine the stability of the output signal as a function of the next iterations. This problem occurs in many neural networks with feedback such as the Hopfield Network [25]. The Figure 3 illustrates the dependence of the fuzzy neuron output in subsequent steps of the time at a constant level of the input signal J.

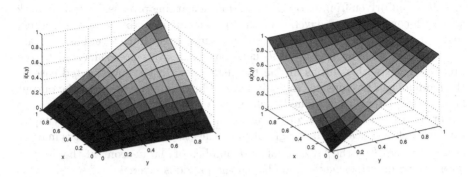

Fig. 2. Graphs of fuzzy trigonometric operations of intersection (t-norm) and union (s-norm) used in J-K Flip-Flop Neuron

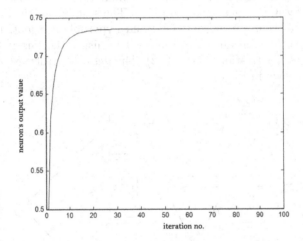

Fig. 3. Stabilization of the output signal of the fuzzy neuron

Such simulations were repeated for different input signal. In all investigated cases the speed of stabilization was almost identical. From these experiments one can conclude that the discrete time in which the stabilization of the output signal was obtained, is between 15-25 iterations. In the present study it has been set as 20 iterations, which corresponds - in digital technique - to 20 steps of clock cycles.

3   Structure of FFF Artificial Neural Network

The neural network is a powerful tool for many scientific and practical problems. The main property of this method is its automatic adjustment to some patterns and consequently a possibility to generalize the relationship between the output and the input driven from the data shown in the learning process. Neural network structure consists of two layers - input and output, in addition, between them some number of layers, so called hidden layers may exist. Each layer has a certain fixed number of neurons. In subsequent layers, neurons are connected to the previous layer with neurons in one to all manner. In the investigated case at the hidden layer neurons are the only Fuzzy Flip-Flop type, while in the output layer classical neurons are found exclusively, with linear activation function.

For the artificial fuzzy neuron presented in the last Section, with each synaptic the real coefficient called the weight of the connections is associated. It is marked as $w_{j,i}^{(k)}$, where k is the layer number, i number of the neuron (in the current layer) and j describes neuron number in the previous layer.

A neuron derive its stimulation from the weighted sum of input signals connected, where the weights inform about the importance of these connections. To this value the so-called bias $b_i^{(k)}$ is added. It is responsible for the shift - the threshold - of the signal. The result of stimulation is converted to the output of neuron by its the activation function. The standard activation functions are threshold function, linear, sigmoidal and hyperbolic tangent. In described methodology, the neuron output is obtained by using the Fuzzy J-K flip-flop with feedback as a activation function (2). The detailed structure of fuzzy neural network is shown in Figure 4.

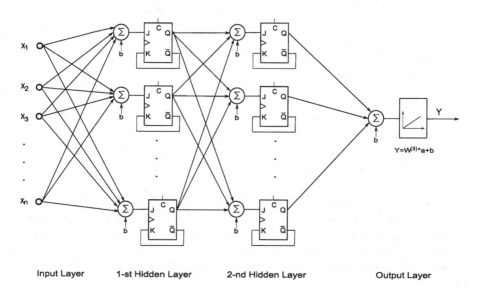

Fig. 4. Fuzzy J-K Flip Flop Neural Network

Due to the strong non-linearity of the activation function - resulting from the fuzzy logic operators used in the hidden layers of neural network, the quality of approximation of function realised by the network, is strongly dependent on the number of neurons in each layer.

4   Evolutionary Strategy for Fuzzy Neural Networks

Evolutionary Strategies (ES) [12] are based on a population of chromosomes that have characteristics related to elements in investigated task. The dimension of strings of genes is directly linked to the considered feature space. Adaptation of the individuals is determined by a target function called a fitness function. In the reported cases the fitness function is the approximation Mean Squared Error (MSE) or in the case of the classification task - number of misclassification on the training data. The population is subjected to crossovers (recombinations) and mutations (perturbations) in general causing improvement of individuals fitness.

In the $(\mu+\lambda)$ strategy population P has μ chromosomes, initially with random characteristics (values for each feature). In each iteration i from the population P randomly selected λ items are copied to the parents population O. First, new individuals are created by making a certain number of recombinations on elements from the population O, consequently they inherit a combination of attributes of their parents. Next, new individuals are created by the mutation operation, which is a random change of genes characteristics. From the combination of μ -the initial chromosomes and the new set of λ individuals (after the recombination and mutation) μ of the fittest are chosen. In this way, the cardinality of the new population is constant. These steps are repeated a certain amount of iterations. Finally from the population the best individual as the solution of the optimization problem is chosen. The whole algorithm was illustrated with the following pseudo-code.

Procedure of the Evolution Strategy $\mu + \lambda$

```
procedure Evolution Strategy (m+l)
    begin
      i = 0
      initialization P(i)
      evaluation P(i)
      while (termination condition not achieved)
        T(i) = reproduction P(i)
        O(i) = recombination /crossover/ and mutation T(i) /perturbation/
        evaluation O(i)
        P(i+1) = m the best chromosomes form set sum of P(i) and O(i)
        i = i+1
      end
end.
```

In the studied case, after setting up the structure of fuzzy neural network, the appearance of chromosome is determined automatically. During the artificial neural network training process, all parameters (like weights and biases) must be considered but also for the genetic operations in ES some additional parameters are required. These include the first order coefficients of standard deviation to determine the range of mutation and also some optional parameters associated with the fuzzy activation function are needed. In the considered case these last were not introduced because of use of trigonometric fuzzy operators, but when in the methodology Dombi's, Frank's, Yager's or Hamacher's operators [13] are used, theirs parameters should be taken into account as well. In some scientific works (e.g.[5]) the parameter which is the initial value in the case for considered network representing by Q_0 has been encoded also in a chromosome. During the study, it was observed that the proposed algorithm is not very sensitive to the above parameter, therefore, constant for each simulation random value from the interval $[0.35, 0.7]$ was assumed.

The data-structure of individuals was referred to ES-chromosomes. Formally a population P of n individuals was described as follows:

$$P = (ch) = (ch_1, ch_2, ..., ch_n) \tag{5}$$

where the i-th ES-chromosome ch_i is defined as

$$ch_i = (ob, ESpar) \tag{6}$$

with parameters describing investigated neural object ob and ES parameters $ESpar$:

$$\begin{aligned} ob &= (W, B, ffun_{par}) \\ ESpar &= (\sigma_1, \sigma_2, ..., \sigma_m) \end{aligned} \tag{7}$$

Here m denotes number of parameters in ob structure. This structure contains all information connected with investigated Fuzzy Flip-Flop Neural Network. Therefore sub-structure W contains all weights, B biases and finally $ffun_{par}$ describe shape of fuzzy norms and co-norms, using some of its parameters. As mentioned before in some fuzzy functions these parameters can be omitted e.g. trigonometrical fuzzy norm.

During evolution, some evolutionary operators as three staged mutation (perturbation), recombination and reproduction (consisting random selection with replacement) were applied [2] .

In real-life biological populations principle, descendants resemble their parents in a certain way and small changes from one generation to another are more often found than significant one. Therefore mutation operator for ES is defined as an addition of normal distributed random numbers to genes values. Both parts of the ES-chromosome: the object-parameters and the strategy-parameters are mutated as follows

$$ob_i^{new} = ob * s(\sigma_i)$$

$$ESpar_i^{new} = ESpar_i * s(\sigma_i) \tag{8}$$

where s is based on random generator with normal distribution and σ_i values (for i=1, 2, ..., m).

Similarly to effects of gene-recombination in nature, several recombination operators are defined for Evolutionary Strategies. At the beginning of studies on ES these operators have not been used. For the study described in this paper, this evolutionary operation is present and it is based on averaged values of vectors ob and $ESpar$ separately. For two chromosomes $ch_1 = (ob_1, ESpar_1)$ and $ch_2 = (ob_2, ESpar_2)$ the recombination operator is defined as follows. In the first step new coefficient $r \in [0, 1]$ is generated using random value generator with uniform distribution. In next step the recombination occurs for each elements of chromosome

$$ob_1^{new} = ob_1 * r + ob_2 * (1 - r)$$
$$ob_2^{new} = ob_2 * r + ob_1 * (1 - r)$$

(9)

$$ESpar_1^{new} = ESpar_1 * r + ESpar_2 * (1 - r)$$
$$ESpar_2^{new} = ESpar_2 * r + ESpar_1 * (1 - r)$$

During the study, it was found that it is disadvantageous to use an algorithm of the recombination based on global crossover methodology i.e. using more than two randomly selected parents to produce one offspring. In this investigated case, it implicates low rates of convergence and obtained networks were characterized by poor generalization. As a simple termination condition, a maximal assumed number of iteration cycles were used.

More details can be found in the bibliography describing the evolutionary algorithms such as [2, 4, 12].

5   Numerical Simulation

Verification of correctness of the method presented in this paper for supervised learning neural network algorithm based on evolutionary strategy $(\mu + \lambda)$ was conducted with numerical simulation. In the numerical verification for testing 4 data sets were used: a single and a double sine functions, a trigonometric functions of two variables and a classification of Iris flowers [14, 18]. Due to editorial constraints selected results of numerical simulations have been shown.

In each of the examined cases of this numerical verification, the main task of the neural network were to obtain the desired response based on a collection training data. In the approximation problem this response is associated with searched approximation formula. During consideration the classification problem the output of neural network corresponds with discrimination function.

At the beginning, the proposed procedure was tested by approximation of one variable function given by the following formula $f(x) = 0.5 \cos(2\pi x) + 0.5$. The training set was generated on the basis of regular points from interval $x \in [0, 1]$ with step 0.02, therefore the set cardinality was equal 51 items. For such formulated task a 1-3-1 Fuzzy Neural Network was used. As a result of numerical tests it was established that the Evolutionary Strategy works best for the following parameters: $\mu = 15$, $\lambda = 5$ during 26 learning epochs with range of mutations 0.1. The best results were equivalent to an error of approximation at level 10^{-6}.

For obvious reasons, not all parameters - studied in this research - and not all aspects of evolution has been reported here.

Next experiment, consisted at approximation of function containing two different components, given by formula $f(x) = 0.5 \sin(2\pi x) \sin(\frac{2\pi}{0.35}x) + 0.5$. A neural network with the structure of 1-5-1 was used. Thus it was characterized by 16 parameters that had to established in the optimization process. 100 training data from the interval $x \in [0, 1]$ were prepared for the learning phase. In the process of learning with use of the Evolutionary Strategy a following result 10^{-6} of MSE approximation was obtained. In this case the best instance of ES algorithm was running with parameters as follow: $\mu = 17$, $\lambda = 4$. The result has been obtained after only 18 iterations of learning.

Another example - with the approximation as a subject task - was a two dimensional function given by following equation $f(x) = 0.5 \sin(2\pi x_1)^5 \sin(\frac{2\pi}{0.35}x_2)^3 + 0.5$. This time the points from training data were generated on a regular square grid ($x \in [-1, 1] \times [-1, 1]$) with the spacing 0.2, therefore, in the simulation 484 learning elements has been used. In this case 2-4-4-1 network structure was chosen, having altogether s 37 parameters. The network was trained by using the evolutionary algorithm with parameters $\mu = 40$, $\lambda = 23$ and 17 learning epochs. As a result of learning seen in Figure 5 approximation error MSE at level 10^{-3} was obtained.

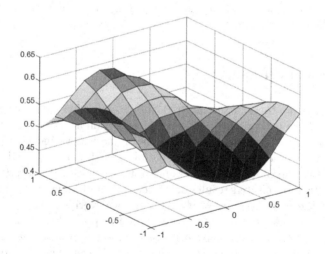

Fig. 5. Result of approximation of two dimensional function

Further research was conducted on the real data set Iris Plants Database [1], taken from the well-known repository the Center for Machine Learning and Intelligent Systems at the University of California, Irvine, at [29]. This data records the lengths and widths of petals and sepals of three species of iris setosa canadensis, versicolor and virginica; the first two classes are linearly separable. Here the task of neural network is to obtain classification function $f : x \mapsto \{1, 2, 3\}$.

The set of data is composed of three classes of equal size represented by 150 elements altogether, but the learning and testing samples have not been defined. The structure of the investigated network was set to 4-3-2-3 and consequently it had 32 parameters (weighs and biases). SE algorithm was used with the parameters $\mu = 50$, $\lambda = 30$ during 25 epochs. Depending on the division between the data sets for learning and testing groups, the quality of the classification ranged from 85 % for the partition ratio of 0.5 to 94.4 % correct classification for training set containing 90% of the examples.

Similar studies were carried out with the Evolutionary Strategies: $(1 + 1)$ as well as (μ, λ) [12]. In these cases obtained results were much worse than presented in this publication.

6 Conclusion

Numerical verification showed the positive property of Fuzzy Flip-Flop Neural Networks with heuristic algorithm applied for the supervised learning.

At this introductory study during verification phase, approximation test of several functions and a simple classification based on data obtained from the collection of benchmark data were under consideration. The results of such evaluation do not differ from other studies [5], and in some cases were found to be better. It must be emphasized that the proposed learning method is much simpler than the existing based on Bacterial Memetic Algorithm. It should also be noted that in the examples of approximation in this study neural network with significantly lower complexity (less number of layers) than in the cited studies were used. For this reason, proposed methodology does not require such a large amount of computing resources and consequently the calculation time was also improved.

The Fuzzy Flip-Flop Neural Network with heuristic algorithm for supervised learning can be applied as a complete tool for modelling dynamic systems, pattern recognition, and other information technology tasks [19] in particular, procedures of analysis and data mining [23]. For the methodology under consideration some new application e.g. the control system in electrical systems (engineering) [15], decision support such as marketing (economics) [20], as well as fault detection [17] will be studied in the near future.

Further basic research will be related to the use of other algorithms inspired by natural biological processes applied to the adaptation of weights and changes in network topology [3] and the creation of procedures employing parallel or distributed approach based on multi-agent systems.

Acknowledgments. The research presented here are co-financed by European Union within European Social Fund, project "Information Technologies: Research And Their Interdisciplinary Applications" in Institute of Computer Science of the Polish Academy of Sciences.

References

1. Angulo, C., Parra, X., Catala, A.: K-SVCR. A Support Vector Machine for Multi-class Classification. Neurocomputing 55, 57–77 (2003)
2. Arabas, J.: Evolutionary Computation for Global Optimization – Current Trends. Journal of Telecommunications and Information Technology 4, 5–10 (2011)
3. Bergh, V.F., Engelbrecht, A.: Cooperative Learning in Neural Networks Using Particle Swarm Optimizers. South African Computer Journal 26, 84–90 (2000)
4. Brownlee, J.: Clever Algorithms: Nature-Inspired Programming Recipes, Lulu Enterprises (2011)
5. Gal, L., Botzheim, J., Koczy, L.T.: Improvements to the Bacterial Memetic Algorithm used for Fuzzy Rule Base Extraction. In: IEEE International Conference on Computational Intelligence for Measurement Systems and Applications, Istanbul, pp. 38–43 (2008)
6. Gal, L., Botzheim, J., Koczy, L.T.: Function Approximation Performance of Fuzzy Neural Networks Based on Frequently Used Fuzzy Operations and a Pair of New Trigonometric Norms. In: IEEE International Conference on Fuzzy Systems, Barcelona, pp. 1–8 (2010)
7. Diamond, J., Pedrycz, W., McLeod, D.: Fuzzy JK Flip-Flops as Computational Structures: Design and Implementation. IEEE Transactions on Circuits and Systems II, Analog and Digital Signal Processing 41(3), 215–226 (1994)
8. Gniewek, L., Kluska, J.: Family of Fuzzy JK Flip-Flops Based on Bounded Product, Bounded Sum and Complementation. IEEE Transactions on Systems, Man, and Cybernetics, Part B: Cybernetics 28(6), 861–868 (1998)
9. Hirota, K., Ozawa, K.: The Concept of Fuzzy Flip-Flop. Man and Cybernetics 19(5), 980–997 (1989)
10. Hirota, K., Pedrycz, W.: Neurocomputations with Fuzzy Flip-Flops. In: Proceedings of International Joint Conference on Neural Networks, Nagoya, vol. 2, pp. 1867–1870 (1993)
11. Jones, A.J.: Genetic Algorithms and Their Applications to the Design of Neural Networks. Neural Computing and Applications, 32–45 (1993)
12. De Jong, K.A.: Evolutionary Computation: A Unified Approach. MIT Press, Cambridge (2006)
13. Kacprzyk, J.: Fuzzy Sets in Systems Analysis. PWN, Warsaw (1986)
14. Kowalski, P.A., Kulczycki, P.: Data Sample Reduction for Classification of Interval Information using Neural Network Sensitivity Analysis. In: Dicheva, D., Dochev, D. (eds.) AIMSA 2010. LNCS, vol. 6304, pp. 271–272. Springer, Heidelberg (2010)
15. Kowalski, P.A., Lukasik, S., Charytanowicz, M., Kulczycki, P.: Data-Driven Fuzzy Modelling and Control with Kernel Density Based Clustering Technique. Polish Journal of Environmental Studies 17, 83–87 (2008)
16. Koczy, L.T., Lovassy, R.: Fuzzy Flip-Flops and Neural Nets? In: IEEE International Fuzzy Systems Conference, London, pp. 1–6 (2007)
17. Kulczycki, P.: Statistical Inference for Fault Detection: A Complete Algorithm Based on Kernel Estimators. Kybernetika 38(2), 141–168 (2002)
18. Kulczycki, P., Kowalski, P.A.: Bayes Classification of Imprecise Information of Interval Type. Control and Cybernetics 40(1), 101–123 (2011)
19. Kulczycki, P., Hryniewicz, O., Kacprzyk, J. (eds.): Information Technologies for Systems Research. WNT, Warsaw (2007) (in Polish)
20. Kulczycki, P., Charytanowicz, M., Kowalski, P.A., Lukasik, S.: The Complete Gradient Clustering Algorithm: Properties in Practical Applications. Journal of Applied Statistics 39(6), 1211–1224 (2012)

21. Lovassy, R., Koczy, L.T., Gal, L.: Multilayer Perception Implemented by Fuzzy Flip-Flops. In: IEEE World Congress on Computational Intelligence, Hong Kong, pp. 1683–1688 (2008)
22. Lovassy, R., Koczy, L.T., Gal, L.: Optimizing Fuzzy Flip-Flop Based Neural Networks by Bacterial Memetic Algorithm. In: IFSA/EUSFLAT, Lisbon, pp. 1508–1513 (2009)
23. Lukasik, S., Kowalski, P.A., Charytanowicz, M., Kulczycki, P.: Fuzzy Model Identification Using Kernel-Density-Based Clustering. In: Atanassov, K., Chountas, P., Kacprzyk, J., Krawczak, M.P., Melo-Pinto, P., Szmidt, E., Zadrozny, S. (eds.) Developments in Fuzzy Sets, Intuitionistic Fuzzy Nets and Related Topics. Applications, vol. II, pp. 135–146. EXIT, Warszawa (2008)
24. Ozawa, K., Hirota, K., Koczy, L.T.: Fuzzy flip-flop. In: Patyra, M.J., Mlynek, D.M. (eds.) Fuzzy Logic Implementation and Applications, pp. 97–236. Wiley (1996)
25. Mandziuk, J.: Solving the N-Queens Problem with a Binary Hopfield-Type Network. Biological Cybernetics 72(5), 439–446 (1995)
26. Marquardt, D.: An Algorithm for Least-Squares Estimation of Nonlinear Parameters. Journal of Applied Mathematics 11, 431–441 (1963)
27. Rutkowski, L.: Computational Intelligence: Methods and Techniques. Springer, Berlin (2008)
28. Whitley, D., Starkweather, T., Bogart, C.: Genetic Algorithms and Neural Networks: Optimizing Connections and Connectivity. Technical Report Department of Computer Science, Colorado State University, pp. 89–117 (1989)
29. Iris Data Set, http://archive.ics.uci.edu/ml/datasets/Iris

Air Traffic Incidents Analysis with the Use of Fuzzy Sets

Michał Lower[1], Jan Magott[1], and Jacek Skorupski[2]

[1] Wrocław University of Technology, Faculty of Electronics, Wrocław, Poland
{michal.lower,jan.magott}@pwr.wroc.pl
[2] Warsaw University of Technology, Faculty of Transport, Warsaw, Poland
jsk@wt.pw.edu.pl

Abstract. In safety, reliability as well as risk analysis and management, information often is uncertain and imprecise. The approach to air incident analysis under uncertain and imprecise information presented in our paper is inspired by the possibility theory. Notably, in such analyses these are both: static and dynamic components that have to be included. As part of this work, static analysis of a serious incident has been performed. In order to do this, probability scale which is based on fuzzy set theory has been given. The scenarios of transformation of incident into accident have been found and their fuzzy probabilities have been calculated. Finally, it has been shown that elimination of one of premises for transformation of the incident into accident significantly reduces the possibility of this transformation.

Keywords: serious incident, fuzzy probability, events tree, fuzzy inference, air traffic safety.

1 Introduction

Air communication is commonly thought as the most safe transport type. Because passenger safety is the main priority of all subjects engaged in air transport, technical, organization, procedure barriers are established in order to avoid air accidents. Sometimes these facilities fail; in most cases because of human error. To learn lessons from these failures, accidents are investigated in order to find their causes. Such investigation is usually qualitative [8].

In the paper, a quantitative analysis of serious incidents is proposed. The "serious incident" is usually a very dangerous event when some barriers against accident have failed to meet their goal. They are very important sources of knowledge about safety assurance systems in air transport. We want to estimate the probability that a given incident would transform into accident. With that kind of study at disposal, one can conclude whether safety facilities are sufficient or have to be extended. In order to evaluate this probability, estimation of safety barrier reliability has to be carried out. Unfortunately, in most cases there are no sufficient data to infer statistically about the frequency of events for the accident scenario. Unfortunately, it is highly unlikely to find that data. There are two reasons of such situation. First is that some of these events occur very rarely, and additionally, in past the events without significant consequences were not usually recorded. The second one is human factor with such

L. Rutkowski et al. (Eds.): ICAISC 2013, Part I, LNAI 7894, pp. 306–317, 2013.
© Springer-Verlag Berlin Heidelberg 2013

measures that are difficult to evaluate as different reactions probabilities and error activity probability. Such measures are charged with uncertainty and subjective estimations. Only methods to obtain such knowledge are expert estimates. These estimations are not precise and not sufficient to probabilistic analysis.

In safety, reliability, and risk analysis and management, information often is uncertain and imprecise. In book [10] three approaches to reliability and safety with uncertain and imprecise information are presented: probability and statistics, fuzzy set theory, possibility theory (inspired by the above).

In paper [1] the following approaches for representation of uncertainty are listed: probability, imprecise (interval) probability, probability bound analysis, possibility theory (foundations: probability, statistics, fuzzy sets), Dempster-Shafer evidence theory.

The approach to air incident analysis presented in our paper is inspired by the possibility theory.

In air incident analysis both types of components have to be included: static and dynamic. Static analysis can be executed by means of fault trees with fuzzy probabilities [16, 17] and event trees with fuzzy probabilities [7]. Fuzzy probability is called possibility. The Dynamic analysis is executed in the time domain. More precisely, the analysis may be carried out using minimal and maximal values of time parameters similarly to the safety study of some railroad crossing in [9]. The other approach is probabilistic when time parameters are represented by probability distributions as in [2] where time coordination of distance protections in high voltage power transmission line was considered. The next kind of analysis will be based upon fuzzy set and will become the topic of the paper.

In this paper, the serious incident which occurred at the Chopin airport in Warsaw in 2007 year would be analyzed. Only static analysis will be executed, while dynamic one will be the topic of the following paper. In order to find the probability that given incident would transform into accident, the analysis of event trees by fuzzy probabilities will be performed.

2   Serious Air Traffic Incident No. 344/07

An analysis of incidents using fuzzy inference is illustrated with the example of a serious air traffic incident which occurred in August 2007 at the Warsaw Chopin airport between Boeing 767 and Boeing 737 aircraft. Its cause was classified as a "human factor" and the causal group H4 – "procedural errors" [18].

2.1   Description of the Circumstances of the Incident

In the incident on 13th of August 2007 participated two aircraft – Boeing 737 (B737) and the Boeing 767 (B767), which more or less at the same time were scheduled for take-off from the Warsaw Chopin airport. As the first, clearance for line-up and wait on runway 29 was issued to B737. As a second, clearance for line-up and wait on runway 33 was given to the B767 crew. The latter aircraft was the first to obtain permission to take-off. A moment after confirmation of permission to take-off, both aircrafts began the start procedure at the same time. The B737 crew wrongly assumed that the start permission was addressed to them. They probably thought that since they had received the permission to line up the runway first, they would be also the first to be permitted to start. In addition, the categories of wake turbulence caused that from the traffic efficiency point of view, it would be better to start B737 before B767. Decision of the controller, however, was different. The air traffic controller (ATC) did not watch the planes taking-off, because at this time he was busy agreeing a helicopter take-off. The situation of simultaneous start was, nevertheless, observed by the pilot of ATR 72, who was waiting in the queue for departure. He reacted over the radio. After this message, B767 pilot looked right and saw B737 taking-off. Then, on his own initiative, braked off and began a rapid deceleration, which led to stopping the plane 200 meters from the intersection of the runways. The assistant controller heard the ATR 72 pilot radio message and informed the controller that B737 operated without authorization. The controller, who originally did not hear the information on the radio, after 16 seconds from the start, recognized the situation and strongly ordered B737 to discontinue the take-off procedure. The B737 crew performed braking and stopped 200 m from the intersection of the runways.

2.2   Premises Conducive for Accident

In the presented example it can be noticed that it is sufficient to impose only one additional risk factor (or a combination of two factors), and the incident would become, in fact, an accident. There are several premises conducive for an accident [15].

1. Weather conditions (visibility) are so bad that it is impossible to see the actual traffic situation. This applies to B767, ATR 72 crews, and the air traffic controller.
2. ATR 72 pilot does not watch the situation on the runways, just waiting for permission to line-up the runway.
3. ATR 72 pilot observes the situation, but does not immediately inform about it on the radio, instead he discusses it with other members of his own crew.
4. B767 crew, busy with their own take-off procedure, does not pay attention to the message transmitted over the radio by the ATR 72 pilot.
5. B767 crew takes a wrong decision to continue the take-off, despite noting B737 aircraft. Such decision could arise, for example, with this reasoning: "there is no possibility to stop before the intersection, let B737 stop - after all, we have a permission to start, maybe we can pass the intersection before the B737", etc.
6. Assistant controller does not pay attention to the information given by radio by the ATR 72 pilot, or does not respond to it properly - does not inform the controller.
7. B737 crew does not react properly to the air traffic controller command and does not interrupt the take-off procedure.

2.3   Scenarios Leading to Accident

As indicated above, only a small number of conducive events is necessary for transformation of an incident into an accident. There are several scenarios that are considered in the context of this work. Logical dependencies between the scenarios leading to accidents and premises conducive for them, are schematically shown in Table 1. In this paper we assume designation of premises E_i, where $i \in \{1, ...,7\}$ and e.g. $E_1 =$

"Insufficient visibility". We also have adopted following designations: 1 - a premise occurred, 0 - a premise did not occur, *n.r.* - the occurrence of premise is irrelevant to the transformation of an incident into an accident or there is only one reasonable premise value.

Table 1. Scenarios of transformation of the incident 344/07 into an accident

	1. Insufficient visibility (E_1)	2. ATR 72 does nt monitor (E_2)	3. ATR 72 does not warn (E_3)	4. B767 does not hear the warning (E_4)	5. B767 does not brake off (E_5)	6. Assistant does not inform (E_6)	7. B737 does not interrupt take-off (E_7)
Scenario 1	1	*n.r.*	*n.r.*	*n.r.*	*n.r.*	*n.r.*	*n.r.*
Scenario 2	0	1	*n.r.*	*n.r.*	*n.r.*	*n.r.*	*n.r.*
Scenario 3	0	0	1	*n.r.*	*n.r.*	*n.r.*	*n.r.*
Scenario 4	0	0	0	1	*n.r.*	1	*n.r.*
Scenario 5	0	0	0	1	*n.r.*	0	1
Scenario 6	0	0	0	0	1	1	*n.r.*
Scenario 7	0	0	0	0	1	0	1

The above scenarios of take-off continuation were determined using the event tree, whom analysis, for the sake of limited paper size, has been omitted.

2.4   Method of Incident Analysis

Estimating the probability of each scenario would allow to determine the probability of the accident occurring as a result of this incident. Unfortunately, realization of most of these scenarios, depends on immeasurable values not available for statistical analysis. For example, in scenario 2 it is impossible to determine, using measurement methods, how often staff focuses exclusively on their procedures and draws little attention to external events. The situation is similar in scenarios 5, 6 or 7, in which we have to deal with human error. Of course, such errors do happen, but it is difficult to estimate the statistical probability of them. We do not know the actual number of such errors (we know at most those errors which have consequences in air traffic events), nor we know the number of opportunities to commit them, so there is no reference necessary to estimate their frequency. In literature we can find some models for estimating the likelihood of operators (pilots and controllers) errors, with respect to the causes of aviation accidents. For example, [3] uses MIDAS human performance model together with a model for estimating the risk of accidents TOPAZ to analyze similar issues - probability of a collision at the junction of the runway and taxiway.

The above mentioned reasons are the basis for seeking probabilities of events conducive for accident in the area of expert assessments. These obviously are often ambiguous and imprecise, which makes us propose the use of fuzzy methods in the analysis of incidents. In this paper, we focus on finding expressions for the fuzzy probability of an accident, given that under these circumstances, the consequences would be catastrophic. For scenarios that lead to the continuation of take-off, formulas for the fuzzy likelihood of their realization will be presented, and the probability will be calculated. The basis will be the event tree analysis by fuzzy probability.

3   Probability Scale

In [13] the example of probability classification scheme was proposed. It is shown in Table 2 which contains both qualitative and quantitative definitions of likelihood categories of aircraft on-board system failure. A similar approach is presented in [5].

Table 2. Probability of occurrence definitions ([13])

	Extremely improbable	Very rare	Rare	Probable	Frequent
Qualitative definition	Should virtually never occur in the whole fleet life	Unlikely to occur when considering several systems of the same type, but nevertheless has to be considered as being possible	Unlikely to occur during the total operational life of each system but may occur several times when considering several systems of the same type	May occur once during total operational life of one system	May occur once or several times during operational life
Quantitative definition	$< 10^{-9}$ per flight hour	10^{-7} to 10^{-9} per flight hour	10^{-5} to 10^{-7} per flight hour	10^{-3} to 10^{-5} per flight hour	1 to 10^{-3} per flight hour

Values of both scales are not precise. Experts can interpret them in different manners. These values can be expressed using fuzzy set theory [9, 12]. Event tree analysis by fuzzy probability has been described in paper [7]. In this paper, fuzzy sets for fuzzy probabilities are expressed by discrete membership functions with a few real values. In our paper, membership functions of fuzzy sets for fuzzy probabilities are trapezoidal. Such functions are used in fault tree analysis by fuzzy probabilities in [16, 17].

Linguistic variable *Probability* is shown in Fig. 1, where it is illustrated in logarithmic scale. The variable has the following values: extremely improbable (*EI*), very rare (*VR*), rare (*RE*), probable (*PR*), frequent (*FR*). For values *VR, RE* i *PR*, trapezoidal functions with parameters (*a,b,c,d*) are as follows:

$$\mu_i(x; a, b, c, d) = \begin{cases} 0, & x \le a \\ \frac{x-a}{b-a}, & a < x \le b \\ 1, & b < x \le c \\ \frac{d-x}{d-c}, & c < x \le d \\ 0, & x > d \end{cases} \qquad (1)$$

where $i \in \{VR, RE, PR\}$

For values *EI* and *FR*, trapezoidal functions are the following:

$$\mu_{EI}(x; a, b, c, d) = \begin{cases} 0, & x < a = b \\ 1, & b \le x \le c \\ \frac{d-x}{d-c}, & c < x \le d \\ 0, & x > d \end{cases} \qquad (2)$$

$$\mu_{FR}(x; a, b, c, d) = \begin{cases} 0, & x \leq a \\ \frac{x-a}{b-a}, & a < x \leq b \\ 1, & < x \leq c = d \\ 0, & x > d \end{cases} \tag{3}$$

In Table 2, probability scale for aircraft on-board system failure in flight is shown. These systems are very reliable. In the analyzed incident, unreliability concerns mainly human factor. In contemporary air traffic systems, human error frequency is much higher than aircraft on-board system failure frequency. Hence, new scale has been accepted with values of linguistic variable *Probability* given by parameters (a,b,c,d) as in Table 3, and illustrated in Fig. 1.

Table 3. Parameters of membership functions of linguistic variable *Probability* values

	a	b	c	d
μ_{EI}	10^{-9}	10^{-9}	10^{-8}	10^{-7}
μ_{VR}	10^{-8}	10^{-7}	10^{-6}	10^{-5}
μ_{RE}	10^{-6}	10^{-5}	10^{-4}	10^{-3}
μ_{PR}	10^{-4}	10^{-3}	10^{-2}	10^{-1}
μ_{FR}	10^{-2}	10^{-1}	1	1

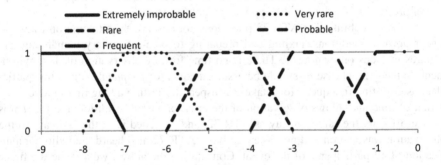

Fig. 1. Linguistic variable *Probability* in logarithmic form

4   Static Analysis of Scenarios Leading to Air Accident

We denote by P_1, P_2, ..., P_7 the probability of occurrence of premises conducive to formation of an aviation accident, and by $P(S_1)$, $P(S_2)$, ..., $P(S_7)$ - the probability of realization of scenarios leading to the transformation of the incident into accident. Fuzzy probabilities P_1, P_2, ..., P_7 will be determined on the basis of the literature, analysis of statistical data and expert assessments obtained for the present study. Such estimates are generally difficult to obtain and subject to a large margin of error, even if they are of fuzzy nature and therefore inherently imprecise. A broader discussion of the problems involved in the risk analysis of complex anthropotechnical systems, particularly in relation to air traffic, can be found in [4].

P_1 - the probability that the weather conditions are unfavorable and do not allow incident participants to notice hazards. Determining this probability will be based on the analysis of meteorological data for the Warsaw Chopin Airport in the last six years. Daily observations from the 33th week of the year and the 8th month of the year (including August 13) were considered together. The results of this analysis are shown in Table 4.

Table 4. Weather conditions for the Chopin Airport [19]

	maximum precipita- tion [mm/h]	minimum precipita- tion [mm/h]	mean precipita- tion [mm/day]	maxi- mum visibility [km]	mini- mum visibility [km]	mean visibility [km]	weather events
8th month	36	0	2,07	30	6	13,7	rain, fog, thunderstorm
33th week	21	0	1,84	27,5	6	13,9	rain, fog, thunderstorm
13.08 2007	4	0	1,8	9,6	9,6	9,6	rain, fog, thunderstorm

Table 4 shows that in spite of fog and precipitation occurring during this period, visibility conditions are good enough that they do not interfere with observation of airfield. Therefore we assume fuzzy probability P_1 equal to "*very rare*". Of course, the analysis taking into account autumn, winter or night conditions will require the adoption of probability P_1 close to the opposite end of the scale.

P_2 - the probability that ATR 72 pilot does not observe the situation on runways. Under normal conditions, taxiing and preparing to take-off is very demanding and requires to focus on own tasks. There is no time for any observation of the environment. In the general case P_2 should be assumed equal to "*frequent*". But in this particular case, waiting in a queue for a take-off (especially lasting a long time) reduces the deficit of time and allows observation of the environment. In addition, the B737 was to take-off from the same runway as ATR 72, and preceded it on the taxiway, so the observation was natural and necessary activity. ATR 72 also heard the radio communication of all participants of the event. Considering the above, we assume the fuzzy probability P_2 to be equal "*probable*".

P_3 - describes the probability of the event, that the pilot who spotted the danger does not inform about it. As in that incident professionally trained pilots were involved, it must be assumed that the fuzzy probability P_3 is set to "*very rare*".

P_4 - the probability of the event, that the B767 crew does not pay attention or does not properly understand the message of danger. ATR 72 pilot's message was not clear - it only indicated the existence of an unusual situation. Somewhat similar probability was estimated in [14], where one of analyzed threats was an undetected warning of runway occupancy sensor. In this paper, we assume that the fuzzy probability P_4 value becomes "*probable*".

P_5 - describes the event of failure of emergency braking maneuver. Given the obviousness of this maneuver, but also proximity of the speed v_1, determining the boundary speed above which one should continue with the take-off, we assume that the fuzzy probability P_5 is equal to "*probable*" .

P_6 - determines the probability of no preventive action from ATC. Given that the controller was busy with other activities, but also the fact that his main task is to ensure the air traffic safety, the probability of failure to respond to the signals of danger P_6 must be considered within the scope of "*very rare*".

P_7 - the probability of refusal to execute the controller's command. Conscious refusal seems impossible. However, the B737 crew could not understand the instructions, or the speed v_1 could be exceeded, in which case an effective response is impossible. Given the above, we assume that the probability of fuzzy probability P_7 is set to "*rare*".

All fuzzy probabilities adopted for analysis are shown in Table 5.

Table 5. Fuzzy probability of premises conducive for accident

Premise	Fuzzy probability
E_1 - Insufficient visibility (P_1)	*very rare* (VR)
E_2 - ATR 72 does not monitor (P_2)	*probable* (PR)
E_3 - ATR 72 does not warn (P_3)	*very rare* (VR)
E_4 - B767 does not hear the warning (P_4)	*probable* (PR)
E_5 - B767 does not brake off (P_5)	*probable* (PR)
E_6 - Assistant controller does not inform (P_6)	*very rare* (VR)
E_7 - B737 does not interrupt take-off (P_7)	*rare* (RE)

Probabilities of realization of scenarios are as follows:

$$P(S_1) = P_1 \tag{4}$$

$$P(S_2) = (1 - P_1) \cdot P_2 \tag{5}$$

$$P(S_3) = (1 - P_1) \cdot (1 - P_2) \cdot P_3 \tag{6}$$

$$P(S_4) = (1 - P_1) \cdot (1 - P_2) \cdot (1 - P_3) \cdot P_4 \cdot P_6 \tag{7}$$

$$P(S_5) = (1 - P_1) \cdot (1 - P_2) \cdot (1 - P_3) \cdot P_4 \cdot (1 - P_6) \cdot P_7 \tag{8}$$

$$P(S_6) = (1 - P_1) \cdot (1 - P_2) \cdot (1 - P_3) \cdot (1 - P_4) \cdot P_5 \cdot P_6 \tag{9}$$

$$P(S_7) = (1 - P_1) \cdot (1 - P_2) \cdot (1 - P_3) \cdot (1 - P_4) \cdot P_5 \cdot (1 - P_6) \cdot P_7 \tag{10}$$

Let us denote by K the event that both aircraft will continue the take-off, and by $P(K)$ the probability of that event, which is given by the expression:

$$P(K) = P_1 + (1 - P_1) \cdot \left(P_2 + (1 - P_2) \cdot \left(P_3 + (1 - P_3) \cdot \left(P_4 \cdot (P_6 + (1 - P_6) \cdot P_7) + (1 - P_4) \cdot P_5 \cdot (P_6 + (1 - P_6) \cdot P_7) \right) \right) \right) \tag{11}$$

Let us consider two trapezoidal fuzzy numbers $P_i = (a_i, b_i, c_i, d_i)$ and $P_j = (a_j, b_j, c_j, d_j)$. Their addition, subtraction, and multiplication, respectively, are represented by trapezoidal fuzzy numbers $(a_i + a_j, b_i + b_j, c_i + c_j, d_i + d_j)$, $(a_i - d_j, b_i - c_j, c_i - b_j, d_i - a_j)$, $(a_i \cdot a_j, b_i \cdot b_j, c_i \cdot c_j, d_i \cdot d_j)$ [16, 17].

Fuzzy probability of realization of scenarios $P(S_1)$, ..., $P(S_7)$ and fuzzy probability that both aircraft will continue the take-off is given in table 6.

Table 6. Fuzzy probabilities of scenarios realization

	a	b	c	d
$P(S_1)$	10^{-8}	10^{-7}	10^{-6}	10^{-5}
$P(S_2)$	$9,9999 \cdot 10^{-5}$	10^{-3}	10^{-2}	10^{-1}
$P(S_3)$	$8,9999 \cdot 10^{-9}$	$9,9 \cdot 10^{-8}$	$9,99 \cdot 10^{-7}$	$9,999 \cdot 10^{-6}$
$P(S_4)$	$8,9998 \cdot 10^{-13}$	$9,9 \cdot 10^{-11}$	$9,99 \cdot 10^{-9}$	$9,999 \cdot 10^{-7}$
$P(S_5)$	$8,9997 \cdot 10^{-11}$	$9,9 \cdot 10^{-9}$	$9,99 \cdot 10^{-7}$	$9,999 \cdot 10^{-5}$
$P(S_6)$	$8,0998 \cdot 10^{-13}$	$9,801 \cdot 10^{-11}$	$9,98 \cdot 10^{-9}$	$9,998 \cdot 10^{-7}$
$P(S_7)$	$8,0998 \cdot 10^{-11}$	$9,801 \cdot 10^{-9}$	$9,98 \cdot 10^{-7}$	$9,998 \cdot 10^{-5}$
$P(K)$	$1,0002 \cdot 10^{-4}$	$1,0002 \cdot 10^{-3}$	$1,0004 \cdot 10^{-2}$	$1,0022 \cdot 10^{-1}$

In order to calculate the value of linguistic variable *Probability* for fuzzy probability $P(K)$, one can apply Jacard's similarity of two fuzzy sets. Jacard's similarity of fuzzy sets A, B with membership functions μ_A, μ_B is defined by [11]:

$$s_J(A, B) = \frac{\int_X min(\mu_A(x), \mu_B(x)) \, dx}{\int_X max(\mu_A(x), \mu_B(x)) \, dx} \tag{12}$$

As we adopted logarithmic scale for linguistic variable *Probability*, the formula for Jacard's similarity calculations was modified to the following form:

$$s_J^{log}(A, B) = \frac{\int_X min(\mu_A(x), \mu_B(x)) \log_{10} dx}{\int_X max(\mu_A(x), \mu_B(x)) \log_{10} dx} \tag{13}$$

For each value of linguistic variable *Probability EI, VR*, etc., similarity with trapezoidal fuzzy number $P(K)$ was calculated and is given in Table 7.

Table 7. Jacard's similarity calculation results

Value of linguistic variable *Probability (ProbVal)*	$s_J^{log}(P(K), ProbVal)$
extremely improbable (EI)	0
very rare (VR)	0
rare (RE)	$6,6646 \cdot 10^{-2}$
probable (PR)	$9,9967 \cdot 10^{-1}$
frequent (FR)	$7,7038 \cdot 10^{-2}$

In the analyzed air traffic incident none of the premises E_i did actually occur. However, there is no certainty that this is a permanent property. Institutions responsible for the air traffic safety take many preventive actions to eliminate the factors that contribute to accidents and incidents. The important question is, which factors should be eliminated first and which merit the most attention. For each premise E_i, we want to find fuzzy probability $P(K|\neg E_i)$ that both aircraft will continue the take-off provided this premise is not true. These fuzzy probabilities will allow evaluation of consequences of preventive activities.

$$P(K|\neg E_1) = P_2 + (1 - P_2) \cdot \left(P_3 + (1 - P_3) \cdot \left(P_4 \cdot (P_6 + (1 - P_6) \cdot P_7) + (1 - P_4) \cdot \right.\right.$$
$$\left.\left. P_5 \cdot (P_6 + (1 - P_6) \cdot P_7)\right)\right) \tag{14}$$

$$P(K|\neg E_2) = P_1 + (1 - P_1) \cdot \left(P_3 + (1 - P_3) \cdot \left(P_4 \cdot (P_6 + (1 - P_6) \cdot P_7) + (1 - P_4) \cdot \right.\right.$$
$$\left.\left. P_5 \cdot (P_6 + (1 - P_6) \cdot P_7)\right)\right) \tag{15}$$

$$P(K|\neg E_3) = P_1 + (1 - P_1) \cdot \left(P_2 + (1 - P_2) \cdot \left(P_4 \cdot (P_6 + (1 - P_6) \cdot P_7) + (1 - P_4) \cdot \right.\right.$$
$$\left.\left. P_5 \cdot (P_6 + (1 - P_6) \cdot P_7)\right)\right) \tag{16}$$

$$P(K|\neg E_4) = P_1 + (1 - P_1) \cdot \left(P_2 + (1 - P_2) \cdot \left(P_3 + (1 - P_3) \cdot P_5 \cdot (P_6 + (1 - P_6) \cdot \right.\right.$$
$$\left.\left. P_7)\right)\right) \tag{17}$$

$$P(K|\neg E_5) = P_1 + (1 - P_1) \cdot \left(P_2 + (1 - P_2) \cdot \left(P_3 + (1 - P_3) \cdot P_4 \cdot (P_6 + (1 - P_6) \cdot \right.\right.$$
$$\left.\left. P_7)\right)\right) \tag{18}$$

$$P(K|\neg E_6) = P_1 + (1 - P_1) \cdot \left(P_2 + (1 - P_2) \cdot \left(P_3 + (1 - P_3) \cdot (P_4 \cdot P_7 + (1 - P_4) \cdot \right.\right.$$
$$\left.\left. P_5 \cdot P_7)\right)\right) \tag{19}$$

$$P(K|\neg E_7) = P_1 + (1 - P_1) \cdot \left(P_2 + (1 - P_2) \cdot \left(P_3 + (1 - P_3) \cdot (P_4 \cdot P_6 + (1 - P_4) \cdot \right.\right.$$
$$\left.\left. P_5 \cdot P_6)\right)\right) \tag{20}$$

Jacard's similarity between $P(K|\neg E_i)$, where $i \in \{1, ..., 7\}$, and values of linguistic variable *Probability* is given in Table 8.

Table 8. Jacard's similarity between $P(K|\neg E_i)$, where $i \in \{1, ..., 7\}$, and values of linguistic variable *Probability*

	$P(K|\neg E_i)$				$s_J^{\log}(P(K|\neg E_i), ProbVal)$				
	a	b	c	d	EI	VR	RE	PR	FR
i=1	1,0001 $\cdot 10^{-4}$	1,0001 $\cdot 10^{-3}$	1,0003 $\cdot 10^{-2}$	1,0021 $\cdot 10^{-1}$	0	0	6,6652 $\cdot 10^{-2}$	9,9971 $\cdot 10^{-1}$	7,7031 $\cdot 10^{-2}$
i=2	2,0192 $\cdot 10^{-8}$	2,201 $\cdot 10^{-7}$	4,019 $\cdot 10^{-6}$	2,2199 $\cdot 10^{-4}$	2,9378 $\cdot 10^{-2}$	5,6335 $\cdot 10^{-1}$	2,7520 $\cdot 10^{-1}$	4,7242 $\cdot 10^{-3}$	0
i=3	1,0001 $\cdot 10^{-4}$	1,0001 $\cdot 10^{-3}$	1,0003 $\cdot 10^{-2}$	1,0021 $\cdot 10^{-1}$	0	0	6,6652 $\cdot 10^{-2}$	9,9971 $\cdot 10^{-1}$	7,7031 $\cdot 10^{-2}$
i=4	1,0002 $\cdot 10^{-4}$	1,0002 $\cdot 10^{-3}$	1,0003 $\cdot 10^{-2}$	1,0012 $\cdot 10^{-1}$	0	0	6,6651 $\cdot 10^{-2}$	9,9979 $\cdot 10^{-1}$	7,6988 $\cdot 10^{-2}$
i=5	1,0002 $\cdot 10^{-4}$	1,0002 $\cdot 10^{-3}$	1,0003 $\cdot 10^{-2}$	1,0012 $\cdot 10^{-1}$	0	0	6,6651 $\cdot 10^{-2}$	9,9979 $\cdot 10^{-1}$	7,6988 $\cdot 10^{-2}$
i=6	1,0002 $\cdot 10^{-4}$	1,0002 $\cdot 10^{-3}$	1,0004 $\cdot 10^{-2}$	1,0022 $\cdot 10^{-1}$	0	0	6,6646 $\cdot 10^{-2}$	9,9967 $\cdot 10^{-1}$	7,7037 $\cdot 10^{-2}$
i=7	1,0002 $\cdot 10^{-4}$	1,0002 $\cdot 10^{-3}$	1,0002 $\cdot 10^{-2}$	1,0002 $\cdot 10^{-1}$	0	0	6,6655 $\cdot 10^{-2}$	9,9991 $\cdot 10^{-1}$	7,3938 $\cdot 10^{-2}$

Calculations for the basic variant (Tables 6 and 7) show that the fuzzy likelihood of take-off continuation is most compliant with a value *"probable"* (*PR*) of linguistic variable *Probability*.

Analysis of the results of calculations in Table 8 shows that elimination of premises E_1, E_3, E_4, E_5, E_6 and E_7 does not change the above mentioned fuzzy evaluation of the possibility of transformation from incident into accident. The most important in this case is the premise E_2 - "ATR72 does not monitor". It turns out that preventive action aiming at the elimination of this premise moves the evaluation of linguistic variable *Probability* into the area between *"rare"* (*RE*) and *"very rare"* (*VR*) values. This means a significant increase in the level of safety. Elimination (or reduction of the likelihood) of the premise E_2 is practically possible. Pilot training should be carried out to increase the understanding of the need to monitor the airfield during the taxiing procedure and while waiting for permission to take-off. One can also consider the introduction of recommendation to carefully observe other traffic into the operating instructions.

5   Summary

In the paper serious incident which occurred at the Chopin airport in Warsaw in 2007 year has been analyzed. While the static analysis has been carried out, the dynamic one will be treated in the next paper. Probability scale for events has been given and it is five values one. For the values the suitable fuzzy sets have been defined. Scenarios of transformation of the incident into an accident have been found using event tree. Fuzzy probability of the transformation has been calculated. Finally, it has been shown that elimination of one of premises for transformation of the incident into accident significantly reduces the possibility of this transformation.

References

1. Aven, T., Zio, E.: Some considerations on the treatment of uncertainties in risk assessment for practical decision making. Reliability Engineering and System Safety 96, 64–74 (2011)
2. Babczyński, T., Łukowicz, M., Magott, J.: Time coordination of distance protections using probabilistic fault trees with time dependencies. IEEE Transaction on Power Delivery 25(3), 1402–1409 (2010)
3. Blom, H., Corker, K., Stroeve, S.: On the integration of human performance and collision risk simulation models of runway operation. National Aerospace Laboratory NLR, Report NLR-TP-2006-682 (2006)
4. Brooker, P.: Air Traffic Management accident risk. Part 1: The limits of realistic modelling. Safety Science 44, 419–450 (2006)
5. Civil Aviation Authority, Air Traffic Safety Requirements CAP 670, CAA Safety Regulation Group (2012)
6. Kacprzyk, J.: Fuzzy Sets in Systems Analysis. National Scientific Publishers, Warsaw (1986) (in Polish)
7. Kenarangui, R.: Event-tree analysis by fuzzy probability. IEEE Transactions on Reliability 40(1), 120–124 (1991)

8. Klich, E.: Flight Safety in Air Transport, Exploitation Problems Library, Exploitation Technology Institute - PIB, Radom (2011) (in Polish)
9. Magott, J., Skrobanek, S.: Timing analysis of safety properties using fault trees with time dependencies and timed state-charts. Reliability Engineering and Systems Safety 97(1), 14–26 (2012)
10. Onisawa, T., Kacprzyk, J. (eds.): Reliability and Safety Analysis under Fuzziness. Physica-Verlag, Springer, Heidelberg (1995)
11. Rajati, M.R., Mendel, J.M., Wu, D.: Solving Zadeh's Magnus challenge problem on linguistic probabilities via linguistic weighted averages. In: IEEE Int. Conf. Fuzzy Systems, FUZZ, June 27-30 (2011)
12. Rutkowska, D., Piliński, M., Rutkowski, L.: Neural Networks, Genetic Algorithms and Fuzzy Systems. Scientific Publishers PWN, Warsaw-Lodz (1997) (in Polish)
13. Safety Management Manual (SMM), 1st edn. International Civil Aviation Organization, Doc 9859, AN/460 (2006)
14. Shortle, J., Xie, Y., Chen, C., Donohue, G.: Simulating Collision Probabilities of Landing Airplanes at Non-towered Airports. Transactions of the Society for Computer Simulation 79(10), 1–17 (2003)
15. Skorupski, J.: Method of analysis of the relation between serious incident and accident in air traffic. In: Berenguer, Grall, Soares (eds.) Advances in Safety, Reliability and Risk Management, pp. 2393–2401. Taylor & Francis Group (2012)
16. Tanaka, H., Fan, L.T., Lai, F.S., Toguchi, K.: Fault-tree analysis by fuzzy probability. IEEE Transactions on Reliability 32(5), 453–457 (1983)
17. Tyagi, S.K., Pandey, D., Tyagi, R.: Fuzzy set theoretic approach to fault tree analysis. International Journal of Engineering, Science and Technology 2(5), 276–283 (2010)
18. Urząd Lotnictwa Cywilnego (Civil Aviation Authority of the Republic of Poland): Statement No. 78 of President of Civil Aviation Authority from 18th of September 2009 on air event No. 344/07, Warszawa (2009) (in Polish)
19. Weather Underground Internet Service, http://polish.wunderground.com

Automatic Design of Interpretable Fuzzy Partitions with Variable Granularity: An Experimental Comparison

Marco Lucarelli, Ciro Castiello, Anna Maria Fanelli, and Corrado Mencar

University of Bari A. Moro, Department of Informatics
via E. Orabona, 4 – 70125 Bari, Italy
{marco.lucarelli,ciro.castiello,corrado.mencar}@uniba.it,
fanelli@di.uniba.it

Abstract. In this paper we compare two algorithms that are capable of generating fuzzy partitions from data so as to verify a number of interpretability constraints: Hierarchical Fuzzy Partitioning (HFP) and Double Clustering with A* (DC*). Both algorithms exhibit the distinguishing feature of self-determining the number of fuzzy sets in each fuzzy partition, thus relieving the user from the selection of the best granularity level for each input feature. However, the two algorithms adopt very different approaches in generating fuzzy partitions, thus motivating an extensive experimentation to highlight points of strength and weakness of both. The experimental results show that, while HFP is on the average more efficient, DC* is capable of generating fuzzy partitions with a better trade-off between interpretability and accuracy, and generally offers greater stability with respect to its hyper-parameters.

1 Introduction

Fuzzy rule-based systems (FRBSs) are tools that enable knowledge representation and inference through fuzzy rules denoted by linguistic terms. The main point of strength of FRBSs is the possibility of establishing a semantic similarity (or co-intension) between the fuzzy sets that are used in their rules and the implicit semantics of the linguistic terms that are used to denote them. In this way the users of a FRBS can read and understand fuzzy rules, as well as revise and integrate rules with domain knowledge. In other words, the FRBS can be *interpretable* for users [1].

However, when FRBSs are acquired from data through some learning scheme, the semantic co-intension between fuzzy sets and linguistic meanings is often lost. This happens because fuzzy sets are usually shaped in order to optimize a specific performance measure, usually defined in terms of accuracy error. Nevertheless, the loss of semantic co-intension in a rule base determines a FRBS that is no longer interpretable. The development of specific learning algorithms is intended to overcome the interpretability loss in FRBSs acquired from data. Mainly, these learning schemes drive the adaption process so that a number of interpretability

L. Rutkowski et al. (Eds.): ICAISC 2013, Part I, LNAI 7894, pp. 318–328, 2013.

constraints is satisfied. The choice of the interpretability constraints used to guide the learning process is usually application-dependent; nevertheless some of them have a general scope and are widely used in literature [2].

Many learning algorithms for acquiring an interpretable FRBS require to fix the *granularity* of fuzzy partitions, i.e. the number of fuzzy sets that partition each input feature: the aim of such algorithms is to find the best shapes of the fuzzy sets in the partition so as to optimally balance accuracy and interpretability of the final system. However, the optimal number of fuzzy sets for each feature is often unknown and could be different for different features. As a result, in many cases a trial-and-error approach is used to select the best granularity for each feature.

An alternative approach is to adopt algorithms that select the best granularity for each feature in the learning scheme. Few algorithms are capable of self-determining the granularity level for each feature: in this paper we consider HI-ERARCHICAL FUZZY PARTITIONING (HFP) [3] and DOUBLE CLUSTERING WITH A* (DC*) [4]. HFP is included in the well-known FisPro tool, which is widely used for modeling interpretable fuzzy systems [5]. It is also used in GUAJE, a suite that involves several tools working together to realize a complete work-flow for designing interpretable fuzzy systems [6]. With respect to HFP, DC* adopts a completely different approach for generating fuzzy partitions. Thus an interesting issue is to evaluate both HFP and DC* on a number of benchmark problems. The aim of this paper is to provide a comparison of the two algorithms in order to highlight points of strength and weakness that can be useful in the selection of the best alternative on the basis of the nature of data. The comparative analysis is performed employing a number of benchmark datasets that can be processed by both algorithms (taking into account that DC* requires numerical features and is limited to classification problems).

In Section 2, both HFP and DC* are briefly sketched and in Section 3 the experimental plan is described. The experimental results are reported in Section 4 along with a comparative discussion of the points of strength and weakness of both algorithms. Some concluding remarks in Section 5 end the paper.

2   Generation of Interpretable Fuzzy Partitions

Both HFP and DC* share the ability of defining interpretable fuzzy partitions from data and do not require any a-priori specification of the granularity of the partitions. The two algorithms tackle the partitioning problem by following very different approaches, but adopt the same set of general-purpose interpretability constraints:

Normality each fuzzy set must have a prototype, i.e. one element with full membership;

Convexity each fuzzy set is convex, i.e. all α-cuts are closed intervals;

Continuity fuzzy sets are defined by continuous membership functions;

Distinguishability the similarity of two fuzzy sets in the partition is less than a threshold;

Completeness each element of the universe of discourse belongs to at least one fuzzy set with a degree greater than a threshold;

Leftmost/rightmost fuzzy sets the bounds of the universe of discourse are prototypes for some fuzzy sets.

Strong fuzzy partitions composed by trapezoidal fuzzy sets[1] are fuzzy partitions where it is guaranteed that, when each element inside the universe of discourse is considered, the sum of its membership degrees to all fuzzy sets of the partition adds up to one. Strong fuzzy partitions are widely used since they satisfy all the previously mentioned interpretability constraints[2]; thus they have been adopted also for the experimentation conducted in this paper.

2.1 Hierarchical Fuzzy Partitioning (HFP)

HFP aims at generating a family of interpretable fuzzy partitions from data. Members of this family are distinguished by their degree of interpretability and accuracy; the user can successively select the partitions that best balance accuracy and interpretability according to his/her needs.

Preliminarily, HFP cycles over each data feature and operates a one-dimensional clustering of data samples to define a first fuzzy partition for each feature. In the worst case a fuzzy set per data sample is generated; however clustering is used to accelerate HFP by generating fuzzy partitions with a number of fuzzy sets considerably smaller than the number of data samples.

The main stage of HFP is to iteratively merge adjacent fuzzy sets so that the new partition is as much similar as the previous partition (the one preceding the merging process). This is accomplished by defining a specific partition measure that is based on computing distances between fuzzy sets: the couple of fuzzy sets to be merged is selected in order to minimize the variation of this partition measure. Fuzzy set merging is carried out so as to guarantee strong fuzzy partitions and the iterative merging process is stopped when only one fuzzy set is defined on each feature.

The merging process is carried out over each input feature independently, resulting in a hierarchy of partitions for each feature. A combination of partitions (one for each feature) defines a granulation of the data space, where each information granule is defined by the Cartesian product of fuzzy sets belonging to different partitions. A selection process of the information granules is carried out by summing the membership degrees of all data samples to each granule (Σ-count): the information granules whose Σ-count is below a threshold are discarded. The remaining information granules can be used to define the rules of a FRBS. To avoid the combinatorial explosion of FRBSs that can be generated by picking a partition in each hierarchy, a heuristic procedure is implemented

---

[1] Triangular fuzzy sets are special cases of trapezoidal fuzzy sets.

[2] It is assumed that similarity is assessed through the possibility measure and the thresholds required for distinguishability and completeness are both fixed to 0.5.

to generate a sequence of FRBSs defined by combinations of partitions with decreasing granularity. The sequence of combinations of partitions is then returned by HFP.

2.2   Double Clustering with A* (DC*)

The objective of DC* is to find the simplest and interpretable fuzzy partition on each input feature that best describes the available data, provided that such data have a class label. Once fuzzy partitions are created, the corresponding fuzzy rules are defined.

As implied by the name, DC* is mainly composed of two phases. Firstly, a quantization process is carried out by the LVQ1 algorithm [7] performed over the whole input space: the process aims at providing a compressed representation of data (given by the code-book vectors, also called prototypes), taking into account class information. In the second phase a clustering on each dimension is performed, taking into account the reciprocal positioning of all the prototypes' projections, together with the related class labels. That leads DC* to face a combinatorial optimization problem which is tackled through the A* search algorithm [8].

A number of elements are relevant to specify the A* algorithm, including the search space, the initial state, a successor operator, the goal test, the cost function and the heuristic function. To characterize the search space in the context of the DC*, the concepts of *cut* and *box* must be introduced. A cut is a midpoint between two adjacent prototypes' projections belonging to different classes; by combining cuts of different features a box is defined, which may include zero or more prototypes. If all prototypes included in a box belong to the same class (or if the box is empty), the box is said *pure*, otherwise it is tagged as *not pure* (see the example in fig. 1).

A candidate solution for the optimization problem at hand is represented by a configuration of cuts, including zero or more cuts for each input feature. The goal test is satisfied if all the boxes corresponding to the cuts of a candidate solution are pure. The search space is the set of all the candidate solutions and the initial state corresponds to the candidate solution with zero cuts for each feature. The successor operator, applied to a candidate solution, generates a set of new candidate solutions: a candidate solution belongs to this set if it has one cut (on any feature) more than the initial candidate solution.

The cost function simply counts the number of cuts in a candidate solution, while the heuristic function estimates the number of cuts that are strictly necessary to obtain a configuration producing pure boxes. The estimate is a lower bound of the real number of cuts that are required, thus making the heuristic function admissible for the convergence and optimality of the A* algorithm.

The A* algorithm uses a priority queue to store the generated candidate solutions that must be evaluated against the goal test. In particular, the specific version of the algorithm implemented for the experimental sessions described in the present paper adopts a multilevel priority queue: this represents an improvement with respect to previous versions of the algorithm [9]. The first level of

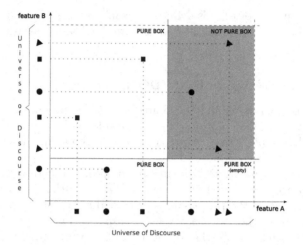

Fig. 1. A bi-dimensional input space with six prototypes of three different classes (square, circle, triangle). The application of two cuts (chosen among the candidate cuts) provides a partition of the input space in four boxes: three pure boxes (one of them is empty) and one not-pure box.

the queue stores the sum of the values related to the cost and heuristic functions, so that candidate solutions can be sorted by considering the number of their cuts and the number of the (estimated) cuts required to achieve a goal solution. Candidate solutions showing the same score at the first level can be further sorted at the second level in order to penalize candidate solutions with cuts that are reciprocally too close. This is achieved by considering the minimum distance of the cut that generated the candidate solution (through the application of the successor operator) from the adjacent cuts. In this way, a ranking is produced where solutions with well separated cuts (and, therefore, wide boxes) are prioritized, thus improving the generalization ability.

The result of the A* search is an optimal configuration of cuts defined over the input features. We have implemented a simple procedure to define strong fuzzy partitions for each input feature based on trapezoidal fuzzy sets[3], so that such partitions can be compared with those obtained by HFP. In fig. 2 an example of fuzzy partition is depicted.

Similarly to HFP, fuzzy sets on each partition are combined together to form multi-dimensional information granules. Clearly, each information granule corresponds to a box of the solution returned by A*; therefore each information granule can be labeled with the class of the corresponding box. As a consequence, fuzzy rules can be immediately defined by taking the information granules that correspond to non-empty boxes as antecedents and the corresponding class labels as consequents.

Few hyper-parameters are required for running DC*: they coincide with those required for running LVQ1. The most important hyper-parameter is the code-book

---

[3] The original version of DC* produces Gaussian fuzzy sets.

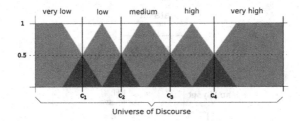

Fig. 2. Example of fuzzy partition obtained from cuts c_1, c_2, c_3, c_4

cardinality, i.e. the number of prototypes to be defined by LVQ1. This value corresponds to the maximum number of fuzzy rules in the final model (more prototypes may belong to the same box, producing a single rule). This hyper-parameter has an immediate interpretation as it regulates the desired granularity of the resulting FRBS: the lower this number, the coarser the rules, which are more readable but possibly less accurate. On the other hand, the higher is the code-book cardinality, the finer is the rule granularity, which may result in a better accuracy counterbalanced by a higher complexity.

3   Experimentation

The overall setup of the experimental sessions is described in this section. The aim of the experimentation is to perform a fair comparative test between HFP and DC*. The test involves the use of two freely available tools: WEKA[4] 3.6.7 [10] and FisPro[5] 3.4 [5]. The first is a suite of machine learning algorithms for data mining tasks: it is used to perform a stratified ten-fold partition of the datasets involved in the experimentation. The latter is an open source software for fuzzy inference system design and optimization: it includes an implementation of HFP and a tool for the subsequent generation of FRBSs. FisPro is also exploited to carry out the performance evaluation of all the derived FRBSs. Figure 3 depicts the comparative experimentation framework highlighting the role of WEKA and FisPro, together with the contribution of DC*.

Ten datasets are involved in the experimental sessions: all of them have been selected from the UCI repository[6] and include numerical, classified data without missing values. The datasets are heterogeneous in their scope, in order to perform the experimentation process on data showing different characteristics. A brief description of the involved datasets is provided in table 1.

In view of the ultimate validation to be accomplished at the end of the experimentation, the first step consists in a stratified ten-fold partition of the datasets, performed using WEKA: given a seed value, the tool randomly creates the data partitions providing the learning sets and the test sets. For each fold a different experiment is carried out.

---

[4] Weka is available at http://www.cs.waikato.ac.nz/ml/weka/

[5] FisPro is available at http://www.inra.fr/mia/M/fispro/FisPro_EN.html

[6] http://archive.ics.uci.edu/ml/

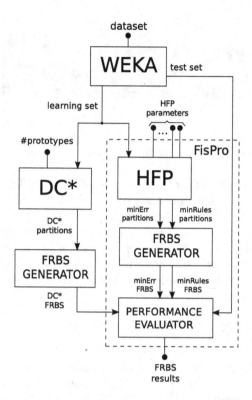

Fig. 3. Comparative experimentation framework

Each learning set is meant to be processed by both HFP and DC*. After the generation of partitions, the corresponding FRBSs are defined. Since HFP generates a family of partitions, only two partitions are eventually selected for comparison: the most accurate —denoted as "minErr"— and the most interpretable (i.e. the partition with the smallest number of rules), denoted as "minRules". Furthermore, HFP requires the specification of a number of hyper-parameters, which have been fixed to their default value.

On the other hand, the behavior of DC* mainly depends on the number of prototypes required by LVQ1, which has been varied for each experimentation, while the following hyper-parameters are fixed for all experimental sessions: a) initial learning rate = 0.01; b) maximum number of epochs = 1000; c) shifting threshold value = 10^{-4}. For each dataset, several executions of DC* are performed, doubling the number of prototypes at each run. In particular, the first run is computed with a number of prototypes equal to the number of classes (one prototype per class). At each successive run, the number of prototypes is doubled and proportionally distributed among the classes. With few exceptions, the process is iterated until the number of prototypes is at least equal to the number of rules of the most accurate FRBS identified by HFP.

Table 1. Dataset characteristics. *The second feature has been removed because it exhibits a constant value. **Class "4" has been removed since it is not represented by any sample.

Dataset	samples	features	classes
Iris	150	4	3
Wine	178	13	3
Breast Cancer Wisconsin	683	9	2
Pima Indians Diabetes	368	8	2
Vertebral Column (2 classes)	310	6	2
Vertebral Column (3 classes)	310	6	3
Ionosphere	351	33(34)*	2
Cardiotocography (CTG)	2126	21	3
Glass Identification	214	9	6(7)**
Statlog-Shuttle	58000	9	7

To evaluate the accuracy of the final FRBSs —both from HFP and DC*— a module within FisPro is applied on the test sets. Since a ten-fold cross validation scheme is adopted, the performance for each dataset can be expressed in terms of average values related to ten different classification models.

4   Results and Discussion

A number of considerations can be drawn from the analysis of the experimental results which are globally illustrated in tables 2 and 3. For each dataset, the table reports the results related to the couple of FRBSs generated by HFP and selected for comparison (the one providing the best accuracy performance and the one including the lower number of rules) and to a number of FRBSs generated by DC* (each of them obtained by doubling the number of prototypes at every new generation).

It can be verified how the simplest models derived (namely, the 2-rules FRBSs produced by HFP and the FRBSs generated by applying DC* with one prototype per class) are characterized by poor values of accuracy performance. On the other hand, by increasing the structural complexity of the models, it is possible to observe a consequent reduction of the error values. In other words, the well known effects connected with the accuracy/interpretability trade-off can be recognized in the results reported in the table.

To allow a fair comparison, the maximum number of DC* prototypes (standing as the upper limit on the maximum number of rules to be generated) is set for each dataset by taking into account the number of rules composing the most effective FRBS derived through HFP (wherever it is possible). In this way, HFP and DC* are oriented to potentially produce models with a similar number of rules so that the accuracy analysis can be more revealing.

In terms of accuracy DC*, outperforms HFP on six datasets. More interestingly, when we turn to consider the accuracy/interpretability trade-off, it can be

Table 2. A general picture of the experimental results (first part). Each column reports the average results (over 10-fold cross validation) ± the standard deviation. For DC* the number p of prototypes used in the first stage is also reported. In **bold**, the best results in terms of accuracy/interpretability tradeoff are highlighted.

Dataset	ALGORITHM		Rules	Features	mean #MF	Err %
Iris	HFP	minErr	8.5±0.81	3±0	2.09±0	5.33±7.20
		minRules	2±0	1±0	2±0	33±14.00
	DC*	$p = 3$	3±0	2±0	2±0	30.7±14.93
		$p = 6$	3.6±0.49	2±0	2±0	21.3±13.27
		$p = 12$	**3±0**	**1.6±0.49**	**2.4±0.49**	**6.67±6.67**
Wine	HFP	minErr	39.6±20.29	5.4±1.11	2.31±0.19	7.22±3.72
		minRules	2±0	1±0	2±0	32±5.41
	DC*	$p = 3$	2.9±0.3	2±0	2±0	43.3±7.50
		$p = 6$	3.1±0.3	2±0	2±0	23.8±5.97
		$p = 12$	3.5±0.5	2±0	2±0	21.3±11.00
		$p = 24$	4.8±1.25	2.3±0.45	2±0	19.1±4.06
WBC	HFP	minErr	34.7±18	4.9±0.83	2.02±0.05	4.85±2.09
		minRules	2±0	1±0	2±0	16.5±6.74
	DC*	$p = 2$	2±0	1±0	2±0	13.7±4.84
		$p = 4$	2±0	1±0	2±0	12.8±4.56
		$p = 8$	2±0	1±0	2±0	13.7±4.84
		$p = 16$	2±0	1±0	2±0	13.7±3.49
		$p = 32$	**3.1±1.58**	**1.5±0.67**	**2±0**	**6.47±3.03**
		$p = 48$	3.5±1.5	1.7±0.64	2±0	6.62±3.56
Pima	HFP	minErr	39±16.64	5.8±1.17	2.29±0.15	28±4.55
		minRules	2±0	1±0	2±0	35±4.03
	DC*	$p = 2$	2±0	1±0	2±0	35.6±4.08
		$p = 4$	2±0	1±0	2±0	36.9±4.83
		$p = 8$	2.2±0.6	1.1±0.3	2±0	37.3±5.64
		$p = 16$	2.6±0.8	1.4±0.49	2±0	32.6±9.38
		$p = 32$	**7.6±2.54**	**3.3±0.46**	**2±0**	**22.2±6.66**
Vertebral 2	HFP	minErr	5.5±3.61	2.3±0.64	2±0	26±7.66
		minRules	2±0	1±0	2±0	33±10.28
	DC*	$p = 2$	2±0	1±0	2±0	34.7±9.53
		$p = 4$	2±0	1±0	2±0	32.2±10.66
		$p = 8$	**2±0**	**1±0**	**2±0**	**25.3±8.31**

observed how the DC* methodology is able to provide the simplest models, exhibiting the smallest numbers of rules and involved features (the average number of MFs per model is almost the same when both algorithms are applied). Such a superiority is verified for each dataset and in some cases the gain in terms of structural complexity is highly appreciable. In this sense, the models produced by DC* appear to be preferable even when their accuracy performance values are slightly lower than those reported by the HFP-generated FRBSs. As a further remark, it can be noticed how DC* provides better results also in terms of model stability, as showed by the standard deviation values reported to complete the information regarding the average numbers of rules, involved features and MFs.

Table 3. (cont'd from table 2)

Dataset	ALGORITHM		Rules	Features	mean #MF	Err %
Vertebral 3	HFP	minErr	4.6±1.28	2.1±0.3	2.05±0.15	43±8.63
		minRules	2±0	1±0	2±0	47±9.16
	DC*	$p = 3$	3±0	2±0	2±0	51.3±7.28
		$p = 6$	**3.9±0.3**	**2±0**	**2±0**	**33.4±11.63**
Ionosphere	HFP	minErr	300±637.02	5±3.02	2±0	16±6.20
		minRules	2±0	1±0	2±0	31±11.43
	DC*	$p = 2$	2±0	1±0	2±0	39.7±8.60
		$p = 4$	2±0	1±0	2±0	23.1±10.26
		$p = 8$	**2.2±0.6**	**1.1±0.3**	**2±0**	**15.7±12.54**
CTG 3	HFP	minErr	120.8±95.21	7.9±1.87	2.16±0.08	17.4±2.48
		minRules	2±0	1±0	2±0	20.4±2.50
	DC*	$p = 3$	2.7±0.46	2±0	2±0	42.3±6.34
		$p = 6$	3±0	2±0	2±0	26.3±7.46
		$p = 12$	**3.3±0.46**	**2.3±0.46**	**2±0**	**13.6±8.50**
Glass	HFP	minErr	15.4±5.28	5.6±0.92	2.13±0.17	51±15.52
		minRules	2±0	1±0	2±0	57±11.38
	DC*	$p = 6$	6±0	3±0	2±0	63.8±15.10
		$p = 12$	**8.4±1.11**	**3.7±0.46**	**2±0**	**43.3±13.71**
Shuttle	HFP	minErr	81.5±22.84	22.83±0.49	2.87±2.76	3.67±1.51
		minRules	2±0	1±0	2±0	21.4±0.43
	DC*	$p = 7$	7±0	3±0	2±0	57.9±19.53
		$p = 14$	10±1.18	4±0	2±0	19.6±2.71

Some additional details, concerning the experiments on particular datasets, can be highlighted. While in a couple of cases (related to the Shuttle and Wine datasets) the iterative application of DC* with doubled number of prototypes has been quit to avoid an excessive growth of the computational burden, in some other circumstances the process has been stopped by reason of the huge number of rules generated by HFP. This is the case, for instance, of the Ionosphere and CTG 3 datasets, where DC* is able to overcome HFP in terms of performance accuracy while producing classifiers with a reduced number of rules. Better results from HFP could be potentially achieved by fine-tuning of the hyper-parameters. However, this would have involved a heavy trial-and-error process further complicated by the need of selecting partitions from the returned sets.

Finally, the overall analysis of the obtained results lets us underline some peculiarities of the DC* algorithm. Firstly, it is able to produce FRBSs with reduced features: their number is lower than both the total number of features in each dataset and the number of features characterizing the HFP-generated models. The second peculiarity of DC* consists in the capability to operate the optimization process mentioned in section 2.2 producing FRBSs with a number of rules which is significantly lower than the number of prototypes (corresponding to the maximum number of attainable rules).

5   Conclusions

The experimental results reported in the paper show that both DC* and HFP exhibit different points of strength that make them valid approaches for generating interpretable FRBSs. In particular, DC* is superior in terms of accuracy/interpretability tradeoff because it is capable of designing very compact FRBSs with appreciable classification errors that are only slightly higher or even smaller than the most accurate models provided by HFP. Furthermore, DC* requires very few hyper-parameters, the most important one regulating the granularity of the acquired knowledge by fixing the upper bound in the number of rules to define. However, DC* is not very sensitive to this hyper-parameter: this avoids the necessity of fine-tuning and guarantees a *descriptive stability* of the resulting FRBSs.

As concerning HFP, this algorithm shows more flexibility since it is not limited to classification problems and, on the average, it is more efficient than DC* because its computational complexity is polynomial on the number of data samples. On the other hand, since the theoretical computational complexity of DC* is exponential in the worst case (on the number of prototypes times the data dimensionality), in some experiments DC* did not terminate in reasonable time. The efficiency of DC* can be improved by a refinement of the heuristic function used in the second stage of DC* where A* is applied; this is matter of current research.

References

1. Mencar, C.: Interpretability of Fuzzy Information Granules. In: Bargiela, A., Pedrycz, W. (eds.) Human-Centric Information Processing. SCI, vol. 182, pp. 95–118. Springer, Heidelberg (2009)
2. Mencar, C., Fanelli, A.M.: Interpretability constraints for fuzzy information granulation. Information Sciences 178, 4585–4618 (2008)
3. Guillaume, S., Charnomordic, B.: Generating an Interpretable Family of Fuzzy Partitions From Data. IEEE Transactions on Fuzzy Systems 12(3), 324–335 (2004)
4. Castellano, G., Fanelli, A.M., Mencar, C., Plantamura, V.L.: Classifying data with interpretable fuzzy granulation. In: Proceedings of the 3rd International Conference on Soft Computing and Intelligent Systems and 7th International Symposium on Advanced Intelligent Systems 2006, Tokyo, Japan, pp. 872–877 (2006)
5. Guillaume, S., Charnomordic, B.: Learning interpretable fuzzy inference systems with FisPro. Information Sciences 181(20), 4409–4427 (2011)
6. Alonso, J.M., Magdalena, L.: Generating Understandable and Accurate Fuzzy Rule-Based Systems in a Java Environment. In: Fanelli, A.M., Pedrycz, W., Petrosino, A. (eds.) WILF 2011. LNCS, vol. 6857, pp. 212–219. Springer, Heidelberg (2011)
7. Kohonen, T.: Self-organizing maps. Information Sciences, vol. 30. Springer (2001)
8. Edelkamp, S., Schrödl, S.: Heuristic Search: Theory and Applications. Morgan Kaufmann (2011)
9. Mencar, C., Consiglio, A., Castellano, G., Fanelli, A.M.: Improving the Classification Ability of DC* Algorithm. In: Masulli, F., Mitra, S., Pasi, G. (eds.) WILF 2007. LNCS (LNAI), vol. 4578, pp. 145–151. Springer, Heidelberg (2007)
10. Hall, M., Frank, E., Holmes, G., Pfahringer, B., Reutemann, P., Witten, I.H.: The WEKA data mining software: an update. SIGKDD Explorations 11(1), 10–18 (2009)

A New Method
for Designing and Complexity Reduction
of Neuro-fuzzy Systems for Nonlinear Modelling

Krystian Łapa, Marcin Zalasiński, and Krzysztof Cpałka

Częstochowa University of Technology,
Institute of Computational Intelligence, Poland
{krystian.lapa,marcin.zalasinski,krzysztof.cpalka}@iisi.pcz.pl

Abstract. In this paper we propose a new method for evolutionary
selection of parameters and structure of neuro-fuzzy system for nonlinear
modelling. This method allows maintain the correct proportions between
accuracy, complexity and interpretability of the system. Our algorithm
has been tested using well-known benchmarks.

1   Introduction

In the fuzzy systems the knowledge is represented in the form of fuzzy rules.
Thanks to that the knowledge can be interpretable. Neuro-fuzzy systems combine
the natural language description of fuzzy systems and the learning properties
of neural-networks (see e.g. [2]-[4], [9]-[12], [24], [27], [31]-[38], [41], [42], [47],
[53]-[57], [68], [69]). Therefore, neuro-fuzzy systems are often used for nonlinear
modelling. Neuro-fuzzy systems are most commonly used for direct modelling
of input-output dependencies ([19], [60], [65]). In other approach neuro-fuzzy
system may be used to generate the coefficients of the matrices of the state-
vector equation ([46]). In both cases the accuracy and interpretability of the
system are important [26].

In the literature various methods have been presented to increase interpretability of the intelligent systems. These methods can be applied in the context of
non-linear modelling. One of the possible approaches is tuning with the use of
genetic algorithms ([33], [37]) or multiobjective optimization ([7], [67]). Other
approach is based on the reduction of the system before or after the learning
process ([25], [58]). In addition, the literature describes many ways of the system initialization (for example by use the clustering algorithms, self-organized
networks etc.) ([1], [63]).

In this paper we propose a new method for designing and complexity reduction
of neuro-fuzzy systems for nonlinear modelling. Our method is based on the
evolutionary strategy (μ, λ). It is used to learn the parameters of the system and
the selection of the structure of the system. In the process of learning we want to
obtain the system with good accuracy of the nonlinear modelling and a simple
and clear rule base. This has been achieved through appropriate design of the
fitness function.

L. Rutkowski et al. (Eds.): ICAISC 2013, Part I, LNAI 7894, pp. 329–344, 2013.

This paper is organized as follows: in Section 2 a neuro-fuzzy system of the Mamdani type for nonlinear modelling is described. In section 3 a description of new method for designing and complexity reduction of neuro-fuzzy systems is shown. Simulation results are described in Section 4. Finally, in Section 5 conclusions are presented.

2   Neuro-fuzzy System for Nonlinear Modelling

We consider multi-input, multi-output neuro-fuzzy system mapping $\mathbf{X} \to \mathbf{Y}$, where $\mathbf{X} \subset \mathbf{R}^n$ and $\mathbf{Y} \subset \mathbf{R}^m$. The fuzzifier performs a mapping from the observed crisp input space $\mathbf{X} \subset \mathbf{R}^n$ to the fuzzy sets defined in $\mathbf{X}$. The most commonly used fuzzifier is the singleton fuzzifier which maps $\bar{\mathbf{x}} = [\bar{x}_1, \dots, \bar{x}_n] \in \mathbf{X}$ into a fuzzy set $A' \subseteq \mathbf{X}$ ([50], [52], [51]). The fuzzy rule base consists of a collection of N fuzzy IF... THEN... rules in the form

$$
R^k : \left[\left(\begin{array}{c} \text{IF } (x_1 \text{ is } A_1^k) \left| w_{k,1}^A \text{ AND} \dots \text{AND } (x_n \text{ is } A_n^k) \left| w_{k,n}^A \right. \right. \\ \text{THEN } (y_1 \text{ is } B_1^k), \dots, (y_m \text{ is } B_m^k) \end{array} \right) \left| w_k^{\text{rule}} \right. \right], \quad (1)
$$

where $\mathbf{x} = [x_1, \dots, x_n] \in \mathbf{X}$, $\mathbf{y} = [y_1, \dots, y_m] \in \mathbf{Y}$, $A_1^k, \dots, A_n^k$ are fuzzy sets characterized by membership functions $\mu_{A_i^k}(x_i)$, $i = 1, \dots, n$, $k = 1, \dots, N$, $B_1^k, \dots,$ B_m^k are fuzzy sets characterized by membership functions $\mu_{B_j^k}(y_j)$, $j = 1, \dots, m$, $k = 1, \dots, N$, $w_{k,i}^A$, $i = 1, \dots, n$, $k = 1, \dots, N$, are weights of antecedents, w_k^{rule}, $k = 1, \dots, N$, are weights of rules.

The fuzzy inference determines a mapping from the fuzzy sets in the input space $\mathbf{X}$ to the fuzzy sets in the output space $\mathbf{Y}$. Each of N rules (1) determines fuzzy sets $\bar{B}_j^k \subset \mathbf{Y}$ ([50], [52], [51]).

The aggregation operator, applied in order to obtain the fuzzy set B_j' is based on fuzzy sets $\bar{B}_j^k$, $k = 1, \dots, N$. The defuzzifier performs a mapping from the fuzzy sets B_j' to a crisp point $\bar{y}_j$, $j = 1, \dots, m$, in $\mathbf{Y} \subset \mathbf{R}$. The center of area (COA) method is defined in the discrete form by the following formula ([50], [48], [52], [51])

$$
\bar{y}_j = \text{def}_j = \frac{\sum_{r=1}^{R} \bar{y}_{j,r}^{\text{def}} \cdot \mu_{B_j'} \left(\bar{y}_{j,r}^{\text{def}} \right)}{\sum_{r=1}^{R} \mu_{B_j'} \left(\bar{y}_{j,r}^{\text{def}} \right)}, \quad (2)
$$

where $\bar{y}_{j,r}^{\text{def}}$, $j = 1, \dots, m$, $r = 1, \dots, R$, are discretization points, R is a number of discretization points [48].

In Mamdani approach formula (2) takes the form

$$
\bar{y}_j = \frac{\sum_{r=1}^{R} \bar{y}_{j,r}^{\text{def}} \cdot \overset{N}{\underset{k=1}{S^*}} \left\{ T \left\{ \overset{n}{\underset{i=1}{T^*}} \left\{ \mu_{A_i^k}(\bar{x}_i); w_{k,i}^A \right\}, \mu_{B_j^k}\left(\bar{y}_{j,r}^{\text{def}} \right) \right\}; w_k^{\text{rule}} \right\}}{\sum_{r=1}^{R} \overset{N}{\underset{k=1}{S^*}} \left\{ T \left\{ \overset{n}{\underset{i=1}{T^*}} \left\{ \mu_{A_i^k}(\bar{x}_i); w_{k,i}^A \right\}, \mu_{B_j^k}\left(\bar{y}_{j,r}^{\text{def}} \right) \right\}; w_k^{\text{rule}} \right\}}, \quad (3)
$$

where t-norm $T\{\cdot\}$ is a generalization of the usual two-valued logical conjunction (studied by classical logic), t-conorm $S\{\cdot\}$ is a generalization of the usual two-valued logical disjunction, $T^*\{\cdot\}$ is a weighted t-norm and $S^*\{\cdot\}$ is a weighted t-conorm ([30], [50], [48], [52], [51]).

In the next section a new learning algorithm for evolution of flexible neuro-fuzzy system (3) is proposed. In the process of evolution (evolution of parameters) we will find all parameters of the neuro-fuzzy system:

- $\{\bar{x}_{i,k}^A, \sigma_{i,k}^A\}$, $i = 1, \ldots, n$, $k = 1, \ldots, N$ - parameters of Gaussian membership functions $\mu_{A_i^k}(x_i)$ of the input fuzzy sets $A_1^k, \ldots, A_n^k$,
- $\{\bar{y}_{j,k}^B, \sigma_{j,k}^B\}$, $k = 1, \ldots, N$, $j = 1, \ldots, m$ - parameters of Gaussian membership functions $\mu_{B_j^k}(y_j)$ of the output fuzzy sets $B_1^k, \ldots, B_m^k$,
- $w_{k,i}^A$, $i = 1, \ldots, n$, $k = 1, \ldots, N$ - weights of antecedents,
- w_k^{rule}, $k = 1, \ldots, N$ - weights of rules,
- $\bar{y}_{j,r}^{\text{def}}$, $j = 1, \ldots, m$, $r = 1, \ldots, R$ - discretization points.

Moreover, in the process of evolution (evolution of structure) we will find number of inputs n, number of antecedents, number of rules N, number of consequents and number of discretization points R.

3 Description of the New Method for Designing and Complexity Reduction of Neuro-fuzzy Systems

The principles of the new method can be summarized as follows:

- The method may be used directly for modelling of dynamic system or it may be used indirectly for modelling proposed in [46].
- The method allows to learn parameters and select automatically the neuro-fuzzy system structure used to nonlinear modelling. The selection of the system structure is based on the selection of number of inputs, number of antecedents, number of rules, number of consequents and number of discretization points in the system. The process is done during system parameters learning process.
- The algorithm was designed in such a way, that in evolution process the unnecessary inputs, antecedents, rules, consequents and discretization points are eliminated. The unnecessary elements of the system are considered elements that reduction does not affect the accuracy of the system.
- The method works to increase the interpretability of the system. It is conducted in such a way that it promoted the results from the whole population in which the input fuzzy sets and the whole rules are the most differentiated (the least similar) and as simple as possible (containing the small number of inputs, antecedents, rules, consequents and discretization points).

The structure of the neuro-fuzzy system is described by formula (3) and its parameters are found using the evolutionary strategy (μ, λ) and the Pittsburgh approach ([5], [13], [21], [40], [48]). The evolutionary strategy (μ, λ) starts with a random generation of the initial parents population $\mathbf{P}$ containing μ individuals. Next, a temporary population $\mathbf{T}$ is created by means of reproduction, whose population contains λ individuals, while $\lambda \geq \mu$. Reproduction consists in a multiple random selection of λ individuals out of population $\mathbf{P}$ (multiple sampling) and placing the selected ones in temporary population $\mathbf{T}$. Individuals of population $\mathbf{T}$ undergo crossover and mutation operations as a result of which an offspring population $\mathbf{O}$ is created, which also has size λ. The purpose of the repair procedure of the population $\mathbf{O}$ is to correct the parameters if they reach inadmissible values. The new population $\mathbf{P}$ containing μ individuals is selected only out of the best λ individuals of population $\mathbf{O}$. For more details on the evolutionary strategy (μ, λ) please see [13], [20], [48].

3.1   Evolution of Parameters

We apply evolutionary strategy (μ, λ) for learning all parameters in the system described by formula (3). In a single chromosome, according to the Pittsburgh approach, a complete linguistic model is coded in the following way

$$
\mathbf{X}^{\mathrm{par}}_{ch} = \left\{
\begin{array}{c}
\bar{x}^A_{1,1}, \sigma^A_{1,1}, \ldots, \bar{x}^A_{n,1}, \sigma^A_{n,1}, \cdots \\
\bar{x}^A_{1,Nmax}, \sigma^A_{1,Nmax}, \ldots, \bar{x}^A_{n,Nmax}, \sigma^A_{n,Nmax}, \\
\bar{y}^B_{1,1}, \sigma^B_{1,1}, \ldots, \bar{y}^B_{m,1}, \sigma^B_{m,1}, \cdots \\
\bar{y}^B_{1,Nmax}, \sigma^B_{1,Nmax}, \ldots, \bar{y}^B_{m,Nmax}, \sigma^B_{m,Nmax}, \\
w^A_{1,1}, \ldots, w^A_{n,1}, \ldots w^A_{1,Nmax}, \ldots, w^A_{n,Nmax}, \\
w^{\mathrm{rule}}_1, \ldots, w^{\mathrm{rule}}_{Nmax} \\
\bar{y}^{\mathrm{def}}_{1,1}, \ldots, \bar{y}^{\mathrm{def}}_{1,Rmax}, \ldots, \bar{y}^{\mathrm{def}}_{m,1}, \ldots, \bar{y}^{\mathrm{def}}_{m,Rmax}
\end{array}
\right\}, \tag{4}
$$

$$
= \left\{ X^{\mathrm{par}}_{ch,1}, \ldots, X^{\mathrm{par}}_{ch,L} \right\}
$$

where $L = Nmax \cdot (3 \cdot n + 2 \cdot m + 1) + Rmax$, $ch = 1, \ldots, \mu$ for the parent population or $ch = 1, \ldots, \lambda$ for the temporary population, $Nmax$ is the maximum number of rules, $Rmax$ is the maximum number of discretization points. The maximum number of rules $Nmax$ should be selected to the problem individually. When the number of the rules $Nmax$ is too hig,h it can decrease the system interpretability. The purpose of the evolution strategy is to automatically select the number of rules from the range $[1, Nmax]$. Analogically, the maximum number of discretization points $Rmax$ should also be selected to the problem individually. The purpose of the evolution strategy is to automatically select the number of discretization points from the range $[1, Rmax]$. The purpose of evolution strategy (μ, λ) is also to select the number of antecedents and consequents within each rule from rule base. The number of antecedents in each of the rules is within the range $[1, n]$, and the number of consequents in each of the rules is within the range $[1, m]$. The reduction of the system is done with the use of additional chromosome $\mathbf{X}^{\mathrm{red}}$, which is described in the detail in the Section 3.2.

The self-adaptive feature of the algorithm is realized by assigning to each gene a separate mutation range described by the standard deviation

$$\sigma_{ch}^{\text{par}} = \left(\sigma_{ch,1}^{\text{par}}, \dots, \sigma_{ch,L}^{\text{par}} \right), \tag{5}$$

where $ch = 1, \dots, \mu$ for the parent population or $ch = 1, \dots, \lambda$ for the temporary population.

For temporary population we use the recombination (crossover) and the mutation operations:

– Crossover with averaging the values of the genes

$$X_{ch1,g}^{\text{par}'} = \tfrac{1}{2} \cdot \left(X_{ch1,g}^{\text{par}} + X_{ch2,g}^{\text{par}} \right), X_{ch2,g}^{\text{par}'} = X_{ch1,g}^{\text{par}'}, \tag{6}$$

and

$$\sigma_{ch1,g}^{\text{par}'} = \tfrac{1}{2} \cdot \left(\sigma_{ch1,g}^{\text{par}} + \sigma_{ch2,g}^{\text{par}} \right), \sigma_{ch2,g}^{\text{par}'} = \sigma_{ch1,g}^{\text{par}'}, \tag{7}$$

where $g = 1, \dots, L$.
– Mutation

$$\sigma_{ch,g}^{\text{par}'} = \sigma_{ch,g}^{\text{par}} \cdot \exp \left(\tau' \cdot N\left(0,1\right) + \tau \cdot N_{ch,g}\left(0,1\right) \right), \tag{8}$$

and

$$X_{ch,g}^{\text{par}'} = X_{ch,g}^{\text{par}} + \sigma_{ch,g}^{\text{par}'} \cdot N_{ch,g}\left(0,1\right), \tag{9}$$

where $\sigma_{ch,g}^{\text{par}}$, $ch = 1, \dots, \lambda$, $g = 1, \dots, L$, denotes current value of the mutation range of the ch-th chromosome of the g-th gene, $\sigma_{ch,g}^{\text{par}'}$, $ch = 1, \dots, \lambda$, $g = 1, \dots, L$, denotes a new value of the mutation range, $N\left(0,1\right)$ is the number drawn from the normal distribution, $N_{ch,g}\left(0,1\right)$ is the number drawn from the normal distribution of the ch-th chromosome, of the g-th gene, and τ', τ denote constants chosen prior to the evolution process. The following formulas can be found in the literature [20]

$$\tau' = \frac{C}{\sqrt{2L}}, \tag{10}$$

and

$$\tau = \frac{C}{\sqrt{2\sqrt{L}}}, \tag{11}$$

where C takes value 1 the most frequently. In order to avoid convergence of the mutation range to 0, we use the following formula

$$\sigma_{ch,g}^{\text{par}'} = \max \left\{ \varepsilon_0, \sigma_{ch,g}^{\text{par}'} \right\}, \tag{12}$$

where ε_0 is a small positive number chosen prior to the evolution process.

3.2   Evolution of Structure

Evolution of structure is based on the evolutionary strategy (μ, λ) and classical genetic algorithm. At the beginning we take the maximum number of rules, antecedents, consequences, inputs, and discretization points. In the next step, we reduce our system using the evolutionary strategy. For this purpose we use an extra chromosome $\mathbf{X}_{ch}^{\mathrm{red}}$. Its genes take binary values and indicate which rules, antecedents, inputs, and discretization points are selected. The chromosome $\mathbf{X}_{ch}^{\mathrm{red}}$ is given by

$$
\mathbf{X}_{ch}^{\mathrm{red}} = \left\{
\begin{array}{c}
A_1^1, ..., A_n^1, ..., A_1^{Nmax}, ..., A_n^{Nmax}, \\
B_1^1, ..., B_m^1, ..., B_1^{Nmax}, ..., B_m^{Nmax}, \\
\mathrm{rule}_1, ..., \mathrm{rule}_N, \\
\bar{y}_{1,1}^{\mathrm{def}}, ..., \bar{y}_{1,Rmax}^{\mathrm{def}}, ..., \bar{y}_{m,1}^{\mathrm{def}}, ..., \bar{y}_{m,Rmax}^{\mathrm{def}}
\end{array}
\right\} = \left\{ X_{ch,1}^{\mathrm{red}}, ..., X_{ch,L^{\mathrm{red}}}^{\mathrm{red}} \right\},
$$
(13)

where $L^{\mathrm{red}} = Nmax \cdot (n+m+1) + m \cdot Rmax$ is the length of the chromosome $\mathbf{X}_{ch}^{\mathrm{red}}$, where $ch = 1, \ldots, \mu$, for the parent population or $ch = 1, \ldots, \lambda$, for the temporary population. Its genes indicate which rules (rule$_k$, $k = 1, \ldots, Nmax$), antecedents (A_i^k, $i = 1, \ldots, n$, $k = 1, \ldots, Nmax$), consequents (B_j^k, $j = 1, ..., m$, $k = 1, ..., Nmax$), inputs ($\bar{x}_i$, $i = 1, \ldots, n$), and discretization points ($\bar{y}^r$, $r = 1, \ldots, Rmax$) are taken to the system.

For temporary population we use the recombination (crossover) and the mutation operations analogically to those in the classical genetic algorithm ([48], [59]):

- Single-point crossover, with probability $p_c \in [0, 1]$ chosen prior to the evolution process.
- Mutation, with probability $p_m \in [0, 1]$ chosen prior to the evolution process.

3.3   Chromosome Population Evaluation after Crossover and Mutation

Each individual $\mathbf{X}_{ch}$ of the parental and temporary populations is represented by sequence of chromosomes $\langle \mathbf{X}_{ch}^{\mathrm{par}}, \sigma_{ch}^{\mathrm{par}}, \mathbf{X}_{ch}^{\mathrm{red}} \rangle$, given by formulas (4), (5) and (13). The genes of the two first chromosomes take real values, whereas the genes of the last chromosome takes integer values.

The system aims to minimize the following fitness function

$$
\mathrm{ff}(\mathbf{X}_{ch}) = \mathrm{ffaccuracy}(\mathbf{X}_{ch}) \cdot \mathrm{ffcomplexity}(\mathbf{X}_{ch}) \cdot \mathrm{ffsimilarity}(\mathbf{X}_{ch}),
$$
(14)

where, individual components are defined as follows:

- The component ffaccuracy $(\mathbf{X}_{ch})$ determines the accuracy of the system (3) i.e. average normalized system error for all outputs and all data from learning sequence

$$\text{ffaccuracy}\left(\mathbf{X}_{ch}\right) = \frac{1}{m_{ch}} \sum_{j=1}^{m_{ch}} \frac{\frac{1}{Z} \sum_{z=1}^{Z} |d_{z,j} - \bar{y}_{z,j}|}{\max\limits_{z=1,\ldots,Z} \{d_{z,j}\} - \min\limits_{z=1,\ldots,Z} \{d_{z,j}\}}, \quad (15)$$

where m_{ch} is a number of output coded in the chromosome ch, Z is the number of samples of learning sequence, $d_{z,j}$ is the desired value of the output signal of the system, $\bar{y}_{z,j}$ is the real value of output signal. The purpose of normalization the component ffaccuracy $(\mathbf{X}_{ch})$ was to ensure even influence on every component of the function (14).

– The component ffcomplexity $(\mathbf{X}_{ch})$ determines complexity of the system (3) i.e. the number of reduced elements of the system in relation to their number

$$\text{ffcomplexity}\left(\mathbf{X}_{ch}\right) = w_{ffcomplexity} + \frac{1}{L^{\text{red}}} \sum_{g=1}^{L^{\text{red}}} \mathbf{X}_{ch,g}^{\text{red}}, \quad (16)$$

where L^{red} is the number of elements of the system which can be reduced, $X_{ch,g}^{\text{red}}$ is a chromosome gene $\mathbf{X}_{ch}$ describes reduction of g gene.

The stability of the component ffcomplexity $(\mathbf{X}_{ch})$ is done by adding the variable $w_{ffcomplexity}$. Then ffcomplexity$(\mathbf{X}_{ch}) \in (w_{ffcomplexity}, w_{ffcomplexity}+1]$. The value of $w_{ffcomplexity}$ was set experimentally.

– The component ffsimilarity $(\mathbf{X}_{ch})$ determines the similarity between the input and output fuzzy sets coded in the tested chromosome

$$\text{ffsimilarity}\left(\mathbf{X}_{ch}\right) = \begin{pmatrix} w_{ffsimilarity} + \\ \dfrac{\displaystyle\sum_{j=1}^{m_{ch}} \sum_{k1=1}^{Nmax_{ch}-1} \sum_{k2=k1+1}^{Nmax_{ch}} \text{sim}\left(\dfrac{\mathbf{X}_{ch}^{\text{par}}\{B_j^{k1}\}}{\mathbf{X}_{ch}^{\text{par}}\{B_j^{k2}\}}\right)}{m_{ch}} + \\ \dfrac{\displaystyle\sum_{i=1}^{n_{ch}} \sum_{k1=1}^{Nmax_{ch}-1} \sum_{k2=k1+1}^{Nmax_{ch}} \text{sim}\left(\dfrac{\mathbf{X}_{ch}^{\text{par}}\{A_i^{k1}\}}{\mathbf{X}_{ch}^{\text{par}}\{A_i^{k2}\}}\right)}{n_{ch}} \\ + \dfrac{}{2\left(\dfrac{Nmax_{ch}}{2}\right)} \end{pmatrix}, \quad (17)$$

where N_{ch} is the number of rules coded by the chromosome ch, n_{ch} is the number of input of particular chromosome ch, $X_{ch}^{\text{par}}\{A_i^k\}$ is the part of the chromosome $\mathbf{X}_{ch}^{\text{par}}$, which codes parameters of the input fuzzy set A_i^k, $\mathbf{X}_{ch}^{\text{par}}\{B_j^k\}$ is the part of the chromosome $\mathbf{X}_{ch}^{\text{par}}$, which codes parameters of the output fuzzy set B_j^k.

The stability of the component ffsimilarity $(\mathbf{X}_{ch})$ is done by adding the variable $w_{similarity}$. Then ffsimilarity $(\mathbf{X}_{ch}) \in (w_{ffsimilarity}, w_{ffsimilarity} + 1]$. The value of $w_{ffcomplexity}$ was set experimentally.

The similarity of fuzzy sets in (17) can be defined with use of many different methods ([15], [28]). In our simulations the method presented in [15] was used.

3.4 Initialization of the Initial Parents Population

Initial values of genes in the initial parent population are the following:

- Genes in chromosome $\mathbf{X}_{ch}^{\text{par}}$, $ch = 1, \ldots, \mu$, corresponding to the input fuzzy sets $A_i{}^k$, $k = 1, \ldots, N$, $i = 1, \ldots, n$, ($\bar{x}_{i,k}^A$ and $\sigma_{i,k}^A$) and genes corresponding to the output fuzzy sets B_j^k, $j = 1, \ldots, m$, $k = 1, \ldots, N$, ($\bar{y}_{j,k}^B$ and $\sigma_{j,k}^B$) were initialized based on the method described in [23].
- Genes in chromosome $\mathbf{X}_{ch}^{\text{par}}$, $ch = 1, \ldots, \mu$, corresponding to discretization points $\bar{y}^r$, $r = 1, \ldots, R$, are chosen as random numbers.
- Genes in chromosome $\mathbf{X}_{ch}^{\text{red}}$, $ch = 1, \ldots, \mu$, are chosen as random numbers from $[0, 1]$.
- Genes in chromosome $\mathbf{X}_{ch}^{\text{red}}$, $ch = 1, \ldots, \mu$, corresponding to weights of antecedents $w_{i,k}^A$, $i = 1, \ldots, n$, $k = 1, \ldots, Nmax$, are chosen as random numbers from $[0, 1]$.

The components of the mutation range σ_{ch}^{par}, $ch = 1, \ldots, \mu$, are equal to 1 before the evolution process.

4 Simulation Results

In the simulations two problems were considered: chemical plant problem [62] and Box and Jenkins gas furnace problem [6]. In both cases system with good accuracy and clear fuzzy rules was searched.

4.1 Chemical Plant Problem

We consider a model of an operator's control of a chemical plant. The plant produces polymers by polymerisating some monomers. Since the start up of the plant is very complicated, men have to perform the manual operations at the plant. Three continuous inputs are chosen for controlling the system: monomer concentration, change of monomer concentration and monomer flow rate. The output is the set point for the monomer flow rate.

The characteristic features of the used evolution strategy (μ, λ) can be summarized as follows:

- The number of parent population $\mu = 128$.
- The number of temporary population $\lambda = 256$.
- Constants $C = 1.2$, $\varepsilon_0 = 0.01$.
- The algorithm performs 2000 steps (generations).
- The mutation probability was set as $p_m = 0.1$.

Table 1. The accuracy of the various methods for chemical plant problem

Method	Average RMSE
Pal and Chakraborty ([43])	0.0092
Lin and Cunningham ([39])	0.0079
Rutkowski ([49]) ($N = 6$)	0.0042
Rutkowski and Cpałka ([14]) ($N = 6$)	0.0035
our result ($N = 3$)	**0.0061**

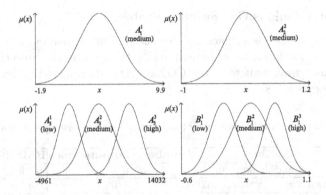

Fig. 1. Inputs and outputs fuzzy sets of the neuro-fuzzy system (3) for the chemical plant problem

- The crossover probability was set as $p_c = 0.8$.
- The value of $w_{ffcomplexity}$ was set as 1.
- The value of $w_{ffsimilarity}$ was set as 1.

The characteristic features of the used neuro-fuzzy system (3) can be summarized as follows:

- As membership function the Gauss function was used.
- The t-norm of the minimum type was used to aggregation of antecedents.
- The t-norm of the minimum type was used as inference operators.
- The t-conorm of the maximum type was used to aggregation of the rules.
- Maximum number of rules was set as $Nmax = 5$.
- Maximum number of discretization points was set as $Rmax = 10$.

The rules of the obtained neuro-fuzzy system are described by the formula:

$$\begin{cases} R^{(1)} : \left[\text{IF} \left(x_1 \text{is} A_1^1 \right) \left| w_{1,1}^\tau \text{AND} \left(x_3 \text{is} A_3^1 \right) \right| w_{1,3}^\tau \text{ THEN} \left(y_1 \text{is} B_1^1 \right) \right] \left| w_1^{\text{rule}} \right. \\ R^{(2)} : \left[\text{IF} \left(x_2 \text{is} A_2^2 \right) \left| w_{2,2}^\tau \text{AND} \left(x_3 \text{Iis} A_3^2 \right) \right| w_{2,3}^\tau \text{ THEN} \left(y_2 \text{is} B_1^2 \right) \right] \left| w_2^{\text{rule}} \right. \\ R^{(3)} : \left[\text{IF} \left(x_3 \text{is} A_3^3 \right) \left| w_{3,3}^\tau \text{ THEN} \left(y_3 \text{is} B_1^3 \right) \right] \left| w_3^{\text{rule}} \right. \end{cases} \quad (18)$$

The simulation results can be summarized as follows:

- In the simulation the good accuracy was achieved with the small number of rules ($N{=}3$).
- In the system working with three rules 4 antecedents was reduced (A_1^2, A_1^3, A_2^1, A_2^3), which additionally increased the interpretability of the system.
- In the evolutionary system remain 4 discretization points ($R{>}N$). Furthermore, the number of discretization points does not decrease the interpretability of the system.
- The system allows to arrange simple and clear fuzzy sets (Fig. 1).

4.2   Box and Jenkins Gas Furnace Problem

The Box and Jenkins gas furnace data consists of 296 measurements of the gas furnace system: the input measurement u(k) is the gas flow rate into the furnace and the output measurement is the CO_2 concentration in the outlet gas. The sampling interval is 9 s.

Table 2. The accuracy of the various methods for Box and Jenkins gas furnace problem

Method	Number of inputs/rules	RMSE
Box and Jenkins [6]	6/-	0.4494
Sugeno and Yasukawa [62]	3/6	0.4358
Wang and Langari [64]	6/2	0.2569
Sugeno and Tanaka [61]	6/2	0.2607
Lin and Cunningham [39]	5/4	0.2664
Kim et al [29]	6/2	0.2190
Delgado et al [18]	2/4	0.4100
Yoshinari [66]	2/6	0.5460
Rutkowski and Cpałka [50]	6/4	0.2416
our result	**4/3**	**0.2956**

The characteristic features of the used evolution strategy (μ, λ) can be summarized as follows:

- The number of parent population $\mu = 128$.
- The number of temporary population $\lambda = 256$.
- Constants $C = 1.2, \varepsilon_0 = 0.01$
- The algorithm performs 2000 steps (generations).
- The mutation probability was set as $p_m = 0.15$.
- The crossover probability was set as $p_c = 0.85$.
- The value of $w_{ffcomplexity}$ was set as 1.
- The value of $w_{ffsimilarity}$ was set as 1.

The characteristic features of the used neuro-fuzzy system can be summarized as follows:

- As membership function the Gauss function was used.
- The t-norm of the algebraic type was used to aggregation of antecedents.

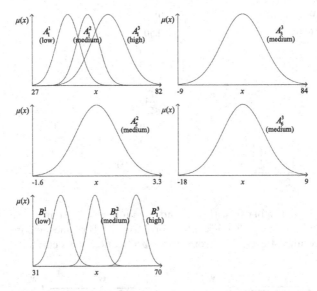

Fig. 2. Inputs and outputs fuzzy sets of the neuro-fuzzy system (3) for Box and Jenkins gas furnace problem

- The t-norm of the algebraic type was used as inference operators.
- The t-conorm of the algebraic type was used to aggregation of rules.
- Maximum number of rules was set as $Nmax = 5$.
- Maximum number of discretization points was set as $Rmax = 10$.

The rules of neuro-fuzzy system are described by the formula:

$$\begin{cases} R^{(1)} : \left[\text{IF} \left(x\,\text{is}A_1^1\right) \middle| w_{1,1}^\tau \text{ THEN} \left(y_1\text{is}B_1^1\right)\right] \middle| w_1^{\text{rule}} \\ R^{(2)} : \left[\text{IF} \left(x_1\text{is}A_1^2\right) \middle| w_{2,1}^\tau \text{AND} \left(x_5\text{is}A_5^2\right) \middle| w_{2,5}^\tau \text{ THEN} \left(y_2\text{is}B_1^2\right)\right] \middle| w_2^{\text{rule}} \\ R^{(3)} : \begin{bmatrix} \text{IF} \left(x_1\text{is}A_1^3\right) \middle| w_{3,1}^\tau \text{ AND} \left(x_3\text{is}A_3^3\right) \middle| w_{3,3}^\tau \text{ AND} \\ \left(x_6\text{is}A_6^3\right) \middle| w_{3,6}^\tau \text{ THEN} \left(y_3\text{is}B_1^3\right) \end{bmatrix} \middle| w_3^{\text{rule}} \end{cases} . \quad (19)$$

The simulation results can be summarized as follows:

- In the simulation the good accuracy was achieved with the small number of rules (N=3) and small number of inputs ($n = 4$).
- In the system working with three rules 6 antecedents (A_3^1, A_5^1, A_6^1, A_3^2, A_6^2, A_5^3) and two inputs ($\bar{x}_2$, $\bar{x}_4$) was reduced, which additionally increased the interpretability of the system.
- In the evolutionary system remain 4 discretization points ($R > N$). Furthermore, the number of discretization points does not decrease the interpretability of the system.
- The system allows to arrange clear and simple fuzzy sets (Fig. 2).

On the Fig. 3 the dependence of the RMSE error and number of L parameters were presented. It can noticed that in case of assumed number of learning steps

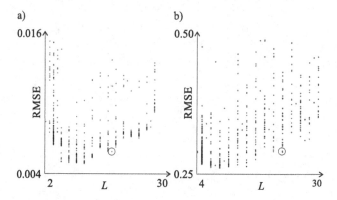

Fig. 3. The dependence between RMSE and the number of system parameters (3) for the following problems: a) chemical plant problem, b) Box and Jenkins gas furnace problem. The results of the best chromosomes are marked with circles.

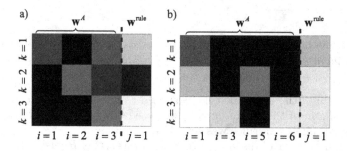

Fig. 4. Exemplary weights representation in the neuro-fuzzy system (3) (dark areas correspond to low values of weights and vice versa) for the following problems: a) chemical plant problem, b) Box and Jenkins gas furnace problem

(generations) the systems which have the smaller number of the parameters work with higher accuracy than the other ones (please see case $L = 18$ on the Fig 3.a and case $L = 20$ on the Fig 3.b). It results from the fact that simpler system is easier to be taught. In both cases the results with best RMSE value wasn't picked. It results from not clearly arranged fuzzy sets and smaller amount of reduced elements in the system.

5   Conclusions

In this paper a new method for learning of neuro-fuzzy systems construction for the nonlinear modelling was proposed. It allows to obtain a good accuracy of system work, possibly simple rules and low complexity of the system. The method is based on the evolution strategy (μ, λ) with the appropriately selected chromosome fitness function. The simulation results confirmed the appropriateness of the work of the system.

Acknowledgment. The project was financed by the National Science Center on the basis of the decision number DEC-2012/05/B/ST7/02138 and by the Częstochowa University of Technology - Faculty of Mechanical Engineering and Computer Science grant for PhD students with number BS/MN 1-109-305/12/P.

References

1. Aziz, D., Ali, M.A.M., Gan, K.B., Saiboon, I.: Initialization of Adaptive Neuro-Fuzzy Inference System Using Fuzzy Clustering in Predicting Primary Triage Category. In: 2012 4th International Conference on Intelligent and Advanced Systems, ICIAS, vol. 1, pp. 170–174 (2012)
2. Bartczuk, Ł., Rutkowska, D.: A new version of the fuzzy-ID3 algorithm. In: Rutkowski, L., Tadeusiewicz, R., Zadeh, L.A., Żurada, J.M. (eds.) ICAISC 2006. LNCS (LNAI), vol. 4029, pp. 1060–1070. Springer, Heidelberg (2006)
3. Bartczuk, Ł., Rutkowska, D.: Medical diagnosis with type-2 fuzzy decision trees. In: Kącki, E., Rudnicki, M., Stempczyńska, J. (eds.) Computers in Medical Activity. AISC, vol. 65, pp. 11–21. Springer, Heidelberg (2009)
4. Bartczuk, Ł., Rutkowska, D.: Type-2 fuzzy decision trees. In: Rutkowski, L., Tadeusiewicz, R., Zadeh, L.A., Zurada, J.M. (eds.) ICAISC 2008. LNCS (LNAI), vol. 5097, pp. 197–206. Springer, Heidelberg (2008)
5. Bentley, P.: Evolutionary Design by Computers. Morgan Kaufmann (1999)
6. Box, G.E.P., Jenkins, G.M.: Time Series Analysis. In: Forecasting and Control, pp. 532–533 (1976)
7. Carlos, A.C.C., Gary, B.L., Van Veldhuizen, D.A.: Evolutionary Algorithms for Solving Multi-Objective Problems (Genetic and Evolutionary Computation). Springer-Verlag, New York, Inc. (2007)
8. Casillas, J., Cordon, O., Herrera, F., Magdalena, L. (eds.): Interpretability Issues in Fuzzy Modeling. STUDFUZZ, vol. 128. Springer, Heidelberg (2003)
9. Cierniak, R.: A new approach to image reconstruction from projections problem using a recurrent neural network. Applied Mathematics and Computer Science 18(2), 147–157 (2008)
10. Cierniak, R.: A novel approach to image reconstruction problem from fan-beam projections using recurrent neural network. In: Rutkowski, L., Tadeusiewicz, R., Zadeh, L.A., Zurada, J.M. (eds.) ICAISC 2008. LNCS (LNAI), vol. 5097, pp. 752–761. Springer, Heidelberg (2008)
11. Cierniak, R.: An image compression algorithm based on neural networks. In: Rutkowski, L., Siekmann, J.H., Tadeusiewicz, R., Zadeh, L.A. (eds.) ICAISC 2004. LNCS (LNAI), vol. 3070, pp. 706–711. Springer, Heidelberg (2004)
12. Cierniak, R.: New neural network algorithm for image reconstruction from fan-beam projections. Elsevier Science: Neurocomputing 72, 3238–3244 (2009)
13. Cordon, O., Herrera, F., Hoffman, F., Magdalena, L.: Genetic Fuzzy Systems: Evolutionary Tuning and Learning of Fuzzy Knowledge Bases. Word Scientific (2001)
14. Cpałka, K., Rutkowski, L.: Flexible Takagi-Sugeno Neuro-Fuzzy Structures for Nonlinear Approximation. WSEAS Transactions on Systems 4(9), 1450–1458 (2005)
15. Cpałka, K.: A New Method for Design and Reduction of Neuro-Fuzzy Classification Systems. IEEE Transactions on Neural Networks 20(4), 701–714 (2009)
16. Cpałka, K.: On evolutionary designing and learning of flexible neuro-fuzzy structures for nonlinear classification. Nonlinear Analysis Series A: Theory, Methods and Applications 71(12), e1659–e1672 (2009)

17. Cpałka, K., Rutkowski, L.: A new method for designing and reduction of neuro-fuzzy systems. In: 2006 IEEE International Conference on Fuzzy Systems, pp. 1851–1857 (2006)
18. Delgado, M., Gómez-Skarmeta, A.F., Martin, F.: Fuzzy clustering-based rapid prototyping for fuzzy rule-based modelling. IEEE Transaction on Fuzzy Systems 5, 223–233 (1997)
19. Diago, L., Kitaoka, T., Hagiwara, I., Kambayashi, T.: Neuro-fuzzy quantification of personal perceptions of facial images based on a limited data set. IEEE Transactions on Neural Networks, 2422–2234 (2011)
20. Fogel, D.B.: Evolutionary Computation: Toward a New Philosophy of Machine Intelligence, 3rd edn. IEEE Press, Piscataway (2006)
21. Freitas, A.: Data Mining and Knowledge Discovery With Evolutionary Algorithms. Springer (2002)
22. Gabryel, M., Cpałka, K., Rutkowski, L.: Evolutionary strategies for learning of neuro-fuzzy systems. In: I Workshop on Genetic Fuzzy Systems, Genewa, pp. 119–123 (2005)
23. Gabryel, M., Rutkowski, L.: Evolutionary Learning of Mamdani-Type Neuro-fuzzy Systems. In: Rutkowski, L., Tadeusiewicz, R., Zadeh, L.A., Żurada, J.M. (eds.) ICAISC 2006. LNCS (LNAI), vol. 4029, pp. 354–359. Springer, Heidelberg (2006)
24. Gabryel, M., Rutkowski, L.: Evolutionary methods for designing neuro-fuzzy modular systems combined by bagging algorithm. In: Rutkowski, L., Tadeusiewicz, R., Zadeh, L.A., Zurada, J.M. (eds.) ICAISC 2008. LNCS (LNAI), vol. 5097, pp. 398–404. Springer, Heidelberg (2008)
25. Gan, L., Laurence, A., Maguib Raouf, N.G., Dadios Elmer, P., Avila Jose Maria, C.: Implementation of GA-KSOM and ANFIS in the classification of colonic histopathological images. In: TENCON 2012 - 2012 IEEE Region 10 Conference, pp. 1–5 (2012)
26. Hisao, I., Yusuke, N.: Discussions on Interpretability of Fuzzy Systems using Simple Examples. In: European Society for Fuzzy Logic and Technology - EUSFLAT, pp. 1649–1654
27. Horzyk, A., Tadeusiewicz, R.: Self-Optimizing Neural Networks. In: Yin, F.-L., Wang, J., Guo, C. (eds.) ISNN 2004. LNCS, vol. 3173, pp. 150–155. Springer, Heidelberg (2004)
28. Kaur, G.: Similarity measure of different types of fuzzy sets. School of Mathematics and Computer Applications, Tharpar University (2010)
29. Kim, E., Park, M., Kimand, S.: A transformed input-domain approach to fuzzy modelling. IEEE Transaction on Fuzzy Systems 6, 596–604 (1998)
30. Klement, E.P., Mesiar, R., Pap, E.: Triangular Norms. Kluwer Academic Publishers (2000)
31. Korytkowski, M., Gabryel, M., Rutkowski, L., Drozda, S.: Evolutionary methods to create interpretable modular system. In: Rutkowski, L., Tadeusiewicz, R., Zadeh, L.A., Zurada, J.M. (eds.) ICAISC 2008. LNCS (LNAI), vol. 5097, pp. 405–413. Springer, Heidelberg (2008)
32. Korytkowski, M., Rutkowski, L., Scherer, R.: On combining backpropagation with boosting. In: Proceedings of the International Joint Conference on Neural Networks, IJCNN, Vancouver, pp. 1274–1277 (2005)
33. Krishnaji, A., Rao, A.A.: Implementation of a hybrid Neuro Fuzzy Genetic System for improving protein secondary structure prediction. In: 2012 National Computing and Communication Systems (NCCCS), pp. 1–5 (2012)
34. Laskowski, Ł.: A novel hybrid-maximum neural network in stereo-matching process. Neural Computing & Applications (2012), doi:10.1007/s00521-012-1202-0

35. Laskowski, Ł.: Objects auto-selection from stereo-images realised by self-correcting neural network. In: Rutkowski, L., Korytkowski, M., Scherer, R., Tadeusiewicz, R., Zadeh, L.A., Zurada, J.M. (eds.) ICAISC 2012, Part I. LNCS (LNAI), vol. 7267, pp. 119–125. Springer, Heidelberg (2012)
36. Laskowski, Ł.: A novel continuous dual mode neural network in stereo-matching process. In: Diamantaras, K., Duch, W., Iliadis, L.S. (eds.) ICANN 2010, Part III. LNCS (LNAI), vol. 6354, pp. 294–297. Springer, Heidelberg (2010)
37. Lin, J., Zheng, Y.B.: Vibration control of rotating plate by decomposed neuro-fuzzy control with genetic algorithm tuning. In: 2012 IEEE International Conference on Control Applications, CCA, pp. 575–580 (2012)
38. Li, X., Er, M.J., Lim, B.S., et al.: Fuzzy Regression Modeling for Tool Performance Prediction and Degradation Detection. International Journal of Neural Systems 20(5), 405–419 (2010)
39. Lin, Y., Cunningham III, G.A.: A New Approach To Fuzzy-Neural System Modeling. IEEE Transactions on Fuzzy Systems 3, 190–198 (1995)
40. Michalewicz, Z.: Genetic Algorithms + Data Structures=Evolution Programs. Springer (1999)
41. Nowicki, R., Pokropińska, A.: Information criterions applied to neuro-fuzzy architectures design. In: Rutkowski, L., Siekmann, J.H., Tadeusiewicz, R., Zadeh, L.A. (eds.) ICAISC 2004. LNCS (LNAI), vol. 3070, pp. 332–337. Springer, Heidelberg (2004)
42. Nowicki, R., Scherer, R., Rutkowski, L.: A method for learning of hierarchical fuzzy systems. In: Sincak, P., Vascak, J., Kvasnicka, V., Pospichal, J. (eds.) Intelligent Technologies - Theory and Applications, pp. 124–129. IOS Press (2002)
43. Pal, N.R., Chakraborty, D.: Simultaneous Feature Analysis and SI. In: Neuro-Fuzzy Pattern Recognition. World Scientific, Singapore (2000)
44. Przybył, A.: Doctoral dissertation: Adaptive observer of induction motor using artificial neural networks and evolutionary algorithms. Poznan University of Technology (2003) (in Polish)
45. Przybył, A., Smoląg, J., Kimla, P.: Real-time Ethernet based, distributed control system for the CNC machine. Electrical Review 2010-2 (2010) (in Polish)
46. Przybył, A., Cpałka, K.: A new method to construct of interpretable models of dynamic systems. In: Rutkowski, L., Korytkowski, M., Scherer, R., Tadeusiewicz, R., Zadeh, L.A., Zurada, J.M. (eds.) ICAISC 2012, Part II. LNCS, vol. 7268, pp. 697–705. Springer, Heidelberg (2012)
47. Rutkowska, D., Nowicki, R., Rutkowski, L.: Neuro-fuzzy architectures with various implication operators. In: Sincak, P., et al. (eds.) The State of the Art in Computational Intelligence, pp. 214–219 (2000)
48. Rutkowski, L.: Computational Intelligence. Springer (2007)
49. Rutkowski, L.: Flexible Neuro-Fuzzy Systems. Kluwer Academic Publishers (2004)
50. Rutkowski, L., Cpałka, K.: Flexible neuro-fuzzy systems. IEEE Trans. Neural Networks 14(3), 554–574 (2003)
51. Rutkowski, L., Cpałka, K.: Flexible weighted neuro-fuzzy systems. In: Proceedings of the 9th Neural Information Processing, pp. 1857–1861 (2002)
52. Rutkowski, L., Przybył, A., Cpałka, K.: Novel Online Speed Profile Generation for Industrial Machine Tool Based on Flexible Neuro-Fuzzy Approximation. IEEE Transactions on Industrial Electronics 59(2), 1238–1247 (2012)
53. Rutkowski, L., Przybył, A., Cpałka, K., Er, M.J.: Online Speed Profile Generation for Industrial Machine Tool Based on Neuro Fuzzy Approach. In: Rutkowski, L., Scherer, R., Tadeusiewicz, R., Zadeh, L.A., Zurada, J.M. (eds.) ICAISC 2010, Part II. LNCS, vol. 6114, pp. 645–650. Springer, Heidelberg (2010)

54. Scherer, R., Rutkowski, L.: A fuzzy relational system with linguistic antecedent certainty factors. In: 6th International Conference on Neural Networks and Soft Computing, Zakopane, Poland. Advances In Soft Computing, pp. 563–569 (2003)
55. Scherer, R., Rutkowski, L.: Connectionist fuzzy relational systems. In: Halgamuge, S.K., Wang, L. (eds.) Computational Intelligence for Modelling and Prediction. SCI, vol. 2, pp. 35–47. Springer, Heidelberg (2005)
56. Scherer, R., Rutkowski, L.: Neuro-fuzzy relational classifiers. In: Rutkowski, L., Siekmann, J.H., Tadeusiewicz, R., Zadeh, L.A. (eds.) ICAISC 2004. LNCS (LNAI), vol. 3070, pp. 376–380. Springer, Heidelberg (2004)
57. Szaleniec, M., Goclon, J., Witko, M., Tadeusiewicz, R.: Application of artificial neural networks and DFT-based parameters for prediction of reaction kinetics of ethylbenzene dehydrogenase. Journal of Computer-Aided Molecular Design 20(3), 145–157 (2006)
58. Rey, M.I., Galende, M., Sainz, G.I., Fuente, M.J.: Checking orthogonal transformations and genetic algorithms for selection of fuzzy rules based on interpretability-accuracy concepts. In: 2011 IEEE International Conference on Fuzzy Systems (FUZZ), pp. 1271–1278 (2011)
59. Sivanandam, S.N., Deepa, S.N.: Introduction to Genetic Algorithms, pp. I-XIX, 1-442. Springer (2008)
60. Subramanian, K., Suresh, S., Venkatesh Babu, R.: Meta-Cognitive Neuro-Fuzzy Inference System for human emotion recognition. In: The 2012 International Joint Conference on Neural Networks (IJCNN), pp. 1–7 (2012)
61. Sugeno, M., Tanaka, K.: Successive identification on a fuzzy model and its applications to prediction of a complex system. Fuzzy Sets and Systems 42, 315–334 (1991)
62. Sugeno, M., Yasakuwa, T.: A Fuzzy-Logic-Based Approach to Qualitative Modeling. IEEE Transactions on Fuzzy Systems, 7–31 (1993)
63. Wang, N., Hu, C., Shi, W.: A Mamdani Fuzzy Modeling Method via Evolution-Objective Cluster Analysis. In: 2012 31st Chinese Control Conference (CCC), pp. 3470–3475 (2012)
64. Wang, L.X., Langari, R.: Building Sugeno-type models using fuzzy discretization and orthogonal parameter estimation techniques. IEEE Transaction on Fuzzy Systems 3, 454–458 (1995)
65. Yong, L., Singh, C.: Evaluation of the failure rates of transmission lines during hurricanes using a neuro-fuzzy system. In: 2010 IEEE 11th International Conference on Probabilistic Methods Applied to Power Systems (PMAPS), pp. 569–574 (2010)
66. Yoshinari, Y., Pedrycz, W., Hirota, K.: Construction of fuzzy models through clustering techniques. Fuzzy Sets and Systems 54, 157–165 (1993)
67. Zitzler, E., Laumanns, M., Bleuler, S.: A Tutorial on Evolutionary Multiobjective Optimization. In: Metaheuristics for Multiobjective Optimisation, pp. 3–38 (2003)
68. Zalasiński, M., Cpałka, K.: A new method of on-line signature verification using a flexible fuzzy one-class classifier. Selected Topics in Computer Science Applications, pp. 38–53. EXIT (2011)
69. Zalasiński, M., Cpałka, K.: Novel algorithm for the on-line signature verification. In: Rutkowski, L., Korytkowski, M., Scherer, R., Tadeusiewicz, R., Zadeh, L.A., Zurada, J.M. (eds.) ICAISC 2012, Part II. LNCS (LNAI), vol. 7268, pp. 362–367. Springer, Heidelberg (2012)

Modelling Financial High Frequency Data Using Ordered Fuzzy Numbers

Adam Marszałek[1] and Tadeusz Burczyński[1,2]

[1] Cracow University of Technology, Institute of Computer Science, Computational Intelligence Department, Warszawska 24, 31-155 Cracow, Poland
amarszalek@pk.edu.pl
[2] Silesian University of Technology, Institute of Computational Mechanics and Engineering, Konarskiego 18A, 44-100 Gliwice, Poland
tadeusz.burczynski@polsl.pl

Abstract. The goal of the paper is to present an original concept of representation of financial high frequency data using Ordered Fuzzy Numbers. This approach allows the transition from high frequency data (e.g. ticks, minutes) to lower frequency data (e.g. daily) while maintaining more information about price movement at assumed time interval than using the popular price charts (e.g. Japanese Candlestick chart). The financial data are modeled using Ordered Fuzzy Numbers called further by Ordered Fuzzy Candlesticks. The use of them allows also modeling uncertainty associated with financial data. How to construct and use Ordered Fuzzy Candlesticks are presented in the main part of this paper.

1 Introduction

Modern financial data sets may contain tens of thousands of quotes in a single day time stamped to the nearest second. Making investment decisions based on observation of each single quotation is very difficult or even impossible. Therefore a large part of investors very often use price charts analysis to make decisions.

The price charts (e.g. Japanese Candlestick chart) are used to illustrate movements in the price of a financial instrument over time. Notice, that using the price chart, a large part of the information about the process is lost, e.g. using Japanese Candlestick chart with daily frequency, for one day, we know only four prices (i.e. open, low, high and close), while in this time the price has changed hundreds of times. In spite of this Japanese Candlestick charting techniques are very popular among traders and allow for achieve more than average profits. More details about the Japanese Candlesticks and trading techniques based on them can be found in [14].

In our previous paper [13] we showed how we can using fuzzy logic (i.e. ordered fuzzy numbers), to model uncertainty associated with financial data and to keep more information about price movement. The idea, construction methods and example of application of Ordered Fuzzy Candlesticks are specifically discussed in this work. In addition some new concepts are also presented.

L. Rutkowski et al. (Eds.): ICAISC 2013, Part I, LNAI 7894, pp. 345–352, 2013.
© Springer-Verlag Berlin Heidelberg 2013

2   From Financial Data to Ordered Fuzzy Candlestick

2.1   Ordered Fuzzy Numbers (OFN)

Ordered Fuzzy Numbers introduced by Kosiński et al. in series of papers [4–8] are defined by ordered pairs of continuous real functions defined on the interval $[0, 1]$ i.e. $A = (f, g)$ with $f, g : [0, 1] \to \mathbb{R}$ as continuous functions. Furthermore, the basic arithmetic operations on ordered fuzzy numbers are defined as the pairwise operations of their elements.

Let $A = (f_A, g_A)$, $B = (f_B, g_B)$ and $C = (f_C, g_C)$ are ordered fuzzy numbers. The sum $C = A + B$, subtraction $C = A - B$, product $C = A \cdot B$, and division $C = A \div B$ are defined by formula

$$f_C(y) = f_A(y) * f_B(y), \qquad g_C(y) = g_A(y) * g_B(y)$$

where $*$ works for $+$, $-$, $\cdot$ and $\div$, respectively, and where $C = A \div B$ is defined, if the functions $|f_B|$ and $|g_B|$ are bigger than zero. In a similar way, multiply an ordered fuzzy number A by a scalar $\lambda \in \mathbb{R}$, i.e. $C = \lambda \cdot A$ is defined by formula

$$f_C(y) = \lambda \cdot f_A(y), \qquad g_C(y) = \lambda \cdot g_A(y)$$

This definition leads to some usefull properties. The one of them is existence of neutral elements of addition and multiplication. This fact causes that not always the result of an arithmetic operation is a fuzzy number with a larger support. This allows to build fuzzy models based on ordered fuzzy numbers in the form of the classical equations without losing the accuracy.

Moreover, a universe $\mathcal{O}$ of all ordered fuzzy numbers can be identified with $\mathcal{C}^0([0,1]) \times \mathcal{C}^0([0,1])$, hence the space $\mathcal{O}$ is topologically a Banach space [7]. A class of defuzzification operators of ordered fuzzy numbers can be defined, as a linear and continuous functionals on the Banach space $\mathcal{O}$, thanks to the general representation theorem (of Banach-Kakutami-Riesz) they are uniquely determined by a pair of Radon measures (ν_1, ν_2) on $[0, 1]$, as

$$Def(A) = \int_0^1 f_A d\nu_1 + \int_0^1 g_A d\nu_2$$

where $Def(A)$ is the value of a defuzzification operator at the ordered fuzzy number $A = (f_A, g_A)$.

In addition, note that a pair of continuous functions (f, g) determines different ordered fuzzy number than the pair (g, f). In this way, we appointed an extra feature to this object, named the orientation. Depending on the orientation, the ordered fuzzy numbers can be divided into two types: a positive orientation, if the direction of ordered fuzzy number is consistent with the direction of the axis

Ox and a negative orientation, if the direction of the ordered fuzzy number is opposite to the direction of the axis Ox.

2.2 Ordered Fuzzy Candlesticks

Generally, in this approach, a fixed time interval of financial high frequency data is identified with ordered fuzzy number and it is called *Ordered Fuzzy Candlestick* (OFC). The general idea is presented in Fig. 1. Notice, that the orientation of the ordered fuzzy number shows whether the ordered fuzzy candlestick is long or short. While the information about movements in the price are contained in the shape of the f and g functions. In the following sections we will show how the ordered fuzzy candlestick can be constructed.

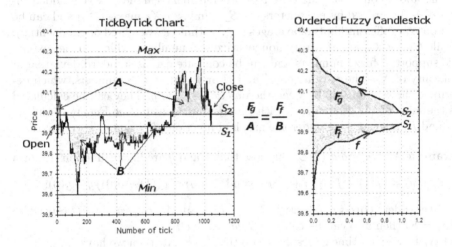

Fig. 1. General idea of concept of Orderd Fuzzy Candlestick

Ordered Fuzzy Candlestick with a Fixed Shape. One possibility is to construct an ordered fuzzy candlestick with assumption fixed shape of f and g functions (e.g. linear, etc.).

Let $\{X_t : t \in T\}$ be a given time series and $T = \{1, 2, \ldots, n\}$. The ordered fuzzy candlestick is defined as an ordered fuzzy number $C = (f, g)$ which satisfies the following conditions 1 - 4 or 5 - 8.

For Long Candlestick

1. $X_1 \leq X_n$
2. $f : [0, 1] \to \mathbb{R}$ is continuous and increasing on $[0, 1]$
3. $g : [0, 1] \to \mathbb{R}$ is continuous and decreasing on $[0, 1]$

4. $S_1 < S_2$, $f(1) = S_1$, $f(0) = \min_{t \in T} X_t - C_1$, $g(1) = S_2$ and $g(0)$ is such that

the ratios $\dfrac{F_g}{A}$ and $\dfrac{F_f}{B}$ are equal.

For Short Candlestick

5. $X_1 > X_n$

6. $f \colon [0,1] \to \mathbb{R}$ is continuous and decreasing on $[0,1]$

7. $g \colon [0,1] \to \mathbb{R}$ is continuous and increasing on $[0,1]$

8. $S_1 < S_2$, $f(1) = S_2$, $f(0) = \max_{t \in T} X_t + C_2$, $g(1) = S_1$ and $g(0)$ is such that

the ratios $\dfrac{F_f}{A}$ and $\dfrac{F_g}{B}$ are equal.

In the above conditions the center of ordered fuzzy candlestick (i.e. added interval) is designated by parameters S_1, $S_2 \in [\min_{t \in T} X_t, \max_{t \in T} X_t]$ and can be compute as different kinds of averages (e.g. arithmetic, weighted or exponential). While C_1 and C_2 are arbitrary nonnegative real numbers, which further extend the support of fuzzy numbers and can be compute e.g. as standard deviation or volatility of X_t. The parameters A and B are positive real numbers, which determine the relationship between the functions f and g. They can be calculated as the mass of the desired area with the assumed density (see Fig. 1). Numbers F_f and F_g are the fields under the graph of functions f^{-1} and g^{-1}, respectively.

Example 1: *Trapezoid OFC.* Suppose that f and g are linear functions in form

$$f(y) = (f(1) - f(0))\, y + f(0) \quad \text{and} \quad g(y) = (g(1) - g(0))\, y + g(0),$$

then the ordered fuzzy candlestick $C = (f, g)$ is called *a trapezoid OFC*, especially if $S_1 = S_2$ then also can be called *a Triangular OFC*.
Let X_t be a given time series. Suppose that $X_1 \leq X_n$ then we have

$$f(y) = (S_1 - \min X_t + C_1) y + \min X_t - C_1$$

$$g(y) = (S_2 - g(0)) y + g(0) \quad \text{where} \quad g(0) = \frac{A}{B}(S_1 - \min X_t + C_1) + S_2.$$

Whereas if $X_1 > X_n$ then we have

$$f(y) = (S_2 - \max X_t + C_2) y + \max X_t + C_2$$

$$g(y) = (S_1 - g(0)) y + g(0) \quad \text{where} \quad g(0) = \frac{B}{A}(S_2 - \max X_t - C_2) + S_1.$$

Example 2: *Gaussian OFC.* The ordered fuzzy candlestick $C = (f, g)$ where the membership relation has a shape similar to the Gaussian function is called *a Gaussian OFC*. It means that f and g are given by functions

$$f(y) = f(z) = \sigma_f \sqrt{-2\ln(z)} + m_f \quad \text{and} \quad g(y) = g(z) = \sigma_g \sqrt{-2\ln(z)} + m_g,$$

where e.g. $z = 0.99y + 0.01$.

Let X_t be a given time series. Suppose that $X_1 \leq X_n$ then we have

$$f(z) = \sigma_f \sqrt{-2\ln(z)} + m_f \text{ where } m_f = S_1, \ \sigma_f = \frac{\min X_t - C_1 - S_1}{\sqrt{-2\ln(0.01)}} \leq 0.$$

$$g(z) = \sigma_g \sqrt{-2\ln(z)} + m_g \text{ where } m_g = S_2, \ \sigma_g = -\frac{A}{B}\sigma_f.$$

Whereas if $X_1 > X_n$ then we have

$$f(z) = \sigma_f \sqrt{-2\ln(z)} + m_f \text{ where } m_f = S_2, \ \sigma_f = \frac{\max X_t + C_1 - S_2}{\sqrt{-2\ln(0.01)}} \geq 0.$$

$$g(z) = \sigma_g \sqrt{-2\ln(z)} + m_g \text{ where } m_g = S_1, \ \sigma_g = -\frac{B}{A}\sigma_f.$$

The examples of realizations of Trapezoid and Gaussian Ordered Fuzzy Candlesticks are presented in Fig. 2.

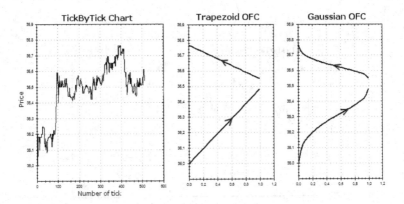

Fig. 2. Examples of Trapezoid and Gaussian OFC

Empirical Ordered Fuzzy Candlestick. In this paper we propose a new type of fuzzy candlesticks, in which functions f and g can be take any shape. The *empirical OFC* is also ordered fuzzy numbers but its member functions are defined in similar way as the empirical distribution in the statistical sciences.

Let $\{X_t : t \in T\}$ be a given time series and $T = \{1, 2, \ldots, n\}$. The values of parameters S_1, S_2 and C_1, C_2 are determined based on a time series of X_t. The new time series of Y_t is created from time series of X_t by sorting in ascending. Next, the two time series $Y_t^{(1)}$ and $Y_t^{(2)}$ are created as

$$Y_t^{(1)} = \{Y_i : Y_0 \leq Y_i \leq S_1\} \qquad t \in \{0, 1, \ldots, K_1\}$$

$$Y_t^{(2)} = \{Y_i : S_2 \leq Y_i \leq Y_n\} \qquad t \in \{0, 1, \ldots, K_2\}$$

Now, based on these time series we define the two discrete functions on interval $[0,1]$ with step $dx = \frac{1}{M}$ (i.e. $M+1$ points) as

$$
\Psi_1(k \cdot dx) = \begin{cases} Y_0^{(1)} - C_1 & \text{if } k = 0 \\ Y_{[\frac{k}{dx}]}^{(1)} & \text{if } k \in \{1, 2, \ldots, M-1\} \\ S_1 & \text{if } k = M \end{cases}
$$

$$
\Psi_2(k \cdot dx) = \begin{cases} Y_{K_2}^{(2)} + C_2 & \text{if } k = 0 \\ Y_{K_2 - [\frac{k}{dx}]}^{(2)} & \text{if } k \in \{1, 2, \ldots, M-1\} \\ S_2 & \text{if } k = M \end{cases}
$$

Then the *empirical OFC* is an ordered fuzzy number $C = (f, g)$ where the functions f and g are continous approximation of functions Ψ_1 and Ψ_2, respectively for long candlestick, whilst for short candlestick Ψ_2 and Ψ_1, respectively. The example of realization of the Empirical Ordered Fuzzy Candlectick is presented in Fig. 3.

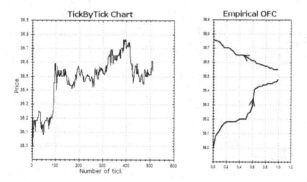

Fig. 3. Example of Empirical OFC

2.3 Ordered Fuzzy Autoregressive Models (OFAR(p))

An classical autoregressive model (AR(p)) is one where the current value of a variable, depends upon only the values that the variable took in previous periods plus an error term [16]. The presented approach, an ordered fuzzy autoregressive model of order p, denoted as OFAR(p), in natural way is fully fuzzy AR(p) and can be expressed as

$$
\overline{X}_t = \overline{\alpha}_0 + \sum_{i=1}^{p} \overline{\alpha}_i \overline{X}_{t-i} + \overline{\varepsilon}_t,
$$

where $\overline{X}_{t-i}$ are the ordered fuzzy candlesticks at a time period t, $\overline{\alpha}_i$ are fuzzy coefficients given by arbitrary ordered fuzzy numbers and $\overline{\varepsilon}_t$ is an error term.

Estimation of OFAR(p) Models. The Least Squares Method is proposed for estimation fuzzy parameters $\overline{\alpha}_i$ in OFAR(p) model and one is defined using a distance measure. The measure of the distance between two ordered fuzzy numbers is expressed by formula

$$d(A, B) = d\left((f_A, g_A), (f_B, g_B)\right) = \|f_A - f_B\|_{L^2} + \|g_A - g_B\|_{L^2},$$

where $\| \cdot \|$ is a metric induced by the L^2-norm. Hence, the least-square method for OFAR(p) is to minimize the following objective function

$$E = \sum_t d\left(\overline{X}_t, \overline{\alpha}_0 + \sum_{i=1}^p \overline{\alpha}_i \overline{X}_{t-i}\right).$$

So-defined function does not guarantee that received coefficients will be ordered fuzzy numbers, so we have to control coefficients in the course of estimation.

Forecasting Using OFAR(p) Models. Forecasts of the OFAR(p) model are obtained recursively in a similar way as for the calssical AR(p) model. Let t be the starting date for forecasting. Then, the 1-step ahead forecast for $\overline{X}_{t+1}$ is

$$\overline{X}_{t+1} = \overline{\alpha}_0 + \sum_{i=1}^p \overline{\alpha}_i \overline{X}_{t+1-i}.$$

The result of forecast is ordered fuzzy number, which includes three kinds of predictions:

- **point forecast:** given by value of a defuzzification operator,
- **interval forecast:** given by subset of support of the ordered fuzzy number in classical meaning,
- **direction forecast:** given by orientation of the ordered fuzzy number.

3   Conclusion and Future Works

The novel approach to modeled financial high frequency data using an ordered fuzzy numbers is presented in this paper. We described the representation of financial data using concept of the ordered fuzzy candlesticks. Moreover, the proposed ordered fuzzy autoregressive models allows to forecasting financial time series in the simple form of classical equations. The future work can be related to the extension of the ordered fuzzy candlesticks concept and some experiments with the prediction of financial time series using proposed time series models based on ordered fuzzy numbers. Our approach can be also successfully applied for many other area of financial modeling, e.g. modeling of volatility and risk management.

References

1. Dubois, D., Prade, H.: Operations on fuzzy numbers. Int. J. System Science 9, 576–578 (1978)
2. Kao, C., Chyu, C.-L.: Least-squares estimates in fuzzy regression analysis. European Journal of Operational Research 148, 426–435 (2003)
3. Kosiński, W., Piechór, K., Prokopowicz, K., Tyburem, K.: On algorithmic approach to operations on fuzzy numbers. In: Burczyński, T., Cholewa, W. (eds.) Methods of Artificial Intelligence in Mechanics and Mechanical Engineering, pp. 95–98. PACM, Gliwice (2001)
4. Kosiński, W., Prokopowicz, P., Ślęzak, D.: Drawback of fuzzy arithmetic - New intuitions and propositions. In: Burczyński, T., Cholewa, W., Moczulski, W. (eds.) Proc. Methods of Artificial Intelligence, pp. 231–237. PACM, Gliwice (2002)
5. Kosiński, W., Prokopowicz, P., Ślęzak, D.: On algebraic operations on fuzzy numbers. In: Kłopotek, M., Wierzchoń, S.T., Trojanowski, K. (eds.) Intelligent Information Processing and Web Mining, Proc. Int. Symp. IIS: IIPWM 2003, Zakopane, Poland, pp. 353–362. Physica Verlag, Heidelberg (2003)
6. Kosiński, W., Prokopowicz, P., Ślęzak, D.: Ordered fuzzy numbers. Bull. Polish Acad. Sci., Ser. Sci. Math. 51(3), 327–338 (2003)
7. Kosiński, W., Prokopowicz, P.: Algebra of fuzzy numbers. Matematyka Stosowana. Matematyka dla Społeczeństwa 5(46), 37–63 (2004) (in Polish)
8. Kosiński, W.: On soft computing and modelling. Image Processing Communications 11(1), 71–82 (2006)
9. Lee, C.L., Liu, A., Chen, W.: Pattern Discovery of Fuzzy Time Series for Financial Prediction. IEEE Trans. on Knowledge and Data Engineering 18(5) (2006)
10. Łachwa, A.: Fuzzy World of Sets, Numbers, Relations, Fazts, Rules and Decisions. EXIT, Warsaw (2001) (in Polish)
11. Łęski, J.: Neuro-fuzzy systems. WNT, Warsaw (2008) (in Polish)
12. Lo, A.W., MacKinlay, A.C.: Stock market prices do not dollow random walks: Evidence from a simple specification test. Review of Financial Studies 1 (1988)
13. Marszałek, A., Burczyński, T.: Financial Fuzzy Time Series Models Based on Ordered Fuzzy Numbers. In: Pedrycz, W., Chen, S.-M. (eds.) Time Series Analysis, Model. & Applications. ISRL, vol. 47, pp. 77–95. Springer, Heidelberg (2013)
14. Nison, S.: Japanese Candlestick Charting Techniques. New York Institute of Finance, New York (1991)
15. Tanaka, H., Uejima, S., Asia, K.: Linear regression analysis with Fuzzy model. IEEE Trans. Systems Man. Cybernet. 12, 903–907 (1982)
16. Tsay, R.S.: Analysis of Financial Time Series, 2nd edn. John Wiley & Sons, Inc, Hoboken (2005)
17. Wagenknecht, M.: On the approximate treatment of fuzzy arithmetics by inclusion, linear regression and information content estimation. In: Chojcan, J., Łęski, J. (eds.) Fuzzy Sets and Their Applications, pp. 291–310. Silesian University of Technology Press, Gliwice (2001)
18. Wagenknecht, M., Hampel, R., Schneider, V.: Computational aspects of fuzzy arithmetic based on Archimedean t-norms. Fuzzy Sets Syst. 123(1), 49–62 (2001)
19. Zadeh, L.A.: The concept of a linguistic variable and its application to approximate reasoning. Part I. Inf. Sci. 8(3), 199–249 (1975)

The Modified Sequential-Binary Approach for Fuzzy Operations on Correlated Assessments

Jacek Pietraszek

Institute of Applied Informatics, Cracow University of Technology
Al. Jana Pawla II 37, 31-864 Kraków, Poland
pmpietra@mech.pk.edu.pl

Abstract. The paper presents modified formalism to perform fuzzy operations on correlated assessments. The application of the standard formalism used in Zadeh's fuzzy logic requires an arbitrary setting of triangular norms and sometimes provides ridiculous results which are inconsistent with the gathered experimental data. The author discovered that the membership function's value may be treated as the mean of statements individually evaluated into YES or NO by a panel of human judges with identifiable identity. It leads to a fundamental change because a pair of triangular norms selected for fuzzy logic is proven and not arbitrarily set. The paper proposes generalization of the fuzzy description into a form of a binary vector. It moves evaluation of statements with fuzzy logic variables into the space of vectors of Boolean components. The new interpretation gives fuzzy variables and values an identity, which is necessary for operations with correlations. Additionally, due to a binary vector data structure, it potentially allows to perform computations utilizing collective intelligence methods such as genetic algorithms.

Keywords: fuzzy sets, fuzzy logic, binomial sequences, subjective assessments.

1   Introduction

The comfort of passengers in vehicles is one of the most significant dynamic performance characteristics of rail vehicles and therefore of utmost importance. The ride comfort is determined by many factors, inner (related to particular person) and outer (related to vehicle environment and ride dynamic). A vibration is the factor recognized with significant importance. The human response to vibration is highly variable and depends on magnitude, frequencies, direction and duration of vibrations.

ISO Standard 2631 [1] and British Standard 6841 [2] precisely define procedures for prediction of vibration discomfort basing on measured vibration at the seat pan, the seat back and the feet of seated person. The standards use RMS (root mean square) of measured acceleration of vibration.

Experimental studies [3] revealed that doubling vibration magnitude requires sixteen-fold reduction of duration to maintain equivalence comfort feeling. It led to introduction of RMQ (root mean quadruple) of measured acceleration of vibration. Both RMS and RMQ are averages of acceleration over time interval. It may lead to false

L. Rutkowski et al. (Eds.): ICAISC 2013, Part I, LNAI 7894, pp. 353–364, 2013.

prediction of discomfort if the vibration signal is not stationery. The remedy for this problem is Vibration Dose Value [1, 4] which is related to RMQ but not averaged over time. It means that VDV measures cumulative dose of vibration. Other approaches to comfort assessment base on whole three-dimensional vector of vibration acceleration like e.g. CEN ENV12299 [5] introducing N_{MV} measure.

BS 6841 and ISO 2631 standards introduce discomfort scale defined as a set of overlapped classes of RMS named: not uncomfortable (less than 0.315), a little uncomfortable (0.315÷0.63), fairly uncomfortable (0.5÷1.0), uncomfortable (0.8÷1.6), very uncomfortable (1.25÷2.5), extremely uncomfortable (greater than 2.0). It clearly leads to fuzzy assessment. Analogically, CEN ENV 12299 defines its discomfort scale as a set of non-overlapped classes of its measure N_{MV} named: very comfortable (less than 1.5), comfortable (1.5÷2.5), medium (2.5÷3.5), uncomfortable (3.5÷4.5), very uncomfortable (greater than 4.5).

Grzegożek, Szczygieł and Król [6] began the study on rail vehicles in 2009. They designed and performed a passive experiment to collect data describing physical conditions of ride and associated subjective assessment of comfort. Fourteen people were driving in a tram and synchronously evaluating ride comfort using electronic panels. The comfort was evaluated on the discrete ordinal scale of 1 to 5. At the same time tram's deck computer were recording through sensors values of acceleration in three perpendicular axes. The analysis of collected data detected the discrepancies between predictions based on standards [1, 2, 4, 5] and empirical results [6]. Standard models clearly proved to be too simplified and building of more complex model is very desirable. Current work is focused on an ordinal logistic regression models [7].

Basing on collected data [6], author start to construct a predicting model involving fuzzy logic into regression like used in similar design of experimts (DoE) approach [8]. In contrast, however, it turned out that the data do not allow the consistent use of a single pair of triangular norms [9-11]. Detailed analysis of the raw data revealed that the significant correlation of collected pairwise data is a cause of the problem. Typical data conversion to the fuzzy form loses information about the correlation. Lack of this information manifests by instability of selection for best-fitting pair of triangular norms.

Bellman and Zadeh [12] has already stated that it is impossible to choose a pair of triangular norms that match all the issues. In the author's opinion, the ambiguity of the choice reflects hidden information about the correlation of variables. In most cases, this information is not available and then remains – as usually – the matching the best pair of triangular norms for the empirical data. In this case, the fuzzy model appears as a latent variables model with hidden information about correlation.

However, if the correlation information is available, it would be a mistake to ignore it. Author proposes a formalism in which a binary vector of assessments is a basic data structure and the scalar fuzzy measure appears at the end of calculations as the average value of this vector's components. The overall idea is that the entire sequence of calculations is carried out with the use of binary assessment vectors, and the scalar fuzzy measure is calculated at the final. The details of this proposal are discussed later in this article.

2   Proposal of the Formalism

2.1   Zadeh's Approach – A Starting Point

Fuzzy sets algebra and coupled fuzzy logic were defined by L. Zadeh in 1965 [13]. The basic element of formalism is a concept of a membership function μ. The function is defined for a particular crisp set taken from a space X:

$$\mu_A : X \rightarrow [0,1] \tag{1}$$

where X is non-empty space and notation μ_A means membership function of a fuzzy set A. Formally, the fuzzy set A is defined as a set of pairs – elements from the space X and assigned memberships:

$$A = \left\{ (x, \mu_A(x)) : x \in X \wedge \mu_A(x) \in [0,1] \right\} . \tag{2}$$

A membership function's value is interpreted as a level of element's belonging to a fuzzy set. The value of 0 means lack of belonging, the value of 1 – a full belonging, intermediate values – partial belonging. There are unary and binary algebraic operations introduced for the such defined fuzzy set. Operations are induced by operations on coupled membership functions:

1. intersection of fuzzy sets

$$A \cap B = \left\{ (x, \mu_{A \cap B}) : x \in X \wedge \mu_{A \cap B}(x) = T(\mu_A(x), \mu_B(x)) \right\} \tag{3}$$

where $T : [0,1] \times [0,1] \rightarrow [0,1]$ is one of so called t-norms [9-11]. An example of t-norm is $\mu_{A \cap B}(x) = \min(\mu_A(x), \mu_B(x))$.

2. union of fuzzy sets

$$A \cup B = \left\{ (x, \mu_{A \cup B}) : x \in X \wedge \mu_{A \cup B}(x) = S(\mu_A(x), \mu_B(x)) \right\} \tag{4}$$

where $S : [0,1] \times [0,1] \rightarrow [0,1]$ is one of so called t-conorm [9-11]. An example of t-conorm is $\mu_{A \cup B}(x) = \max(\mu_A(x), \mu_B(x))$.

3. complement of fuzzy set

$$\overline{A} = \left\{ (x, \mu_{\overline{A}}) : x \in X \wedge \mu_{\overline{A}}(x) = 1 - \mu_A(x) \right\} \tag{5}$$

The pair of triangle norms should be selected for a particular problem depending on its specific features. It is a known difficulty noticed already by Bellman and Zadeh [12]. There is no possibility to define fuzzy sets algebra operations in a form being universal and applicable in all situations. Restrictions originated from this difficulty were identified and analyzed by Klement, Mesiar and Pap [14]. There are dual pairs defined for triangle norms: t-norm and t-conorm. They must comply with general assumptions of norm in metric spaces. Comprehensive descriptions based on functional equations theory results may be found in [15, 16]. Such defined fuzzy sets algebra has some features of classic sets algebra: idempotency, commutativity, associativity although the law of excluded middle and law of contradiction do not hold: $A \cup \overline{A} \neq X$ and $A \cap \overline{A} \neq \varnothing$.

The algebra $(F(X), \cup, \cap, ^-)$, where $F(X)$ denotes family of all fuzzy sets in space X, is not Boolean algebra but weaker De Morgan algebra [17, 18]. The algebra $(Fz(X), \vee, \wedge, ^-)$, where $Fz(X)$ denotes family of all membership functions over space X, is not Boolean algebra but also De Morgan algebra [17, 18]. There is alternative concept around fuzzy sets involving two functions. Atanassov [19, 20] proposed to couple two features with element from space X: membership and non-membership. The completeness up to 1 is named hesitance. This concept is known as intuitions fuzzy sets (IFS). Difficulties with continuous membership function in clustering problems lead to three-level discretised membership which is known as shadowed fuzzy sets (SFS), proposed by Pedrycz [21]. Fuzzy sets in R^1 have a main technical importance and if such sets comply with special assumptions then they are named fuzzy numbers [22]. The implementation of fuzzy number algebra is difficult to utilize and many different approaches were proposed e.g. trapezoidal and its derivatives [23-24]. Regardless of successes, the concept of fuzziness and its relatives are strongly criticized by many mathematicians and statisticians e.g. de Finetti [25]. The main objections are imprecision in 'fuzziness' definition and redundancy in comparison to well-known probabilistic uncertainty. On the other way, the users' objections are focused on calculus difficulties and choice of triangular norms what are arbitrary selected to a particular problem.

2.2   Difficulties in Fuzzy Numbers Calculus

The main purpose of author's investigation was adoption of fuzzy methods into design of experiment domain. During this work many difficulties were found in implementation of calculus but more fundamentally also. The existing fuzzy number theory mutations could not allow to evaluate expression where the same fuzzy variable is involved in many places. All appearances of the variable are treated as completely uncorrelated and it generates results for contextually forbidden combinations of fuzzy number elements. There are many ridiculous contradictions not allowed in classic arithmetic.

The main problem is identity of the value. For a real number its identity is its value, position on R^1 scale. There is not equivalent identity for a fuzzy set. Thus all possible combinations of elements are involved while evaluating fuzzy expression. It has no sense for any physical variable. Fuzzy set describes uncertainty about value of the variable, but the variable itself can be in only one state at the moment, not in two or more different states. Adoptions of fuzzy number calculus are mainly concentrated on fuzzy functions of real (crisp) arguments. This allows to avoid mentioned correlation problem [26]. Regardless of this imperfect arithmetic, there are many trials to build even formal fuzzy statistics [27]. Author assessed that the reason of his efforts failing was the lack of fuzzy value identity and the loss of correlation information. Thus the constructing of fuzzy value identity should be the first. The fuzzy sets algebra (and derived fuzzy numbers algebra also) recognize two fuzzy sets as equal if and only if for each element of the space X membership functions are equal also:

$$A = B \quad \Leftrightarrow \quad \forall x \in X \; \mu_A(x) = \mu_B(x) \; . \tag{6}$$

Such defined fuzzy sets equality disallows identity assigning to fuzzy values and consideration of correlation levels. The scalar membership function is insufficient for such description of a fuzzy value. It is necessary to create a formalism which allows $\forall x \in X \; \mu_A(x) = \mu_B(x)$ even though $A \neq B$. The substitute should be consistent with existing fuzzy sets and fuzzy logic formalism in asymptotic form or particular case.

2.3   Outline of Proposed Sequential-Binary Concept

Author proposes that value of membership function should be treated as a weighted result of voting where some human voting panel is involved. Individual vote is binary as only 'YES' or 'NO'. Theoretically number of the panel may be even infinite but countable. The main proposal is an assumption: a sequence of votes on the truth of 'p' sentence is the only description of this truth. The membership function is replaced with potentially infinite binary sequence. The membership function becomes only simpler form of the sequence presentation but without sequence pattern information. Equality of two membership functions should be replaced by an equality of two binary sequences in all positions. Additionally it allows to differentiate behavior of fuzzy values in binary operations between them.

In such approach, fuzzy sets algebra and fuzzy logic algebra operations are induced as Boolean operations on paired elements of binary sequences. It quite similar to operations involved during fuzzy sets aggregations described by Klement, Mesiar and Pap [14]. Properties of similar Bernoulli infinite sequences was investigated by de Finetti [25]. In the remaining part of the article, the proposed formalism will be named YAAFL (*Yet Another Approach to Fuzzy Logic*).

2.4   Formal Definition of Proposed Formalism

Let triple (Ω, S, P) is a probabilistic space. Let elementary events space $\Omega = \{\omega_0, \omega_1\}$, where ω_0 denotes decision 'NO' and ω_1 – 'YES'. Let S denotes σ-field on Borel sets in Ω. Every set belonging to S is named event. Let P denotes non-negative real function on domain S and co-domain [0, 1] with following values for events from S: $P(\varnothing) = 0$, $P(\{\omega_0\}) = 1 - \mu$, $P(\{\omega_1\}) = \mu$, $P(\{\omega_0\} \cup \{\omega_1\}) = 1$. P is named probability distribution. Let B denotes binary subset of $\mathbf{R}^1$: $B = \{0, 1\}$.

Let $X_1, ..., X_n$ denotes binomial independent random variables which comply with following conditions: $\forall i \leq n \; X_i : \Omega \to B \; \forall i \leq n \; \forall x \in \mathbf{R} \; \{\omega : X_i(\omega) < x\} \in S$.

Let $\{X_n\}$ denotes n-element random sequence. The membership n-bit sequence is defined as a realization of random sequence for particular event $\{X_n\}(\omega) \in B^n$, where B_n is a space of all possible n-bit membership sequences. For such defined sequences algebra operations may be induced from Boolean algebra operations on sequences elements' pair:

1. intersection of membership sequences $\{X_n\}$ and $\{Y_n\}$

$$\left(\{X_n\} \cap \{Y_n\}\right)(\omega) = \left\{X_n(\omega) \wedge Y_n(\omega)\right\},\tag{7}$$

2. union of membership sequences $\{X_n\}$ and $\{Y_n\}$

$$\left(\{X_n\} \cup \{Y_n\}\right)(\omega) = \left\{X_n(\omega) \vee Y_n(\omega)\right\},\tag{8}$$

3. negation of the membership sequence $\{X_n\}$

$$\overline{\{X_n\}}(\omega) = \left\{\overline{X_n(\omega)}\right\}.\tag{9}$$

Such defined algebra $(B^n, \cap, \cup, \overline{})$ is Boolean algebra. The weighted Hamming measure for membership sequence $\{X_n\}(\omega)$ is formulated:

$$\mu\left(\{X_n\}(\omega)\right) = \frac{1}{n}\sum_{i=1}^{n} X_n(\omega).\tag{10}$$

Semantically such defined weighted measure μ is consistent with existing Zadeh's membership function but it is necessary to note that all operations of YAAFL formalism should be provided on membership sequences. A projection of the sequence into scalar value may be used only for synthetic information.

3   Description of Achieved Results

3.1   Logic Laws Complying

Let $\{X_n\}$ denotes membership sequence in B_n space. The law of excluded middle $A \cup \overline{A} = X$ and law of contradiction $A \cap \overline{A} = \varnothing$ hold. This is the main difference in comparison to existing Zadeh's formalism. The proof is presented below.

Consider the product of this sequence and its negation:

$$\left(\{X_n\} \cap \{\overline{X}_n\}\right)(\omega) = \left\{X_n(\omega) \wedge \overline{X}_n(\omega)\right\}.\tag{11}$$

The right side of equality is calculated according to the rules of Boolean algebra, so finally:

$$\left(\{X_n\} \cap \{\overline{X}_n\}\right)(\omega) = \left\{0_n\right\}.\tag{12}$$

The value of membership function for this expression is also scalar zero:

$$\mu\Big(\big(\{X_n\}\cap\{\overline{X}_n\}\big)(\omega)\Big)=0 \quad \forall\omega, \tag{13}$$

which is different from the result obtained in the case of scalar membership function. On the other hand, consider the sum of the sequence and its negation:

$$\big(\{X_n\}\cup\{\overline{X}_n\}\big)(\omega)=\{X_n(\omega)\vee\overline{X}_n(\omega)\}. \tag{14}$$

The right side of equality is calculated according to the rules of Boolean algebra, so:

$$\big(\{X_n\}\cup\{\overline{X}_n\}\big)(\omega)=\{1_n\}. \tag{15}$$

The value of membership function for this expression is also scalar one:

$$\mu\Big(\big(\{X_n\}\cup\{\overline{X}_n\}\big)(\omega)\Big)=1 \quad \forall\omega, \tag{16}$$

This result is also different than in the case of scalar membership function.

3.2   Conformity with Triangular Norms

Min-max Norms
Let $\{X_n\}$ and $\{Y_n\}$ denotes membership sequences in B_n space. If both sequences are sorted in the same direction (it means that all 1's are on heads or tails of sequences) then weighted Hamming measures for intersection and union of both sequences are equal to min-max norms. It describes variables with correlations close to +1. The proof is presented below.

Let the mapping $\mathrm{Desc}: B_n \rightarrow B_n$ sorts membership sequence in descending order (1s – firstly, 0s – later), where the effect of the mapping is defined by the formula:

$$\mathrm{Desc}\big(\{x_n\}\big)=\Big\{z_n: \ \forall 1\leq i\leq k \ z_i=1\wedge\forall k<j\leq n \ z_j=0\wedge k=\sum_{m=1}^{n}x_m\Big\}. \tag{17}$$

Let $\{X_n\}$ and $\{Y_n\}$ be any n-element sequences in the space B_n. Consider the product of sorted sequences:

$$\mathrm{Desc}\big(\{x_n\}\big)\cap\mathrm{Desc}\big(\{y_n\}\big)=$$
$$=\Big\{z_n: \ \forall 1\leq i\leq k \ z_i=1\wedge\forall k<j\leq n \ z_j=0\wedge k=\min(\sum_{m=1}^{n}x_m,\sum_{m=1}^{n}y_m)\Big\} \tag{18}$$

The membership function of such product is equal to:

$$\mu\left(\mathrm{Desc}\left(\{x_n\}\right)\cap\mathrm{Desc}\left(\{y_n\}\right)\right)=\min\left(\mu\left(\mathrm{Desc}\left(\{x_n\}\right)\right),\mu\left(\mathrm{Desc}\left(\{y_n\}\right)\right)\right) \tag{19}$$

as it was to prove. Now consider the sum of sorted sequences:

$$\mathrm{Desc}\left(\{x_n\}\right)\cup\mathrm{Desc}\left(\{y_n\}\right)=$$
$$=\left\{z_n:\ \forall 1\le i\le k\ z_i=1\wedge\forall k<j\le n\ z_j=0\wedge k=\max(\sum_{m=1}^{n}x_m,\sum_{m=1}^{n}y_m)\right\} \tag{20}$$

The membership function of such product is equal to:

$$\mu\left(\mathrm{Desc}\left(\{x_n\}\right)\cup\mathrm{Desc}\left(\{y_n\}\right)\right)=\max\left(\mu\left(\mathrm{Desc}\left(\{x_n\}\right)\right),\mu\left(\mathrm{Desc}\left(\{y_n\}\right)\right)\right) \tag{21}$$

as it was to prove. Such case maximizes the Hamming norm of the product and minimizes the Hamming norm of the sum.

Łukasiewicz's Norms

Let $\{X_n\}$ and $\{Y_n\}$ denotes membership sequences in B_n space. If both sequences are sorted in the reverse order (it means that all 1's are on head of the one sequence and tail of the latter) then weighted Hamming measures for intersection and union of both sequences are equal to Łukasiewicz's (logical) norms. It describes variables with correlations close to -1. The proof is presented below.

Let the mapping $\mathrm{Asc}:B_n\to B_n$ sorts membership sequence in ascending order (0s – firstly, 1s – later), where the effect of the mapping is defined by the formula:

$$\mathrm{Asc}\left(\{x_n\}\right)=\left\{z_n:\ \forall 1\le i\le k\ z_i=0\wedge\forall k<j\le n\ z_j=1\wedge k=n-\sum_{m=1}^{n}x_n\right\}. \tag{22}$$

Let the mapping $\mathrm{Desc}:B_n\to B_n$ sorts membership sequence in descending order and be defined as in formula (eq.17). Let $\{X_n\}$ and $\{Y_n\}$ be any n-element sequences in the space B_n. Consider the product of sorted sequences $\mathrm{Desc}\left(\{x_n\}\right)\cap\mathrm{Asc}\left(\{y_n\}\right)$. The result of this product is highly dependent on whether the subsequences of 1s will overlap or not. If subsequences are not overlapped, then the product will be sequence of 0s:

$$\sum_{i=1}^{n}x_i+\sum_{j=1}^{n}y_j<n\ \Rightarrow\ \mathrm{Desc}\left(\{x_n\}\right)\cap\mathrm{Asc}\left(\{y_n\}\right)=\{0\}. \tag{23}$$

Similarly, a membership function take the value of zero:

$$\mu\left(\mathrm{Desc}\{x_n\}\right)+\mu\left(\mathrm{Asc}\{y_n\}\right)<1\ \Rightarrow\ \mu\left(\mathrm{Desc}\left(\{x_n\}\right)\cap\mathrm{Asc}\left(\{y_n\}\right)\right)=0. \tag{24}$$

If subsequences are overlapped, then the products will be in the following form:

$$\sum_{i=1}^{n} x_i + \sum_{j=1}^{n} y_j \geq n \quad \Rightarrow \quad \text{Desc}\big(\{x_n\}\big) \cap \text{Asc}\big(\{y_n\}\big) = \{z_n\}, \tag{25}$$

where z values are defined by the formula:

$$z_i = \begin{cases} 0 & i \leq n - \sum_{k=1}^{n} y_n \\ 1 & n - \sum_{k=1}^{n} y_n < i \leq \sum_{k=1}^{n} x_n \\ 0 & i > \sum_{k=1}^{n} x_n \end{cases} \tag{26}$$

Membership function takes the value:

$$\mu\big(\text{Desc}\{x_n\}\big) + \mu\big(\text{Asc}\{y_n\}\big) \geq 1 \quad \Rightarrow$$
$$\Rightarrow \quad \mu\big(\text{Desc}\big(\{x_n\}\big) \cap \text{Asc}\big(\{y_n\}\big)\big) = \mu\big(\text{Desc}\{x_n\}\big) + \mu\big(\text{Asc}\{y_n\}\big) - 1 \tag{27}$$

In conclusion, combining both results, the membership function for the product of reverse sorted sequences is:

$$\mu\big(\text{Desc}\big(\{x_n\}\big) \cap \text{Asc}\big(\{y_n\}\big)\big) = \max\big(0, \mu\big(\text{Desc}\{x_n\}\big) + \mu\big(\text{Asc}\{y_n\}\big) - 1\big) \tag{28}$$

as it was to prove. Now consider the sum $\text{Desc}\big(\{x_n\}\big) \cap \text{Asc}\big(\{y_n\}\big)$ of reverse sorted sequences. The result of this sum is also highly dependent on whether the subsequences of 1s will overlap or not. If subsequences are overlapped, then the sum will be sequence of 1s:

$$\sum_{i=1}^{n} x_i + \sum_{j=1}^{n} y_j \geq n \quad \Rightarrow \quad \text{Desc}\big(\{x_n\}\big) \cup \text{Asc}\big(\{y_n\}\big) = \{1\}. \tag{29}$$

The membership function of such sum is equal to:

$$\mu\big(\text{Desc}\{x_n\}\big) + \mu\big(\text{Asc}\{y_n\}\big) \geq 1 \quad \Rightarrow \quad \mu\big(\text{Desc}\big(\{x_n\}\big) \cup \text{Asc}\big(\{y_n\}\big)\big) = 1. \tag{30}$$

If subsequences are not overlapped, then the products will be in the following form:

$$\sum_{i=1}^{n} x_i + \sum_{j=1}^{n} y_j < n \quad \Rightarrow \quad \text{Desc}\big(\{x_n\}\big) \cup \text{Asc}\big(\{y_n\}\big) = \{z_n\}, \tag{31}$$

where z values are defined by the formula:

$$z_i = \begin{cases} 1 & i \le \sum\limits_{k=1}^{n} x_n \\ 0 & \sum\limits_{k=1}^{n} x_n < i \le n - \sum\limits_{k=1}^{n} y_n \\ 1 & n - \sum\limits_{k=1}^{n} y_n < i \end{cases} \tag{32}$$

Similarly, the sum of membership function takes the following form:

$$\mu\big(\mathrm{Desc}\{x_n\}\big) + \mu\big(\mathrm{Asc}\{y_n\}\big) < 1 \quad \Rightarrow$$
$$\Rightarrow \quad \mu\big(\mathrm{Desc}(\{x_n\}) \cup \mathrm{Asc}(\{y_n\})\big) = \mu\big(\mathrm{Desc}(\{x_n\})\big) + \mu\big(\mathrm{Asc}(\{y_n\})\big) \tag{33}$$

In conclusion, combining both results, the membership function for the sum of reverse sorted sequences is:

$$\mu\big(\mathrm{Desc}(\{x_n\}) \cap \mathrm{Asc}(\{y_n\})\big) = \min\big(1, \mu\big(\mathrm{Desc}\{x_n\}\big) + \mu\big(\mathrm{Asc}\{y_n\}\big)\big) \tag{34}$$

as it was to prove. Such case minimizes the Hamming norm of the product and maximizes the Hamming norm of the sum.

Algebraic Norms

If both sequences have random pattern of sequence then expected value of weighted Hamming measures for intersection and union of both sequences are equal to algebraic norms. It describes uncorrelated variables i.e. with correlations close to 0. Let $\{X_n\}$ and $\{Y_n\}$ denotes two randomly independent membership sequences in probabilistic space (Ω, S, P) with probability respectively:

$$\forall i \quad P(X_i = 1) = \mu_x, \tag{35}$$

$$\forall i \quad P(Y_i = 1) = \mu_y.$$

Expected values of Hamming measure for the product and the sum of membership sequences are equal to algebraic norms:

$$E\big(\mu(\{X_n(\omega)\} \cap \{Y_n(\omega)\})\big) = \mu_x \mu_y, \tag{36}$$

$$E\big(\mu(\{X_n(\omega)\} \cup \{Y_n(\omega)\})\big) = \mu_x + \mu_y - \mu_x \mu_y.$$

The proof is presented below. The expected value of Hamming measure for the product of sequences is given by:

$$E\left(\mu\left(\left\{X_n(\omega)\right\}\cap\left\{Y_n(\omega)\right\}\right)\right)=E\left(\frac{1}{n}\sum_{i=1}^{n}X_n(\omega)Y_n(\omega)\right). \tag{37}$$

Any two elements in each sequence are independent. Similarly, between the strings. Therefore:

$$E\left(\mu\left(\left\{X_n(\omega)\right\}\cap\left\{Y_n(\omega)\right\}\right)\right)=\frac{1}{n}\sum_{i=1}^{n}E(X_n(\omega))E(Y_n(\omega)) \tag{38}$$

and then:

$$E\left(\mu\left(\left\{X_n(\omega)\right\}\cap\left\{Y_n(\omega)\right\}\right)\right)=\mu_x\mu_y \tag{39}$$

as it was to prove. The proof for the sum is carried out similarly.

4   Conclusions

In this paper is presented the modified fuzzy logic algebra. There is a replacement of membership function: n-element binary membership sequence. Such description allows to describe fuzzy value by membership sequence pattern (if identifiable) or by traditional scalar membership function. The fuzzy logic for membership sequences is formally Boolean algebra as opposed to Zadeh's fuzzy logic for scalar membership functions being De Morgan algebra. There is introduced a mathematical formulation of the proposed formalism, the induced algebraic operations are also defined. A weighted Hamming measure for membership sequences is defined as semantically equivalent to Zadeh's membership function. There are shown binary patterns of membership sequences where weighted Hamming measure for intersection and union of membership sequences is equal to typical pairs of triangular norms such as the min-max, the logical and the algebraic ones. It appears that a binary vector data structure allows to utilize collective intelligence methods such as genetic algorithms.

It would be desirable to investigate the following problems:

- an identification of other possible sequence patterns leading to known triangular norms,
- an estimation of the minimal length of a membership sequence for an assumed precision of evaluations and an assumed risk of two fuzzy values identity collision in B_n space.

References

1. ISO2631: Mechanical vibration and shock – Evaluation of human exposure to whole-body vibration – Part 1: General requirements. ISO, Geneve (1997)
2. BS6841: Guide to measurement and evaluation of human exposure to whole-body mechanical vibration and repeated shoc. BSI, London (1987)
3. Griffin, M.J.: Discomfort from feeling vehicle vibration. Vehicle Syst. Dyn. 45, 679–698 (2007)

4. BS6472-1: Guide to evaluation of human exposure to vibration in buildings. Vibration sources other than blasting. BSI, London (2008)
5. CEN_ENV12299: Railway applications - Ride comfort for passengers - Measurement and evaluation. CEN-CENELEC, Brussels (2009)
6. Grzegożek, W., Szczygieł, J., Król, S.: An Attempt of an Employment of a Continuous Wavelet Transform for Evaluation of Temporary Comfort Distrubances. Journal of KONES Powertrain and Transport 16, 165–172 (2009)
7. Pietraszek, J., Grzegożek, W., Szczygieł, J.: Forecasting of Subjective Comfort in Tram Using Ordinal Logistic Regression and Manifold Learning. Journal of KONES Powertrain and Transport 19, 403–410 (2012)
8. Pietraszek, J.: Fuzzy Regression Compared to Classical Experimental Design in the Case of Flywheel Assembly. In: Rutkowski, L., Korytkowski, M., Scherer, R., Tadeusiewicz, R., Zadeh, L.A., Zurada, J.M. (eds.) ICAISC 2012, Part I. LNCS (LNAI), vol. 7267, pp. 310–317. Springer, Heidelberg (2012)
9. Ling, C.H.: Representation of associative functions. Publ. Math., Debrecen 6, 167–173 (1973)
10. Paalman de Miranda, A.B.: Topological semigroups. Math. Centre Tracts 11 Math. Centrum, Amsterdam (1964)
11. Schweizer, B., Sklar, A.: Statistical metric spaces. Pac. J. Math. 10, 313–334 (1960)
12. Bellman, R.E., Zadeh, L.A.: Local and fuzzy logics. In: Dunn, J.M., Epstein, D. (eds.) Modern Uses of Multiple Valued Logic, pp. 103–165. D. Reidel, Dordrecht (1977)
13. Zadeh, L.A.: Fuzzy Sets. Inform Control 8, 338–353 (1965)
14. Klement, E.P., Mesiar, R., Pap, E.: Fuzzy Set Theory: 'AND' is more than just the Minimum. In: Hryniewicz, O. (ed.) Issues in Soft Computing. Decisions and Operations Research, pp. 39–52. EXIT Press, Warszawa (2005)
15. Aczel, J.: Lectures on functional equations and their applications. Academic Press, New York (1966)
16. Fuchs, L.: Partially ordered algebraic systems. Pergamon Press, Oxford (1963)
17. Cignoli, R.: Injective De-Morgan and Kleene Algebras. P. Am. Math. Soc. 47, 269–278 (1975)
18. Negoita, C.V., Ralescu, D.A.: Applications of fuzzy sets to systems analysis. Birkhäuser Verlag, Stuttgart (1975)
19. Atanassov, K.T.: Intuitionistic Fuzzy-Sets. Fuzzy Set Syst. 20, 87–96 (1986)
20. Szmidt, E., Kacprzyk, J.: Intuitionistic fuzzy events and their probabilities. Notes on Intuitionistic Fuzzy Sets 4, 68–72 (1999)
21. Pedrycz, W.: Shadowed sets: bridging fuzzy and rough sets. In: Pal, S.K., Skowron, A. (eds.) Rough Fuzzy Hybridization. A New Trend in Decision-Making, pp. 179–199. Springer, Singapore (1999)
22. Dubois, D., Prade, H.: Operations on Fuzzy Numbers. Int. J. Syst. Sci. 9, 613–626 (1978)
23. Grzegorzewski, P., Mrówka, E.: Trapezoidal approximations of fuzzy numbers. In: De Baets, B., Kaynak, O., Bilgiç, T. (eds.) IFSA 2003. LNCS, vol. 2715, pp. 237–244. Springer, Heidelberg (2003)
24. Grzegorzewski, P.: Fuzzy number approximation via shadowed sets. Inform. Sciences 225, 35–46 (2012)
25. de Finetti, B.: Foresight: its logical laws, its subjective sources. In: Kyburg, H.E., Smokler, H.E. (eds.) Studies in Subjective Probability. John Wiley & Sons, New York (1964)
26. Tyrala, R.: Linear Systems with Fuzzy Solution. In: Grzegorzewski, P. (ed.) Issues in Soft Computing. Theory and Applications, pp. 277–288. EXIT Press, Warszawa (2005)
27. Buckley, J.J.: Fuzzy Probability and Statistics. Springer, Berlin (2006)

Flexible and Simple Methods of Calculations on Fuzzy Numbers with the Ordered Fuzzy Numbers Model

Piotr Prokopowicz

Institute of Mechanics and Applied Computer Science
Kazimierz Wielki University, Bydgoszcz, Poland
piotrekp@ukw.edu.pl
http://www.imis.ukw.edu.pl

Abstract. The publication shows the way of implementing arithmetic operations on fuzzy numbers based on Ordered Fuzzy Numbers calculation model [12], [13], [14]. This model allows to perform calculations on fuzzy numbers in a way that the outcomes meet the same criteria as the outcomes of calculations on real numbers. In this text, to the four basic operations with Ordered Fuzzy Numbers, a logarithm and exponentiation was added. Several examples of the calculations are included, the results of which are obvious and typical of real numbers but not achievable with the use of conventional computational methods for fuzzy numbers. From these examples one can see that the use of Ordered Fuzzy Numbers allows to obtain outcomes for real numbers in spite of using the fuzzy values.

Keywords: fuzzy number, Ordered Fuzzy Numbers, arithmetic calculations on fuzzy numbers, logarithm of fuzzy numbers, exponent of fuzzy numbers.

1 Introduction

The abilities to analyze and process information is an important factor in the development in every field. In many real problems, however, we find cases where the data that we are able to obtain are imprecise or uncertain. People deal with such data by linguistic description such as heavy weight, cold, little water, far away, etc. The need for using more formal methods appears when one needs to save such data in a digital way in order to automate further processing.

More appropriate tool in such situations is the theory of fuzzy sets [1], which allows to describe imprecise information mathematically. Furthermore, in the case of modeling imprecise quantitative data such as: about 4, more or less 2, etc. fuzzy numbers are used.

There are many mathematical models for analyzing the data. A large number of numerical methods supporting processing the information were defined. Unfortunately, the existing computational model of fuzzy numbers makes it difficult to apply all the tools in the processing of imprecise data. This is due to the fact

L. Rutkowski et al. (Eds.): ICAISC 2013, Part I, LNAI 7894, pp. 365–375, 2013.

that in most applications numerical operations on fuzzy values, are based on the so-called Zadehs extension principle [2]. It introduces a formal apparatus for transferring operations (also arithmetic) from ordinary sets to fuzzy sets. Unfortunately, the use of the extension principle involves inconvenient consequences, particularly in the case of repeating series of actions. The main problem here is the expansion of the fuzzy number support with the subsequent actions. Regardless of whether we add or subtract numbers, they becoming "fuzzier". Consequently, after a few calculations we can receive impractical outcomes with a very wide support. These operations properties are also related to other negative consequences, such as the difference $A - A$ does not allow to obtain the neutral element of addition, which is the number zero. Another important drawback is the lack of a simple method for solving the elementary equation of $A + X = B$ (where A and B are non-singleton fuzzy numbers). These negative calculations characteristics impede the application of even basic calculations in the numerical analysis of the imprecise data, not to mention the more complex ones.

Remark 1. Crisp values can be represented as fuzzy numbers with the use of the so-called singletons. This publication focuses, however, on the general characteristic of fuzzy values, so any further discussion in the context of fuzzy numbers will apply to situations in which we are dealing with the general form of a fuzzy number, not its particular case - a singleton.

One of the commonly accepted models of fuzzy numbers is the proposal introduced by Dubois and Prade [3]. It is based on the fact of considering the membership function of fuzzy numbers as a pair of two shape functions describing the left and right fuzzy spread. This model is called (L, R) fuzzy numbers. (L, R) numbers gained great popularity due to good interpretation and relatively easy implementation of basic operations such as adding. Calculations are also based on the Zadehs extension principle, which as mentioned before is connected with several significant adverse consequences.

To improve the computational properties of fuzzy numbers several additional solutions were introduced. They are usually connected with defining additional operations or constraints ([6][7][11]).

An alternative solution is to use Ordered Fuzzy Numbers mathematical model [12] [13]. This publication focuses precisely on this model, and in particular on methods of carrying out calculations. A better understanding of the OFN model requires a new approach to modeling fuzzy values, which can cause some difficulties. However, an important benefit is the ability to perform all arithmetical calculations with the same relations between the results, as in the case of operations on real numbers.

2   Ordered Fuzzy Numbers (OFN)

In the series of papers [12], [13], [14],[16],[18],[19], [21], [22] were introduced and developed main concepts of the idea of Ordered Fuzzy Numbers. Following these papers fuzzy number will be identified with the pair of functions defined on the interval $[0, 1]$.

Definition 1. *The Ordered Fuzzy Number (OFN in short) A is an ordered pair of two continuous functions*

$$A = (f_A, g_A) \tag{1}$$

called the UP-part and the DOWN-part, respectively, both defined on the closed interval $[0,1]$ with values in $\mathbf{R}$.

If the both functions f and g are monotonic (Fig.1 a)), they are also invertible and possess the corresponding inverse functions defined on a real axis with the values in $[0,1]$. Now, if these two opposite functions are not connected, we linking them with constant function (with the value 1). In such way we receive an object which directly represents the classical fuzzy number. For the finalization of transformation, we need to mark an order of f and g with an arrow on the graph (see Fig.1 b)). Notice that pairs (f,g) and (g,f) are the two different Ordered Fuzzy Numbers, unless $f = g$. They differ by their orientation.

The interpretations for this orientation and its relations with the real world problems are explained in the [21] and [22].

It is worth to point out that a class of Ordered Fuzzy Numbers (OFNs) represents the whole class of convex fuzzy numbers ([4],[8],[9],[10],[17], with continuous membership functions.

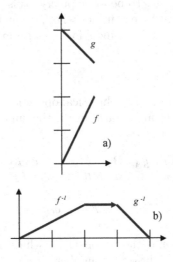

Fig. 1. a)Ordered Fuzzy Number from definition, b)Ordered Fuzzy Number as convex fuzzy number with an arrow

There are publications about OFNs, where propositions of the new methods for the fuzzy systems can be found. The papers [18],[19],[20] contains examples of the new inference methods based on the OFNs. The works [15],[23] are about defuzzyfication methods.

3 Arithmetic Operations

Operations on Ordered Fuzzy Numbers we define as operations with the UP and DOWN parts as follows:

Definition 2. *Let* $A = (f_A, g_A), B = (f_B, g_B)$ *and* $C = (f_C, g_C)$ *are mathematical objects called Ordered Fuzzy Numbers. The sum* $C = A + B$, *subtraction* $C = A - B$, *product* $C = A \cdot B$, *and division* $C = A \div B$ *are defined by formula*

$$f_C(y) = f_A(y) \star f_B(y) \qquad \wedge \qquad g_C(y) = g_A(y) \star g_B(y) \qquad (2)$$

where "$\star$" replaces operations "$+$", "$-$", "$\cdot$", and "$/$". Moreover A/B *s determined only if the OFN* B *does not contain zero. The* $y \in [0,1]$ *is the domain of functions* f *and* g.

It is also worth noting that the subtraction is equal to the addition of the opposite number, where the opposite number is obtained by multiplying the given value by the -1 (real number - singleton). By using the above-mentioned method in calculation of $A - A$ we obtain exact zero (crisp number).

Remark 2. Determining whether a given OFN contains (or not) r value (real number) is a mental shortcut. To be more precise, this phrase should be understood as a situation in which we consider whether any of the functions (UP or DOWN part) forming OFN have value r for any argument.

3.1 More Operations

Going further in the direction of arithmetical operations, we can offer definition of exponentiation and counting logarithms in the similar way as in basic four operations.

Definition 3. *Let* $A = (f_A, g_A), B = (f_B, g_B)$ *and* $C = (f_C, g_C)$ *are OFNs. The result of exponentation* A *raised to the power of* B *written* A^B *is defined by formula*

$$f_C = f_A{}^{f_B} \qquad \wedge \qquad g_C = g_A{}^{g_B}. \qquad (3)$$

The logarithm of a number is the exponent by which another fixed value, the base, has to be raised to produce that number.

Definition 4. *Let* $A = (f_A, g_A), B = (f_B, g_B)$ *and* $C = (f_C, g_C)$ *are OFNs. The logarithm of a number* A *with respect to base* B *written* $\log_B^A$ *is defined by formula*

$$f_C = \log_{f_B}(f_A) \qquad \wedge \qquad g_C = \log_{g_B}(g_A). \qquad (4)$$

Of course, as in the case of real numbers as with the OFNs, appropriate restrictions should be applied. During exponentiation when the exponent is not an integer, the main limitation is the exclusion as a base these OFNs that contain negative values. With logarithms, in turn, the limitations are as follows:

- OFN which is a base and an exponent can contain only non-negative values;
- in addition, the base of the logarithm cannot include number 1.

4   Calculations on OFNs

In this chapter a number of examples showing the arithmetic sequences of calculations will be presented. Examples focus on such transformations, which in cases of real numbers could be reduced and brought to one of the numbers that is a part of the transformation. However, because OFN was used in the calculations, partial results will be presented in order to make it easier to keep track of what is happening at each stage of the calculations.

4.1   Solving Equations

These examples show the solution of the equation $X = A + B$ where A and B are known values. Here ones attention should be drawn to two options:

a) when B has a grater support than A (Fig.2),
b) when A has a greater support than B (Fig.3).

It is inasmuch important that in the set of convex fuzzy numbers for option a) there is a solution, although it cannot be obtained by a simple arithmetic operation. However, for the option b) the solution does not exist, because there is no such fuzzy number, which could be added to the value A, to obtain the outcome of the number with "narrow" support. With the use of the OFN model both options are resolved in the same manner, by simple calculation of $X = B - A$, which is presented in the examples on Fig.2 and Fig.3.

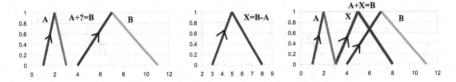

Fig. 2. Equation where B is wider than A

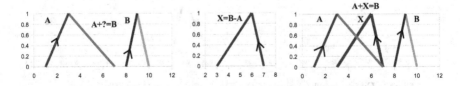

Fig. 3. Equation where A is wider than B

4.2   Distributivity

The following two examples should be considered together. The first one (Fig.4) shows as the result of calculation $A(B - C)$, and the next $AB - AC$ (Fig.5). With the use of OFN model the two results are the same, which corresponds to similar computation on real numbers. However, it would not provide us such results with the use of typical calculations with fuzzy numbers.

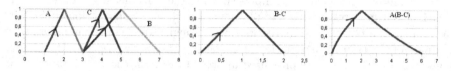

Fig. 4. Result of $A(B - C)$

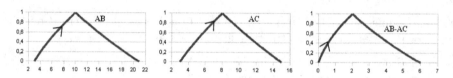

Fig. 5. Result of $AB - AC$ is the same like in Fig.4

4.3   Sum of Fractions

In this example (Fig.6), we see a situation where the sum of fractions $\frac{B}{C} + \frac{(C-B)}{C}$ comes down to the number 1 with the use of real numbers. The same thing also happens when in the same way we operate with OFNs.

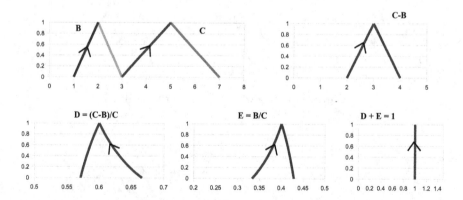

Fig. 6. Example when sum of the OFNs fractions is equal to crisp 1

4.4 Multiplication of Fractions

The next example (Fig.7) shows the calculations $\frac{3A}{2} \cdot \frac{2B}{3A}$ for a situation, in which the actual outcome with real numbers can be achieved by reducing repeated numerators and denominators without any calculations. After investigating the specific actions we can see that by using OFNs we could also simplify the calculations.

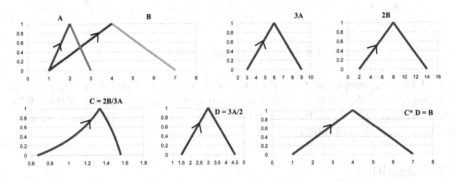

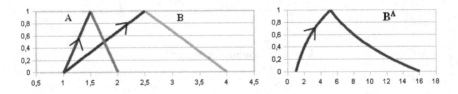

Fig. 7. Result of $\frac{3A}{2} \cdot \frac{2B}{3A}$

4.5 Exponentiation

This example shows (Fig.8) the calculations of exponential function A^B where the base and the exponent is a fuzzy number.

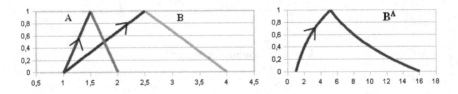

Fig. 8. OFN to the power of OFN

4.6 Exponentiation and Multiplying

The following two examples can be considered together. The first example shows the calculation, in which for the real numbers as a result we get a base of operation raising number to the power $A^{1/4} \cdot A^{3/4}$. As anyone can see on the Fig.9 the same is obtained when A is OFN.

Next example refers to the previous one but here are OFNs in the place of real numbers. Between exponents, there is the following relationship: the first exponent is $\frac{B}{C}$, and the other is $\frac{(C-B)}{C}$. In one of the previous examples (see Fig.6) it has already been shown that their sum is 1 (crisp). Additionally we

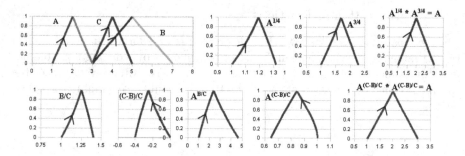

Fig. 9. Multiplying exponents which sum is equal 1

expect that, an every number raised to the power 1 gives in a result the base of exponentiation. We see (Fig.9) that is true also, with multiplication of the OFNs, where we have the same base and the exponents sum to unity, the outcome is the base, as with real numbers.

4.7 Logarithm

Here we have two examples also. First example (Fig.10) shows calculations on OFNs with the use of logarithmic function. In the next example we see (Fig.11) a series of transformations that for real numbers should generate an outcome which equals number A. The same thing is obtained when we use the OFN model.

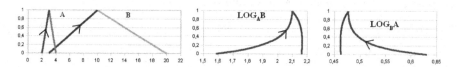

Fig. 10. Example of logarithm

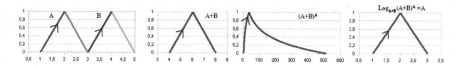

Fig. 11. Properties of logarithm preserved with OFNs

4.8 Comments for Examples

It is worth noting that the presentation of these few examples does not intend to prove mathematical relationships between calculations on OFN model and calculations on real numbers. The purpose of these examples is to show OFNs computational mechanisms and the fact that the outcomes are also fuzzy numbers, which can be interpreted as imprecise data.

However, when it comes to the accordance of the operations in OFN model with the ones on real numbers, it is a consequence of the definition of mathematical operations. Such results can be achieved because when introducing a new model, operations on fuzzy numbers were moved directly to operations on real numbers. After a closer investigation of the definitions (Def.2 and Def.3) it can be noted that the operations on the parts of OFN are executed through operations on functions representing these parts. The operations on the functions are, in turn, operations on their values. Thus, if the space of function value is the space of real numbers (as with all OFNs), then, in fact, operations on functions are carried out through operations on those numbers.

4.9   Improper OFNs

It is worth noting that the objects as shown in the figure (Fig.12) are also consistent with the definition of OFN. As one can see, their shape can not be defined as a function. They are called improper OFNs. In case when there is a need to read the membership values in the form of classical fuzzy number, one can use the definition of membership function for OFNs (see [22]), which indicates a clear solution for such structures. Here it should be also noted that despite the unusual (as for fuzzy numbers) shape, such OFNs still contain important information needed for the calculations. Moreover, according to the interpretation proposed in [22], this information may have a broader meaning depending on the context of carried out operations.

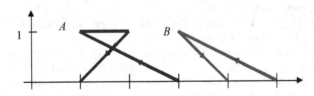

Fig. 12. Examples of results

5   Summary

OFNs constitute an important step in the development of calculation apparatus for uncertain or imprecise data. The new model is a tool allowing to transfer calculation characteristics from real numbers to fuzzy numbers, without defining separate follow-up actions, which are not in real numbers set, and avoiding the continuous expansion of the support with subsequent arithmetic operations.

Presented examples demonstrate the easiness and flexibility of calculations that can be applied to imprecise data processing. Although we operate on objects representing fuzzy numbers, we obtain the same relationships between the calculations and the outcomes of operations as with real numbers.

Such calculation properties allow taking the next step in processing imprecise values. With the use of OFNs we can transfer known mathematical models created for describing the world with the help of precise figures under the circumstances when we have data available only in the form of fuzzy numbers. Calculations of such relationships, apart from introducing a new model do not require further actions to improve the outcomes or to define new actions.

To sum up, it can be stated that by using the OFN model in terms of calculations we bring together possibilities of processing precise and imprecise data.

References

1. Zadeh, L.A.: Fuzzy sets. Information and Control 8, 338–353 (1965)
2. Zadeh, L.A.: The concept of a linguistic variable and its application to approximate reasoning, Part I, II, III. Information Sciences 8, 199–249 (1975)
3. Dubois, D., Prade, H.: Operations on fuzzy numbers. Int. J. System Science 9(6), 613–626 (1978)
4. Nguyen, H.T.: A note on the extension principle for fuzzy sets. J. Math. Anal. Appl. 64, 369–380 (1978)
5. Kaucher, E.: Interval analysis in the extended interval space IR. Computing, Suppl. 2, 33–49 (1980)
6. Sanchez, E.: Solutions of fuzzy equations with extended operations. Fuzzy Sets and Systems 12, 237–248 (1984)
7. Klir, G.J.: Fuzzy arithmetic with requisite constraints. Fuzzy Sets and Systems 91(2), 165–175 (1997)
8. Wagenknecht, M.: On the approximate treatment of fuzzy arithmetics by inclusion, linear regression and information content estimation. In: Chojcan, J., Łęski, J. (eds.) Fuzzy Sets and their Applications, pp. 291–310. Wydawnictwo Politechniki Śląskiej, Gliwice (2001) (in Polish)
9. Guanrong, C., Tat, P.T.: Fuzzy Sets, Fuzzy Logic, and Fuzzy Control Systems. CRS Press, Boca Raton (2001)
10. Drewniak, J.: Fuzzy numbers. In: Chojcan, J., Łęski, J. (eds.) Fuzzy Sets and their Applications, pp. 103–129. WPŚ, Gliwice (2001) (in Polish)
11. Wagenknecht, M., Hampel, R., Schneider, V.: Computational aspects of fuzzy arithmetic based on archimedean t-norms. Fuzzy Sets and Systems 123(1), 49–62 (2001)
12. Kosiński, W., Prokopowicz, P., Ślęzak, D.: Ordered fuzzy number. Bulletin of the Polish Academy of Sciences, Ser. Sci. Math. 51(3), 327–338 (2003)
13. Kosiński, W., Prokopowicz, P., Ślęzak, D.: On algebraic operations on fuzzy numbers. In: Kłopotek, M., Wierzchoń, S.T., Trojanowski, K. (eds.) Intelligent Information Processing and Web Mining, Proc. of Int. IIS: IIPWM 2003, Conference held in Zakopane, Poland, June 2-5, pp. 353–362. Physica-Verlag (2003)
14. Kosiński, W., Prokopowicz, P., Ślęzak, D.: Calculus with fuzzy numbers. In: Bolc, L., Michalewicz, Z., Nishida, T. (eds.) IMTCI 2004. LNCS (LNAI), vol. 3490, pp. 21–28. Springer, Heidelberg (2005)
15. Kosiński, W.: On defuzzyfication of ordered fuzzy numbers. In: Rutkowski, L., Siekmann, J.H., Tadeusiewicz, R., Zadeh, L.A. (eds.) ICAISC 2004. LNCS (LNAI), vol. 3070, pp. 326–331. Springer, Heidelberg (2004)
16. Koleśnik, R., Prokopowicz, P., Kosiński, W.: Fuzzy Calculator – usefull tool for programming with fuzzy algebra. In: Rutkowski, L., Siekmann, J.H., Tadeusiewicz, R., Zadeh, L.A. (eds.) ICAISC 2004. LNCS (LNAI), vol. 3070, pp. 320–325. Springer, Heidelberg (2004)

17. Buckley James, J., Eslami, E.: An Introduction to Fuzzy Logic and Fuzzy Sets. Physica-Verlag, A Springer-Verlag Company, Heidelberg (2005)
18. Prokopowicz, P.: Methods based on the ordered fuzzy numbers used in fuzzy control. In: Proc. of the Fifth International Workshop on Robot Motion and Control, RoMoCo 2005, Dymaczewo, Poland, pp. 349–354 (June 2005)
19. Prokopowicz, P.: Using Ordered Fuzzy Numbers Arithmetic in Fuzzy Control. In: Cader, A., Rutkowski, L., Tadeusiewicz, R., Zurada, J.M. (eds.) Proc. of the 8th International Conference on Artificial Intelligence and Soft Computing, Zakopane, Poland, pp. 156–162. Academic Publishing House EXIT, Warsaw (2006)
20. Prokopowicz, P.: Adaptation of Rules in the Fuzzy Control System Using the Arithmetic of Ordered Fuzzy Numbers. In: Rutkowski, L., Tadeusiewicz, R., Zadeh, L.A., Zurada, J.M. (eds.) ICAISC 2008. LNCS (LNAI), vol. 5097, pp. 306–316. Springer, Heidelberg (2008)
21. Kosiński, W., Prokopowicz, P.: Fuzziness - Representation of Dynamic Changes, Using Ordered Fuzzy Numbers Arithmetic, New Dimensions in Fuzzy Logic and Related Technologies. In: Stepnicka, M., Novak, V., Bodenhofer, U. (eds.) Proc. of the 5th EUSFLAT Conference, Ostrava, Czech Republic, September 11-14, vol. I, pp. 449–456. University of Ostrava (2007)
22. Kosiński, W., Prokopowicz, P., Kacprzak, D.: Fuzziness – representation of dynamic changes by ordered fuzzy numbers. In: Seising, R. (ed.) Views on Fuzzy Sets and Systems. STUDFUZZ, vol. 243, pp. 485–508. Springer, Heidelberg (2009)
23. Kosiński, W., Wilczyńska-Sztyma, D.: Defuzzification and implication within ordered fuzzy numbers. In: WCCI 2010 IEEE World Congress on Computational Intelligence, July 18-23, pp. 1073–1079. CCIB, Barcelona (2010)

The Use of Fuzzy Numbers in the Process of Designing Relational Fuzzy Cognitive Maps

Grzegorz Słoń

Kielce University of Technology,
al. Tysiąclecia P. P. 7, 25-314 Kielce, Poland
g.slon@tu.kielce.pl

Abstract. The paper presents a certain approach to the design and operation of fuzzy cognitive maps (FCM) of a new type, which is specified by the name of Relational Fuzzy Cognitive Map (RFCM). This approach is based on the introduction into the model a description, which is based on fuzzy numbers and fuzzy relations, so you can avoid some of the problems related to the designing (especially learning) classical structures of FCMs. Properties of fuzzy numbers arithmetic cause that the learning process as well as the subsequent operation of such a model run differently than in classical models known from the literature. There are conceptual and technical difficulties connected with this issue, but that can be overcome with the use of the methods described in the work. The proposed approach provides a complete fuzziness of all parameters at every stage of designing the model.

Keywords: fuzzy relations, fuzzy numbers, fuzzy numbers arithmetic, relational fuzzy cognitive map, intelligent modeling.

1 Introduction

The idea of Fuzzy Cognitive Map (FCM) was introduced in 1986 [4] with regard to the model, which used a descriptive approach to fuzzy logic [14]. In later years, as the appearance of subsequent modifications of this approach (eg [6]) new methods of learning have been developed and FCMs have been implemented to further areas [1,2,10,12,13]. Today it is one of the important branches of computational intelligence, which is applicable to the classification, prediction, and monitoring of complex systems with incomplete or imprecise information. It is particularly useful in the analysis of the impact of selected parameter on the other parameters of the system. Incompleteness of information may result from the high complexity of the analyzed system, or from the lack of knowledge about its structure (which makes it difficult to build a classical mathematical model based on systems of differential equations). Imprecision is defined as the use of the description or the use of subjective, linguistic measures, which may be offset by the introduction of fuzzy techniques. The basis of work of most modern applications of FCMs was construction based on sets of decision rules such as:

$$IF \ (X_1 = LV_1)AND(X_2 = LV_2)AND \ ... \ (X_n = LV_n) \ THEN \ X_j = LV_j \quad (1)$$

L. Rutkowski et al. (Eds.): ICAISC 2013, Part I, LNAI 7894, pp. 376–387, 2013.

where: LV – one of linguistic values used in the model of FCM.

Rule-based method for the construction of the FCM, the principle of which is shown by (1), is effective, but its use is associated with a number of practical problems. First, a set of rules, in principle, must be created by an expert, what makes it difficult to fully automate the design process. Secondly, the FCM learning is a difficult process because it also should be based on the constructions of the $IF - THEN$ type. In most modern learning methods for FCM various "subterfuges" are applied to replace fuzzy linguistic values with their numerical equivalents, allowing you to convert a rule-based structure (1) on a set of algebraic equations, but such ways legitimize a departure from primary advantages of fuzzy logic, which is the mapping of concept values using string variables expressing imprecision. Thirdly, the modification of FCM model (1) is difficult because of the assumption implies the need to modify all the rules, which implies the re-engagement of experts to develop actually the entire model from the ground, and this is a time-consuming and prone to errors. In addition, there is also the difficulty of choosing the correct number of linguistic values describing both linguistic concepts and causal connections between them. In fact, the only way is to rely on the opinions of experts, which greatly limits the ability to automate the process of selection of parameters.

The proposed structure of RFCM, in which the basis of the operation is a set of: fuzzy numbers, fuzzy relations and operations of arithmetic on fuzzy numbers and fuzzy relations, allows to obtain the final structure similar, in a sense, to the FCM. The main difference is keeping the fuzzy nature of all elements of the model at each stage of the process of its designing and operation. This is possible by using a special mathematical apparatus that allows to automate the design and learning of the model, so this model is more flexible and easier to practical application. In the RFCM model normalized values of concepts are represented by fuzzy numbers, and causal connections between concepts – by fuzzy relations. Such solutions have not been previously used due to the difficulty of practical application of the mathematical apparatus of fuzzy algebra in discrete environment of computer algorithms. Moreover, there weren't methods of automated design of fuzzy relations with the desired properties. The presented approach includes solutions for both those problems.

2   Basic Operations of Fuzzy Numbers Algebra

Fuzzy number is a fuzzy set with the specified characteristics [3]. Fuzzy arithmetic provides tools [3] to perform algebraic operations (such as addition, subtraction, etc.) on such sets. Thanks to its application one can move away from rule-based principles of creation and work of models of fuzzy cognitive maps and replace them with partially automated approach based on algebraic equations. Analyzed type of the model has a discrete nature (due to computer processing algorithms), and hence the discrete nature of such equations. In described solution three algebraic operations on fuzzy numbers and relations are used: addition and subtraction of fuzzy numbers and fuzzy composition of fuzzy number and fuzzy relation:

– fuzzy addition (operator $\oplus$):

$$\mu_{A \oplus B}(y) = \max_{\substack{y_1, y_2 \\ y = y_1 + y_2}} \min\{\mu_A(y_1), \mu_B(y_2)\} \ , \tag{2}$$

– fuzzy subtraction (operator $\ominus$):

$$\mu_{A \ominus B}(y) = \max_{\substack{y_1, y_2 \\ y = y_1 - y_2}} \min\{\mu_A(y_1), \mu_B(y_2)\} \ , \tag{3}$$

– fuzzy composition (operator $\circ$):

$$\mu_{A \circ R}(y) = \max_{x \in A} \{\min [\mu_A(x), \mu_R(x, y)]\} \ . \tag{4}$$

where: A, B – fuzzy numbers; $\mu_X(y)$ – value of a membership function of the fuzzy number X in point y of the support; R – fuzzy relation; $\mu_R(x, y)$ – value of a membership function of the fuzzy relation R in point (x, y) of the relation base.

Operations (2)-(4) concern the discrete models. Particularly noteworthy is max-min fuzzy composition operation (4). This operation is known in the theory of discrete mathematics, but rather refers to operations on vectors and matrices. It has been adapted to the needs of fuzzy arithmetic in such a way that the input vector is created with the "numerators" of fuzzy singletons describing the fuzzy number A. A natural consequence of this approach is, of course, assumption that the dimension of the matrix describing the fuzzy relation R is the same as cardinality of the support of the fuzzy number A.

3   General Form of Relational Fuzzy Cognitive Map

The general structure of a Relational Fuzzy Cognitive Map (RFCM) is similar to the FCM. It can be presented in the form of a digraph as shown in Fig. 1.

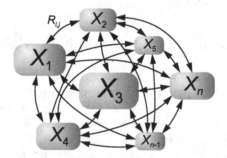

Fig. 1. Graphical representation of RFCM structure. X_1-X_n – fuzzy (normalized) values of concepts; n – number of concepts; $R_{i,j}$ – representation of the set of fuzzy relations between concepts; $i, j = 1, ..., n$.

Occuring in Fig. 1 "Concepts" are selected, key (from the point of view of the modeling purposes) quantities that describe the analyzed system. These can be physical quantities, but they can also be of abstract nature and play a supporting role. In general, input and output concepts are not distinct, though, if the need arises, one can enter such a division.

Such a model can be described by a pair of sets (5):

$$< \mathbf{X}, \mathbf{R} > \tag{5}$$

where: $\mathbf{X} = [X_1, X_2, ..., X_n]^T$ – vector of fuzzyfied values of concepts (in the form of fuzzy numbers); $\mathbf{R} = \{R_{i,j}\}_{i,j=1,...,n}$ – RFCM parameters – matrix of fuzzy relations between concepts ($R_{i,j}$ – fuzzy relation between concepts X_i and X_j).

Mathematical description of work of the model from Fig. 1 lies in calculating the fuzzy values of individual concepts in the subsequent steps of discrete time. Presented model of RFCM has, essentially, dynamic character (due to multi-directional closed-loop feedbacks between concepts) and therefore, though different methods are possible, it looks like the best approach is the one based on taking into account the non-linear rate of change of concept values (6):

$$X_j(t+1) = X_j(t) \oplus \bigoplus_{\substack{i=1 \\ i \neq j}}^{n} [(X_i(t) \ominus X_i(t-1)) \circ R_{i,j}] \tag{6}$$

where: $X_j(t)$ – fuzzy value of analyzed (j-th) concept in step t of discrete time; $R_{i,j}$ – fuzzy relation between concepts i-th and j-th; n – number of concepts; $i, j = 1, ..., n$.

RFCM model described by equation (6) gives the impression of a simple, but the setting of its key elements can present difficulties which make its practical implementation impossible. The rest of the work will be devoted to this very issue.

3.1 Designing Fuzzy Relations

For proper operation of the RFCM model described by equation (6) proper design of the shapes of fuzzy relations between the concepts has crucial meaning. The general form of such a relation between sets A and B is shown in Fig. 2.

As can be seen, each element of such a structure must be separately set to achieve the desired effect. This task would be much easier if one could develop a functional dependence being the basis for the constructing such a relation. It is possible with a comprehensive treatment of methods of fuzzyfication for all quantities in the model – the values of the concepts and relations. The basis of the arithmetic approach to constructing the RFCM is a developed method of creating fuzzy relations on the base of certain general functional form (7):

$$\mu_R(a, b) = f_R\left(\frac{p_1 \cdot b - p_2 \cdot r(a)}{p_3 \cdot \sigma}\right) \tag{7}$$

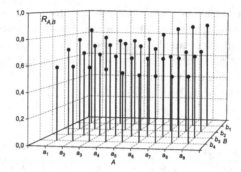

Fig. 2. Graphical representation of fuzzy relation $R_{A,B}$ between two sets: $A = \{a_1, a_2, ..., a_9\}$ and $B = \{b_1, b_2, b_3, b_4\}$ - in the form of points determining levels of the relation.

where: a, b – corresponding points of supports of fuzzy numbers A i B connected with relation R (in RFCM models these supports are identical); f_R – base function dependent on the selected class of the membership function; σ – fuzziness coefficient; $r(a)$ – functional coefficient of power of fuzzy relation R; p_1, p_2, p_3 – coefficients dependent on the selected class of the membership function.

The "class" of a membership function mentioned in (7) should be understood as one of the main types of characteristic functions of a fuzzy set [5,8,9]. Functions of the classes: Λ, Π, π and a Gauss function, hereinafter called a function of class **G**, are best suited for this purpose. The function of class **G** has the advantage of easiness of modification of the fuzziness coefficient. For a single fuzzy relation between concepts i and j it can be written as (8):

$$\mu_{R_{i,j}}(s_i, s_j) = e^{-x^2} \tag{8}$$

where: $x = \frac{s_j - r_{i,j}(s_i)}{\sigma_{i,j}}$; $\mu_{R_{i,j}}$ – membership function of the fuzzy relation $R_{i,j}$ between concepts i and j; s_i, s_j – supports of fuzzy values of concepts i and j; $r_{i,j}(s_i)$ – coefficient of power of fuzzy relation $R_{i,j}$ (in the functional form); $\sigma_{i,j}$ – fuzziness coefficient of fuzzy relation $R_{i,j}$.

It should be stressed that coefficient of power of relation $r_{i,j}(s_i)$ appearing in equation (8) is a function of the support, and the supports are sets of the same k points, that are: $s_i = \{s_{i(1)}, s_{i(2)}, ..., s_{i(k)}\} = s_j = \{s_{j(1)}, s_{j(2)}, ..., s_{j(k)}\}$, where k – number of the uviversum sampling points.

The simplest form of function $r_{i,j}$ is a linear form (9):

$$r_{i,j}(s_i) = \overline{r}_{i,j} \cdot s_i \tag{9}$$

where: $\overline{r}_{i,j}$ – directional coefficient of function of power coefficient of fuzzy relation between concepts i and j.

An exemplary graphical representation of a fuzzy relation with the membership function of class **G**, for which the power coefficient $r_{i,j}$ is defined according to (9) is shown in Fig. 3:

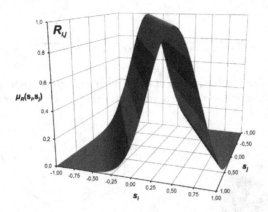

Fig. 3. Graphical representation of fuzzy relation with the membership function of class **G** from (8), in which: $\bar{r}_{i,j} = 0.5$, $\sigma_{i,j} = 0.4$, $k = 41$, fuzzyfied on the support of the range $[-1, 1]$.

Using a similar technique one can create fuzzy relations based on membership functions of other classes, it should be remembered, however, that the change of class of the fuzzy relation will change the result of the max-min composition from equation (4), as shown in Figs. 4 and 5. On the other hand, regardless of the assumed classes (each fuzzy relation can be built based on the membership function of any class), this method of creating fuzzy relations facilitates automation of learning algorithms whose job it is to adapt the model parameters to the needs of the current goal of the modeling.

The above-described approach is comprehensive, i.e. it must include not only the creation of fuzzy relations, but also an adequate method of fuzzyfication of values of concepts and proper selection of the other parameters of the model.

3.2 Fuzzyfication of Values of Concepts

The values of concepts are, in general, fuzzyfied with known methods which use membership functions, however, as fuzzy numbers, used to describe the concepts, are fuzzy sets of a certain specificity [5], can use for this purpose only the membership functions of the classes: **G**, **Λ** or **π**. Class **G**, as described by the smallest number of parameters, seems to be the most convenient for the purposes of the automation of the design process (the membership function of fuzzy number A in Fig. 4 is of class **G**). Due to the discrete nature of computer processing, the value of the concepts are presented as sets of fuzzy singletons whose membership

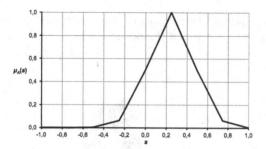

Fig. 4. Exemplary fuzzy value of concept A – membership function of class **G**, center $\overline{A} = 0.25$, fuzziness coefficient $\sigma_A = 0.3$, support range $[-1, 1]$, number of the universum sampling points $k = 9$.

a)

b)

c)

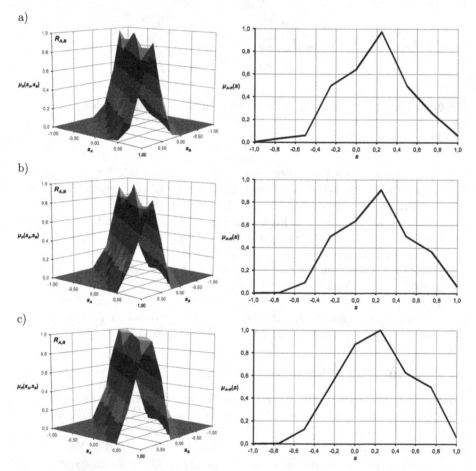

Fig. 5. Results of max-min fuzzy composition of fuzzy number A from Fig. 4 with fuzzy relations characterized by the same power coefficients ($\overline{r} = 0.8$ and comparable dispersions for different types of the membership functions. a) relation of type **G**, b) relation of type **Λ**, c) relation of type **Π**.

levels are determined on the basis of appropriate membership function of, for example, class **G** – such as (10):

$$\mu_{X_i}(s) = e^{-\left(\frac{s-\overline{X}_i}{\sigma_i}\right)^2} \tag{10}$$

where: X_i – fuzzy value of the i-th concept; s – the support; $\overline{X}_i$ – the center (normalized real value) of the i-th concept; σ_i – fuzziness coefficient of the i-th concept; $i = 1, ..., n$; n – number of concepts.

The graphical representation of the concept value fuzzyfied according to (10) is presented in Fig. 6.

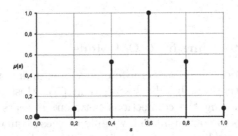

Fig. 6. The graphical representation of fuzzy value of a concept with the membership function of class **G**, where: $\overline{X} = 0.6$; $\sigma = 0.25$; $k = 6$; the support of the range $[0, 1]$.

The points marked in Fig. 6 illustrate consecutive fuzzy singletons of fuzzy number that represent fuzzy value X of a certain concept, where, on the support $[0, 1]$, 6 consecutive sampling points were evenly placed.

3.3 The Support Parameters

As mentioned earlier, the model structure must be created comprehensively. This applies mainly to the support parameters which must be common to all the concepts and fuzzy relations. This is due to the specific nature of fuzzy arithmetic operations, described by equations (2)-(4). From the general assumptions of the RFCM model, that the cores (centers) of fuzzy numbers describing concepts need to be in the range $[-1, 1]$, but the use of such a range of the support would be insufficient. The method of defuzzyfication of fuzzy numbers based on weighted average, that is proposed for use in the model, is sensitive to asymmetry of the fuzzy number relative to its center. Such asymmetry (and hence - defuzzyfication error) increases as the center moves toward the limit of the support range. The support should therefore be wide enough to membership levels of fuzzy singletons of concept values were at the edge of a low enough so as not to have a major impact on the outcome of defuzzyfication. On the other hand, although there are other methods, defuzzyfication by the weighted average method has certain advantages connected with representing the physical properties of the fuzzy number and it is convenient to use this method. Of course, the support can not be expanded freely, because increasing the span will lengthen the time of calculation. The experiments have shown that the support range $[-2, 2]$ is sufficient. Number of the support sampling points k is equivalent to the number of linguistic values used for the description of all fuzzy quantities in the model. It must be constant and the same for all quantities. The choice of k value is an important issue because its increase improves the accuracy of the model but increases the calculation time.It is therefore advantageous use of a low value of k, however, it is related to the deterioration of the model accuracy. Basically, the parameters of initially created model must be undergone an additional adaptation in order to increase the accuracy. This is done by the way of supervised learning.

3.4   Supervised Learning in RFCM Model

For classic construction of FCM there were developed many, mainly supervised learning methods (they are briefly described in [7]). Most of them employ a simplified model showing the connections between concepts in the form of a matrix of real numbers containing the weights of these connections. Then, the learning mechanism modifies the weights in order to help the selected concepts to achieve assumed values. Such an approach is not feasible in RRMK model, in which each causal connection between concepts is represented by a discrete fuzzy relation built on the basis of more than one parameter (from at least 2 (for membership function type $\mathbf{G}$) to at least 4 (for membership function type π)). The general idea is similar, i.e. it is based on the analysis of a certain criterion – the closeness coefficient, which may take the form of (11):

$$J(Q) = \Phi\left(\|\overline{X}_i(t) - Z_i(t)\|\right) \Rightarrow \min_Q \tag{11}$$

where: $\Phi()$ – selected optimization function (e.g. square); $\overline{X}_i(t)$, $Z_i(t)$ – defuzzyfied and crisp (given) trajectories of changes of value of the i-th concept; $\| \ \|$ – selected norm; t - discrete time.

Quantity Q, that appears in (11), is a vector of the changed parameters dependent on the assumed method of creating the fuzzy relations. For the relation of type $\mathbf{G}$ it can take the form (12):

$$Q = [\{\overline{r}_{i,j}\}, \{\sigma_{i,j}\}, k]^T \tag{12}$$

where: k – number of the support sampling points; $\{\overline{r}_{i,j}\}$ – directional coefficients of functional power coefficients of fuzzy relations $R_{i,j}$; $\{\sigma_{i,j}\}$ - fuzziness coefficients of fuzzy relations $R_{i,j}$; $i, j = 1, ..., n$; n – number of concepts in the model.

For the purposes of the RFCM learning there was developed algorithm of successive approximations with variable step of changes of the parameters that can be included into the group of population methods. Generally speaking, his work lies in making successive small changes in selected elements of vector Q with simultaneous tracking the criterion (11). Its formal form is shown in equation (13):

$$R_{i,j}(t+1) = R_{i,j}(t) \oplus \Delta R_{i,j}(t) \tag{13}$$

where: $\Delta R_{i,j}(t)$ – "increment" of fuzzy relation $R_{i,j}$; $R_{i,j}(0)$ – fuzzy relation with initial values of parameters.

Due to the volume limitations, this paper doesn't contain closer description of the learning algorithm. More details were presented in [11].

4   Exemplary Model of RFCM

The study involved a hypothetical system consisting of four concepts. In this system, the concept no 1 was stimulated with a signal of a value of 0.5, which caused a change in the values of all the concepts. Obtained in this way normalized reference waveforms are shown in Fig. 7.

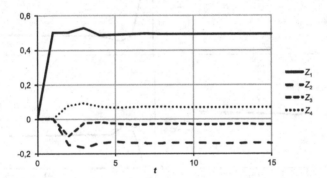

Fig. 7. Reference courses of the analyzed system. Z_1-Z_4 – normalized values of concepts.

Then the initial RFCM structure was designed, in which all fuzzy relations are of class **G** and have a common initial values of parameters: $\bar{r}_{i,j} = 0$, $\sigma_{i,j} = 0.4$. There was assumed the support with the range $[-2, 2]$, $k = 17$ and, for simplicity, there were assumed common parameters for fuzzyfying the concepts: class of the membership function **G** and fuzziness coefficient $\sigma_I = 0.6$. Such prepared model was subjected to a process of learning using algorithm of successive approximations with a variable step of parameter changes - basing on the reference waveforms, using function in the form of (14) as a learning criterion in accordance with (11).

$$J(Q) = \sqrt{\frac{1}{n}\sum_{i=1}^{n}\frac{1}{T}\sum_{t=1}^{T}\left(\overline{X}_i(t) - Z_i(t)\right)^2} \tag{14}$$

where: T – the total number of discrete time t steps taken into account; n – number of concepts.

The result is the model with the parameters presented in Tab. 1.

Table 1. Final results of the RFCM learning process

$\bar{r}$	X_1	X_2	X_3	X_4	σ	X_1	X_2	X_3	X_4
X_1	0.00	-0.31	-0.17	0.13	X_1	0.40	0.36	0.32	0.38
X_2	0.08	0.00	-0.19	0.03	X_2	0.43	0.40	0.35	0.40
X_3	-0.12	0.16	0.00	-0.20	X_3	0.43	0.53	0.40	0.60
X_4	0.15	-0.06	0.16	0.00	X_4	0.45	0.64	0.40	0.40

The model, obtained in the way of the learning process, was stimulated with the use of the same set of signals as the reference system. The resulting waveforms, together with waveforms of reference, are shown in Fig. 8.

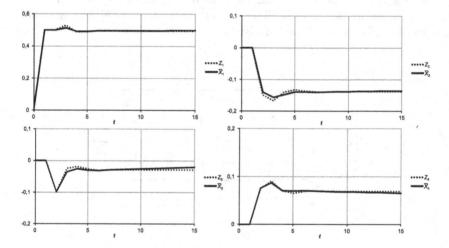

Fig. 8. Courses obtained by the RFCM model in comparison with adequate reference courses. Z_1-Z_4 – reference values; $\overline{X}_1$-$\overline{X}_4$ – RFCM values (after defuzzyfication).

5   Conclusion

The use of fuzzy numbers arithmetic to the design and operation of Relational Fuzzy Cognitive Map allows creating the effectively working models of complex systems characterized by a high degree of uncertainty or imprecision, especially systems with dynamic internal structure. Its use enables the construction of a fully automated algorithms of designing (especially in terms of learning) the fuzzy structure of the model. Such an approach, however, requires the use of new methods to design fuzzy relations between fuzzy concepts. A study of selected classes of membership functions showed high efficiency of presented method. Work is currently underway on improving the methods of adaptation of fuzzy relations.

References

1. Carvalho, J.P., Tomé, J.A.: Rule-based fuzzy cognitive maps - Expressing Time in Qualitative System Dynamics. In: Proc. of the FUZZ-IEEE 2001, Melbourne, Australia, pp. 280–283 (2001)
2. Dickerson, J.A., Kosko, B.: Virtual worlds as fuzzy cognitive maps. Presence 3(2), 173–189 (1994)
3. Kosiński, W., Prokopowicz, P., Ślęzak, D.: On algebraic operations on fuzzy numbers. In: Kłopotek, M., et al. (eds.) Intelligent Information Processing and Web Mining, pp. 353–362. Physica Verlag, Heidelberg (2003)
4. Kosko, B.: Fuzzy cognitive maps. Int. Journal of Man-Machine Studies 24, 65–75 (1986)
5. Łachwa, A.: Fuzzy world of sets, numbers, relations, facts, rules and decisions. Akademicka Oficyna Wydawnicza EXIT, Warsaw (2001) (in Polish)
6. Mamdani, E.H.: Application of fuzzy algorithms for the control of a simple dynamic plant. IEE Proceedings 121(12), 1585–1588 (1974)
7. Papageorgiou, E.I.: Learning Algorithms for Fuzzy Cognitive Maps - A Review Study. IEEE Transactions on Systems, Man and Cybernetics, Part C: Applications and Reviews 42(2), 150–163 (2012)
8. Rutkowska, D., Piliński, M., Rutkowski, L.: Neural networks, genetic algorithms and fuzzy systems. PWN, Warsaw (1997) (in Polish)
9. Rutkowski, L.: Methods and techniques of artificial intelligence. PWN, Warszaw (2005) (in Polish)
10. Siraj, A., Bridges, S.M., Vaughn, R.B.: Fuzzy Cognitive Maps for Decision Support in an Intelligent Intrusion Detection System. In: IFSA World Congress and 20th NAFIPS International Conference, Vancouver, Canada, pp. 2165–2170 (2001)
11. Słoń, G., Yastrebov, A.: Optimization and Adaptation of Dynamic Models of Fuzzy Relational Cognitive Maps. In: Kuznetsov, S.O., Ślęzak, D., Hepting, D.H., Mirkin, B.G. (eds.) RSFDGrC 2011. LNCS (LNAI), vol. 6743, pp. 95–102. Springer, Heidelberg (2011)
12. Stylios, C.D., Georgopoulos, V.C., Groumpos, P.P.: The Use of Fuzzy Cognitive Maps in Modeling Systems. In: Proc. of 5th IEEE Mediterranean Conference on Control and Systems, Paphos, Paper No. 67 (1997)
13. Stylios, C.D., Groumpos, P.P.: Fuzzy cognitive maps in modeling supervisory control systems. Journal of Intelligent & Fuzzy Systems 8(2), 83–98 (2000)
14. Takagi, H., Sugeno, M.: Fuzzy Identification of Systems and Its Application to Modeling and Control. IEEE Transactions on Systems, Man and Cybernetics SMC-15(1), 116–132 (1985)

Metasets, Intuitionistic Fuzzy Sets and Uncertainty

Bartłomiej Starosta and Witold Kosiński

Polish-Japanese Institute of Information Technology,
ul. Koszykowa 86,
02-008 Warsaw, Poland
{barstar,wkos}@pjwstk.edu.pl

Abstract. Metaset is a new concept of set with partial membership relation. It is directed towards computer implementations and applications. The degrees of membership for metasets are expressed as binary sequences and they may be evaluated as real numbers too.

The forcing mechanism discussed in this paper is used to assign certainty values to sentences involving metasets. It turns out, that for a sentence involving finite first order metasets only its certainty value complements the certainty value of its negation. This is not true in general: sentences expressing properties of metasets may have positive uncertainty value. We supply an example of a sentence which is totally uncertain.

Keywords: metaset, partial membership, classical set theory, intuitionistic fuzzy set.

1 Introduction

Metaset is a new concept of set with partial membership relation [6]. It is based on the classical set theory [3], [4] and it is directed towards computer implementations. Its scope of practical applications [5] are similar to intuitionistic fuzzy sets [1].

In this paper we investigate certainty values of sentences expressing facts concerning metasets. In particular we focus on their significant feature which is the capability of expressing uncertainty. We present the example of the sentence whose certainty value and the certainty value of its negation are equal 0. The uncertainty value of such sentence is equal 1. We then show that for sentences involving finite first order metasets only, the certainty value complements the certainty value of its negation, i.e., they sum up to unity – the truth value. This means that such sentences admit no uncertainty.

The capability of expressing uncertainty allows for representing intuitionistic fuzzy sets [1] by metasets [7]. By the main result of this paper – which says that the uncertainty value vanishes for finite first order metasets – we claim that we cannot directly represent arbitrary intuitionistic fuzzy sets by metasets in computers, i.e., using finite metasets. However, we can represent [8] finite fuzzy sets [11].

L. Rutkowski et al. (Eds.): ICAISC 2013, Part I, LNAI 7894, pp. 388–399, 2013.

2 Metasets

Informally, a metaset is a set whose elements have associated degrees of membership. We formalize this idea by means of ordered pairs. Each member of a metaset – viewed as a classical set – is encapsulated in an ordered pair. The first element of the pair is the member and the second element is a node of the binary tree, which specifies its degree of membership. For simplicity, we present results for first order metasets here. A generalization is outlined in the section 6.

Definition 1. *A set which is either the empty set $\emptyset$ or which has the form:*

$$\tau = \{\, \langle \sigma, p \rangle : \sigma \text{ is a set}, \ p \in \mathbb{T} \,\}$$

is called a first order metaset (fo-metaset).

The binary tree $\mathbb{T}$ is the set of all finite binary sequences, i.e., functions whose domains are finite ordinals, valued in 2:[1]

$$\mathbb{T} = \bigcup_{n \in \mathbb{N}} 2^n \,. \tag{1}$$

We define the ordering $\leq$ in the tree $\mathbb{T}$ to be the reverse inclusion of functions seen as sets. Thus, for $p, q \in \mathbb{T}$ such, that $p \colon n \mapsto 2$ and $q \colon m \mapsto 2$, we have $p \leq q$ whenever $p \supseteq q$, i.e., $n \geq m$ and $p_{\restriction m} = q$. The root $\mathbb{1}$ is the largest element of $\mathbb{T}$ in this ordering: it is included in each function and for all $p \in \mathbb{T}$ we have $p \leq \mathbb{1}$.

A *level* in $\mathbb{T}$ is the set of all sequences with the same length. Each level has a number. The level with the number n is the set 2^n. The level 0 consists of the empty sequence $\mathbb{1}$ only.

A *branch* in $\mathbb{T}$ is an infinite binary sequence, i.e., a function $\mathbb{N} \mapsto 2$. A branch intersects all levels in $\mathbb{T}$, and each of them only once.

Nodes of the tree $\mathbb{T}$ are sometimes called *conditions*. If $p \leq q \in \mathbb{T}$, then we say that the condition p is *stronger* than the condition q, and q is *weaker* than p. A stronger condition is meant to designate a stipulation which is harder to satisfy than the one described by a weaker condition. For instance, "very cold" and "slightly cold" are stronger conditions than just "cold", since they carry more information concerning the temperature.

The class of first order metasets is denoted by $\mathfrak{M}^1$. The first element σ of an ordered pair $\langle \sigma, p \rangle$ contained in a fo-metaset τ is called a *potential element* of τ, since it is a member of τ to a degree p which usually is less than certainty. A potential element may be simultaneously paired with multiple different conditions which taken together comprise its membership degree in the fo-metaset. From the point of view of the set theory a fo-metaset is a relation between a crisp set and a set of nodes of the binary tree. Therefore, we adopt the following terms and notation concerning relations. For the given metaset τ, the set of its potential elements:

$$\mathrm{dom}(\tau) = \{\, \sigma : \exists_{p \in \mathbb{T}} \ \langle \sigma, p \rangle \in \tau \,\} \tag{2}$$

---

[1] For $n \in \mathbb{N}$, let $2^n = \{\, f \colon n \mapsto 2 \,\}$ denote the set of all functions with the domain n and the range $2 = \{\, 0, 1 \,\}$ – they are binary sequences of the length n.

is called the *domain* of the metaset τ, and the set:

$$\mathrm{ran}(\tau) = \{\, p\colon \exists_{\sigma \in \mathrm{dom}(\tau)}\ \langle \sigma, p \rangle \in \tau \,\} \tag{3}$$

is called the *range* of the metaset τ.

The class of finite first ordered metasets is denoted by $\mathfrak{MF}^1$. Metasets in this class are particularly important for computer applications, where representable entities are naturally finite. Thus,

$$\tau \in \mathfrak{MF}^1 \quad \text{iff} \quad |\mathrm{dom}(\tau)| < \aleph_0 \wedge |\mathrm{ran}(\tau)| < \aleph_0 . \tag{4}$$

3   Interpretations

An interpretation of a first order metaset is a crisp set extracted out of the metaset by means of a branch in the binary tree. For the given fo-metaset, each branch in $\mathbb{T}$ determines a different interpretation. All the interpretations taken together make up a collection of sets with specific internal dependencies, which represents the fo-metaset by means of its crisp views. In practical applications these particular views are treated as various experts' opinions on some vague term represented by the fo-metaset.

Properties of crisp sets which are interpretations of the given first order metaset determine the properties of the fo-metaset itself. We use the forcing mechanism (sec. 4) for transferring relationships between sets which are interpretations onto the fo-metaset. A good example is the definition of the membership relation which relies on membership among interpretations (sec. 4.2).

Definition 2. *Let τ be a first order metaset and let $\mathcal{C} \subset \mathbb{T}$ be a branch. The set*

$$\tau_\mathcal{C} = \{\, \sigma \in \mathrm{dom}(\tau)\colon \langle \sigma, p \rangle \in \tau \wedge p \in \mathcal{C} \,\}$$

is called the interpretation of the first order metaset τ given by the branch $\mathcal{C}$.

Any interpretation of the empty fo-metaset is the empty set, independently of the branch. The process of producing the interpretation of a fo-metaset consists in two stages. In the first stage we remove all the ordered pairs whose second elements are conditions which do not belong to the branch $\mathcal{C}$. The second stage replaces the remaining pairs – whose second elements lie on the branch $\mathcal{C}$ – with their first elements. As the result we obtain a crisp set.

A fo-metaset may have multiple different interpretations – each branch in the tree determines one. Usually, many of them are pairwise equal, so the number of different interpretations is much less than the number of branches. Finite fo-metasets always have a finite number of different interpretations. There are metasets whose interpretations are all equal, even when they are not finite.

In this paper we deal with finite first order metasets. For such metasets we consider the greatest level number of the level whose conditions may affect interpretations.

Definition 3. *The deciding level for a finite first order metaset τ, denoted by $\mathfrak{l}_\tau$, is the greatest level number of conditions in* $\operatorname{ran}(\tau)$:

$$\mathfrak{l}_\tau = \max\{\,|p|: p \in \operatorname{ran}(\tau)\,\} \ .$$

If $\tau = \emptyset$, then we take $\mathfrak{l}_\tau = 0$.

Since $p \in \mathbb{T}$ is a function, then $|p|$ is its cardinality – the number of ordered pairs which is just the length of the binary sequence p. It is also equal to the level number to which it belongs. Thus, $\mathfrak{l}_\tau$ is the length of the longest sequence in $\operatorname{ran}(\tau)$. Conditions on levels below $\mathfrak{l}_\tau$ do not affect interpretations of τ.

Lemma 1. *Let τ be a finite first order metaset and let $\mathcal{C}'$ and $\mathcal{C}''$ be branches. If initial segments of size $\mathfrak{l}_\tau$ of $\mathcal{C}'$ and $\mathcal{C}''$ are equal:*

$$\forall_{n \leq \mathfrak{l}_\tau} \mathcal{C}'(n) = \mathcal{C}''(n) \ ,$$

then $\tau_{\mathcal{C}'} = \tau_{\mathcal{C}''}$.

Proof. Since there are no conditions on levels below $\mathfrak{l}_\tau$ in $\operatorname{ran}(\tau)$, and by the assumption, we obtain $\{\,\langle \sigma, p \rangle \in \tau: p \in \mathcal{C}'\,\} = \{\,\langle \sigma, p \rangle \in \tau: p \in \mathcal{C}''\,\}$. Therefore, $\tau_{\mathcal{C}'} = \{\,\sigma: \langle \sigma, p \rangle \in \tau \wedge p \in \mathcal{C}'\,\} = \{\,\sigma: \langle \sigma, p \rangle \in \tau \wedge p \in \mathcal{C}''\,\} = \tau_{\mathcal{C}''}$.

4   Forcing

In this section we define and investigate a relation between a condition and a sentence. This relation, called *forcing* relation [2], is designed to describe the level of confidence or certainty assigned to the sentence. The level is evaluated by means of nodes of $\mathbb{T}$. The root condition $\mathbb{1}$ specifies the absolute certainty, whereas its descendants represent less certain degrees. The sentences are classical set theory formulas, where free variables are substituted by fo-metasets and bound variables range over the class of first order metasets.

Given a branch $\mathcal{C}$, we may substitute particular fo-metasets in the sentence $\sigma \in \tau$ with their interpretations which are ordinary crisp sets, e.g.: $\sigma_{\mathcal{C}} \in \tau_{\mathcal{C}}$. The resulting sentence is a set-theory sentence expressing some property of the sets $\tau_{\mathcal{C}}$ and $\sigma_{\mathcal{C}}$, the membership relation in this case. Such sentence may be either true or false, depending on $\tau_{\mathcal{C}}$ and $\sigma_{\mathcal{C}}$.

For the given fo-metaset τ each condition $p \in \mathbb{T}$ specifies a family of interpretations of τ: they are determined by all the branches $\mathcal{C}$ containing this particular condition p. If for each such branch the resulting sentence – after substituting fo-metasets with their interpretations – has the same logical value, then we may think of conditional truth or falsity of the given sentence, which is qualified by the condition p. Therefore, we may consider p as the certainty degree for the sentence.

Let Φ be a formula built using some of the following symbols: variables $(x^1, x^2, \ldots)$, the constant symbol $(\emptyset)$, the relational symbols $(\in, =, \subset)$, logical connectives $(\wedge, \vee, \neg, \rightarrow)$, quantifiers $(\forall, \exists)$ and parentheses. If we substitute each free variable x^i $(i = 1 \ldots n)$ with some metaset ν^i, and restrict the range of each quantifier to the class of first order metasets $\mathfrak{M}^1$, then we get as the result the sentence $\Phi(\nu^1, \ldots, \nu^n)$ of the metaset language, which states some property of the metasets $\nu^1, \ldots, \nu^n$. By the *interpretation* of this sentence, determined by the branch $\mathcal{C}$, we understand the sentence $\Phi(\nu^1_{\mathcal{C}}, \ldots, \nu^n_{\mathcal{C}})$ denoted shortly with $\Phi_{\mathcal{C}}$. The sentence $\Phi_{\mathcal{C}}$ is the result of substituting free variables of the formula Φ with the interpretations $\nu^i_{\mathcal{C}}$ of the metasets ν^i, and restricting the range of bound variables to the class of all sets $\mathbf{V}$. In other words, we replace the metasets in the sentence Φ with their interpretations. The only constant $\emptyset$ in Φ as well as in $\Phi_{\mathcal{C}}$ denotes the empty set which is the same set in both cases: as a crisp set and as a metaset.

Definition 4. *Let $x^1, x^2, \ldots x^n$ be all free variables of the formula Φ and let $\nu^1, \nu^2, \ldots \nu^n$ be first order metasets. We say that the condition $p \in \mathbb{T}$ forces the sentence $\Phi(\nu^1, \nu^2, \ldots \nu^n)$, whenever for each branch $\mathcal{C} \subset \mathbb{T}$ containing the condition p, the sentence $\Phi(\nu^1_{\mathcal{C}}, \nu^2_{\mathcal{C}}, \ldots \nu^n_{\mathcal{C}})$ is true. We denote the forcing relation with the symbol $\Vdash$. Thus,*

$$p \Vdash \Phi(\nu^1, \ldots \nu^n) \quad \text{iff} \quad \text{for each branch } \mathcal{C} \ni p \text{ holds } \Phi(\nu^1_{\mathcal{C}}, \ldots \nu^n_{\mathcal{C}}) \,.$$

We use the abbreviation $p \nVdash \Phi$ for expressing the negation $\neg(p \Vdash \Phi)$. In such case, not for each branch $\mathcal{C}$ containing p the sentence $\Phi_{\mathcal{C}}$ holds, however, such branches may exist. Furthermore, the symbol $\notin$ in the formula $\mu \notin \tau$ will stand for $\neg(\mu \in \tau)$, and similarly, $\mu \neq \tau$ will stand for $\neg(\mu = \tau)$.

The key idea of the forcing relation lies in transferring properties from crisp sets onto fo-metasets. Let a property described by a formula $\Phi(x)$ be satisfied by all crisp sets of the form $\nu_{\mathcal{C}}$, where ν is a metaset and $\mathcal{C}$ is a branch in $\mathbb{T}$. In other words, $\Phi(\nu_{\mathcal{C}})$ holds for all the sets which are interpretations of the metaset ν given by all branches $\mathcal{C}$ in $\mathbb{T}$. Then we might think that this property also "holds" for the metaset ν, and we formulate this fact by saying that $\mathbb{1}$ forces $\Phi(\nu)$. If $\Phi(\nu_{\mathcal{C}})$ holds only for branches $\mathcal{C}$ containing some condition p, then we might think that it "holds to the degree p" for the metaset ν; we say that p forces $\Phi(\nu)$ in such case. Since we try to transfer – or force – satisfiability of some property from crisp sets onto fo-metasets, we call this mechanism *forcing*.[2] The next example shows how to transfer the property of being equal onto two specific fo-metasets.

The following two lemmas expose the most fundamental and significant features of the forcing relation. The first says that forcing is propagated down the branch, i.e., if a condition p forces Φ, then stronger conditions force Φ too. However, weaker conditions do not have to force it. It should be understood that the stronger conditions carry more detailed information above the weaker ones.

Lemma 2. *Let $p, q \in \mathbb{T}$ and let Φ be a sentence. If p forces Φ and q is stronger than p, then q forces Φ too:*

$$p \Vdash \Phi \wedge q \leq p \quad \rightarrow \quad q \Vdash \Phi \,.$$

---

[2] This mechanism is similar to, and in fact was inspired by the method of forcing in the classical set theory [2]. It has not much in common with the original.

Proof. If $q \leq p$, then each branch containing q also contains p. If C is any such branch and $p \Vdash \Phi$, then Φ_C holds. Because it is true for all $C \ni q$, then we have $q \Vdash \Phi$.

A finite maximal antichain of conditions stronger than $p \in \mathbb{T}$ propagates forcing upwards to the condition p. A set $R \subset \mathbb{T}$ is called an antichain when all its members are pairwise incomparable. It is a maximal antichain in $\mathbb{T}$, when each $q \in \mathbb{T}$ is comparable to some element of R. It is a maximal antichain below p, when each $q \leq p$ is comparable to some element of R and all the members of R are stronger than p.

Lemma 3. *Let $p \in \mathbb{T}$, $R \subset \mathbb{T}$ and let Φ be a sentence. If R is a finite maximal antichain below p and each $q \in R$ forces Φ, then p also forces Φ.*

Proof. $p \Vdash \Phi$ whenever for each branch $C \ni p$ holds Φ_C. Since R is a finite maximal antichain whose elements are stronger than p, then each branch containing p must also contain some element $q \in R$. Each such q forces Φ, so for any branch $C \ni p$ we have Φ_C.

4.1   Forcing and Certainty Degrees

If we treat conditions as certainty degrees for sentences, then the stronger condition specifies the degree which is less than the degree specified by the weaker one (assuming the conditions are different). Indeed, by the above lemmas $r \Vdash \Psi$ is equivalent to the conjunction $r \cdot 0 \Vdash \Psi \wedge r \cdot 1 \Vdash \Psi$ (where $r \cdot 0$ and $r \cdot 1$ denote the direct descendants of r) meaning that the certainty degree specified by r is equal to the "sum" of certainty degrees specified by both $r \cdot 0$ and $r \cdot 1$ taken together. But if it happens that $r \cdot 0 \Vdash \Psi$ and $r \cdot 1 \nVdash \Psi$, then also $r \nVdash \Psi$. In such case the $r \cdot 0$ contributes only a half of the certainty degree specified by r – another half of it could be contributed by $r \cdot 1$, but is not in this case. The root $\mathbb{1}$, being the largest element in $\mathbb{T}$, specifies the highest certainty degree. The ordering of certainty degrees is consistent with the ordering of conditions in $\mathbb{T}$. We stress that the term certainty degree is used informally in this paper. We define now other precise terms for measuring the certainty of sentences.

For the given sentence Φ, the following set $\mathcal{T}_\Phi$ is called the *certainty set* for Φ.

$$\mathcal{T}_\Phi = \{ p \in \mathbb{T} : p \Vdash \Phi \} . \tag{5}$$

It contains all the conditions which force the given sentence and it gives a measure of certainty that the sentence is true. Members of this set are called *certainty factors* for Φ. Each certainty factor contributes to the overall degree of certainty that the sentence is true, which is represented by the certainty set.

By the lemma 2, if there exists a $p \in \mathbb{T}$ which forces Φ, then there exist infinitely many other conditions which force Φ too. Among them are all those stronger than p. Therefore, the whole certainty set is equivalent to the set of its maximal elements. Since,

$$p \Vdash \Phi \quad \rightarrow \quad \exists_{q \geq p} \, q \in \max\{\mathcal{T}_\Phi\} \wedge q \Vdash \Phi , \tag{6}$$

then each $p \in \mathcal{T}_\Phi \setminus \max\{\mathcal{T}_\Phi\}$ is redundant. The substantial information concerning the conditions which force Φ is contained in $\max\{\mathcal{T}_\Phi\}$ exclusively. Forcing of Φ by any stronger conditions may be concluded by applying the lemma 2. Thus we come to the following concept of certainty degree for sentences.

Definition 5. *Let Φ be a sentence. The set of maximal elements of the certainty set for Φ:*

$$\|\Phi\| = \max\{p \in \mathbb{T} : p \Vdash \Phi\}$$

is called the certainty grade for Φ. If the certainty set is empty, then the certainty grade is empty too.

When the certainty set is equal to the whole tree $\mathbb{T}$, then the certainty grade is the singleton containing only the root: $\|\Phi\| = \{\mathbb{1}\}$. We may evaluate certainty of sentences numerically too.

Definition 6. *Let Φ be a sentence. The following value is called the certainty value for Φ:*

$$|\Phi| = \sum_{p \in \|\Phi\|} \frac{1}{2^{|p|}} .$$

One may easily see that whenever no p forces Φ, then $|\Phi| = 0$ and if each $p \in \mathbb{T}$ forces Φ, then $|\Phi| = 1$. Therefore, $|\Phi| \in [0,1]$.

4.2   Membership and Non-membership

We do not give thorough presentation of relations for metasets in this paper. For completeness, we supply only the definitions of conditional membership and non-membership. Other relations, like conditional equality and non-equality, are defined similarly – by means of the forcing mechanism.

In fact, we define an infinite number of membership relations. Each of them designates the membership satisfied to some degree specified by a node of the binary tree. Moreover, any two fo-metasets may be simultaneously in multiple membership relations qualified by different conditions.

Definition 7. *We say that the metaset μ belongs to the metaset τ under the condition $p \in \mathbb{T}$, whenever $p \Vdash \mu \in \tau$. We use the notation $\mu \in_p \tau$.*

In other words, $\mu \in_p \tau$ whenever for each branch $\mathcal{C} \subset \mathbb{T}$ containing p holds $\mu_{\mathcal{C}} \in \tau_{\mathcal{C}}$. The conditional membership reflects the idea that a metaset μ belongs to a metaset τ whenever some conditions are fulfilled. The conditions are represented by nodes of $\mathbb{T}$.

Each $p \in \mathbb{T}$ specifies another relation $\in_p$. Different conditions specify membership relations which are satisfied with different certainty factors. The lemmas 2 and 3 prove that the relations are not independent. For instance, $\mu \in_p \tau$ is equivalent to $\mu \in_{p \cdot 0} \tau \wedge \mu \in_{p \cdot 1} \tau$, i.e., being a member under the condition p is equivalent to being a member under both conditions $p \cdot 0$ and $p \cdot 1$ which are the direct descendants of p.

We introduce another set of relations for expressing non-membership. The reason for this is due to the fact that $p \not\Vdash \mu \in \tau$ is not equivalent to $p \Vdash \mu \notin \tau$. Indeed, $p \not\Vdash \mu \in \tau$ means, that it is not true that for each branch $\mathcal{C}$ containing p holds $\mu_\mathcal{C} \in \tau_\mathcal{C}$, however such branches may exist. On the other hand, $p \Vdash \mu \notin \tau$ means that for each $\mathcal{C} \ni p$ holds $\mu_\mathcal{C} \notin \tau_\mathcal{C}$. That is why we need another relation "is not a member under the condition p".

Definition 8. *We say that the metaset μ does not belong to the metaset τ under the condition $p \in \mathbb{T}$, whenever $p \Vdash \mu \notin \tau$. We use the notation $\mu \notin_p \tau$.*

Thus, $\mu \notin_p \tau$, whenever for each branch $\mathcal{C}$ containing p the set $\mu_\mathcal{C}$ is not a member of the set $\tau_\mathcal{C}$. Contrary to the classical case, where a set is either a member of another or it is not at all, for two fo-metasets it is possible that they are simultaneously in different membership and non-membership relations.

For metasets σ, τ, the membership grade of σ in τ is just the certainty grade of the sentence $\sigma \in \tau$, represented by the set $\|\sigma \in \tau\|$. The membership value is $|\sigma \in \tau|$. Similarly, the non-membership grade is $\|\sigma \notin \tau\|$ and non-membership value is $|\sigma \notin \tau|$. The membership and non-membership values, when considered as functions of σ, resemble membership and non-membership functions of an intuitionistic fuzzy set [1]. We now investigate the problem of uncertainty, in particular uncertainty of membership, which is the core of intuitionistic fuzzy set idea.

5   Certainty and Uncertainty

Let $\Phi(x_1, \ldots, x_n)$ be a formula with all free variables shown and let $\mu_1, \ldots, \mu_n$ be finite first order metasets. If we substitute each free variable x_i in the formula Φ with the corresponding metaset μ_i and restrict the range of each quantifier to the class $\mathfrak{MF}^1$ then we call the resulting sentence $\Phi(\mu_1, \ldots, \mu_n)$ a $\mathfrak{MF}^1$-*sentence*.

If a sentence involves metasets which are not finite, then it is possible, that neither the sentence nor its negation is forced by any condition. The following example demonstrates fo-metasets σ, τ such, that both $p \not\Vdash \sigma \in \tau$ and $p \not\Vdash \sigma \notin \tau$, for all $p \in \mathbb{T}$. Of course, each interpretation of the sentence is either true or false.

Example 1. Let $\sigma = \{ \langle n, p \rangle : p \in \mathbb{T} \wedge n = \Sigma_{i \in \text{dom}(p)} \, p(i) \}$, $\tau = \{ \langle \mathbb{N}, \mathbb{1} \rangle \}$. Recall, that conditions are functions $p \colon m \mapsto 2$ with domains in $\mathbb{N}$. Each ordered pair in σ is comprised of an arbitrary condition $p \in \mathbb{T}$ and the natural number $n \in \mathbb{N}$, which is equal to the number of occurrences of 1 in the binary representation of $p \colon n = \Sigma_{i \in \text{dom}(p)} \, p(i)$. In other words

$$\sigma = \{ \langle n, p_n \rangle : n \in \mathbb{N} \text{ and } p_n \text{ has exactly } n \text{ occurrences of } 1 \} .$$

For instance: p_0 may be $[0]$, $[00]$, etc., p_1 may be of form $[100]$, $[01]$, $[0010]$.

If $\mathcal{C}$ is a branch containing a finite number of 1s and infinite number of 0s, i.e., $\Sigma_{i \in \omega} \mathcal{C}(i) = n < \infty$, then $\sigma_\mathcal{C} = \{0, \ldots, n\}$, so $\sigma_\mathcal{C} \notin \tau_\mathcal{C} = \{\mathbb{N}\}$. If, on the other hand, $\mathcal{C}$ contains infinite number of 1s, then $\sigma_\mathcal{C} = \mathbb{N}$, since for any $n \in \mathbb{N}$

there exists at least one condition $p_n \in C$ such, that $n = \Sigma_{i\in\mathrm{dom}(p_n)}\, p_n(i)$ and $\langle n, p_n \rangle \in \sigma$. In such case we have $\sigma_C \in \tau_C$. Thus, for an arbitrary $p \in \mathbb{T}$ holds $p \not\Vdash \sigma \in \tau$ as well as $p \not\Vdash \sigma \notin \tau$, since for C containing infinitely may 1s the membership holds in interpretations, whereas for the remaining ones – it does not hold.

Let Φ denote the sentence $\sigma \in \tau$. The example shows that although for each branch C either Φ_C or $\neg\Phi_C$ holds, the certainty sets for both Φ and $\neg\Phi$ are empty. Therefore, also certainty values $|\Phi|$ and $|\neg\Phi|$ are equal 0. The difference $1 - (|\Phi| + |\neg\Phi|)$ is the measure of uncertainty of the sentence Φ. Since it is equal to 1 in this case, then we say that Φ is totally uncertain – we cannot say anything about truth or falsity of Φ. The example 1 may be modified so, that both certainty values $|\Phi|$, $|\neg\Phi|$, as well as the uncertainty value $1 - (|\Phi| + |\neg\Phi|)$ are positive [7].

We now show that for any $\mathfrak{MF}^1$-sentence Φ the certainty value for Φ complements the certainty value for $\neg\Phi$, i.e., their sum is equal to 1. It means that $\mathfrak{MF}^1$-sentences admit no uncertainty.

Let $\Phi(x^1, \ldots, x^n)$ be a formula with all free variables shown and let $\tau^i \in \mathfrak{MF}^1$, for $i = 1, \ldots, n$. Let $\mathfrak{l}_\Phi$ denote the greatest of the deciding levels of all τ^i:

$$\mathfrak{l}_\Phi = \max\left\{ \mathfrak{l}_{\tau^i} : i = 1, \ldots, n \right\} . \tag{7}$$

We call $\mathfrak{l}_\Phi$ the *deciding level* for the $\mathfrak{MF}^1$-sentence Φ. It has the following property.

Theorem 1. *If Φ is a $\mathfrak{MF}^1$-sentence and $\mathfrak{l}_\Phi$ is the deciding level for Φ, then the following holds*

$$p \in 2^{\mathfrak{l}_\Phi} \quad \rightarrow \quad p \Vdash \Phi \lor p \Vdash \neg\Phi .$$

Proof. Let $\tau^1, \ldots, \tau^n \in \mathfrak{MF}^1$ be all fo-metasets occurring in Φ (not bound by quantifiers). Take arbitrary $p \in 2^{\mathfrak{l}_\Phi}$ and let us assume that $p \not\Vdash \Phi$. By the definition there exists a branch $C \ni p$ such, that $\neg\Phi_C$ is true. Let C' be another branch containing p. There are no elements which are less than p in any of the sets $\mathrm{ran}(\tau^i)$, $i = 1, \ldots, n$. Therefore, $C \cap \mathrm{ran}(\tau^i) = C' \cap \mathrm{ran}(\tau^i)$ and by the lemma 1 we conclude $\tau^i_C = \tau^i_{C'}$ for each τ^i. Clearly, $\neg\Phi(\tau^1_C, \ldots, \tau^n_C) \land \bigwedge_{i=1}^{i=n} \tau^i_C = \tau^i_{C'}$ implies $\neg\Phi(\tau^1_{C'}, \ldots, \tau^n_{C'})$. Since for each branch $C' \ni p$ holds $\neg\Phi(\tau^1_{C'}, \ldots, \tau^n_{C'})$, then $p \Vdash \neg\Phi$.

Lemma 4. *Let Φ be a $\mathfrak{MF}^1$-sentence and let $\mathfrak{l}_\Phi$ be the deciding level for Φ. Let $F_\Phi = \{ p \in 2^{\mathfrak{l}_\Phi} : p \Vdash \Phi \}$. The following holds:*

$$|\Phi| = \sum_{p \in F_\Phi} \frac{1}{2^{|p|}} .$$

Proof. By the definition 6 we have $|\Phi| = \sum_{p \in \|\Phi\|} \frac{1}{2^{|p|}}$. If $p \in F_\Phi$, then there exists a $q \in \|\Phi\|$ such, that $p \leq q$. Let $F_\Phi \!\restriction_q = \{ p \in F_\Phi : p \leq q \}$. We claim, that

$$\frac{1}{2^{|q|}} = \sum_{p \in F_\Phi \restriction_q} \frac{1}{2^{|p|}} . \tag{8}$$

Indeed, by the lemma 2, $F_\Phi \!\restriction_q$ contains all the conditions in the deciding level 2^{l_Φ}, which are stronger than q, since all of them force Φ. Applying the formula $\frac{1}{2^{|p|}} = \frac{1}{2^{|p \cdot 0|}} + \frac{1}{2^{|p \cdot 1|}}$ appropriate number of times we obtain (8). To complete the proof note, that $F_\Phi = \bigcup_{q \in \|\Phi\|} F_\Phi \!\restriction_q$.

Corollary 1. *If Φ is a $\mathfrak{MF}^1$-sentence, then $|\Phi| + |\neg\Phi| = 1$.*

We may easily calculate certainty values for $\mathfrak{MF}^1$-sentences applying the theorem 1. Let $T_\Phi = \{\, p \in 2^{l_\Phi} : p \Vdash \Phi \,\}$ and $N_\Phi = \{\, p \in 2^{l_\Phi} : p \Vdash \neg\Phi \,\}$. By the theorem we have $T_\Phi \cup N_\Phi = 2^{l_\Phi}$ – these sets fill the whole deciding level. Since there are 2^{l_Φ} elements on the l_Φ-th level, then

$$|\Phi| = \frac{|T_\Phi|}{2^{l_\Phi}} \quad \text{and} \quad |\neg\Phi| = \frac{|N_\Phi|}{2^{l_\Phi}} . \tag{9}$$

We apply here lemmas 2, 3 and take into account that $\frac{1}{2^{|p|}} = \frac{1}{2^{|p \cdot 0|}} + \frac{1}{2^{|p \cdot 1|}}$ for any $p \in \mathbb{T}$.

6 Generalization

For the sake of simplicity, we presented results for the class of first order metasets. However, they are valid for metasets in general. Details, as well as other generalizations of these results can be found in [10]. For completeness, we mention the general definition of metaset and interpretation.

Definition 9. *A set which is either the empty set $\emptyset$ or which has the form:*

$$\tau = \{\, \langle \sigma, p \rangle : \sigma \text{ is a metaset}, \ p \in \mathbb{T} \,\}$$

is called a metaset.

Formally, this is a definition by induction on the well founded relation $\in$. By the Axiom of Foundation in the Zermelo-Fraenkel set theory (ZFC) there are no infinite branches in the recursion as well as there are no cycles.[3] Therefore, no metaset is a member of itself. From the point of view of ZFC a metaset is a particular case of a $\mathbb{P}$-name (see also [4, Ch. VII, §2] for justification of such type of definitions).

The definition of interpretation for general metasets is recursive too.

Definition 10. *Let τ be a metaset and let $C \subset \mathbb{T}$ be a branch. The set*

$$\mathrm{int}(\tau, C) = \{\, \mathrm{int}(\sigma, C) : \langle \sigma, p \rangle \in \tau \wedge p \in C \,\}$$

is called the interpretation of the metaset τ given by the branch C.

---

[3] The Axiom of Foundation in ZFC says that every non-empty set x contains an element y which is disjoint from x:

$$\forall_{x \neq \emptyset} \, \exists_{y \in x} \, \neg \exists z \, (z \in x \wedge z \in y) .$$

The definition 4 of forcing applies without change to metasets in general – the restriction to first order metasets was not really necessary.

With the above general definitions we prove in [10], that for a $\mathfrak{MF}$-sentence Φ the union $\|\Phi\| \cup \|\neg\Phi\|$ is a maximal finite antichain in $\mathbb{T}$. A $\mathfrak{MF}$-sentence differs from a $\mathfrak{MF}^1$-sentence in that all metasets involved are hereditarily finite sets[4] instead of just first order finite. Note, that a maximal finite antichain in $\mathbb{T}$ intersects all branches in the tree, so in such case each branch contains a condition which either forces Φ or $\neg\Phi$. This result is more general and it implies the theorem 1.

7   Metasets and Intuitionistic Fuzzy Sets

If $\sigma, \tau \in \mathfrak{MF}^1$, then the membership value of σ in τ is equal to $|\sigma \in \tau|$ and the non-membership value of σ in τ is equal to $|\sigma \notin \tau|$. By the corollary 1 we know that $|\sigma \in \tau| + |\sigma \notin \tau| = 1$. However, if any of σ, τ is not a finite fo-metaset, then this sum may be less than 1, or even equal 0, like in the example 1. The complement to 1 of this sum: $1 - |\sigma \in \tau| - |\sigma \notin \tau|$, is called the *uncertainty value* of membership. This resembles intuitionistic fuzzy sets [1]. An intuitionistic fuzzy set is a triple $\langle X, \mu, \nu \rangle$, where $\mu \colon X \mapsto [0,1]$ is the membership function and $\nu \colon X \mapsto [0,1]$ is the non-membership function. They satisfy requirement $\mu(x) + \nu(x) \leq 1$, for each $x \in X$. The difference $1 - (\mu(x) + \nu(x))$ is called the *hesitancy degree*. In [7] we demonstrate the method for representing intuitionistic fuzzy sets by means of metasets. For the given intuitionistic fuzzy set $\langle X, \mu, \nu \rangle$ we construct a sequence of metasets $\{\rho_x\}_{x \in X}$ and an additional metaset Ω such, that $|\rho_x \in \Omega| = \mu(x)$ and $|\rho_x \notin \Omega| = \nu(x)$, for each $x \in X$. We also show how to evaluate the uncertainty grade to obtain the uncertainty value of membership for the metasets $\{\rho_x\}_{x \in X}$ and Ω. We conclude, that the uncertainty value of membership of ρ_x in Ω is equal $1 - (\mu(x) + \nu(x))$, for each $x \in X$.

By the corollary 1, the metasets ρ_x and Ω cannot be finite first order metasets. Indeed, the uncertainty of membership vanishes for such metasets. Therefore, we conclude that intuitionistic fuzzy sets cannot be directly represented by metasets in computers, where all representable entities are naturally finite.

On the other hand, it is possible to represent ordinary finite fuzzy sets [11] by means of metasets either using the method outlined above [7] and assuming that the hesitancy degree is 0, or with another method introduced in [8].

8   Summary

We have introduced the concept of metaset – set with partial membership relation. We have defined the fundamental techniques of interpretation and forcing and we have shown how to evaluate certainty values for sentences of the metaset language, in particular certainty values of membership and non-membership.

---

[4] A set is hereditarily finite whenever it is a finite set and all its members are hereditarily finite sets.

We have proved, that for sentences involving finite first order metasets exclusively, the certainty value of a sentence complements the certainty value of its negation. We have demonstrated the example showing, that it is not true in general: a sentence involving infinite metasets may have positive uncertainty value. For sentences expressing membership this resembles the hesitancy degree of intuitionistic fuzzy sets [1].

The class of finite metasets is especially important due to the fact, that metasets implementable in computers are naturally finite. Therefore, the presented results are significant for computer applications of metasets [5].

References

1. Atanassov, K.T.: Intuitionistic Fuzzy Sets. Fuzzy Sets and Systems 20, 87–96 (1986)
2. Cohen, P.: The Independence of the Continuum Hypothesis 1. Proceedings of the National Academy of Sciences of the United States of America 50, 1143–1148 (1963)
3. Jech, T.: Set Theory: The Third Millennium Edition, Revised and Expanded. Springer, Heidelberg (2006)
4. Kunen, K.: Set Theory, An Introduction to Independence Proofs. Studies in Logic and Foundations of Mathematics, vol. 102. North-Holland Publishing Company, Amsterdam (1980)
5. Starosta, B.: Application of Meta Sets to Character Recognition. In: Rauch, J., Raś, Z.W., Berka, P., Elomaa, T. (eds.) ISMIS 2009. LNCS (LNAI), vol. 5722, pp. 602–611. Springer, Heidelberg (2009)
6. Starosta, B.: Metasets: A New Approach to Partial Membership. In: Rutkowski, L., Korytkowski, M., Scherer, R., Tadeusiewicz, R., Zadeh, L.A., Zurada, J.M. (eds.) ICAISC 2012, Part I. LNCS (LNAI), vol. 7267, pp. 325–333. Springer, Heidelberg (2012)
7. Starosta, B.: Representing Intuitionistic Fuzzy Sets as Metasets. In: Atanassov, K.T., et al. (eds.) Developments in Fuzzy Sets, Intuitionistic Fuzzy Sets, Generalized Nets and Related Topics. Foundations, vol. I, pp. 185–208. Systems Research Institute, Polish Academy of Sciences, Warsaw (2010)
8. Starosta, B.: Fuzzy Sets as Metasets. In: Proc. of XI International PhD Workshop (OWD 2009), Conference Archives PTETIS, vol. 26, pp. 11–15 (2009)
9. Starosta, B., Kosiński, W.: Meta Sets – Another Approach to Fuzziness. In: Seising, R. (ed.) Views on Fuzzy Sets and Systems. STUDFUZZ, vol. 243, pp. 509–532. Springer, Heidelberg (2009)
10. Starosta, B., Kosiński, W.: Metasets, Certainty and Uncertainty. In: Atanassov, K.T., et al. (eds.) Developments in Fuzzy Sets, Intuitionistic Fuzzy Sets, Generalized Nets and Related Topics. Systems Research Institute, Polish Academy of Sciences, Warsaw (in printing, 2013)
11. Zadeh, L.A.: Fuzzy Sets. Information and Control 8, 338–353 (1965)

A New Similarity Function for Generalized Trapezoidal Fuzzy Numbers

E. Vicente, A. Mateos, and A. Jiménez

Artificial Intelligence Department, Technical University of Madrid, Spain
e.vicentecestero@upm.es, {amateos,ajimenez}@fi.upm.es

Abstract. Numerous authors have proposed functions to quantify the degree of similarity between two fuzzy numbers using various descriptive parameters, such as the geometric distance, the distance between the centers of gravity or the perimeter. However, these similarity functions have drawbacks for specific situations. We propose a new similarity measure for generalized trapezoidal fuzzy numbers aimed at overcoming such drawbacks. This new measure accounts for the distance between the centers of gravity and the geometric distance but also incorporates a new term based on the shared area between the fuzzy numbers. The proposed measure is compared against other measures in the literature.

1 Introduction

The *theory of fuzzy sets* was first introduced by Zadeh [14]. It is a multivalued logic developed to deal with imprecise or vague data based on degrees of truth rather than the usual Boolean true or false logic. It is useful for modeling concepts in a environment concerning inaccurate or vague measurements.

Fuzzy logic is useful for building a linguistic terms scale that experts will use to measure imprecise parameters. For instance, a nine-member linguistic terms set is introduced in [12]. These linguistic terms are usually associated with a triangular or trapezoidal fuzzy number [15]. Fuzzy number arithmetic, defined in conformity with the model in question, is then used to make computations (addition, multiplication, substraction, ranking...) using the fuzzy information provided by experts (see, e.g. the arithmetic proposed in [13] for linguistic values trapezoidal fuzzy numbers or the one in [4,6] for generalized trapezoidal fuzzy numbers). For advance in research in fuzzy number arithmetic and logical operators, see [11].

Partial or final results of computations with fuzzy numbers lead to new (triangular or trapezoidal) fuzzy numbers that often need to be expressed again by a linguistic term. Consequently, we have to identify the linguistic term on the previously defined scale whose associated fuzzy number is most similar to the one derived from computations.

Different metrics can be used to establish the similarity between fuzzy numbers, based on their distance, form or size. These parameters can be aggregated in mathematical expressions that define the degree of similarity between two fuzzy numbers.

L. Rutkowski et al. (Eds.): ICAISC 2013, Part I, LNAI 7894, pp. 400–411, 2013.

However, all similarity measures proposed by different authors have drawbacks, because the parameters used are not always best suited to the circumstances of the problem and the type of fuzzy number that the model uses. In this paper, we propose a similarity measure for generalized trapezoidal fuzzy numbers with good properties that overcomes the drawbacks of other similarity measures proposed in the literature.

In Section 2, we review the similarity measures proposed in the literature, analyzing their advantages and drawbacks. In Section 3, we propose a new similarity measure. We demonstrate that the new similarity measure has the same good properties as earlier measures and other additional properties that overcome their drawbacks. In Section 4, we compare the proposed measure with the measures outlined in this section, taking as a reference the set of 30 pairs of generalized fuzzy numbers provided in [13]. Finally, some conclusions are provided in Section 5.

2   Overview of Similarity Measures

First we introduce preliminary concepts to formalize similarity measures. We then review the major similarity measures proposed in the literature and more recent measures derived from them in chronological order, identifying their most interesting properties, as well as their drawbacks.

Generalized trapezoidal fuzzy numbers were first proposed by Chen [4,5]. A generalized trapezoidal fuzzy number with support in the interval $[0,1]$ is a tuple $(a_1, a_2, a_3, a_4; w_{\widetilde{A}})$ with $0 \leq a_1 \leq a_2 \leq a_3 \leq a_4 \leq 1$, and $w_{\widetilde{A}} \in [0,1]$ together with a membership function $(\mu_{\widetilde{A}} : \mathbb{R} \longrightarrow [0, w_{\widetilde{A}}])$,

$$\mu_{\widetilde{A}} = \begin{cases} 0 & \text{if } x < a_1 \\ \frac{w_{\widetilde{A}}(x-a_1)}{a_2-a_1} & \text{if } a_1 < x < a_2 \\ w_{\widetilde{A}} & \text{if } a_2 < x < a_3 \\ \frac{w_{\widetilde{A}}(x-a_4)}{a_3-a_4} & \text{if } a_3 < x < a_4 \\ 0 & \text{if } a_4 < x \end{cases}$$

indicating the degree of membership of any value $x \in \mathbb{R}$ to the fuzzy number $\widetilde{A}$. We denote by $TF[0,1]$ the set of all these fuzzy numbers.

In particular, if $w_{\widetilde{A}} = 1$, then we say that $\widetilde{A}$ is a *normalized fuzzy number*, and denote by $TF[0,1;1]$ the set of these fuzzy numbers.

A *similarity measure* is a function $S : TF[0,1] \times TF[0,1] \longrightarrow [0,1]$ indicating the degree of similarity between two fuzzy numbers. This value must match the intuitive perception that we have of the fuzzy numbers that we are comparing. The closer this value is to 1, the more similar the fuzzy numbers will be.

The first ideas about the similarity of normalized fuzzy numbers with support in $[0,1]$ stemmed, of course, from the distance notion. If we define a distance $d(\widetilde{A}, \widetilde{B}) \in [0,1]$ between fuzzy numbers $\widetilde{A}, \widetilde{B} \in TF[0,1;1]$, then generally $S = 1 - d$ is a similarity function. Chen [5] defined the degree of similarity between two normalized fuzzy numbers $\widetilde{A} = (a_1, a_2, a_3, a_4; 1)$ and $\widetilde{B} = (b_1, b_2, b_3, b_4; 1)$ using the geometric distance as

$$S(\widetilde{A}, \widetilde{B}) = 1 - \frac{\sum\limits_{i=1}^{4} |a_i - b_i|}{4}. \tag{1}$$

This measure has a number of interesting properties: *Property 1* $(S(\widetilde{A}, \widetilde{B}) = S(\widetilde{B}, \widetilde{A}))$, *Property 2* $(S(\widetilde{A}, \widetilde{B}) = 1 \Leftrightarrow \widetilde{A} = \widetilde{B})$ and *Property 3* (if $\widetilde{A} = (a, a, a, a; 1)$, $\widetilde{B} = (b, b, b, b; 1)$ then $S(\widetilde{A}, \widetilde{B}) = 1 - |a - b|$).

Tran and Duckstein [11] defined a distance, which was computed as a weighted sum of distances between two intervals across all the α-cuts from 0 to 1. This distance was also used in [8] to measure the intensity of dominance between trapezoidal fuzzy weights representing the preferences of DMs within MAUT. However, neither Chen's nor Tran and Duckstein's measures can be used to determine the similarity between generalized fuzzy numbers.

Chen and Chen [2] extended the similarity measure to the set $TF[0, 1]$ adding to Eq. (1) the distance between the centers of gravity of the compared numbers [1]. Thus, the similarity measure between the numbers $\widetilde{A} = (a_1, a_2, a_3, a_4; w_{\widetilde{A}})$ and $\widetilde{B} = (b_1, b_2, b_3, b_4; w_{\widetilde{B}})$ is determined by the expression

$$S(\widetilde{A}, \widetilde{B}) = \left[1 - \frac{\sum\limits_{i=1}^{4} |a_i - b_i|}{4}\right] \times \left[1 - |X_{\widetilde{A}} - X_{\widetilde{B}}|\right]^{B(S_{\widetilde{A}}, S_{\widetilde{B}})} \times \left[\frac{min\{Y_{\widetilde{A}}, Y_{\widetilde{B}}\}}{max\{Y_{\widetilde{A}}, Y_{\widetilde{B}}\}}\right], \tag{2}$$

where $(X_{\widetilde{A}}, Y_{\widetilde{A}})$ and $(X_{\widetilde{B}}, Y_{\widetilde{B}})$ are the centroids of $\widetilde{A}$ and $\widetilde{B}$, respectively, i.e.

$$X_{\widetilde{A}} = \begin{cases} \frac{Y_{\widetilde{A}}(a_3+a_2)+(w_{\widetilde{A}}-Y_{\widetilde{A}})(a_4+a_1)}{2w_{\widetilde{A}}}, & \text{if } w_{\widetilde{A}} \neq 0 \\ \frac{a_4+a_1}{2}, & \text{if } w_{\widetilde{A}} = 0 \end{cases}, \quad Y_{\widetilde{A}} = \begin{cases} \frac{w_{\widetilde{A}}\left(\frac{a_3-a_2}{a_4-a_1}+2\right)}{6}, & \text{if } a_4 \neq a_1 \\ \frac{w_{\widetilde{A}}}{2}, & \text{if } a_4 = a_1 \end{cases}, \tag{3}$$

$$B(S_{\widetilde{A}}, S_{\widetilde{B}}) = \begin{cases} 1, & \text{if } S_{\widetilde{A}} + S_{\widetilde{B}} > 0 \\ 0, & \text{otherwise} \end{cases}, \quad S_{\widetilde{A}} = a_4 - a_1 \text{ and } S_{\widetilde{B}} = b_4 - b_1.$$

The factor $[1 - |X_{\widetilde{A}} - X_{\widetilde{B}}|]^{B(S_{\widetilde{A}}, S_{\widetilde{B}})}$ is used to distinguish pairs of the form $\widetilde{A} = (a, a, a, a; w_{\widetilde{A}})$ and $\widetilde{B} = (b, b, b, b; w_{\widetilde{B}})$ from the remaining pairs of generalized fuzzy numbers. This extends the previous measures published in 1996 to generalized fuzzy numbers, and provides a fourth property: *Property 4* (if $\widetilde{A} = (a, a, a, a; 0)$, $\widetilde{B} = (a, a, a, a; 1)$ then $S(\widetilde{A}, \widetilde{B}) = 0$).

Indeed, the first fuzzy number is clearly not the real number a, whereas the second fuzzy number clearly is the real number a. So, the similarity between them is evidently zero.

However, this measure has a small drawback since it assigns a degree of similarity $S(\widetilde{A}, \widetilde{B}) = 0$ to fuzzy numbers $\widetilde{A} = (a, a, a, a; 0)$ and $\widetilde{B} = (a, a, a, a; 10^{-10^{10}})$.

Can we be sure that these numbers are completely different?, i.e. as different as the numbers of property 4? Obviously not. Then, we need a measure that distinguishes these numbers in a fairer way.

Wei and Chen [12] proposed a new measure using the perimeter concept of generalized trapezoidal fuzzy numbers:

$$S(\widetilde{A}, \widetilde{B}) = \left[1 - \frac{\sum\limits_{i=1}^{4} |a_i - b_i|}{4} \right] \times \left[\frac{min\{P(\widetilde{A}), P(\widetilde{B})\} + min\{w_{\widetilde{A}}, w_{\widetilde{B}}\}}{max\{P(\widetilde{A}), P(\widetilde{B})\} + max\{w_{\widetilde{A}}, w_{\widetilde{B}}\}} \right], \quad (4)$$

where $P(\widetilde{A}) = \sqrt{(a_1 - a_2)^2 + w_{\widetilde{A}}^2} + \sqrt{(a_3 - a_4)^2 + w_{\widetilde{A}}^2} + (a_3 - a_2) + (a_4 - a_1)$, and analogously for $P(\widetilde{B})$.

Like the measure proposed by Chen and Chen [2], this new measure also verifies the four properties but again has the above drawback. This was the ground proffered by Xu et al. [13] for proposing a new measure based, like the measure published by Chen and Chen [2], on the concept of center of gravity. Xu et al. consider two weights $w, 1 - w \in (0, 1)$ to attach more or less importance to the concepts used:

$$S_w(\widetilde{A}, \widetilde{B}) = 1 - w \frac{\sum |a_i - b_i|}{4} - (1 - w) \frac{\sqrt{(X_{\widetilde{A}} - X_{\widetilde{B}})^2 + (Y_{\widetilde{A}} - Y_{\widetilde{B}})^2}}{\sqrt{1.25}}.$$

This action effectively mitigates the drawback of the measures by Chen and Chen[2] and Wei and Chen [12], since it assigns a high degree of similarity to fuzzy numbers of the form $(a, a, a, a, 0)$ and (a, a, a, a, ϵ) with ϵ near zero, and also provides a new property: *Property 5* ($S(\widetilde{A}, \widetilde{B}) = 0$ (and $\widetilde{A} < \widetilde{B}$) $\Leftrightarrow \widetilde{A} = (0, 0, 0, 0; 0)$ and $\widetilde{B} = (1, 1, 1, 1; 1)$).

However, Xu et al. sacrificed properties 3 and 4 to achieve this fifth property. For example, if we consider $w = 0.5$, then the degree of similarity of $(0.1, 0.1, 0.1, 0.1; 1)$ and $(0.1, 0.1, 0.1, 0.1; 0)$ is 0.7763 with respect to the fourth property. For $(a, a, a, a; 1)$ and $(b, b, b, b; 1)$, we have $S(\widetilde{A}, \widetilde{B}) = 1 - 0.5 | a - b | -0.5 \frac{|a-b|}{\sqrt{1.25}} \neq 1 - | a - b |$, with respect to the third property.

Another drawback of Xu et al.'s measure is as follows. If we consider the trapezoidal fuzzy numbers shown in Fig. 1, $\widetilde{A} = (0, 0.1, 0.3, 0.4; 1)$, $\widetilde{B} = (0.25, 0.4, 0.6, 0.75; 1)$ and $\widetilde{C} = (0.75, 0.775, 0.825, 0.85; 1)$, then the degree of similarity of $\widetilde{C}$ and $\widetilde{A}$ with respect to $\widetilde{B}$, with $w = 0.5$, is 0.7156 in both cases. Therefore, the numbers $\widetilde{C}$ and $\widetilde{A}$ are just similar to the central number $\widetilde{B}$. However, $\widetilde{B}$ should clearly be more similar to $\widetilde{A}$ than $\widetilde{C}$ on the basis of its shape, size, and more importantly, the shared area.

Apart from Chen and Xu et al.'s measures, numerous authors have defined the degree of similarity between two trapezoidal fuzzy numbers, without giving up any of the five described properties. Note, for example, the Sridevi and Nadarajan's extension [10], a fuzzy distance that replaces the geometric distance

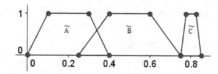

Fig. 1. A drawback of Xu et al.'s measure

in the measure proposed by Chen and Chen[2],

$$S(\widetilde{A}, \widetilde{B}) = \left[\frac{\sum\limits_{i=1}^{4} \mu_d(x)}{4} \right] \times \left[1 - |X_{\widetilde{A}} - X_{\widetilde{B}}| \right]^{B(S_{\widetilde{A}}, S_{\widetilde{B}})} \times \left[\frac{min\{Y_{\widetilde{A}}, Y_{\widetilde{B}}\}}{max\{Y_{\widetilde{A}}, Y_{\widetilde{B}}\}} \right],$$

with $\mu_d(x) = \begin{cases} 1 - \frac{x}{d}, & \text{if } 0 \leq x \leq d \\ 0, & \text{otherwise} \end{cases}$, $d \in (0, 1]$, $x = | a_i - b_i |$ and $(X_{\widetilde{A}}, Y_{\widetilde{A}})$ and
$(X_{\widetilde{B}}, Y_{\widetilde{B}})$ the centroids of the compared fuzzy numbers. Parameter d represents
the level of precision required to measure the similarity between the two fuzzy
numbers. The measure by Sridevi and Nadarajan sacrifices the third and the
fifth property.

More recently, Gomathi and Sivaraman [7] proposed a new measure. This
measure sacrifices only the fifth property but again has the same the drawback
as the measures by Chen and Wei and Chen. It modifies the measure proposed
by Wei and Chen by using the geometric instead of the arithmetic mean of the
difference of the vertices of the fuzzy numbers under comparison. Moreover, it
considers a straightforward function including the vertices and heights of the
fuzzy numbers rather than their perimeters in order to reduce computational
time with respect to the measure by Wei and Chen but achieve similar results:

$$S(\widetilde{A}, \widetilde{B}) = \left[\sqrt[4]{\prod_{i=1}^{4} (1 - | a_i - b_i |)} \right] \times \left[\frac{min\{Q(\widetilde{A}), Q(\widetilde{B})\} + min\{w_{\widetilde{A}}, w_{\widetilde{B}}\}}{max\{Q(\widetilde{A}), Q(\widetilde{B})\} + max\{w_{\widetilde{A}}, w_{\widetilde{B}}\}} \right],$$

$$(5)$$

where $Q(\widetilde{A}) = \sqrt{(a_2 - a_1)^2 + (a_3 - a_2)^2 + (a_4 - a_3)^2 + w_{\widetilde{A}}^2}$.

3   A New Similarity Function

The most common parameters in the similarity measures are the geometric distance, the distance between the centers of gravity and the perimeter. In the
measure that we propose, we incorporate the shared area between the generalized fuzzy numbers with respect to the total area of these fuzzy numbers. The
closer this value is to 1, the more similar are the compared fuzzy numbers.

We also directly use the difference between the height of the generalized
fuzzy numbers, since although the distance between the centroids to some extent

already considers this parameter, failures have been observed when measuring the similarity between some pairs of fuzzy numbers whose height is close to zero, as discussed in Section 2.

We define the degree of similarity of the generalized trapezoidal fuzzy numbers $\widetilde{A} = (a_1, a_2, a_3, a_4; w_{\widetilde{A}})$ and $\widetilde{B} = (b_1, b_2, b_3, b_4; w_{\widetilde{B}})$ as follows:

– if $\max\{(a_4 - a_1), (b_4 - b_1)\} \neq 0$, then

$$S(\widetilde{A},\widetilde{B}) = (1- \mid w_{\widetilde{A}}-w_{\widetilde{B}} \mid) \times \left(1 - (1 - \alpha - \beta) \times \left(1 - \frac{\int_0^1 \mu_{\widetilde{A}\cap\widetilde{B}}(x)dx}{\int_0^1 \mu_{\widetilde{A}\cup\widetilde{B}}(x)dx}\right) \right.$$
$$\left. -\alpha\frac{\sum \mid a_i - b_i \mid}{4} - \beta\frac{d[(X_{\widetilde{A}}, Y_{\widetilde{A}}), (X_{\widetilde{B}}, Y_{\widetilde{B}})]}{M}\right),$$

– otherwise,

$$S(\widetilde{A},\widetilde{B}) = (1- \mid w_{\widetilde{A}}-w_{\widetilde{B}} \mid) \times \left(1 - \left(\frac{1 - \alpha - \beta}{2} + \alpha\right) \times \frac{\sum \mid a_i - b_i \mid}{4}\right.$$
$$\left. - \left(\frac{1 - \alpha - \beta}{2} + \beta\right) \times \frac{d[(X_{\widetilde{A}}, Y_{\widetilde{A}}), (X_{\widetilde{B}}, Y_{\widetilde{B}})]}{M}\right),$$

where $\alpha + \beta < 1$, $\mu_{\widetilde{\chi}}$ is the membership function of $\widetilde{\chi}$, $M = \max\limits_{[0,1] \times [0,\frac{1}{2}]} \{d(x, y), (x', y'))\}$, $\mu_{\widetilde{A}\cap\widetilde{B}}(x) = \min\limits_{0 \leq x \leq 1} \{\mu_{\widetilde{A}}(x), \mu_{\widetilde{B}}(x)\}$, $\mu_{\widetilde{A}\cup\widetilde{B}}(x) = \max\limits_{0 \leq x \leq 1} \{\mu_{\widetilde{A}}(x), \mu_{\widetilde{B}}(x)\}$, $(X_{\widetilde{A}}, Y_{\widetilde{A}})$, $(X_{\widetilde{B}}, Y_{\widetilde{B}})$ are computed as in Eqs. (3), and d is a distance in $\mathbb{R}^2$.

From now on, we analyze the properties of the proposed similarity measure

Proposition 1. $S(\widetilde{A}, \widetilde{B}) \in [0, 1]$.

Proof. Since the weights sum 1, it suffices to see that $(1- \mid w_{\widetilde{A}} - w_{\widetilde{B}} \mid) \leq 1$, $\frac{\int_0^1 \mu_{\widetilde{A}\cap\widetilde{B}}(x)dx}{\int_0^1 \mu_{\widetilde{A}\cup\widetilde{B}}(x)dx} \leq 1$, $\frac{\sum \mid a_i - b_i \mid}{4} \leq 1$, $\frac{d[(X_{\widetilde{A}}, Y_{\widetilde{A}}), (X_{\widetilde{B}}, Y_{\widetilde{B}})]}{M} \leq 1$, which is trivial. $\square$

Proposition 2. $S(\widetilde{A}, \widetilde{B}) = S(\widetilde{B}, \widetilde{A})$.

Proof. Trivial. $\square$

Proposition 3. $S(\widetilde{A}, \widetilde{B}) = 1 \Leftrightarrow \widetilde{A} = \widetilde{B}$.

Proof. The reverse implication is obvious. Consider the direct implication. If $max\{(a_4 - a_1), (b_4 - b_1)\} \neq 0$, then $S(\widetilde{A},\widetilde{B}) = 1$, and, since both factors of $S(\widetilde{A},\widetilde{B})$ are less than or equal to 1, theoretically

$$1 - (1-\alpha-\beta)\left(1 - \frac{\int_0^1 \mu_{\widetilde{A}\cap\widetilde{B}}(x)dx}{\int_0^1 \mu_{\widetilde{A}\cup\widetilde{B}}(x)dx}\right) - \alpha\frac{\sum \mid a_i - b_i \mid}{4} - \beta\frac{d[(X_{\widetilde{A}}, Y_{\widetilde{A}}), (X_{\widetilde{B}}, Y_{\widetilde{B}})]}{M} = 1$$

$$\Rightarrow (1-\alpha-\beta)\left(1 - \frac{\int_0^1 \mu_{\widetilde{A}\cap\widetilde{B}}(x)dx}{\int_0^1 \mu_{\widetilde{A}\cup\widetilde{B}}(x)dx}\right) + \alpha\frac{\sum \mid a_i - b_i \mid}{4} + \beta\frac{d[(X_{\widetilde{A}}, Y_{\widetilde{A}}), (X_{\widetilde{B}}, Y_{\widetilde{B}})]}{M} = 0,$$

and, as the three summands are positive or zero, necessarily: $\frac{\int_0^1 \mu_{\tilde{A} \cap \tilde{B}}(x)dx}{\int_0^1 \mu_{\tilde{A} \cup \tilde{B}}(x)dx} = $
1, $\frac{\sum |a_i - b_i|}{4} = 0$ and $\frac{d[(X_{\tilde{A}}, Y_{\tilde{A}}),(X_{\tilde{B}}, Y_{\tilde{B}})]}{M} = 0$. Thus, $\tilde{A} = \tilde{B}$.

If $max\{(a_4 - a_1), (b_4 - b_1)\} = 0$, then we have analogously that $\frac{\sum |a_i - b_i|}{4} = $
0 and $\frac{d[(X_{\tilde{A}}, Y_{\tilde{A}}),(X_{\tilde{B}}, Y_{\tilde{B}})]}{M} = 0$. Thus, $\tilde{A} = \tilde{B}$. $\qquad\square$

Proposition 4. *If $M = 1$ and $\tilde{A} = (a, a, a, a; 1)$ and $\tilde{B} = (b, b, b, b; 1)$, then*
$S(\tilde{A}, \tilde{B}) = 1 - |a - b|$.

Proof. Trivial. $\qquad\square$

We will see afterwards that the use of distances with $M=1$ has additional
advantages.

Proposition 5. *If $\tilde{A} = (a, a, a, a; 0)$ and $\tilde{B} = (a, a, a, a; 1)$, then $S(\tilde{A}, \tilde{B}) = 0$.*

Proof. Trivial. $\qquad\square$

Proposition 6. *If $S(\tilde{A}, \tilde{B}) = 0$ and $\tilde{A} \leq \tilde{B}$, then $|w_{\tilde{A}} - w_{\tilde{B}}| = 1$ or $\tilde{A} = (0, 0, 0, 0; w_{\tilde{A}})$ and $\tilde{B} = (1, 1, 1, 1; w_{\tilde{B}})$, with $w_{\tilde{A}}, w_{\tilde{B}} \in [0, 1]$.*

Proof. Let us assume that $|w_{\tilde{A}} - w_{\tilde{B}}| \neq 1$, then if $max\{(a_4 - a_1), (b_4 - b_1)\} \neq 0$

$$S(\tilde{A}, \tilde{B}) = 0 \Rightarrow (1 - \alpha - \beta) \left(1 - \frac{\int_0^1 \mu_{\tilde{A} \cap \tilde{B}}(x)dx}{\int_0^1 \mu_{\tilde{A} \cup \tilde{B}}(x)dx} - 1\right) + \alpha \left(\frac{\sum |a_i - b_i|}{4} - 1\right) +$$
$$+ \beta \left(\frac{d[(X_{\tilde{A}}, Y_{\tilde{A}}),(X_{\tilde{B}}, Y_{\tilde{B}})]}{M} - 1\right) = 0$$

and, since they are summands of $[0, 1]$, they must each be zero, i.e.

$$\frac{\int_0^1 \mu_{\tilde{A} \cap \tilde{B}}(x)dx}{\int_0^1 \mu_{\tilde{A} \cup \tilde{B}}(x)dx} = 0, \quad \frac{\sum |a_i - b_i|}{4} = 1 \quad \text{and} \quad \frac{d[(X_{\tilde{A}}, Y_{\tilde{A}}),(X_{\tilde{B}}, Y_{\tilde{B}})]}{M} = 1.$$

It follows from the second expression that $|a_i - b_i| = 1 \ \forall i$, and, as $\tilde{A} \leq \tilde{B}$, we
have $b_i = a_i + 1 \ \forall i$, and, since $a_i, b_i \in [0, 1]$, necessarily $a_i = 0, b_i = 1 \ \forall i$.
If $max\{(a_4 - a_1), (b_4 - b_1)\} = 0$, then:

$$1 - (\frac{1 - \alpha - \beta}{2} + \alpha)\frac{\sum |a_i - b_i|}{4} - (\frac{1 - \alpha - \beta}{2} + \beta)\frac{d[(X_{\tilde{A}}, Y_{\tilde{A}}),(X_{\tilde{B}}, Y_{\tilde{B}})]}{M} = 0$$

and an analogous analysis would be applied. $\qquad\square$

Other noteworthy observations about the proposed measure are:

1. For $\alpha + \beta = 1$, and d the Euclidean distance on $\mathbb{R}^2$, we have Xu et al.'s
   measure for trapezoidal fuzzy numbers such that $|w_{\tilde{A}} - w_{\tilde{B}}| = 0$.
2. The measure penalizes the fact that two sets are disjoint using a weight
   $(1 - \alpha - \beta)$.

3. As demonstrated in propositions 2-5, the proposed measure verifies the first four properties if we use a distance d with $M = \max\limits_{[0,1]\times[0,\frac{1}{2}]} \{d((x,y),$ $(x',y'))\} = 1$, like, for example, the distance $l_\infty((x_1,y_1),(x_2,y_2)) = \max$ $\{|x_1 - x_2|,|y_1 - y_2|\}$. The fifth property holds only partially, since there are other pairs of fuzzy numbers whose similarity is zero in addition to the numbers $\widetilde{A} = (0,0,0,0;0)$ and $\widetilde{B} = (1,1,1,1;1)$

4. The proposal has the following property: $\lim\limits_{\varepsilon \to 0} S((a,a,a,a;0),(a,a,a,a;\varepsilon)) =$ 1 and $\lim\limits_{\varepsilon \to 1} S((a,a,a,a;0),(a,a,a,a;\varepsilon)) = 0$, which overcomes that drawback of the measures proposed by Chen and Chen[2] and Wei and Chen [12], outlined in Section 2.

   For example, the similarity between $\widetilde{A} = (a,a,a,a;0)$ and $\widetilde{B} = (a,a,a,a;$ $10^{-10^{10}})$ is $S(\widetilde{A},\widetilde{B}) \approx 1$, which appears to be more reasonable than the null value assigned by the measures proposed by Chen and Chen[2] and Wei and Chen [12].

5. The set $TF[0,1;1] = \{(a,b,c,d;1) \in TF[0,1]\}$ is a subset of $TF[0,1]$, especially interesting in many domains of decision theory, since experts will often identify a linguistic term scale represented by numbers in $TF[0,1;1]$. However, certain considerations are required regarding the distance d used in the similarity measure. For convenience's sake we write $(a,b,c,d) \equiv (a,b,c,d;1)$ to denote the elements in $TF[0,1;1]$. Suppose that the spheres identified by the distance d are not rectangular[1]. If we restrict to $TF[0,1;1]$, a good measure of similarity should identify $(0,0,0,0)$ and $(1,1,1,1)$ as the most different elements. However, there exists $\widetilde{A} \in TF[0,1;1]$ such that $S((0,0,0,0),\widetilde{A}) <$ $S((0,0,0,0),(1,1,1,1))$. For example, if we take Xu et al.'s measure (2010), S_w, with $w = 0.5$, $S_{0.5}((0,0,0,0),(1,1,1,1)) = 0.052$.

   As the spheres in the Euclidean distance in $\mathbb{R}^2$ are circles, if we represent the circle centered at the centroid of $(0,0,0,0)$, i.e. at $(0,0.5)$, whose radius is the distance to the centroid of $(1,1,1,1)$, i.e. at $(1,0.5)$, we obtain a region beyond this circumference containing the centroid of another number in $TF[0,1;1]$. This number will be farther from $(0,0,0,0)$ than $(1,1,1,1)$ itself.

   More specifically, we know that the centroid of any number in $TF[0,1;1]$ is located in the band $[0,1] \times [1/3,1/2]$, [4]. The circle intersects the line $y = \frac{1}{3}$ at $x = \sqrt{\frac{35}{36}}$. Then, any number $(a,1,1,1)$ with $a > \sqrt{\frac{35}{36}}$ is less similar to $(0,0,0,0)$ than $(1,1,1,1)$ itself. For instance, $S_{0.5}((0.99,1,1,1),(0,0,0,0)) =$ $0.049 < 0.52 = S_{0.5}((0,0,0,0),(1,1,1,1))$. However, this is not a problem if the spheres defined by a distance are rectangular. For example, with the distance l_∞, whose spheres are square, we can ensure that the elements that differ most from $TF[0,1;1]$ are $(0,0,0,0)$ and $(1,1,1,1)$.

   Another appropriate pseudo-distance is $d((x_1,y_1),(x_2,y_2)) = |x_1 - x_2|$, whose spheres are vertical bands. We denote this distance by l_*. As the

---

[1] The sphere with center a and radius r with distance d is $A(a,r) = \{x \in \mathbb{R}^n :$ $d(x,a) = r\}$.

centroids are located in the band $[0, 1] \times [1/3, 1/2]$ [1], the range of variation on the abscissa is much greater than the ordinate. These distances mostly attach more importance to the position on the horizontal axis of the trapezoidal fuzzy numbers, which is, together with the shared area, one of the main parameters to be taken into account when identifying a linguistic term from the given fuzzy scale.

4 Comparative Analysis

We have compared the proposed measure using the distance l_∞ and the pseudo-distance l_*, with $\alpha = \beta = \frac{1}{3}$, with the measures by Chen and Chen [2], Wei and Chen [12], Xu et al. [13] and Gomathi and Sivaraman [7], outlined in Section 1. We have applied the measures to compute the similarity of 30 pairs of fuzzy numbers previously proposed by Xu et al. in [13], see Fig. 2. The results are shown in Table 1.

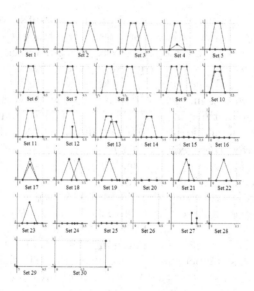

Fig. 2. Sets of fuzzy pairs for comparison

First, there are not great differences in the proposed measure when using l_* and l_∞, see Table 1, since

$$l_\infty\left((X_{\widetilde{A}}, Y_{\widetilde{A}}), (X_{\widetilde{B}}, Y_{\widetilde{B}})\right) \neq l_*\left((X_{\widetilde{A}}, Y_{\widetilde{A}}), (X_{\widetilde{B}}, Y_{\widetilde{B}})\right) \Leftrightarrow \left|Y_{\widetilde{A}} - Y_{\widetilde{B}}\right| > \left|X_{\widetilde{A}} - X_{\widetilde{B}}\right|.$$

However, $\left|Y_{\widetilde{A}} - Y_{\widetilde{B}}\right| < \frac{1}{2} - \frac{1}{3} = \frac{1}{6}$, and therefore $\left|X_{\widetilde{A}} - X_{\widetilde{B}}\right| > \frac{1}{6}$, is a sufficient condition for both measures to coincide [1]. Also, whenever $\left|X_{\widetilde{A}} - X_{\widetilde{B}}\right| < \frac{1}{6}$, both measures will be very similar but not necessarily equal.

We also realize that there are missing values in Table 1. The similarity of the fuzzy numbers involved in cases 24, 25, 26 and 28 cannot be computed using the measure proposed by Chen and Chen [2] since the height of both fuzzy numbers is 0. Then, the term $max\{Y_{\widetilde{A}}, Y_{\widetilde{B}}\}$ would be 0, leading to a division by 0, see Eq. (2). On the other hand, cases 26 and 28 cannot be addressed by the measures proposed by Wei and Chen [12] and Gomathi and Sivaraman [7], since the perimeter of both fuzzy numbers is also 0 and, again, we would have division by 0, see Eqs. (4) and (5), respectively.

In Fig. 5 we graphically compare the similarity measures. The proposed measures (with l_* and l_∞, respectively) are always located at the ordinate axe, while the compared measure is located at the abscissa. Each point represent the degree of similarity output by the two compared measures for one out of the 30 pairs of fuzzy numbers. The farther the points are from the bisector of the first quadrant, the greater the difference between the measures compared.

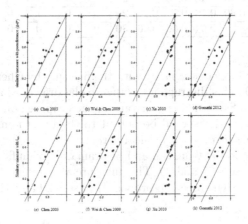

Fig. 3. Charts comparing measures

Most of points in the graphs are located between the lines $y = x$ and $y = x - \frac{1}{3}$. It can be easily explained since the proposed measures penalize with weight $1 - \alpha - \beta = \frac{1}{3}$ the similarity of pairs of disjoint fuzzy numbers, as pointed out in the observations about the proposed method in Section 3.

We see that the biggest controversy is output when comparing the proposed measure with the measure proposed by Xu et al. [13], in which a large number of points considerably away from the bisector of the first quadrant. This matches up with the data in Table 1, in which values in the column corresponding to this measure are quite higher than the corresponding to the other. The higher differences appear when the two fuzzy numbers considered have very different heights, like cases 14, 19 and 24, where the values output by all measures are quite similar but for the measure by Xu et al.

Table 1. Comparison with other similarity measures

Set	[2]	[12]	[13]	[7]	l_*	l_∞	Set	[2]	[12]	[13]	[7]	l_*	l_∞
1	0.84	0.95	0.96	0.97	0.91	0.89	16	1	1	1	1	1	1
2	0.31	0.58	0.62	0.60	0.40	0.40	17	0.75	0.78	0.97	0.76	0.73	0.72
3	0.55	0.78	0.81	0.80	0.54	0.54	18	0.48	0.63	0.81	0.61	0.56	0.55
4	0.17	0.31	0.84	0.24	0.14	0.12	19	0	0.17	0.75	0.10	0.10	0.10
5	0	0.16	0.77	0.09	0	0	20	0	0.79	1	0.95	0.66	0.66
6	0	0	0.67	0	0	0	21	0.76	0.59	0.92	0.66	0.49	0.49
7	1	1	1	1	1	1	22	0	0	0.83	0	0.12	0.11
8	0.36	0.6	0.62	0.6	0.40	0.40	23	0	0.19	0.82	0.12	0.12	0.18
9	0.64	0.8	0.81	0.8	0.55	0.55	24	*	0.9	0.90	0.73	0.60	0.5998
10	0.8	0.82	0.96	0.80	0.75	0.72	25	*	0	0.93	0	0.61	0.62
11	0	0.16	0.77	0.08	0	0	26	*	*	0.81	*	0.53	0.53
12	0.44	0.32	0.86	0.36	0.25	0.23	27	0.45	0.45	0.89	0.45	0.48	0.48
13	0.40	0.52	0.89	0.46	0.56	0.56	28	*	*	1	*	1	1
14	0	0.19	0.80	0.10	0.12	0.11	29	0	0	1	0	1	0.99
15	0	0.98	1	0.94	0.66	0.66	30	0	0	0	0	0	0

We also note the large discrepancy with the measure by Chen and Chen [2] in cases 15, 20 and 29. This discrepancy is due to the drawback associated to this measure, outlined in Section 2, is overcome in the proposed one (Section 3), i.e., a high degree of similarity should be output to the fuzzy numbers of the form $(a, a, a, a, 0)$ and (a, a, a, a, ϵ) with ε near zero.

Finally, the measure by Gomathi and Sivaraman [7] significantly differs from the proposed in the sets 25 and 29. This measure also differs with the measures by Chen (even more than with the proposed) in sets 20 and 15.

5   Conclusions

Quantifying the degree of similarity between two fuzzy numbers is necessary in a great variety of applications of fuzzy logic, specially when a linguistic terms scale has been defined and a fuzzy number resulting from different computations has to be compared with the fuzzy numbers associated to the linguistic terms to identify the most similar one.

We have proposed a new similarity measure for generalized trapezoidal fuzzy numbers based on the difference of heights and the shared area between the numbers involved in relation to the total area of both, in addition to the distance between the centers of gravity and the geometric distance, which have already been considered by other authors. The result is a measure of similarity with many good properties, which outperforms the other measures in the sense that it can properly compare pairs of fuzzy numbers that the other methods can not address or do not fit well. Specifically, the proposed measure outperforms the measure by Chen since fuzzy numbers with null height can now be compared. It also outperforms measures by Wei and Chen and by Gomathi and Sivaraman since it can compare fuzzy numbers with null perimeter. Moreover, the proposed measure keeps good properties of the other measures and establishes a more realistic similarity when comparing fuzzy numbers of the form $(a, a, a, a, 0)$ and (a, a, a, a, ϵ), with ε near zero. Regarding the measure by Xu et al., it is outperformed by the proposed measure since properties 3 and 4 are accomplished and the additional drawback of this method illustrated in Section 2 is overcome.

However, the proposed measure does not necessarily identify the fuzzy numbers $\tilde{A} = (0, 0, 0, 0, 0)$ and $\tilde{B} = (1, 1, 1, 1, 1)$ as the most different, i.e., there are other numbers in $TF[0, 1]$ whose similarity is zero as well, i.e. property 5 is only satisfied in one direction. In any case, both the number and quality of the properties we won and the difficulties that the proposed measure exceeds represent benefits greater than the losses from the partially satisfaction of property 5.

Acknowledgment. The paper was supported by Madrid Government project S-2009/ESP-1685 and the Ministry of Science project MTM2011-28983-CO3-03.

References

1. Chen, S.J., Chen, S.M.: A new simple center-of-gravity method for handling the fuzzy ranking and the defuzzification problems. In: 8th National Conf. Fuzzy Theory Applications, Taipei, Republic of China (2000)
2. Chen, S.J., Chen, S.M.: Fuzzy risk analysis based on similarity measures of generalized fuzzy numbers. IEEE Fuzzy Syst. 11, 45–56 (2003)
3. Chen, S.J., Chen, S.M.: Fuzzy risk analysis based on the ranking of generalized trapezoidal fuzzy numbers. Appl. Intell. 26, 1–11 (2007)
4. Chen, S.M.: Operations on fuzzy numbers with function principle. Tamkang J. Manage. Sc. 6, 13–25 (1985)
5. Chen, S.M.: New methods for subjective mental workload assessment and fuzzy risk analysis. Cybernet. Syst. 27, 449–472 (1996)
6. Chen, S.M.: Ranking generalized fuzzy number with graded mean integration. In: Proceedings of IFSA 1999, vol. 2, pp. 899–902 (1999)
7. Gomathi Nayagam, V.L., Sivaraman, G.: A novel similarity measure between generalized fuzzy numbers. Int. J. Comput. Theor. Eng. 4, 448–450 (2012)
8. Jiménez, A., Mateos, A., Sabio, P.: Dominance intensity measure within fuzzy weight oriented MAUT: an application. OMEGA 41, 397–405 (2013)
9. Ross, T.J.: Fuzzy logic with engineering applications. John Wiley & Sons, Chichester (2010)
10. Sridevi, B., Nadarajan, R.: Fuzzy similarity measure for generalized fuzzy numbers. Int. J. Open Probl. Comput. Sc. Math. 2, 111–116 (2009)
11. Tran, L., Dukstein, L.: Comparison of fuzzy numbers using a fuzzy distance measure. Fuzzy Set. Syst. 130, 331–341 (2002)
12. Wei, S.H., Chen, S.M.: A new approach for fuzzy risk analysis based on similarity measures of generalized fuzzy numbers. Expert Syst. Appl. 36, 589–598 (2009)
13. Xu, Z., Shang, S., Qian, W., Shu, W.: A method for fuzzy risk analysis based on the new similarity of trapezoidal fuzzy numbers. Expert Syst. Appl. 37, 1920–1927 (2010)
14. Zadeh, L.A.: Fuzzy sets. Inform. Control 8, 338–353 (1965)
15. Zhang, W.R.: Knowledge representation using linguistic fuzzy relations. PhD. Dissertation, University of South Carolina, USA (1986)

Fuzzy Granulation Approach to Color Digital Picture Recognition

Krzysztof Wiaderek and Danuta Rutkowska

Institute of Computer and Information Sciences, Czestochowa University of
Technology, Dabrowskiego Street 73, 42-201 Czestochowa, Poland
krzys@icis.pcz.pl, drutko@kik.pcz.czest.pl

Abstract. This paper presents a new approach to color digital picture
recognition, especially classification of pictures described by linguistic
terms. Fuzzy granulation is proposed to express a picture as a composition of fuzzy granules that carry information about color, location, and
size, each of these attributes represented by fuzzy sets characterized by
membership functions. With regard to the color, the CIE chromaticity
triangle is applied, with the concept of fuzzy color areas. The classification result is obtained based on fuzzy IF-THEN rules and fuzzy logic
inference employed in a fuzzy system.

1 Introduction

Color digital pictures are very popular nowadays. The number of such pictures we
collect are still growing. In addition, the picture resolution increases. Therefore,
we need new methods for searching, recognition, and retrieving a particular
picture from a large collection of them.

Color is a very important attribute of digital pictures. It carries significant
information that helps to distinguish, recognize, compare, and classify different
pictures or objects presented on various pictures. As a matter of fact, color
should be considered as a triplet, i.e. hue (pure color), saturation, and lightness;
we describe the color properties in Section 2. However, the name "color" is
commonly used as a synonym of "hue". Hence, in the case where it can be
accepted, sometimes we also treat these two terms interchangeably.

In this paper, with regard to the color digital pictures, fuzzy granulation
approach – introduced by Zadeh [19] – is proposed to describe fuzzy location of
pixels as well as fuzziness of their color. Thus, we can consider a color digital
picture as a collection of pixels or groups of pixels which we call macropixels,
and treat them as fuzzy sets [16]. In the framework of the fuzzy granulation,
the macropixels can be viewed as fuzzy granules that carry information about
the color, location, as well as size of the macropixels. Hence, a color digital
picture is a composition of the fuzzy granules that represent fuzzy relations
(see e.g. [11]) between the attributes of color, location, and size. In addition,
interactions between the granules are expressed by their fuzziness that results in
the overlapping of the granules within the picture.

L. Rutkowski et al. (Eds.): ICAISC 2013, Part I, LNAI 7894, pp. 412–425, 2013.

The fuzzy granulation approach applied to color digital pictures may be very useful for problems of picture classification where classes are distinguished based on linguistic description. Such a problem is considered in Section 8, and its solution can be obtained based on fuzzy IF-THEN rules formulated in this section and applied to a fuzzy inference system (see e.g. [11]).

In Section 7, the fuzzy granulation approach is outlined, with regard to image processing and color digital picture recognition, referring to other sections, especially to Section 6 where the idea of macropixels is introduced. The new approach, based on the fuzzy granulation, is more precisely described, including some mathematical formulas, in Section 8.

Sections 2, 3, and 4 concern the color attribute while Section 5 as well as Section 6 are interested in the location of pixels in a digital picture. As mentioned earlier, Section 2 provides general information about color, hue, and color models (that take into account saturation and lightness). Section 3 describes a particular type of color models that is the CIE chromaticity triangle which is applied in the problem considered in this paper. In Section 4, we focus our attention on the color areas of the CIE chromaticity triangle, viewed as fuzzy regions (fuzzy sets) characterized by membership functions. In Section 5, fuzzy sets and their membership functions are proposed to represent the pixel locations. Section 6 refers to the third attribute of the granules, i.e. size.

In Section 9, some conclusions and final remarks are included, as well as further research directions outlined. This paper presents a new concept of fuzzy granulation approach to color digital picture recognition that can be extended in many directions and applied to various new problems formulated in the area of image processing and recognition.

2 Color Properties and Models

The pure color is called "hue". Usually, colors with the same hue are distinguished with descriptive adjectives such as "light blue", "pastel blue", "vivid blue", "dark blue", which refer to their lightness and/or chroma (saturation). Exceptions inlude "brown" which is a dark "orange", and "pink" that is a light red with reduced chroma. Hue is one of the main properties of a color. Saturation (also called chroma) and lightness (also called brightness, value, or tone) are two additional properties of a color. Hue is the term for the pure spectrum of colors that appear in the rainbow as well as in the visible spectrum of white light separated by a prism.

Theoretically all hues can be mixed from three basic hues, known as primaries. There are different definitions of the primary colors. i.e. painters primaries, printers primaries, and light primaries; for details, see e.g. [1].

However, the visible spectrum consists of much more colors than a computer monitor can display. The well known RGB (red, green, blue) refers to the application in computer screens where colored light is mixed. If all three light primaries are mixed the theoretical result is white light. The RGB is an additive color model, combining red, green, and blue light. In computers the RGB color model is used in numerical color specifications.

It has been observed that the RGB colors have some limitaitons. The RGB is hardware-oriented and non-intuitive which means that people can easily learn how to use the RGB but they rather think of hue, saturation and lightness, and how to translate them to the RGB.

Two most common representations of points in the RGB color model, based on hue, saturation and lightness, are HSL and HSV. The former stands for "hue", "saturation", and "lightness", while the latter for: "hue", "saturation", and "value". The HSV is also called HSB (where B stands for "brightness"). A third model, common in computer vision applications, is HSI, for "hue", "saturation", and "intensity". The HSV, HSB, HSL color models are slight variations on the HSI theme.

Saturation defines a range from pure color to gray at a constant lightness level. A pure color is fully saturated. Lightness indicates the level of illumination, and defines a range from dark (no light) to fully illuminated.

In a color space, colors can be identified numerically by their coordinates. There are precise rules for converting between the HSL and HSV spaces, defined as mappings of the RGB. The convertion between them should remain the same color; however it is not always true with regard to different color spaces (e.g. RGB to CMYK that is a subtractive color model, used in color printing). Since RGB and CMYK are both device-dependent spaces, there is no simple or general conversion formula that converts between them. The CMYK color model is based on the printers primaries, i.e. cyan, magenta, and yellow. In addition, the key (black) component is used. Color printing typically employ ink of the four colors (including black). Mixing the three printers primaries theortically results in black, but imperfect ink formulations do not give true black, which is why the additional key component is needed. It is worth noticing that secondary mixtures of the CMY primaries (cyan, magenta, yellow) results in red, green, blue.

It is worth emphasizing that the RGB model is usually employed for production of colors while the HSI for description of colors. Conversion between RGB and HSI is also possible; see e.g. [4], [5].

Some color spaces separate the three dimensions of color into one luminance dimension and a pair of chromaticity dimension. For example, the chromaticity coordinates x and y are used in the xyY space, in the CIE color model, described in the next section.

Luminance is the physical measure of brightness; the standard unit of luminance is candela per square meter. Luminance is the amount of visible light leaving a point on a surface in a given direction. We can simply say that luminance is the amount of light reflected from a hue (on a physical surface or an imaginary plane). Brightness is the perception elicited by the luminance of a visual target. A given target luminance can elicit different perceptions of brightness in different contexts.

Formerly the term "brightness" was used as a synonym for "luminance". Lightness was the term used in the CIE world (see Sections 3), and thought of as synonym for reflectivity as well as intensity.

The CIE procedure converts the spectral power distribution of light from an object into a brightness parameter Y and two chromaticity coordinates x, y. The brightness parameter Y is a measure of luminance which is light intensity factored by the sinsitivity of the normal human eye.

Chromaticity is an objective specification of the quality of a color regardless of its luminance. The CIE diagram removes all intensity information, and uses its two dimensions to describe hue and saturation.

More information on this subject we can find in many publications refering to color theory, computer vision, etc.; many interesting details are available on the Internet, including Wikipedia.

3   The CIE Chromaticity Triangle and Fuzzy Color Areas

The CIE color model was developed to be completely independent of any device or other means of emission or reproduction and is based as closely as possible on how humans perceive color. This model was introduced in 1931 by the CIE that stands for Comission Internationale de l'Eclairage (International Commission on Illumination).

The CIE chromaticity diagram represents the mapping of human color perception in terms of two CIE parameters x and y, called the chromaticity coordinates, which map a color with respect to hue and saturation.

Color names have been assigned to different regions of the CIE color space (chromaticity triangle) by various researchers; see e.g. [3], [4]. These are approximate colors that represent rough categories, and not to be taken as precise statements of color. Therefore, we can treat them as fuzzy sets, and boundaries between the regions may be viewed as not crisp but belonging to the distinct areas with a certain membership value.

The original CIE 1931 color space was updated in 1960 and 1976 so that the chromacity spacing would be more perceptually uniform, and also more convenient for industrial applications (e.g. food, paint, etc.). The main advantage of the 1976 CIE chromaticity diagram is that the distance between points on the diagram is approximately proportional to the perceived color difference.

In this paper, we apply the original CIE chromaticity triangle, with the labeled regions presented in [3], [4]. Thus, we employ 23 fuzzy regions of the CIE color space, assosiated with the following colors (hues): red, pink, reddish orange, orange pink, orange, yellowish orange, yellow, greenish yellow, yellow green, yellowish green, green, bluish green, bluegreen, greenish blue, blue, purplish blue, bluish purple, purple, reddish purple, purplish pink, red purple, purplish red, white.

The CIE chromaticity diagram shows the range of perceivable hues for the normal human eye. We can say that the chromaticity diagram plots the entire gamut of human-perceivable colors by their x, y coordinates. The inverted-U shaped locus boundary (that is the upper part of the horseshoe shaped boundary) represents spectral colors (wavelengths in nm). The lower-bound of the locus is known as the "line of purples" and represents non-spectral colors obtained by mixing light of red and blue wavelengths. Colors on the periphery of the locus are saturated, and become progressively desaturated in the direction towards white somewhere in the middle of the plot.

Any color within a triangle defined by three primaries (red, green, blue) can be created (or recreated) by additive mixing of varying proportion of those primary colors. The area of the triangle is much less than the entire chromaticity diagram. The triangle (located in the CIE diagram), which is the gamut of additive coverage with RGB primaries, represents the colors that can be displayed by a particular monitor (not including any brightness information). Another gamut (a smaller area), included in the RGB triangle, indicates the range available to commercial four-color printing process; see [15]. It is important knowing that different display technologies (e.g. CRT, LCD, plasma, inkjet printers, laser printers) may have inherently different color gamuts. Printers can display much less colors than monitors. It is worth noticing that in some areas the RGB gamut is "outside" that of the CMYK space (applied in color printing).

As a matter of fact, there are different types of RGB spaces depending on the technical reasons, professional requirements, and display devices. The most common are Adobe, Apple, ProPhoto, and sRGB (created cooperatively by HP and Microsoft in 1996), as well as CIE RGB i.e. the above mentioned gamut located in the CIE diagram. For details, see e.g. [6], [8].

4   Membership of Pixels to the Color Areas of the CIE Triangle

Color digital pictures are composed of pixels (picture elements, i.e. smallest units of 2-dimensional images). The pixels have a color associated with each of them. Using the RGB color model in computers, the color of a pixel is expressed as an RGB triplet (r, g, b) where each of the components (RGB coordinates) can vary from zero to a defined maximum value (e.g. 1 or 255). An RGB triplet (r, g, b) represents the 3-dimensional coordinate of the point of the given color within the cube created by 3 axes (red, blue, and green) with values within [0,1] range. In this model, every point in the cube denotes the color from black (0,0,0) to white (1,1,1). The triplets (r, g, b) are viewed as ordinary Cartesian coordinates in a euclidean space.

The (r, g, b) coordinates can be transformed into the CIE chromaticity triangle, i.e. to the color areas located on the 2-dimensional space (of the CIE diagram) with (x, y) coordinates. Detailed information concerning the transformation from RGB to XYZ space and vice versa as well as color gamut representation in the CIE diagram of different RGB color spaces is presented e.g. in [6]. It is also possible to convert RGB coordinates between sRGB and other types of RGB spaces; see [7]. Mathematical formulas describing the transformation from XYZ space to xyz and then to xy can be found in many publications, e.g. [4]. The transformation is also explained and the mathematical equations are included in [14].

For considerations in this paper, it is sufficient to use the following equations

$$x = f_1(r, g, b), \quad y = f_2(r, g, b) \tag{1}$$

which in this general form describe the transformation from the RGB color space (3-dimensional) to the 2-dimensional xy space of the CIE chromaticity diagram. Of course, for the calculations we employ the precisely defined functions (1), presented in the publications cited above.

Knowing the functions (1), we can transform each triplet (r, g, b) associated with particular pixels of a digital color picture to the CIE chromaticity triangle (the gamut). In this way, we can assign a proper color area of the CIE diagram to every pixel of the picture.

Each pixel of the picture (color image) is characterized by two attributes: color and location. The former refers to the (r, g, b) and (x, y) in the corresponding area of the CIE gamut. The latter concerns the spatial location within the picture and will be discussed in the next section.

Let us denote:

Ω – digital color picture

M – number of pixels in the picture Ω

p_j – j-th pixel in the picture Ω, where $j = 1, ..., M$

$c_j = (r_j, g_j, b_j)$ – triplet (r, g, b) for pixel p_j, where $j = 1, ..., M$

As mentioned in Section 3, the color areas (regions) of the CIE chromaticity triangle may be treated as fuzzy regions, with fuzzy boundaries between those areas. This means that the fuzzy color areas are fuzzy sets of points (x, y) that belong to them with membership grades expressed by a value from the interval $[0.1]$. Thus, a point (x, y) may fully belong to a color region (membership value equals 1), partially belong (membership greater than 0 and less than 1) or not belong (membership equals 0). The membership functions of the fuzzy sets may be defined in different ways. An algorithm for creation such membership functions for the fuzzy color areas of the CIE triangle is proposed in [14].

Let Δ_{CIE} denotes the CIE chromaticity triangle, and $\{H_1, H_2, ..., H_n\}$ - crisp color areas (regions with sharp boundaries) of the Δ_{CIE}. Hence, we have the following equation

$$\Delta_{CIE} = \bigcup_{i=1}^{n} H_i \tag{2}$$

In the case of the regions presented in [3], [4] and mentioned in Section 3, the number of the color areas, $n=23$, and there are 23 labels (color names) listed in Section 3 assigned to each region H_i, for $i = 1, ..., 23$.

As explained in Section 3, the color areas H_i, for $i = 1, ..., n$, can be viewed as fuzzy regions. Let us denote them as $\{\widetilde{H}_1, \widetilde{H}_2, ..., \widetilde{H}_n\}$. The fuzzy sets $\{\widetilde{H}_i\}$, for $i = 1, ..., 23$, like the corresponding crisp sets $\{H_i\}$, are defined in the 2-dimensional space (of the CIE diagram) with (x, y) coordinates. This space is called the universe of discourse for the fuzzy sets. Both the crisp sets $\{H_i\}$ and fuzzy sets $\{\widetilde{H}_i\}$ are sets of points (x, y). Each of these points (elements, objects) may belong to only one of the crisp sets $\{H_i\}$ but can partially belong to more than one fuzzy set $\{\widetilde{H}_i\}$, for $i = 1, ..., n$, where $n=23$. When the fuzzy sets are considered, their membership functions must be known (see [16], [11]). Let us denote them as $\mu_{\widetilde{H}_i}(x, y)$. As mentioned earlier, those membership functions are determined in [14].

With regard to a digital color picture, Ω, for every pixel, p_j, $j = 1, ..., M$, its color atribute value, $c_j = (r_j, g_j, b_j)$, can easily be transformed to the point (x_j, y_j) in the Δ_{CIE}, by use of formulas (1). Hence, we can determine the membership values of c_j to the fuzzy sets $\{\widetilde{H}_i\}$, for $i = 1, ..., n$, as $\mu_{\widetilde{H}_i}(c_j) = \mu_{\widetilde{H}_i}(x_j, y_j)$.

In [12], the CIE chromaticity triangle is employed, and membership degrees of particular hues in color digital pictures are used in a classification task. However, with regard to the practical application under consideration in that case, we are not interested in the location of pixels of particular color. Thus, this is a different problem; in this paper, the pixel location is very important.

5   Fuzzy Location of Pixels in a Digital Picture

Let us again consider a digital picture, Ω, composed of pixels, p_j, for $j = 1, ..., M$, but in this case we are interested in locations of the pixels within the image. Moreover, the locations will be viewed as fuzzy areas reprezented by fuzzy sets. This concept is shown in Fig. 1 where membership functions that define the fuzzy regions are portrayed. Trapezoidal membership functions are assumed to characterize the left, central, and right parts of the picture, respectively, denoted as S_L, S_M, S_R and W_D, W_C, W_U, for both s and w axes. As a matter of fact,

$$S^\Omega = \{S_L, S_M, S_R\}, \quad W^\Omega = \{W_U, W_C, W_D\} \tag{3}$$

are fuzzy sets with following membership functions:
$\{\mu_{S_L}(s), \mu_{S_M}(s), \mu_{S_R}(s)\}$ and $\{\mu_{W_U}(w)), \mu_{W_C}(w)), \mu_{W_D}(w)\}$, respectively, for the picture Ω. Now, let us consider the Cartesian product

$$Q^\Omega = S^\Omega \times W^\Omega \tag{4}$$

and the fuzzy sets depicted in Table 1. The 2-dimensional fuzzy sets presented in this table are Cartesian products of 1-dimensional fuzzy sets (3). These fuzzy sets are characterized by membership functions obtained as the minimum or product of two corresponding membership functions of the fuzzy sets (3); according to the definition of the Cartesian product of two fuzzy sets (see e.g. [18], [11]). The fuzzy sets portrayed in Table 1 describe the fuzzy locations of pixels in a digital picture Ω.

In Section 4, we considered the color attribute, c_j, of pixels p_j, for $j = 1, ..., M$, of a digital picture Ω. Now we focus our attention on the location attribute of the pixels. Let us denote: $S = \{1, 2, ..., M_s\}$, $W = \{1, 2, ..., M_w\}$, where $M = M_s M_w$; see Fig. 1. Then, the location attribute of a pixel p_j in the picture Ω, denoted

Table 1. Two-dimensional fuzzy sets that represent pixel locations in a digital picture

Left Upper	Left Central	Left Down
$S_L \times W_U$	$S_L \times W_C$	$S_L \times W_D$
Middle Upper	Middle Central	Middle Down
$S_M \times W_U$	$S_M \times W_C$	$S_M \times W_D$
Right Upper	Right Central	Right Down
$S_R \times W_U$	$S_R \times W_C$	$S_R \times W_D$

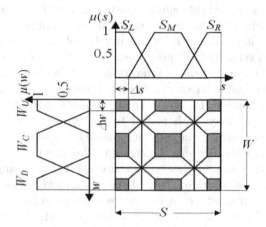

Fig. 1. Membership functions of fuzzy locations

as q_j, is expressed by coordinates (s, w) that determine the point in the space $S \times W$ corresponding to the pixel location. It is very easy to assign the proper coordinates (s, w) to every pixel p_j, where $s \in S$ and $w \in W$. It is obvious that, for all $j = 1, ..., M$, the pixel location $q_j(s, w) \in Q^\Omega$. In particular, this attribute of a pixel p_j belongs to the fuzzy sets illustrated in Table 1 and Fig. 1, with different membership values, depending on their membership functions.

6   An Idea of Macropixels

In Sections 4 and 5, single pixels of a digital picture have been considered with regard to two attributes: color and location, respectively. However, nowadays the number of pixels employed to represent digital pictures are usually very large. Moreover, we observe that it becomes larger and larger in digital cameras. This means that we collect more and more digital color pictures of hight spatial resolution of the images. Processing a large number of hight resolution images requires so many mathematical operations per pixel that is often a hight computational load even for today's powerful computers. Therefore, in this section, instead of individual pixels an idea of groups of pixels, called "macropixels", is proposed.

A digital color picture is viewed as a 2-dimensional array of single pixels arranged in columns and rows. In this way, the digital pictures discussed in Sections 4 and 5 have been described; see Fig. 1. To create the macropixels, we divide the whole image (digital picture) to identical rectangles that play the role of the macropixels. This means that the width and hight of the picture, S and W, respectively, are divided into intervals that build the rectangles (macropixels). Two algorithms may be proposed: incremental and decremental. The former means that the algorithm starts with individual pixels and then the rectangles that contain neighboring pixels are created. The latter algorithm starts with the whole image that is divided into smaller parts (rectangular macropixels). In the incremental algorithm, at the first iteration many small macropixels are constructed. The next iterations produce less number of macropixels of bigger size. In the decremental version of this algorithm, we start with the large macropixele equal to the whole picture, then next iterations produce smaller macropixels. We can say that on the one hand we can treat the macropixels as individual pixels while on the other hand we can view the macropixels as the whole picture.

Speaking more precisely, with regard to the decremental algorithm, every macropixel is treated as the whole picture, in each iteration, when it is divided into macropixels of a smaller size. Referring to the incremental algorithm, new macropixels of bigger size are viewed as the whole picture composed of pixels. This case concerns the proces of creating the macropixels. When the macropixels have already been constructed we can treat them as individual pixels that are characterized by two attributes: color and location. In this way, in many applications, we can focus our attention on the macropixels of specific color and location, instead of every pixel of the image.

Like with regard to the pixels, the color and location attributes of macropixels are viewed as fuzzy concepts. The color attribute of macropixels can be considered in the same way as presented for pixels in Section 4, with regard to the CIE chromaticity diagram. However, we should explain how to determine the color of macropixels based on the color attribute values, c_j, of the pixels p_j that belong to these macropixels. Every macropixel is composed of the individual pixels that are subsets of the pixels $\{p_j\}$, for $j = 1, ..., M$, that form the whole picture Ω.

Let us assume that the picture Ω consists of M_k macropixels, Ω_k, for $k = 1, ..., M_k$. Every macropixel, Ω_k, can be viewed as an individual pixel reffering to its membership to the color regions, $\{\tilde{H}_i\}$, for $i = 1, ..., n$, in the CIE diagram.

We can propose several methods to determine the color value of the macropixel, Ω_k, for $k = 1, ..., M_k$. Among others, we can take into consideration the average value of the membership of the individual pixels that create the macropixel to the CIE color regions. In this paper, we focus our attention on an approximate color of a group of neighboring pixels (macropixel) rather than the color of individual pixels.

The location attribute of the macropixels can be considered with regard to the approach presented in Section 5 for individual pixels. The macropixels, Ω_k, for $k = 1, ..., M_k$, may be viewed as fuzzy pixels that belong to the fuzzy sets portrayed in Fig. 1 and Table 1.

In this section, we propose the macropixels of rectangular shape and the same size. However, we can introduce another attribute of the macropixels, in addition to the color and location, that is the size. Taking into account a group of pixels (macropixel) of a specific color and location (expressed by fuzzy values), the third attribute, i.e. the size may include very useful information with regard to the problem described in Section 8.

7   Fuzzy Granulation

Fuzzy granulation approach, as mentioned in Section 1, has been introduced by Zadeh [19]. Some information one can also find in e.g. [11]. New ideas concerning the fuzzy granulation approach have been developed by Pedrycz, especially with regard to neural networks (see e.g. [9]), also in application to pattern recognition [10].

According to Zadeh [17], [18], [19], linguistic variables are concomitant with the concept of granulation. As the author explained in [18], granulation, in fuzzy logic, involves a grouping of objects into fuzzy granules, with a granule being a clump of objects drawn together by similarity. In efect, granulation may be viewed as a form of fuzzy quantization, which in turn may be seen as an instance of fuzzy data compression. In the non-fuzzy case, quantization is the same as crisp granulation where granules are not fuzzy.

Image processing is one of examples where information granulation may be applied and play an important role in pattern recognition [10]. In this case, the similarity of objects that are candidats for grouping into a granule usually refers to the closeness of pixels located spatially close to each other. In the concept of information granulation, the granules can take a form of sets, fuzzy sets, rough sets, etc., but most often are concentrated on the use of fuzzy sets.

In this paper, we apply the concept of fuzzy granulation to digital color pictures. The idea of macropixels, described in Section 6, is strictly related to the fuzzy granulation approach. The fuzzy color areas of the CIE diagram, discussed in Sections 3 and 4, as well as the fuzzy locations, proposed in Section 5, can be considered in the framework of the fuzzy granulation.

The macropixels may be viewed as fuzzy granules that represent groups of pixels similar with regard to their location in a digital picture. When pixels of the same (or similar) color are located within a macropixel, we have a granule of the same color and location. In addition, as mentioned in Section 6, the third attribute, i.e. the size of the macropixels may be taken into account. Thus, we can see a digital color picture as a collection of macropixels associated with corresponding granules that carry information about color, location, and size. This concept is especially useful with regard to the problem considered in this paper and discribed in Section 8.

From the color point of view, the fuzzy regions of the CIE chromaticity triangle may be treated as fuzzy granules. In this case, the granules are groups of points with similar color (hue). Referring to the location, the fuzzy sets defined in the space (4) and presented in Table 1 with the illustration in Fig. 1, form fuzzy granules of the points (pixels) characterized by the same fuzzy location. Both kinds of the fuzzy granules are labeled with values of linguistic variables, i.e. linguistic names of color and location. Fuzzy IF-THEN rules with these linguistic variables are applied in the fuzzy granulation approach. Thus, information concerning colors and locations of pixels are granulated in a fuzzy way in order to inference a result of the picture recognition problem, formulated in Section 8.

8   A New Approach to Color Digital Picture Recognition

Let us consider the following problem. Having a large collection of color digital pictures, we would like to find a picture (or pictures) presenting an object characterized by three attributes – size, color, and location – with fuzzy values (e.g. a big object of a color close to red, located somewhere in the center). In order to recognize such a picture (or a group of similar pictures), we can employ the idea of macropixels (described in Section 6) along with the fuzzy approach to color (see Section 4) and location (see Section 5). The fuzzy granulation, as mentioned in Section 7, is especially useful with regard to this problem. Information granules, in this case, contain information about size, color, and location. Macropixels of different sizes and the same (or similar) color and location form the information granules.

Referring to the color, location, and size, we have the following fuzzy granules:

- For the color — $\{C_i\} = \{\tilde{H}_i\}$, for $i = 1, ..., n$, where $n = 23$, with the membership functions $\mu_{\tilde{H}_i}(c_j) = \mu_{\tilde{H}_i}(x_j, y_j)$, for $j = 1, ..., M$, see Section 4
- For the location — $\{Q_l\}$, for $l = 1, ..., L$, where $Q_1 = S_L \times W_U$, $Q_2 = S_L \times W_C$, $Q_3 = S_L \times W_D$, $Q_4 = S_M \times W_U$, $Q_5 = S_M \times W_C$, $Q_6 = S_M \times W_D$, $Q_7 = S_R \times W_U$, $Q_8 = S_R \times W_C$, $Q_9 = S_R \times W_D$, where $L = 9$, in Table 1, with the membership functions of fuzzy sets (3) shown in Fig. 1; for details concerning the membership functions of 2-dimensional fuzzy sets (3) see Section 5, of course – we can consider the case of more than 9 fuzzy sets for the location
- For the size — $\{Z_m\}$, for $m = 1, ..., K$, i.e. fuzzy sets with membership functions that describe the size of macropixel Ω_k, for $k = 1, ..., M_k$ (see Section 6) as e.g. "small", "medium", "big" ($K = 3$) or "very small", "small", "medium", "big", "very big" ($K = 5$), relatively to the size of the digital color picture Ω.

Now, we assume that we have M_k macropixels of different sizes, created in the way described in Section 6. The membership functions of the macropixel size can be defined as trapezoidal-shaped functions (like in Fig. 1) or e.g. triangular or Gaussian functions. Precise definitions of the membership functions have to correspond to the above mentioned linguistic names e.g. big or small size.

The fuzzy granules, for the color, location, and size, deal with a single dimension (attribute). When a granule of the 3-dimension is considered, we take the Cartesian product of the corresponding fuzzy sets (1-dimensional granules) in each dimension (coordinate). In this way, we obtain the following fuzzy granules:

$$G^k = C^k \times Q^k \times Z^k, \quad k = 1, ..., M_k \tag{5}$$

where $C^k \subset \{\tilde{H}_i\}$, for $i = 1, ..., n$, $Q^k \subset \{Q_l\}$, for $l = 1, ..., L$, $Z^k \subset \{Z_m\}$, for $m = 1, ..., K$.

According to the definition of the Cartesian product of fuzzy sets, a triangular norm (t-norm) must be applied to determine the fuzzy granule (5); for details, see e.g. [11].

The fuzzy granule (5) is a multidimensional fuzzy set that represents a fuzzy relation between color, location, and size (attributes of the macropixels). In the fuzzy granulation approach, a digital color picture is viewed as a composition of the fuzzy granules that carry information about the color, location, and size, as well as interactions between them (expressed by the fuzziness that results in overlapping of the granules).

With regard to the problem of picture recognition, described at the begining of this section, fuzzy IF-THEN rules of the following form can be formulated:

IF c is C_i **AND** q is Q_l **AND** z is Z_m **THEN** class D_r

where (c, q, z) is a point belonging to the space of fuzzy granules (5), and D_r, for $r = 1, ..., R$, denotes distinguished classes in the classification problem of the digital color pictures. For example, D_r may be a class of the pictures presenting a big object of a color close to red, located somewhere in the center.

The classification problem can be solved by use of a fuzzy system with the inference method based on fuzzy logic and the fuzzy IF-THEN rules; for details see e.g. [11]. In this way, we expect to obtain a group of pictures belonging to the specific class (e.g. with a big object of a color close to red, somewhere in the center of the picture). Then, having relatively small number of such a pictures (after the classification), it is much easier to find the one that we are searching for. Of course, it is possible to get just the only one picture from a large collection of others.

It is worth emphasizing that the approach proposed in this paper is granular oriented rather than pixel processing. Fuzziness of the granules enables to use linguistic descriptions of digital color pictures and the inference based on fuzzy IF-THEN rules. In the classification problem of picture recognition, considered in this section, it is not necessary to process every pixel of the digital picture. Instead, we can take into account only macropixels of a specific location and size, e.g. a big macropixel in the center of the picture, and classify them with regard to their color.

Referring to the color of macropixels, we can employ the method presented in [12], where an amount of specific colors (hues) in the whole digital picture is determined based on the CIE chromaticity triangle, ignoring the location of the color pixels. Now, we can apply this method to macropixels treated as the whole picture in the algorithm described in [12].

9 Conclusions and Final Remarks

The problem addressed in Section 8 may be treated as an example of a group of problems concerning recognition of color digital pictures. Various specific tasks can be formulated and solved within the framework of the fuzzy granulation approach. Among others, it seems to be very useful in image segmentation, where a digital image is partitioned into segments (groups of pixels, known as superpixels); see e.g. [2].

In this paper, we consider the problem of color digital pictures recognition that can be viewed as a special case of image processing and image recognition. As mentioned in Section 1, we are interested in a large collection of the color digital pictures that are images, of course, but typical, taken by popular digital cameras, not e.g. medical images. Therefore, we use the name "picture" rather that "image", in order to focus our attention on the application to usual photos. Moreover, the important issue is that we are now not going to recognize the exact image presented in the picture but only its specific part described by an approximate color and location.

It should be emphasized that the main idea concerning the problems considered in this paper is to describe a picture by linguistic terms that refer to color, location, and size, i.e. the attributes of macropixels. Then, our task is to recognize (and e.g. classify) pictures with specific features, expressed by the linguistic description, such as "a big object of a color close to red, located somewhere in the center of the picture". Thus, our aim is not to recognize details of the image but only selected features with approximate (fuzzy) values.

Further research on this subject may concern to include the third dimension of the CIE chromaticity triangle, that is the luminance. We expect that this can improve the recognition results with regard to the color attribute.

In addition, different shapes of the macropixels may be considered, so other shapes of their membership functions must be applied. In this way, we can obtain a better model of interactions between the granules. This should result in better representation of an image included in a digital color picture.

Then, we can extend our research to the very interesting problem of image understanding (see e.g.[13]) based on the fuzzy granulation approach introduced in this paper.

The granulation approach that we propose to color digital picture recognition differs from the granular computing in pattern recognition, presented in [10]. However, we can adopt some ideas in our future research, and use fuzzy granules to summarize a collection of pictures.

References

1. Briggs, D.: The Dimensions of Colour (2012), available on the Internet
   http://www.huevaluechroma.com
2. Felzenszwalb, P., Huttenlocher, D.: Efficient graph-based image segmentation. International Journal of Computer Vision 59(2), 167–181 (2004)
3. Fortner, B.: Number by color. Part 5. SciTech Journal 6, 30–33 (1996)
4. Fortner, B., Meyer, T.E.: Number by Color. A Guide to Using Color to Undersdand Technical Data. Springer (1997)
5. Moeslund, T.B.: Introduction to Video and Image Processing. Building Real Systems and Applications. Springer, London (2012)

6. Pascale, D.: A Review of RGB Color Spaces ... from xyY to R'G'B'. The BabelColor Company (2003), available on the Internet http://www.babelcolor.com
7. Pascale, D.: The RGB Code: The Mysteries of Color Revealed. Part 3: Color Differences and Converting Colors (2004), available on the Internet http://www.graphics.com
8. Pascale, D.: RGB Coordinates of the Macbeth ColorChecker. The BabelColor Company (2006), available on the Internet http://www.babelcolor.com
9. Pedrycz, W.: Neural networks in the framework of granular computing. International Journal of Applied Mathematics and Computer Science 10(4), 723–745 (2000)
10. Pedrycz, W., Vukovich, G.: Granular computing in pattern recognition. In: Bunke, H., Kandel, A. (eds.) Neuro-Fuzzy Pattern Recofnition, pp. 125–143. World Scientific (2000)
11. Rutkowska, D.: Neuro-Fuzzy Architectures and Hybrid Learning. Springer (2002)
12. Rutkowska, D., Wiaderek, K.: Fuzzy classification of color patterns. In: Proceedings of the 5th Conference on Neural Networks and Soft Computing, Zakopane, Poland, pp. 368–373 (2000)
13. Tadeusiewicz, R., Ogiela, M.R.: Why Automatic Understanding? In: Beliczynski, B., Dzielinski, A., Iwanowski, M., Ribeiro, B. (eds.) ICANNGA 2007, Part II. LNCS, vol. 4432, pp. 477–491. Springer, Heidelberg (2007)
14. Wiaderek, K.: Fuzzy sets in colour image processing based on the CIE chromaticity triangle. In: Rutkowska, D., Cader, A., Przybyszewski, K. (eds.) Selected Topics in Computer Science Applications, pp. 3–26. Academic Publishing House EXIT, Warsaw (2011)
15. Williamson, S.J., Cummins, H.Z.: Light and Color in Nature and Art. Wiley (1983)
16. Zadeh, L.A.: Fuzzy sets. Information and Control 8, 338–353 (1965)
17. Zadeh, L.A.: Fuzzy sets and information granularity. In: Gupta, M., Ragade, R., Yager, R. (eds.) Advances in Fuzzy Set Theory and Applications, pp. 3–18. North Holland, Amsterdam (1979)
18. Zadeh, L.A.: Fuzzy logic and calculi of fuzzy rules and fuzzy graphs: a precis. Multiple Valued Logic 1, 1–38 (1996)
19. Zadeh, L.A.: Toward a theory of fuzzy information granulation and its centrality in human reasoning and fuzzy logic. Fuzzy Sets and Systems 90, 111–127 (1997)

Pruning One-Class Classifier Ensembles by Combining Sphere Intersection and Consistency Measures

Bartosz Krawczyk and Michał Woźniak

Department of Systems and Computer Networks,
Wroclaw University of Technology, Wyb. Wyspianskiego 27, 50-370 Wroclaw, Poland
{bartosz.krawczyk,michal.wozniak}@pwr.wroc.pl

Abstract. One-class classification is considered as one of the most challenging topics in the contemporary machine learning. Creating Multiple Classifier Systems for this task has proven itself as a promising research direction. Here arises a problem on how to select valuable members to the committee - so far a largely unexplored area in one-class classification. This paper introduces a novel approach that allows to choose appropriate models to the committee in such a way that assures both high quality of individual classifiers and a high diversity among the pool members. We aim at preventing the selection of both too weak or too similar models. This is achieved with the usage of an multi-objective optimization that allows to consider several criteria when searching for a good subset of classifiers. A memetic algorithm is applied due to its efficiency and less random behavior than traditional genetic algorithm. As one-class classification differs from traditional multi-class problems we propose to use two measures suitable for this problem - consistency measure that allow to rank the quality of one-class models and introduced by us sphere intersection measure that serves as a diversity metric. Experimental results carried on a number of benchmark datasets proves that it outperforms traditional single-objective approaches.

Keywords: machine learning, one-class classification, ensemble pruning, classifier selection, diversity, random subspace, memetic algorithm, multi-objective optimisation.

1 Introduction

One-class classification (OCC) is a specific subfield of machine learning. During the classifier training step there are at disposal only objects from a single class, called the target concept. It is assumed that at the exploitation phase of such a classifier there may appear new, unseen objects, called outliers. Therefore OCC aims at establishing a boundary that separates the target objects from possible outliers [22]. The term single-class classification was introduced in [11], but also outlier detection or novelty detection [3] are used to name this field of study.

L. Rutkowski et al. (Eds.): ICAISC 2013, Part I, LNAI 7894, pp. 426–436, 2013.

OCC is a difficult task and there are many open problems related to it. One of the most prominent is how the target class boundary should be tuned - in case of being too general unwanted outliers would be accepted, in case of being too matched to the training set a strong overfitting may occur. From this one may see that it is risky to rely only on a single given model. In recent years there have been several successful attempts on how to improve the quality of one-class recognition systems. One of them is the ensemble approach utilizing outputs of more than one model.

Multiple classifier systems (MCSs) despite the well established status they are the subject of ongoing intense research. Among many factors entangled in the design process of MCS one of the uttermost importance is how to select classifiers to ensure the high quality of the ensemble. Combining similar classifiers do not contribute to the system being constructed, apart from increasing the computational complexity. In some cases (e.g. voting fusion methods) it may even decrease the quality of the committee. Therefore selected members should display characteristics unique to each of them in order to improve the quality of the collective decision. There are two main research trends in this area - how to assure the diversity among the individual classifiers in the pool [14] and how to measure it efficiently [2].

One should bore in mind that diversity itself is not the perfect criterion for classifier selection. It is easy to imagine a situation in which two classifiers have a high diversity in comparison to each other but at the same time one of them (or even both) is of low quality. When using diversity for the ensemble pruning such models would be selected but at the same time the quality of the MCS will drop. In an ideal situation the committee should consist of models that are competent and mutually complementary i.e., each of the classifiers should display a high individual accuracy and a high diversity when compared to other members.

It must be mentioned that there are two different views on the applications of one-class classifiers:

- as a tool for solving problems in which objects other than the ones originating from the target class are hard or even impossible to obtain, e.g. in machine fault diagnosis where generating all possible malfunctions of the system is too cost and time consuming - the paper follow this view on the OCC,
- as a tool for decomposition of a multi-class classification task [24].

The paper proposes a new way of the classifier selection designed for the specific nature of OCC. We propose to utilize simultaneously two criteria - one responsible for the predictive quality of classifiers and one for the diversity of the ensemble. This way we prevent our committee from consisting of models too weak or too similar to each other. Due to the specific nature of OCC accuracy itself cannot be used - instead we utilize an unsupervised consistency criterion that is suitable for this task. For measuring the diversity we introduce a novel measure based on minimization of the intersection between the spherical classifiers. A multi-objective memetic algorithm is used to chose the best subset of classifiers from the available pool. The extensive experimental results, backed up with the test of a statistical significance prove the usefulness of our proposition.

2   Combining One-Class Classifiers

The problem of building MCSs on the basis of one-class still awaits for proper attention. There are some papers dealing with the proposals on how to combine one-class classifiers [24], but most of them are oriented on the practical application [5], not on theoretical advances.

One-class boundary methods, such as used in this paper Support Vector Data Description (SVDD) [20], are based on computing the distance between the object x and the decision boundary that encloses the target class ω_T. To apply fusion methods we require the support function of object x for a given class. We propose to use the following heuristic solution:

$$\widehat{F}(x, \omega_T) = \frac{1}{c_1} exp(-d(x|\omega_T)/c_2), \qquad (1)$$

which models a Gaussian distribution around the classifier, where $d(x|\omega_T)$ is an Euclidean distance metric between the considered object and a decision boundary, c_1 is the normalization constant and c_2 is the scale parameter. Parameters c_1 and c_2 should be fitted to the target class distribution. One may easily see that used distance metric plays an important role in the process of combining one-class classifiers [16].

After such a mapping it is possible to combine OCC models based on their support functions [19]. Let us assume that there are L OCC classifiers in the pool. In this paper we use the mean of the estimated probabilities which is expressed by:

$$y_{mp}(x) = \frac{1}{L} \sum_{k} (P_k(x|\omega_T). \qquad (2)$$

This fusion method assumes that the outliers distribution is independent of x and thus uniform in the area around the target concept.

3   Model Selection for One-Class Classification

Classifier selection (known also as ensemble pruning) plays an important role in the process of the MCS design. There are two main criteria that should be considered while choosing models for the committee:

- accuracy - adding weak classifiers with a low competence will decrease the overall quality of the MCS;
- diversity - adding similar classifiers will contribute nothing to the ensemble apart from increasing the computational cost.

One should note that both of them have some drawbacks - highly accurate classifiers may be similar to each other, while highly diverse classifiers may display a weak individual quality. Both of these criteria are commonly used in the process of classifier selection for multi-class cases. Yet for the specific nature of OCC there is little work so far on how to evaluate usefulness of a pool of models to a committee. In [4] it is suggested to prune the ensemble according to the individual accuracies of classifiers, while authors of this paper introduced dedicated diversity measures for this task [12,15].

In this paper we use two independent criteria - consistency measure to rank classifiers according to their quality (as we have no outlier objects at the classifier building step we cannot use simple accuracy measure) and sphere intersection which we introduce as a novel diversity measure tuned to the nature of OCC.

3.1 Consistency Measure

The consistency measure indicates how consistent a pool of classifiers is in rejecting fraction f of the target data [21]. One may compute it by comparing the rejected fraction f with an estimate of the error on the target class $\widehat{\varepsilon^t}$:

$$Cons(\Pi^l) = |\widehat{\varepsilon^t} - f|, \tag{3}$$

where Π^l is the tested pool of classifiers. This is an unsupervised measure well suitable for OCC problems as we need only the estimation of error on the target class - no information about outliers is required.

3.2 Sphere Intersection Measure

Intuitively a high diversity of an ensemble may be achieved when each of the classifiers have a different area of competence. From this one may easily see that two classifiers with similar areas of competence will not contribute much to the quality of the committee. Taking into consideration the specific nature of boundary one-class classifiers we may assume that two predictors with high overlap of decision boundaries may be deemed as ones with a low diversity. Therefore we propose a diversity measure designed specifically for spherical one-class classifiers (such as considered in this paper SVDD), based on a degree of overlap between individual classifiers [9].

In case of classifier overlapping there may be two situations - where classifiers overlap pairwise and when more than a pair of classifiers overlap. Examples of such situations are presented in Fig. 1.

We propose to measure the diversity of the ensemble by measuring the overall degree of overlap between all classifiers in the pool. Firstly we need to calculate the volume of a single spherical classifier:

$$V_S(a, R) = \frac{2\pi^{\frac{D}{2}} R^D}{\Gamma(D/2 + 1)}, \tag{4}$$

where D is the dimensionality of the training set $\mathcal{TS}$, a is the center of the sphere, R is the radius the sphere and Γ is the gamma function.

Therefore the volume of all L classifiers from the pool is equal to the sum of their individual volumes:

$$V_{sum} = \sum_{i=1}^{L} V_S(a_i, R_i). \tag{5}$$

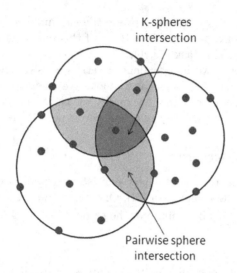

Fig. 1. Example of possible sphere intersections - two spheres overlapping (pairwise) and more than two spheres overlapping (K-spheres intersection)

In case of a lack of overlap between the spheres in the committee the volume of an ensemble is equal to the sum of the volumes of all individual classifiers:

$$V_{ens} = V_{sum} \Leftrightarrow$$
$$\forall_{i \neq j} \quad _{i,j=1,...,L} \quad V_{\mathcal{S}}(a_i, R_i) \cap V_{\mathcal{S}}(a_j, R_j) = \emptyset. \tag{6}$$

We assume that maximum diversity is achieved for the situation presented in (6) i.e. when no overlap between individual classifiers exist.

In case of E pairwise overlaps the volume of an ensemble is given by the following formulae:

$$V_{ens} = \sum_{i=1}^{L} V_{\mathcal{S}}(a_i, R_i) - \sum_{e=1}^{E} V_{\mathcal{O}_e} \Leftrightarrow$$
$$\exists_{i \neq j} \quad _{i,j=1,...,L} \quad V_{\mathcal{S}}(a_i, R_i) \cap V_{\mathcal{S}}(a_j, R_j) \neq \emptyset. \tag{7}$$

The spherical cap [7] is a part of a hypersphere defined by its height $h_c \in [0, 2R]$ and its radius $r_c \in [0, 2R]$. In the [9] a following equation for D dimensional spherical cap has been proposed:

$$V_{cap}(R, h_c, D) = \frac{\pi^{(D-1)/2} R^{D-1}}{\Gamma((D-1)/2 + 1)} \int_0^{\beta_{max}(R, h_c)} sin^{D-1}(\beta) d\beta, \tag{8}$$

where

$$\beta_{max}(R, h_c) = arcsin(\sqrt{(2R - h_c)(h_c/R^2)}). \tag{9}$$

From this we may write the volume of a single pairwise overlap $V_{\mathcal{O}_e}$ as a sum of their spherical caps:

$$V_{\mathcal{O}_e}(R, h_c) = V_{cap1} + V_{cap2}. \tag{10}$$

In case when more than two classifiers overlap the computation of the volume of the overlap becomes more complex. One may simplify this problem by counting only pairwise overlaps, but this would lead to counting some parts of the overlapping region K times for K intersecting spherical classifiers.

The volume of non-pairwise overlap can be bounded between the volume of classifiers with only pairwise overlaps and the volume of classifiers with no overlapping:

$$\sum_{i=1}^{L} V_S(a_i, R_i) - \sum_{e=1}^{E} V_{\mathcal{O}_e} \leq V_{ens} \leq \sum_{i=1}^{L} V_S(a_i, R_i). \tag{11}$$

Basing on the presented upper and lower bound one may derive an approximation of the volume of the ensemble with non-pairwise overlapping:

$$V_{ens} \approx \sum_{i=1}^{L} V_S(a_i, R_i) - \frac{1}{2} \sum_{e=1}^{E} V_{\mathcal{O}_e}. \tag{12}$$

The maximum error of such an approximation is no greater than $\frac{1}{2} \sum_{e=1}^{E} V_{\mathcal{O}_e}$.

With presented above equations we propose to measure the diversity by comparing the volume of the ensemble to the sum of all individual classifiers, assuming that with increase of the intersection degree the diversity falls down:

$$DIV_{SI_{oc}}(\Pi^l) = \frac{V_{ens}}{V_{sum}}. \tag{13}$$

4   Proposed Method

In this paper we propose to select OCC classifiers to the committee according to the combination of both of these criteria, hoping that this will allow to combine their strong points while becoming more robust to flaws exhibited by each of them. To achieve this we propose to use a multi-objective optimization, conducted with the usage of a memetic algorithm (MA) [6].

MAs may be seen as a hybrid solution that fuses together different meta-heuristics in hope to use gain advantage from combining their strong points. The idea of MAs is based on the individual improvement plus population co-operation. Unlike traditional Evolutionary Algorithms (EA), MAs are biased towards exploiting all the knowledge about the problem under study. By this they may be seen as less random and more directed search method. The so-called No-Free-Lunch Theorem for optimization [25] proven that the quality of the search algorithm lies on the amount and quality of the knowledge that is available. MAs start slowly to gain the attention of machine learning filed [17].

In this paper we use a MA that is a hybrid approach using both EA and tabu search to exclude re-visiting previously checked points in solution space. Additionally to allow for searching simultaneously for classifiers with high consistency and diversity we use a multi-objective MA [10], aiming at maximizing both of these criteria.

Let us formulate the multi-objective optimization criterion as:

$$minimize\ g(\Pi^l) = (-Cons(\Pi^l) + DIV_{SI_{oc}}(\Pi^l)),, \qquad (14)$$

where Π^l is the given pool of classifiers that will undergo an ensemble pruning procedure, $Cons(\Pi^l)$ stands for the overall consistency of the given ensemble and $DIV_{SI_{oc}}(\Pi^l)$ is the diversity of the considered ensemble expressed by the mentioned Sphere Intersection Measure. The revert sign before the consistency value is due to the fact that it should be maximized while the lowest value of sphere intersection shows the highest ensemble diversity.

An individual in the MA population represents a classifier ensemble Ch=[C], where component C represents L classifiers at our disposal in the pool:

$$C = [C_1, C_2, ..., C_L], \qquad (15)$$

and is a binary vector with 1s indicating the chosen individual classifiers (i.e., if we have 10 classifiers then 0010110010 would indicate that classifiers 3, 5, 6, and 9 are chosen for the ensemble).

For this MA standard operators for EAs such as individual selection, mutation, cross-over etc. apply. Additionally a tabu search is applied at the end of each iteration to additionally tune the available individuals.

The control parameters of the MA algorithm are as follows:

- N_c - the upper limit of algorithm cycles,
- N_p - the population quantity,
- β - the mutation probability,
- γ - the crossover probability,
- Δ_m - the mutation range factor,
- V - the upper limit of algorithm iterations without quality improvement.
- T - the size of the tabu list.
- N_T - the number of cycles for improvement of individuals via the tabu search.

By this we achieve two goals: we use a more stable search procedure than in our previous works [13] and we utilize two criteria for classifier selection in hope to find the most suitable candidates for the OCC ensemble.

In the next section we present the experimental evaluation of our proposal.

5   Experimental Results

5.1   Aims of the Experiment

The aims of the experiment was to check the quality of the proposed method on several benchmark datasets and compare the multi-objective classifier selection for one-class ensembles with other approaches - based only on the diversity criterion and only on the consistency criterion. This way we may easily see if increasing the complexity of the OCC MCS by including a multi-objective optimization is a worthwhile task.

5.2   Set-Up

For the experiment a Support Vector Data Description [20] with a polynomial kernel is used as a base classifier. The pool of classifiers were homogeneous, i.e. consisted of classifiers of the same type.

The pool of classifiers consisted in total of 30 models build on the basis of a Random Subspace [8] approach with each subspace consisting of 60 % of original features.

The parameters used for the weight optimisation were set as follows: $N_c = 300$, $N_p = 50$, $\beta = 0.7$, $\gamma = 0.3$, $\Delta_m = 0.2$, $V = 20$, $T = 7$ and $N_T = 15$.

The combined 5x2 cv F test [1], tuned to OCC problems according to a scheme presented in [12], was carried out to asses the statistical significance of obtained results.

All experiments were carried out in the R environment [23] and computer implementations of the classification methods used were taken from dedicated packages built into the above mentioned software. This ensured that results achieved the best possible efficiency and that performance was not diminished by a bad implementation. Diversity measures and combination methods were implemented by authors.

5.3   Datasets

We have chosen 10 binary datasets in total - 9 coming from UCI Repository and an additional one, originating from chemoinformatics domain and describing the process of discovering pharmaceutically useful isoforms of CYP 2C19 molecule. The dataset is available for download at [18].

The objects from the minor class were used as the target concept, while objects from the major class as outliers.

Details of the chosen datasets are given in Table 1.

Table 1. Details of datasets used in the experimental investigation. Numbers in parentheses indicates the number of objects in the minor class in case of binary problems.

No.	Name	Objects	Features	Classes
1	Breast-cancer	286 (85)	9	2
2	Breast-Wisconsin	699 (241)	9	2
3	Colic	368 (191)	22	2
4	Diabetes	768 (268)	8	2
5	Heart-statlog	270 (120)	13	2
6	Hepatitis	155 (32)	19	2
7	Ionosphere	351(124)	34	2
8	Sonar	208 (97)	60	2
9	Voting records	435 (168)	16	2
10	CYP2C19 isoform	837 (181)	242	2

5.4   Results

The results are presented in Tab. 2. *ALL* stands for a committee consisting of all available models' *CONS* for a classifier selection approach according to the consistency criterion, *DIV* for a classifier selection according to the diversity criterion and *CONS + DIV* for the proposed multi-objective approach. Small numbers under each method stands for the indexes of models from which the considered one is statistically better.

Table 2. Results of the experimental results with the respect to the accuracy [%] and statistical significance

No.	ALL[1]	CONS[2]	DIV[3]	CONS+DIV[4]
1.	53.24	55.53	57.74	60.03
	–	1	1,2	1,2,3
2.	86.09	87.98	88.01	89.91
	–	1	1	1,2,3
3.	69.20	74.35	76.02	76.02
	–	1	1,2	1,2
4.	58.54	59.62	61.45	63.85
	–	–	1,2	1,2,3
5.	83.12	87.33	84.22	89.57
	–	1,3	–	1,2,3
6.	57.72	62.94	63.41	68.00
	–	1	1	1,2,3
7.	71.94	74.56	74.07	76.29
	–	1	1	1,2,3
8.	85.23	88.80	90.11	92.45
	–	1	1,2	1,2,3
9.	86.81	89.54	87.05	90.13
	–	1,3	–	1,3
10.	73.09	77.78	80.31	82.06
	–	1	1,2	1,2,3

5.5   Results Discussion

The experimental investigations clearly prove the quality of the proposed method. In 8 out of 10 benchmark tests the multi-objective classifier selection outperformed in a statistically significant way both of the methods based on a single criterion. This shows that combining two criteria increases the robustness of the OCC MCS to selection of weak classifiers, reducing the drawbacks of both methods.

In case of two benchmarks there were no statistical differences between the proposed approach and one of the reference. Yet the multi-criteria solution never displayed worser performance than any of the single-criterion selectors.

In case of several datasets (e.g. Breast-Wisconsin) there were no difference when using the accuracy or diversity criterion - but the proposed approach allowed for further boost of the final accuracy of the MCS. This proves that one may overcome the weak sides of both competence measures when using them together.

Finally the pruned ensemble (regardless which criterion was used) always outperformed in a statistically significant way the committee with all classifiers combined. This shows that classifier selection in OCC ensembles is a very important step towards improving their quality.

6 Conclusions

The paper discussed the idea of pruning one-class ensembles. In this work we have introduced a novel approach for selecting OCC models to the committee using the fusion of two separate criteria - consistency and diversity. A multi-objective memetic algorithm was used to select classifiers to the OCC ensemble in such a way that they at the same time display a high recognition quality and are not similar to each other. This was done to check if using more than one criterion simultaneously will allow to better exploit the available pool of classifiers.

Experimental investigations, executed on benchmark datasets, proved the quality of our approach. The multi-objective classifier selection in 8 out of 10 cases it outperformed the single-criterion methods in a statistically significant way. This shows that using both diversity and consistency for OCC classifier selection is a promising research direction.

Acknowledgment. The work was supported in part by the statutory funds of the Department of Systems and Computer Networks, Wroclaw University of Technology and by the Polish National Science Centre under the grant N N519 650440 which is being realized in years 2011-2014.

References

1. Alpaydin, E.: Combined 5 x 2 cv f test for comparing supervised classification learning algorithms. Neural Computation 11(8), 1885–1892 (1999)
2. Bi, Y.: The impact of diversity on the accuracy of evidential classifier ensembles. International Journal of Approximate Reasoning 53(4), 584–607 (2012)
3. Bishop, C.M.: Novelty detection and neural network validation. IEE Proceedings: Vision, Image and Signal Processing 141(4), 217–222 (1994)
4. Cheplygina, V., Tax, D.M.J.: Pruned random subspace method for one-class classifiers. In: Sansone, C., Kittler, J., Roli, F. (eds.) MCS 2011. LNCS, vol. 6713, pp. 96–105. Springer, Heidelberg (2011)
5. Giacinto, G., Perdisci, R., Del Rio, M., Roli, F.: Intrusion detection in computer networks by a modular ensemble of one-class classifiers. Inf. Fusion 9, 69–82 (2008)
6. Harman, M., McMinn, P.: A theoretical and empirical study of search-based testing: Local, global, and hybrid search. IEEE Transactions on Software Engineering 36(2), 226–247 (2010)
7. Harris, J.W., Stocker, H.: Handbook of mathematics and computational science. Springer, New York (1998)
8. Ho, T.K.: The random subspace method for constructing decision forests. IEEE Trans. Pattern Anal. Mach. Intell. 20, 832–844 (1998)

9. Juszczak, P.: Learning to recognise. A study on one-class classification and active learning. PhD thesis, Delft University of Technology (2006)

10. Knowles, J., Corne, D.: Memetic algorithms for multiobjective optimization: Issues, methods and prospects, pp. 325–332. IEEE Press (2004)

11. Koch, M.W., Moya, M.M., Hostetler, L.D., Fogler, R.J.: Cueing, feature discovery, and one-class learning for synthetic aperture radar automatic target recognition. Neural Networks 8(7-8), 1081–1102 (1995)

12. Krawczyk, B.: Diversity in ensembles for one-class classification. In: Pechenizkiy, M., Wojciechowski, M. (eds.) New Trends in Databases & Inform. AISC, vol. 185, pp. 119–129. Springer, Heidelberg (2012)

13. Krawczyk, B., Woźniak, M.: Designing cost-sensitive ensemble – genetic approach. In: Choraś, R.S. (ed.) Image Processing and Communications Challenges 3. AISC, vol. 102, pp. 227–234. Springer, Heidelberg (2011)

14. Krawczyk, B., Woźniak, M.: Analysis of diversity assurance methods for combined classifiers. In: Choraś, R.S. (ed.) Image Processing and Communications Challenges 4. AISC, vol. 184, pp. 177–184. Springer, Heidelberg (2013)

15. Krawczyk, B., Woźniak, M.: Combining diverse one-class classifiers. In: Corchado, E., Snášel, V., Abraham, A., Woźniak, M., Graña, M., Cho, S.-B. (eds.) HAIS 2012, Part II. LNCS, vol. 7209, pp. 590–601. Springer, Heidelberg (2012)

16. Krawczyk, B., Woźniak, M.: Experiments on distance measures for combining one-class classifiers. In: Proceedings of the FEDCISIS 2012 Conference, pp. 88–92 (2012)

17. Liu, B., Zhao, D., Reynaert, P., Gielen, G.G.E.: Synthesis of integrated passive components for high-frequency rf ics based on evolutionary computation and machine learning techniques. IEEE Transactions on Computer-Aided Design of Integrated Circuits and Systems 30(10), 1458–1468 (2011)

18. SIAM: Proceedings of the Eleventh SIAM International Conference on Data Mining, SDM 2011, Mesa, Arizona, USA, April 28-30. SIAM, Omnipress (2011)

19. Tax, D.M.J., Duin, R.P.W.: Combining one-class classifiers. In: Kittler, J., Roli, F. (eds.) MCS 2001. LNCS, vol. 2096, pp. 299–308. Springer, Heidelberg (2001)

20. Tax, D.M.J., Duin, R.P.W.: Support vector data description. Machine Learning 54(1), 45–66 (2004)

21. Tax, D.M.J., Müller, K.: A consistency-based model selection for one-class classification. In: Proceedings - International Conference on Pattern Recognition, vol. 3, pp. 363–366 (2004)

22. Tax, D.M.J., Duin, R.P.W.: Characterizing one-class datasets. In: Proceedings of the Sixteenth Annual Symposium of the Pattern Recognition Association of South Africa, pp. 21–26 (2005)

23. R Development Core Team: R: A Language and Environment for Statistical Computing. R Foundation for Statistical Computing, Vienna, Austria (2008)

24. Wilk, T., Woźniak, M.: Soft computing methods applied to combination of one-class classifiers. Neurocomput. 75, 185–193 (2012)

25. Wolpert, D.H., Macready, W.G.: No free lunch theorems for optimization. IEEE Transactions on Evolutionary Computation 1(1), 67–82 (1997)

SUCCESS: A New Approach for Semi-supervised Classification of Time-Series

Kristóf Marussy and Krisztian Buza

Department of Computer Science and Information Theory
Budapest University of Technology and Economics
1117 Budapest, Magyar tudósok körútja 2.
kris7topher@gmail.com, buza@cs.bme.hu
http://www.cs.bme.hu

Abstract. The growing interest in time-series classification can be attributed to the intensively increasing amount of temporal data collected by widespread sensors. Often, human experts may only review a small portion of all the available data. Therefore, the available labeled data may not be representative enough and semi-supervised techniques may be necessary. In order to construct accurate classifiers, semi-supervised techniques learn both from labeled and unlabeled data. In this paper, we introduce a novel semi-supervised time-series classifier based on constrained hierarchical clustering and dynamic time warping. We discuss our approach in the framework of graph theory and evaluate it on 44 publicly available real-world time-series datasets from various domains. Our results show that our approach substantially outperforms the state-of-the-art semi-supervised time-series classifier. The results are also justified by statistical significance tests.

Keywords: time-series, semi-supervised classification, constrained clustering, hubs, dynamic time warping.

1 Introduction

In the last decades, various types of sensors became cheaper and spread widely. Most of them record the values of some attributes continuously over time which results in extremely high number of very large time series. While such huge amounts of temporal data have never been seen before, they motivate the growing interest in time-series research. In the financial domain, for example, due to their huge volume, even storage of temporal data is challenging [14]. In general, one of the most prominent problems associated with temporal data is *classification* of time-series which is the common theoretical background of various recognition and prediction tasks ranging from handwriting, speech [20] and sign language recognition over signature verification [8] to problems related to medical diagnosis such as classification of electroencephalogram (EEG, "brain wave") and electrocardiograph (ECG) signals [2].

While the amount of temporal data grows drastically, in many cases, human experts only have the chance to review and label a small portion of all the

L. Rutkowski et al. (Eds.): ICAISC 2013, Part I, LNAI 7894, pp. 437–447, 2013.
© Springer-Verlag Berlin Heidelberg 2013

available data. Therefore, the labeled data may not be representative enough which may result in suboptimal classifiers. This problem is amplified by the high intrinsic dimensionality of time-series [16],[17]. As in high dimensional spaces the data becomes inherently sparse – a phenomenon often referred to as the curse of dimensionality – it is even more difficult to find a representative training set. In order to alleviate this problem, besides learning from the labeled data, we aim to use additional unlabeled data to construct more accurate time-series classifiers.

In this paper, we introduce a novel semi-supervised time-series classifier based on constrained hierarchical clustering [13] and dynamic time warping [20]. We call our approach SUCCESS: Semi-sUpervised ClassifiCation of timE SerieS. We discuss semi-supervised classification in the framework of graph theory: in particular, we show that semi-supervised classification is analogous to the minimal spanning tree problem. We explain our algorithm within this framework and explain its differences to the state-of-the-art semi-supervised time-series classifier. We evaluate our approach on 44 publicly available real-world time-series datasets from various domains. Our results show that our approach substantially outperforms the state-of-the-art semi-supervised time-series classifier. The results are also justified by statistical significance tests.

The remainder of the paper is organized as follows. In Section 2, we introduce the field of semi-supervised time-series classification and review the most important related works. Section 3 presents our approach followed by the experiments in Section 4. We conclude in Section 5.

2   Background

Both semi-supervised learning and time-series classification have been actively researched in the last decades. From the point of view of our current study, most relevant works deal with constrained clustering, cluster-and-label paradigm, self-training and semi-supervised classification of time-series. We will review these fields in the subsequent sections.

For an overview of further semi-supervised techniques and time-series classification approaches we refer to [3], [21], [25] and the references therein.

2.1   Constrained Clustering

With clustering the data, we mean the automatic identification of groups of similar instances. Such groups are called clusters. In case of constrained clustering, the algorithm is provided with some pieces of *a priori* information in the form of *cannot-link-constraints* (or *must-link-constraints*) that describe that some instances *can not be* (or *must be*) in the same cluster. In case of *hierarchical agglomerative clustering* (HAC) algorithms, each instance initially belongs to a separate cluster. Clusters are then merged in an iterative process. In each iteration, the two most similar clusters are merged. The process is finished when the number of clusters has reached the expected number of clusters (or when

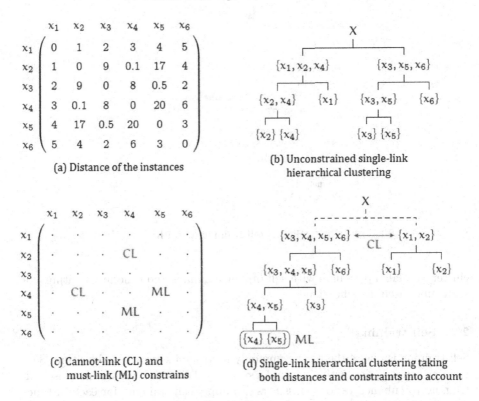

(a) Distance of the instances

(b) Unconstrained single-link
hierarchical clustering

(c) Cannot-link (CL) and
must-link (ML) constrains

(d) Single-link hierarchical clustering taking
both distances and constraints into account

Fig. 1. Unconstrained and constrained single-link hierarchical agglomerative clustering with the dendograms illustrating the merge steps performed during the iterative process

the two most similar clusters are too far from each other respectively). The expected number of clusters (or the distance threshold) is an external parameter set by the user. In case of *single link*, the similarity of two clusters is determined by the distance of their closest instances. Must-link (ML) and cannot-link (CL) constraints were shown to improve clustering accuracy and robustness [11], [13] compared to the case of unconstrained hierarchical clustering. Unconstrained and constrained single-link hierarchical agglomerative clustering algorithms are illustrated in Figure 1.

2.2   Cluster-and-Label

In the cluster-and-label approach, unconstrained or constrained clustering is performed first. Clusters are then mapped to classes by some algorithm. A possible mapping can be constructed by majority vote, i.e., each cluster gets mapped to the class of which the most labeled instances it contains.

Cluster-and-label performs well if the particular clustering algorithm captures the true structure of the data. Dara et al. [5] and Demiriz et al. [6] applied the

```
Self-Training(L, U)
1   L_0 = L
2   U_0 = U
3   t = 0
4   repeat
5       M = Supervised-Learning(L_t)
6       x_best = arg max Certainty(M, x)
                 x∈U_t
7       ŷ = Classify(M, x_best)
8       L_{t+1} = L_t ∪ {(x_best, ŷ)}
9       U_{t+1} = U_t \ {x_best}
10      t = t + 1
11  until |U_t| == 0
12  return M
```

Fig. 2. Simple self-training algorithm

cluster-and-label paradigm with self-organizing maps and genetic algorithms for semi-supervised classification.

2.3   Self-training

Self-training is one of the most commonly used semi-supervised algorithm. Self-training is a wrapper method around a supervised classifier, i.e., one may use self-training to enhance various classifiers. To apply self-training, for each instance x to be classified, besides its predicted class label, the classifier must be able to output a certainty score, i.e., an estimation of how likely the predicted class label is correct.

Self-training is an iterative process during which the set of labeled instances is grown until all the instances become labeled. Let L_1 denote the set of initially labeled instances, and, more generally, let L_t denote the set of labeled instances in the t-th iteration ($t \geq 1$). In each iteration of self-training, the base classifier is trained on the labeled set L_t. Then, the base classifier is used to classify the unlabeled instances. Finally, the instances with highest certainty scores are selected. These instances, together with their predicted labels, are added to the set of labeled instances, in order to construct L_{t+1} the set of labeled instance for the next iteration. In the simplest case, one instance is added in each iteration, the pseudocode of this algorithm is shown in Figure 2. In context of nearest neighbor classification, the algorithm are illustrated in Figure 3. Other variants of self-training include e.g. Yarowsky's algorithm [23].

2.4   Semi-supervised Classification of Time-series

One of the most surprising recent results in the time-series classification domain is that simple nearest neighbor classifiers using a special distance measure called dynamic time warping (DTW) are generally competitive with, if not better than, many complicated approaches [7]. Therefore, we build our approach on

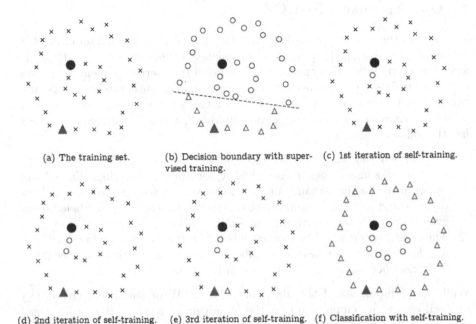

(a) The training set.

(b) Decision boundary with supervised training.

(c) 1st iteration of self-training.

(d) 2nd iteration of self-training.

(e) 3rd iteration of self-training.

(f) Classification with self-training.

Fig. 3. Self-training with nearest neighbor. There are two classes, circles and triangles. Bold symbols correspond to instances of the initially labeled training set L_1, while unlabeled instances are marked with crosses, see Subfigure (a). Subfigures (c) – (e) show the first three iterations of Self-Training. The final output of self-training is shown in Subfigure (f).

the DTW-based nearest neighbor classification of time-series. DTW was originally introduced for speech recognition [20]. The key feature of DTW is that is allows for siftings and elongations while it compares two time-series. We refer to [3] for a detailed description of DTW.

Despite its relevance, there are just a few works on the semi-supervised classification of time-series. Wei and Keogh proposed a self-training based approach [22] which was enhanced by Ratanamahatana et al. [18] by the introduction of a new stopping criterion. Nguyen et al. used k-Means and principal component analysis for semi-supervised time-series classification [15]. All these works focused on the case when labeled instances are only available for one of the classes. In contrast, we assume that there are some labeled instances for each class, like in the example shown in Figure 3. Furthermore, our approach is much simpler than that of Nguyen et al., as we do not use dimensionality reduction. Instead, we compare time-series directly by DTW. Zhong used self-training with Hidden Markov Models [24] for the semi-supervised classification of small time-series datasets. In contrast to previous works, we base our approach on the cluster-and-label paradigm and use a constrained hierarchical single link clustering algorithm.

3   Our Approach: SUCCESS

We consider the semi-supervised classification problem, in which a set of labeled time-series $L = \{(x_i, y_i)\}_{i=1}^{l}$ and a set of unlabeled time-series $U = \{x_i\}_{i=l+1}^{n}$ is available as train data to a classifier. The labeled time series (elements of L) are called *seeds*. We wish to construct a classifier that can accurately classify any time-series, i.e., not only elements of U. For this problem, we propose a novel semi-supervised time-series classification approach, called SUCCESS. SUCCESS has the following phases:

1. The labeled and unlabeled instances of the training set are clustered with constrained single-linkage hierarchical agglomerative clustering. While doing so, we measure the distance of two instances (time-series) as their DTW-distance and we include cannot-link constraints for *each* pair of labeled seeds even if the both seeds have the same class labels.
2. The resulting top-level clusters are labeled by their corresponding seeds.
3. The final classifier is 1-nearest neighbor trained on the resulting labeled data. This classifier can be applied to *unseen* test data.

While the components of the algorithm (like DTW or single-link clustering) are well-known, we emphasize that the algorithm as a whole is new for semi-supervised time-series classification. Next, we explain the difference between self-training and our approach using the framework of graph theory.

3.1   A Graph-Theoretic View of Semi-supervised Time-Series Classification

The presented semi-supervised time-series classification algorithms can be considered as algorithms that aim at finding the minimum spanning tree of a graph.

Consider the set of all, labeled and unlabeled, train instances $X = L \cup U = \{x_i\}_{i=1}^{n}$. Let $G = (X, V)$ be an undirected *complete* graph, the vertices of which correspond the instances of the database, and the weights of the edges correspond the distance of two instances (DTW-distance in our case): $w_{i,j} = d(x_i, x_j)$.

We define a *spanning forest* as a set of trees $\mathcal{T} = \{T_i\}_{i=1}^{l}$ that satisfy the following properties:

- The trees are disjoint, i.e. $\forall i : x_i \in V(T_a) \wedge x_i \in V(T_b) \Rightarrow a = b$.
- The trees together span the entire set of instances, i.e. $\bigcup_{i=1}^{l} V(T_i) = X$.
- The ith tree contains the i labeled instances, i.e. $\forall 1 \leq i \leq l : x_i \in V(T_i)$.

Note that we consider forests where the number of trees equals the number of labeled instances, and each tree corresponds to a labeled instance.

A spanning forest is a *minimum spanning forest* if the sum of its edge weights $W(\mathcal{T}) = \sum_{i=1}^{l} \sum_{e \in E(T_i)} w(e)$ is minimal.

Let us define the graph $G^{\star} = (X \cup \{\star\}, E^{\star})$, which is an extension of G with a super-vertex $\star$. This super-vertex $\star$ is connected to the labeled examples with 0-weight edges, i.e., $E^{\star} = E \cup \{\{x_i, \star\} : 1 \leq i \leq l\}$, and $w(\{x_i, \star\}) = 0$ for all vertices x_i.

Consider the tree T^* which contains $\star$ and the new edges from $\star$, ant the union of the trees in a minimum spanning forest $\mathcal{T}$ of G. The sum of edge-weights in T^* is not greater than that of a minimum spanning tree of G^*, therefore, T^* is a minimum spanning tree of G^*.

The self-training algorithm with the 1-nearest neighbor classifier can be viewed as a specific way of finding a minimum spanning tree of G^*. In particular, if all the edge weights $w_{i,j}$ in G are strictly positive, except the weights of edges that connect $\star$ and the seeds, instance based self-training is equivalent to running Prim's algorithm [4] with $\star$ as the root node. In the first l iterations, the algorithm adds the labeled instances $\{x_i\}_{i=1}^l$ to the tree. In every subsequent iteration, the set nodes in the growing tree equals the set of already labeled instances.

Therefore, we can see that self-training corresponds to Prim's minimal spanning tree algorithm. Next, we show that our approach, SUCCESS, in contrast, corresponds Kruskal's algorithm [4].

Notice that the forest which is gradually joined by Kruskal's algorithm is a set of clusters at some level of a *single-linkage* (SLINK) *hierarchical agglomerative clustering* dendrogram.

Due to $\star$ and the 0-weight edges connecting $\star$ with the labeled instances, in the first l iterations, Kruskal's greedy algorithm will select all the labeled instances into the minimal spanning tree. Therefore, after the l-th iteration, the tree has l branches, each one corresponding to a labeled instance. In the subsequent iterations the tree grows along these branches, however, no new branch is created from node $\star$ as all of the edges of $\star$ are already contained in the tree after the l-th iteration. We call the aforementioned branches *main branches*. When the algorithm terminates, each of the main branches corresponds to a cluster. This is analogous to having cannot-link constraints in the hierarchical clustering between each pair of labeled instances.

4   Experiments

In order to assist reproducibility, we provide a detailed description of the experiments we performed.

Methods – We compared our approach, SUCCESS, against Wei's approach [22], which is one the most prominent state-of-the-art semi-supervised time-series classifiers. While Wei's approach is based on self-training, SUCCESS is based on the cluster-and-label paradigm as explained before.

Datasets – We evaluated both Wei's approach and SUCCESS on 44 publicly available real-world datasets from the UCR time-series repository [10]. These datasets originate from various domains ranging from handwriting recognition [19] and user identification with graphical passwords [1] over biological shape recognition [9] and electrocardiograph classification to gesture recognition [12].

Table 1. Summary of the results. The number of datasets on which our approach wins/looses against Wei's approach. The numbers in parenthesis show how many times the difference is statistically significant.

	Unlabeled Train	Test
Wins	29 (14)	30 (6)
Ties	-	2
Looses	15 (5)	12 (3)

The names of these datasets as well as the number of classes are shown in the first two columns of Table 2.

Comparison Protocol – We run experiments separately on each of the 44 datasets. For each experiment, we split the data into 3 disjoint subsets: the first one, denoted as L, contains around 10% of the instances. The second split, U, contains around 80% of the instances while the remaining instances are in the third split. We used the first split, L, as the initially labeled instances of the semi-supervised algorithm. U served as the set of unlabeled training instances the labels of which were unavailable to the algorithm but the instances themselves were available at training time. The third split was used as test data that was completely unavailable to the algorithm at the training time. The instances of the test set were classified one by one without updating the classification model. We measured the performance both on the set of unlabeled training instances (U) and on the test set. This allowed us to simulate two, slightly different, real-world situations. Measuring the performance on U corresponds to the case of having a large set of unlabeled instances and a small set of labeled instances with the goal of correctly classifying the unlabeled instances. Measuring the performance on the test set simulates the situation where we have a large set of unlabeled instances and a small set of labeled instances and we aim at constructing a classifier that should be used to classify *new* instances that may be different from the unlabeled instances available at training time.

We used misclassification ratio to measure the performance of the baseline and our approach. For each dataset, we repeated all experiments 10 times, i.e., we split the data into the above three splits 10 times by random and measured the performances of our approach and the baseline. In Table 2, we report average performances. In order to check whether the differences are statistically significant, we used t-tests at significance level $\alpha = 0.05$.

Results – We show the average misclassification ratios on the 44 datasets in Table 2. We use the $+$ symbol to denote that an approach statistically significantly outperformed its competitor. The results of our experiments are summarized in Table 1. As it can be seen, in clear majority of the datasets, our approach, SUCCESS, outperforms Wei's approach. For each dataset, we also performed experiments with 20% of the data being labeled train data L (and 70% being the unlabeled train data U respectively) and we observed very similar results.

Table 2. Misclassification ratio of Wei's approach and SUCCESS. Bold font denotes the winner, + denotes statistically significant difference. (While determining the winner, we took the non-shown digits into account as well.)

Dataset	Number of classes	Unlabeled train Wei	SUCCESS	Test Wei	SUCCESS
50 Words	50	0.432	**0.398+**	0.436	**0.414**
Adiac	37	0.607	**0.582+**	0.601	**0.595**
Beef	5	0.683	**0.656**	0.617	**0.600**
Car	4	0.484	**0.457**	0.458	**0.450**
CBF	3	0.007	**0.002**	0.005	**0.003**
ChlorineConcentration	3	0.373	**0.062+**	0.350	**0.101+**
CinC ECG Torso	4	0.021	**0.001+**	0.019	**0.001+**
Coffee	2	0.429	**0.368+**	0.460	**0.440**
Cricket_X	12	0.477	**0.425+**	0.465	**0.444**
Cricket_Y	12	0.463	**0.405+**	0.433	**0.396+**
Cricket_Z	12	0.443	**0.395+**	0.459	**0.423+**
DiatomSizeReduction	4	0.018	**0.017**	0.031	**0.025**
ECG200	2	0.237	**0.225**	0.239	**0.195**
ECGFiveDays	2	0.051	**0.021+**	0.053	**0.030**
FaceFour	4	0.201	**0.191**	**0.182**	0.200
FacesUCR	14	0.080	**0.062+**	0.083	**0.070+**
Fish	7	**0.424**	0.449	**0.403**	0.434
GunPoint	2	0.089	**0.039**	0.075	**0.045**
Haptics	5	**0.671+**	0.706	**0.704**	0.730
InlineSkate	7	0.693	**0.679**	0.683	**0.663**
ItalyPowerDemand	2	**0.063**	0.073	**0.066**	0.076
Lighting2	2	0.355	**0.322**	0.342	**0.317**
Lighting7	7	**0.463**	0.477	0.536	**0.529**
Mallat	8	0.042	**0.041**	0.042	**0.037**
MedicalImages	10	**0.379**	0.386	0.394	**0.393**
MoteStrain	2	**0.124**	0.129	0.115	**0.107**
OliveOil	4	**0.300**	0.315	**0.367**	0.383
OSULeaf	6	0.550	**0.512+**	0.532	**0.466+**
Plane	7	0.050	**0.049**	0.038	**0.038**
SonyAIBORobotS.	2	**0.052+**	0.090	**0.060+**	0.110
SonyAIBORobotS.II	2	**0.088**	0.094	**0.079**	0.087
StarLightCurves	3	**0.119+**	0.200	**0.140+**	0.200
SwedishLeaf	15	**0.330+**	0.369	**0.364**	0.379
Symbols	6	0.033	**0.022+**	0.025	**0.019**
SyntheticControl	6	0.051	**0.029**	0.065	**0.045**
Trace	4	0.054	**0.001+**	0.050	**0.000**
TwoLeadECG	2	0.004	**0.001**	0.003	**0.001**
TwoPatterns	4	0.000	**0.000**	0.000	**0.000**
uWaveGestureX	8	**0.276**	0.284	**0.284**	0.286
uWaveGestureY	8	**0.356**	0.368	**0.377**	0.377
uWaveGestureZ	8	**0.359+**	0.378	**0.368+**	0.385
Wafer	2	0.009	**0.009**	0.009	**0.009**
WordsSynonyms	25	0.414	**0.378+**	0.410	**0.382**
Yoga	2	**0.148**	0.149	0.152	**0.151**

5   Conclusion

In this paper, we proposed SUCCESS, a novel semi-supervised time-series classifier. We discussed the relation between the minimal spanning tree problem and semi-supervised classification. We pointed out the analogy between a state-of-the-art semi-supervised time-series classifier and Prim's algorithm as well as our approach and Kruskal's greedy algorithm. We performed exhaustive experimental evaluation that showed that our approach is able to outperform that state-of-the-art semi-supervised time-series classifier on many real-world datasets.

Besides time-series, huge amounts of other types of sequential data are being collected, e.g., DNA-sequence of a persons and other organisms. Therefore, as future work, one may consider to use similar approaches for the semi-supervised classification of other types of sequential data.

Acknowledgments. The work reported in the paper has been developed in the framework of the project "Talent care and cultivation in the scientific workshops of BME". This project is supported by the grant TÁMOP-4.2.2.B-10/1–2010-0009. We acknowledge the DAAD-MÖB Researcher Exchange Program.

References

1. Malek, B., Orozco, M., Saddik, A.E.: Novel shoulder-surfing resistant haptic-based graphical password. In: Proceedings of EuroHaptics 2006 (2006)
2. Buza, K., Nanopoulos, A., Schmidt-Thieme, L., Koller, J.: Fast Classification of Electrocardiograph Signals via Instance Selection. In: First IEEE Conference on Healthcare Informatics, Imaging, and Systems Biology (HISB) (2011)
3. Buza, K.A.: Fusion Methods for Time-Series Classification. Ph.D. thesis (2011)
4. Cormen, T., Leiserson, C., Rivest, R., Stein, C.: Introduction to Algorithms. The MIT Press (2001)
5. Dara, R., Kremer, S., Stacey, D.: Clustering unlabeled data with soms improves classification of labeled real-world data. In: Proceedings of the 2002 International Joint Conference on Neural Networks, IJCNN 2002, vol. 3, pp. 2237–2242 (2002)
6. Demiriz, A., Bennett, K., Embrechts, M.J.: Semi-supervised clustering using genetic algorithms. In: Artificial Neural Networks in Engineering, ANNIE 1999, pp. 809–814. ASME Press (1999)
7. Ding, H., Trajcevski, G., Scheuermann, P., Wang, X., Keogh, E.J.: Querying and mining of time series data: experimental comparison of representations and distance measures. PVLDB 1(2), 1542–1552 (2008)
8. Gruber, C., Coduro, M., Sick, B.: Signature Verification with Dynamic RBF Networks and Time Series Motifs. In: 10th International Workshop on Frontiers in Handwriting Recognition (2006)
9. Jalba, A., Wilkinson, M., Roerdink, J., Bayer, M., Juggins, S.: Automatic diatom identification using contour analysis by morphological curvature scale spaces. Machine Vision and Applications 16, 217–228 (2005),
   http://dx.doi.org/10.1007/s00138-005-0175-8
10. Keogh, E.J., Xi, X., Wei, L., Ratanamahatana, C.A.: The UCR Time Series Classification/Clustering Homepage (2006),
    http://www.cs.ucr.edu/~eamonn/time_series_data/

11. Kestler, H.A., Kraus, J.M., Palm, G., Schwenker, F.: On the effects of constraints in semi-supervised hierarchical clustering. In: Schwenker, F., Marinai, S. (eds.) ANNPR 2006. LNCS (LNAI), vol. 4087, pp. 57–66. Springer, Heidelberg (2006)
12. Ko, M.H., West, G., Venkatesh, S., Kumar, M.: Using dynamic time warping for online temporal fusion in multisensor systems. Information Fusion 9(3), 370–388 (2008), special Issue on Distributed Sensor Networks, http://www.sciencedirect.com/science/article/pii/S1566253506000674
13. Miyamoto, S., Terami, A.: Semi-supervised agglomerative hierarchical clustering algorithms with pairwise constraints. In: FUZZ-IEEE, pp. 1–6. IEEE (2010)
14. Nagy, G.I., Buza, K.: SOHAC: Efficient storage of tick data that supports search and analysis. In: Perner, P. (ed.) ICDM 2012. LNCS, vol. 7377, pp. 38–51. Springer, Heidelberg (2012), http://dx.doi.org/10.1007/978-3-642-31488-9_4
15. Nguyen, M.N., Li, X., Ng, S.K.: Positive unlabeled leaning for time series classification. In: Walsh, T. (ed.) IJCAI, pp. 1421–1426. IJCAI/AAAI (2011)
16. Radovanovic, M., Nanopoulos, A., Ivanovic, M.: Hubs in space: Popular nearest neighbors in high-dimensional data. Journal of Machine Learning Research 11, 2487–2531 (2010)
17. Radovanovic, M., Nanopoulos, A., Ivanovic, M.: Time-series classification in many intrinsic dimensions. In: SDM, pp. 677–688. SIAM (2010)
18. Ratanamahatana, C.A., Wanichsan, D.: Stopping criterion selection for efficient semi-supervised time series classification. In: Lee, R.Y. (ed.) Soft. Eng., Arti. Intel., Net. Para./Distr. Comp. SCI, vol. 149, pp. 1–14. Springer (2008)
19. Rath, T., Manmatha, R.: Word Image Matching using Dynamic Time Warping. In: Proceedings of the IEEE Computer Society Conference on Computer Vision and Pattern Recognition, vol. 2, pp. II-521–II-527. IEEE (2003)
20. Sakoe, H., Chiba, S.: Dynamic Programming Algorithm Optimization for Spoken Word Recognition. Acoustics, Speech and Signal Processing 26(1), 43–49 (1978)
21. Seeger, M.: Learning with labeled and unlabeled data. Tech. rep., University of Edinburgh (2001)
22. Wei, L., Keogh, E.J.: Semi-supervised time series classification. In: Eliassi-Rad, T., Ungar, L.H., Craven, M., Gunopulos, D. (eds.) KDD, pp. 748–753. ACM (2006)
23. Yarowsky, D.: Word-sense disambiguation using statistical models of roget's categories trained on large corpora. In: COLING, pp. 454–460 (1992)
24. Zhong, S.: Semi-supervised sequence classification with hmms. IJPRAI 19(2), 165–182 (2005)
25. Zhu, X.: Semi-supervised learning literature survey (2007)

A New Method of Improving Classification Accuracy of Decision Tree in Case of Incomplete Samples

Bartosz A. Nowak, Robert K. Nowicki, and Wojciech K. Mleczko

Institute of Computational Intelligence, Czestochowa University of Technology,
Al. Armii Krajowej 36, 42-200 Czestochowa, Poland
{bartosz.nowak,robert.nowicki,wojciech.mleczko}@iisi.pcz.pl

Abstract. In the paper a new method is proposed which improves the classification accuracy of decision trees for samples with missing values. This aim was achieved by adding new nodes to the decision tree. The proposed procedure applies structures and functions of well-known C4.5 algorithm. However, it can be easily adapted to other methods, for forming decision trees. The efficiency of the new algorithm has been confirmed by tests using eleven databases from UCI Repository. The research has been concerned classification but the method is not limited to classification tasks.

Keywords: missing values, C4.5, classification, decision tree.

1 Introduction

In the current stage of the development of computer science, especially computational intelligence, we dispose of many methods designed to data processing and decision making. The important positions are occupied by non-parametric techniques [8,24,25,26], neural networks [1,10,11,23], fuzzy systems [12,22], relational systems [30], classifiers based on Pawlak rough sets [17,19] and decision trees [1,4,27] as well as any hybrid methods [6,7,18,29,31,32]. Actually, all of them have been already adapted to process also incomplete input data. In this area hybrid solutions play important role, especially rough fuzzy systems [15,16] and other high level fuzzy methods [33,34,35]. However, this paper concerns decision trees only.

As in the case of many other decision system, structure of the decision tree is determined by a set of samples applied at design time, i.e. learning set. Each sample concerns single state or observation, and described by a defined set of attributes. Generally, separated samples belong to one or more class, or to none of considered classes. In the paper we assume that every learning sample belongs to exactly one of the considered classes. Moreover, we accept that values of some attributes describing the samples are missing. This subject has been considered by a lot of authors. In many papers there are many various solutions for it. Among others, in [36,37] authors use the internal node strategy in building cost-sensitive decision trees. Another proposition has been formulated in [2]. Authors

L. Rutkowski et al. (Eds.): ICAISC 2013, Part I, LNAI 7894, pp. 448–458, 2013.
© Springer-Verlag Berlin Heidelberg 2013

use a fuzzy random forest, which is an ensemble of fuzzy decision trees. In a case of missing values on the attribute used in a branch, the sample is further processed by every sub-node with degree of fulfilment divided by number of sub-nodes. A similar solution is proposed in [9], but in application for classification data streams by a fuzzy decision tree. A little more sophisticated approach exist in a popular algorithm C4.5 [20], where degrees of fulfilment are multiplied by factors equal to probabilities of use corresponding sub-nodes.

In the paper authors propose an algorithm that adds alternative nodes to a decision tree in order to improve accuracy of classification in the case when the sample have missing values of attributes. This approach differs from the method in CART [3], where surrogate splits are used, but no new nodes are added to the decision tree. The proposed method applies algorithm C4.5 [20,21], but it is independent from C4.5, therefore authors in the paper have omitted description of C4.5, and the proposed bellow algorithm may also work slightly changed with different methods for building and pruning of decision trees.

The paper is organised as follow. Section 2 contains the genesis of the proposed algorithm, the main idea and details of the method. Section 3 presents the process of experiments and obtained results. It contains also the example of wrapped tree for the simplest benchmark - well known iris classification. The last section is a summary, conclusions and final remarks.

2   Proposed Method

This section presents genesis of proposed algorithm and details of them. We called them WrapTree, because it wrapped the original decision tree by additional branches and nodes which improve the classification accuracy of decision in the case of missing values.

The starting point of the research was the idea of decision tree forest. In this solution many decision trees are created, each for different set of available features. In such ensemble, during classification of a sample only one decision tree is active. It is the tree prepared for work with specific set of attributes compatible with set of available attributes in current sample. If the compatible tree is unavailable, e.g. due to limited system size, the sample is rejected or processed by most appropriate tree using some more sophisticate methods.

During the preliminary studies about forests of trees the following observations have been done:

1. There are many cases when decision trees, which were created with different set of attributes (V_a, V_b) are the same, because they use the same subset of attributes $(V_c, V_c \subseteq V_a \land V_c \subseteq V_b)$
2. In some cases decision tree, created with some set of attributes (V_a), contains only one leaf, mainly because of the pruning. In that case there seems to be no reason to create trees with smaller sets of attributes $(V_b \subsetneq V_a)$ than mentioned one-element tree.
3. In the most cases the parts of decision trees close to the root are identical in trees made for various sets of available attributes.

Our goal is to propose the algorithm creating a single tree wrapped by supplementary branches and nodes dedicated to serving the samples with missing features. The reference tree is built for serving complete samples by any known method e.g. C4.5. After wrapping process the resultant tree should assume classification accuracy comparable to mentioned above tree forest. It occurs also in the case of missing features. The total number of branches and nodes should be significantly lower.

Due to mentioned cases, our algorithm does not store identical trees more than once, use original tree as a base for new decision trees, and does not add new nodes for any branches, when it is unnecessary. These features reduce greatly time and resources needed to create the decision tree in comparison to a method, which create decision trees separately for each chosen sets of available attributes.

Because final decision tree is the equivalent to composition of many decision trees, which have been created with different sets of attributes, there is necessity to add proper method checking if chosen attribute has non-missing value.

2.1 Extending of Reference Tree

As was mentioned above, the reference decision tree is prepared by any known algorithm, e.g. C4.5. However, such a tree must be extended to be able to work with supplementary branches and nodes which will be prepared by the proposed algorithm. As a result the reference decision tree will contain four types of branches, i.e.

- Numerical — determine if the value of examined attribute is greater than defined threshold or not. This type of branches occurs only when former branches on the processed path excluded case of inaccessibility of examined attribute value, i.e. the examined in branch attribute has been former examined for the same sample.
- Symbolic — determine if the attribute takes defined value or label or not. As previous one this type of branch occurs if, basing on previous branches, we are sure that value of examined feature is available in the processed sample.
- Numerical or lack — if value of the examined attribute is available they determine if the value of examined attribute is greater than the defined threshold or not. When value of examined attribute is not available the alternative subtree is assigned.
- Symbolic or lack — if value of examined attribute is available they determine if the attribute takes the defined value or label or not. When value of the examined attribute is not available, the alternative subtree is assigned.

Both types of numerical branches have applied in a reference tree shown in Fig. 1.

2.2 Adding of New Nodes

The alternative subtrees, wrapped the reference tree, are created by the proposed procedure (WrapTree) presented below. This procedure is recursive. It adds to

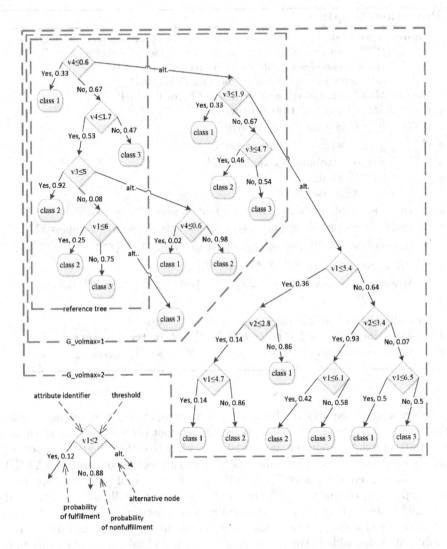

Fig. 1. Results of the algorithm for $G\_volmax = 0, 1, 2$, iris database, 135 samples

some branches of existing decision tree an alternative node. These newly created nodes are used afterwards as a root of a new decision tree, which are created by C4.5, but with limited set of available attributes.

Procedure. WrapTree

Input: a node of decision tree ($tree\_node^{(act)}$), set of already used attributes ($P^{(act)}$), set of excluded attributes ($G^{(act)}$), set of samples ($X^{(act)}$), vector of samples weights ($\mathbf{w}^{(act)}$), maximal size of the $G^{(act)}$ and intensity of a algorithm (constant G_volmax).

Result: Modification of the node $tree\_node^{(act)}$ or its child.

1   **if** $tree\_node^{(act)}$ *is a leaf* **then return**;
2   **if** $\|G^{(act)}\| \geq G\_volmax$ **then return**;
3   **if** $\sum_{x_s:x_s \in X^{(act)}} w_s^{(act)} < 1$ **then return**;
4   $v^{(act)} =$ decision attribute of $tree\_node^{(act)}$;
5   **if** $v^{(act)} \notin P^{(act)}$ **then**
    // new attribute
6   create an empty node ($tree\_node^{(alt)}$) alternative to $tree\_node^{(act)}$;
7   create a decision sub-tree using $tree\_node^{(alt)}$ as a root, with samples $X^{(act)}$, their weights $\mathbf{w}^{(act)}$ and set of available attributes $V - \left\{ G^{(act)} \cup \left\{ v^{(act)} \right\} \right\}$;
8   PruneTree($tree\_node^{(alt)}$, $X^{(act)}$, $\mathbf{w}^{(act)}$);
9   WrapTree($tree\_node^{(alt)}$, $P^{(act)}$, $G^{(act)} \cup \{v^{(act)}\}$, $X^{(act)}$, $\mathbf{w}^{(act)}$, G_volmax);
10    $P^{(act)} = P^{(act)} \cup \{v^{(act)}\}$;
11 **foreach** *child node* $tree\_node^{(sub)}$ *of* $tree\_node^{(act)}$ **do**
12   determine $X^{(sub)}$, $\mathbf{w}^{(sub)}$ for $tree\_node^{(sub)}$; // in two variants
13   WrapTree($tree\_node^{(sub)}$, $P^{(act)}$, $G^{(act)}$, $X^{(act)}$, $\mathbf{w}^{(act)}$, G_volmax);

The procedure requires the following input parameters set by operator: constant integer parameter G_volmax greater than 0, but not greater than the number of attributes (n), pointer to node of a decision tree ($tree\_node^{(act)}$), sets of already used ($P^{(act)}$) and excluded ($G^{(act)}$) attributes, set of samples ($X^{(act)}$) and vector of their weights ($\mathbf{w}^{(act)}$). In the first execution of the procedure, root node is pointed, all samples with their initial weights (usually all of them equal to 1) and empty sets of already used and excluded attributes.

Parameter G_volmax defines the intensity of the algorithm, and affects the number of nodes added. We can estimate that the obtained by our procedure wrapped tree is equivalent of an ensemble (forest) of $1 + \binom{n}{1} + \binom{n}{2} \ldots + \binom{n}{G\_volmax}$ trees, created using various sets of attributes. The first tree of such forest is created using complete samples. The other trees are build using samples with combination of $n - G\_volmax$ to $n - 1$ available attributes. When $G\_volmax = 1$, then proposed algorithm create one decision tree, that is

Table 1. Properties of the used data sets

data set	no. of samples	no. of attributes	no. of classes
dermatology	366	34	6
ecoli	336	7	8
glass	214	9	2
ionosphere	351	34	2
iris	150	4	3
page-blocks	5473	10	5
parkinsons	195	22	2
pendigits	10992	16	10
pima diabetes	768	8	2
vowel	528	10	11
wisconsin	699	9	2

equivalent to a composition of $n + 1$ trees $(Tree_a, a = 1 \ldots n + 1)$. The first one is the reference tree, prepared for complete samples served. The following trees $(Tree_a, a = 2 \ldots n + 1)$ are created omitting one attribute (v_{a-1}). When $G\_volmax = n$, the algorithm makes tree that is equivalent to composition of decision trees created for every possible combination of available sets, including empty set.

Procedure WrapTree in each execution concerns on the single node of the decision tree and may recursively execute itself on sub-nodes. In the beginning (commands 1-3) WrapTree checks if at least one of stopping condition is fulfilled. These stopping conditions are: verify if the current node is a leaf, and does not have sub-nodes; check if defined maximal level of recursion (G_volmax) has been achieved, verify if a sum of samples weights is too small. After that, the procedure checks if an attribute in the current node has been already used (command 5), if not, then: adds a new empty node $(tree\_node^{(alt)})$, and connects it to current node; create a new sub tree (command 7) using the same set of samples and their weights, but set of attributes reduced by excluded attributes $(G^{(act)})$ and attribute of current node $(v^{(act)})$; then prune that tree (command 8), after that execute WrapTree (command 9) for created and pruned sub-tree with the same settings, but with set of forbidden attributes enlarged by the current attribute $(v^{(act)})$; later adds current attribute to set of already used attributes (command 10). It is worth to mention, that commands 7-8 use C4.5 algorithm, but they can be easily substituted by other decision tree building algorithms. After creation of alternative node procedure processes each sub-node (command 11), which are not the alternative node. At first, procedure determine set of samples and their weights, which should be directed to this sub-node (command 12), and then execute WrapTree (command 13) with determined before set of samples and their weights. In the paper two variants of the method to determine samples and their weights for sub-node (command 12) are proposed, which differ when learning samples have missing values:

1. $X^{(sub)}$ = all samples, that have available current attribute $(v^{(act)})$ and fulfilled condition in $tree\_node^{(act)}$ for child node $tree\_node^{(sub)}$.

$$w_s^{(sub)} = \begin{cases} w_s^{(act)} & \text{if } x_s \in X^{(sub)} \\ 0 & \text{else,} \end{cases}$$

where x_s is a sample with index s.

2. $X^{(sub)}$ = all samples, that have available value for current attribute $(v^{(act)})$ and fulfilled condition in $tree\_node^{(act)}$ for child node $tree\_node_{sub}$; or missing value for current attribute $(v^{(act)})$.

$$w_s^{(sub)} = \begin{cases} w_s^{(cur)} & \text{if } x_s \in X^{(sub)} \wedge v^{(act)} \in P_s \\ w_s^{(cur)} \cdot p^{(cur,sub)} & \text{if } x_s \in X^{(sub)} \wedge v^{(act)} \in G_s \\ 0 & \text{else,} \end{cases}$$

where P_s is a set of attributes with non-missing values for sample x_s, G_s is a set of attributes with missing values for sample x_s, $p^{(cur,sub)}$ is a probability, that learning samples which reached $tree\_node^{(act)}$, and had available values for attribute $v^{(act)}$, were sent to $tree\_node^{(sub)}$. This method is similar to used in C4.5 [20].

By default the first method were used, which has lower accuracy of classification samples in learning set in case of missing values in learning and testing set, but produce smaller decision trees.

Table 2. Efficiency of classification

number of missing values in sample	1		3		
G_volmax	0	1	0	1	3
dataset					
dermatology	.883	**.894**	.863	.892	**.892**
ecoli	.594	**.656**	.465	.486	**.528**
glass	.882	**.882**	.790	.837	**.838**
ionosphere	**.881**	.879	**.871**	.853	.845
iris	.947	**.953**	.767	.693	**.813**
page-blocks	.766	**.825**	.614	.646	**.714**
parkinsons	**.851**	.838	.778	**.838**	**.838**
pendigits	.941	**.959**	.910	.921	**.929**
pima diabetes	**.687**	.681	.628	**.657**	.637
vowel	.703	**.765**	.510	.566	**.605**
wisconsin	.929	**.948**	.946	.943	**.946**
winner	3	8	1	2	9

3   Experiments and Results

All experiments performed to 10-fold cross validation. It states, that whole set of samples is divided into 10 subsets with nearly equal number of samples. All experiments are repeated 10 times and every final result are average for 10 tests.

In each test consecutive subset is chosen as the testing set and remaining 9 subsets as the learning set.

The algorithm was tested using data sets (Table 1) from UCI Repository [14]. Each sample belonged to exactly one class and all attributes were numerical. In the paper efficiency of classification is computed not as simple accuracy of classification but as average accuracy of classification for samples in each class,

$$efficiency = \frac{1}{m} \sum_{j=1...m} \left(\frac{1}{||\omega_j||} \sum_{x_s:x_s \in \omega_j} correctly\_classified(x_s) \right), \qquad (1)$$

where m is a number of samples, ω_j is j class, $||\omega_j||$ is number of testing samples that belongs to ω_j, $correctly\_classified(x_s)$ is a logical function, which states if sample x_s was properly classified.

For testing purposes databases were prepared in two variants (a number of missing values in sample = {1,3}), according to number of attributes with missing values for each sample. Distribution of missing values within data sets was pseudo-random, but constructed system tried to enforce the same number of missing values for each attribute.

Table 3. Number of nodes in decision tree

number of missing values in sample	1		3		
G_volmax	0	1	0	1	3
dataset					
dermatology	32.2	179.0	54.8	239.4	2236.7
ecoli	57.4	216.1	76.8	207.5	664.2
glass	14.0	53.7	19.8	60.4	204.2
ionosphere	27.2	153.1	27.4	143.0	1294.1
iris	21.2	44.5	39.8	63.5	100.8
page-blocks	128.8	627.7	131.2	534.4	2914.1
parkinsons	22.6	89.0	20.4	79.8	457.0
pendigits	908.0	5737.6	1796.8	7782.7	61448.3
pima diabetes	24.0	88.8	12.8	50.4	271.3
vowel	190.0	875.0	302.0	994.0	4695.0
wisconsin	33.2	131.5	51.8	167.1	563.9
average difference	−	+338,9%	−	+261,0%	+2045,3%

Experiments were performed with standard for C4.5 parameters of building tree and pruning. Parameter G_volmax was set to values: 0, which means that algorithm WrapTree was disabled; 1 and 3. Parameter $G\_volmax = 3$ was tested only for samples with 3 missing parameters, because all decision tree created with G_volmax greater than number of missing values in testing sample works exactly the same.

Table 4. Number of the used nodes during classification

number of missing values in sample	1		3		
G_volmax	0	1	0	1	3
dataset					
dermatology	5.4	5.2	7.3	6.0	5.9
ecoli	8.3	6.0	17.6	10.3	6.3
glass	4.0	3.8	7.6	5.6	4.8
ionosphere	5.6	5.4	6.6	6.0	5.9
iris	6.4	4.3	23.3	10.2	4.9
page-blocks	11.8	8.6	19.1	11.0	7.8
parkinsons	4.6	4.3	5.1	4.3	4.2
pendigits	13.2	10.3	28.7	15.5	11.0
pima diabetes	5.3	4.4	5.6	5.0	4.4
vowel	11.8	8.3	29.7	14.2	9.0
wisconsin	5.3	4.4	11.1	7.0	5.4
average difference	$-$	-17.5%	$-$	-32.3%	-44.6%

Results of the experiments are shown in tables: Table 2 – average efficiency of classification of each class according to 1, Table 3 – mean number of nodes in decision tree, Table 4 – average number of nodes used during classification of testing samples.

4   Final Remarks

In the paper, authors presented a new method for improving accuracy of classification by decision trees in case of samples with missing values. The effectiveness of a solution has been confirmed by series computer simulations. As expected, the tests showed that size of decision trees significantly increased after proposed procedure execution. The size is notwithstanding smaller than corresponding tree forest. Moreover, the wrapped tree use smaller number of nodes than other solution designed to process samples with missing features.

The future works with presented idea will concerns extending the interpretability of the knowledge contained in the tree. In this subject the inspiration could be a proposition that comes from fuzzy systems [5]. Also the ensembles of wrapped trees combined with other types of classification [28] could be promising. They could use e.g. AdaBoost or bagging metaalgorithms [13].

References

1. Bartczuk, L., Rutkowska, D.: Type-2 fuzzy decision trees. In: Rutkowski, L., Tadeusiewicz, R., Zadeh, L.A., Zurada, J.M. (eds.) ICAISC 2008. LNCS (LNAI), vol. 5097, pp. 197–206. Springer, Heidelberg (2008)
2. Bonissone, P., Cadenas, J.M., Carmen Garrido, M., Andrés Díaz-Valladares, R.: A fuzzy random forest (2010)

3. Breiman, L., Friedman, J., Olshen, R., Stone, C.: Classification and Regression Trees. Wadsworth Int. Group (1984)
4. Brodley, C.E., Utgoff, P.E.: Multivariate decision trees (1995)
5. Cpalka, K.: A method for designing flexible neuro-fuzzy systems. In: Rutkowski, L., Tadeusiewicz, R., Zadeh, L.A., Żurada, J.M. (eds.) ICAISC 2006. LNCS (LNAI), vol. 4029, pp. 212–219. Springer, Heidelberg (2006)
6. Cpałka, K.: On evolutionary designing and learning of flexible neuro-fuzzy structures for nonlinear classification. Nonlinear Analysis: Theory, Methods & Applications 71(12), 1659–1672 (2009)
7. Gabryel, M., Scherer, R.: Determining fuzzy relation by evolutionary learning in neuro-fuzzy systems. In: Rutkowski, L., Tadeusiewicz, R., Zadeh, L.A., Zurada, J. (eds.) Computational Intelligence: Methods and Applications, pp. 176–182. Academic Publishing House EXIT (2008)
8. Greblicki, W., Rutkowski, L.: Density-free bayes risk consistency of nonparametric pattern recognition procedures. Proceedings of the IEEE 69(4), 482–483 (1981)
9. Hashemi, S., Yang, Y.: Flexible decision tree for data stream classification in the presence of concept change, noise and missing values. Data Mining and Knowledge Discovery 19, 95–131 (2009)
10. Haykin, S., Network, N.: A comprehensive foundation. Neural Networks 2 (2004)
11. Horzyk, A., Tadeusiewicz, R.: Self-optimizing neural networks. In: Yin, F.-L., Wang, J., Guo, C. (eds.) ISNN 2004. LNCS, vol. 3173, pp. 150–155. Springer, Heidelberg (2004)
12. Korytkowski, M., Rutkowski, L., Scherer, R.: From ensemble of fuzzy classifiers to single fuzzy rule base classifier. In: Rutkowski, L., Tadeusiewicz, R., Zadeh, L.A., Zurada, J.M. (eds.) ICAISC 2008. LNCS (LNAI), vol. 5097, pp. 265–272. Springer, Heidelberg (2008)
13. Korytkowski, M., Scherer, R., Rutkowski, L.: On combining backpropagation with boosting. In: 2006 International Joint Conference on Neural Networks, IEEE World Congress on Computational Intelligence, Vancouver, BC, Canada, pp. 1274–1277 (2006)
14. Mertz, C.J., Murphy, P.M.: UCI machine learning repository, http://archive.ics.uci.edu/ml/datasets.html
15. Nowicki, R.: On combining neuro–fuzzy architectures with the rough set theory to solve classification problems with incomplete data. IEEE Trans. on Knowledge and Data Engineering 20(9), 1239–1253 (2008)
16. Nowicki, R.: Rough–neuro–fuzzy structures for classification with missing data. IEEE Trans. on Systems, Man, and Cybernetics—Part B: Cybernetics 39(6), 1334–1347 (2009)
17. Pawlak, Z.: Rough sets. International Journal of Computer and Information Sciences 11(5), 341–356 (1982)
18. Przybył, A., Cpałka, K.: A new method to construct of interpretable models of dynamic systems. In: Rutkowski, L., Korytkowski, M., Scherer, R., Tadeusiewicz, R., Zadeh, L.A., Zurada, J.M. (eds.) ICAISC 2012, Part II. LNCS, vol. 7268, pp. 697–705. Springer, Heidelberg (2012)
19. Qian, Y., Dang, C., Liang, J., Zhang, H., Ma, J.: On the evaluation of the decision performance of an incomplete decision table. Data & Knowledge Engineering 65(3), 373–400 (2008)
20. Quinlan, J.: C4.5: Programs for Machine Learning. Morgan Kaufmann (1993)
21. Quinlan, J.R.: Improved use of continuous attributes in c4.5. Journal of Artificial Intelligence Research 4, 77–90 (1996)

22. Rutkowska, D., Nowicki, R.: Implication-based neuro–fuzzy architectures. International Journal of Applied Mathematics and Computer Science 10(4), 675–701 (2000)
23. Rutkowska, D., Rutkowski, L., Nowicki, R.: On processing of noisy data by fuzzy inference neural networks. In: Proceedings of the IASTED International Conference, Signal and Image Processing, Nassau, Bahamas, pp. 314–318 (October 1999)
24. Rutkowski, L.: Sequential estimates of probability densities by orthogonal series and their application in pattern classification. IEEE Transactions on Systems, Man and Cybernetics SMC-10(12), 918–920 (1980)
25. Rutkowski, L.: Adaptive probabilistic neural networks for pattern classification in time-varying environment. IEEE Transactions on Neural Networks 15(4), 811–827 (2004)
26. Rutkowski, L.: Generalized regression neural networks in time-varying environment. IEEE Transactions on Neural Networks 15(3), 576–596 (2004)
27. Rutkowski, L., Pietruczuk, L., Duda, P., Jaworski, M.: Decision trees for mining data streams based on the McDiarmid's bound. IEEE Transactions on Knowledge and Data Engineering 25 (2013)
28. Scherer, R.: Boosting ensemble of relational neuro-fuzzy systems. In: Rutkowski, L., Tadeusiewicz, R., Zadeh, L.A., Żurada, J.M. (eds.) ICAISC 2006. LNCS (LNAI), vol. 4029, pp. 306–313. Springer, Heidelberg (2006)
29. Scherer, R., Korytkowski, M., Nowicki, R., Rutkowski, L.: Modular rough neuro-fuzzy systems for classification. In: Wyrzykowski, R., Dongarra, J., Karczewski, K., Wasniewski, J. (eds.) PPAM 2007. LNCS, vol. 4967, pp. 540–548. Springer, Heidelberg (2008)
30. Scherer, R., Rutkowski, L.: A fuzzy relational system with linguistic antecedent certainty factors. In: Rutkowski, L., Kacprzyk, J. (eds.) Proceedings of the Sixth International Conference on Neural Network and Soft Computing. Advances in Soft Computing, pp. 563–569. Springer, Heidelberg (2003)
31. Scherer, R., Rutkowski, L.: Neuro-fuzzy relational classifiers. In: Rutkowski, L., Siekmann, J.H., Tadeusiewicz, R., Zadeh, L.A. (eds.) ICAISC 2004. LNCS (LNAI), vol. 3070, pp. 376–380. Springer, Heidelberg (2004)
32. Scherer, R., Rutkowski, L.: Connectionist fuzzy relational systems. In: Hagamuge, S.K., Wang, L. (eds.) Computational Intelligence for Modelling and Prediction. SCI, vol. 2, pp. 35–47. Springer, Heidelberg (2005)
33. Starczewski, J.T.: On defuzzification of interval type-2 fuzzy sets. In: Rutkowski, L., Tadeusiewicz, R., Zadeh, L.A., Zurada, J.M. (eds.) ICAISC 2008. LNCS (LNAI), vol. 5097, pp. 333–340. Springer, Heidelberg (2008)
34. Starczewski, J.T.: A type-1 approximation of interval type-2 FLS. In: Di Gesù, V., Pal, S.K., Petrosino, A. (eds.) WILF 2009. LNCS, vol. 5571, pp. 287–294. Springer, Heidelberg (2009)
35. Starczewski, J.T.: General type-2 fls with uncertainty generated by fuzzy rough sets. In: FUZZ-IEEE, pp. 1–6 (2010)
36. Zhang, S.: Decision tree classifiers sensitive to heterogeneous costs. Journal of Systems and Software 85(4), 771–779 (2012)
37. Zhang, S., Qin, Z., Ling, C., Sheng, S.: "Missing is useful": missing values in cost-sensitive decision trees. IEEE Transactions on Knowledge and Data Engineering 17(12), 1689–1693 (2005)

Adaptation of Decision Trees
for Handling Concept Drift

Lena Pietruczuk, Piotr Duda, and Maciej Jaworski

Institute of Intelligent Systems, Czestochowa University of Technology,
Armii Krajowej 36, 42-200 Czestochowa, Poland
{lena.pietruczuk,piotr.duda,maciej.jaworski}@iisi.pcz.pl

Abstract. The problem of data stream mining is widely studied in the
literature. Especially difficult to solve is the problem of mining data with
occurring concept drift. The most commonly used algorithms are those
based on decision trees. In this article we investigate the performance of
a few algorithms of constructing decision trees for data stream classification, not explicitly designed to deal with changing distribution of data.
We show how to adapt these methods to deal with concept drift and we
compare the obtained results.

1 Introduction

In the data mining community one of the most challenging tasks is the extraction
of knowledge from data streams [1]-[3], [19], [20], [23]. Data stream is a possibly
infinite sequence of data. Therefore traditional data mining algorithms are not
applicable in this field and they need to be modified significantly to handle data
streams. Data stream mining algorithms can be divided into a few categories.
One of them consist of one-pass algorithms in which each data element is processed at most once. An example of such an algorithm is the Very Fast Decision
Tree algorithm (VFDT) [6]. The another group are algorithms working on data
chunks. Data elements are collected in the chunk, on which a traditional data
mining algorithm is applied. The obtained results are then either synthesized
with output from previous chunk or have an effect on data elements in the following data chunk. Most ensemble algorithms belong to this group. The next
group worth consideration are algorithms with the sliding window. The sliding
window is an object in which only the number $|W|$ of recent elements from the
stream is collected. If a new data element is read from the stream, it updates the
current results and is put inside the sliding window. If the sliding window is of
fixed volume, the oldest element from the window is deleted and its effect on the
results is canceled out at this point. If the volume of the window changes over
time, the oldest element is deleted every time the number of elements in the window exceeds its currently desired size. An example of an algorithm with sliding
window technique is the Concept-adapting Very Fast Decision Tree algorithm
(CVFDT) [8].

As in the case of traditional data mining, the most important techniques
used to extract information from data streams are clustering and classification.

L. Rutkowski et al. (Eds.): ICAISC 2013, Part I, LNAI 7894, pp. 459–473, 2013.

This paper is focused only on the latter. The task of classification can be defined as follows: given the training dataset $Z = \{X_i = (x_i, y_i), \ i \in \{1, \ldots, N\}\}$, $x_i = [x_i^1, \ldots, x_i^D] \in A_1 \times \cdots \times A_D$, $y_i \in \Lambda$, where A_j is the set of possible values of attribute a_j and $\Lambda = \{k_1, \ldots, k_K\}$ is the set of K different classes, find a function $h : A_1 \times \cdots \times A_D \longrightarrow \Lambda$ which for any element $x \in A_1 \times \cdots \times A_D$ returns its corresponding class $y \in \Lambda$ with probability as high as possible. If the class of the element x is unknown, the classifier h is used to predict the corresponding class. There are many methods for data classification, e.g. artificial neural networks, decision trees or the k-nearest neighbor algorithm. Among them decision trees stand out mainly with two desired features: they provide satisfactorily high accuracies and are easily interpretable by the user.

Decision tree consists of nodes and leaves. To each node l_q (where l_1 is the root of the tree) one of the attributes a_j, $j \in \{1, \ldots, D\}$, is assigned. The node is split according to chosen attribute into its children nodes. If the tree is non-binary, the number of children is equal to the cardinality of set A_i (therefore non-binary trees make sense only for attributes with nominal values). In this case each children corresponds to a single possible value v_j^λ, $\lambda \in \{1, \ldots, |A_j|\}$, from set A_i. If the tree is binary, the number of children is equal to 2. In this case the set A_i is partitioned into two disjoint subsets A_i^L and $A_i^R = A_i \backslash A_i^L$. The two children nodes correspond to these two subsets.

In each node l_q sufficient statistics $n_{j\lambda}^r(l_q)$ of data elements are stored, denoting the number of elements of the class k_r, with the value of attribute a_j equal to v_j^λ. If the attribute is numerical, its domain is divided into B_j bins and each bin is considered as one discrete value. Sufficient statistics represent the subset $Z(l_q)$ of the training set Z, which is collected in node l_q. They are used to determine the best attribute to split the node. The choice is made on a basis of some impurity measure function. For example in the ID3 algorithm an information entropy is used. In the Classification and Regression Tree algorithm (CART) the Gini index is used as the impurity measure and this measure is considered in presented paper. If $n^r(l_q)$ denotes the number of elements with class k_r in set $Z(l_q)$ and $n(l_q)$ is the cardinality of set $Z(l_q)$, then the Gini index of set $Z(l_q)$ is given by

$$Gini(Z(l_q)) = 1 - \sum_{r=1}^{K} \left(\frac{n^r(l_q)}{n(l_q)} \right)^2. \tag{1}$$

Let us now define the set $Z_{A_j^L}(l_q)$ as a subset of elements from set $Z(l_q)$ for which the value of attribute a_j belongs to A_j^L. Then the weighted Gini index for attribute a_j and partition of its values (A_j^L, A_j^R) for set $Z(l_q)$ (in case of binary trees) is given by

$$Gini_{A_j^L}(Z(l_q)) = \frac{n_{A_j^L}(l_q)}{n(l_q)} Gini(Z_{A_j^L}(l_q)) + \frac{n_{A_j \backslash A_j^L}(l_q)}{n(l_q)} Gini(Z_{A_j \backslash A_j^L}(l_q)), \tag{2}$$

where $n_{A_j^L}(l_q)$ is the cardinality of set $Z_{A_j^L}(l_q)$. Then the weighted Gini index for attribute a_j is defined as the maximum of (2) over all possible partitions of set A_j

$$Gini_{a_j}(Z(l_q)) = \max_{A_j^L \in \mathcal{P}_j} \{Gini_{A_j^L}(Z(l_q))\}, \tag{3}$$

where $\mathcal{P}_j$ is the set of all possible subsets of A_j.

At this point one can define the Gini gain function, which is simply a difference between formulas (1) and (3)

$$\overline{G}_{l_q}(a_j) = Gini(Z(l_q)) - Gini_{a_j}(Z(l_q)). \tag{4}$$

Finally, an attribute a_{MAX}, which maximizes formula (4), is chosen to split the node

$$a_{MAX} = \arg \max_{a_j} \{\overline{G}_{l_q}(a_j)\}. \tag{5}$$

If all elements in the considered node are of the same class, then the node is not split and becomes a leaf. Leaves are used to assign a class to unlabeled data elements.

In case of traditional algorithms for decision trees construction the attribute a_{MAX} is determined on a basis of set $Z(l_q)$, which size depends only on the size of the whole training set Z. In case of data streams the set Z is potentially infinite and in the specified moment in time obviously only finite subset of it is available in the considered node. Therefore, the main problem is to establish the number of elements $n(l_q)$ sufficient to determine if the best attribute derived from the available data sample is the same as it would be in the case of infinite data set. The recipe for how to do it is presented in section 2. In particular, the McDiarmid Tree (McDT) algorithm is presented.

Another problem encountered in data stream mining is the concept drift. This problem was widely considered in literature [3], [7], [11]-[18], [22]. As the subsequent data elements from the stream arrive sequentially to the system, their concept, i.e. the probability distribution of attribute values and classes, can change over time. Therefore, the decision tree built in a basis of past data elements can be inappropriate to classify future elements. The decision tree should posses the ability to rebuild its structure dynamically if the data concept changes. Several techniques for concept drift handling in case of decision trees are presented in section 3. A special attention is paid for the concept-adaptive version of the McDT algorithm (CMcDT). The modification is based on the idea of the CVFDT algorithm. In section 4 the experimental results are presented. Section 5 draws the conclusions.

2   The McDiarmid Tree Algorithm

Well known in the scientific community algorithm the Hoeffdings Decision Trees, presented by P. Domingos and G. Hulten in [6], was the basis for many existing algorithms. To solve the problem of determining the best attribute to make a split authors used statistical tool called the Hoeffding's bound. However it was shown in [19] that this method can not be applied in this case. Authors pointed the fact that this bound is applicable only for numerical data while the incoming data could be categorical. Moreover this bound can not be used in conjunction with split measures like information gain or Gini index. This is due to the fact that those measures can not be expressed as a sum of independent random variables and use only the frequencies of data elements. Therefore authors propose to use the McDiarmid's inequality instead of Hoeffding's bound (see [19]). The presented algorithm is based on the Hoeffding Tree algorithm. The difference is the value of parameter ϵ. When for the purpose of determining the quality of a split the impurity measure information gain is used, then the value of parameter ϵ is obtained as follows [19]

$$\epsilon = C_{Gain}(K, n(l_q)) \sqrt{\frac{\ln(1/\delta)}{2n(l_q)}}, \tag{6}$$

where

$$C_{Gain}(K, n(l_q)) = 6(K \log_2 en(l_q) + \log_2 2n(l_q)) + 2 \log_2 K. \tag{7}$$

If the impurity measure Gini index is applied then the value of parameter ϵ is calculated from the formula [19]

$$\epsilon = 8 \sqrt{\frac{\ln(1/\delta)}{2n(l_q)}}. \tag{8}$$

The pseudocode of the McDiarmid tree algorithm is placed below. For convenience the following notations will be introduced:

- $\mathcal{A}$ - set of all attributes
- a_j - the j-th attribute from set $\mathcal{A}$
- a_{MAX1} - attribute with the highest value of $G(\cdot)$
- a_{MAX2} - attribute with the second highest value of $G(\cdot)$

The McDiarmid tree algorithm

Inputs: Z	is a sequence of examples,
$\mathcal{A}$	is a set of discrete attributes,
$G(\cdot)$	is a split evaluation function,
δ	is one minus the desired probability of choosing the correct attribute at any given node.

Output: $McDT$ is a decision tree.

Procedure $McDiarmidTree(Z, \mathcal{A}, G, \delta)$
Let $McDT$ be a tree with a single leaf l_1 (the root).
For each class k_r

For each attribute $a_j \in \mathcal{A}$
    For each value v_j^λ of attribute a_j
        Let $n_{j\lambda}^r(l_1) = 0$.
For each example X in $\check{Z}$
    Sort X into a leaf l using $McDT$.
    For each attribute $a_j \in \mathcal{A}$
        For each value v_j^λ of attribute a_j
            If value of example X for attribute a_j equals v_j^λ
            and X comes from class k_r
                Increment $n_{j\lambda}^r(l)$.
    Label l with the majority class among the examples
    seen so far at l.
    If the examples seen so far at l are not of the same class
        Compute $\overline{G}_l(a_j)$ for each attribute $a_j \in \mathcal{A}$ using
        the counts $n_{j\lambda}^r(l)$.
        Let a_{MAX1} be the attribute with the highest $\overline{G}_l$.
        Let a_{MAX2} be the attribute with the second-highest $\overline{G}_l$.
        Compute ϵ using equation (6) for
        information gain or (8) for Gini gain.
        If $\overline{G}_l(a_{MAX1}) - \overline{G}_l(a_{MAX2}) > \epsilon$, then
            Replace l by an internal node that splits on a_{MAX1}.
            For each branch of the split
                Add a new leaf l_m
                For each class k_r
                    For each attribute $a_j \in \mathcal{A}$
                        For each value v_j^λ of a_j
                            Let $n_{j\lambda}^r(l_m) = 0$.
Return $McDT$.

3 Concept Drift Handling with Decision Trees

In [8] the authors proposed a method for classification of data streams called the CVFDT algorithm. This method is designed to handle the concept drift. In line with construction of the main decision tree, the algorithm tries to develop alternative subtrees in some nodes. If the alternative tree occurs to provide higher accuracy than the original subtree, then the latter is simply replaced by the former. Another important modification introduced in the CVFDT algorithm is the sliding window. The temporary state of the decision tree is based only on the $|W|$ recently read data elements, where $|W|$ is the size of the window. If the data element stored in the window becomes deprecated its effect on the classifier is immediately canceled. Based on the pseudocode of the McDT algorithm presented in previous section, its concept-adapting version, the CMcDT algorithm, can be described in several points:

a) The classifier consists of the original tree and of potential alternative subtrees. The number of alternative trees in each node is not limited. Moreover, nodes in alternative trees can itself contain alternative subtrees. As in the McDT algorithm, data elements are sorted through the original tree according to their values of attributes. If any node l_q on the path from the root to the leaf contains non empty set of alternative subtrees $ALT(l_q)$, the data element is recursively sorted through each element from set $ALT(l_q)$.

b) Nodes created in the tree (also in the alternative trees) receive their own unique, monotonically increasing ID number. For each data element X_i the maximum identifier $ID_{max,i}$ among all visited nodes is noticed. The element X_i and the number $ID_{max,i}$ are then put together as one record into the sliding window.

c) If the number of elements stored in the window exceeds its currently desired volume $|W|$, the last record from it is taken, i.e. X_{last}, $ID_{max,last}$. Then the *ForgetExample* procedure, described below, is executed.

> *Procedure ForgetExample($McDT$,$\mathcal{A}$,X_{last},$ID_{max,last}$)*
>   Sort X_{last} through $McDT$
>   Let P be the set of nodes traversed in the sort
>   For each node l in P
>   If ID number of node l is not greater that $ID_{max,last}$, then
>   For each attribute a_j in $\mathcal{A}$
>   For each value v_j^λ of attribute a_j
>   If value of example X_{last} for attribute a_j equals v_j^λ and X_{last} comes from class k_r, then
>   Decrement $n_{j\lambda}^r(l)$
>   For each tree T_{alt} in $ALT(l)$
>   ForgetExample(T_{alt},$\mathcal{A}$,X_{last},$ID_{max,last}$)

Next the record X_{last}, $ID_{max,last}$ is deleted from the window. The procedure *ForgetExample* cancels the effect of old data elements on the state of classifier, as they may not correspond to the current data concept.

d) After every f data elements from the stream are processed, algorithm checks at each node l (which is not a leaf) if a new alternative subtree should be created. This is done by executing the procedure *CheckSplitValidity* described below. The procedure is run for the original tree and recursively for all the alternative trees.

> *Procedure CkeckSplitValidity($McDT$,$\mathcal{A}$,δ)*
>   For each node l in $McDT$ that is not a leaf
>   For each tree T_{alt} in $ALT(l)$
>   CheckSplitValidity(T_{alt},δ)
>   For each attribute a in $\mathcal{A}$
>   Compute $\overline{G}_l(a)$
>   Let a_{split} be the split attribute at l

Let a_{m1} be the attribute with the highest $\overline{G}_l$ other than a_{split}
Let a_{m2} be the attribute with the highest $\overline{G}_l$ other than a_{m1}
Let $\Delta \overline{G}_l = \overline{G}_l(a_{m1}) - \overline{G}_l(a_{m2})$
If $\Delta \overline{G}_l \geq 0$ and no tree in $ALT(l)$ already splits on a_{m1} with
the same partition A_{m1}^L at its root, then
    Compute ϵ using equation (8) and δ
    If $\Delta \overline{G}_l > \epsilon$, then
        Create a new node l_{new}, for which the parent
        is the same as for node l
        $ALT(l) = ALT(l) + \{l_{new}\}$
        For each children node (leaf) l_m of l_{new}
           $ALT(l_m) = \emptyset$
           For each class k_r, each attribute a_j and each value v_j^λ
              $n_{j\lambda}^r(l_m) = 0$

For each node l the value of Gini gain is computed. Then the attribute a_{m1} with the highest value of Gini gain, without taking into account the split attribute a_{split} of node l, is considered. If attribute a_{m1} provides higher value of Gini gain than attribute a_{split} does and there is no tree in $ALT(l)$ that already splits on a_{m1}, then the procedure continues. Let a_{m2} denote the attribute with the highest value of Gini gain, without taking into account attribute a_{m1} (in particular a_{m2} may be equal to a_{split}). If the difference between $\overline{G}_l(a_{m1})$ and $\overline{G}_l(a_{m2})$ is greater than the value of ϵ computed from equation (8), then it is a signal that a_{m1} may be, with great certainty, better attribute to split node l than the current attribute a_{split}. A new subtree is created, with root l_{new} which splits according to attribute a_{m1}, and it is inserted into set $ALT(l)$.

e) Each existing alternative tree has to be checked from time to time whether it provides higher accuracy than the corresponding original subtree. For this reason each node l, containing nonempty set of alternative trees, is switched to the test mode after collecting m_{start} data elements. When the node is in this mode, which is held until m_{stop} data elements are collected, it updates its sufficient statistics $n_{j\lambda}^r(l)$ but does not produce new alternative trees. For this m_{stop} data elements accuracy of the subtree with root at node l is calculated. The accuracy is also calculated, on the same m_{stop} data elements, for each alternative tree from $ALT(l)$. If the most accurate alternative tree $T_{alt,max}$ occurs to be more accurate than the original subtree, the node l is simply replaced by $T_{alt,max}$ and the other alternative trees are deleted. After the m_{stop} data elements the test mode in node l is switched off. The algorithm is equipped with the pruning mechanism to discard alternative trees which are not promising. If the test mode ends with no replacement, for each alternative tree $T_i(l)$ from $ALT(l)$ the difference between the accuracies achieved for T_i and for the original subtree is calculated. If the current difference is greater than the smallest difference ever achieved for considered tree $T_i(l)$ in previous tests by more than 1%, then $T_i(l)$ is pruned from the set $ALT(l)$ and is not considered in future tests.

Another method to deal with streaming data with concept drift is to apply the ensemble of algorithms [4], [9], [10]. It is used to improve the accuracy of a simple algorithm. There are number of ways of building and connecting basic algorithms to obtain better accuracy. In this paper the performance of the ensemble modified FID3 algorithm (emFID3), presented in [10], on the streaming data with occurrence of a change of class distribution is analyzed.

4   Experimental Results

In this section efficiency of the McDT, CMcDT and emFID algorithms in handling concept drift is examined. The McDT and CMcDT algorithms are applied with configuration $\delta = 0.1$, $f = 100$, m_{start}=500, m_{stop}=100. The CMcDT algorithm is used in both versions, with and without sliding windows. The emFID algorithm is applied with the size of data chunk equal to 1000, number of trees in ensemble fixed to 50 and the maximum depth of the tree set to 20.

In each experiment a two class problem is considered and synthetic data are used. The data are generated from uniform distribution on a previously defined D-dimensional hypercube. A class of an instance is assigned by location of elements relative to the hyperplane given by

$$\sum_{d=1}^{D} w_d \mathbf{x}_d = w_0, \tag{9}$$

where $[\mathbf{x}_1, \ldots, \mathbf{x}_D]$ is a point in D-dimensional Euclidean space and $[w_1, \ldots, w_D]$ is the vector perpendicular to the hyperplane. Data elements X_i for which $\sum_{d=1}^{D} w_d x_i^d \geq w_0$ are assigned to the first class, in other case elements are assigned to the second class. The values w_d, for $d = 0, 1, \ldots, D$, evolve during each experiment to simulate a change of data concept. The number and type of changes is different for each of the experiments.

To evaluate performance of the McDT and CMcDT algorithms, the testing set of 2000 data elements is generated from current distribution when it is required.

4.1   Experiment 1

In the first experiment the 2-dimensional data are considered. The data are generated from the cube $[0, 1]^2$. The number of instances in the experiment is set to 500000 and the distribution of data is changed 3 times. The hyperplane changes over every 125000 data elements. It starts from hyperplane given by equation

$$\mathbf{x}_1 = 0.5 \tag{10}$$

and every change is a rotation of the hyperplane by 45 degrees relative to the point $(0.5, 0.5)$. In the CMcDT algorithm the sliding window size is set to 10000.

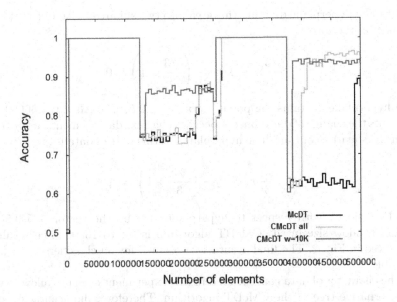

Fig. 1. Accuracy obtained for the classifiers for 2-dimensional data with concept drift described in 4.1

Table 1. Final accuracies of classifiers for 2-dimensional data with concept drift described in 4.1

Algorithms	McDT	CMcDT all	CMcDT w=10K	emFID3
Accuracy	0.8735	**0.9505**	0.9335	0.9334

In Figure 1 the accuracies obtained for subsequent data elements are presented. For data from 1 to 125000 and from 250000 to 375000 only one split is required to achieve high accuracy very close to 100%. Therefore all the classifiers obtain the high accuracy very fast. In the last part of data the alternative tree mechanism allows the CMcDT algorithm to outperform the McDT algorithm. The CMcDT algorithm replaces a part of original tree by the alternative tree, what results with immediate gain of accuracy. On the other hand the McDT algorithm has many more nodes in the tree, therefore it needs many more data elements to fit to the current data concept. In Table 1 the final accuracies of classifiers are summarized. As can be seen the highest accuracy is obtained for the CMcDT algorithm.

4.2 Experiment 2

In a second experiment the 2-dimensional data are considered. The set of 10^6 data elements is generated. The first 500000 data elements come from the square

$[0,1]^2$. The hyperplane dividing this area into two subareas with different classes is taken in the form

$$\frac{\sqrt{3}}{3}x_1 + x_2 - \frac{1}{2}\left(\frac{\sqrt{3}}{3}+1\right) = 0. \tag{11}$$

The hyperplane contains the point $(x_1, x_2) = (0.5, 0.5)$. After the 500000 data elements the change of data concept occurs. The next data elements are generated from the square $[0.5, 1.5]^2$. The hyperplane for this part of data is given by

$$\frac{\sqrt{3}}{3}x_1 + x_2 - \left(\frac{\sqrt{3}}{3}+1\right) = 0, \tag{12}$$

which is moved with respect to hyperplane (11) by the vector $[0.5, 0.5]$. The sliding window size in the CMcDT algorithm is set to 10000. The results are presented in Fig. 2. The final accuracies obtained for all classifiers are collected in Table 2.

The character of data concept used in this experiment does not allow to create an alternative tree in the CMcDT algorithm. Therefore, the accuracies for the McDT and the CMcDT (without window) algorithms are the same (since the

Table 2. Final accuracies of classifiers for 2-dimensional data with concept drift described in 4.2

Algorithms	McDT	CMcDT all	CMcDT w=10K	emFID3
Accuracy	0.8932	0.9116	0.8458	**0.92**

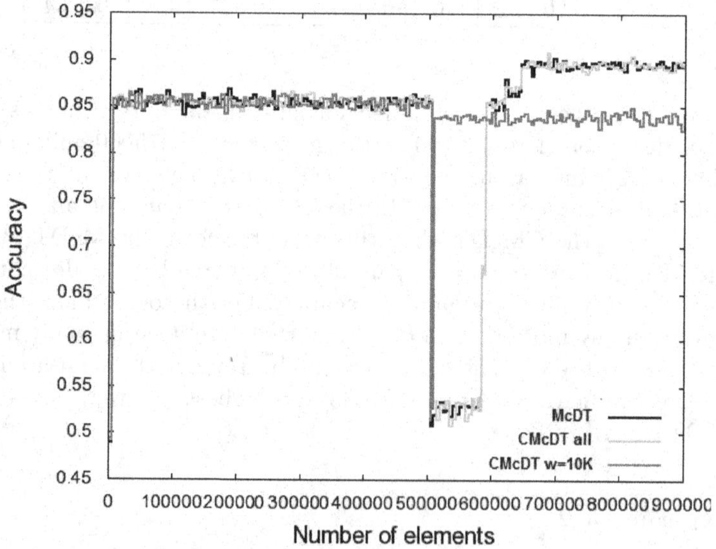

Fig. 2. Accuracy obtained for the classifiers for 2-dimensional data with concept drift described in 4.2

created trees in both cases are exactly the same). The difference is in the CMcDT algorithm with sliding window. The window cancels the effect of deprecated data. Hence, after the occurrence of concept drift, the acceptable accuracy could be quickly restored in this case. The final accuracy, according to Table 2, is the highest for the emFID3 algorithm. However, the value obtained for the CMcDT algorithm is comparable.

4.3 Experiment 3

In a third experiment the 15-dimensional data are considered. The 10^6 data are generated from the cube $[0, 1]^{15}$. The hyperplane is chosen randomly and is changed 3 times every 250000 data elements. Each hyperplane passes through the point $[0.3, \ldots, 0.3]$. In the CMcDT algorithm the sliding windows size is set to 50000. The results are presented in Fig. 3 and Table 3.

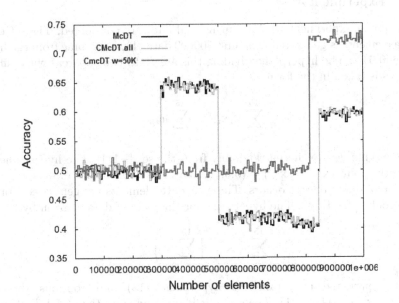

Fig. 3. Accuracy obtained for the classifiers for 15-dimensional data with concept drift described in 4.3

Table 3. Final accuracies of classifiers for 15-dimensional data with concept drift described in 4.3

Algorithms	McDT	CMcDT all	CMcDT w=50K	emFID3
Accuracy	0.588	0.5796	0.7142	**0.8818**

The performance of the algorithm depends heavily on distribution of data. For the considered distributions data allow to make a split and to increase accuracy only twice. Moreover in the CMcDT algorithm no alternative trees are created. In such a case both the McDT and the CMcDT algorithms have drawbacks caused by expired data elements. After every split a set of data is divided into two subsets. Hence each children node is reached by data elements less often than its parent node. That makes it more difficult to fit the tree to a current concept by expansion. Moreover it needs a lot of data to update sufficient statistics in nodes. Use of sliding windows allows to follow the trend of data. However, because of bounded number of considered data elements, it permits a split only in favorable situations, like in the last concept. The emFID3 algorithm does not manifest the problems mentioned above and, as a result, obtains the highest final accuracy.

4.4   Experiment 4

In a fourth experiment the 15-dimensional data are considered. The set of 10^6 data elements is generated. The first 500000 data elements come from the hypercube $[0, 1]^{15}$. The hyperplane dividing this area into two subareas with different classes is taken in the form

$$\sum_{i=1}^{15} w_i \mathbf{x}_i - \frac{1}{2} \sum_{i=1}^{15} w_i = 0. \tag{13}$$

The weights w_i are chosen randomly from the set $[-1, 1]$. The hyperplane contains the point $(\mathbf{x}_1, \ldots, \mathbf{x}_{15}) = (0.5, \ldots, 0.5)$. After the 500000 data elements the change of data concept occurs. The next data elements are generated from the hypercube $[0.5, 1.5]^{15}$. The hyperplane for this part of data is given by

$$\sum_{i=1}^{15} w_i \mathbf{x}_i - \left(\sum_{i=1}^{15} w_i \right) = 0. \tag{14}$$

This hyperplane is parallel to hyperplane (13) and contains the point $(\mathbf{x}_1, \ldots, \mathbf{x}_{15}) = (1, \ldots, 1)$. The size of sliding window in the CMcDT algorithm is set to 10000.

As can be seen in Fig. 4 the McDT algorithm needs a lot more data to fit to the current concept. The CMcDT algorithm creates an alternative tree after the change of concept, what allows to obtain higher accuracy. Use of sliding window provides faster adaptation to the new data concept and ensures higher final accuracy.

In Table 4 the final accuracies obtained for different classifiers are presented. The results for the McDT and the CMcDT algorithms are similar. The ensemble algorithm outperforms the others.

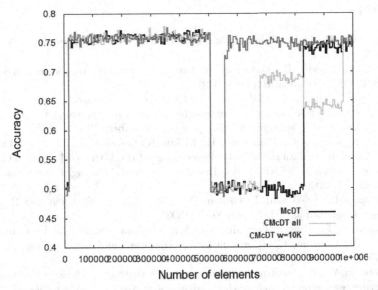

Fig. 4. Accuracy obtained for the classifiers for 15-dimensional data with concept drift described in 4.4

Table 4. Final accuracies of classifiers for 15-dimensional data with concept drift described in 4.4

Algorithms	McDT	CMcDT all	CMcDT w=10K	emFID3
Accuracy	0.7486	0.7688	0.7818	**0.88**

5 Conclusions

In this paper the task of data stream classification was considered. Specifically the problem of concept drift handling in decision trees was investigated. The McDiarmid Tree algorithm was combined with methods put forward formerly in the CVFDT algorithm. Particularly the sliding window and the alternative trees mechanisms were applied. Performance of the proposed algorithm (i.e. the CM-cDT algorithm) was then compared with the McDT algorithm and the emFID3 algorithm. The experimental results show that the methods presented in this paper make the concept drift handling by decision trees possible. Simulations also showed that the ensemble algorithm provides higher accuracy than the one-pass algorithm or the algorithm with sliding window. However, the emFID3 algorithm is much more time and memory consuming.

Acknowledgments. The work presented in this paper was supported by a grant from Switzerland through the Swiss Contribution to the enlarged European Union.

L. Pietruczuk, P. Duda, and M. Jaworski

References

1. Aggarwal, C.: Data Streams. Models and Algorithms. Springer, LLC, New York (2007)
2. Bifet, A., Kirkby, R.: Data Stream Mining a Practical Approach, University of WAIKATO, Technical Report (2009)
3. Bifet, A., Holmes, G., Pfahringer, B., Gavaldà, R.: Improving Adaptive Bagging Methods for Evolving Data Streams. In: Zhou, Z.-H., Washio, T. (eds.) ACML 2009. LNCS, vol. 5828, pp. 23–37. Springer, Heidelberg (2009)
4. Bifet, A., Holmes, G., Pfahringer, B., Kirkby, R., Gavalda, R.: New ensemble methods for evolving data streams. In: Proceedings of the 15th ACM SIGKDD International Conference on Knowledge Discovery and Data Mining, Paris, France, June 28-July 01 (2009)
5. Breiman, L., Friedman, J., Olshen, R., Stone, C.: Classification and Regression Trees. Chapman and Hall, New York (1993)
6. Domingos, P., Hulten, G.: Mining high-speed data streams. In: Proc. 6th ACM SIGKDD Internat. Conf. on Knowledge Discovery and Data Mining, pp. 71–80 (2000)
7. Greblicki, W., Rutkowska, D., Rutkowski, L.: An orthogonal series estimate of time-varying regression. Annals of the Institute of Statistical Mathematics 35, 215–228 (1983)
8. Hulten, G., Spencer, L., Domingos, P.: Mining time-changing data streams. In: Proc. 7th ACM SIGKDD Internat. Conf. on Knowledge Discovery and Data Mining, pp. 97–106 (2001)
9. Kuncheva, L.I.: Classifier Ensembles for Changing Environments. In: Roli, F., Kittler, J., Windeatt, T. (eds.) MCS 2004. LNCS, vol. 3077, pp. 1–15. Springer, Heidelberg (2004)
10. Pietruczuk, L., Duda, P., Jaworski, M.: A New Fuzzy Classifier for Data Streams. In: Rutkowski, L., Korytkowski, M., Scherer, R., Tadeusiewicz, R., Zadeh, L.A., Zurada, J.M. (eds.) ICAISC 2012, Part I. LNCS (LNAI), vol. 7267, pp. 318–324. Springer, Heidelberg (2012)
11. Rutkowski, L.: On Bayes risk consistent pattern recognition procedures in a quasi-stationary environment. IEEE Transactions on Pattern Analysis and Machine Intelligence PAMI-4(1), 84–87 (1982)
12. Rutkowski, L.: On nonparametric identification with prediction of time-varying systems. IEEE Transactions on Automatic Control AC-29, 58–60 (1984)
13. Rutkowski, L.: Nonparametric identification of quasi-stationary systems. Systems and Control Letters 6, 33–35 (1985)
14. Rutkowski, L.: Real-time identification of time-varying systems by non-parametric algorithms based on Parzen kernels. International Journal of Systems Science 16, 1123–1130 (1985)
15. Rutkowski, L.: Application of multiple Fourier series to identification of multivariable nonstationary systems. International Journal of Systems Science 20(10), 1993–2002 (1989)
16. Rutkowski, L.: Non-parametric learning algorithms in the time-varying environments. Signal Processing 18(2), 129–137 (1989)
17. Rutkowski, L.: New Soft Computing Techniques for System Modelling. Pattern Classification and Image Processing, Springer (2004)
18. Rutkowski, L.: Adaptive probabilistic neural-networks for pattern classification in time-varying environment. IEEE Trans. Neural Networks 15, 811–827 (2004)

19. Rutkowski, L., Pietruczuk, L., Duda, P., Jaworski, M.: Decision Trees for Mining Data Streams Based on the McDiarmid's Bound. IEEE Transactions on Knowledge and Data Engineering 25 (2013)
20. Rutkowski, L., Jaworski, M., Pietruczuk, L., Duda, P., Decision Trees for Mining Data Streams Based on the Gaussian Approximation. IEEE Transactions on Knowledge and Data Engineering 99(PrePrints) (2013)
21. Quinlan, J.R.: Learning efficient classification procedures and their application to chess end games. In: Michalski, R.S., Garbonell, J.G., Mitchell, T.M. (eds.) Machine Learning: an Artificial Inteligence Approach, pp. 463–482. Morgan Kaufmann, San Francisco (1983)
22. Wang, H., Fan, W., Yu, P., Han, J.: Mining concept-drifting data streams using ensemble classifiers. In: Proc. 9th ACM SIGKDD Internat. Conf. on Knowledge Discovery and Data Mining, pp. 226–235 (2003)
23. Wang, T., Li, Z., Hu, X., Yan, Y., Chen, H.: A New Decision Tree Classification Method for Mining High-Speed Data Streams Based on Threaded Binary Search Trees. In: Washio, T., et al. (eds.) PAKDD 2007. LNCS (LNAI), vol. 4819, pp. 256–267. Springer, Heidelberg (2007)

Hesitant Neural Gas for Supervised and Semi-supervised Classification

Piotr Płoński and Krzysztof Zaremba

Institute of Radioelectronics, Warsaw University of Technology,
Nowowiejska 15/19,00-665 Warsaw, Poland
{pplonski,zaremba}@ire.pw.edu.pl

Abstract. Neural Gas is a neural network algorithm for vector quantization. It has not arbitrary established network topology, instead its topology is changing dynamically during training process. Originally, the Neural Gas is an unsupervised algorithm. However, there are several extensions that enables Neural Gas to use the information about sample's class. This significantly improves the accuracy of obtained clusters. Therefore, the Neural Gas was successfully used in classification problems. In this paper we present a novel method to learn the Neural Gas with fully and partially labelled data sets. Proposed method simulates the neuron's hesitation between membership to the classes during the learning. Hesitation process is based on neuron's class membership probability and Metropolis-Hastings algorithm. The proposed method was compared with state-of-art extensions of Neural Gas on supervised and semi-supervised classification tasks on benchmark data sets. Experimental results yield better or the same classification accuracy on both types of supervision.

Keywords: Neural Gas, Supervised clustering, Semi-supervised clustering, Classification, Metropolis-Hastings algorithm.

1 Introduction

Neural Gas (NG) is an algorithm for cluster analysis [2], first presented by Martinez and Shulten [11]. In contrary to well known Self-Organising Maps [10] it has not arbitrary established network topology, instead its topology is changing dynamically during the training process. There are many extensions of NG mainly focused on finding optimal neurons number [3] or using more sophisticated similarity measures than Euclidean [14], [5]. Originally, NG optimises clusters in unsupervised way, although there are various examples that use NG in classification tasks [14], [17]. The methods that enables use of NG for classification can be divided into three groups.

The first group of methods uses standard NG in an unsupervised manner. After training for each neuron the class label is designated based on major vote of sample's class, which belongs to the neuron. This method is also so-called 'winner-takes-all' (WTA) strategy [14].

L. Rutkowski et al. (Eds.): ICAISC 2013, Part I, LNAI 7894, pp. 474–482, 2013.

The second approach combines information about class label in binary coded manner in attribute vector [13]. Each neuron has two types of weights, corresponding to attributes and class. The part of input vector with class information is presented only during training. In testing phase, the information of neuron class label is coded in class weights. This can be interpreted as a fuzzy class membership. There are several approaches to measure similarity between neuron's weights and input vector [18], [19].

Third group of methods arbitrary assigns neurons to the class label [14]. The neuron is learned only with samples from the corresponding class. During the testing, the output class label is designed upon the closest neuron's class. There are some more sophisticated methods of learning with arbitrary assigned neurons in NG[5], [7], [4].

Contemporary, more often in data mining are situations that class labels are not available for all samples in data set. This is because labelling data by human expert can be expensive. Learning with partially labelled data is so-called semi-supervised [8].

In this paper we present a novel method for controlling supervision in Neural Gas algorithm. It is based on neuron's class membership probability and Metropolis-Hastings (MH) algorithm [12], [6]. The MH is well known from Simulated Annealing (SA) method [9]. Proposed method can be used on both data type: fully and partially labelled. We so-called proposed method as 'Hesitant Neural Gas' (HNG). Recently, we proposed a similar method for controlling learning of neurons in Self-Organising Maps [15].

Firstly, we provide a description of Neural Gas algorithm and three methods to use it for classification (one from each group). Secondly, the Hesitant Neural Gas algorithm is described. Then, the comparison of the HNG with other methods is presented on fully and partially labelled sets. Additionally, on fully labelled sets HNG is compared to Learning Vector Quantization (LVQ) algorithm [10], which is a state-of-art method in prototype-based supervised classification.

2   Methods

Let's denote data set as $D = \{(\boldsymbol{x_i}, c_i)\}$, where $\boldsymbol{x_i}$ is an attribute vector, $\boldsymbol{x} \in \mathcal{R}^d$ and c_i is a discrete class number of i-th sample, $i = [1, 2, ..., M]$ and $c = [1, 2, ..., C]$. Sometimes the class number will be encoded as a binary vector and denoted as $\boldsymbol{y_i}$, where $\boldsymbol{y_{ij}} = 1$ for $j = c_i$ and $\boldsymbol{y_{ij}} = 0$ otherwise.

2.1   Neural Gas

In the Neural Gas algorithm each neuron is described by weights vector $\boldsymbol{w_j}$, where $j = \{1, 2, .., N\}$. For each input sample D_i are computed distances to neurons by following equation:

$$Dist(\boldsymbol{w_j}, D_i) = (\boldsymbol{x_i} - \boldsymbol{w_j})^T (\boldsymbol{x_i} - \boldsymbol{w_j}). \tag{1}$$

Then distances are sorted and for each neuron a k_j rank is assigned, $k = \{0, 1, 2, .., N-1\}$. The rank $k_j = 0$ is assigned to the closest neuron, whereas consecutive k are for neurons with greater distance. The $k_j = N-1$ is for the furthest neuron. Then, weight update step is executed. The weights of each neuron are updated with the following formula:

$$w'_j = w_j + \eta e^{-k_j/\lambda}(x_i - w_j), \tag{2}$$

where η is a learning rate and λ is a neighbourhood range. The η is decreasing during learning:

$$\eta = \eta_0 e^{-t/\sigma}, \tag{3}$$

where t is a current epoch number and σ controls speed of decreasing. Network is trained till chosen number of learning procedure iterations t_{stop} is exceeded. In original Neural Gas presented by Martinez and Schulten [11] there were also optimised edges, which connect similar neurons. This can be useful for visualization purposes. However, this is not in the scope of this paper.

2.2 WTA Neural Gas

In the WTA Neural Gas after unsupervised training process the class membership for each neuron is computed. The neuron's class label is designated base on major votes of sample's class for which neuron was selected as the closest ($k_j = 0$). The disadvantage of this method are so-called 'empty neurons', when neuron has no assigned label. This situation is observed, when neuron has never been selected as the closest during training but is selected for the testing sample. In case of partially labelled data set, only labelled samples participate in class voting.

2.3 Fuzzy Neural Gas

The other approach to use NG as classifier is so-called 'Fuzzy Neural Gas'. In the training process, it takes into consideration the class vector y_j additionally to input attributes. Each neuron contains part of weights corresponding to the attributes w_j^x and class w_j^y. The similarity measure between input sample and neuron is computed during learning process by equation:

$$Dist_{train}(w_j, D_i) = \gamma(w_j^x - x_i)^T(w_j^x - x_i) + (1-\gamma)(w_j^y - y_i)^T(w_j^y - y_i). \tag{4}$$

The γ coefficient controls the balance between distance from attributes and class. The update step is performed with equations:

$$w_j^{x'} = w_j^x + \eta\gamma e^{-k_j/\lambda}(x_i - w_j^x), \tag{5}$$

$$w_j^{y'} = w_j^y + \eta(1-\gamma)e^{-k_j/\lambda}(y_i - w_j^y). \tag{6}$$

In the testing phase, to the network is presented an input vector only with attributes. This step is also so-called 'exploitation phase'. The distance is computed by:

$$Dist_{test}(\boldsymbol{w}_j, D_i) = (\boldsymbol{w}_j^x - \boldsymbol{x}_i)^T (\boldsymbol{w}_j^x - \boldsymbol{x}_i). \tag{7}$$

The output class label is designated based on position of maximum value in the $\boldsymbol{w}_j^y$ weights of the closest neuron. For semi-supervised learning, the second part of equation (4) is considered only when sample's class label is available, otherwise is omitted.

2.4 Class Neural Gas

The last approach arbitrary assigns neurons to the classes. In the training process neurons take part in the learning only with samples from corresponding class. During testing, all neurons are considered for distance computation. The output class label is designated from the closest neuron. We so-called this method as 'Class Neural Gas' (CNG). In case of learning with samples without class label all neurons participate in the distance computation during training and testing.

2.5 Proposed Method - Hesitant Neural Gas

In the proposed method, neuron's class membership is described by a probability. We note $P_j(h)$ as a probability of j-th neuron's membership in class number h. In the training phase, for each sample is selected a group of neurons that will take part in the weights optimisation. Selection is described by a matrix T, where $T_j^i = 1$ means that j-th neuron will participate in the learning with i-th sample, $T_j^i = 0$ otherwise. Neurons are selected in two steps. First choose neurons having maximum probability for the class matching the class c_i of the input sample:

$$T_j^{i(1)} = \begin{cases} 1 & \text{if } \arg\max_h(P_j(h)) = c_i; \\ 0 & \text{otherwise.} \end{cases} \tag{8}$$

In the second step, remaining neurons are considered, with $T_j^{i(1)} = 0$. The decision on joining into the training with i-th sample is taken upon MH algorithm. The probability of joining is computed using following equation:

$$J_j^i = 1 - exp(-\rho P_j(c_i)t_{stop}/t), \tag{9}$$

where ρ is the parameter that controls the intensity of hesitation, $\rho \in [0,1]$. The greater ρ value, the more neurons are selected additionally to learning in the MH step. In the eq.(9) the number of training iteration t is used, therefore neurons will be selected less frequently at the end of learning process than at its beginning. This can be interpreted as a hesitation of the neuron, which decreases during the training. Whether the MH decision will be positive ($T_j^{i(2)} = 1$), we draw random number a from an uniform distribution, $a \in [0,1]$. The neuron will be added to the training group if a value is smaller than J_j^i:

$$T_j^{i(2)} = \begin{cases} 1 & \text{if } a < J_j^i; \\ 0 & \text{otherwise.} \end{cases} \tag{10}$$

The final decision on neuron selection is a logical 'or' of the decisions from two steps: $T_j^i = T_j^{i(1)} \vee T_j^{i(2)}$. Neurons with $T_j^i = 0$ will not take part in distance computation step neither in weights update step. After all training samples presentation, neuron's class membership probability is updated. During the training for each i-th sample the neighbourhood value $e^{-k_j/\lambda}$ is added to the neuron's probability of membership in a given class:

$$P_j'(h) = \sum_i^N T_j^i e^{-k_j/\lambda}, \text{ for } h = c_i. \tag{11}$$

Note, that the neighbourhood is considered only if j-th neuron was selected for training with i-th sample. The neighbourhood value represents the belonging of the neuron to the input sample's class. After all iterations in a given epoch, the probability is normalized and updated with formula:

$$P_j(h) = \frac{P_j'(h)}{\sum_{l=1}^C P_j'(l)}. \tag{12}$$

In case of partially labelled data, we assume that all neurons take part in the training for samples without class label, thus $T_j^i = 1$ for all neurons. However, unlabelled samples do not take part in probability of class membership update (eq. 11). For labelled samples the procedure described above is used.

3   Results

To test performance of the Hesitant Neural Gas method on fully labelled data, we will compare it to the Learning Vector Quantization algorithm (LVQ) [10], WTA NG, Fuzzy NG, Class NG, Hesitant NG. The LVQ is not used in comparison on partially labelled data sets. The comparison is made on 6 real data sets. We used data sets 'Wine', 'Ionosphere', 'Iris', 'Sonar', 'Glass' from the 'UCI Machine Learing Repository' [1] [1], and set 'Faces' are from the 'The ORL Database of Faces'[2]. Data sets are described in Table 1. In all experiments we train algorithms with number of iterations $t_{stop} = 200$. We use learning rate $\eta_1 = 0.1$, exponentially decreasing to $\eta_{200} = 0.001$. The neighbourhood range was $\lambda = 1$. All algorithms were initialized with random samples. For all data sets, we arbitrarily chose the neurons number - selecting optimal network size is not in the scope of this paper. The selected values are presented in Table 1. The total number of neurons for each algorithm type is equal. Additionally, the ρ parameter for the HNG must be tuned. We checked several values of ρ, $\rho = \{0.05, 0.25, 0.5, 0.75, 1.0\}$. The optimal value was selected by cross-validation. Selected ρ values for each data set are presented in Table 1. To demonstrate the impact on number of positive MH decision depending on different ρ values, we count the number of positive MH decisions in each learning epoch for all neurons in the network for all considered

[1] http://archive.ics.uci.edu/ml/

[2] http://www.cl.cam.ac.uk/research/dtg/attarchive/facedatabase.html

Table 1. Description of data sets used to test performance, number of neurons used to each data set and optimal ρ in the Hesitant Neural Gas. (*In 'Faces' data set, the number of attributes was reduced with PCA.)

	Train examples	Test examples	Attributes	Classes	# neurons	MH ρ
Faces	320	80	50*	40	80	0.75
Sonar	166	42	60	2	36	1
Glass	171	43	9	6	24	0.05
Iris	120	30	4	3	12	0.25
Ionosphere	280	71	34	2	24	0.5
Wine	142	36	13	3	12	0.25

ρ values. The demonstration is made on 'Iris' set and presented in the Fig.1. It can be observed that, the greater ρ value is, the more positive MH decisions are made and the more frequently neuron takes part in the training with the sample from the class different than its major class. For each data set we made 10 repetitions to avoid effect of local minima. At each time training and testing subsets were redrawn. For comparison measure, we take a percentage of incorrect classifications. The obtained mean results on testing subsets are presented in the Table.2. The results were obtained using all labels from data sets in the training.

Table 2. Percent of incorrect classification on the testing subsets. Networks were learned with fully labelled samples. Results are mean and σ over 10 runs.

	LVQ	WTA Neural Gas	Fuzzy Neural Gas	Class Neural Gas	Hesitant Neural Gas
Faces	8.25±3.34	21.38±4.62	18.50±6.66	**4.00±2.55**	4.50±2.44
Sonar	14.52±7.48	23.1±5.39	19.76±6.92	**13.33±6.07**	13.57±5.50
Glass	31.16±6.95	34.42±5.98	37.67±9.29	35.35±5.46	**29.77±9.79**
Iris	4.00±2.11	4.33±4.46	**3.67±1.89**	4.00±2.11	4.00±2.11
Ionosphere	10.99±2.95	9.44±3.26	8.73±3.44	8.17±2.18	**7.89±2.75**
Wine	5.00±3.66	5.28±2.76	**3.06±2.43**	3.06±2.43	3.33±2.87
All sets error	73.92	97.95	91.39	67.91	**63.06**

The overall classification error on all data sets was the smallest for the proposed HNG method. However, the CNG was the best method on three sets. It gains the lowest error on 'Faces', 'Sonar' and 'Wine' sets. The HNG was the best method on two sets: 'Sonar' and 'Ionosphere'. The FNG method was the best on two data sets, namely: 'Iris' and 'Wine'. The HNG and CNG obtained smaller overall error than the LVQ algorithm. Although, the LVQ method was better than WTA-NG and FNG. The WTA-NG has the poorest accuracy on all sets, which can be expected as only this method does not use information about class labels directly in the learning.

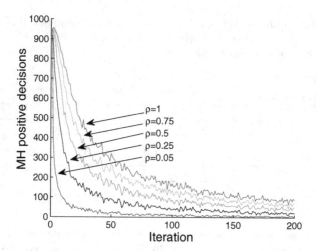

Fig. 1. Number of positive MH decisions in Hesitant Neural Gas algorithm taken in each training iteration for different ρ values on 'Iris' data set

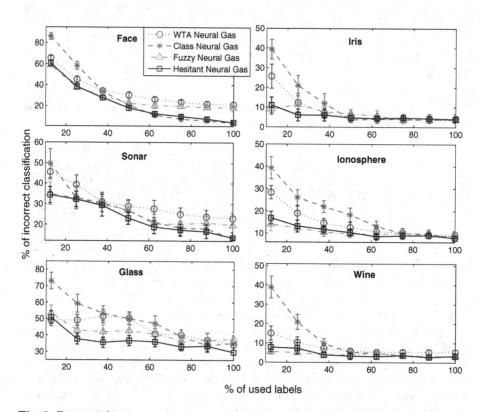

Fig. 2. Percent of incorrect classification on the testing subsets. Networks were learned with partially labelled samples. Results are mean and σ over 10 runs.

To test performance of the proposed HNG method on partially labelled data, we used only part of available labels from the training subsets in the learning process, in per cent $r = \{12.5, 25, 37.5, 50, 75, 87.5, 100\}$. The results are presented in the Fig.2. The HNG method achieved the smallest classification error for 'Faces', 'Sonar', 'Glass' and 'Iris' data sets when less than a half of available labels were used during the learning, $r < 50$. For 'Ionosphere' and 'Wine' data sets when r was smaller than 50, the FNG has the slightly better performance than the HNG. When small number of labels was used ($r < 50$), it can be observed that the CNG has the largest classification error on all data sets. Though, when the number of used labels grows the performance of the CNG significantly increases. This can be caused by arbitrary assigning class labels to the neuron. When the number of samples with class labels is smaller than number of samples without labels, the impact of labelled samples on neurons' weights is not enough to force unlabelled samples to belong to correct neurons. For 'Iris' and 'Wine' data sets, for $r > 50$ all methods seems to give similar results. These sets are rather simple, therefore all methods obtained similar local minima.

4   Conclusions

In this paper we present a novel method that extends Neural Gas algorithm for supervised and semi-supervised learning. It is so-called the 'Hesitant Neural Gas'. It controls the neuron's weights optimisation by selecting a group of neurons which will participate in the training of the presented sample. At first, neurons with the same as sample's class are selected. In the next step, the hesitation mechanism is introduced, which enables neurons with different class to take part in weights optimisation. The hesitation is based on neuron's class membership probability and Metropolis-Hastings algorithm. The hesitation intensity is controlled by ρ parameter and current training epoch number. The number of MH positive decisions decrease during learning, which can be interpreted as making neurons more confident. For unlabelled samples all neurons participate in the training. The proposed HNG method was compared to other state-of-art extensions of NG and LVQ algorithm on classification tasks. The results confirm that proposed method obtains better or similar accuracy than other methods on both types of supervision. Matlab implementation of the HNG algorithm is available at http://home.elka.pw.edu.pl/~pplonski/hesitant_neural_gas.

References

1. Asuncion, A., Newman, D.J.: UCI machine learning repository. University of California, Irvine, School of Information and Computer Sciences (2007)
2. Du, K.-L.: Clustering: A neural network approach. Neural Networks 23, 89–107 (2010)
3. Fritzke, B.: A Growing Neural Gas Network Learns Topologies. In: Advances in Neural Information Processing Systems (NIPS 1994), pp. 625–632 (1994)

4. Hammer, B., Hasenfuss, A., Schleif, F.-M., Villmann, T.: Supervised Batch Neural Gas. In: Schwenker, F., Marinai, S. (eds.) ANNPR 2006. LNCS (LNAI), vol. 4087, pp. 33–45. Springer, Heidelberg (2006)
5. Hammer, B., Strickert, M., Villmann, T.: Supervised Neural Gas with General Similarity Measure. Neural Processing Letters 21, 21–44 (2005)
6. Hastings, W.K.: Monte Carlo Sampling Methods Using Markov Chains and Their Applications. Biometrika 57, 97–109 (1970)
7. Herrmann, M., Villmann, T.: Vector Quantization by Optimal Neural Gas. In: Gerstner, W., Hasler, M., Germond, A., Nicoud, J.-D. (eds.) ICANN 1997. LNCS, vol. 1327, pp. 625–630. Springer, Heidelberg (1997)
8. Kästner, M., Villmann, T.: Fuzzy Supervised Self-Organizing Map for Semi-supervised Vector Quantization. In: Rutkowski, L., Korytkowski, M., Scherer, R., Tadeusiewicz, R., Zadeh, L.A., Zurada, J.M. (eds.) ICAISC 2012, Part I. LNCS, vol. 7267, pp. 256–265. Springer, Heidelberg (2012)
9. Kirkpatrick, S., Gelatt, C.D., Vecchi, M.P.: Optimization by Simulated Annealing. Science 220, 671–680 (1983)
10. Kohonen, T.: The Self-Organizing Map. Proceedings of the IEEE 78, 1464–1480 (1990)
11. Martinetz, T., Schulten, K.: A Neural-Gas Network Learns Topologies. Artificial Neural Networks 1, 397–402 (1991)
12. Metropolis, N., Rosenbluth, A.W., Rosenbluth, M.N., Teller, A.H., Teller, E.: Equations of State Calculations by Fast Computing Machines. Journal of Chemical Physics 21, 1087–1092 (1953)
13. Midenet, S., Grumbach, A.: Learning Associations by Self-Organization: The LASSO model. Neurocomputing 6, 343–361 (1994)
14. Möller, R., Hoffmann, H.: An extension of neural gas to local PCA. Neurocomputing 62, 305–326 (2004)
15. Płoński, P., Zaremba, K.: Self-Organising Maps for Classification with Metropolis-Hastings Algorithm for Supervision. In: Huang, T., Zeng, Z., Li, C., Leung, C.S. (eds.) ICONIP 2012, Part III. LNCS, vol. 7665, pp. 149–156. Springer, Heidelberg (2012)
16. Schenck, W., Welsch, R., Kaiser, A., Möller, R.: Adaptive learning rate control for neural gas principal component analysis. In: European Symposium on Artificial Neural Networks (ESANN 2010), pp. 213–218. d-side pub. (2010)
17. Schleif, F.-M., Villmann, T., Hammer, B.: Supervised Neural Gas for Classification of Functional Data and Its Application to the Analysis of Clinical Proteom Spectra. In: Sandoval, F., Prieto, A.G., Cabestany, J., Graña, M. (eds.) IWANN 2007. LNCS, vol. 4507, pp. 1036–1044. Springer, Heidelberg (2007)
18. Villmann, T., Geweniger, T., Kästner, M., Lange, M.: Fuzzy Neural Gas for Unsupervised Vector Quantization. In: Rutkowski, L., Korytkowski, M., Scherer, R., Tadeusiewicz, R., Zadeh, L.A., Zurada, J.M. (eds.) ICAISC 2012, Part I. LNCS, vol. 7267, pp. 350–358. Springer, Heidelberg (2012)
19. Villmann, T., Hammer, B., Schleif, F.-M., Geweniger, T., Hermann, W.: Fuzzy classification by fuzzy labeled neural gas. Neural Networks 19, 772–779 (2006)

Intuitionistic Fuzzy Classifier for Imbalanced Classes

Eulalia Szmidt[1,2], Janusz Kacprzyk[1,2], and Marta Kukier[1]

[1] Systems Research Institute, Polish Academy of Sciences,
ul. Newelska 6, 01–447 Warsaw, Poland
[2] Warsaw School of Information Technology, ul. Newelska 6, 01-447 Warsaw, Poland
{Eulalia.Szmidt,Janusz.Kacprzyk}@ibspan.waw.pl

Abstract. Imbalanced classes are a real challenge for the classifiers. Imbalanced classes are the classes smaller than other classes but not necessary small ones. Most often the smaller classes are more interested from an user point of view but more difficult to be seen by a classifier. In this paper, which is a continuation of our previous works, we discuss a classifier using some inherited features of Atanassovs intuitionistic fuzzy sets (A-IFSs for short) making them a good tool for recognizing imbalanced classes. We illustrate our considerations on benchmark examples paying attention to detailed behavior of the classifier proposed (several measures besides general accuracy are examined). We use simple cross validation method (with 10 experiments). Results are compared with a fuzzy classifier known as a good one from literature. We also consider a problem of granulation (symmetric or asymmetric granulation, and a number of the intervals used) and its influence on the results.

Keywords: Classification, imbalanced classes, intuitionistic fuzzy sets, intuitionistic fuzzy classifier.

1 Introduction

Constructing a good classifier for the imbalanced classes is a difficult task. An imbalanced class does not need to be a small class – it may be a class with lots of elements but still far less that the other class. Usually, a two-category problem (Duda [15]) *positive/negative* called also *legal/illegal* classification problem with a relatively small class is considered. Constructing a classifier for such classes is both an interesting theoretical challenge and a problem often met in different types of real tasks. Examples are given by Kubat at al. [19], Fawcett and Provost [16], Japkowicz [18], Lewis and Catlett [20], Mladenic and Grobelnik [21], He and Garcia [17]. To solve the imbalance problems usually up-sampling and down-sampling are used but both methods interfere in the structure of the data, and in a case of overlapping classes even the artificially obtained balance does not solve the problem (some data points may appear as valid examples in both classes).

This paper is a continuation of our previous works (cf. Szmidt and Kukier [34], [35], [36]) on intuitionistic fuzzy approach to the problem of classification of imbalanced and overlapping classes. We consider a two–class classification problem (*legal* – relatively small class, and *illegal* – a bigger class).

L. Rutkowski et al. (Eds.): ICAISC 2013, Part I, LNAI 7894, pp. 483–492, 2013.

The classifier using A-IFSs has its roots in the fuzzy set approach proposed by Baldwin at al. [10]. In that approach the classes are represented by fuzzy sets generated from the relative frequency distributions representing the data points used as examples of the classes [10]. In the process of generating fuzzy sets a mass assignment based approach is adopted (Baldwin at al. [7], [10]). For the obtained model (fuzzy sets describing the classes), using a chosen classification rule, a testing phase is performed to assess the performance of the proposed method.

Considering the intuitionistic fuzzy classifier we perform the same steps as in a case of the above mentioned fuzzy classifier. The main difference lies in making use of A-IFSs for the representation of classes, and in exploiting A-IFSs structure to obtain a classifier which better recognizes the relatively small classes.

The crucial step of the method is a representation of the classes by A-IFSs (first, training phase). The A-IFSs are generated from the relative frequency distributions representing the data considered – according to the procedure given by Szmidt and Baldwin [24]. Having in mind recognition of the smaller class as good as possible we use the information about the hesitation margins making it possible to improve the results of data classification in the (second) testing phase.

The obtained results in the testing phase were examined using confusion matrices making possible to explore detailed behavior of the classifiers (not only in the sense of general error/accuracy). We have used simple cross validation method (with 10 experiments). Obtained results are compared with a fuzzy classifier. Two benchmark data sets are used - "Glass", and "Wine" (cf. [41]).

We have also taken into account other measures of classifier errors, namely, geometric mean, and so called F-*value* (Section 3.1). The last two measures were used to assess the influence of the parameters used in one of the important steps when constructing the classifier, namely, granulation. We compared results for symmetric and asymmetric granulation, and for increasing number of intervals. The influence of granulation on the results has been verified using data sets "Glass", and "Wine", "Heart" and "Breast Cancer" (cf. [41]).

2   Brief Introduction to A-IFSs

One of the possible generalizations of a fuzzy set in X (Zadeh [39]) given by

$$A^{'} = \{< x, \mu_{A'}(x) > | x \in X\} \qquad (1)$$

where $\mu_{A'}(x) \in [0, 1]$ is the membership function of the fuzzy set $A^{'}$, is an A-IFS (Atanassov [1], [3], [4]) A is given by

$$A = \{< x, \mu_A(x), \nu_A(x) > | x \in X\} \qquad (2)$$

where: $\mu_A : X \to [0, 1]$ and $\nu_A : X \to [0, 1]$ such that

$$0 \leq \mu_A(x) + \nu_A(x) \leq 1 \qquad (3)$$

and $\mu_A(x)$, $\nu_A(x) \in [0, 1]$ denote a degree of membership and a degree of non-membership of $x \in A$, respectively.

Obviously, each fuzzy set may be represented by the following A-IFS

$$A = \{< x, \mu_{A'}(x), 1 - \mu_{A'}(x) > | x \in X\} \qquad (4)$$

An additional concept for each A-IFS in X, that is not only an obvious result of (2) and (3) but which is also relevant for applications, we will call (Atanasov [3])

$$\pi_A(x) = 1 - \mu_A(x) - \nu_A(x) \qquad (5)$$

a *hesitation margin* of $x \in A$ which expresses a lack of knowledge of whether x belongs to A or not (cf. Atanassov [3]). It is obvious that $0 \leq \pi_A(x) \leq 1$, for each $x \in X$.

The hesitation margin turns out to be important while considering the distances (Szmidt and Kacprzyk [26], [27], [31], entropy (Szmidt and Kacprzyk [28], [32]), similarity (Szmidt and Kacprzyk [33]) for the A-IFSs, etc. i.e., the measures that play a crucial role in virtually all information processing tasks.

Hesitation margins turn out to be relevant for applications - in image processing (cf. Bustince et al. [12], [11]) and classification of imbalanced and overlapping classes (cf. Szmidt and Kukier [34], [35], [36]), group decision making, negotiations, voting and other situations (cf. Szmidt and Kacprzyk papers).

In our further considerations we will use operator $D_\alpha(A)$ (Atanassov [3]) with $\alpha \in [0, 1]$:

$$D_\alpha(A) = \{\langle x, \mu_A(x) + \alpha\pi_A(x), \nu_A(x) + (1 - \alpha)\pi_A(x)\rangle | x \in X\} \qquad (6)$$

Operator $D_\alpha(A)$ makes it possible to "see" better imbalanced classes (information about hesitation margins is most important here).

3   Intuitionistic Fuzzy Classifier

Details concerning construction of an intuitionistic fuzzy classifier are presented in Szmidt and Kukier [34], [35], [36]. Here we only remind the basic steps. First, it is necessary to convert training data expressed as relative frequency distributions into A-IFSs (cf. Szmidt and Baldwin [22], [23], [24]) describing *legal* and *illegal* classes in the space of all the attributes. The problem of granulation (symmetric or asymmetric model, number of intervals for the attributes) is described in details in Szmidt and Kukier [34], [35], [36]) In effect each data instance is described as an intuitionistic fuzzy element (all three terms are taken into account: membership value μ, non-membership value ν, and hesitation margin π). Taking into account that the hesitation margins assign (the width of the) intervals where the unknown values of memberships lie, we use operator $D_\alpha(A)$ (6) so that the elements of the class we are interested in, could be seen as good as possible (details in Szmidt and Kukier [34], [35], [36]). For our purposes, i.e., to "see" better the smaller class, the values of α (6) are from interval $[0.5, 1]$. For $\alpha = 0.5$ we obtain a fuzzy classifier. It is worth stressing that the case $\alpha = 1$ does not produce the best results. We built such models for each attribute separately, and next, aggregate the results (see Szmidt and Kukier [34], [35], [36]).

3.1   The Models of a Classifier Error

Traditionally *accuracy* of a classifier is measured as the percentage of instances that are correctly classified, and *error* is measured as the percentage of incorrectly classified instances (unseen data). But when the considered classes are imbalanced or when misclassification costs are not equal both the accuracy and the error are not sufficient.

Confusion Matrix
The confusion matrix (Table 1) is often used to assess a two–class classifier. The meaning of the symbols is

Table 1. The Confusion Matrix

	Tested Legal	Tested Illegal
Actual Legal	a	b
Actual Illegal	c	d

a – the number of correctly classified legal points,
b – the number of incorrectly classified legal points,
c – the number of incorrectly classified illegal points,
d – the number of correctly classified illegal points,
In result, the most often used measures to assess a classifier are:

$$Acc = \frac{legalls\ and\ illegals\ correctly\ classified}{total} = \frac{a+d}{a+b+c+d} \qquad (7)$$

$$TPR = \frac{legalls\ correctly\ classified}{total\ legalls} = \frac{a}{a+b} \qquad (8)$$

$$FPR = \frac{illegals\ incorrectly\ classified}{total\ illegals} = \frac{c}{c+d} \qquad (9)$$

Another, often used measure of error is geometric mean (Kubat et al. [19]):

$$GM = \sqrt{TPR * PPV} \qquad (10)$$

where $PPV = \frac{legalls\ correctly\ classified}{total\ legalls} = \frac{a}{a+c}$. Measure GM "treats" the same TPR and PPV.

If we wish to point out which one of TPR and PPV is most important for us, we may use another measure, so called $F - value$:

$$FV = \frac{(1 + \beta^2)TPR * PPV}{\beta^2 PPV * TPR} \qquad (11)$$

For better recognizing relatively small classes, parameter β should be greater than 1.

Table 2. Results for Glass, $\alpha = 0.7$, asymmetric granulation

No class		Acc FS	Acc IFS	TPR FS	TPR IFS	FPR FS	FPR IFS
1	average	79.4	76.3	0.56	0.9	0.09	0.31
	standard deviation	3.3	3.3	0.12	0.04	0.05	0.05
2	average	74.8	60.9	0.48	0.85	0.48	0.85
	standard deviation	3.6	4.2	0.11	0.09	0.11	0.09
3	average	90.8	84.9	0	0.21	0.01	0.09
	standard deviation	1.0	3.7	0	0.14	0.01	0.04
5	average	93.3	93.3	0.09	0.17	0.01	0.01
	standard deviation	1.0	1.2	0.09	0.12	0.01	0.01
6	average	95.6	97.0	0.12	0.42	0	0
	standard deviation	1.2	1.1	0.18	0.23	0	0
7	average	92.7	94.7	0.44	0.68	0.01	0.02
	standard deviation	1.4	1.7	0.14	0.17	0.01	0.01

3.2 Results Obtained

First, we present the results obtained from an intuitionistic fuzzy classifier recognizing elements from two benchmark data sets – "Glass", and "Wine" (cf. [41]). To verify the classifier we use simple cross validation method (with 10 experiments). The examined data set was separated in each iteration into a training set and test set (50/50) by selecting examples randomly. For each experiment the mean of the accuracy measures, and their standard deviation were calculated. Results obtained by an intuitionistic fuzzy classifier are compared with the results obtained by a fuzzy classifier.

In Tables 2–3 there are results for "Glass" identification database (cf. [41]) with 214 instances, 7 classes (4th class is empty), 10 attributes.

Table 3. Results for Glass, $\alpha = 0.7$, symmetric granulation

no class		Acc FS	Acc IFS	TPR FS	TPR IFS	FPR FS	FPR IFS
1	average	71.5	60.3	0.25	0.94	0.05	0.57
	standard deviation	2.8	3.2	0.13	0.06	0.04	0.05
2	average	73.0	54.0	0.46	0.91	0.11	0.67
	standard deviation	2.6	3.2	0.14	0.07	0.07	0.07
3	average	89.4	44.4	0.06	0.84	0.03	0.59
	standard deviation	2.6	4.1	0.09	0.12	0.04	0.05
5	average	94.0	92.4	0.56	0.74	0.03	0.06
	standard deviation	2.2	3.3	0.2	0.15	0.02	0.04
6	average	96.2	94.3	0.48	0.64	0.01	0.04
	standard deviation	1.5	2.6	0.22	0.22	0.01	0.03
7	average	94.7	92.5	0.8	0.86	0.03	0.07
	standard deviation	1.9	1.5	0.12	0.1	0.02	0.02

In Table 2 asymmetric granulation was applied with $\alpha = 0.7$. Accuracy (7) for fuzzy classifier $AccFS$ is better than for intuitionistic fuzzy classifier $AccIFS$ for classes 1–3, is the same for both classifiers for class 5, and is better for intuitionistic fuzzy classifier for classes 6–7. But in all cases $TPRIFS$ is better than $TPRFS$ which means that intuitionisticc fuzzy classifier "sees" better the class we are interested in. Improving of TPR for intuitionistic fuzzy classifier is at cost of bigger values of FPR for classes 1–3. But it is worth stressing that for classes 5–7 we obtain both better accuracy and TPR for intuitionistic classifier whereas FPR is practically the same.

Table 4. Results for intuitionistic fuzzy classifier as a function of number of intervals, symmetric granulation

data base	no of intervals	Acc IFS	GM	TPR	FV
Wine 3	3	28.1	0.522	1.0	0.652
	5	79.775	0.775	1.000	0.870
	7	89.888	0.866	1.000	0.930
	10	94.382	0.926	1.000	0.960
	15	96.629	0.961	1.000	0.976
	20	96.629	0.980	1.000	0.976
	25	96.629	0.980	0.958	0.950
	30	95.506	0.980	0.958	0.943
Heart 2	3	34.228	0.381	1.000	0.479
	5	40.940	0.416	1.000	0.506
	7	40.940	0.416	1.000	0.506
	10	42.953	0.428	1.000	0.514
	15	46.980	0.445	0.944	0.509
	20	55.034	0.467	0.944	0.548
	25	61.745	0.511	0.889	0.559
	30	62.416	0.541	0.833	0.536
Glass 5	3	80.769	0.509	1.000	0.636
	5	83.654	0.540	1.000	0.673
	7	81.731	0.463	0.857	0.577
	10	93.269	0.655	0.857	0.750
	15	93.269	0.655	0.857	0.750
	20	93.269	0.598	0.714	0.658
	25	93.269	0.598	0.714	0.658
	30	94.231	0.630	0.714	0.676

In Table 3 there are results for the same database "Glass", with the same parameter $\alpha = 0.7$ but with symmetric granulation. The *accuracy* of intuitionistic fuzzy classifier $AccIFS$ is lower than *accuracy* of fuzzy classifier $AccFS$ with symmetric granulation for classes 1–3. On the other hand, the values of $PRIFS$ are considerably better than the counterpart values of $TPRFS$. Unfortunately, better values of $TPRIFS$, i.e., better recognition of relatively smaller class by intuitionistic fuzzy classifier, accompany considerably bigger values of of $FPRIFS$. In other words, intuitionistic fuzzy classifier with symmetric granulation better recognizes relatively small classes but general accuracy, and recognition of other classes is worse.

It is also interesting to notice the problem of granulation in the sense of the number of the intervals used. Results of experiments with several data bases (chosen classes) are in Tables 4 and 5. We can see both for a symmetric (Table 4) and an asymmetric granulation (Table 4) that in general it is not the truth in a case of the imbalanced classes that the more intervals used the better. When we start from small number of intervals, even general accuracy of the classifier for some tested classes increases first (Wine 3, Glass 5, Glass 3), gains its maximum, and next decreases. The situation is even worse for TPR – practically, for all the tested classes, the best values of TPR are obtained for small number of the intervals, and the more intervals the values of TPR decrease.

Table 5. Results for intuitionistic fuzzy classifier as a function of number of intervals, asymmetric granulation

data base	no of intervals	Acc IFS	GM	TPR	FV
Heart 3	3	30.201	0.376	0.944	0.443
	5	34.228	0.395	0.944	0.457
	7	39.597	0.410	0.944	0.478
	10	42.953	0.421	0.944	0.491
	15	57.047	0.476	0.889	0.533
	20	61.074	0.508	0.611	0.410
	25	69.128	0.561	0.444	0.345
	30	71.812	0.615	0.444	0.357
Glass 3	3	23.077	0.318	0.318	0.360
	5	39.423	0.208	0.208	0.250
	7	61.538	0.214	0.214	0.267
	10	79.808	0.298	0.272	0.238
	20	92.308	0.385	0.385	0.256
	25	91.346	N/A	N/A	N/A
	30	91.346	N/A	N/A	N/A
Breast Cancer 1	3	79.532	0.903	1.000	0.941
	5	95.029	0.954	0.991	0,980
	7	95.614	0.966	0.986	0,979
	10	95.322	0.966	0.982	0.975
	15	95.906	0.971	0.982	0.977
	20	96.199	0.971	0.986	0.980
	25	95.906	0.971	0.982	0.977
	30	96.199	0.971	0.986	0.977

Observations of GM confirm the fact that just increasing the number of intervals is not the best practice while constructing a classifier for recognizing imbalanced classes. The same conclusion is confirmed when observing FV values (for parameter $\beta = 2$ which means slight preference for relatively smaller class). The situation described is the result of the fact that when using more intervals during granulation, instances from relatively smaller classes are even more substantially dominated in a separate interval (worse "visible"). The only solution is a careful process of assigning the number of the intervals when constructing the classifier as each data base, and each class in a data base is specific.

4 Conclusions

A simple yet effective intuitionistic fuzzy classifier was tested on some imbalanced and overlapping data. Results obtained confirm that the intuitionistic fuzzy classifier fulfills our main demand, i.e., "sees" better relatively smaller classes. The results are better than for a fuzzy classifier known from literature as a good one for recognizing imbalanced classes. We may pay for it in lower accuracy of recognizing all instances because bigger classes might be seen worse. But it is not a rule – sometimes both relatively smaller class and bigger classes are recognized better by intuitionistic fuzzy classifier than by the counterpart fuzzy classifier.

We have also tested an influence of the number of the intervals applied (in the process of granulation) on the results. Several measures were tested. It turns out that increasing the number of intervals does not mean improving the results as the elements of the smaller classes can be even more dominated in very narrow intervals.

Acknowledgment. Partially supported by the Ministry of Science and Higher Education Grant UMO-2012/05/B/ST6/03068.

References

1. Atanassov, K.: Intuitionistic Fuzzy Sets. VII ITKR Session. Sofia (Deposed in Centr. Sci.-Techn. Library of Bulg. Acad. of Sci., 1697/84) (1983) (in Bulgarian)
2. Atanassov, K.: Intuitionistic Fuzzy Sets. Fuzzy Sets and Systems 20, 87–96 (1986)
3. Atanassov, K.: Intuitionistic Fuzzy Sets: Theory and Applications. Springer (1999)
4. Atanassov, K.T.: On Intuitionistic Fuzzy Sets Theory. STUDFUZZ, vol. 283. Springer, Heidelberg (2012)
5. Baldwin, J.F.: Combining Evidences for Evidential Reasoning. International Journal of Intelligent Systems 6, 569–616 (1991)
6. Baldwin, J.F.: The Management of Fuzzy and Probabilistic Uncertainties for Knowledge Based Systems. In: Shapiro, S.A. (ed.) Encyclopaedia of AI, 2nd edn., pp. 528–537. John Wiley (1992b)
7. Baldwin, J.F., Martin, T.P., Pilsworth, B.W.: FRIL – Fuzzy and Evidential Reasoning in Artificial Intelligence. John Wiley (1995)
8. Baldwin, J.F., Lawry, J., Martin, T.P.: A Mass Assignment Theory of the Probability of Fuzzy Events. ITRC Report 229, University of Bristol, UK (1995a)
9. Baldwin, J.F., Coyne, M.R., Martin, T.P.: Intelligent Reasoning Using General Knowledge to Update Specific Information: A Database Approach. J. of Intel. Inf. Syst. 4, 281–304 (1995b)
10. Baldwin, J.F., Lawry, J., Martin, T.P.: The Application of generalized Fuzzy Rules to Machine Learning and Automated Knowledge Discovery. Int. Journal of Uncertainty, Fuzzyness and Knowledge-Based Systems 6(5), 459–487 (1998)
11. Bustince, H., Mohedano, V., Barrenechea, E., Pagola, M.: Image thresholding using intuitionistic fuzzy sets. In: Atanassov, K., Kacprzyk, J., Krawczak, M., Szmidt, E. (eds.) Issues in the Representation and Processing of Uncertain and Imprecise Information. Fuzzy Sets, Intuitionistic Fuzzy Sets, Generalized Nets, and Related Topics. EXIT, Warsaw (2005)
12. Bustince, H., Mohedano, V., Barrenechea, E., Pagola, M.: An algorithm for calculating the threshold of an image representing uncertainty through A-IFSs. In: IPMU 2006, pp. 2383–2390 (2006)
13. Dubois, D., Prade, H.: Unfair coins and necessity measures: towards a possibilistic interpretation of histograms. Fuzzy Sets and Systems 10, 15–20 (1983)
14. Dubois, D., Prade, H.: The three semantics of fuzzy sets. Fuzzy Sets and Systems 90, 141–150 (1997)
15. Duda, R.O., Hart, P., Stork, D.: Pattern Classification. John Wiley and Sons, Inc. (2000)
16. Fawcett, T., Provost, F.: Adaptive Fraud Detection. Data Mining and Knowledge Discovery 3(1), 291–316 (1997)
17. He, H., Garcia, E.A.: Learning from Imbalanced Data. IEEE Trans. on Knowledge and Data Engineering 21(3), 1263–1284 (2009)

18. Japkowicz, N.: Class Imbalances: Are we Focusing on the Right Issue? In: ICML, Washington (2003)
19. Kubat, M., Holte, R., Matwin, S.: Machine Learning for the Detection of Oil Spills in Satellite Radar Images. Machine Learning 30, 195–215 (1998)
20. Lewis, D., Catlett, J.: Heterogeneous Uncertainty Sampling for Supervised Learning. In: Proc. 11th Conf. on Machine Learning, pp. 148–156 (1994)
21. Mladenic, D., Grobelnik, M.: Feature Selection for Unbalanced Class Distribution and Naive Bayes. In: 16th Int. Conf. on Machine Learning, pp. 258–267 (1999)
22. Szmidt, E., Baldwin, J.: New Similarity Measure for Intuitionistic Fuzzy Set Theory and Mass Assignment Theory. Notes on IFSs 9(3), 60–76 (2003)
23. Szmidt, E., Baldwin, J.: Entropy for Intuitionistic Fuzzy Set Theory and Mass Assignment Theory. Notes on IFSs 10(3), 15–28 (2004)
24. Szmidt, E., Baldwin, J.: Assigning the parameters for Intuitionistic Fuzzy Sets. Notes on IFSs 11(6), 1–12 (2005)
25. Szmidt, E., Baldwin, J.: Intuitionistic Fuzzy Set Functions, Mass Assignment Theory, Possibility Theory and Histograms. In: 2006 IEEE World Congress on Computational Intelligence, pp. 237–243 (2006)
26. Szmidt, E., Kacprzyk, J.: On measuring distances between intuitionistic fuzzy sets. Notes on IFS 3(4), 1–13 (1997)
27. Szmidt, E., Kacprzyk, J.: Distances between intuitionistic fuzzy sets. Fuzzy Sets and Systems 114(3), 505–518 (2000)
28. Szmidt, E., Kacprzyk, J.: Entropy for intuitionistic fuzzy sets. Fuzzy Sets and Systems 118(3), 467–477 (2001)
29. Szmidt, E., Kacprzyk, J.: An Intuitionistic Fuzzy Set Base Approach to Intelligent Data Analysis (an application to medical diagnosis). In: Abraham, A., Jain, L., Kacprzyk, J. (eds.) Recent Advances in Intelligent Paradigms and Applications. STUDFUZZ, vol. 113, pp. 57–70. Springer, Heidelberg (2002)
30. Szmidt, E., Kacprzyk, J.: A new concept of a similarity measure for intuitionistic fuzzy sets and its use in group decision making. In: Torra, V., Narukawa, Y., Miyamoto, S. (eds.) MDAI 2005. LNCS (LNAI), vol. 3558, pp. 272–282. Springer, Heidelberg (2005)
31. Szmidt, E., Kacprzyk, J.: Distances Between Intuitionistic Fuzzy Sets: Straightforward Approaches may not work. In: IEEE IS 2006, pp. 716–721 (2006)
32. Szmidt, E., Kacprzyk, J.: Some problems with entropy measures for the Atanassov intuitionistic fuzzy sets. In: Masulli, F., Mitra, S., Pasi, G. (eds.) WILF 2007. LNCS (LNAI), vol. 4578, pp. 291–297. Springer, Heidelberg (2007)
33. Szmidt, E., Kacprzyk, J.: A New Similarity Measure for Intuitionistic Fuzzy Sets: Straightforward Approaches may not work. In: 2007 IEEE Conf. on Fuzzy Systems, pp. 481–486 (2007a)
34. Szmidt, E., Kukier, M.: Classification of Imbalanced and Overlapping Classes using Intuitionistic Fuzzy Sets. In: IEEE IS 2006, London, pp. 722–727 (2006)
35. Szmidt, E., Kukier, M.: A New Approach to Classification of Imbalanced Classes via Atanassov's Intuitionistic Fuzzy Sets. In: Wang, H.-F. (ed.) Intelligent Data Analysis: Developing New Methodologies Through Pattern Discovery and Recovery, pp. 85–101. Idea Group (2008)
36. Szmidt, E., Kukier, M.: Atanassov's intuitionistic fuzzy sets in classification of imbalanced and overlapping classes. In: Chountas, P., Petrounias, I., Kacprzyk, J. (eds.) Intelligent Techniques and Tools for Novel System Architectures. SCI, vol. 109, pp. 455–471. Springer, Heidelberg (2008)
37. Yager, R.R.: Level sets for membership evaluation of fuzzy subsets. Tech. Rep. RRY-79-14, Iona Colledge, New York (1979)

38. Yamada, K.: Probability–Possibility Transformation Based on Evidence Theory. In: Proc. IFSA–NAFIPS 2001, pp. 70–75 (2001)
39. Zadeh, L.A.: Fuzzy sets. Inf. and Control 8, 338–353 (1965)
40. Zadeh, L.A.: Fuzzy Sets as the Basis for a Theory of Possibility. Fuzzy Sets and Systems 1, 3–28 (1978)
41. http://archive.ics.uci.edu/ml/machine-learning-databases

Novel Algorithm
for the On-Line Signature Verification
Using Selected Discretization Points Groups

Marcin Zalasiński and Krzysztof Cpałka

Częstochowa University of Technology,
Institute of Computational Intelligence, Poland
{marcin.zalasinski,krzysztof.cpalka}@iisi.pcz.pl

Abstract. Identity verification based on on-line signature is a commonly known biometric task. Some methods based on the on-line signature biometric attribute used for identity verification use information from partitions of the signature. Efficiency of these methods is relatively high. In this paper we would like to present a new approach to signature trajectories partitioning, based on selection of the discretization points groups. The new method was compared to other methods, with use of the SVC2004 public on-line signature database.

1 Introduction

Signature is a biometric attribute commonly used in identity verification process. This attribute may be categorized into two groups - off-line (static) signature and on-line (dynamic) signature. Off-line signature contains only information about shape of the signature. Systems which use this type of signature may be used for example for verification identity of person who signed some kind of documents. On-line signature contains many additional information about dynamics of signing process. This kind of signatures are acquired with use of some digital input device, e.g. graphic tablet. Dynamic signatures are more reliable than static ones, because they are more difficult to forge (see e.g. [6]).

One of the most effective method of identity verification with use of dynamic signature is method based on signature trajectories partitioning (see e.g. [9], [11]). In [11] velocity signal is split into three bands and strokes which belong to the medium-velocity band are used for discrimination purposes. Method presented in [9] assumes division of velocity and pressure signals into two parts. After this process four partitions are created. Each partition contains template created from trajectories of training signatures which belong to the partition. Then selection of the most discriminative partition (called stable partition) is performed. Stable partition is selected on the basis of similarities between each training signature of the user and the template. The template from selected partition is compared to the test signature during verification process. Identity verification is performed on the basis of this comparison, signature is classified as genuine or forgery. Our approach to identity verification, presented in [31],

L. Rutkowski et al. (Eds.): ICAISC 2013, Part I, LNAI 7894, pp. 493–502, 2013.

also refers to partitioning of signature trajectories. In our method all partitions are considered during verification process, because we assume that all partitions may contain useful information about signer. All partitions have also weights of importance calculated individually for each signer, therefore partitions which are more characteristic for the user will be more important during verification process. During classification phase classifier based on the t-conorm with the weights of arguments is used (see [1]-[4], [23]). This approach is more effective than approach with use only one partition.

In this paper we present a new method of signature partitioning based on selection of discretization points groups. This method also divide signature trajectories into few partitions which are weighted by weights of importance and are used during classification process. Classification is performed with use a neuro-fuzzy system (see e.g. [2]-[3], [7], [12]-[15], [17]-[18], [22]-[28]).

This paper is organized into four sections. In Section 2 the new approach to signature trajectories partitioning with selection of the discretization points groups is presented. Simulation results are presented in Section 3. Conclusions are drawn in Section 4.

2   Signature Verification Based on discretization Points Groups

2.1   General Idea of the Algorithm

In this paper we propose a new method of signature partitioning. The method may be summarized as follows: (a)In our approach partitions are used during the training and classification phase. (b)Classification process is performed with use of weights of importance. Weights are calculated individually for each signer and for each partition. Partitions are created in a new way, so that the interpretation of weights is different from the weights considered in [31]. (c)Proposed classifier bases on flexible neuro-fuzzy system with weights of antecedents (see e.g. [2]-[3], [22]). The weights of importance are associated with the parts of the signatures. The conception of use of weights in triangular norms and neuro-fuzzy systems is described in [5], [22].

The algorithm is performed as follows:

- **Step 1. Partitioning of signatures.** Signatures are partitioned with use of the method which creates vertical partitions, selecting best discretization points groups. Each of vertical partitions has the same width. Number of vertical partitions is the same for each user (see Fig. 1).
- **Step 2. Template generation.** In this step templates for each partition are generated. Templates are created on the basis of signatures generated by signer during training data acquisition phase. Each template contains average values of signature signals. This step is performed only during training phase.

- **Step 3. Calculation of signatures similarity in each partition.** In this phase similarities between each signature of the user and template are calculated. The similarities are calculated for each partition.
- **Step 4. Computation of the weights of importance.** During this step weights of importance for each partition are created. Values of weights are based on mean distance between training signatures and template and also on similarity in distances between training signatures and template. This step is performed only during training phase.
- **Step 5. Creation decision boundary for each partition.** During this step linear decision boundary between genuine signatures and forged signatures is created individually for the user (see [31]). This step is performed only during training phase. Genuine signatures of the other users may be used as forged signatures (see e.g. [29]).
- **Step 6. Determination of the fuzzy rules used in classification phase.** Fuzzy rules describe a way of test signature classification. The rules based on the fuzzy sets, which use decision boundaries determined in the step 5. Therefore they may be interpretable.
- **Step 7. Classification.** In this step signature is classified as genuine or forgery. Classification process is performed on the basis of distances between template and sample signature in the partitions. This step is performed only during test phase. In the verification process flexible neuro-fuzzy system of the Mamdani type is used. Each of the antecedents of this classifier is associated with the weight determined in Step 2.

We can see that steps 1-6 are performed during training phase, while steps 1,3,7 are performed during test phase.

2.2   Determination of Partitions and Weights of Partitions

First, partitioning of the signatures is performed. The new approach presented in this paper assumes partitioning based on selected time intervals of signing. This approach is possible to implement because lengths of the all signature signals are the same through the pre-processing. Pre-processing of the signatures is performed after the acquisition phase. Lengths of the signatures are fitted by the Dynamic Time Warping algorithm (see e.g. [16]) which use velocity or pressure signal. Next, each signal is divided into parts of the same width. Membership of the k-th sample of the j-th signature of the i-th user to the p-th partition is described as follows:

$$
part_{i,j,k}^{\{s\}} = \begin{cases} 1 & \text{for} \quad 0 < k \le \frac{K}{PN^{\{s\}}} \\ 2 & \text{for} \quad \frac{K}{PN^{\{s\}}} < k \le \frac{2K}{PN^{\{s\}}} \\ \vdots \\ PN^{\{s\}} & \text{for} \quad \frac{(PN^{\{s\}}-1)K}{PN^{\{s\}}} < k \le K \end{cases} \tag{1}
$$

where s is a signal type (velocity or pressure) used during alignment phase, i is the user number ($i = 1, 2, \ldots, I$), j is the signature number ($j = 1, 2, \ldots, J$), K

is a number of samples, k is the sample number $(k = 1, 2, \ldots, K)$ and $PN^{\{s\}}$ is a number of partitions. In this method we have assumed, that $PN^{\{v\}} = PN^{\{z\}}$. Partitioning method is shown in Fig. 1.

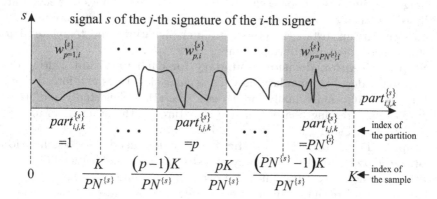

Fig. 1. Signature partitioning

After partitioning, templates of the signatures are generated. Generation of the templates is based on the training signatures. Templates are concerned with the user and assigned to the partition. Generation of an element of template $ta_{p,i,k}^{\{s\}}$, $p = 1, 2, \ldots, PN^{\{s\}}$, $i = 1, 2, \ldots, I$, $k = 1, 2, \ldots, K$, for the k-th time step of the p-th partition of the i-th signer for signatures aligned with use of s signal (v velocity or z pressure) and a trajectory (x or y) is calculated by the formula:

$$ta_{p,i,k}^{\{s\}} = \frac{1}{J} \sum_{j=1}^{J} a_{p,i,j,k}^{\{s\}}, \tag{2}$$

where $a_{p,i,j,k}^{\{s\}}$, $p = 1, 2, \ldots, PN^{\{s\}}$, $i = 1, 2, \ldots, I$, $j = 1, 2, \ldots, J$, $k = 1, 2, \ldots, K$, is trajectory (x or y) value in the k-th sample of the p-th partition of the j-th signature of the i-th signer. Template $\mathbf{ta}_{p,i}^{\{s\}}$, $p = 1, 2, \ldots, PN^{\{s\}}$, $i = 1, 2, \ldots, I$, of the p-th partition of the i-th signer for signatures aligned with use of s signal (v velocity or z pressure) and a trajectory (x or y) is described by the following equation:

$$\mathbf{ta}_{p,i}^{\{s\}} = \left[ta_{p,i,1}^{\{s\}}, ta_{p,i,2}^{\{s\}}, \ldots, ta_{p,i,k}^{\{s\}} \right]. \tag{3}$$

Next, distances between each template and each signature trajectory are calculated. Distance $da_{p,i,j}^{\{s\}}$, $p = 1, 2, \ldots, PN^{\{s\}}$, $i = 1, 2, \ldots, I$, $j = 1, 2, \ldots, J$, between template of the p-th partition of the i-th signer generated for signatures aligned with use of s signal (v velocity or z pressure) and a trajectory (x or y), and the j-th signature of the i-th signer is described as follows:

$$da_{p,i,j}^{\{s\}} = \sqrt{\sum_{k=1}^{K} \left(ta_{p,i,k}^{\{s\}} - a_{p,i,j,k}^{\{s\}} \right)^2}, \tag{4}$$

where $a_{p,i,j,k}^{\{s\}}$, $p = 1, 2, \ldots, PN^{\{s\}}$, $i = 1, 2, \ldots, I$, $j = 1, 2, \ldots, J$, $k = 1, 2, \ldots, K$, is a a trajectory (x or y) value in the k-th sample of the p-th partition of the j-th signature of the i-th signer.

Next, distances between templates and signatures in two dimensional space are calculated. Distance $d_{p,i,j}^{\{s\}}$, $p = 1, 2, \ldots, PN^{\{s\}}$, $i = 1, 2, \ldots, I$, $j = 1, 2, \ldots, J$, between the j-th signature trajectory of the i-th signer and template of the i-th signer in the p-th partition generated for signatures aligned with use of s signal is calculated by the formula:

$$d_{p,i,j}^{\{s\}} = \sqrt{\left(dx_{p,i,j}^{\{s\}} \right)^2 + \left(dy_{p,i,j}^{\{s\}} \right)^2}. \tag{5}$$

Next, weights of importance for each partition are calculated. First step to compute weights of importance is calculation of mean distances between signatures and template in partitions. Mean distance between signatures of the i-th signer and template of the i-th signer in the p-th partition $\bar{d}_{p,i}^{\{s\}}$, $p = 1, 2, \ldots, PN^{\{s\}}$, $i = 1, 2, \ldots, I$, related to signal s (v velocity or z pressure) is calculated by the formula:

$$\bar{d}_{p,i}^{\{s\}} = \frac{1}{J} \sum_{j=1}^{J} d_{p,i,j}^{\{s\}}. \tag{6}$$

Then, standard deviation of distances in each partition should be calculated. Standard deviation of signatures $\sigma_{p,i}^{\{s\}}$, $p = 1, 2, \ldots, PN^{\{s\}}$, $i = 1, 2, \ldots, I$, of the i-th user from the p-th partition related to signal s (*velocity* or *pressure*) is calculated using the following equation:

$$\sigma_{p,i}^{\{s\}} = \sqrt{\frac{1}{J} \sum_{j=1}^{J} \left(\bar{d}_{p,i}^{\{s\}} - d_{p,i,j}^{\{s\}} \right)^2}. \tag{7}$$

Next, weights of importance are calculated. Weight $w_{p,i}^{'\{s\}}$, $p = 1, 2, \ldots, PN^{\{s\}}$, $i = 1, 2, \ldots, I$, of the p-th partition of the i-th user related to signal s (*velocity* or *pressure*) is calculated by the following formula:

$$w_{p,i}^{'\{s\}} = \bar{d}_{p,i}^{\{s\}} \sigma_{p,i}^{\{s\}}. \tag{8}$$

After that, weights should be normalized. Normalization of weight is used to simplify the classification phase. Weight $w_{p,i}^{\{s\}}$, $p = 1, 2, \ldots, PN^{\{s\}}$, $i = 1, 2, \ldots, I$, of the p-th partition of the i-th user related to signal s (*velocity* or *pressure*) is normalized by the following equation:

$$w_{p,i}^{\{s\}} = 1 - \frac{0.9 \cdot w_{p,i}^{'\{s\}}}{\max\left\{w_{1,i}^{'\{s\}}, \ldots, w_{PN^{\{s\}},i}^{'\{s\}}\right\}}. \tag{9}$$

Use of coefficient 0.9 in formula (9) causes that partition with the lowest value of weight of importance is also used in classification process.

Next, selection of location of decision boundary and determination of the value $dlrnmax_{p,i}^{\{s\}}$, $p = 1, 2, \ldots, PN^{\{s\}}$, $i = 1, 2, \ldots, I$, $s \in \{v, z\}$ is performed (see [31]). The determined values have an impact on spacing of fuzzy sets, which represent values $\{low, high\}$ assumed by the $PN^{\{v\}} + PN^{\{z\}}$ linguistic variables "the truth of the i-th user signature from p-th partition of s signal" $(p = 1, 2, \ldots, PN^{\{s\}}, s \in \{v, z\})$.

2.3   Signature Classification

In the last step signature verification is performed. In this step flexible Mamdani-type neuro-fuzzy system is used (see e.g. [2]-[3], [22]). Our system works on the basis of two fuzzy rules presented as follows:

$$\left\{ \begin{array}{l} R^1 : \left[\begin{array}{l} \text{IF}\left(dtst_{1,i}^{\{s\}} \text{is} A_{1,i}^{1\ \{s\}}\right) \Big| w_{1,i}^{\{s\}} \text{ OR} \ldots \\ \left(dtst_{PN^{\{s\}},i}^{\{s\}} \text{is} A_{PN^{\{s\}},i}^{1\ \{s\}}\right) \Big| w_{PN^{\{s\}},i}^{\{s\}} \text{THEN} y_i \text{is} B^1 \end{array} \right] \\ R^2 : \left[\begin{array}{l} \text{IF}\left(dtst_{1,i}^{\{s\}} \text{is} A_{1,i}^{2\ \{s\}}\right) \Big| w_{1,i}^{\{s\}} \text{ OR} \ldots \\ \left(dtst_{PN^{\{s\}},i}^{\{s\}} \text{is} A_{PN^{\{s\}},i}^{2\ \{s\}}\right) \Big| w_{PN^{\{s\}},i}^{\{s\}} \text{THEN} y_i \text{is} B^2 \end{array} \right] \end{array} \right., \tag{10}$$

where

- $dtst_{p,i}^{\{s\}}$, $s \in \{v, z\}$, $p = 1, 2, \ldots, PN^{\{s\}}$, $i = 1, 2, \ldots, I$, are input linguistic variables, whose numeric value is a distance between the test signature trajectory of the i-th signer and decision boundary in the p-th partition for signatures aligned with use of s signal.
- $A_{p,i}^{1\ \{s\}}$, $A_{p,i}^{2\ \{s\}}$, $p = 1, 2, \ldots, PN^{\{s\}}$, $i = 1, 2, \ldots, I$, are input fuzzy sets related to the signal $s \in \{v, z\}$ shown in Fig. 2.
- y_i, $i = 1, 2, \ldots, I$, is input linguistic variable interpreted as reliability of signature.
- B^1, B^2 are output fuzzy sets shown in Fig. 2.
- $w_{p,i}^{\{s\}}$, $p = 1, 2, \ldots, PN^{\{s\}}$, $i = 1, 2, \ldots, I$, $s \in \{v, z\}$, are weights of the p-th partition of the i-th user related to signal s.

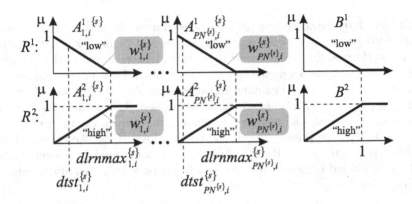

Fig. 2. Input and output fuzzy sets of the flexible neuro-fuzzy system of the Mamdani type for signature verification

Signature is considered true if the following assumption is satisfied:

$$
\bar{y}_i = \frac{S^* \left\{ \begin{array}{c} \mu_{A^2_{1,i}}^{\{s\}} \left(dtst^{\{s\}}_{1,i} \right), \ldots, \\ \mu_{A^2_{PN\{s\},i}}^{\{s\}} \left(dtst^{\{s\}}_{PN\{s\},i} \right); w^{\{s\}}_{1,i}, \ldots, w^{\{s\}}_{PN\{s\},i} \end{array} \right\}}{\left(S^* \left\{ \begin{array}{c} \mu_{A^2_{1,i}}^{\{s\}} \left(dtst^{\{s\}}_{1,i} \right), \ldots, \\ \mu_{A^2_{PN\{s\},i}}^{\{s\}} \left(dtst^{\{s\}}_{PN\{s\},i} \right); w^{\{s\}}_{1,i}, \ldots, w^{\{s\}}_{PN\{s\},i} \end{array} \right\} + \right.} > cth_i,
\left. S^* \left\{ \begin{array}{c} \mu_{A^1_{1,i}}^{\{s\}} \left(dtst^{\{s\}}_{1,i} \right), \ldots, \\ \mu_{A^1_{PN\{s\},i}}^{\{s\}} \left(dtst^{\{s\}}_{PN\{s\},i} \right); w^{\{s\}}_{1,i}, \ldots, w^{\{s\}}_{PN\{s\},i} \end{array} \right\} \right)
$$

$$(11)$$

where

- $S^* \{\cdot\}$ is a weighted t-conorm of the algebraic type (see [2]).
- $\bar{y}_i$, $i = 1, 2, \ldots, I$, is the value of the output signal of applied neuro-fuzzy system described by rules (10). Detailed description of the system can be found in [2]. Formula (11) is the result of the general relationship describing the transformation of the input signal of Mamdani-type system.
- $cth_i \in [0, 1]$ - coefficient determined experimentally during training phase for each user to eliminate disproportion between FAR and FRR error (see [29]). The parameters $cth_i \in [0, 1]$, computed individually for the i-th user, $i = 1, 2, \ldots, I$, are used during verification process in the test phase.

In future research we plan to use probabilistic neural networks for classification of dynamic signature ([8], [19]-[21]).

3   Simulation Results

Public SVC 2004 database (see [29]) was used during simulation. The database contains 40 signers and for each signer 20 genuine and 20 forgery signatures. The test was performed five times, every time for all signers stored in the database. During training phase 5 genuine signatures (numbers 1-10) of each signer were used. During test phase 10 genuine signatures (numbers 11-20) and 20 forgery signatures (numbers 21-40) of each signer were used. All the methods were implemented in the authorial testing environment to compare the results.

In the Table 1 we present simulation results. FAR (False Acceptance Rate) and FRR (False Rejection Rate) values are commonly used in biometrics (see e.g. [10]). It should be noted, that method based on vertical partitions achieves the best results.

Table 1. Results of simulation performed by our system

Method	Average FAR	Average FRR	Average error
Khan et al. [9]	12.30 %	13.90 %	13.10 %
Zalasiński and Cpałka [31]	11.13 %	11.45 %	11.29 %
Our method	**11.35 %**	**9.80 %**	**10.57 %**

4   Conclusions

In this paper a new method of signature partitioning is presented. The method assumes division of signals on the basis of discretization points time index values. All partitions are used during training and verification process. They are described by weights of importance which contain information about reliability of the partition. Achieved high accuracy of signature verification proves the correctness of the proposed method.

Acknowledgment. The project was financed by the National Science Center on the basis of the decision number DEC-2011/01/N/ST6/06964.

References

1. Cpałka, K., Rutkowski, L.: A new method for designing and reduction of neuro-fuzzy systems. In: IEEE Int. Conference on Fuzzy Systems, pp. 1851–1857 (2006)
2. Cpałka, K.: A method for designing flexible neuro-fuzzy systems. In: Rutkowski, L., Tadeusiewicz, R., Zadeh, L.A., Żurada, J.M. (eds.) ICAISC 2006. LNCS (LNAI), vol. 4029, pp. 212–219. Springer, Heidelberg (2006)
3. Cpałka, K., Rutkowski, L.: Neuro-fuzzy structures for pattern classification. WSEAS Trans. on Computers, 697–688 (2005)
4. Cpałka, K., Rutkowski, L.: Neuro-fuzzy systems derived from quasi-triangular norms. In: IEEE International Conference on Fuzzy Systems, vol. 2, pp. 1031–1036 (2004)

5. Cpałka, K.: On evolutionary designing and learning of flexible neuro-fuzzy structures for nonlinear classification. Nonlinear Analysis series A: Theory, Methods & Applications, vol. 71. Elsevier (2009)

6. Faundez-Zanuy, M.: On-line signature recognition based on VQ-DTW. Pattern Recognition 40 (2007)

7. Gabryel, M., Rutkowski, L.: Evolutionary methods for designing neuro-fuzzy modular systems combined by bagging algorithm. In: Rutkowski, L., Tadeusiewicz, R., Zadeh, L.A., Zurada, J.M. (eds.) ICAISC 2008. LNCS (LNAI), vol. 5097, pp. 398–404. Springer, Heidelberg (2008)

8. Greblicki, W., Rutkowski, L.: Density-free Bayes risk consistency of nonparametric pattern recognition procedures. Proceedings of the IEEE 69(4), 482–483 (1981)

9. Ibrahim, M.T., Khan, M.A., Alimgeer, K.S., Khan, M.K., Taj, I.A., Guan, L.: Velocity and pressure-based partitions of horizontal and vertical trajectories for on-line signature verification. Pattern Recognition 43 (2010)

10. Jain, A.K., Ross, A.: Introduction to Biometrics. In: Jain, A.K., Flynn, P., Ross, A.A. (eds.) Handbook of Biometrics. Springer (2008)

11. Khan, M.A.U., Khan, M.K., Khan, M.A.: Velocity-image model for online signature verification. IEEE Trans. Image Process 15 (2006)

12. Korytkowski, M., Gabryel, M., Rutkowski, L., Drozda, S.: Evolutionary methods to create interpretable modular system. In: Rutkowski, L., Tadeusiewicz, R., Zadeh, L.A., Zurada, J.M. (eds.) ICAISC 2008. LNCS (LNAI), vol. 5097, pp. 405–413. Springer, Heidelberg (2008)

13. Korytkowski, M., Rutkowski, L., Scherer, R.: On combining backpropagation with boosting. In: Proceedings of the International Joint Conference on Neural Networks (IJCNN), Vancouver, pp. 1274–1277 (2005)

14. Li, X., Er, M.J., Lim, B.S., et al.: Fuzzy Regression Modeling for Tool Performance Prediction and Degradation Detection. International Journal of Neural Systems 20(5), 405–419 (2010)

15. Nowicki, R., Pokropińska, A.: Information criterions applied to neuro-fuzzy architectures design. In: Rutkowski, L., Siekmann, J.H., Tadeusiewicz, R., Zadeh, L.A. (eds.) ICAISC 2004. LNCS (LNAI), vol. 3070, pp. 332–337. Springer, Heidelberg (2004)

16. Pravdova, V., Walczak, B., Massart, D.L.: A comparison of two algorithms for warping of analytical signals. Analytica Chimica Acta 456, 77–92 (2002)

17. Przybył, A., Cpałka, K.: A new method to construct of interpretable models of dynamic systems. In: Rutkowski, L., Korytkowski, M., Scherer, R., Tadeusiewicz, R., Zadeh, L.A., Zurada, J.M. (eds.) ICAISC 2012, Part II. LNCS, vol. 7268, pp. 697–705. Springer, Heidelberg (2012)

18. Rutkowska, D., Nowicki, R., Rutkowski, L.: Neuro-fuzzy architectures with various implication operators. In: Sincak, P., et al. (eds.) The State of the Art in Computational Intelligence, pp. 214–219 (2000)

19. Rutkowski, L.: Sequential estimates of probability densities by orthogonal series and their application in pattern classification. IEEE Transactions on Systems, Man, and Cybernetics SMC-10(12), 918–920 (1980)

20. Rutkowski, L.: On Bayes risk consistent pattern recognition procedures in a quasi-stationary environment. IEEE Transactions on Pattern Analysis and Machine Intelligence PAMI-4(1), 84–87 (1982)

21. Rutkowski, L.: Adaptive probabilistic neural-networks for pattern classification in time-varying environment. IEEE Transactions on Neural Networks 15, 811–827 (2004)

22. Rutkowski, L.: Computational intelligence. Springer (2007)
23. Rutkowski, L., Cpałka, K.: Flexible weighted neuro-fuzzy systems. In: Proceedings of the 9th International Conference on Neural Information Processing, ICONIP 2002, pp. 1857–1861 (2002)
24. Rutkowski, L., Przybył, A., Cpałka, K., Er, M.J.: Online Speed Profile Generation for Industrial Machine Tool Based on Neuro Fuzzy Approach. In: Rutkowski, L., Scherer, R., Tadeusiewicz, R., Zadeh, L.A., Zurada, J.M. (eds.) ICAISC 2010, Part II. LNCS, vol. 6114, pp. 645–650. Springer, Heidelberg (2010)
25. Rutkowski, L., Przybył, A., Cpałka, K.: Novel Online Speed Profile Generation for Industrial Machine Tool Based on Flexible Neuro-Fuzzy Approximation. IEEE Transactions on Industrial Electronics 59(2), 1238–1247 (2012)
26. Scherer, R., Rutkowski, L.: A fuzzy relational system with linguistic antecedent certainty factors. In: 6th International Conference on Neural Networks and Soft Computing, Zakopane, Poland. Advances In Soft Computing, pp. 563–569 (2003)
27. Scherer, R., Rutkowski, L.: Connectionist fuzzy relational systems. In: Halgamuge, S.K., Wang, L. (eds.) Computational Intelligence for Modelling and Prediction. SCI, vol. 2, pp. 35–47. Springer, Heidelberg (2005)
28. Scherer, R., Rutkowski, L.: Neuro-fuzzy relational classifiers. In: Rutkowski, L., Siekmann, J.H., Tadeusiewicz, R., Zadeh, L.A. (eds.) ICAISC 2004. LNCS (LNAI), vol. 3070, pp. 376–380. Springer, Heidelberg (2004)
29. Yeung, D.-Y., Chang, H., Xiong, Y., George, S., Kashi, R., Matsumoto, T., Rigoll, G.: SVC2004: First International Signature Verification Competition. In: Zhang, D., Jain, A.K. (eds.) ICBA 2004. LNCS, vol. 3072, pp. 16–22. Springer, Heidelberg (2004)
30. Zalasiński, M., Cpałka, K.: A new method of on-line signature verification using a flexible fuzzy one-class classifier. Selected Topics in Computer Science Applications, pp. 38–53. EXIT (2011)
31. Zalasiński, M., Cpałka, K.: Novel algorithm for the on-line signature verification. In: Rutkowski, L., Korytkowski, M., Scherer, R., Tadeusiewicz, R., Zadeh, L.A., Zurada, J.M. (eds.) ICAISC 2012, Part II. LNCS (LNAI), vol. 7268, pp. 362–367. Springer, Heidelberg (2012)

Speech Enhancement in Noisy Environments in Hearing Aids Driven by a Tailored Gain Function Based on a Gaussian Mixture Model

Lorena Álvarez, Enrique Alexandre, Cosme Llerena, Roberto Gil-Pita, and Lucas Cuadra

Departamento de Teoría de la Señal y Comunicaciones
Escuela Politécnica Superior. Universidad de Alcalá
28805 - Alcalá de Henares, Madrid, Spain
{lorena.alvrezp,enrique.alexandre,cosme.llerena,
roberto.gil,lucas.cuadra}@uah.es
http://www.uah.es

Abstract. This paper centers on a novel approach aiming at speech enhancement in hearing aids. It consists in creating -by making use of perceptual concepts, and a supervised learning process driven by a genetic algorithm (GA)- a gain function ($\mathcal{G}$) that not only does it enhance the speech quality but also the speech intelligibility in noisy environments. The proposed algorithm creates the enhanced gain function by using a Gaussian mixture model fueled by the GA. To what extent the speech quality is enhanced is quantitatively measured by the algorithm itself by using a scheme based on the perceptual evaluation of speech quality (PESQ) standard. In this "blind" process, it does not use any initial information but that iteratively quantified by the PESQ measurement. The GA computes the optimized parameters that maximize the PESQ score. The experimental work, carried out over three different databases, shows how the computed gain function assists the hearing aid in enhancing speech, when compared to the values reached by using a standard hearing aid based on a multiband compressor-expander algorithm.

Keywords: Gaussian mixture model, genetic algorithms, perceptual evaluation of speech quality, speech enhancement, digital hearing aids.

1 Introduction

According to the latest scientific statistics of the World Health Organization, hearing loss has become a global major healthcare concern. Nowadays, almost 275 million people worldwide, which amounts to approximately 4 % of the total population, suffer from hearing loss [1], and regrettably, this number of deaf and hard of hearing people is increasing at an alarm rate not only because of the aging of the world's population, but also because of the growing exposure to excessive noise in their quotidian life.

The good news is that 90 % of hearing loss cases could be mitigated by using some kind of hearing aid, whereas 10 % of them would require medical or surgical

L. Rutkowski et al. (Eds.): ICAISC 2013, Part I, LNAI 7894, pp. 503–514, 2013.
© Springer-Verlag Berlin Heidelberg 2013

intervention. The bad news is that only about 5 % of people, who could be benefited from hearing aids, wear it in their daily life. In this regard, it has been shown that hearing-aid users repeatedly complain about the difficulty of understanding speech when they are immersed in background noise [2]. Many times, the users can "hear" but they cannot understand the speech signal. They typically require a signal-to-noise-ratio (SNR) of about 5-10 dB higher than that required by normal hearing listeners to achieve the same level of speech understanding [3]. With this in mind, it seems evident that there is a latent reason to work towards the objective of enhancing speech in digital hearing aids.

A common approach aiming at speech enhancement in hearing-aid users, when they are surrounded by environmental sounds, is based on "noise reduction schemes". These methods are divided into two groups: single- and multi- microphone noise reduction algorithms [4]. They both aim at increasing the SNR and thereby increasing the speech intelligibility, lowering the listening effort and improving the perceived quality of the acoustic environment. However, both approaches suffer from serious drawbacks for being implemented in real time in an in-the-market, average-performance hearing aids. On the one hand, a crucial requirement of most single-microphone noise reduction algorithms is the estimation of the noise spectrum. Since most realistic noisy environments are characterized by non-stationarity, it is necessary to frequently adjust the noise spectrum to maintain an effective noise reduction processing. A reasonable way is to perform this adjustment whenever target speech is absent. This obviously demands to develop a speech pause detection algorithm, which is strongly limited by some design restrictions, imposed by the digital signal processor (DSP) on which digital hearing aids are based. On the other hand, multi-microphone schemes need to wirelessly transmit to the left and right ears some parameters involved in the noise reduction algorithm, which has not been efficiently solved yet at a reasonable computational cost in average-performance digital hearing aids.

These are the main reasons why we propose in this paper a *novel* approach aiming at speech enhancement in noisy environments in hearing aids. It basically consists in automatically generating by making use of a supervised learning process, driven by a genetic algorithm (GA), a "gain function" $\mathcal{G}$ (also called "gain matrix"), which aims at enhancing speech in hearing-aid users when they are immersed in environmental noise. In the effort of designing the mentioned gain function, the proposed approach measures objectively the quality of a set of speech signals generated by the hearing aid, which depend on the gain function, by using a scheme based on the perceptual evaluation of speech quality (PESQ) [5]. Fig. 1 will assist us in more clearly introducing our approach, along with the structure of the paper. As it is illustrated, the aforementioned algorithm compares the amplified output signal produced by the hearing aid, s_o (subscript o meaning "output"), with a reference, high quality signal, s_c (subscript c meaning "clean"). Please note that this reference signal is included in a database, and consequently, the process of designing the gain function must be accomplished by an adequate database of speech-in-quiet signals. The output signal s_o is basically the reference signal s_c after 1) having been corrupted with noise (n), and 2) after having been modified by the hearing aid. Using both signals (s_c and s_o), the PESQ block generates a score ranging from -0.5 ("bad") to 4.5 ("excellent"). The higher the score is, the better the speech "perceived by the human auditory system" is. The output signal produced by the hearing aid (s_o) depends on the gain function of the hearing aid. As it will be explained in Section 2, the proposed approach creates the gain function, $\mathcal{G}$, by using a Gaussian mixture model (GMM) driven by a GA. This model (and in turns, the PESQ score) depends on a number of parameters. This GA computes the optimized parameters that maximize the global PESQ score for the speech sounds included in the database. The paper is completed with a variety of experimental work that suggests the feasibility of the mentioned approach to enhance speech in hearing aids.

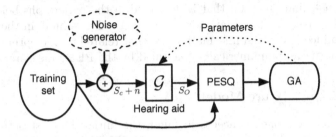

Fig. 1. Simplified block diagram illustrating the way the proposed method works

2 Blind Modeling of the Gain Function

2.1 Motivation

Put it simple, a digital hearing aid consists of a bank of sound compressors, one for each frequency band $k = 1, \ldots, N_B$, where N_B is the number of frequency bands available in the DSP. With this in mind, the sound signal that enters the hearing aid, labeled $s_c(t)$, is divided into a number of L frames and the DSP computes the short-time-Fourier-transform (STFT) of each frame. Thus, for the sake of simplicity, $S_C(k, l)$ will represent here the k-th frequency component of the STFT of the l-th frame corresponding to $s_c(t)$. Note that $l = 1, \ldots, L$ labels the index over the L frames into which any sound signal is segmented. Within this scenario, each sample $S_C(k, l)$ is multiplied in the DSP by a gain value that depends on the level (dB) of the input sound frame and the frequency band.

Thus, the gain matrix $\mathcal{G}$ which contains all the parameters required to completely compute the gain value for any level of the input signal in any frequency band, can be formally expressed as follows:

$$\mathcal{G} = f(X, k) \tag{1}$$

where X is the level (dB) of the input signal (frame, in the context of the application at hand), and $k = 1, \ldots, N_B$ labels the index over the N_B frequency components of the STFT of the input frame.

Computing the gain, as a function of the level of the input frame (X) and the frequency band (k), can require intensive computational cost. To illustrate this statement, we can imagine a standard hearing aid in which the compression-expansion technique in each frequency band, in the easiest form, is performed by means of piecewise linear approximation strategies (this is commonly known as "multiband compressor-expander algorithm" [6]), and using, for instance, three segments. This simple scenario would demand to compute five parameters to define the gain curve for each frequency band. If $N_B = 64$ bands are considered, the total number of parameters included in matrix $\mathcal{G}$ would be $64 \times 5 = 320$.

In the effort of reducing this number of parameters to be optimized, we propose to model the complete gain $\mathcal{G}$ (and not its separate pieces), as a "smooth" function in a "blind" method that is described in the paragraphs below. Prior to this, it is convenient to remark we say the method is "blind" in the sense we do not introduce any initial information but that related to perceptual concepts (just those that can be numerically quantified by the PESQ measurement).

2.2   Gaussian Mixture Model

With the aforementioned concepts in mind, the initial, blind structure of the gain $\mathcal{G}$ can be formally expressed by using a GMM [7], which basically consists in a properly weighted combination of Gaussian components as shown below:

$$\mathcal{G} \approx p(\mathbf{x}) = \sum_{i=1}^{M} w_i \cdot \mathcal{N}(\mathbf{m}_i, \mathbf{C}_i) \tag{2}$$

where:

- $p(\mathbf{x})$ is the probability density function of the Gaussian mixture
- $\mathbf{x} = [x_1, x_2, \ldots, x_d]$ is a d-dimensional data vector
- M represents the number of Gaussian components
- w_i labels the amplitude or weight of the i-th Gaussian component
- $\mathcal{N}$ is a multivariate normal or Gaussian distribution (with mean value $\mathbf{m}_i$ and covariance matrix $\mathbf{C}_i$), whose density function is as follows:

$$\mathcal{N} = \frac{1}{(2\pi)^{(d/2)}|\mathbf{C}_i|^{1/2}} exp \left\{ -\frac{1}{2}(\mathbf{x} - \mathbf{m}_i)^T \mathbf{C}_i^{-1}(\mathbf{x} - \mathbf{m}_i) \right\}. \tag{3}$$

The complete GMM is thus parameterized by the mean vectors, the covariance matrices and the mixture weights from all Gaussian component densities. These aforementioned unknown parameters will be computed by making use of a GA. Please note that in this work, the mixture model has to approximate the gain matrix $\mathcal{G}$ as a function of the level (dB) of the input frame and the frequency band (k). Thus, the data vector **x** results here in a 2-dimensional continuous vector (that is, $d = 2$), in which the first dimension represents the level (dB) of the input frame and the second dimension represents the frequency band.

Completing this section demands to emphasize that a key advantage of this approach is that the number of parameters to be optimized is drastically reduced since now that number does not depend either on the number of frequency bands available in the DSP or the different levels of the input frame. This can be clearly noticed by having a look at the number of parameters to be optimized when using, for instance, a 3-piece linear approximation which results in 320 (see Section 2.1 for further details), and the number of parameters demanded when modeling the gain function by making use of a GMM that results in 6 parameters (in the case of a two dimensional 1-GMM[1]), 12 parameters (in the case of a two dimensional 2-GMM) or 18 parameters (in the case of a two dimensional 3-GMM). Finally, it is worth mentioning here that it has been shown experimentally that a number of Gaussian components higher than 3 (that is, $M > 3$) does not cause a significant improvement in the results although it would require larger computational resources.

2.3 Case-Study: Real-Time Implementation

The DSP used to carry out the experiments is Toccata Plus [9]. This DSP is composed of two coprocessors: 1) the weighted overlapp-add (WOLA) filter-bank coprocessor that performs the time/frequency decomposition and 2) the "core processor" dealing with the remaining tasks, such as, for instance, compensating the hearing loss.

At a first glance, implementing in the DSP the gain function ($\mathcal{G}$) could be approached from the two viewpoints that follow. The first one consists in storing in data-memory the *optimized* parameters of the GMM found by the GA, and by making use of Equation (2), computing in the DSP the proper value of the gain to be applied to reduce the noise. The main advantage of this approach is that it requires less use of data-memory storage. The very serious associated drawback is, however, that it is very difficult its practical implementation in a DSP because it requires intensive computational cost. The second approach is as follows: 1) computing $\mathcal{G}$ *offline*; 2) tabulating $\mathcal{G}$ for any level (dB) of the input sound frame and any frequency band; and 3) storing the tabulated values of $\mathcal{G}$ in the DSP data-memory. The main advantage of this second approach is that it requires much lower computational cost at the expense of increasing the amount of data-memory used. However, as it will be shown later on, this stronger use of data-memory is perfectly feasible. These are basically the reasons why we have chosen this approach in order to illustrate the feasibility of the core idea we propose in this paper.

Thus, using this second approach, the subsequent questions arising are *how many different levels (dB) of the input frame and frequencies should be considered?* And consequently, *how many different values of gain should be considered?*

---

[1] Henceforth, M-GMM labels a Gaussian mixture model with M Gaussian components.

Since the WOLA filter-bank output provides $N_B = 64$ frequency bands and the 16-bit A/D and D/A converters exhibit a dynamic range of 96.3 dB, we have set the dynamic margin ranging from 1 to 96 dB for the level of the input signal (in steps of 1 dB, which has been found to have enough precision in our experiments), and ranging from 1 to 64 for the frequency bands involved. Within this framework, the total number of tabulated values for $\mathcal{G}$ to be stored in the data memory has been found to be $64 \times 96 = 6144$. Since, each value requires 2 bytes (1 word), the total memory required would be 12288 bytes ($\sim$ 12 Kbytes, or equivalently, $\sim$ 6 Kwords). Since the total data-capacity of the DSP is 8-Kword, this approach does not exceed the restrictions imposed by the DSP.

Finally, for properly completing this section, Table 1 shows the computational cost, $\mathcal{C}$ (clock cycles), and the average load, $\mathcal{L}$ (%), required for programming in the Toccata Plus DSP each functional block involved in a hearing loss compensation algorithm that makes use of a gain matrix as the one proposed in this paper. As shown, the total computational cost and load average (%) needed to implement the whole digital hearing aid functionalities (including the gain function $\mathcal{G}$) has been found to be 3.931 clock cycles and 51.2 %, respectively.

Table 1. Total computational cost (in clock cycles) and load average (%) required, for implementing in the Toccata Plus DSP, the hearing loss compensation algorithm including the gain function ($\mathcal{G}$) proposed in this work

Block/assembler instruction	Total cost (clock cycles)	Load average (%)
Call	2	0.03
Push	21	0.27
Hearing loss compensation algorithm including the gain matrix ($\mathcal{G}$)	3885	50.58
Call	21	0.27
Ret	2	0.03
Total	3931	51.18

3   Experimental Work and Results

Prior to the description of the experimental work and the results obtained in this paper (Section 3.2), it is worth having a look at the experimental setup and the databases used for the experiments (Section 3.1).

3.1   Experimental Setup

A total of three speech-in-noise databases have been used. These databases are described in the following paragraphs.

- **Database 1**. This database is made of 30 clean speech sentences, randomly selected from [10]. These 30 clean speech sentences have been degraded by additive white Gaussian noise at SNR $= 0, 5, 10$ and 15 dB, as schematically illustrated in Fig. 1. These values of SNRs have been taken from [11]. With this in mind, this database actually consists of 120 speech-in-noise files. For properly training and testing the proposed approach, it is necessary for the database to be divided into two different sets. For this reason, for each study-case SNR, 10 files (35 %) have been picked randomly as training data, and the remaining 20 files (65 %) have been used for the purpose of testing. This division has been made ensuring that the relative proportion of files of each category is preserved for each set.
- **Database 2**. It is composed of 30 clean speech sentences extracted from the noisy speech corpus (NOIZEUS), available in [11]. As in "database 1", these clean speech sentences have been degraded by additive white Gaussian noise at SNR $= 0, 5, 10$ and 15 dB. This database has been used because it contains *phonetically balanced* sentences with relatively low word-context predictability.
- **Database 3**. This database is composed of the same 30 clean speech sentences used to design "database 2", but in this case, these clean speech sentences have been corrupted by eight different *real-world* noises at SNR $= 0, 5, 10$ and 15 dB. The real-world noises have been taken from the AURORA database [12]. This database was compiled by Loizou [11].

The files included in the three aforementioned databases have been properly modified by using a hearing aid simulator, modeled in [13], and by using a subject with a flat 40 dB hearing loss. The results obtained by using this hearing aid simulator have been labelled "Mult. compressor-expander HA" in the numerical results. In the effort of exploring the performance of the gain function proposed in this work, we have compared these results with those obtained when the hearing aid simulator makes use of the gain function proposed here (instead of using a multiband compressor-expander algorithm). In order to obtain this gain function, "database 1" has been used to train the algorithm described in Section 2, whereas both "database 2" and "database 3" have been used to assess the performance of the obtained solutions with "database 1".

Regarding the GA context, any *individual* is a real-number vector with the structure $I \equiv [v_1, v_2, v_3, \ldots, v_6]$, for the easiest case in which $M = 1$ (that is, only 1 Gaussian component has been used for the GMM). In this regard, v_1 designates the weight of the Gaussian mixture, v_2 and v_3 represent the elements of the mean vector and finally, v_4, v_5 and v_6 label the elements of the covariance matrix. If the mixture consists of a greater number of components, such as, for instance, $M = 2$, the dimension of each individual is 12 (the first six parameters define the parameters of one Gaussian component and the following six parameters define the parameters of the second Gaussian component) and so on. Table 2 summarizes the main design parameters the GA makes use of, where M labels the number of Gaussian components used in the mixture.

Table 2. Design parameters the GA makes use of

Parameters	Value
Initial population (p_0)	$150 \times M$
Crossover probability (p_c)	0.8
Mutation probability (p_m)	0.1
Max. no. of generations	50
Max. no. of iterations in which the score remains unchanged	20

Completing this description of the batches of experiments demands to mention that the experiments have been repeated 10 times. It has been found that the variance of the results obtained by 10 runs of the GA is kept below 0.01, and consequently, aiming at saving computational resources, it is not worthwhile to run the experiments a larger number of repetitions.

3.2   Numerical Results

Fig. 2(a), 2(b) and 2(c) represent the mean value and the standard deviation of the computed PESQ scores as a function of the SNR when the number of Gaussian components in the obtained gain function is $M = 1, 2$ and 3, respectively. These results correspond to a batch of experiments carried out by training the approach using the design speech-in-noise files at SNR $= 0$ dB, included in "database 1" (discussed in Section 3.1). The results shown in the three mentioned figures correspond to the test speech-in-noise files included in "database 1". The solid lines in the sequence of figures correspond to the mean value and standard deviation of the PESQ scores, when the gain matrix ($\mathcal{G}$) is used in the hearing aid. For comparative purposes, the dashed, monotonously increasing lines in the mentioned figures correspond to the mean and standard deviation values of the PESQ scores reached when the gain programmed in the hearing aid is based on a multiband compression-expansion strategy (labeled "Mult. compressor-expander HA" in the pictures).

Fig. 2(a), 2(b) and 2(c) provide the following valuable information:

- The computed gain function ($\mathcal{G}$) makes the hearing aid reach better results in terms of speech quality, regardless of the number of Gaussian components (M) used to model the gain matrix, than those achieved by using a standard hearing aid in which the gain function in each frequency band is based on a multiband compression-expansion strategy.
- Regardless of the SNR level of the speech-in-noise files, the results obtained with $M = 3$ Gaussian components are always better than those obtained with $M = 1$ or 2 components.
- These figures clearly illustrate to what extent the proposed method enhances the speech quality, especially in the worst scenario in which the level of noise equals the level of speech, or in other words, when SNR $= 0$ dB.

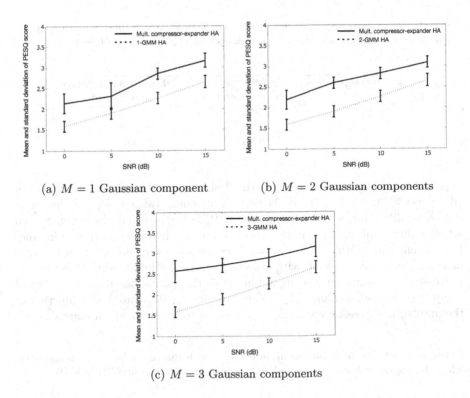

(a) $M = 1$ Gaussian component   (b) $M = 2$ Gaussian components

(c) $M = 3$ Gaussian components

Fig. 2. Mean and standard deviation values of PESQ scores, as a function of the SNR. It is also illustrated the case in which the hearing-aid user makes use of a standard hearing aid in which the gain is based on a multiband compressor-expander algorithm.

One important question that could arise is whether improvements in terms of speech intelligibility are also reported. In order to answer this question, we have made use of a standardized measure that is the so-called speech intelligibility index (SII) [14] to predict speech intelligibility. Table 3 lists the mean speech quality improvement (in terms of PESQ score) and the mean speech intelligibility improvement (in terms of SII score), when the test speech-in-noise files included in "database 1" are processed by a hearing aid in which the gain matrix is based on a GMM, with respect to the situation in which the mentioned files are processed by a standard hearing aid in which the gain is based on a multiband compression-expansion algorithm. These results, illustrated as a function of the number of Gaussian components used (M) in the mixture model, correspond to the situation in which the approach has been trained with the design speech-in-noise files included in "database 1" at SNR = 0 dB. It seems clear to note that speech intelligibility is also increased, especially when $M = 3$ components are used in the mixture model.

In order to explore the influence of other SNRs in the training process of the approach, we have carried out a similar batch of experiments in which the

Table 3. Mean speech enhancement, in terms of both speech quality and intelligibility, when the approach has been trained with speech-in-noise files at SNR = 0 dB

Gaussian components (M)	Speech quality improvement (%)	Speech intelligibility improvement (%)
1	10.3	5.7
2	11.4	8.9
3	14.5	11.9

approach has been trained by using the design speech-in-noise files included in "database 1" at SNR = 5 dB. With this in mind, Table 4 depicts the mean speech quality improvement (in terms of PESQ score) and the mean speech intelligibility improvement (in terms of SII score), when the test speech-in-noise files included in "database 1" are processed by a hearing aid in which the gain matrix is based on a GMM, with respect to the situation in which the files are processed by a standard hearing aid in which the gain is based on a multiband compression-expansion algorithm. These results are illustrated as a function of the number of Gaussian components (M) used to model the gain matrix.

Table 4. Mean speech enhancement, in terms of both speech quality and intelligibility, when the approach has been trained with speech-in-noise files at SNR = 5 dB

Gaussian components (M)	Speech quality improvement (%)	Speech intelligibility improvement (%)
1	11.0	6.8
2	14.7	9.6
3	15.1	12.2

Note that, as in the former batch of experiments, the best result is achieved when $M = 3$ Gaussian components are used in the mixture model leading to achieve 15.1 % and 12.2 % improvement in terms of speech quality and speech intelligibility, respectively.

Finally, and for comparative purposes in order to evaluate the influence of the database used in the experiments, we have tested the results obtained with "database 1", using now "database 2" and "database 3" (both described in Section 3.1). Or in other words, we have tested the gain function obtained with "database 1", using now the speech-in-noise files included in "database 2" and "database 3". The results below correspond to those obtained when the approach has been trained with the design speech-in-noise files included in "database 1" at SNR = 5 dB and by using $M = 3$ Gaussian components. Fig. 3(a) and 3(b) represent the mean speech quality improvement, as a function of the SNR, obtained when the speech-in-noise files, included in "database 2" and "database 3", respectively, are processed by the study-case hearing aid (labeled "3-GMM HA" in the picture). It is also illustrated the case in which the mentioned files are processed by a standard hearing aid in which the gain is based on a multiband compressor-expander algorithm. The mean speech quality improvement has been found to be about 15 % and 8 %, respectively.

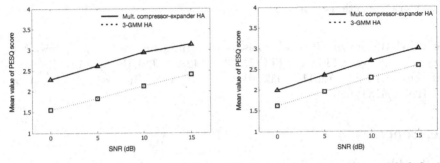

(a) Speech-in-noise files included in "database 2"

(b) Speech-in-noise files included in "database 3"

Fig. 3. Mean values of PESQ score, as a function of the SNR, when the speech-in-noise files are processed by the study-case hearing aid with $M = 3$ Gaussian components. It is also illustrated the case in which the mentioned files are processed by a standard hearing aid in which the gain is based on a multiband compressor-expander algorithm.

4   Conclusions

This paper focuses on a novel approach aiming at speech enhancement in hearing aids. It consists in creating -by using a supervised learning process driven by a GA- a gain function that not only does it enhance speech quality, but also speech intelligibility in noisy environments in hearing aids.

The experimental work has been carried out by using three different speech-in-noise databases. The main results can be summarized as follows:

1. The computed gain function makes the hearing aid reach better results in terms of speech quality, regardless of the number of Gaussian components used (M) to model the gain function, than those achieved by using a standard hearing aid in which the gain function in each frequency band is based on a multiband compression-expansion strategy.
2. Regardless of the SNR level of speech-in-noise files, the results obtained with $M = 3$ Gaussian components are always better than those obtained with $M = 1, 2$ components.
3. The results clearly show to what extent the proposed algorithm enhances the speech quality and speech intelligibility, especially in the worst scenario in which the level of noise equals the level of speech (SNR $= 0$ dB).

It has been also shown that the total load average required to implement this approach in the Toccata Plus DSP is about 52 %.

These results point out to a new field of research in the jointly use of perceptual and artificial intelligent concepts applied on speech enhancement in hearing aids. Besides the obvious improvement in the quality of the speech perceived by the user, the key point consists in its lower computational cost because, once the gain function is programmed in the DSP, it is no longer necessary to run any other noise reduction algorithm.

Acknowledgments. This work has been partially funded by the Spanish Ministry of Economy and Finance (TEC2012-38142-C04-02), the Spanish Ministry of Defence (DEFENSA2011-10032110035) and the Universidad de Alcala (UAH2011/EXP-026)

References

1. World Health Organization, http://www.who.int/pbd/deafness/news/en/
2. Kochkin, S.: MarkeTrak V: Why my hearing aids are in the drawer: The consumers' perspective. Hear. J. 53(2), 34–42 (2000)
3. Van den Bogaert, T., Doclo, S., Wouters, J., Moonen, M.: Speech enhancement with multichannel Wiener filter techniques in multimicrophone binaural hearing aids. J. Acoust. Soc. Am. 125(1), 360–371 (2009)
4. Hendriks, R.C., Gerkmann, T.: Noise Correlation Matrix Estimation for Multi-Microphone Speech Enhancement. IEEE T. Audio Speech 20(1), 223–233 (2012)
5. Rix, A.W., Hollier, M.P., Hekstra, A.P., Beerends, J.G.: Perceptual Evaluation of Speech Quality (PESQ), the new ITU standard for end-to-end speech quality assessment, part I - time-delay compensation. J. Audio Eng. Soc. 50(10), 755–764 (2002)
6. Cummins, K.L., Hecox, K.E., Williamson, M.J.: Adaptive, programmable signal processing hearing aid. US Patent 4,887,299, Google Patents (1989)
7. Reynolds, D.: Gaussian mixture models. Encyclopedia of Biometric Recognition, 12–17 (2008)
8. Falk, T.H., Chan, W.Y.: Objective speech quality assessment using Gaussian mixture models. In: 22nd Biennial Symposium on Communications (2004)
9. Dspfactory Ltd.: Toccata Plus Evaluation and Development Board Manual. Dspfactory Ltd. (2002)
10. Scheirer, C., Slaney, M.: Construction and evaluation of a robust multi feature speech/music discriminator. In: IEEE International Conference on Acoustics, Speech and Signal Processing, ICASSP 1997, pp. 1331–1334 (1997)
11. Loizou, P.C.: Speech Enhancement. Theory and Practice. CRC (2007)
12. Hirsch, H.G., Pearce, D.: The Aurora Experimental Framework for the Performance Evaluation of Speech Recognition Systems Under Noisy Conditions. In: ASR2000-Automatic Speech Recognition: Challenges for the new Millenium ISCA Tutorial and Research Workshop (ITRW) (2000)
13. Vicen-Bueno, R., Gil-Pita, R., Utrilla-Manso, M., Álvarez-Pérez, L.: A Hearing Aid Simulator to Test Adaptive Signal Processing Algorithms. In: 10th IEEE International Symposium on Intelligent Signal Processing, pp. 1–6 (2007)
14. National Standards Institute: Method for the Calculation of the Speech Intelligibility Index, New York (1997)

Two-Dimensional Hidden Markov Models for Pattern Recognition

Janusz Bobulski and Lukasz Adrjanowicz

Czestochowa University of Technology
Institute of Computer and Information Science
Dabrowskiego Street 73, 42-200 Czestochowa, Poland
{januszb,lukasz.adrjanowicz}@icis.pcz.pl

Abstract. Hidden Markov models are well-known methods for image processing. They are used in many areas where 1D data are processed. In the case of 2D data, there appear some problems with application HMM. There are some solutions, but they convert input observation from 2D to 1D, or create parallel pseudo 2D HMM, which is set of 1D HMMs in fact. This paper describes authentic 2D HMM with two-dimensional input data, and its application for pattern recognition in image processing.

Keywords: hidden Markov model, pattern recognition, image processing.

1 Introduction

Hidden Markov models (HMM) are widely apply in data classification. They are used in speech recognition, character recognition, biological sequence analysis, financial data processing, texture analysis, face recognition, etc. [1]This widely application of HMM is result of its effectiveness. An extension of the HMM to work on two-dimensional data is 2D HMM. A 2D HMM can be regarded as a combination of one state matrix and one observation matrix, where transition between states take place according to a 2D Markovian probability and each observation is generated independently by the corresponding state at the same matrix position. It was noted that the complexity of estimating the parameters of a 2D HMMs or using them to perform maximum a posteriori classification is exponential in the size of data. Similar to 1D HMM, the most important thing for 2D HMMs is also to solve the three basic problems, namely, probability evolution, optimal state matrix and parameters estimation.

When we process one-dimensional data, we have good tools and solution for this. Unfortunately, this is unpractical in image processing, because the images are two-dimensional. When you convert an image from 2D to 1D , you lose some information. So, if we process two-dimensional data, we should apply two-dimensional HMM, and this 2D HMM should works with 2D data. One of solutions is pseudo 2D HMM[2],[3],[4]. This model is extension of classic 1D HMM. There are super-states, which mask one-dimensional hidden Markov models (Fig. 1). Linear model is the topology of superstates, where only self transition

L. Rutkowski et al. (Eds.): ICAISC 2013, Part I, LNAI 7894, pp. 515–523, 2013.

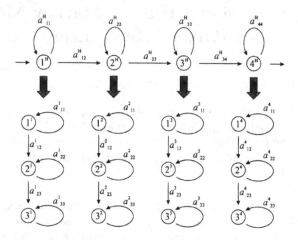

Fig. 1. Pseudo 2D HMM [1]

and transition to the following superstate are possible. Inside the superstates there are linear 1D HMM. The state sequences in the rows are independent of the state sequences of neighboring rows. Additional, input data are divided to the vector. So, we have 1D model with 1D data in practise.

Other approach to image processing use two-dimensional data present in works [5] and [6]. The solutions base on Markov Random Fields (MRF) and give good results for classification and segmentation, but not in pattern recognition. Interesting results showed in paper [7]. This article presents analytic solution and proof of correctness two-dimensional HMM. But this 2D HMM is similar to MRF, works with one-dimensional data and can be apply only for left-right type of HMM. This article presents real solution for 2D problem in HMM. There is show true 2D HMM which processes 2D data.

2   Classic 1D HMM

HMM is a double stochastic process with underlying stochastic process that is not observable (hidden), but can be observed through another set of stochastic processes that produce a sequence of observation [8]. Let $O = \{O_1, .., O_T\}$ be the sequence of observation of feature vectors, where T is the total number of feature vectors in the sequence. The statistical parameters of the model may be defined as follows [9]:

- The number of states of the model, N
- The number of symbols M
- The transition probabilities of the underlying Markov chain, $A = \{a_{ij}\}, 1 \leq i, j \leq N$, where a_{ij} is the probability of transition from state i to state j

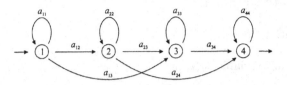

Fig. 2. One-dimensional HMM

- The observation probabilities, $B = \{b_{jm})\}$ $1 \leq j \leq N, 1 \leq m \leq M$ which represents the probability of gnerate the m_{th} symbol in the j_{th} state.
- The initial probability vector, $\Pi = \{\pi_i\}$ $1 \leq i \leq N$.

Hence, the HMM requires three probability measures to be defined, A, B, Π and the notation $\lambda = (A, B, \Pi)$ is often used to indicate the set of parameters of the model. In the proposed method, one model is made for each part of the face. The parameters of the model are generated at random at the beginning. Then they are estimated with Baum-Welch algorithm, which is based on the forward-backward algorithm. The forward algorithm calculates the coefficient $\alpha_t(i)$ (probability of observing the partial sequence $(o_1, , o_t)$ such that state q_t is i). The backward algorithm calculates the coefficient $\beta_t(i)$ (probability of observing the partial sequence $(o_{t+1}, , o_T)$ such that state q_t is i). The Baum-Welch algorithm, which computes the λ, can be described as follows [9]:

1. Let initial model be λ_0
2. Compute new λ based on λ_0 and observation O
3. If $log(P(O|\lambda) - log(P(O)|\lambda_0) < DELTA$ stop
4. Else set $\lambda \rightarrow \lambda_0$ and go to step 2.

The parameters of new model λ, based on λ_0 and observation O, are estimated from equation of Baum-Welch algorithm [8], and then are recorded to the database.

3   Three Basic Problems

There are three fundamental problems of interest that must be solved for HMM to be useful in some applications. These problems are the following:

1. Given observation $O = (o_1, o_2, , o_T)$ and model $\lambda = (A, B, \Pi)$, efficiently compute $P(O|\lambda)$
2. Given observation $O = (o_1, o_2, , o_T)$ and model λ find the optimal state sequence $q = (q_1, q_2, , q_T)$
3. Given observation $O = (o_1, o_2, , o_T)$, estimate model parameters $\lambda = (A, B, \Pi)$ that maximize $P(O|\lambda)$

3.1   Solution to Problem 1

Forward Algorithm [9]

- Define forward variable $\alpha_t(i)$ as:

$$\alpha_t(i) = P(o_1, o_2,, o_t, q_t = i | \lambda) \tag{1}$$

- $\alpha_t(i)$ is the probability of observing the partial sequence $(o_1, o_2,, o_t)$ such that the the state q_t is i
- Induction
  1. Initialization:

$$\alpha_1(i) = \pi_i b_i(o_1) \tag{2}$$

  2. Induction:

$$\alpha_{t+1}(i) = \left[\sum_{i=1}^{N} \alpha_t(i) a_{ij} \right] b_j(o_{t+1}) \tag{3}$$

  3. Termination:

$$P(O|\lambda) = \sum_{i=1}^{N} \alpha_T(i) \tag{4}$$

Backward Algorithm [9]

- Define backward variable $\beta_t(i)$ as:

$$\beta_t(i) = P(o_{t+1}, o_{t+2},, o_T, q_t = i | \lambda) \tag{5}$$

- $\beta_t(i)$ is the probability of observing the partial sequence $(o_1, o_2,, o_t)$ such that the the state q_t is i
- Induction
  1. Initialization:

$$\beta_T(i) = 1 \tag{6}$$

  2. Induction:

$$\beta_t(i) = \sum_{i=1}^{N} a_{ij} b_j(o_{t+1} \beta_{t+1}(j), \tag{7}$$

$$1 \le i \le N, t = T - 1, ..., 1$$

  3. Termination:

$$P(O|\lambda) = \sum_{i=1}^{N} \beta_1(i) \tag{8}$$

3.2   Solution to Problem 2

Viterbi Algorithm [10]

– Initialization:

$$\delta_1(i) = \pi_i b_i(o_1), 1 \le i \le N \tag{9}$$

$$1 \le i \le N$$

$$\psi_1 = 0 \tag{10}$$

– Recursion:

$$\delta_t(j) = \max_{1 \le i \le N} [\delta_{t-1}(i) a_{ij}] b_j(o_t) \tag{11}$$

$$\psi_t(j) = arg \max_{1 \le i \le N} [\delta_{t-1}(i) a_{ij}] b_j(o_t) \tag{12}$$

$$1 \le j \le N, 2 \le t \le T$$

– Termination:

$$P^* = \max_{1 \le i \le N} [\delta_t(i)] \tag{13}$$

$$q_t^* = arg \max_{1 \le i \le N} [\delta_t(i)] \tag{14}$$

– Backtracking:

$$q_t^* = \psi_t(q_{t+1}^*) \tag{15}$$

$$t = T - 1, T - 2, ..., 1$$

3.3   Solution to Problem 3

Baum-Welch Algorithm [9]:

– Define $\xi(i, j)$ as the probability of being in state i at time t and in state j at time $t + 1$

$$\xi(i, j) = \frac{\alpha_t(i) a_{ij} b_j(o_{t+1}) \beta_{t+1}(j)}{P(O|\lambda)} = \frac{\alpha_t(i) a_{ij} b_j(o_{t+1}) \beta_{t+1}(j)}{\sum_{i=1}^{N} \sum_{j=1}^{N} \alpha_t(i) a_{ij} b_j(o_{t+1}) \beta_{t+1}(j)} \tag{16}$$

– Define $\gamma(i)$ as the probability of being in state i at time t, given observation sequence.

$$\gamma_t(i) = \sum_{j=1}^{N} \xi_t(i, j) \tag{17}$$

– $\sum_{t=1}^{T} \gamma_t(i)$ is the expected number of times state i is visited
– $\sum_{t=1}^{T-1} \xi_t(i, j)$ is the expected number of transition from state i to j

Update rules:

– $\bar{\pi}_i = $ expected frequency in state i at time $(t = 1) = \gamma_1(i)$

- $\bar{a}_{ij}$ = (expected number of transition from state i to state j)/(expected number of transitions from state i:

$$\bar{a}_{ij} = \frac{\sum_t \xi_t(i,j)}{\sum_t \gamma_t(i)} \tag{18}$$

- $\bar{b}_j(k)$ = (expected number of times in state j and oserving symbol k)/(expected number of times in state j:

$$\bar{b}_j(k) = \frac{\sum_{t,o_t=k} \gamma_t(j)}{\sum_t \gamma_t(j)} \tag{19}$$

4   2D HMM

In paper [7], Yujian proposed definitions and proofs of 2D HMM. He has presented several analytic formulae for solving the three basic problems of 2-D HMM. Solution to Problem 2 is usefull., and Viterbi algorithm can be easily adopted to image recognition with two dimensional input data. Unfortunetly, solution to problem 1 and 3 may be use only with one dimensional data - observation vector. Besides presented solutions are for Markov model type "left-right", and not ergodic. So, I present solution to problems 1 and 3 for two dimensional data. The statistical parameters of the 2D model (Fig. 3):

- The number of states of the model N^2
- The number of data streams k_1 x $k_2 = K$
- The number of symbols M
- The transition probabilities of the underlying Markov chain, $A = \{a_{ijl}\}, 1 \leq i, j \leq N, 1 \leq l \leq N^2$, where a_{ij} is the probability of transition from state ij to state l
- The observation probabilities, $B = \{b_{ijm})\}, 1 \leq i, j \leq N, 1 \leq m \leq M$ which represents the probability of gnerate the m_{th} symbol in the ij_{th} state.
- The initial probability, $\Pi = \{\pi_{ijk}\}, 1 \leq i, j \leq N, 1 \leq k \leq K$.
- Oservation sequence $O = \{o_t\}, 1 \leq t \leq T, o_t$ is square matrix simply observation with size k_1 x $k_2 = K$

4.1   Solution to 2D Problem 1

Forward Algorithm

- Define forward variable $\alpha_t(i,j,k)$ as:

$$\alpha_t(i,j,k) = P(o_1, o_2,, o_t, q_t = ij|\lambda) \tag{20}$$

- $\alpha_t(i,j,k)$ is the probability of observing the partial sequence $(o_1, o_2,, o_t)$ such that the the state q_t is i, j for each k_{th} strem of data
- Induction

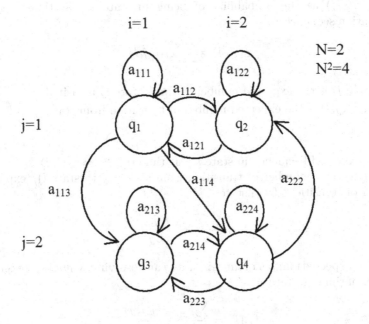

Fig. 3. Two-dimensional ergodic HMM

1. Initialization:

$$\alpha_1(i, j, k) = \pi_{ijk} b_{ij}(o_1) \tag{21}$$

2. Induction:

$$\alpha_{t+1}(i, j, k) = \left[\sum_{l=1}^{N} \alpha_t(i, j, k) a_{ijl} \right] b_{ij}(o_{t+1}) \tag{22}$$

3. Termination:

$$P(O|\lambda) = \sum_{t=1}^{T} \sum_{k=1}^{K} \alpha_T(i, j, k) \tag{23}$$

4.2   Solution to 2D Problem 3

Parameters reestimation Algorithm:

- Define $\xi(i, j, l)$ as the probability of being in state ij at time t and in state l at time $t + 1$ for each k_{th} strem of data

$$\xi_t(i, j, l) = \frac{\alpha_t(i, j, k) a_{ijl} b_{ij}(o_{t+1}) \beta_{t+1}(i, j, k)}{P(O|\lambda)} = \frac{\alpha_t(i, j, k) a_{ijl} b_{ij}(o_{t+1}) \beta_{t+1}(i, j, k)}{\sum_{k=1}^{K} \sum_{l=1}^{N^2} \alpha_t(i, j, k) a_{ijl} b_{ij}(o_{t+1}) \beta_{t+1}(i, j, k)} \tag{24}$$

- Define $\gamma(i,j)$ as the probability of being in state i,j at time t, given observation sequence.

$$\gamma_t(i,j) = \sum_{l=1}^{N^2} \xi_t(i,j,l) \tag{25}$$

- $\sum_{t=1}^{T} \gamma_t(i,j)$ is the expected number of times state ij is visited
- $\sum_{t=1}^{T-1} \xi_t(i,j,l)$ is the expected number of transition from state ij to l

Update rules:

- $\overline{\pi_{ij}}k$ = expected frequency in state i,j at time $(t=1) = \gamma_1(i,j)$
- $\bar{a}_{ij}$ = (expected number of transition from state i,j to state l)/(expected number of transitions from state i,j:

$$\bar{a}_{ijl} = \frac{\sum_t \xi_t(i,j,l)}{\sum_t \gamma_t(i,j)} \tag{26}$$

- $\bar{b}_{ij}(k)$ = (expected number of times in state j and oserving symbol k)/(expected number of times in state j:

$$\bar{b}_{ij}(k) = \frac{\sum_{t,o_t=k} \gamma_t(i,j)}{\sum_t \gamma_t(i,j)} \tag{27}$$

5   Experimenting

The image database *Amsterdam Library of Object Images* was used in experimenting. It is a color image collection of one-thousand small objects, recorded for scientific purposes. In order to capture the sensory variation in object recordings, they systematically varied viewing angle, illumination angle, and illumination color for each object, and additionally captured wide-baseline stereo images. They recorded over a hundred images of each object, yielding a total of 110,250 images for the collection [11],[12].

In order to verify the method has benn selected fifty objects. Three images for learning and three for testing has been chosen for each object. The 2D HMM has been implemented with parameters $N = 5, N^2 = 25, K = 25, M = 50$. Wavelet transform has been chosen as features extraction technigue. Table 1 presents The results of experiments.

Table 1. Comparison of recognition rate

Method	Recognition rate [%]
Eigenvector	94
1D HMM	84
2D HMM	92

6   Conclusion

Article presents real solution for 2D problem in HMM. There is show true 2D HMM which processes 2D data. Hidden Markov models are well-known methods for image processing, but in most cases they convert input observation from 2D to 1D, or create parallel pseudo 2D HMM, which is set of 1D HMMs in fact. This paper describes authentic 2D HMM with two-dimensional input data, and its application for pattern recognition in image processing. The advantage of this solution is that it does not lose the information. In addition, it reduces the complexity of the system because it omitted data conversion step.

References

1. Kompanets, L., Kubanek, M., Rydzek, S.: Czestochowa-Faces and Biometrics of Asymmetrical Face. In: Rutkowski, L., Siekmann, J.H., Tadeusiewicz, R., Zadeh, L.A. (eds.) ICAISC 2004. LNCS (LNAI), vol. 3070, pp. 742–747. Springer, Heidelberg (2004)
2. Eickeler, S., Müller, S., Rigoll, G.: High Performance Face Recognition Using Pseudo 2-D Hidden Markov Models. In: European Control Conference (1999), http://citeseer.ist.psu.edu
3. Vitoantonio Bevilacqua, V., Cariello, L., Carro, G., Daleno, D., Mastronardi, G.: A face recognition system based on Pseudo 2D HMM applied to neural network coefficients. Soft Comput. 12(7), 615–621 (2008)
4. Kubanek, M.: Automatic Methods for Determining the Characteristic Points in Face Image. In: Rutkowski, L., Scherer, R., Tadeusiewicz, R., Zadeh, L.A., Zurada, J.M. (eds.) ICAISC 2010, Part I. LNCS (LNAI), vol. 6113, pp. 523–530. Springer, Heidelberg (2010)
5. Li, J., Najmi, A., Gray, R.M.: Image classification by a two dimensional Hidden Markov model. IEEE Transactions on Signal Processing 48, 517–533 (2000)
6. Joshi, D., Li, J., Wang, J.Z.: A computationally Efficient Approach to the estimation of two- and three-dimensional hidden Markov models. IEEE Transactions on Image Processing 15(7), 1871–1886 (2006)
7. Li, Y.: An analytic solution for estimating two-dimensional hidden Markov models. Applied Mathematics and Computation 185, 810–822 (2007)
8. Rabiner, L.R.: A tutorial on hidden Markov models and selected application in speech recognition. Proc. IEEE 77, 257–285 (1989)
9. Kanungo, T.: Hidden Markov Model Tutorial (1999), http://www.kanungo.com/software/hmmtut.pdf
10. Forney, G.D.: The Viterbi Algorithm. Proc. IEEE 61(3), 268–278 (1973)
11. Geusebroek, J.M., Burghouts, G.J., Smeulders, A.W.M.: The Amsterdam library of object images. Int. J. Comput. Vision 61(1), 103–112 (2005)
12. Amsterdam Library of Object Images, http://www.science.uva.nl/~aloi

Video Compression Algorithm Based on Neural Networks

Robert Cierniak and Michal Knop

Institute of Computational Intelligence, Czestochowa University of Technology
Armii Krajowej 36, 42-200 Czestochowa, Poland

Abstract. This paper describes a concept of algorithm dedicated to video compression. In our approach we use an algorithm named the predictive vector quantization (PVQ). Into this scheme of image compression a competitive neural networks quantizer and a neural networks predictor are incorporated. In our paper, we extend this neural image compression approach to a new method of video compression. We also used the image histogram method to detect scene changes, what have to improve the video compression performance. The experimental results are presented and discussed.

1 Introduction

Video and image compression is commonly used in todays multimedia data transmission. There are various techniques of coding the data in order to reduce video data redundancy. Most of the algorithms and codecs combine a spatial compensation of images as well as movement compensation in time. They can be found in following applications:

1. broadcast, subscription, and pay-per-view services over satellite, cable, and terrestrial transmission channels (e.g., using H.222.0 / MPEG-2 systems [1]);
2. wire-line and wireless real-time conversational services (e.g., using H.32x [2] or Session Initiation Protocol (SIP) [3]);
3. Internet or local area network (LAN) video streaming (using Real-Time Protocol/Internet Protocol (RTP/IP) [4]);
4. storage formats (e.g., digital versatile disk (DVD), digital camcorders, and personal video recorders) [5].

Currently, there are many compression standards. The most popular are JPEG and MPEG. They differ in the level of compression as well as application. JPEG and JPEG2000 standards are used for image compression with an adjustable compression rate. MPEG standard contains a whole family of international compression standards of audiovisual digital data compression. The best known standards are MPEG-1, MPEG-2, and MPEG-4. More information on the MPEG standards can be found in literature [6].

In our work, we used a PVQ (Predictive Vector Quantization) algorithm to compress a video sequence. It is a combination of a VQ (Vector Quantization)

L. Rutkowski et al. (Eds.): ICAISC 2013, Part I, LNAI 7894, pp. 524–531, 2013.

[7], [8], and DPCM (Differential Pulse Code Modulation). More information on the techniques can be found in sources [9], [10], [11]. Additionally, we used image histograms in order to detect a scene change [12], which is necessary to change parameters of the predictor and the codebook.

2   Video Compression Algorithm

This paper describes a compression algorithm which is designed based on the existing algorithm described in [9], [10], [11]. It also has been extended to include a scene change detection algorithm, based on a comparison of histograms of each frame of a film. Diagram of the proposed algorithm is shown in Fig. 1.

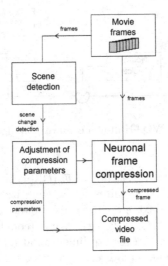

Fig. 1. Neronal video compression algorithm

2.1   Neuronal Compression VQDPCM

The architecture of the predictive vector quantization algorithm (PVQ), as depicted in fig. 2 [11] is a vector extension of the scalar differential pulse code modulation scheme [9], [10] combined with Huffman coding.

The following elements form the block diagram of the PVQ algorithm: encoder and decoder, each containing an identical neural-predictor, codebook and neural vector quantizer (other approaches are possible too, for example using neuro-fuzzy systems, see e.g. [13]-[19]), and Huffman coder. The successive input vectors $\mathbf{V}(t)$ are introduced to the encoder. The difference $\mathbf{E}(t) = [e_1(t), e_2(t), ..., e_q(t)]^T$ given by the equation

$$\mathbf{E}(t) = \mathbf{V}(t) - \overline{\mathbf{V}}(t) \tag{1}$$

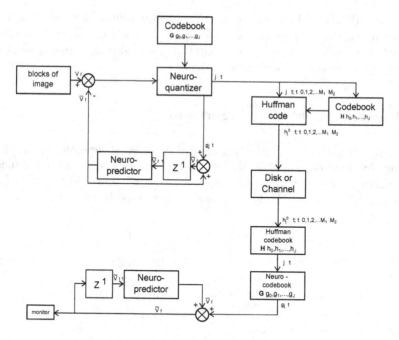

Fig. 2. PVQ+Huffman compression algorithm

is formed, where: $\overline{\mathbf{V}}(t) = [\overline{v}_1(t), \overline{v}_2(t), ..., \overline{v}_q(t)]^T$ is the predictor of $\mathbf{V}(t)$. Statistically, the difference $\mathbf{E}(t)$ requires fewer quantization bits than the original subimage $\mathbf{V}(t)$. The next step is vector quantization of $\mathbf{E}(t)$ using the set of reproduction vectors $\mathbf{G} = [\mathbf{g}_0, \mathbf{g}_1, ..., \mathbf{g}_J]$ (codebook), where $\mathbf{g}_j = [g_{1j}, g_{2j}, ..., g_{qj}]^T$ (codewords). For every q-dimensional difference vector $\mathbf{E}(t)$, the distortion (usually the mean square error) between $\mathbf{E}(t)$ and every codeword $\mathbf{g}_j$, $j = 0, 1, ..., J-1$ is computed. The codeword $\mathbf{g}_{j^0}(t)$ is selected as the representation vector for $\mathbf{E}(t)$ if

$$d_{j^0} = \min_{0 \le j \le J} d_j, \tag{2}$$

a measure d in expression (2) we can take e.g. the Euclidean distance. Observe that by adding the prediction vector $\overline{\mathbf{V}}(t)$ to the quantized difference vector $\mathbf{g}_{j^0}(t)$ we get the reconstructed approximation $\widetilde{\mathbf{V}}(t)$ of the original input vector $\mathbf{V}(t)$, i.e.

$$\widetilde{\mathbf{V}}(t) = \overline{\mathbf{V}}(t) + \mathbf{g}_{j^0}(t). \tag{3}$$

The prediction vector $\overline{\mathbf{V}}(t)$ of the input vector $\mathbf{V}(t)$ is made from past observation of reconstructed vector $\widetilde{\mathbf{V}}(t-1)$. In our approach, the predictor is a nonlinear neural network specifically designed for this purpose. Finally, the set of the $j^0(t)$ is coded by the Huffman coder. The codebook of the Huffman coder is designed using a set of counters f_j which count how frequently given label $j^0(t)$ araises after presentation of all vectors $\mathbf{V}(t)$. The appropriate codewords $h^0(t)$

from the Huffman codebook are broadcasted via the transmission channel to the decoder. In the decoder, first the codewords $h^0(t)$ transmitted by the channel are decoded using the Huffman codebook and then inverse vector-quantized. Next, the reconstructed vector $\tilde{V}(t)$ is formed in the same manner as in the encoder (see formula (3)).

2.2 Scene Detection

Let us assume that the function $d(j_i, f_j)$ is calculated by comparison of histograms of each color space of two frames (f_i, f_j) [20], [21], and it is defined by equation

$$d(f_i, f_j) = (|H_i r(k) - H_j r(k)| + |H_i g(k) - H_j g(k)| + |H_i b(k) - H_j b(k)|) \quad (4)$$

where $H_i r(k), H_i g(k), H_i b(k)$ describe value of color k in the histogram for individual color space (r,g,b) of frame f_i [12]. Using weight of brightness for each color space from (4), equation can be defined as

$$d(f_i, f_j) = (|H_i r(k) - H_j r(k)| * \alpha + |H_i g(k) - H_j g(k)| * \beta + |H_i b(k) - H_j b(k)| * \gamma) \quad (5)$$

where α, β, γ describe constant value of brightness level for digital image and have a value of $\alpha = 0.3$, $\beta = 0.59$, $\gamma = 0.11$. Using statistical analysis to emphasize the differences in two frames, comparison test $X^2(dx^2(f_i, f_j))$ is an effective method for scene change detection by comparison of image histograms. Equation can be defined as

$$dx^2(f_i, f_j) = \begin{cases} \sum \frac{(H_i(k) - H_j(k))^2}{MAX(H_i(k), H_j(k))} & , if H_i, H_j \neq 0 \\ 0 & , otherwise \end{cases} \quad (6)$$

Methods based on image histograms may have a problem to detect differences in the two images with similar color distribution, because histograms do not store information about the space. The solution to this problem could be a comparison of the distributions of the histogram in the local area of the frame. The value of differences of the frame by comparing the color histograms for each block and its accumulation is determined as follows

$$d(f_i, f_j) = \sum_{bl=1}^{m} DP(f_i, f_j, bl), \quad (7)$$

where

$$DP(f_i, f_j, bl) = \sum_{k=1}^{N} |H_i(k, bl) - H_j(k, bl)| \quad (8)$$

$H_i(k, bl)$ describes the color value k in the histogram in the block bl in frame(f_i), and m is the total number of blocks. Divided into local distribution histogram has a lot of the previously mentioned advantages. In addition, equation (5) can apply a weighting for each color space. Equation (6) allows to use statistical methods, and the equation (7) split the image into blocks. Combining all these methods we obtain the equation to determine the difference in the compared frames and define it as follows

$$d(f_i, f_j, bl) = \sum_{bl=1}^{m} Dx^2(f_i, f_j, bl) \tag{9}$$

where

$$Dx^2(f_i, f_j, bl) = \sum_{k=1}^{N} \left[\frac{(H_i r(k) - H_j r(k))^2}{MAX(H_i r(k), H_j r(k))} * \alpha \right] + \tag{10}$$

$$\left[\frac{(H_i g(k) - H_j g(k))^2}{MAX(H_i g(k), H_j g(k))} * \beta \right] + \left[\frac{(H_i b(k) - H_j b(k))^2}{MAX(H_i b(k), H_j b(k))} * \gamma \right]$$

In the equation above, $H_i r(k)$, $H_i g(k)$, $H_i b(k)$ describe the color value k in the histogram for each of the color space (r, g, b), N denotes the maximum value of the color in the image, and m is a total number of blocks in the image. The difference value computed from eq. (10) was divided by the number of pixels within an image block, and the sum of the differences in eq. (9) was divided by the number of blocks m of the image division. The obtained results were then normalized to values between 0 and 1. The diagram of the algorithm is presented in Fig. 3.

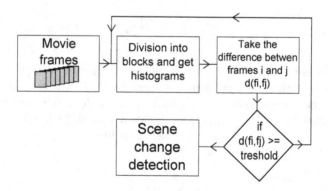

Fig. 3. Scene change detection algorithm

3   Experimental Result

In the presented solution, we used frames extracted directly from a video file which had a resolution of 576x416 and 256 levels of grey. Next, we performed four tests of the efficiency of the algorithm. In the first and second case, the frames were compressed within single scene. In the first experiment we compressed frames creating a separate codebook and a predictor for each of them (Fig.4b). In the second approach we applied a single codebook and a predictor to all frames (Fig.4c).

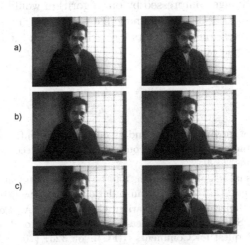

Fig. 4. a)original sequence b)compressed sequence test 1 c)compressed sequence test 2

In the third and fourth tests the compressed frames were in a transit between scenes. The third experiment assumed the use of the same codebook and a predictor when the scenes changed (Fig.5b). The results show that this approach is insufficient in case of a major change of the scene. In the last case, when a scene change was detected a new codebook and a predictor were created (Fig.5c).

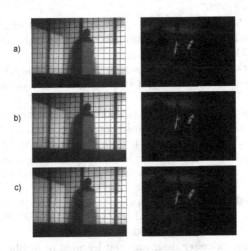

Fig. 5. a)original sequence b)compressed sequence test 3 c)compressed sequence test 4

4   Conclusions

The simulations have shown the usefulness of scene change detection algorithm for the presented compression algorithm. Our experiments show that without scene detection an image compressed by our algorithm would be saddled with a big mistake. On the other hand, the image file would contain too much information about the compression parameters for each frame, in the case of appending that information to the output file.

References

1. Generic coding of moving pictures and associated audio information–Part 1: Systems. Int. Telecommun. Union-Telecommun. (ITU-T), Recommendation H.222.0 (MPEG-2 Systems) (1994)
2. Narrow-band visual telephone systems and terminal equipment. Int. Telecommun. Union-Telecommun. (ITU-T), Recommendation H.320 (1999)
3. Rosenberg, J., Schulzrinne, H., Camarillo, G., Johnston, A., Peterson, J., Sparks, R., Handley, M., Schooler, E.: SIP: Session Initiation Protocol. Internet Eng. Task Force (IETF). Request for Comments (RFC), vol. 3261 (2002)
4. Schulzrinne, H., Casner, S., Frederick, R., Jacobson, V.: RTP: A transport protocol for real-time applications. Internet Eng. Task Force (IETF). Request for Comments (RFC), vol. 1889 (1996)
5. Sullivan, G.J., Wiegand, T.: Video Compression–From Concepts to the H.264/AVC Standard. Proceedings of the IEEE 93, 18–31 (2005)
6. Clarke, R.J.: Digital compression of still images and video. Academic Press, London (1995)
7. Gray, R.: Vector quantization. IEEE ASSP Magazine 1, 4–29 (1984)
8. Gersho, A., Gray, R.M.: Vector quantization and signal compression. Kluwer Academic Publishers (1992)
9. Rutkowski, L., Cierniak, R.: Image compression by competitive learning neural networks and predictive vector quantization. Applied Mathematics and Computer Science 6, 706–711 (1996)
10. Cierniak, R., Rutkowski, L.: On image compression by competitive neural networks and optimal linear predictors. Signal Processing: Image Communication 15, 559–565 (2000)
11. Cierniak, R.: An Image Compression Algorithm Based on Neural Networks. In: Rutkowski, L., Siekmann, J.H., Tadeusiewicz, R., Zadeh, L.A. (eds.) ICAISC 2004. LNCS (LNAI), vol. 3070, pp. 706–711. Springer, Heidelberg (2004)
12. Patel, K., Tiwari, M., Singh, J.: Video water marking using abrupt scene detection. International Journal of Computer Technology and Electronics Engineering 1, 187–189 (2011)
13. Cpałka, K.: A method for designing flexible neuro-fuzzy systems. In: Rutkowski, L., Tadeusiewicz, R., Zadeh, L.A., Żurada, J.M. (eds.) ICAISC 2006. LNCS (LNAI), vol. 4029, pp. 212–219. Springer, Heidelberg (2006)
14. Cpałka, K.: On evolutionary designing and learning of flexible neuro-fuzzy structures for nonlinear classification. Nonlinear Analysis Series A: Theory, Methods and Applications 71, e1659–e1672 (2009)

15. Przybył, A., Cpałka, K.: A new method to construct of interpretable models of dynamic systems. In: Rutkowski, L., Korytkowski, M., Scherer, R., Tadeusiewicz, R., Zadeh, L.A., Zurada, J.M. (eds.) ICAISC 2012, Part II. LNCS (LNAI), vol. 7268, pp. 697–705. Springer, Heidelberg (2012)
16. Zalasiński, M., Cpałka, K.: Novel algorithm for the on-line signature verification. In: Rutkowski, L., Korytkowski, M., Scherer, R., Tadeusiewicz, R., Zadeh, L.A., Zurada, J.M. (eds.) ICAISC 2012, Part II. LNCS, vol. 7268, pp. 362–367. Springer, Heidelberg (2012)
17. Rutkowski, L.: Real-time identification of time-varying systems by non-parametric algorithms based on Parzen kernels. International Journal of Systems Science 16, 1123–1130 (1985)
18. Rutkowski, L.: Application of multiple Fourier series to identification of multivariable nonstationary systems. International Journal of Systems Science 20(10), 1993–2002 (1989)
19. Rutkowski, L.: Generalized regression neural networks in time-varying environment. IEEE Trans. Neural Networks 15, 576–596 (2004)
20. Lam, C.F., Lee, M.-C.: Video segmentation using color difference histogram. In: Ip, H.H.-S., Smeulders, A.W.M. (eds.) MINAR 1998. LNCS, vol. 1464, pp. 159–174. Springer, Heidelberg (1998)
21. Yeo, B.L., Liu, B.: Rapid scene analysis on compressed video. IEEE Transactions on Circuits and Systems for Video Technology 5, 533–544 (1995)

Online Crowdsource System Supporting Ground Truth Datasets Creation

Paweł Drozda, Krzysztof Sopyła, and Przemysław Górecki

Department of Mathematics and Computer Sciences,
University of Warmia and Mazury, Olsztyn, Poland
ksopyla@uwm.edu.pl, {pdrozda,pgorecki}@matman.uwm.edu.pl

Abstract. This paper proposes a design of a system for creating image similarity datasets which are necessary for testing the quality of supervised ranking algorithms. In particular, the main goal is to facilitate the creation of similar images rankings for given a imaginary dataset. The system was designed in a manner that involves user feedback in the process of creating the rankings. In each iteration of ranking construction, the query image and twelve candidates are presented to the user, who is intended to select the most similar one. Moreover, in order to accelerate the method convergence the approach based on simulated annealing is adapted. It initially chooses the images randomly from a dataset and in the later stages the images with rank rate above zero are chosen with certain probability.

Keywords: System Design, CBIR, Simulated Annealing.

1 Introduction

The dynamic development of artificial intelligence methods and particularly learning from data techniques causes continuous increase in the volume of learning datasets. Such datasets contain elements each composed of particular objects with a specified decision. Learning algorithms, based on the data from the dataset, form the decision model. With the use of the decision model, for any new object the correct decision is taken with high probability. Among the supervised learning techniques, there can be distinguished:

- classification, where the training set contains the objects assigned to the one of the predefined classes,
- multi-label classification, where the object is identified by a number of classes,
- regressions, where the object contains the real-value label,
- ranking, where the feedback is designated as the order of the relevant collection of objects.

The creation of an adequate training dataset is a challenging and time consuming task. Firstly, it is necessary to collect a sufficiently large number of data samples which carry out full latent information about the considered domain.

L. Rutkowski et al. (Eds.): ICAISC 2013, Part I, LNAI 7894, pp. 532–539, 2013.

Collecting the required number of data in many cases becomes difficult, as in the medical field where frequently we only have a few positive instances (patients with a particularly rare disease). On the other hand, we can be flooded with noisy data obtained from sensors. Another important issue during the dataset creation is tagging all objects in an appropriate manner. The problems at this stage may be: the lack of the necessary expertise knowledge to carry out object evaluation or assessment by a too narrow group of users resulting in biased labeling.

To overcome the above-mentioned problems, systems supporting the process of creating training dataset were developed, where the power of crowd is exploited. Humans are treated as computational units for solving hard AI problems. The crowdsourcing idea involves encouraging people from all over the world via the web system to tag data, create or collect new instances. This approach is beginning to be used by research centers or large corporations, for instance, the platform prepared by Amazon - Mechanical Turk [12], [13] allows to delegate many tasks in the field of artificial intelligence to Internet community, such as identifying objects in a photo or video, performing data de-duplication and transcribing audio recordings. These kinds of systems were also widely used in the field of bioinformatics, where data is large and have many spatial relations. For example, the Foldit system [2], [9] is directed to protein structure prediction, EteRNA - was design to find and create RNA knots, polyhedra, and other shapes never before seen, while PHYLO [8] helps to create better algorithms for multiple sequence alignments.

This paper describes the PicRank system, which supports the process of creating rankings for visually similar images. The system uses human recognition capabilities for assessing image similarity and applies AI techniques to obtain image ordering. The creation of a full ranking for the group of N images involves determining for each query image the order of the remaining images in terms of their visual similarity. The most commonly used methods are based on similarity relations. The system presents the query image and certain number of randomly selected elements to the user and the user's task is to select the most similar picture. Combining feedback from all users, the partial order relation on the set of objects is received, on the basis which the final images ranking is formed. Such a procedure for a single query requires the display of $O(N^2)$ examples, and in order to obtain unbiased results, many users should be involved in ranking creation.

To accelerate convergence of the ranking creation process in PicRank the selective procedure of images choice was implemented, which was inspired by Simulated Annealing. It enables increasing the accuracy of the ranking established while keeping the ability to explore whole image dataset.

The paper is organized as follows. Next section presents different approaches to ranking creation. In section 3 a detailed description of the proposed method is presented. Section 4 shows PicRank system architecture and explains design concepts. Conclusions and future directions are pointed out in Section 5.

2   Ranking Algorithms

The ranking creation could be considered in two aspects. The first one connected with scoring and ordering query results in information retrieval systems and the second one for player evaluation in games or tournaments. Both have to compute the score for each object. These computations however take into account different components.

Search rankings are mainly based on the object's features and its connections to other documents [11]. Most algorithms use different similarity measures to determine how close each relevant instance is to the query specified by the user. Having previously recoded ranking data collected from a narrow group of users, the common practice is to apply machine learning techniques[7,16,10] to re-rank documents and predict ordering for future, unseen data [14,1,5]. Considering this aspect of ranking creation, our paper tries to deal with the problem of gathering ordered data relying on user feedback. Having ordered data, the ranked image dataset essential for the evaluation of new ranking algorithms is built.

The second group of methods is related to ranking players for different kinds of games. In this group, the score is computed on the basis of the player's and its opponents' game statistics, such as number of wins, losses, draws and current ranking position. These methods have been used for chess player rankings for a long time and presently, they have attracted a lot of attention due to their suitability for player or team matching in online multi-player games [6]. Good scoring system provides useful information about players skills and thus, team matching algorithm could create balanced games. The well known chess ranking system ELO [3] is based on statistical foundations, where the model tries to asses which of the two players is likely to win. The correct ranking should be a good estimator of the game expected value. When the game is finished, the ranking is updated and the different amount of points can be granted depending on the opponent's ranking. In particular, a win against a high rated player results in a greater number of points than winning against a low rated competitor. When considering a defeat, analogous rules are applied. The TrueSkill ranking system [6] follows a different approach, where rather than assuming a single fixed score for the player, the system estimates its belief using a Gaussian distribution and associates its mean μ ranking position and standard deviation σ with the user. With the increase of the number of games played, the estimation of μ and σ is closer to true values and thus the belief of user rank is stronger.

This paper adopts game rankings in creating datasets, as it turned out to be a useful technique for improving and accelerating the process of creating the datasets where all the information about objects similarity comes from user feedback. Each user session could be treated as a game, where the game participants are images. The winning image, pointed out by the user, is the most similar to the query image. When all wins, losses and draws in all games associated with query image are counted, we are able to assign the score to each image and assess the visual similarity (aggregated from many users feedback).

3   Process of Ranking Creation

In order to obtain a complete ranking for the particular dataset, it is necessary to find partial order for each query image ' $\prec_q$ ' where $q \in 1 \ldots N$ and N is the size of the dataset. The vast majority of methods try to make approximation by pairwise comparison. For example, query image (pic_q) and two other random pictures (pic_i, pic_j) from the dataset are shown to the user and his task is to choose the most similar one to pic_q. This gives information about order between pic_i, pic_j, if pic_i is more similar than pic_j than $pic_i \prec_q pic_j$. This approach scales poorly for big sets: firstly, for one ranking we have to asses ($\frac{N*(N-1)}{2}$) image pairs and secondly, we have to obtain N such rankings and finally in order to get unbiased results this procedure should be repeated for many users. To sum up, we found that procedure for creating complete ranking has $O(M * N^3)$ complexity, where N - dataset size, M- number of involved users.

The above-mentioned difficulties could be overcome by making some approximations. In particular, during ranking creation procedure, only first k ranked elements are taken into account, which significantly reduces creation time. This observation leads to the method which firstly finds coarse ordering and in the latter stages focuses only on improving ranking of first k positions. We found that this approach is analogous to Simulated Annealing, where at the beginning of the algorithm we are likely to accept bad candidates and in the later stages we focus only on better solutions. Acceptance of bad solutions is associated with specified probability distribution and parameter T (temperature), where the parameter T decreases during algorithm execution. It results in a constantly decreasing probability of bad solutions acceptance.

In the context of ranking creation, the initial stages should ensure a relevant set of candidates in terms of similarity to the query image, and not necessarily well-ordered. Then, further phases should focus on intra-ranking ordering. For this reason our approach oscillates between showing the user random images and the images coming from the partial ranking created before. Inspired by Simulated Annealing the probability associated with choosing random pictures decreases with the particular cooling scheme. Each picture set presented to the user contains 12 examples and forms a game for the particular query image. The game winner (the image most similar to the query) is specified by the user and the rest of examples are marked as losers. Rankings are created on the basis of the number of game wins and losses associated with the particular query image. The summary of presented procedure in this section is shown in Algorithm 1.

4   System Architecture and Design

In order to enable multiple users to participate in the creation of datasets the system is available via Internet http://picrank.eastgroup.pl and for the purpose of assessing the similarity the user is not forced to log in. No necessity of logging into the system was intended to attract users to take part in generating collections of rankings. The system was built according to the Model View

---

Algorithm 1. Ranking creation procedure

Require: $T-$ initial temperature parameter
Require: $DataSet-$ imaginary dataset
Require: $CoolingScheme-$ chosen temperature decreasing schedule
Require: $RankingMethod-$ chosen ranking score algorithm
1: **repeat**
2:     $queryImage = RandomImage(DataSet)$
3:     $rankingGame = CreateRankingGame(queryImage)$
4:     **if** $P_{accept\_rand}(iter, T) > random()$ **then**
5:         $gameParticipants = AddGameParticipiants(rankingGame, DataSet, 12)$
6:     **else**
7:         $partialRankingSet = GetRanking(queryImage)$
8:         $gameParticipants = AddGameParticipiants(rankingGame, partialRankingSet, 12)$
9:     **end if**
10:     $GenerateGameView(rankingGame)$
11:     $mostSimilarImg = WatiForUserFeedback()$
12:     $MarkAsGameWinner(rankingGame, queryImage, mostSimilarImg)$
13:     $MarkAsGameLoser((rankingGame, queryImage, mostSimilarImg)$
14:     $iter = iter + 1$
15:     $T = CalculateTemperature(CoolingScheme, iter, T)$
16: **until** Ranking created
17: **for all** $queryImage$ in $DataSet$ **do**
18:     **for all** $image$ in $DataSet$ **do**
19:         $score = ComputeRankingScore(image, queryImage, RankingMethod)$
20:     **end for**
21: **end for**

Controller (MVC) standard with the use of ASP. Net MVC 3.0 framework. The entire infrastructure is based on Windows Server 2008, IIS 7.0 web server and database management server MS SQL Server 2008.

The system was divided into independent modules in a flexible mode, which would make it possible to easily modify, replace, expand and add any modules or algorithms. A crucial role in the system is played by the candidates selection mechanisms for a particular game and the method in which the ranking is created, since they significantly affect the relevance of the considered dataset. In case of the system described in this paper, the mechanism of candidates selection is based on the Simulated Annealing method (as described in section 3), while the position in the ranking is determined by sorting the ratios of the games won to the sum of all games played in relation to the considered query image. It is worth a notice that each of the images is on the ranking lists of all the other images from the dataset.

In the PicRank system there are two types of actors: the first, the standard user, who is intended to rank similarity of images and the administrator, who in addition to participating in ranking creation, should manage datasets and generate the current ranking based on the votes of all users. In order to create a new dataset, the administrator has to load a compressed folder with images to the server. At the time of loading the dataset to the server all the basic information about the dataset in question are added to the table DataSets (see database diagram on Figure 1), while the image data go to the table Pictures. It should be noted, that each image has a reference to the dataset it belongs. Among the available collections on the server, the administrator selects all the datasets for which the evaluation may be conducted.

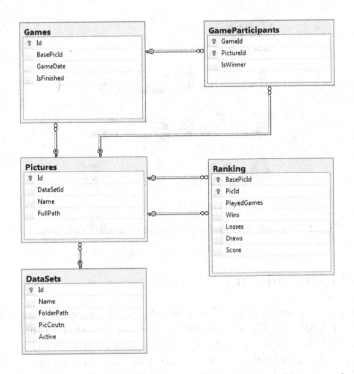

Fig. 1. Part of database diagram connected with ranking procedure

At the time when the user enters the page, a randomly selected query image and twelve candidates from one of the available datasets are displayed to him and a game associated with the query image is created. This is illustrated in Games table by adding appropriate entries of the game, while in the table GameParticipants the selected candidates are added. One of the candidates designated by the user as the most similar to the query image, is regarded as the game winner and IsWinner field is set to true for him and for the rest of images IsWinner field is set to false. On the basis of the games played, the number of wins, losses and draws the Score field from the table Ranking (from 0 to 1) is calculated. The value of the Score field indicates the position in the ranking for the query image (BasePicId), where a higher value means a better place in the ranking.

The created system was used to produce a set of rankings in a far shorter time when comparing to the time needed for creating a ranking in a standard manner by a single user. In addition, due to the feedback from many different users, the global user preference and final results are unbiased. An example of a ranking dataset was created for different types of shoes. Dataset contains 200 images in 4 shoe categories. A sample ranking for particular sneakers is shown on Figure 2, which can be obtained through the administration panel.

Fig. 2. Example of a generated sneaker ranking with scores

5   Conclusion and Future Work

This paper presents the PicRank [15] system for creating ranked image datasets based on user feedback. The crowdsourcing idea improved the ranking quality and accelerated the whole process. Our approach is inspired by the Simulated Annealing algorithm where in order to speed up the convergence to the final ranking, decreasing probability was used in a similar manner. During ranking creation the system shows the images for which the user has to assess similarity from a random collection or from a partial ranking created before.

Further research will focus on implementation of new ranking scores such as Elo chess ranking [3] and methods of choosing game participants. It is important to test and evaluate different cooling schedules like: logarithmic [4] or geometric.

Acknowledgments. The research has been supported by grant N N516 480940 from The National Science Center of the Republic of Poland and by grant 1309-802 from Ministry of Science and Higher Education of the Republic of Poland.

References

1. Collins, M., Duffy, N.: New ranking algorithms for parsing and tagging: Kernels over discrete structures, and the voted perceptron. In: ACL, pp. 263–270 (2002)
2. Cooper, S., Khatib, F., Treuille, A., Barbero, J., Lee, J., Beenen, M., Leaver-Fay, A., Baker, D., Popović, Z., Foldit Players: Predicting protein structures with a multiplayer online game. Nature 466(7307), 756–760 (2010)

3. Elo, A.E.: The Rating of Chess Players, Past and Present. Ishi Press (2008)
4. Geman, S., Geman, D.: Stochastic relaxation, Gibbs distributions and the Bayesian restoration of images. IEEE Transactions on Pattern Analysis and Machine Intelligence 6(6), 721–741 (1984)
5. Górecki, P., Sopyła, K., Drozda, P.: Ranking by K-means voting algorithm for similar image retrieval. In: Rutkowski, L., Korytkowski, M., Scherer, R., Tadeusiewicz, R., Zadeh, L.A., Zurada, J.M. (eds.) ICAISC 2012, Part I. LNCS, vol. 7267, pp. 509–517. Springer, Heidelberg (2012)
6. Herbrich, R., Minka, T., Graepel, T.: TrueSkill(TM): A Bayesian Skill Rating System, vol. 20 (2007)
7. Joachims, T.: Optimizing search engines using clickthrough data. In: Proceedings of the Eighth ACM SIGKDD International Conference on Knowledge Discovery and Data Mining, KDD 2002, pp. 133–142. ACM, New York (2002)
8. Kawrykow, A., Roumanis, G., Kam, A., Kwak, D., Leung, C., Wu, C., Zarour, E., Sarmenta, L., Blanchette, M., Waldispühl, J., Phylo players: Phylo: A citizen science approach for improving multiple sequence alignment. PLoS ONE 7(3), e31362 (2012)
9. Khatib, F., Cooper, S., Tyka, M.D., Xu, K., Makedon, I., Popović, Z., Baker, D., Foldit Players: Algorithm discovery by protein folding game players. Proceedings of the National Academy of Sciences 108(47), 18949–18953 (2011)
10. Korytkowski, M., Nowicki, R., Rutkowski, L., Scherer, R.: Adaboost ensemble of DCOG rough–neuro–fuzzy systems. In: Jędrzejowicz, P., Nguyen, N.T., Hoang, K. (eds.) ICCCI 2011, Part I. LNCS, vol. 6922, pp. 62–71. Springer, Heidelberg (2011)
11. Page, L., Brin, S., Motwani, R., Winograd, T.: The pagerank citation ranking: Bringing order to the web. Technical Report 1999-66, Stanford InfoLab. Previous number = SIDL-WP-1999-0120 (November 1999)
12. Paolacci, G., Chandler, J., Ipeirotis, P.G.: Running experiments on amazon mechanical turk. Judgment and Decision Making 5(5), 411–419 (2010)
13. Ross, J., Irani, L., Silberman, M.S., Zaldivar, A., Tomlinson, B.: Who are the crowdworkers?: shifting demographics in mechanical turk. In: Proceedings of the 28th of the International Conference Extended Abstracts on Human Factors in Computing Systems, CHI EA 2010, pp. 2863–2872. ACM, New York (2010)
14. Shen, L., Joshi, A.K.: Ranking and reranking with perceptron. Machine Learning, 73–96 (2005)
15. Sopyła, K., Drozda, P., Górecki, P.: Picrank - online crowdsource system for image ranking creation (2012)
16. Sopyła, K., Drozda, P., Górecki, P.: SVM with CUDA accelerated kernels for big sparse problems. In: Rutkowski, L., Korytkowski, M., Scherer, R., Tadeusiewicz, R., Zadeh, L.A., Zurada, J.M. (eds.) ICAISC 2012, Part I. LNCS, vol. 7267, pp. 439–447. Springer, Heidelberg (2012)

Object Detection by Simple Fuzzy Classifiers Generated by Boosting

Marcin Gabryel, Marcin Korytkowski, Rafał Scherer, and Leszek Rutkowski

Institute of Computational Intelligence, Częstochowa University of Technology
al. Armii Krajowej 36, 42-200 Częstochowa, Poland
{marcin.gabryel,marcin.korytkowski,rafal.scherer,
leszek.rutkowski}@iisi.pcz.pl
http://iisi.pcz.pl

Abstract. Finding key points based on SURF and SIFT and size of their vector reduction is a classical approach for object recognition systems. In this paper we present a new framework for object recognition based on generating simple fuzzy classifiers using key points and boosting meta learning to distinguish between one known class and other classes. We tested proposed approach on a known image dataset.

1 Introduction

The problem of image recognition on the basis of its content is a one of the most important computer science challenges [12][13][14]. Finding keypoints based on SURF [2] and SIFT [9] and keypoint vectors dimensionality reduction is the classical approach for object recognition systems. The main contribution of this paper is to find the set of fuzzy rules which are representative for some class of objects. Fuzzy systems are very efficient method for describing partial membership to a set [3][4][5][11][16]. This approach could be very useful for the search based on the image content in a set of complex graphical objects in a database. In addition, creating an optimal set of indexes could accelerate this process. The general scheme of our approach is as follows:

- Determining key points for a set of images, the content of which belong to the same class (e.g. airplanes) using SURF or SIFT algorithms (positive examples),
- Determining key points for different classes using SURF or SIFT algorithms (negative examples),
- Dimensionality reduction using principal component analysis (PCA) algorithm by using both the positive and negative samples (vector size of 128 numbers is reduced to 36),
- Design of a fuzzy classifier based on the AdaBoost algorithm and assigning weights to each of its rules.

The main idea of this paper is suggested in papers [17] and [20] where the authors changed slightly the basis of Adaboost algorithm. They use the whole set

L. Rutkowski et al. (Eds.): ICAISC 2013, Part I, LNAI 7894, pp. 540–547, 2013.
© Springer-Verlag Berlin Heidelberg 2013

of training examples to build many classifiers, then they choose the best model according to the error value. We are going back to the original AdaBoost. In each step we randomly choose one positive example according to their weights. This example is a base to build final classifiers. We also introduced other changes to the original concept where the authors searched for the most important samples. We are going to find the most important classes of descriptors representing objects of certain type. In our case, all classifiers are neuro-fuzzy models.

The paper is organized as follows. In the first section we present basis of algorithms which are used to build the proposed solution. It consists of algorithms to generate keypoints (SURF, SIFT etc.), algorithms for size of keypoints reduction (PCA), algorithms for modular systems building (AdaBoost) and fuzzy logic. Next section describes the proposed method and Section 3 provides simulation results.

2 Methods Used in Proposed Approach

2.1 Boosting

This section describes the AdaBoost algorithm which is the most popular boosting method [15]. The algorithm described here is designed for binary classification. Let us denote the l-th learning vector by $\mathbf{z}^l = [x_1^l, ..., x_n^l, y^l]$, $l = 1...m$ is the number of a vector in the learning sequence, n is the dimension of input vector $\mathbf{x}^l$, and y^l is the learning class label. Weights D^l assigned to learning vectors, have to fulfill the following conditions

$$(i)\ 0 < D^l < 1\ ,$$
$$(ii)\ \sum_{l=1}^{m} D^l = 1\ . \tag{1}$$

The weight D^l is the information how well classifiers were learned in consecutive steps of an algorithm for a given input vector x^l. Vector $\mathbf{D}$ for all input vectors is initialized according to the following equation

$$D_t^l = \frac{1}{m}, \quad \text{for } t = 0, ..., T\ , \tag{2}$$

where t is the number of a boosting iteration (and a number of a classifier in the ensemble). Let $\{h_t(\mathbf{x}) : t = 1, ..., T\}$ denotes a set of hypotheses obtained in consecutive steps t of the algorithm being described. For simplicity we limit our problem to a binary classification (dichotomy) i.e. $y \in \{-1, 1\}$ or $h_t(\mathbf{x}) = \pm 1$. Similarly to learning vectors weights, we assign a weight c_t for every hypothesis, such that

$$(i)\ \sum_{t=1}^{T} c_t = 1\ ,$$
$$(ii)\ c_t > 0\ . \tag{3}$$

Now in the AdaBoost algorithm we repeat steps 1-4 for $t = 1, ..., T$:

1. Create hypothesis h_t and train it with a data set with respect to a distribution d_t for input vectors.
2. Compute the classification error ε_t of a trained classifier h_t according to the formula

$$\varepsilon_t = \sum_{l=1}^{m} D_t^l(z^l) I(h_t(\mathbf{x}^l) \neq y^l) , \qquad (4)$$

where I is the indicator function

$$I(a \neq b) = \begin{cases} 1 \text{ if } a \neq b \\ 0 \text{ if } a = b \end{cases} . \qquad (5)$$

If $\varepsilon_t = 0$ or $\varepsilon_t \geq 0.5$, stop the algorithm.
3. Compute the value

$$\alpha_t = 0.5 \ln \frac{1 - \varepsilon_t}{\varepsilon_t} . \qquad (6)$$

4. Modify weights for learning vectors according to the formula

$$D_{t+1}(\mathbf{z}^l) = \frac{D_t(\mathbf{z}^l) \exp\{-\alpha_t I(h_t(\mathbf{x}_l) = y^l)\}}{N_t} , \qquad (7)$$

where N_t is a constant such that $\sum_{l=1}^{m} D_{t+1}(\mathbf{z}^l) = 1$. To compute the overall output of the ensemble of classifiers trained by AdaBoost algorithm, the following formula is used

$$f(\mathbf{x}) = \sum_{t=1}^{T} c_t h_t(\mathbf{x}) , \qquad (8)$$

where

$$c_t = \frac{\alpha_t}{\sum_{t=1}^{T} \alpha_t} \qquad (9)$$

is classifier importance for a given training set, $h_t(\mathbf{x})$ is the response of the hypothesis t on the basis of feature vector $\mathbf{x} = [x_1, ..., x_n]$. The coefficient c_t value is computed on the basis of the classifier error and can be interpreted as the measure of classification accuracy of the given classifier. Moreover, the assumption (1) should be met. As we see, the AdaBoost algorithm is a meta-learning algorithm and does not determine the way of learning for classifiers in the ensemble.

2.2   Image Descriptors for Interest Regions

Local image descriptors for interest regions are utilized in applications such as image matching, image or texture recognition. There are many local descriptors developed to date [18]. The most common are SIFT (Scale Invariant Feature Transformation) [8] and SURF (Speeded Up Robust Features) [2]. Generally, SURF is faster than SIFT thanks to lower dimensionality (64 vs. 128 dimensions. SIFT

[9], consists of four major stages: (1) scale-space peak selection; (2) keypoint localization; (3) orientation assignment; (4) keypoint descriptor. A SIFT descriptor is constituted of a 128-dimensional vector (8 orientation bins for each 4x4 location bins). This representation allows significant levels of local distortions and changes in illumination. Vector of 128 key points is reduced in our approach to a 36-dimensional feature vector [6].

3   Proposed Approach

The main idea of this paper is suggested in [17], however we introduced many changes to the original concept. The authors of [17] used boosting algorithm to find a set of representative keypoints for selected class of images. They also changed the basis of the Adaboost algorithm: in each step of their modified algorithm they use the whole set of training examples to build many classifiers, then they choose the best model according to error value. We revert to the original AdaBoost. In each step we randomly choose one positive example according to their weight. Such an example $c = [c_1, \ldots, c_n] = [x, \ldots, x_n]$ is a base to build the final classifier. This classifier is a very simple nonstandard neuro-fuzzy model, because it consists of one fuzzy rule. Thus we construct for every element of a vector c a Gaussian function $G_i(c_i, \delta_i)$. Each Gaussian function has the center in the value of x_i, $i = 1, .., n$. Then we train our classifier in the following way:

1. We calculate the distance from the point designated by the selected vector c to each of the remaining positive examples x.
2. During this process we have to check whether this distance is less than the threshold chosen by user (in our simulations we chose 0.5).
3. In this case (distance is less then threshold) we record for each of coordinates of vector c how far a coordinate is distant from it to the right or left, that is we calculate
   If ($LeftMargin_i > c_i$) then $LeftMargin_i = c_i$
   If ($RightMargin_i < c_i$) then $RightMargin_i = c_i$
   And at the start of the algorithm $RightMargin_i = LeftMargin_i = c_i$
4. After training process, we modify parameters of each of the Gaussian functions which constitute the classifier in this step. The new centers are designated using formula $c_i = |RightMargin_i - LeftMargin_i|/2$. The second parameter of the Gaussian functions is their width. Due to the fact that our Gaussian functions are equated with membership functions of fuzzy sets we assume that throughout the interval $|LeftMargin, RightMargin|$ it must take values greater than 0.5; classifier assigned samples from this area to the class of positive samples. Hence, we set the width of the Gaussian functions by

$$\delta_i = \frac{|RightMargin_i - LeftMargin_i|}{\sqrt{-\ln 0.5}} \tag{10}$$

5. After determining the parameters of the new Gaussian functions we also obtain a set of fuzzy rules antecedents. For the entire set of samples (positive

and negative ones) we test the performance of the classifier by treating it as a single neuro-fuzzy rule. The aggregation of rules antecedents is made with the minimum operator according to $\varepsilon = \sum_j w_j \left| r\left(\mathbf{x}_j\right) - y_j \right|$ which corresponds to (4) and r is the output of a given classifier (rule). In this step, we determine also the importance of the rule, according to the formula (6). Now we modify weights of all samples depending on the classification quality

$$w_{t+1,j} = w_{t,j}\beta_t^{1-e_j} \tag{11}$$

which corresponds to the formula 7 and $e_j = 0$ when the sample is classified correctly and $e_j = 1$ otherwise and $\beta_t = \ln \frac{1-\varepsilon_t}{\varepsilon_t}$ where t is a boosting step.

In [17] the membership to the a given classifier h is determined by computing distance d and then checking if d is smaller than threshold θ:

$$h\left(f,\theta\right) = \begin{cases} 1, d < \theta \\ 0, d \geq \theta \end{cases}, \tag{12}$$

where $h\left(f,\theta\right)$ is the response of a classifier, f – vector of features, which is identified with a classifier. The operation of this classifier can be presented in two-dimensional feature space as a circle with a radius of θ within which all samples are similar (in the sense of close proximity) to the feature vector f (Fig. 1c). In the figure a circle and a cross denote the position of the feature vectors of the two classes of objects in two-dimensional space. Despite its simplicity, the classifier has a major disadvantage, as it requires the selection of an appropriate threshold value θ. In the case of high-value threshold θ, the classifier can be extended to reach samples from a different class (Fig. 1d). On the other hand, lower threshold θ may not include all of the samples.

Our approach, consisting in the formation of the Gaussian functions, is more immune to the relative position of the samples in the feature space. Each Gaussian function is determined during learning, constantly changing its width as learning new samples. Since every dimension of the feature vector is represented by one Gaussian function, the space is divided into rectangles of varying width, the shape of which is better suited to the distribution of samples in space. Figure 1 a and b show how the shape of the Gaussian functions fits to the next sample during the learning process, not including samples from other classes in its range.

4   Results

Two hundred images was scaled to the size of 120x80. The files were taken from the Corel Database [19]. Images are divided into two classes – the first class consists of the pictures of dinosaurs. The second class consists of randomly selected images from the other ones. Figure 2 shows nine examples of positive samples used for learning. After training process described in Section 3 we obtained a set of ten classifiers. The examples of Gaussian functions for one feature after pruning process is shown in Figure 3. All positive images were classified correctly.

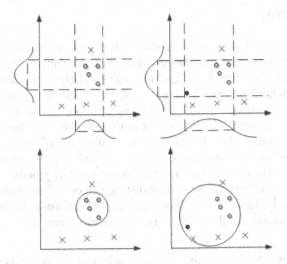

Fig. 1. Effect of change of the way of key point comparison, a) based on the distance b) using fuzzy logic

Fig. 2. Example of positive samples used for learning

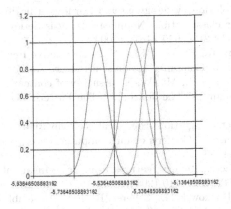

Fig. 3. Example of Gaussian functions of one feature for three simple classifiers after pruning process

5 Conclusions

The presented method is a starting point for further work on the fuzzy representation of similar feature vectors (key points). Gaussian functions acquired during learning can be reduced by finding similar ones and their merging. It will allow to reduce the number of parameters describing all the key points of the class. These functions are assigned with labels describing images that contain specific data points. This in turn will allow easier storage in the database and index generation for faster search for similar images. Similar sets of key points described by sets of Gaussian functions allow to perform some fuzzy logic operations and will also allow for the calculation of the degree of similarity between images. The system presented in this paper can only distinguish one class of objects from the other ones. If we build several such classifier systems, we can combine them with appropriate assumptions about fuzzy rules normalization [10].

Acknowledgments. The project was funded by the National Center for Science under decision number DEC-2011/01/D/ST6/06957.

References

1. Bay, H., Tuytelaars, T., Van Gool, L.: SURF: Speeded Up Robust Features. In: European Conference in Computer Vision, pp. 404–417 (2006)
2. Bay, H., Ess, A., Tuytelaars, T., Van Gool, L.: Speeded-Up Robust Features (SURF). International Journal of Computer Vision and Image Understanding (CVIU) 110(3), 346–359 (2008)
3. Cpałka, K.: A method for designing flexible neuro-fuzzy systems. In: Rutkowski, L., Tadeusiewicz, R., Zadeh, L.A., Żurada, J.M. (eds.) ICAISC 2006. LNCS (LNAI), vol. 4029, pp. 212–219. Springer, Heidelberg (2006)
4. Cpałka, K., Rutkowski, L.: Flexible Takagi Sugeno fuzzy systems. In: Proceedings of the International Joint Conference on Neural Networks, IJCNN 2005, Montreal, pp. 1764–1769 (2005)
5. Cpałka, K.: On evolutionary designing and learning of flexible neuro-fuzzy structures for nonlinear classification. Nonlinear Analysis Series A: Theory, Methods and Applications 71(12), e1659–e1672 (2009)
6. Ke, Y., Sukthankar, R.: PCA-SIFT: A More Distinctive Representation for Local Image Descriptors. In: Computer Vision and Pattern Recognition (2004)
7. Liu, Y., Zhang, D., Lu, G., Ma, W.-Y.: Asurvey of content-based image retrieval with high-level semantics. The Journal of The Pattern Recognition 40, 262–282 (2007)
8. Lowe, D.G.: Object recognition from local scale-invariant features. In: Proceedings of the International Conference on Computer Vision, vol. 2, pp. 1150–1157, doi:10.1109/ICCV.1999
9. Lowe, D.G.: Distinctive Image Features from Scale-Invariant Keypoints. Int'l J. Computer Vision 60(2), 91–110 (2004)
10. Korytkowski, M., Rutkowski, L., Scherer, R.: From Ensemble of Fuzzy Classifiers to Single Fuzzy Rule Base Classifier. In: Rutkowski, L., Tadeusiewicz, R., Zadeh, L.A., Zurada, J.M. (eds.) ICAISC 2008. LNCS (LNAI), vol. 5097, pp. 265–272. Springer, Heidelberg (2008)

11. Nowicki, R., Rutkowski, L.: Soft Techniques for Bayesian Classification. In: Rutkowski, L., Kacprzyk, J. (eds.) Neural Networks and Soft Computing. Advances in Soft Computing, pp. s.537–s.544. Springer Physica-Verlag (2003)
12. Ogiela, L., Tadeusiewicz, R., Ogiela, M.R.: Cognitive Computing in Intelligent Medical Pattern Recognition Systems. In: Huang, D.-S., Li, K., Irwin, G.W. (eds.) ICIC. LNICST, vol. 344, pp. 851–856. Springer, Heidelberg (2006)
13. Ogiela, M.R., Tadeusiewicz, R.: Syntactic pattern recognition for X-ray diagnosis of pancreatic cancer. IEEE Engineering in Medicine and Biology Magazine 19(6), 94–105 (2000)
14. Ogiela, M.R., Tadeusiewicz, R., Ogiela, L.: Intelligent Semantic Information Retrieval in Medical Pattern Cognitive Analysis. In: Gervasi, O., Gavrilova, M.L., Kumar, V., Laganá, A., Lee, H.P., Mun, Y., Taniar, D., Tan, C.J.K. (eds.) ICCSA 2005. LNCS, vol. 3483, pp. 852–857. Springer, Heidelberg (2005)
15. Schapire, R.E.: A Brief Introduction to Boosting. In: Conference on Artificial Intelligence, pp. 1401–1406 (1999)
16. Starczewski, J.T.: On defuzzification of interval type-2 fuzzy sets. In: Rutkowski, L., Tadeusiewicz, R., Zadeh, L.A., Zurada, J.M. (eds.) ICAISC 2008. LNCS (LNAI), vol. 5097, pp. 333–340. Springer, Heidelberg (2008)
17. Tieu, K., Viola, P.: Boosting Image Retrieval. International Journal of Computer Vision 56(1/2), 17–36 (2004)
18. Tuytelaars, T., Mikolajczyk, K.: Local Invariant Feature Detectors: A Survey. In: Foundation and Trends in Computer Graphics and Vision, pp. 177–280 (2008)
19. Wang, J.Z., Li, J., Wiederhold, G.: SIMPLIcity: Semantics-Sensitive Integrated Matching for Picture Libraries. IEEE Transactions on Pattern Analysis and Machine Intelligence (TPAMI) 23(9), 947–963 (2001)
20. Zhang, W., Yu, B., Zelinsky, G., Samaras, D.: Object class recognition using multiple layer boosting with heterogenous features. In: Proc. CVPR, pp. 323–330 (2005)

Road Surface Recognition System
Based on Its Picture

Michal Jankowski[1] and Jacek Mazurkiewicz[2]

[1] OPTOPOL Technology S.A. Wroclaw Branch
ul. Promien 4, 51-659 Wroclaw, Poland
mikimicha@gmail.com
[2] Institute of Computer Engineering, Control and Robotics,
Wroclaw University of Technology, ul. Janiszewskiego 11/17, 50-372 Wroclaw, Poland
Jacek.Mazurkiewicz@pwr.wroc.pl

Abstract. A grip of the road finding seems to be very solid problem in case of self-driven cars. It can be done by recognition of surface the car is moving on. The photos of the road taken while driving a vehicle can be the solid data source for the detection process. It is rather difficult to extract information from pictures that provide data necessary for classifier to distinguish patterns. Apparently simple preprocessing is not enough since a neural network was not able to learn anything. To resolve the problem of the road recognition entirely new picture preprocessing type has been developed. It fits circles of uniformly brightness areas then counts them and measures their sizes. The learning of the multilayer perceptron realised by such data gives very good results. The new way of extracting data from pictures is a promising solution and was named as "Growing Bubbles Algorithm". The algorithm was implemented as part of a real system to support the on-line driver decision. The system was tested in the real car in real traffic with very promising results.

1 Introduction

It is very likely that in the soon future there will be no need to drive a car as it will drive itself. There are already sophisticated far-reaching experiments with vehicles like this [10]. Now Google is promoting their Driverless Car and strongly lobbying in Nevada for creating a law to use the self driven cars on a public roads [7]. The next step of this technology is to know - in the automatic way - what kind of surface the car is driven on. Such info seems to be crucial to predict the maximum safety-speed of the car. Systems like Auto Brake, City Safety or Collision Warning also would need data about grip of the road [3] [6] [9].

The paper describes a part of a system which is realised and tested at real traffic. The system is predicting distance needed to stop a car based on the actual speed and the grip of a tires. Of course the grip depends on type of the road surface. The surface is distinguished as asphalt, sett, wet asphalt, snow, etc. While getting information about speed is relatively easy because it can be just read from car sensor finding the grip is a topic of the paper.

L. Rutkowski et al. (Eds.): ICAISC 2013, Part I, LNAI 7894, pp. 548–558, 2013.

2   System Description

A specialised hardware and the unique software is necessary to implement the problem described above. The working system has been build up from several components: a speed sensor, a brake pedal position sensor, a microcontroller (MCU), a camera and a PC computer. The MCU constantly reads signals and stores them for later sending. The computer requests data from microcontroller device every 20 milliseconds. Also a special application running on PC is controlling a camera and takes a photo every second. Information about the speed and about the surface type is enough to predict stopping distance.

The data describing the speed are ready to use just after the end of the reading procedure. The surface recognition is more time consuming process and needs next "solid steps" for implementation. Firstly already taken photo is normalized then preprocessed and a neural network is used as classifier of the presented surface [1] [5]. Lastly - based on obtained data and knowledge acquired from learning data - the stopping distance is computed.

Although the system is designed to work properly in any situation it has one solid hardware limitation. The surfaces are recognized based on static photos and the camera is not always able to take a photo in dark scene. The high quality camera can improve the situation and solve the problem. Therefore photos of various roads were collected for test of the system.

3   Learning Data

We can point two special areas for collected data. The stopping distance prediction is the main goal of the system the data about retardation on each surface was needful. Using this information a square function was discovered for each surface that system is recognising. The functions describe the relation between the speed and the stoping distance.

The main topic is to learn the neural network to recognize a road surfaces based on the photos of the road. So the pictures for each type of the road surface for different types of weather conditions have been collected. As a result the data describing: asphalt, sett, snow, and off-road in 22 different variations like: day, night wet, dry, good quality, bad quality. The road surface is recognised not based on the entire view but using only the piece of the photo, patterns are populated by copying the different areas of the same picture. The neural network is trained using around 150 patterns for the each type of the road [1] [9].

4   Image Recognition

The surface recognition is only a part of a bigger project - so the actual functionality of this part is limited. In the current state the system can recognize three types of surfaces: a snow, an asphalt and a sett. On the other hand we can prove that the surface can be recognised precisely. Moreover the discovered preprocessing approach can be easily extended for more types of the road.

The process runs as follow. The camera takes the photos of the road. The photos are processed to detect the surface type. Firstly the square is cut out from the photo in a place where the right car wheel is going to contact the road surface. It cannot be taken from the area between wheels as there could be different type of the surface. For example in winter time we can find a snow is in a middle of a road but the car wheels go on the clean asphalt surface.

Before the image cropping the thresholds for image normalization are calculated. After the cropping the small square is normalized using previously found thresholds. Next the histogram equalisation is used. This way the picture seems to be more clear and unequivocal [5]. At the end the prepared square is ready for subsequent processing.

4.1   Snow Recognition

The snow recognition seems to be the easiest task. The average colour of the picture square creates the basis of the solution. It is little bit surprising that a snow surface is not always the brightest surface. Sometimes the sett can be brighter and it depends only on auto exposition of a camera. Therefore lightens is not something that the algorithm can rely on. The key observation is that snow has one dominating colour component. This is usual situation, many times something what we recognize as white it is a bit blue e.g. white paper for printer is also blue [5]. Lastly as a result of dominating component also saturation of the colour is noticeable.

Putting all of the mentioned steps together we create the snow recognition algorithm. The average colour in picture square is calculated for all R, G and B channels separately. For the RGB colour the HSL representation is also computed. If the B (blue) is dominating component and H (hue) is greater than 6% the picture is recognized as a snow.

4.2   Asphalt and Set Recognition

The snow recognition is very accurate and do not require a lot of computation. This is the reason why it can be used as the initial process of the road surface detection. If the picture is not pointed as snow the next step is made and the neural network gives and answer if the presented photo includes the sett or the asphalt probe.

Apparently the distinguish between the asphalt and the sett is unexpectedly difficult. It seems that pattern of relatively smooth and uniform asphalt differs from the sett significantly and therefore it is trivial to make the classifier for it. However simple preprocessing gives no valuable results. The neural network is trained with the following types of images: grayscale, B&W, B&W using the median algorithm to remove the ragged edges. We tried to build the input based on the already detected corners or based on the B&W image with detected corners. The approaches are the completely blind ways - the neural network is not able to learn. It is clear that the completely new way of data extracting is necessary.

5 Growing Bubbles Algorithm

The "Growing Bubbles Algorithm" is developed especially to find an answer: is presented image the probe of the asphalt or the probe of the sett. Apparently differences between patterns for the same type of the road are so significant that the neural networks are not able to recognize it properly [1].

The following observation can be converted to a solution. The proportion of black and white areas analysis and the frequency of appearance can potentially point to correct answers. In this case place and rotation of pattern are ignored and it is the issue with the previous preprocessing types. As a consequence, a unique algorithm is developed.

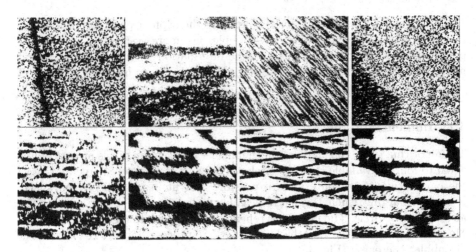

Fig. 1. Example of Black and White crops of a surface (asphalt - top, sett - bottom)

The photos of a sett contains quite significant white areas divided by the dark lines. In general it is difficult to find these lines as a result of bad image quality. For the asphalt probe the only common pattern are the little black spots (Fig. 1). The mentioned observations create a base of the "Growing Bubbles Algorithm".

Therefore a task for the algorithm is to extract only the information about the sizes and the frequency of the appearance for solid colour areas. The idea is to fill the white and black areas, to count them and to measure its sizes. It could be the key information for detecting the sett. However usually the stones presented in the photos stick together in such a way that there is no gap between them and simple filling will fail in a such situation. We have to limit an expansion of the filling areas and this is exactly what bubbles do. The areas are filled by the bubbles instead of the simple colour. The bubbles cannot grow bigger than the sett stones and consequently are able to preserve its sizes. The bubbles size for black and white areas analysis can be the device to distinguish between the sett probe and the asphalt probe [4].

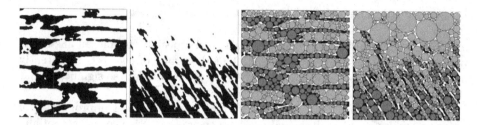

Fig. 2. Comparison of simple B&W with median algorithm to bubbles preprocessing. Counting from left: 1 - B&W with median sett, 2 - B&W with median asphalt, 3 - bubbles sett, 4 - bubbles asphalt

(Fig. 2) shows the example for the sett and the asphalt probe preprocessing. It can be easily noticed that sizes of bubbles are more systematic for the sett pattern than for the asphalt pattern. The information about bubbles sizes and numbers allows to remove the noise recorded in the plane images: the angle of sett, the shape of sett, etc.

5.1 Implementation

The algorithm goes true all pixels in the image. If the white pixels area of radius equal to four is available it draws circle there. Next it tries to enlarge and move the circle around the white area to possibly best fit in the solid colour space. It stops enlarging when the circle is going to overlay the black zone or the already drown circle. The process is repeated until all white regions are touched. Meanwhile in analogical way the black areas are processed where the second set of bubbles is created (Fig. 3).

In fact the process of enlarging is not stopped immediately if the circle overlaps the single pixel. A little bit of overlapping is allowed and thanks to that the circles can fit better ragged edges. As the consequence - the circles are filled with colour. Later when new circle is looking for a place it calculates how many pixels overlaps already.

Fig. 3. Growing bubble is moving to fit the space and filled with a gry scale at the end

1. Set R to 4.
2. Iterate through all of the pixels.
3. If actual pixel is white then take red (lighter) colour, If it is black then take the blue (darker) colour, otherwise go to Point 2.
4. Set error variable to zero.
5. In place pointed by the actual pixel draw the circle of radius R pixels with a chosen colour.
6. For each pixel out of the picture or overlapping different colour increment error variable and save average error place.
7. If error variable not larger then increment R and go back to Point 4.
8. If error is to big then move circle in an opposite side to the average error place and draw again.
9. If error variable is less than before then increment R and go to Point 4.
10. If error variable is bigger than draw the previous circle and fill it with chosen colour.
11. If it was not the last pixel in the picture go to Point 2.
12. Calculate pattern - count bubbles grouped by sizes and colours.

5.2   Retrieving Pattern

When all bubbles are drawn it is a time for the actual data retrieving. All circles are grouped by intervals of sizes and colours. The members of each group are counted and the cardinalities of groups are the classifier input.

There is one more factor to extract from the picture. The photos of the asphalt probe can provide the direction of a light as one corner is usually lighter than the other. This effect is as strong as strong the light is and is not noticeable in cloudy weather. In a process of thresholding almost all information in the light zone is removed as a result of low dynamic range. It is because the asphalt is the kind of dark texture that is close to solid colour. At the same time dynamic range for the sett probe is high as stone is light and gaps are usually dark. The thresholding do not lose any important information in consequence of scene lightening.

In order to preserve information about the asphalt light direction the picture is splitted by four squares [4]. The counting bubbles algorithm is done for each of the square separately (Fig. 4).

In (Fig. 5) there is print out for the obtained data calculated by the bubbles preprocessing. It is found for top left square and white areas: 37 circles of size 4-5, 31 circles of size 6-7 ... 5 circles of size greater than 26.

6   Results

6.1   Snow Recognition

The snow recognition algorithm works with very promising accuracy of 100% correctly recognized patterns of the collected data. There is only one condition

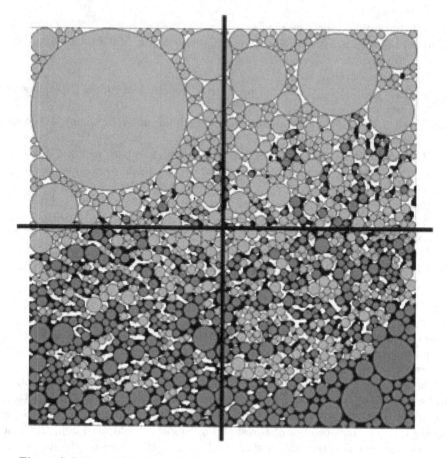

Fig. 4. Splitting picture in order to preserve data about the lightens direction

Black Top Left:	8	5	2	0	0	0	0	0	0	0	0	0
White Top Left:	37	31	13	6	2	2	4	0	0	1	2	5
Black Top Right:	43	26	12	3	2	0	2	2	0	1	0	2
White Top Right:	45	34	15	3	2	2	0	1	1	1	2	1
Black Bottom Left:	38	31	8	6	4	2	1	0	0	1	3	5
White Bottom Left:	24	22	6	2	0	0	1	0	0	1	0	0
Black Bottom Right:	8	12	5	2	2	3	0	0	0	1	1	1
White Bottom Right:	30	22	9	5	1	1	2	1	0	0	0	5

Fig. 5. Example of classifier data input

for the proper recognition of the snow. The white balance ought to be correct. The cameras set it in automatic way but it gives appropriate results rarely. The way to solve it is to put some neutral colour object in a view of a camera. It would be possible then to correct the white balance based on registered colour of the neutral object.

input	hidden	step	mom.	epochs	train	accuracy gener.	valid.	MSE train	gener.	valid.
1600	2	0,001	0,8	20000	99,36	50	73,08	0,00652	0,2753	0,1666
1600	4	0,001	0,8	20000	100	53,85	73,08	0,000044	0,2741	0,1429
1600	6	0,001	0,8	20000	100	50	61,54	0,000016	0,3211	0,2109
1600	8	0,001	0,8	20000	100	48,08	59,62	0,00001	0,3148	0,1822
1600	10	0,001	0,8	20000	100	48,08	63,46	0,000006	0,3024	0,1804
1600	12	0,001	0,8	20000	100	50	46,15	0,000003	0,2947	0,1998
1600	14	0,001	0,8	20000	100	40,38	38,46	0,000021	0,2637	0,2872
1600	16	0,001	0,8	20000	100	44,23	42,31	0,000011	0,2768	0,2990
1600	18	0,001	0,8	20000	100	48,08	46,15	0,000007	0,2698	0,2965
1600	19	0,001	0,8	20000	100	59,62	53,85	0,000005	0,2186	0,2631
1600	21	0,001	0,8	20000	100	59,62	53,85	0,000005	0,2180	0,2601
1600	23	0,001	0,8	20000	100	57,69	50	0,000011	0,2206	0,2665
1600	25	0,001	0,8	20000	100	40,38	51,92	0,000002	0,3589	0,2950
1600	27	0,001	0,8	20000	100	40,38	50	0,000002	0,3605	0,2889
1600	29	0,001	0,8	20000	100	36,54	53,85	0,000003	0,3596	0,2927
1600	31	0,001	0,8	20000	100	36,54	53,85	0,000003	0,3596	0,2927
1600	33	0,001	0,8	20000	100	36,54	46,15	0,000005	0,3561	0,2838
1600	35	0,001	0,8	20000	100	34,62	46,15	0,00001	0,3479	0,2755

Fig. 6. B&W + median algorithm - looking for the proper number of hidden neurons, 1600 pixel picture as input

input	hidden	step	mom.	epochs	train	gener.	valid.	train	gener.	valid.
400	8	0,001	0,8	6000	100	40,38	50	0,000119	0,3287	0,2940
400	10	0,001	0,8	6000	100	42,31	50	0,000056	0,3366	0,2966
400	12	0,001	0,8	6000	100	42,31	51,92	0,000028	0,3388	0,2985
400	14	0,001	0,8	6000	100	42,31	50	0,000021	0,3484	0,3021
400	16	0,001	0,8	6000	100	40,38	50	0,000015	0,3289	0,2980
400	18	0,001	0,8	6000	100	42,31	50	0,000013	0,3476	0,2994
400	20	0,001	0,8	6000	100	40,38	50	0,00001	0,3430	0,3031
400	22	0,001	0,8	6000	100	44,23	51,92	0,000008	0,3494	0,3034
400	24	0,001	0,8	6000	100	42,31	50	0,000008	0,3404	0,2978
400	26	0,001	0,8	6000	100	42,31	50	0,000006	0,3593	0,3091
400	28	0,001	0,8	6000	100	44,23	51,92	0,000006	0,3476	0,3086
400	30	0,001	0,8	6000	100	42,31	51,92	0,000005	0,3426	0,3014
400	32	0,001	0,8	6000	100	44,23	51,92	0,000005	0,3561	0,3047
400	34	0,001	0,8	6000	100	44,23	51,92	0,000004	0,3603	0,3214
400	36	0,001	0,8	6000	100	44,23	51,92	0,000004	0,3585	0,3032

Fig. 7. B&W + median algorithm - looking for the proper number of hidden neurons, 400 pixel picture as input

input	hidden	step	mom.	epochs	accuracy			MSE		
					train	gener.	valid.	train	gener.	valid.
96	20	0,001	0,8	150000	98,08	90,38	82,69	0,00065	0,0501	0,0782
96	20	0,001	0,8	150000	100	90,38	88,46	0,000153	0,0477	0,0574
96	20	0,001	0,8	150000	94,44	90,38	76,92	0,025761	0,0517	0,1281
96	19	0,001	0,8	150000	99,36	90,38	86,54	0,001198	0,0451	0,0277
96	19	0,001	0,8	150000	99,36	90,38	84,62	0,006379	0,0679	0,0842
96	19	0,001	0,8	150000	100	88,46	86,54	0,000006	0,0546	0,1032
96	18	0,001	0,8	150000	95,51	90,38	92,31	0,036066	0,0843	0,0500
96	18	0,001	0,8	150000	98,72	90,38	94,23	0,000491	0,0427	0,0339
96	18	0,001	0,8	150000	100	88,46	84,62	0,000005	0,1025	0,0958
96	17	0,001	0,8	150000	100	86,54	88,46	0,000005	0,0539	0,1009
96	17	0,001	0,8	150000	100	90,38	92,31	0,000301	0,0557	0,0247

Fig. 8. Training for Growing Bubbles Algorithm

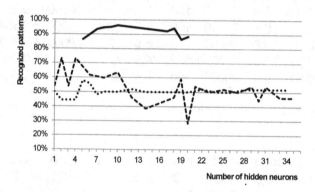

Fig. 9. The best learning results for different numbers of hidden neurons. The chart describes the percentage of the correct recognized patterns from the validation set. The Dash and the dot lines shows best results for the standard - simple preprocessing types. The dot line was for 400 input pixels (line closest to 50%) and the dash line for 1600 input pixels. The solid line - over 90% - shows learning process for "Growing Bubbles Algorithm"

6.2   Asphalt and Set Recognition

The recognition of the sett and the asphalt is quite difficult. The patterns for the asphalt and the sett differ significantly although the neural network training based on the traditional preprocessing methods gives no sensible results. The three-layer MLP is used as a device for recognition process. The output layer includes two neurons, the number of neurons in the input layer is fixed to the actual size of the input signal. The number of neurons in the hidden layer is tuned by the experimental way. The backpropagation algorithm with momentum parameter is used for the training procedure. The momentum parameter and the speed of the training is fixed by the set of experiments: momentum equals to

0.8, step - 0.001. The results are grouped in the tables. The following names are in use for the columns description: *input* - number of input neurons, *hidden* - number of hidden neurons, *step* - speed of the space exploring the of solutions, *mom* - momentum parameter, *epochs* - number of training iterations, *train* - training set accuracy, *gener.* - generalization set accuracy, *valid.* - validation set accuracy.

Figure 6 shows the training results for input signal as 1600 pixels pictures for different sizes of the hidden layer. Figure 7 illustrates the same experiment but for 400 pixels pictures. In the Figure 8 we can see the table of results for "Growing Bubbles Algorithm" used for input signal preprocessing.

Figure 9 compares simple preprocessing with discovered "bubbles" solution. It can be easily noticed that in most cases of traditional preprocessing the accuracy is more guess then actual recognition. "Growing Bubbles Algorithm" with best result of **96,15%** of recognized photos has clear advantage over other solutions in recognition between the asphalt and the sett.

7   Conclusion

Although a bit more types of the road surfaces could be recognized it is possible to make surface recognition with good results based on the photo taken "on-line" during the car movement. The recognition between the good quality asphalt and the bad quality asphalt could be also done with use of bubbles algorithm. When thinking about a final product ready for customers, there will be need for a way of calibrating the system. While the road recognition will be the same for each vehicle and speed reading can be customized for different cars, the retardation quadratic functions will have to be discovered automatically by each user. There are too many variables to customize this product for each car, tires and brakes [2]. It will be enough when the user brakes on each road and the system collects the data by removing the skidding effect and discovering the functions. Probably, by calibrating system on asphalt, it will be possible to estimate functions for other surfaces. However, to perform that, the speed will have to be read from all ABS sensors as it will be easy to remove errors caused by sliding [3].

The system of braking distance prediction is satisfactory and could be developed up to customer ready product. However the most interesting part of it is the "Growing Bubbles Algorithm". It is suitable for surface recognition and potentially for many other areas [8]. The algorithm was implemented as part of a real system to support the on-line driver decision. The system was tested in the real car in real traffic with very promising results.

References

1. Du, K.L., Swamy, M.N.S.: Neural Networks in a Softcomputing Framework. Springer, London (2010)
2. Han, J., Kamber, M., Pei, J.: Data Mining. Morgen Kaufmann, Walthman (2012)

3. Anti-lock Braking System (ABS), Traction Control (2012),
   http://www.samarins.com/glossary/abs.html#.T-2dSLV1Dj8
4. Circle-Drawing Algorithms (2012), http://groups.csail.mit.edu/graphics/
   classes/6.837/F98/Lecture6/circle.html
5. Levine, M.D., Gandhi, M.R., Bhattacharyya, J.: Image Normalization for Illumination Compensation in Facial Images (2012),
   http://wwwhomes.uni-bielefeld.de/ggoetze/B/IlluminationReport.pdf
6. Li, H., Nashashibi, F.: Multi-Vehicle Cooperative Perception and Augmented Reality for Driver Assistance: A Possibility to "See" Through Front Vehicle. In: 14th
   International IEEE Conference on Inteligent Transportation Systems, Washington,
   DC (2011)
7. Lindner, F., Kressel, U., Kaelberer, S.: Robust Recognition of Traffic Signals. In:
   IEEE Intelligent Vehicles Symposium, University of Parma (2004)
8. Narzt, W., Pomberger, G., Ferscha, A., Kold, D., Muller, R., Wieghardt, J., Hort-
   ner, H., Lindinger, C.: Augmented Reality Navigation Systems. Springer (2005)
9. Serafin, T.P., Mazurkiewicz, J.: IDEA - Intelligent Driving E-Assistant System.
   In: Problems of Dependability and Modelling, Oficyna Wydawnicza Politechniki
   Wroclawskiej, Wroclaw (2011)
10. World first: Automated Driving in Real Urban Traffic,
    http://www.dlr.de/en/desktopdefault.aspx/tabid-6216/10226_read-26991/

Landmine Detection in 3D Images from Ground Penetrating Radar Using Haar-Like Features[*]

Przemysław Klęsk[1], Andrzej Godziuk[2], Mariusz Kapruziak[1,2], and Bogdan Olech[1,2]

[1] Faculty of Computer Science
West Pomeranian University of Technology
ul. Żołnierska 49, 71-210, Szczecin, Poland
{pklesk,mkapruziak,bolech}@wi.zut.edu.pl
[2] Autocomp Management
ul. Władysława IV 1, 70-651 Szczecin, Poland
andrzej@godziuk.pl, {mkapruziak,bolech}@autocomp.com.pl

Abstract. A prototype landmine detecting vehicle is presented. The vehicle is equipped with a Ground Penetrating Radar working in the frequency domain. The device collects 3D images defined over coordinates system: along track × across track × time, where the time (which can be associated with the depth) is obtained from frequency measurements via FFT. Learning of the detector is carried out by a boosting algorithm and is based on our proposition of *3D Haar-like features*. Algorithmic details and experimental results are described, in particular: obtained accuracy, sensitivity, false-alarms rate and ROC curve.

1 Introduction

In the recent decade the Ground Penetrating Radar and its applications seem to be a popular research subject. Some of application areas are: groundwater contamination, sedimentology, archeology, military technology [7]. As regards the landmine detection problem, Yarovoy [13] reports that at least 67 countries are contaminated by landmines with estimates of the number of mines laid from 50 to 150 million[1]. The electromagnetic induction (EMI) metal detector, one of the most common demining tools, suffers from problems such as insufficient detection depth and a high false-alarm rate (FAR) due to subsurface roots, rocks, and water pockets for antipersonnel (AP) mines with low metal content[2].

---

[*] Agreement no. 0091/R/TOO/2010/12 for R&D project no. 0 R00 0091 12, dated on 30.11.2010, signed with the Ministry of Science and Higher Education in Poland (consortium of Military Institute or Armament Technology in Zielonka and Autocomp Management Sp. z o.o.).

[1] According to Ottawa Treaty (http://www.un.org/Depts/mine/UNDocs/ban_trty.htm), which entered into force in 1999, all stockpiles of mines should be destroyed within 4 years and all minefields lifted in 10 years; which did not happen [13].

[2] Example of metal-detector performance in Cambodia between 1992 and 1998: only 0.3% of the 200 million items excavated by deminers were AP mines or UXO [6].

L. Rutkowski et al. (Eds.): ICAISC 2013, Part I, LNAI 7894, pp. 559–567, 2013.

As regards GPR applications for landmine detection, most studies are focused on different GPR imaging techniques and feature extraction techniques. Some of them work directly on obtained radar images — radagrams, where (in time domains) the target pattern to detect is a *hyperbola* shape, see the Fig. 2. Obviously, any object non-transparent to GPR produces a hyperbola shape in the image. Therefore, the goal is to distinguish hyperbolas characteristic for mines from other hyperbolas. Some of feature extraction techniques try to recover physical quantities related to mines from images, e.g.: depth of burial, size, radius or height (as the distance between mine top and bottom estimated from two hyperbolas). Other approaches transform the images using e.g. Hyperbola Flattening Transform [5] or try to derive some graphically-oriented features as descriptors. To enumerate some examples the following names can be given: blob[3] detection [5], seeded growing segmentation [1], hyperbola detection via Hough Transform [10][4], searching for maxima along hyperbolas and polynomial curve-fitting [14], estimation of diagonal and antidiagonal edges strengths [14].

2   Motivation

In many published research results, a common observation to be made is that although three-dimensional GPR images are at disposal e.g. in a form $i(x, y, t)$ being the image intensity over a point (x, y) for the time moment t, such an information is not used directly. Instead, different simplifications are made in order to use only two-dimensional information. For example, only few slices (B scans) are picked from the 3D image with the highest mean intensity, or hyperbola curve-fitting is carried out separately in (x, t) and (y, t) projections [5,14,4].

The most likely reason behind such simplifications is to reduce the computational cost. Think of a scanning procedure which traverses a 3D image (e.g. of resolution $100 \times 100 \times 512$ over each $1 \, m^2$) with a certain 3D subwindow, and for each its position the features extraction and the detection must be done. Note that analogical procedures in computer vision problems (e.g. face/human detection), where a 2D image is analyzed and 2D features are extracted, are cheaper roughly speaking by a factor related to the resolution along additional time axis.

Our motivation is to make a direct use of three-dimensional information, *not* to simplify the analysis to a two-dimensional, and simultaneously to maintain a fast performance. The main idea behind the paper was to propose *3D Haar-like features*, as an extension of known 2D ones, and to check their applicability to landmine detection problem. We remind that fast performance of Haar-like features is owed to their coupling with a trick called the *integral image*, due to Viola and Jones [11,12] for face detection applications, which allows to calculate each feature in $O(1)$ time (constant) regardless of its scale.

---

[3] Binary Large Objects — object in the image with highest size × intensity product.
[4] Application of GPR to underground pipes and cables detection.

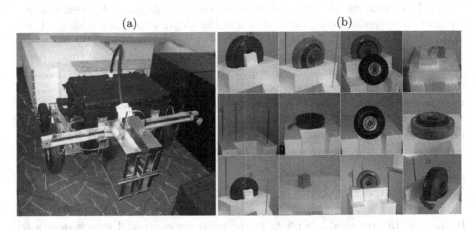

Fig. 1. (a) Remotely controlled vehicle with the GPR. (b) Examples of scanned scenes.

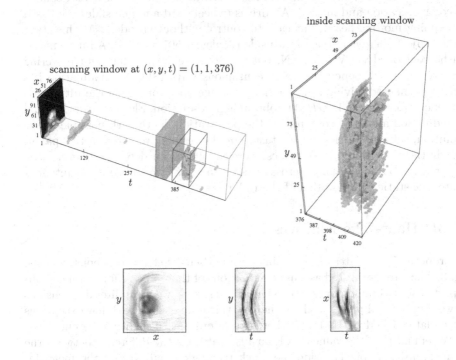

Fig. 2. Exemplary detection of a mine. First row shows: a scanning 3D window zoomed out and in; second row shows: slices through the middle of the scanning window.

We must clearly remark that at the present initial stage of our research project, the GPR measurements were taken in indoor conditions and objects under recognition were *not buried* but exposed in the air. In experiments we used two anti-tank mine models (plastic and metal) and various negative objects: metal boxes, plates, rods, wheels, see the Fig. 1b. Therefore, the purpose of this paper is mainly to present the methodology/approach we propose and to report experimental results for the simplified experimental setting. Our plan for future research is to build a container filled with the ground, in which objects would be buried, and over which the vehicle would travel. Obviously, we are aware that 'air conditions' can be significantly easier for the detection than subsurface conditions due to ground permittivity, clutter, air-ground interface, etc.

3   Hardware Set-Up

In the Fig. 1a presented is a photo of the remotely controlled vehicle dedicated to scan subsurface of the ground (in the future), being used as the prototype platform in this project. The big black case contains all electronics and control for communication and motion. All drives (wheels and antenna slide) are based on stepping motors, heavy, but easy to control without encoders. At this stage of the project there is also a VNA inside (Agilent E5071C-4K5). All movements can be controlled via Wi-Fi LAN, but the VNA requires cabling for powering at present state. Stepped frequency continuous wave (SFCW) modulation has been implemented, giving a high dynamic range and working in the ultra-wide frequency range (up to $18\,GHz$) to obtain high resolution. Flexibility of this kind of modulation allows to compromise the penetration depth with possible image resolution, suitably to the specific task. For the results presented in this paper, steps in the resolution (of 3D images) were as follows: for depth — $10\,mm$ (scan A), for scans B and C (along, across track) — $5\,mm$. Two Vivaldi type antennas create a bi-static configuration of the radar.

4   3D Haar-Like Features

We propose 17 templates of three-dimensional Haar-like features, depicted in the Fig. 3. They are generated as simple extensions of their 5 two-dimensional counterparts (most common ones). By 'simple extensions' we mean literal extensions of two dimensional patterns along the new third dimension, with few exceptions of templates: 7 and $14, 15, 16, 17$ where extensions have a slightly different sense.

We remind that the value of a Haar-like feature is the difference between the mean intensity of pixels inside the black rectangles (cubes) and the mean intensity of pixels inside the white rectangles (cubes). Let ii denote the integral image defined as: $ii(x, y, t) = \sum_{1 \leqslant j \leqslant x} \sum_{1 \leqslant k \leqslant y} \sum_{1 \leqslant l \leqslant t} i(j, k, l)$. Then, for a cube spanned from (x_1, y_1, t_1) to (x_2, y_2, t_2), the sum of intensities in the cube can

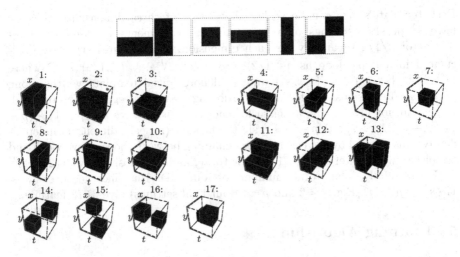

Fig. 3. Illustration of 3D Haar-like template features. The top row shows 5 common 2D patterns, further rows show groups of proposed 3D extensions.

be calculated using only 8 key points of the integral image (regardless of cube's size), for example in the following manner:

$$\sum_{x_1 \leqslant j \leqslant x_2} \sum_{y_1 \leqslant k \leqslant y_2} \sum_{t_1 \leqslant l \leqslant t_2} i(j,k,l) =$$

$$ii(x_2, y_2, t_2) - ii(x_1 - 1, y_2, t_2) - ii(x_2, y_1 - 1, t_2) + ii(x_1 - 1, y_1 - 1, t_2)$$

$$- \Big(ii(x_2, y_2, t_1 - 1) - ii(x_1 - 1, y_2, t_1 - 1) - ii(x_2, y_1 - 1, t_1 - 1) + ii(x_1 - 1, y_1 - 1, t_1 - 1) \Big).$$

3D Integral Image. A 3D integral image can be effectively calculated by the following algorithm (induction):

1. Create arrays: $ii_{n_x \times n_y \times n_t}$, $jj_{n_y \times n_t}$, kk_{n_t}.
2. For $x = 1, \ldots, n_x$
   2.1. For $y = 1, \ldots, n_y$
      2.1.1. For $t = 1, \ldots, n_t$
         2.1.1.1. if $t > 1$ $s := kk(t-1) + i(x,y,t)$, otherwise $s := i(x,y,t)$.
         2.1.1.2. $kk(t) := s$.
         2.1.1.3. if $y > 1$ $s := s + jj(y-1,t)$.
         2.1.1.4. $jj(y,t) := s$.
         2.1.1.5. if $x > 1$ $ii(x,y,t) := ii(x-1,y,t) + s$, otherwise $ii(x,y,t) := s$.
3. Return ii.

Number of Features (Parametrization). As regards the total number of features we used in experiments, it was implied by two parameters: the number of scale levels $s = 1, 2, \ldots$, and the number of position levels $p = 1, 2, \ldots$.

Each template's size can be scaled along each of three dimensions, thus we have s^3 possible scalings of a template. In experiments we used the scaling factor $\sqrt[3]{1/2}$ separately for each dimension, thus features sizes were calculated in a triple loop as: $(\sqrt[3]{1/2})^j \cdot w_x, (\sqrt[3]{1/2})^k \cdot w_y, (\sqrt[3]{1/2})^l \cdot w_t$, where $(j,k,l) \in \{(1,1,1),\ldots,(s,s,s)\}$ and w. denote initial template widths along particular dimensions. For features positioning we used a regular centered grid. In general, for given p the abscissa for each dimension were: $\{-(p-1),-(p-2)\ldots,-1,0,1,\ldots,p-2,p-1\} \times$ a shift. The shift (for each dimension independently) was implied by the free margin remaining between the window width and template's width after scaling. Thus, the total number of positions was $(2p-1)^3$.

Hence finally, the total number of our 3D Haar-like features was: $17 \cdot s^3 \cdot (2p-1)^3$. E.g. $s=2$ and $p=2$ (our final settings) give $3\,672$ features.

5   Learning Algorithm

After experimenting with three boosting algorithms: *AdaBoost* [2,11], *RealBoost* [9,3] and *Response Binning Boost* [8], we finally decided for the last one yielding the best results. Firstly, the **Response Binning Boost** algorithm approximates postive/negative class distributions by piece-wise constant functions instead of normals (as it is the case in former two algorithms), which is more adequate for multimodal distributions. Secondly, it does not look for a single threshold value to separate classes (as *AdaBoost* does) but applies the maximum a posteriori rule (similarly to *RealBoost*). The response of each weak classifier for an input vector $\mathbf{x}$ is real (not binary): $h(x) = 1/2 \log\left(P(+|\mathbf{x})/P(-|\mathbf{x})\right)$ [5].

Notation. Let $\{(\mathbf{x}_i, y_i)\}$, $i = 1,\ldots,m$, denote the set of training examples, with input feature vectors $\mathbf{x}_i = (x_{i1},\ldots,x_{in})$ and class labels $y_i \in \{-1,1\}$. Let w_i denote the weight of i-th example at current step of the boosting procedure. Let B denote the number of bins. For simplification we use bins of equal widths. Given an interval $[a_1, a_2]$ and a number x, the bin index $\beta(x) \in \{1,\ldots,B\}$ that x belongs to is: $\beta(x) = \lceil B(x - a_1)/(a_2 - a_1) \rceil$ for $a_1 < x \leqslant a_2$; with border cases: $\beta(x) = 1$ for $x \leqslant a_1$ and $\beta(x) = B$ for $a_2 < x$. When pixel intensities are normalized to $[0, 1]$ then Haar-like features are bounded to $[-1, 1]$. The interval $[-1, 1]$ can serve as $[a_1, a_2]$. However, in our GPR data, most features were rarely distributed outside the $[-0.25, 0.25]$ interval, and it was the one finally chosen.

Let $\widehat{P}(+,j \text{ in } b) = \sum_{\{i:\, y_i=+1, \beta(x_{ij})=b\}} w_i$ denote the estimated probability (using current weights) that an example is positive and its j-th feature belongs to bin b; analogically for $\widehat{P}(-,j \text{ in } b)$. For the input vector $\mathbf{x}_i$ the result of a weak classifier using the j-th feature is [3,8]:

$$h(\mathbf{x}_i; j) = 1/2 \log\left(\widehat{P}(+,j \text{ in } \beta(x_{ij})) \Big/ \widehat{P}(-,j \text{ in } \beta(x_{ij}))\right). \tag{1}$$

---

[5] This way also, the weighting of weak classifiers is internally incorporated into this formula. Note that for *AdaBoost* $h(x) = \pm 1$ and the ensemble-classifier is $\sum_k \alpha_k h_k(x)$, where $\alpha_k = 1/2 \log(1 - \epsilon_k)/(\epsilon_k)$ with ϵ_k being the training error of k-th classifier.

Boosting Procedure

1. Start with uniform weights distribution for data examples

$$w_i := 1/m, \quad i = 1, \ldots, m.$$

2. For $k = 1, \ldots, K$ repeat:

   2.1. Select the best feature j_k (and thus the best weak classifier h_k) which minimizes

   $$Z_k := \sum_{i=1}^{m} w_i \exp\left(-y_i h_k(\mathbf{x}_i; j_k)\right).$$

   2.2. Update weights distribution

   $$w_i := w_i \exp\left(-y_i h_k(\mathbf{x}_i; j_k)\right) / Z_k.$$

3. The final classifier is

$$H(\mathbf{x}) = \text{sgn}\left(\sum_{k=1}^{K} h_k(\mathbf{x}; j_k)\right).$$

6 Experiments and Results

For data acquisition, learning and detection experiments, we have developed a combined software environment in *C#* and *Wolfram Mathematica 7.0*. As positive objects (to be detected) we used two anti-tank mine models: a metal one and a plastic one. As negative objects we used various objects non-transparent to GPR: metal boxes, plates, rods, wheels. We set up scenes with different configurations of these objects, see the Fig. 1b, and took GPR measurements from them at resolution $240 \times 200 \times 512$.

After scanning GPR 3D images with a sliding window[6], we obtained a data set consisting in total of: 234 positive window examples and 17 583 negative window examples. It is worth to remark that while scanning we memorized *all* positive windows, but *not all* negative windows, because many of them were repeating 'air examples'. Thus, not all such examples are necessary for the classifier to learn from[7]. For every window 3 672 Haar-like features were calculated. The data was split into training and testing subsets approximately in a proportion $\frac{3}{4} : \frac{1}{4}$.

After being trained via boosting (we imposed at max. 100 weak classifiers, and the number of bins $B = 16$), our prototype mine detector (for indoor 'air' conditions) was tested on the hold-out data set (39 postives, 4 357 negatives). The final results were as follows — **accuracy: 99.91%, sensitivity: 97.43%, FAR: 0.06885%.** This means that only 1 positive window out of all 39, and 3 negative windows out of all 4357 were misclassified.

---

[6] The window size was experimentally set to $45 \times 45 \times 95$ in order to fit mine hyperbolas.

[7] Precisely: if the mean intensity in a negative window was above the typical mean intensity for air (indicating something interesting in it) we kept the window with probability 10%; otherwise, we kept it with probability 1%.

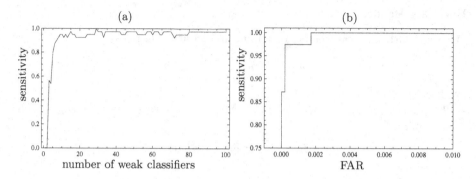

Fig. 4. (a) Sensitivity as the number of weak classifiers grows. (b) Final ROC curve.

In the Fig. 4a we illustrate the influence of the number of weak classifiers on obtained sensitivity measure. The Fig. 4b shows the ROC curve obtained for the ensemble classifier. The curve indicates that the sensitivity can be lifted up to 100% at the cost of FAR increased to 0.17081%.

7   Conclusions and Future Work

Experiments carried out on the prototype detector demonstrate that the proposed approach based on 3D Haar-like features is a promising one. The accuracy level was satisfactorily high, and simultaneously the main motivation — fast performance — has been achieved. Execution times of the overall procedure (for $240 \times 200 \times 512$ images) consisting of: integral image calculation, scanning with a subwindow, multiple extractions of features and detections were of order $800\,ms \div 1200\,ms$ (C#, Intel i7 1.6 GHz CPU, 8 GB RAM). Thus, the mean analysis time per each subwindow was $0.11\,ms \div 0.17\,ms$. Obviously, the learning procedure must be done offline and in our case was taking $\approx 0.5\,h$.

The major future research direction for us is the transition to realistic subsurface conditions. Clearly, all types of inhomogeneities and clutter that can be met underground may cause relevant problems. As additional future work we plan certain construction improvements on the vehicle. Finally, definitely more numeric experiments have to be conducted, involving e.g.: more measurements on various objects 'pretending' to be landmines, tests on greater number of Haar-like features and different learning settings.

References

1. Bhuiyan, A., Nath, B.: Anti-personnel mine detection and classification using GPR image. In: 18th Int. Conf. on Pattern Recognition, ICPR 2006, vol. 2, pp. 1082–1085. IEEE Computer Society, Los Alamitos (2006)
2. Freund, Y., Schapire, R.E.: A decision-theoretic generalization of on-line learning and an application to boosting. Journal of Computer Science and System Sciences 55, 119–139 (1997)

3. Friedman, J., Hastie, T., Tibshirani, R.: Additive logistic regression: a statistical view of boosting. The Annals of Statistics 28(2), 337–407

4. Frigui, H., et al.: Context-dependent multisensor fusion and its application to land mine detection. IEEE Trans. on Geoscience and Remote Sensing 48(6) (2010)

5. Marble, J.A.: Advances in Surface Penetrating Technologies for Imaging, Detection and Classification. PhD thesis, University of Michigan, Michigan, USA (2007)

6. McDonald, J., et al.: Alternatives for landmine detection. Technical report, RAND Corporation (2003)

7. Mol, H.M.: Ground Penetrating Radar: Theory and Applications. Elsevier, Oxford (2009)

8. Rasolzadeh, B., et al.: Response binning: Improved weak classifiers for boosting. In: IEEE Intelligent Vehicles Symposium, pp. 344–349 (2006)

9. Schapire, R.E., Singer, Y.: Improved boosting using confidence-rated predictions. Machine Learning 37(3), 297–336

10. Seyfried, D., et al.: Information extraction from ultrawideband ground penetrating radar data: A machine learning approach. In: 7th German Microwave Conference (GeMiC 2012), pp. 1–4 (2012)

11. Viola, P., Jones, M.: Rapid object detection using a boosted cascade of simple features. In: Conference on Computer Vision and Pattern Recognition, CVPR 2001, pp. 511–518. IEEE (2001)

12. Viola, P., Jones, M.: Robust real-time face detection. International Journal of Computer Vision 57(2), 137–154 (2004)

13. Yarovoy, A.: Landmine and unexploaded ordnance detection and classification with ground penetrating radar. In: Mol, H.M. (ed.) Ground Penetrating Radar: Theory and Applications, pp. 445–478. Elsevier, Oxford (2009)

14. Zhu, Q., Collins, L.M.: Application of feature extraction methods for landmine detection using the Wichmann/Niitek Ground-Penetrating Radar. IEEE Transactions on Geoscience and Remote Sensing 43(1) (2005)

Synchronizing Speech Mixtures in Speech Separation Problems under Reverberant Conditions

Cosme Llerena, Roberto Gil-Pita, Lorena Álvarez, and Manuel Rosa-Zurera

Polytechnic School, University of Alcalá,
Ctra. Madrid-Barcelona Km 33.200, 28850 Alcalá de Henares, Spain
{cosme.llerena,roberto.gil,lorena.alvrezp,manuel.rosa}@uah.es
http://portal.uah.es/portal/page/portal/politecnica/

Abstract. Blind Source Separation (BSS) techniques aim at recovering unobserved source signals from observed mixtures (typically, the outputs of an array of sensors). Practically all classical BSS techniques do not work properly under reverberant conditions and therefore, it still remains an open problem. In this sense, we propose in this document the use of synchronization of speech mixtures in order to improve the results of classical BSS techniques. Specifically, we have applied the synchronization of mixtures combined with one of the most well-known and robust BSS algorithms that works under non-reverberant conditions, the Degenerate Unmixing Estimation Technique (DUET). In the aim of synchronizing speech mixtures prior to the speech source separation, the suitability of working with seven Time Delay Estimation (TDE) techniques has been analyzed. Results show the feasibility of using synchronization since the results of DUET are improved and additionally, it has been observed what is the most useful TDE algorithm in this framework.

Keywords: Speech Source Separation, Time-Delay Estimation, Convolutive Mixing Model, Reverberant Conditions.

1 Introduction

Blind Source Separation (BSS) [1], which was firstly proposed in [2], consists in recovering unobserved source signals from observed mixtures received at a set of sensors. This problem is named as "blind" since: 1) the mixing process is unknown and, 2) there is not much information about the characteristics of the source signals. In order to compensate this lack of information, different techniques and assumptions about the nature of the sources are made. There is a powerful technique underlying BSS algorithms, which is based on spatial diversity. Put it very simple, spatial diversity is a property of sensor arrays that relies on the fact of having more than one sensor and has been exploited in many applications such as, wireless communications [3]. With respect to the different assumptions, the mutual statistical independence of the source signals is broadly supposed [4]; the Independent Component Analysis (ICA) method [5] being a

L. Rutkowski et al. (Eds.): ICAISC 2013, Part I, LNAI 7894, pp. 568–579, 2013.

good example of a BSS algorithm working under this assumption. Apart from this realistic hypothesis, sparsity, which is another property of source signals, is commonly used. Sparsity has different definitions [6] and it is commonly assumed that a signal is sparse when all its energy is concentrated in just one coefficient and all others are zero (or almost zero). In the particular case at hand, since the signals correspond to speech sources[1], an appropriate transformation must be carried out aiming at achieving an adequate sparse representation of them. In this regard, it is well-known that a speech signal represented in the Time-Frequency (T-F) domain can be considered as sparse, since the energy due to speech is contained in a reduced number of time-frequency points and, in general, these points do not overlap with points due to other sources. With this in mind, the Short-Time-Fourier-Transform (STFT) may be applied to the speech sources.

In this sense, the popular Degenerate Unmixing Estimation Technique (DUET) [7] is a good example of a BSS algorithm that makes use of the STFT and aims at assigning each T-F point to one source. In the effort of associating each T-F point with one source or another, it calculates a binary mask that helps the algorithm decide whether a point belongs to a source or the other. These masks are obtained by means of two different ratios computed from the STFT. Being more explicit, these measures include the Inter-sensor Level Difference (ILD) and Inter-sensor Time Difference (ITD). From a mathematical point of view, let us suppose two mixtures ($\mathbf{x}_1$ and $\mathbf{x}_2$) and their STFTs ($X_1(\omega, k)$ and $X_2(\omega, k)$), the mentioned ratios are calculated as shown in Equations (1) and (2)

$$ILD = a_{21} = \frac{|X_2(\omega, k)|}{|X_1(\omega, k)|} \tag{1}$$

$$ITD = \delta_{21} = -\frac{1}{\omega} arg \left(\frac{X_2(\omega, k)}{X_1(\omega, k)} \right) \tag{2}$$

where ω is the index over the frequency bins and k labels the one over the time frames. In this point, it is highlight to mention a certain problem arising in this context when the mixtures are delayed more than the length of a time frame, what basically involves the T-F points do not coincide and then, the information extracted from the abovementioned ratios is wrong. Aiming at overcoming this problem, we propose in this paper, prior to the speech source separation problem carried out by means of DUET algorithm, to firstly synchronize the speech mixtures captured at the set of sensors (microphones in this case). In this sense, in [8], it is studied how clock synchronization affects the performance of sound source separation with a distributed microphone array.

The first step to synchronize the mixtures is to identify the delays. In the particular case at hand, speech mixtures can experiment two different delays. The first one is the propagation delay which involves the time required for the signal to propagate from the source to the microphones and, the second one is due to the synchronization of the microphones since, in a real study-case, it

---

[1] The task of recovering speech sources from audio mixtures is the so-called Blind Audio Source Separation (BASS) in the literature.

seems clear to note that the microphones involved in a set of sensors will not start the recording of the signal at the same time. Note that this latter delay should not exceed the length of a time frame. An example of a scheme to overcome the synchronization problem of distributed audio capture devices is shown in [9].

In this regard, the synchronization of single speech signals by means of Time Delay Estimation (TDE) algorithms has been widely studied in the literature [10,11]. Put it very simple, TDE is the process of determining the relative time shift between a reference signal and a delayed signal and lies at the core of many modern signal-processing algorithms. Different TDE algorithms have been proposed in both time and frequency domain. In this paper, we will focus on a set of very well-known TDE algorithms proposed for time domain.

Within these algorithms, the cross-correlation-based TDE algorithms are the most popular ones. In this kind of algorithms, the goal is to search the maximum value of the cross-correlation, since that value indicates when a signal and the shifted version of another signal have the maximum similarity. Aiming at enhancing the performance of these methods, a large number of improvements have been proposed [12] and they basically consist in introducing a filter or weighting function in the expression of the cross-correlation. These algorithms are known as Generalized Cross-Correlation (GCC) methods [13]. The objective of these algorithms is to make easier the search of the aforementioned maximum value. Examples of GCC methods include the Phase Transform Algorithm (PHAT) or the Roth Processor (ROTH), which both have been studied in this paper. Apart from these two methods, it has been also explored here the use of other algorithms such as, for instance, the Average Square Difference Function (ASDF) method or an adaptive algorithm like the Maximum Likelihood (ML) method.

In the speech signals framework, it is important to point out that the vast majority of the aforementioned TDE algorithms aim at estimating the delay under the assumption of *single* source signals, or in other words, only one speech source is contained in the signal or, at most, the speech signal with a signal due to noise. In the problem at hand, multiple signals are presented in the mixtures, and consequently, speech mixtures are more complex. Note that TDE algorithms for speech mixtures has seen little treatment in the literature so far. For illustrative purposes, in [14] can be found a TDE algorithm working with speech mixtures. It must also be mentioned a interesting work [15], where a very efficient scheme of synchronization combined with a BSS [16] method is proposed.

To sum up, we propose in this paper the synchronization of speech mixtures aiming at improving the results obtained with DUET algorithm in scenarios of convolutive mixtures, paying special attention to situations under reverberant effects. To be more precise, the speech mixtures are firstly synchronized by means of TDE algorithms and after that, the DUET algorithm is carried out. In order to evaluate the feasibility of using the study-case TDE algorithms, we have made use of the so-called signal-to-noise-ratio (SNR) between source signals and the estimated ones as will be shown in the numerical results.

The remainder of this paper is organized as follows. In Section 2, the speech separation problem is described. Section 3 contains the description of the TDE methods that have been implemented in this paper. In Section 4, the experimental setup and the database used for the experiments are explained, along with the results obtained. Finally, Section 5 summarizes the conclusions of this work.

2   Speech Separation Problem

2.1   The Mixing Model

Fig. 1 illustrates the particular speech separation problem explored in this paper. As shown, $N = 2$ speech sources and $M = 2$ microphones are presented, what involves an even-determined case. Although it will be better understood later on, we can say in advance that this figure depicts the typical scenario in which two people are speaking in a room.

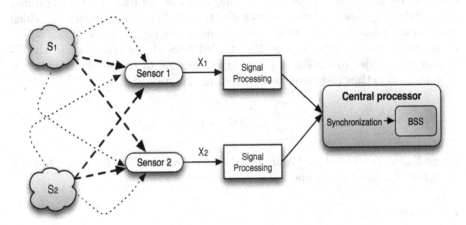

Fig. 1. An illustrative representation of the particular speech separation problem explored in this paper, that is, convolutive mixing model with noise and reverberation effects. Note that prior to the speech separation, mixtures are synchronized in a central processor by means of TDE methods.

In order to carry out the speech source separation, it is necessary to previously understand the way the mixing process happens. In our particular study-case, we suppose a convolutive mixing model in a noisy and reverberant environment. Convolutive mixing process refers here to the fact that the differences of delays that a speech source suffers among the different microphones are taken into account. Regarding the noise, it has been assumed an additive Gaussian noise with mean equals to zero and variance equals to σ^2. In addition, echoes of the target's reflected waves also have been considered due to the reverberant conditions.

Put it in a more mathematical way, it is assumed that at the discrete-time t, a set of N sources signals, that is, $\mathbf{s}(t) = [s_1(t), \ldots, s_N(t)]$ is received at M sensors that are part of an array sensor, $\mathbf{x}(t) = [x_1(t), \ldots, x_M(t)]$ being thus the received mixtures at the time t. This can be clearly observed in Equation (3)

$$x_m(t) = \sum_{n=1}^{N} a_{mn}(t) * s_n(t), \ \forall \ m = 1, \ldots, M, \tag{3}$$

where any mixed signal is a linear mixture of filtered versions of each source signal and $a_{mn}(t)$ label the mixing filter coefficients which basically depend on the position of sources and microphones. And since noise and reverberation effects are considered, Equation (3) can be rewritten as shown in Equation (4)

$$x_m(t) = \sum_{n=1}^{N} a_{mn}(t) * s_n(t) + i_m(t), \ \forall \ m = 1, \ldots, M. \tag{4}$$

$i_m(t)$ being the sum of interfering signals at the discrete time t and at the microphone m. These interference signals may occur because of 1) the background noise and/or 2) echoes of the sources due to reverberation phenomena, which result in attenuated and delayed copies of the sources $s_n(t), \forall \ n = 1, \ldots, N$.

As stated in the Introduction, the studied BSS algorithms work in the T-F domain in order to obtain a sparse representation of the source signals and Equation (4) is thus re-written as depicted in Equation (5)

$$X_m(\omega, k) = \sum_{n=1}^{N} A_{mn}(\omega) \cdot S_n(\omega, k) + I_m(\omega, k), \tag{5}$$

where $X_m(\omega, k)$ and $S_n(\omega, k)$ represent the STFT for the ω-th frequency bin and m-th time frame of $x_m(t)$ and $s_n(t)$, respectively.

2.2   Source Demixing

As succinctly mentioned in the Introduction, DUET makes use of a time-frequency mask $(M_{\omega k})$ to separate speech sources in the T-F domain and this mask is calculated from Inter-sensor Level Differences and Inter-sensor Time Differences as explained in [7]. From a mathematical point of view, this mask is used as follows:

$$\widehat{S}_n(\omega, k) = M_{\omega k} \cdot X_m(\omega, k), \tag{6}$$

where $\widehat{S}_n(\omega, k)$ is the estimation of the n-th source and $X_m(\omega, k)$ labels the mixture at ω-th frequency bin and k-th frame for the m-th microphone.

Regrettably, in the case of speech mixtures, this mask may not work properly since the sparse property is not always correct because of the fact that there are contributions of different sources, echoes of these sources and so on.

3   Time Delay Estimation

The study-case TDE algorithms are explained in a detailed way in the paragraphs that follow. As previously mentioned, they have been chosen because they are well-known and robust methods for estimating delays between different kinds of signals. In Section 4, we will explore how well these algorithms work in estimating delays for the case of speech mixtures. In order to explain the methods, it is worth mentioning that we denote the two speech mixtures of our study-case by (x_1 and x_2) and the delay between them by D_{12}.

3.1 Cross-Correlation (CC) Method

The cross-correlation between speech mixtures is calculated. If the length of the mixtures is T, the expression of the cross-correlation is shown in Equation (7)

$$R_{x_1x_2}(\tau) = E\left[x_1(t)x_2(t-\tau)\right], \; \forall \, 1 \le t \le T. \tag{7}$$

It is well-known that the delay between both mixtures can be obtained from the position of the maximum peak of the cross-correlation [12].

3.2 Phase Transform (PHAT) Method

This algorithm has been chosen since it has been widely used for estimating delays between acoustic signals arriving at spatially distributed microphones. PHAT method can be classified into the group of Generalized Cross-Correlation (GCC) methods, or in other words, a weighting function (ψ_p) is introduced in the expression of the cross-correlation, as it can be observed in Equation (8)

$$R_{x_1x_2}(\tau) = \int_{-\infty}^{\infty} \psi_p(f)G_{x_1x_2}(f)e^{j2\pi f\tau}df \tag{8}$$

where $G_{x_1x_2}(f)$ labels the cross-spectrum of the received signals and the weighting function responds to Expression (9)

$$\psi_p(f) = \frac{1}{|G_{x_1x_2}(f)|}. \tag{9}$$

This new weighting function can be very useful since it aims to sharpen the peaks of the cross-correlation by means of whitening the input mixtures, making easier to find the location of the maximum peak. Having a look at Expression (9), it seems clear to note that the information related to phase is preserved.

3.3 Modified Phase Transform (PHAT-β) Method

This modified version [17] of PHAT algorithm has been also studied. It has been shown that it provides very good results in estimating delays when signals are corrupted by both independent noise and reverberation effects. Within this algorithm, the weighting function is very similar to that of PHAT algorithm but in this case, a new parameter (β) is taken into account. The expression of this new weighting function can be observed in Equation (10)

$$\psi_{p\beta}(f) = \frac{1}{\left|G_{x_1x_2}^{\beta}(f)\right|}. \tag{10}$$

This parameter allows us to control the degree of whitening and limit the amount of degradation from the independent noise. Please note that β is a real number ranging from 0 to 1. If β is equal to 0, the algorithm is equivalent to CC method and if β is set to be 1, the algorithm is equivalent to PHAT method. In the case of intermediate values, a process of partial whitening occurs.

3.4   Maximum Likelihood (ML) Method

ML method [18] is also included in GCC methods and it has been selected since it works in systems where multipath effects are considered. It tends to obtain maximum likelihood solutions for TDE problems. Within this method, the weighting function responds to the expression shown in Equation (11)

$$\psi_{ML}(f) = \frac{1}{|G_{x_1 x_2}(f)|} \frac{|\gamma_{x_1 x_2}(f)|^2}{1 - |\gamma_{x_1 x_2}(f)|^2} \tag{11}$$

where $|\gamma_{x_1 x_2}(f)|^2$ is the magnitude squared coherency and it responds to Equation (12)

$$|\gamma_{x_1 x_2}(f)|^2 = \frac{|G_{x_1 x_2}(f)|^2}{G_{x_1 x_1}(f) \cdot G_{x_2 x_2}(f)}. \tag{12}$$

The ML function aims at increasing the accuracy of the calculation of the delay. It can be observed that the greater weight is assigned to frequency bands that give near-unity coherence. In the same line of reasoning as that in the previous methods, the maximum of the cross-correlation must be computed.

3.5   Roth Processor (ROTH)

ROTH processor [19] has been chosen since it has been proven to be very efficient in scenarios where additive noise is presented [13], by means of suppressing the frequency regions where noise is clearly presented. Within this algorithm, the weighting function has been found to be as follows:

$$\psi_{roth}(f) = \frac{1}{G_{x_1 x_1}(f)}. \tag{13}$$

3.6   Smoothed Coherence Transform (SCOT)

SCOT method [20] has been used in many TDE applications where the presence of noise is important. In this case, the expression of the weighting function is as indicated in Equation (14)

$$\psi_{scoth}(f) = \frac{1}{\sqrt{G_{x_1 x_1}(f) \cdot G_{x_2 x_2}(f)}}. \tag{14}$$

It can be considered as a pre-whitening filter followed by a process of cross-correlation. Having a look at Equation (13), it seems clear to note that if $G_{x_1 x_1}(f) = G_{x_2 x_2}(f)$, SCOT method is equivalent to ROTH algorithm.

3.7   Average Square Difference Function (ASDF) Method

ASDF [21] method does not belong to GCC methods, since instead of using the cross-correlation function, it uses a difference function what involves lower usage of computational load, since multiplications are not needed. This difference function is the square error between the signals as shown in Equation (15)

$$R_{ASDF}(\tau) = \frac{1}{T} \sum_{t=0}^{T-1} |x_1(t) - x_2(t - \tau)|^2. \tag{15}$$

By searching the minimum of the previous function, the delay between the signals is determined from its corresponding τ.

To sum up, it can be mentioned that these classical TDE algorithms have been chosen because they have demonstrated to have several advantages in classical TDE problems, not only in terms of computational cost, but also in robustness against the presence of noise, reverberations or multipath effects, etc. Then, we are interested in exploring their performances in our BSS problem.

4   Results

4.1   Experimental Setup

The sound database has been created from TIMIT database [22]. TIMIT database includes a total of 630 speakers (70 % male and 30 % female) of American English. The signals are 16-bit with a sampling frequency of 16000 Hz. From these speech signals, signals of different lengths have been obtained (0.25, 0.5, 1, 2, 4, 8 and 16 seconds). Frame size of the STFT (L_f) has also been set to different values (128, 256, 512, 1024 and 2048 samples), aiming at exploring the performance of DUET using the study-case TDE algorithms.

To carry out the experiments, we have set up a simple scenario that simulates the situation of two people talking simultaneously in a room of dimensions $6 \times 6 \times 3$ m. A 2-microphone array has been used and in order to simulate its response, the model that we use is the so-called Mirror Image model [23], which performs the microphone impulse response including room impulse response calculation. It considers both directivity pattern of the microphone and attenuation due to distance. For a number of N sources, the mentioned model considers that there are $(2 \cdot N + 1)^3$ virtual sources to simulate the echoes of the speech sources. In this model, we have modified the reflection coefficient (C_r), from 0 (non-reverberant environment) to 0.2 in steps of 0.1 (reverberant environments).

To evaluate the performance of BSS algorithms, we have chosen a metric that considers the quality of the separated signals, to be more precise, the SNR between original and separated sources.

4.2   Numerical Results

In the aim of demonstrating the advantages of synchronizing the input speech mixtures in DUET algorithm, different experiments are carried out considering a large number of parameter combinations (length of mixtures, STFT frame size, reflection coefficient, ...). Due to the large number of parameter combinations, all the results cannot be shown, nevertheless, the most important ones are presented. For example, it has been observed that the longer the length signal is, the better the results obtained are and this is the reason why the results for signals of 16 seconds length are shown in Table 1 and Table 2. Specifically, these tables show the mean SNR of 60 experiments between the separated and original sources in a non-reverberant and in a reverberant environment, respectively.

Deepening a little more in the results depicted in Table 1, the first row shows the values obtained by using DUET algorithm without synchronizing the speech mixtures, in the scenario proposed in Section 4.1. As illustrated, these values basically range from 3.26 to 3.54 dB, which are low in terms of speech quality and motivate us to explore the performance of synchronizing the speech mixtures. In the rest of rows in Table 1, the outcomes achieved thanks to the combination of the synchronization of the speech mixtures and DUET algorithm are shown, for different STFT frame sizes (L_f). Note that the TDE algorithms used in the synchronization process are explained in Section 3. It is also worth mentioning that for PATH-β algorithm, β is varied from 0.1 to 0.9 in steps of 0.1, although Table 1 only shows the cases in which the highest SNR is obtained, that is, for $\beta = 0.1, 0.2, 0.3, 0.4$ and 0.9. Looking at the SNRs obtained, it seems clear to note that an important increase of the SNR has been obtained when compared to those values obtained without synchronization, leading to reach values of SNR higher than 7 dB, what represents significant improvements. For the cases of shorter STFT frame sizes, especially for $L_f = 128$ and 256, an improvement of more than 70 % is obtained, reaching more than 100 % of improvement when longer STFT frame sizes are used, like, for example, for $L_f = 1024$ and 2048. Then, it is clear to note that the longer the STFT frame size is, the better the SNR obtained is and roughly speaking, this increase of SNR for longer frame sizes occurs with all the study-case TDE methods. For illustrative purposes, PATH-0.2 obtains a SNR equals to 5.80 dB for $L_f = 128$, whereas it reaches a SNR equals to 7.39 dB for $L_f = 2048$. It is interesting to note that PATH-β obtains in general very good results for all the frame sizes for low values of β (from 0.1 to 0.4), what it makes sense since PATH-β is especially designed for cases in which reverberation effects and noise are presented. Note that ASDF method decreases drastically its performance as the STFT frame size increases.

Table 2 illustrates very interesting information since a speech separation problem in a room under reverberation effects ($C_r = 0.2$, a typical reflection coefficient) is considered. Speech separation in reverberant conditions still remains an open problem since, due to its complexity, the vast majority of BSS algorithms do not achieve good results. Table 2 represents the same information as Table 1 but for a reverberant case. Looking at the first row of Table 2, DUET algorithm without synchronizing speech mixtures obtains lower SNRs than for the same situation without reverberation, these values ranging from 2.17 to 2.67 dB. It is important to note that, despite reverberation effects, an improvement close to 65 % has been obtained for the shorter STFT frame sizes and reaching an

Table 1. Mean SNR obtained by DUET without (first row) and using (the rest of rows) the different TDE algorithms, for the even-determined convolutive case of two mixtures and two sources, with noise and without reverberation effects ($Cr = 0$). 60 speech separation experiments have been carried out per each combination of parameters.

TDE	$L_f=128$	$L_f=256$	$L_f=512$	$L_f=1024$	$L_f=2048$
-	3.31	3.33	3.26	3.30	3.54
CC	5.79	5.82	6.11	6.84	7.37
PHAT	5.61	5.73	5.88	6.47	6.93
PHAT-0.1	5.79	5.82	6.11	6.84	7.35
PHAT-0.2	5.80	5.78	6.02	6.97	7.39
PHAT-0.3	5.85	5.78	6.03	6.84	7.24
PHAT-0.4	5.80	5.76	6.01	6.80	7.18
PHAT-0.9	5.56	5.54	5.85	6.58	6.92
ML	5.47	5.69	5.75	6.47	6.93
ASDF	5.79	5.82	6.29	5.32	4.39
ROTH	5.44	5.52	5.62	6.23	6.69
SCOT	5.72	5.66	6.00	6.50	7.01

Table 2. Mean SNR obtained by DUET without (first row) and using (the rest of rows) the different TDE algorithms, for the even-determined convolutive case of two mixtures and two sources, with noise and reverberation effects ($Cr = 0.2$). 60 speech separation experiments have been carried out per each combination of parameters.

TDE	$L_f=128$	$L_f=256$	$L_f=512$	$L_f=1024$	$L_f=2048$
-	2.39	2.17	2.41	2.67	2.56
CC	3.81	3.85	3.90	3.96	4.66
PHAT	3.84	3.89	3.92	3.99	4.47
PHAT-0.1	3.81	3.83	3.86	3.94	4.68
PHAT-0.2	3.84	3.83	4.03	3.97	4.65
PHAT-0.3	3.84	3.83	4.03	3.97	4.65
PHAT-0.4	3.81	3.81	3.96	4.04	4.64
PHAT-0.9	3.84	3.89	3.92	3.99	4.47
ML	3.83	3.88	3.89	4.01	4.46
ASDF	3.81	3.85	4.09	3.55	3.43
ROTH	3.73	3.68	3.81	3.83	4.52
SCOT	3.87	3.87	3.74	3.99	4.42

improvement of approximately 80 % for STFT frames of $L_f = 2048$. Unexpectedly, for the particular case of $L_f = 1024$, the improvement is lower, being about 50 %. Note that when $C_r = 0.2$, there is not a most appropriate TDE algorithm, since the results depend on the STFT frame size. As the reader can note, despite that DUET algorithm does not work properly for reverberant problems as the one proposed here, its results have been significantly increased (reaching more than 4.5 dB for the best cases), what leads to think about the idea of applying synchronization of speech mixtures with other BSS algorithms.

5 Conclusions

This paper focuses on applying synchronization of speech mixtures prior to the speech separation problem for BSS algorithms that use ILDs and ITDs, DUET being a very representative example. We have studied a convolutive mixing case with additive Gaussian noise and with or without reverberation effects, specifically, we have implemented a problem in a room using the Mirror Image Model to simulate the reverberation and multipath effects. We pay special attention to speech separation problems under reverberation effects due to its difficulty.

We have tested seven TDE methods in order to synchronize speech mixtures and different results have been obtained depending on some parameters as the reflection coefficient, STFT frame size, etc. Both in the non-reverberant case as in the reverberant one, an important improvement of the SNR has been obtained.

In the case without reverberation, a considerable increase of the SNR has been achieved, in some cases, *doubling* the value of SNR. According the STFT frame size increases, the SNR increases, for example, the 7.39 dB obtained by PATH-0.2 for a STFT frame size of 2048. We also realize that broadly, PATH-β method for values of β equal to 0.1, 0.2 and 0.3, achieves the better results, while ASDF method performs worse results with longer STFT frame sizes. The rest of TDE methods work achieving similar results. With reverberation effects, we have also improved the outcomes of the DUET algorithm, increasing the SNR close to 70% when longer STFT frame sizes. Unlike the non-reverberant case, all the algorithms achieve very similar results except ASDF method.

Therefore delays such as, the propagation delay of the sources or the delay due to synchronization of the microphones, do not affect the results of our BSS algorithm. To sum up, these results point out to a new filed of research in the jointly use of TDE and better adapted BSS algorithms to reverberant cases.

Acknowledgments. This work has been funded by the Spanish Ministry of Science (project TEC2012-38142-C04-02) and the Spanish Ministry of Defence (DEFENSA2011-10032110035).

References

1. Cao, X.R., Liu, R.: General approach to blind source separation. IEEE Transactions on Signal Processing, 562–571 (1996)
2. Hérault, J., Jutten, C., Ans, B.: Détection de grandeurs primitives dans un message composite par une architecture de calcul neuromimétique en apprentissage non supervisé. In: 10 Colloque sur le Traitement du Signal et Des Images, France (1985)
3. Diggavi, S.N., Al-Dhahir, N., Stamoulis, A., Calderbank, A.R.: Great expectations: The value of spatial diversity in wireless networks. Proceedings of the IEEE, 219–270 (2004)
4. Cichocki, A., Georgiev, P.: Blind source separation algorithms with matrix constraints. IEICE Transactions on Fundamentals of Electronics, Communications and Computer Sciences, 522–531 (2003)

5. Te-Won, L.: Independent component analysis: theory and applications. Kluwer Academic Publishers, Boston (1998)
6. Hurley, N., Rickard, S.: Comparing measures of sparsity. IEEE Transactions on Information Theory, 4723–4741 (2009)
7. Yilmaz, O., Rickard, S.: Blind separation of speech mixtures via time-frequency masking. IEEE Transactions on Signal Processing, 1830–1847 (2004)
8. Zicheng, L.: Sound source separation with distributed microphone arrays in the presence of clock synchronization errors. In: Proc. Int. Workshop Acoustic Echo and Noise Control, IWAENC (2008)
9. Lienhart, R., Kozintsev, I., Wehr, S., Yeung, M.: On the importance of exact synchronization for distributed audio signal processing. In: IEEE International Conference on Acoustics, Speech, and Signal Processing, ICASSP, vol. 4, pp. IV-840–IV-843. IEEE (2003)
10. Brandstein, M.S., Adcock, J.E., Silverman, H.F.: A practical time-delay estimator for localizing speech sources with a microphone array. Computer Speech and Language, 153–170 (1995)
11. Yegnanarayana, B., Prasanna, S.R.M., Duraiswami, R., Zotkin, D.: Processing of reverberant speech for time-delay estimation. IEEE Transactions on Speech and Audio Processing, 1110–1118 (2005)
12. Carter, G.C.: Coherence and time delay estimation. Proceedings of the IEEE, 236–255 (1987)
13. Knapp, C., Carter, G.: The generalized correlation method for estimation of time delay. IEEE Transactions on Acoustics, Speech and Signal Processing, 320–327 (1976)
14. Emile, B., Comon, P., Le Roux, J.: Estimation of time delays with fewer sensors than sources. IEEE Transactions on Signal Processing, 2012–2015 (1998)
15. Wehr, S., Kozintsev, I., Lienhart, R., Kellermann, W.: Synchronization of acoustic sensors for distributed ad-hoc audio networks and its use for blind source separation. In: Proceedings of the IEEE Sixth International Symposium on Multimedia Software Engineering, pp. 18–25. IEEE (2004)
16. Francourt, C., Parra, L.: The coherence function in blind source separation of convolutive mixtures of non-stationary signals. In: IEEE Workshop on Neural Networks for Signal Processing, pp. 303–312 (2001)
17. Donohue, K.D., Agrinsoni, A., Hannemann, J.: Audio signal delay estimation using partial whitening. In: Proceedings of the IEEE SoutheastCon, pp. 466–471. IEEE (2007)
18. Saarnisaari, H.: ML time delay estimation in a multipath channel. In: Proceedings of the IEEE 4th International Symposium on Spread Spectrum Techniques and Applications, pp. 1007–1011. IEEE (1996)
19. Roth, P.R.: Effective measurements using digital signal analysis. IEEE Spectrum 8, 62–70 (1971)
20. Carter, G.C., Nuttall, A.H., Cable, P.G.: The smoothed coherence transform. Proceedings of the IEEE, 1497–1498 (1973)
21. Jacovitti, G., Scarano, G.: Discrete time techniques for time delay estimation. IEEE Transactions on Signal Processing, 525–533 (1993)
22. Seneff, S., Zue, V.: Transcription and alignment of the timit database, TIMIT CD-ROM Documentation (1998)
23. McGovern, S.G: A model for room acoustics, http://www.2pi.us/rir.html

Neuronal Model-Based Image Reconstruction from Projections Method

Anna Lorent, Michał Knaś, and Piotr Dobosz

Institute of Computational Intelligence, Czestochowa University of Technology,
Armii Krajowej 36, 42-200 Czestochowa, Poland

Abstract. The presented paper describes a model-based approach to the image reconstruction from projections problem, which takes into consideration the statistical properties of the measurements in tomographic system with parallel x-ray beams. The reconstruction problem is formulated as an optimization problem. Different forms of objectives of this optimization are tested. The optimization process is carried out using a recurrent neural network. Experimental results show that the exactly statistically tailored objective yields the best results, and appropriately designed neural network is able to reconstruct an image with better quality than a conventional algorithm with convolution and back-projection.

1 Introduction

The image reconstruction problem is a popular research topic in various fields. It is especially relevant to medicine, in particular to the medical imaging techniques, e.g. computed tomography (CT) (see e.g. [1]). The images obtained with this technique are often blurred because the real measurements of X-ray intensity, which are used to perform the reconstruction, are distorted by physical noise. The quality of the reconstructed image in the presence of noise can be measured using the low-level resolution parameter evaluated using a physical phantom. One of the possible solutions to overcome the problem mentioned above is to increase the intensity of X-rays emitted by an X-ray tube. Unfortunately, this approach undoubtedly has negative effects on the health of the patient and conflicts with the current safety requirements for radiation protection. Therefore, this situation presents a challenge for the scientists concerned with the image reconstruction problem. The main goal of these efforts is to formulate reconstruction algorithms in which the statistical nature of the measured signals is taken into consideration. It is likely to result in a significant improvement of the reconstructed images or in a decrease of intensity of the X-ray radiation used.

Analytical reconstruction methods, e.g. filtered back-projection method (FBP), and algebraic reconstruction techniques (ART) [2] are the most popular reconstruction methods in computed tomography. Statistical reconstruction methods are being currently developed, because they are adapted to the specific statistics of a given technique so they can yield a reduction in radiation dose during an examination. The most interesting statistical algorithms are based on the statistical model of a given medical imaging system, e.g. the maximum *a posteriori* probability (MAP) approach (see [3]) which is a development of the maximum likelihood (ML) concept. This model is included in

L. Rutkowski et al. (Eds.): ICAISC 2013, Part I, LNAI 7894, pp. 580–587, 2013.

the design of the iterative coordinate descent (ICD) reconstruction method. Other approaches are also based on this methodology, such as conjugate gradient (CG) approach [4] [5] and ordered-subsets (OS) algorithms [6] [7]. Contrary to IDC, in CG and OS all the pixels are updated in parallel, but these methods need considerably more iterations to achieve a solution. It worth noting that in all these algorithms the optimization procedures are performed, where the primary term of the cost function is formulated in the algebraic way. An analytical approach (see e.g. [8], [9], [10], [11]) would eliminate most of the problems related to the algebraic background of those algorithms, first of all, the computational complexity of the method.

In this paper we present the use of an analytical model-based iterative reconstruction method, which takes a few thousand steps to converge and improves image quality.

2 Neural Network Statistical Image Reconstruction Algorithm

The analytical statistical reconstruction algorithm was previously described in [12]. In the paper presented here, we develop this idea, taking into consideration the time of reconstruction process and the calculation complexity of the algorithm. The proposed reconstruction method using the recurrent neural network is shown in Fig.1, where the parallel-beam geometry of collected projections is used.

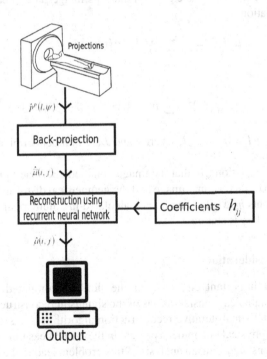

Fig. 1. An image reconstruction algorithm with parallel-beam geometry of the scanner

2.1   The Back-Projection Operation

The first step of the considered reconstruction algorithm is a back-projection operation. Let us define the function $\mu(x,y)$ which describes a distribution of the attenuation coefficient of X-rays in an investigated cross-section of the human body. This operation is carried out according to the following relation:

$$\tilde{\mu}(x,y) = \int_0^\pi \dot{p}(s,\alpha)\,d\alpha. \tag{1}$$

During this operation we use the measurements $p(s,\alpha)$ obtained in a physical way by the scanner. It is highly possible that for a given projection no ray passes through a certain point (x,y) of the reconstructed image. To evaluate a projection value for a virtual ray passing through this point we can apply interpolation, as follows:

$$\dot{p}(\dot{s},\alpha) = \int_{-\infty}^{+\infty} p(s,\alpha)\cdot int\,(\dot{s}-s)\,ds, \tag{2}$$

where $int\,(\Delta s)$ is an interpolation function, and $s = x\cos\alpha + y\sin\alpha$. After the back-projection operation we obtain a strongly blurred image $\tilde{\mu}(x,y)$.

It is shown in the literature (see e.g. [11]) that this image $\tilde{\mu}(x,y)$ can be expressed by the following relation:

$$\hat{\mu}(i,j) \approx \sum_k \sum_l \hat{\mu}(l,k)\cdot h(i-k,j-l), \tag{3}$$

where

$$h(\Delta i,\Delta j) = \Delta_\alpha\,(\Delta_s)^2 \cdot \sum_{\psi=0}^{\Psi-1} int\,(i\Delta_s\cos\psi\Delta_\alpha + j\Delta_s\sin\psi\Delta_\alpha), \tag{4}$$

and $i,k = 0,1,\ldots,I$; $j,l = 0,1,\ldots,J$, where I and J are numbers of pixels in horizontal and vertical directions.

One can see from equation (3), that the image obtained after back-projection operation is a convolution of the original image and the geometrical distortion element given by (4). The coefficients $h(\Delta i,\Delta j)$ can be precalculated in a numerical way, before the reconstruction procedure is started.

2.2   Statistical Considerations

Currently, the most important challenge in the field of computed tomography is concerned with the statistical considerations of the signals in reconstruction algorithms (see e.g. [3]). Our statistical iterative reconstruction algorithm is based on the probabilistic model of the physical phenomena present in the x-ray measurement system. The detailed considerations regarding an analysis of this problem lead to the conclusion that it is justified to use an appropriate form of the error measure during reconstruction process. The following model-based loss function for the reconstruction algorithm has been proposed in [12]:

$$L1 = -\frac{1}{2} \sum_{i=1}^{I} \sum_{j=1}^{J} \frac{1}{\sigma_\Sigma^2(i,j)} \cdot f\left(\sum_{\bar{i}} \sum_{\bar{j}} \hat{\mu}^*(\bar{i},\bar{j}) \cdot h(\Delta i, \Delta j) - \hat{\mu}(i,j)\right), \qquad (5)$$

The equation involves the term $\sigma_\Sigma^2(i,j)$ related to the values of variations of signals measured by the X-ray detectors. The values of this term need to be computed and stored in the memory for all pixels of the image being reconstructed. The use of the value $\sigma_\Sigma^2(i,j)$ in such a form contributes to the increase of the computational cost of the algorithm as a large number of multiplications for this term is needed in each iteration, i.e. equal to the number of pixels in the image. Our goal in this paper is to examine the influence of the constant for all pixels value of this coefficient on the performance of the algorithm. We will consider a modified loss function in the following form:

$$L2 = -\frac{1}{2} \sum_{i=1}^{I} \sum_{j=1}^{J} \frac{1}{\bar{\sigma}^2} \cdot f\left(\sum_{\bar{i}} \sum_{\bar{j}} \hat{\mu}^*(\bar{i},\bar{j}) \cdot h(\Delta i, \Delta j) - \hat{\mu}(i,j)\right), \qquad (6)$$

where $\sigma_\Sigma^2(i,j)$ from equation (5) is replaced with a value averaged for all pixels:

$$\bar{\sigma}^2 = \frac{1}{I \cdot J} \sum_{i=1}^{I} \sum_{j=1}^{J} \sigma_\Sigma^2(i,j) \qquad (7)$$

This will enable us to move the coefficient $\bar{\sigma}^2$ outside the sum in the equation (6), which will significantly reduce the number of multiplications performed during each iteration of the algorithm.

It is worth noting that the form of the function $f(\bullet)$ we use is as follows:

$$f(e(i,j)) = c\lambda \cdot \ln \cosh\left(\frac{e(i,j)}{\lambda}\right). \qquad (8)$$

where: c and λ are constant coefficients.

2.3 Reconstruction Process Using Recurrent Neural Network

The recurrent neural network used for realizing the reconstruction process performs the image reconstruction from projection in 2D by optimization of the objective determined by relation (5) or (6) (other approaches are possible too, for example using neuro-fuzzy systems, see e.g. [13], [14]). This can be formulated as the following optimization problem:

$$\min_{\mathbf{M}} \left(w \cdot \sum_{i=1}^{I} \sum_{j=1}^{J} \frac{1}{\sigma_\Sigma^2(i,j)} \cdot f(e(i,j)(\mathbf{M})) \right), \qquad (9)$$

or

$$\min_{\mathbf{M}} \left(w \cdot \sum_{i=1}^{I} \sum_{j=1}^{J} \frac{1}{\bar{\sigma}^2} \cdot f\left(e\left(i,j\right)\left(\mathbf{M}\right)\right) \right), \tag{10}$$

where: $\mathbf{M} = [\hat{\mu}(i,j)]$ is a matrix of pixels from the original image; w is a suitable large positive coefficient; $f(\bullet)$ is the penalty function

Having above described the methodology of the approach to the optimization problem we can assume the form of distance $e(i,j)$, as follows

$$e\left(i,j\right) = \sum_{\bar{i}} \sum_{\bar{j}} \hat{\mu}^* \left(\bar{i}, \bar{j}\right) \cdot h\left(\Delta i, \Delta j\right) - \hat{\mu}\left(i,j\right). \tag{11}$$

Hence, we can determine the following relation:

$$\frac{d\hat{\mu}^t\left(i,j\right)}{dt} = -w \sum_{\bar{i}=1}^{I} \sum_{\bar{j}=1}^{J} \frac{1}{\sigma_{\Sigma}^2\left(i,j\right)} \cdot f'\left(e\left(i,j\right)\right) h\left(\Delta i, \Delta j\right), \tag{12}$$

or

$$\frac{d\hat{\mu}^t\left(i,j\right)}{dt} = -w \sum_{\bar{i}=1}^{I} \sum_{\bar{j}=1}^{J} \frac{1}{\bar{\sigma}^2\left(i,j\right)} \cdot f'\left(e\left(i,j\right)\right) h\left(\Delta i, \Delta j\right), \tag{13}$$

Taking into consideration the origin of the distance $e(i,j)$ we can expect good results of image reconstruction using described algorithm measure of projections in x-ray computed tomography. The pair of equations (11) and (12)/(13) is a starting point to construct recurrent neural network structure (see e.g. [15]) realising the image reconstruction process depicted in Fig. 1.

3   Experimental Results

Computer simulations were carried out to analyse the effects of using the constant value of coefficient $\bar{\sigma}^2$ on the running time of the algorithm and the quality of the reconstructed image. For the purposes of testing the approach proposed here, we have used a mathematical model of the human head, the well-known FORBILD phantom, which can be seen in its original form in Table 1c. In our experiments the image size was 1024 $\times$1024 pixels. The quality of the reconstruction has been evaluated by computing the MSE error measure between the original and the reconstructed images.

The simulations were implemented for GPUs with the NVIDIA CUDA framework and executed on the GeForce GTX 680 graphics card. The results obtained for 3000 iterations of the algorithm are presented in Table 1.

Table 1. View of the images: a) original image; b) image reconstructed using the original loss function (5); c) image reconstructed using the loss function with constant $\bar{\sigma}^2$ (6); d) reconstructed image using the standard FBP with Shepp-Logan kernel

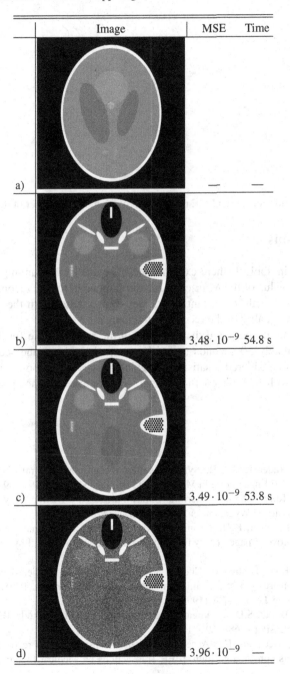

	Image	MSE	Time
a)		—	—
b)		$3.48 \cdot 10^{-9}$	54.8 s
c)		$3.49 \cdot 10^{-9}$	53.8 s
d)		$3.96 \cdot 10^{-9}$	—

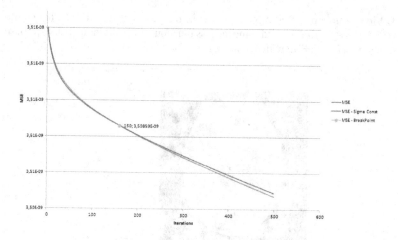

Fig. 2. The value of the MSE plotted as a function of the number of iterations

4 Conclusions

As can be seen in Table 1, there exits a trade-off between the running time of the algorithm and the value of the MSE error measure obtained for the reconstructed image. Replacing $\sigma_\Sigma^2(i, j)$ with a constant coefficient $\bar{\sigma}^2$ decreases both the run-time of the algorithm and the quality of the reconstructed image.

However, it should be noted that the gain in the running time for 3000 iterations, taking approximately 50 seconds to finish, is equal to about one second. If such a difference is not considered a satisfactory gain for specific purposes, it is justified to use statistically well-founded coefficient $\sigma_\Sigma^2(i, j)$ computed for each pixel of the image separately.

References

1. Ogiela, M.R., Tadeusiewicz, R.: Syntactic pattern recognition for X-ray diagnosis of pancreatic cancer. IEEE Engineering in Medicine and Biology Magazine 19(6), 94–105 (2000)
2. Cierniak, R.: Tomografia komputerowa. Budowa urzadzen CT. Algorytmy rekonstrukcyjne. Akademicka Oficyna Wydawnicza EXIT, Warszawa (2005)
3. Thibault, J.-B., Sauer, K.D., Bouman, C.A., Hsieh, J.: A three-dimensional statistical approach to improved image quality for multislice helical CT. Medical Physics 11, 4526–4544 (2007)
4. Muncuoglu, E.U., Leahy, R., Cherry, S.R., Zhou, Z.: Fast gradient-based methods for bayesian reconstruction of transmission and emission PET images. IEEE Transactions on Medical Imaging 13, 687–701 (1994)
5. Fessler, J.A., Booth, S.D.: Conjugate-gradient preconditioning methods. IEEE Transactions on Image Processing 8, 688–699 (1999)
6. Kamphuis, C., Beekman, F.J.: Accelerated iterative transmission CT reconstruction using an ordered subsets convex algorithm. IEEE Transactions on Medical Imaging 17, 1001–1005 (1998)

7. Erdogan, H., Fessler, J.A.: Ordered subsets algorithm for transmission tomography. Physics in Medicine and Biology 44, 2835–2851 (1999)
8. Cierniak, R.: A 2D approach to tomographic image reconstruction using a Hopfield-type neural network. International Journal Artificial Intelligence in Medicine 43, 113–125 (2008)
9. Cierniak, R.: A new approach to image reconstruction from projections problem using a recurrent neural network. Applied Mathematics and Computer Science 18, 147–157 (2008)
10. Cierniak, R.: A novel approach to image reconstruction problem from fan-beam projections using recurrent neural network. In: Rutkowski, L., Tadeusiewicz, R., Zadeh, L.A., Zurada, J.M. (eds.) ICAISC 2008. LNCS (LNAI), vol. 5097, pp. 752–761. Springer, Heidelberg (2008)
11. Cierniak, R.: New neural network algorithm for image reconstruction from fan-beam projections. Neurocomputing 72, 3238–3244 (2009)
12. Cierniak, R., Lorent, A.: A neuronal approach to the statistical image reconstruction from projections problem. In: Nguyen, N.-T., Hoang, K., Jędrzejowicz, P. (eds.) ICCCI 2012, Part I. LNCS, vol. 7653, pp. 344–353. Springer, Heidelberg (2012)
13. Cpałka, K.: A method for designing flexible neuro-fuzzy systems. In: Rutkowski, L., Tadeusiewicz, R., Zadeh, L.A., Żurada, J.M. (eds.) ICAISC 2006. LNCS (LNAI), vol. 4029, pp. 212–219. Springer, Heidelberg (2006)
14. Przybył, A., Cpałka, K.: A new method to construct of interpretable models of dynamic systems. In: Rutkowski, L., Korytkowski, M., Scherer, R., Tadeusiewicz, R., Zadeh, L.A., Zurada, J.M. (eds.) ICAISC 2012, Part II. LNCS (LNAI), vol. 7268, pp. 697–705. Springer, Heidelberg (2012)
15. Horzyk, A., Tadeusiewicz, R.: Self-Optimizing Neural Networks. In: Yin, F.-L., Wang, J., Guo, C. (eds.) ISNN 2004. LNCS, vol. 3173, pp. 150–155. Springer, Heidelberg (2004)

Representation of Edge Detection Results Based on Graph Theory

Patryk Najgebauer, Tomasz Nowak, Jakub Romanowski,
Janusz Rygał, and Marcin Korytkowski

Institute of Computational Intelligence, Częstochowa University of Technology
al. Armii Krajowej 36, 42-200 Częstochowa, Poland
{patryk.najgebauer,tomasz.nowak,jakub.romanowski,janusz.rygal,
marcin.korytkowski}@iisi.pcz.pl
http://iisi.pcz.pl

Abstract. This paper describes a concept of image retrieval method based on graph theory, used to speed up the process of edge detection and to represent results in more efficient way. We assume that result representation of edge detection based on graph theory is more efficient than standard map-based representation. Advantages of graph-based representation are direct access to edge nodes of the shape without search and segmentation of edges points as is the case with map-based representations. Another advance is less data consumption, only data for nodes and their connections are needed, what is important in large database applications for good scalability.

In the described approach we reduce the amount of necessary image data to examine by modifying some standard edge detection method. To obtain that, we use an auxiliary grid to detect points of edge intersections with grid lines. Each intersection point becomes a node of graph that is a base element of the graph-based representation. Finally, our method based on edge segmentation creates connections between graph nodes determined in the previous steps of the algorithm. The method analyzes an image independently in squares determined by an auxiliary grid, which can be fork and parallel processed. We motivate the idea of our work that it will be used to develop a method for image feature extraction in CBIR for database applications.

Keywords: edge detection, edge representation, graph theory, image processing.

1 Introduction

A family of edge detection methods is one of the first developed and most commonly used in content based image processing. The main goal of edge detection is to detect locations of rapid changes in image brightness. These changes are typical for edges that make boundaries between different regions of images. In most cases, boundaries between regions are created between overlapping objects, objects and background or content over objects. The edge detection process massively reduce the amount of data to be analyzed as usually only significant shape

L. Rutkowski et al. (Eds.): ICAISC 2013, Part I, LNAI 7894, pp. 588–601, 2013.

elements of the image remain. Edge detection is the first step in many computer vision algorithms such as shape recognition, object detection, feature extraction, face recognition, image compression etc. [4][5][11][12][14][15][7][6][8].

Edge detection is a low level operation on image pixels and in most cases uses some operators. The operators in many variants are used to identify horizontal, vertical or diagonal edges and also to identify corner of edges. Operators are matrixes of coefficient values that are used to analyze neighbor pixels values. Frequently, the operator matrix size is of 3x3 pixels. The resulting value of the operator is the sum of multiplications between pixels value and operator coefficient values. Edge detection operators are classified into two general categories: first-order derivative and second-order derivative.

Operators of first-order derivative generate image gradient value thus they are also called gradient operators. Formula (1) shows value determination method of first-order derivatives of image. G_x is a horizontal component of local derivative and the G_y is vertical component of local derivative. G_x and G_y values are determined by the mask of operator.

$$G = G_x + G_y = \frac{\delta I}{\delta x} + \frac{\delta I}{\delta y} \tag{1}$$

In this group we have most of classic operators such as Prewitt (Fig. 1a), Sobel (Fig. 1b), and Robert Cross (Fig. 1c) [9]. To compute the gradient two operators in opposite orientation are used, usually horizontal and vertical. Edges points are determined by thresholding and localization of local extrema values in a set of operator results.

Operators of second-order derivative are based on detecting points of zero-crossing values. These points indicate local extreme pixels values of image. Formula (2) shows value determination method of second-order derivatives of the image, where L is determined by a single mask of the operator.

$$L = \frac{\delta^2 I}{\delta x^2} + \frac{\delta^2 I}{\delta y^2} \tag{2}$$

Results of edge detection with use of this operator are relatively similar to operators of first-order derivative. In contrast to the first order, we use only one operator but in this case we lose information about orientation of the edge and also this type of operators are more sensitive to sharp noise. The most popular is the Laplasian of a Gaussian (LoG) (Fig. 1d) filter that assumes use of Gaussian operator for smoothing and Laplacian second-order operator [10]. This operators also are used to blob detection and to designate key points of image in many image comparing algorithms. The described operators are presented in Fig. 1. Results of edge detection process is a map with identical size as input image with marked points of detected edges. Usually maps are presented as images, what is easily readable for human.

Most of the standard edge detection methods are vulnerable to blur noise. It is caused by the size of operator matrix that analyze only small area of the image. This problem can be eliminated by using operators with larger matrix,

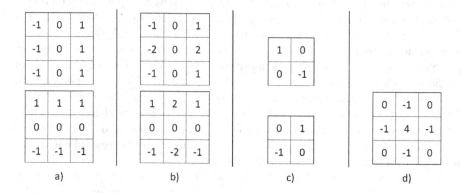

Fig. 1. Typical edge detection operators (a - Prewitt, b - Sobel, c - Roberts Cross, d - Laplacian)

but it increases inaccuracy of detected edges and increase the number of pixel that must be analyzed by the operator in one step. Sharp noise also creates distortion in detected edges but that can be easily eliminated by Gaussian or median image pre-filtering [1]. Edges can also be detected after the process of image segmentation. In this way, edges points are designed by selecting the shape of image segments.

Graphs are structures (3) consisting of a non-empty set of vertices **V** called nodes and a set of edges **E** defining connections between nodes.

$$G = (V, E) \tag{3}$$

Using graphs we can map data structures in a natural way and create links between them to eventually perform actions on them. By graphs we can represent and form many difficult dependencies that exist in real life. Graphs are used in many areas of computer science such as databases, text processing, determination of optimal path or tasks optimization. The structure of the graph is also very legible and intuitive for humans, so it is also used in representing data dependencies in graphical interfaces.

In our solution, graphs were used for two purposes: as data organization in detected edges description as well as the graphical representation of the edges by displaying the graph structure.

2   Problem Description

As mentioned earlier, results of standard edge detection process is represented by a map of edges points. Map-based representation gives precise position of edges points and their nearest content. This type of representation allows for efficient access to points values by their position. This approach is well legible for human mind, but in computer image processing that approach creates some difficulties in subsequent operations.

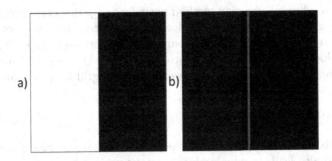

Fig. 2. Example of map based edge representation. Left input image. Right result of edge detection method.

Map representation method causes that we have a large amount of data to examine. In most cases only small part of resulting map is marked as edges points. For example, for the image of the size 200x200 pixels presented in (Fig. 2), edge detection process produce 40,000 result values as two-dimensional map of size 200x200 points. Detected edge consists of only 200 points, other map space are unused. As we can see only 0.5% of result map is marked as detected edges points. This is not optimal solution to store results of edge detection especially in case of database applications.

Another problem is that in most solutions edge tracking is performed after edge detection. Edge tracking most often is made by segmentation of detected edges. In the first step, fragments of edges must be localized in the resultant map. After that, in each step of segmentation, edge pixels are grouped by comparing with other neighboring pixels. This approach slows the algorithm and additionally there is a problem on the edge forks. Many of contacting or intersecting edges share the same segments which makes it difficult to further semantically evaluate segmentation results.

As we can see, most of algorithms might be more efficient after elimination or reducing process of edge segmentation. Our approach assumes replacement of the map representation by a graph. Graph representation dramatically reduce the amount of data required for edges representation. All required data is used to represent only the significant edges by nodes. There is also potential for compression by setting maximal distance between nodes. For example, a graph created from an image (Fig. 2) with preselected 10 pixel maximal distance between nodes, contains only 20 nodes connected with 19 edges links. Each node required only position value.

Second advantage of graph representation is immediate access to edge shape by nodes. Using graph representation we do not need to localize edges in edge preprocessing step. That accelerate and reduce memory requirements of the method.

The proposed graph creation method optimizes edge detection process by use of auxiliary grid. In the process of edge detection most of space between grid lines is omitted because our method searches edges intersections with grid lines. After edge localization, the method proceeds with edge segmentation between detected intersections, so only space over edges and grid lines is analyzed.

3   Existing Solutions

Most of methods that use graph theory is focused on image segmentation [3] [13]. This method also leads to edge detection by determining segment borders. This approach is based on image conversion to a graph. Pixels of image are represented by graph nodes and connected with neighboring pixels via graphs links. For each link, magnitude value is calculated by operators similar to gradients operators. Segments are determined by link removing that corresponds to minimum cut with the smallest cut value among all minimum cuts between every pair of vertices.

In the case of this approach, all pixels of the image are examined. Not only all of them are examined, but they are examined multiple times, depending on the size of the mask currently used. Generated graph is large and consists of thick and vast grid of nodes. Each pixel is mapped by one node and connected with several neighbor pixel nodes. The methods are focused on precise image segmentation. Their results graph representation contains more elements than the input image.

None of the previous work was dedicated to use graph theory in purpose for edge representation. Our approach unlike the existing works is focused to speed up the edge detection and to reduce amount of data needed for storing the results. The presented method assumes significant edges extraction and representation with minimal accuracy decrease of the mapped edges.

4   Proposed Method

Presented method assumes a different way of edge detection and data representation. Graph representation of detected edges will accelerate the search process, storage and operations on the set of edges.

The main assumption of the presented approach is edge detection followed by graph generation on the basis of the detected edges. The method searches for edges and determines nodes points with the use of an auxiliary grid. Use of the auxiliary grid is an important part of the proposed solution. Image analysis is performed over the line of the auxiliary grid to detect the collision points of objects edges with grid lines. For each detected collision point algorithm assigns graph node that represent point of the detected edge, as demonstrated in the Fig. 3a. The use of the auxiliary grid allows for regular graph nodes distribution depending on the used density of the grid. The generated graphs are rare graphs that mean they usually have only two connections to neighboring nodes located on the edge line as shown in the image (Fig. 3c). The only exception to this rule

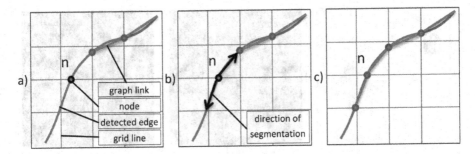

Fig. 3. Graph preparing schema. a) - graph nodes determination, b) - edges segmentation between nodes, c) - node path.

are the points of edges intersections or forks where more nodes is connected. This feature simplifies further analysis process of generated graphs and their store process, because most of the nodes can be represented in similar form to the two-way list that groups node in the edge path.

Application of the auxiliary grid and the graph based representation makes operations independent between nodes, thus it allows to generate the graph by parallel programming between image segments defined by the auxiliary grid lines.

4.1   Edge Node Detection

Determination of graph nodes takes place over the lines of the auxiliary grid. For each point of the image under the auxiliary grid lines, gradient vector $\vec{g}$ is designated by formula (4), where $\mathbf{G_x}$ and $\mathbf{G_y}$ are the values calculated by Prewitt gradient operator.

$$\vec{g} = [\mathbf{G_x}, \mathbf{G_y}] \tag{4}$$

The length of gradient vector $\vec{g}$ determines the strength of the edge at a given point, and the same vector also indicates the direction of the edge. In practice, the vector indicates the direction where the pixels of the image are brighter.

The presented method uses operators of 5x5 pixels kernel size. This improves the coverage of the image between the auxiliary grid lines. This is important in cases where the auxiliary grid line passes through the point where the edge of the image is weakened or even broken.

Gradient vector $\vec{g}$ value of each point is compared with the other vectors of the adjacent points, located on the auxiliary grid line. Point of the largest vector value becomes a node if the vector orientation is not too close to the orientation of the auxiliary grid line. It prevents the problem of creating multiple nodes at the edge that is tangent to the auxiliary grid line.

4.2   Edge Nodes Combining

The next step is to connect the resulting edges nodes. Our approach uses edge segmentation method for this purpose. Another possibility is to connect nodes

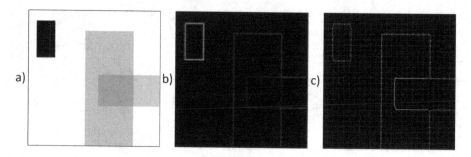

Fig. 4. Graph making result. a) input image, b) edge map-based representation, c) graph-based representation.

basing on searching the nearest neighboring nodes by examining the correlations between their positions and orientation determined by the gradient vectors. This approach is faster but unfortunately some problems occur, especially in the case of lines that run parallel and close together, they may be combined into one. Another problematic case are lines that will be connected when, in fact, they are two different edges of which ends are located between grid lines. Presented segmentation provides high accuracy identical to conventional edge detection methods.

Segmentation proceeds in two opposite directions from the starting point (Fig. 3b) designated by the node position. Segmentation in two directions determines only the strongest connections with other nodes. During segmentation branched edges are ignored but, if they are significantly important than they will be connected from other node. This causes the omission of many fragments of an insignificant edge that can make the graph less readable for human. This action can also be considered to the operations forming the salient edges [2] that assumes reduction of edges points that are not local extremes. In contrast to the standard salient edges method we do not process existing maps of detected edges points, because in the proposed method salient edges are a side effect of the edge representation by a graph.

After determining the opposite points the edge segmentation process begins that aims to set new segmentation points up to cross the line of the auxiliary grid. In each step for each of the two points of segmentation three neighboring edges points are tested which values are calculated on-demand by using gradient operators that designating the orientation vector. The point of the highest gradient vector length is a new point of segmentation.

Gradient vector of the edge orientation is also used to properly select positions of three neighboring pixels that are compared in the second step. All combinations create 8 variants of 3x3 kernels. Mask represents neighboring pixels group in vertical, horizontal and diagonal edge segmentation directions.

If the current segmentation point is localized at the grid line, continuation of segmentation is interrupted. Then the algorithm searches for the most closely located node of the graph, but is restricted to the distance of 3 units. This value of the maximal distance results from the fact that the segmentation is conducted between the grid lines. After this segmentation process, resulting position on the grid line can be slightly different from the position of earlier determined nodes of neighbors grid lines. If at the segmentation point there not exists any node of graph then a new one is created at this point. After that, a new connection is created between start and the newly determined node of segmentation.

New connected nodes are assigned to the appropriate paths. Paths in our solution are a very important part because their form is ideally suited to represent the image edges. Paths and edges are objects that consist of the following nodes, which are connected one by one without branching. For this reason, all of free nodes are assigned to suitable permanent path. With this approach we also get a set of predefined paths representing each independent image edges.

4.3   Post-processing

The final step is post-processing designed to eliminate unnecessary insignificant nodes of the resulting graph. This process removes isolated nodes and nodes that are part of the one-element paths. Single nodes in most cases are elements of textures, stains, or noise, that have been cut by the single grid line, and do not make connections between other nodes located on the neighboring grid lines. Image of the final result is shown in Fig. 4c and to compare both methods, Fig. 4b shows results of the standard map-based edge detection.

5   Experiments

In order to present the characteristics and capabilities of our method, we performed two types of experiments: the first comparing our solution with the solution of the traditional map-based representation of the edge, and a second one showing the dependence between created graph in response to change of density value of the auxiliary grid. All photos are resized to 400x400 pixels size only to improve readability.

5.1   Comparison of Map-Based and Graph-Based Representation

To present a comparison of two methods of edges representation we decided to conduct comparative tests between the methods. For the purpose of the test, we used five randomly selected images from the Internet. In both cases, Prewitt operator with 5x5 pixels kernel size is used to perform edge detection. The drawing (Fig. 5) presents visual effect of the two methods of edge representation. The first column represents the input images, the next edge detected map-based representation, and the last shows resulting image of the graphs-based representation method. On images of graph-based representation, the nodes are represented by white pixels. Graph connection between nodes are represents by grey lines. Regular horizontal and vertical dark-grey lines represent lines of auxiliary grid used to edge detection and node determination. For all images we preset 10 pixels

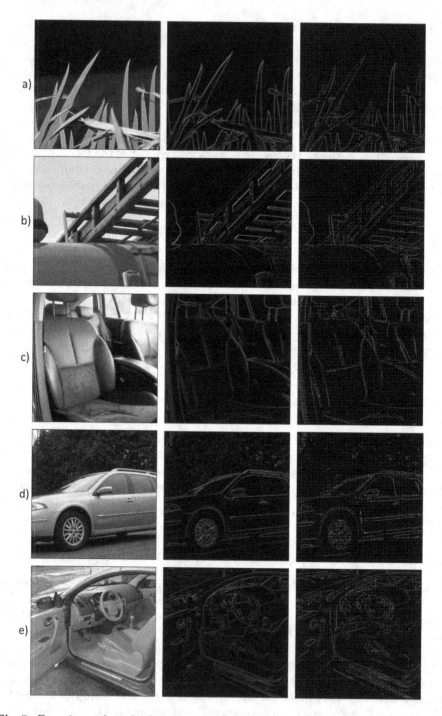

Fig. 5. Experimental results for edge detection on 5 real images. First column, original images; second column, map representation; third column, graph representation.

Table 1. Summary of map-based representation

Image number.	No. of map points.	No. of edge points.	Edge / map points ratio.
Fig. 4a 160000	24843	15,53%
Fig. 4b 160000	24069	15,04%
Fig. 4c 160000	27592	17,25%
Fig. 4d 160000	28515	17,82%
Fig. 4e 160000	33946	21,22%

Table 2. Summary of graph-based representation compared with map-based representation

Image number.	No. of graph nodes	No. of graph links	Nodes / map points ratio	Nodes / edge points ratio
Fig. 4a 989	797	0,62%	3,98%
Fig. 4b 1166	1010	0,73%	4,84%
Fig. 4c 1239	1001	0,77%	4,49%
Fig. 4d 1307	1030	0,82%	4,58%
Fig. 4e 1865	1427	1,17%	5,49%

density value of auxiliary grid and 0.05 value of edge threshold. At first sight both of representation methods are very similar. Table 1 and Table 2 present a comparison of two methods. All images have been scaled to a resolution of 400x400 pixels, so map-based representation consists of 160 thousand points.

Conventional map-based algorithm after image processing with using Prewitt operator classified on average about 28 thousand points as points of edges. Points classification were made by thresholding with a threshold value of 0.05 that is the same as we used in the graph-based method. Map of points that represents the edges is the same size as the image. Map is composed of 160 thousand points from which only about 28 thousand is marked as true edge points. Number of edge points is only about 17% of the map, the other pixels are not used.

The graph-based method allows to represent all of significant image edges with use about 1.3 thousand nodes and 1 thousand of node connections. Average number of used nodes is only about 0.8% of the amount of image pixels. This is enormous difference, especially that in the case of the graph-based method, unlike to map-based one, there is no need to use large map of edge points. As far as result storage is concerned, the graph-based method need only about 0.8% amount of data that the map-based method required.

Finally, we can also compare the value of the average number of graph nodes to the average number of map points marked as edges. In this case the number of graph nodes is only 4.5% of the number of points marked as edges. This comparison shows great capabilities offered by the graph-based representation.

5.2   The Relationship between Density of the Auxiliary Grid and the Number of Graph Nodes

To introduce another property of the proposed method which is the ability to compress, or reduce the number of points, we perform an experiment on the photo by a gradually reducing the density of the auxiliary grid and observing the size of result graph and changes in readability of generated graph on the basis of their original images. We decided to use six different density of auxiliary grid starting from the highest 5, 10, 15, 20, 25 and 30 pixels space between grid lines. Images (Fig. 6) and (Fig. 5c) represent graphic results of the graph-based method in this experiment. Table 3 presents the values describing the number of the graph nodes and their connections depending on the density of the auxiliary grid. As we can see in the resulting images, the most optimal image results are obtained for the density value of the auxiliary grid between 10 and 15 pixels. We can see on them a slight lack of detail, and also a large decrease in the size of the generated graph. Below this density value we can observe total loss of small image details. Only the most distinct edges of largest objects remain. A less dense auxiliary grid can be used in the processing or pyramidal image analysis or analyze images of larger sizes.

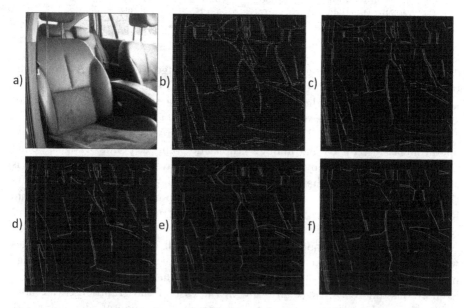

Fig. 6. Results of the graph-based representation of different density of auxiliary grid. a) input image, b) 5px grid density, c) 15px grid density, d) 20px grid density, e) 25px grid density, d) 30px grid density.

Table 3. Representation of the difference in the size of the graph, depending on the density of the auxiliary grid

Image number.	Density of auxiliary grid.	No. of nodes.	No. of nodes links.
Fig. 5a 5		2074	1791
Fig. 4c2 10		1239	1001
Fig. 5c 15		723	571
Fig. 5d 20		580	444
Fig. 5e 25		436	332
Fig. 5f 30		338	297

6 Conclusions

From the experiments and results of the comparison between the map-based representation and the graph-based method we can see quite significant difference between the methods. The map-based method is characterized by the following features:

1. Highly detailed. By analyzing the edges we can read their precise shape and texture. This is especially important if searched or analyzed objects have a large amount of small details. It is also possible to read strength and direction of the gradient vector so it allow to create detailed image local descriptors typical used to search for the same image structures.
2. The method also represents areas that not classified as edges points. This property allows to determine the width or blur of detected edge that is effect of local gradient rising. It also allows to analyze object convexity.
3. Direct access to the values of the gradient by reference to the position. It is instant access, the same as two dimensional array access.
4. No relationship between the points. Map is a set of points defining the value of the local gradient. There is no information about the exact location of the edge. To determine the shape of the edge, at first it must be located at least one point of edge and then must be performed edge segmentation.
5. Many no-edges points. Map-based representation contains many points which are not edges of objects such as fragments of textures, smudges, spots. It makes difficult to properly localize and segment edges.
6. Large memory requirements. The amount of necessary memory depends only on the size of the photo, not on the amount of edge points. High ratio of amount of map points to the number of edge points.

The graph-based method is characterized by the following features:

1. Direct access to the node of the edge with the relation between the other nodes. There is no need to search for edge points. Determination of the edges shape is sufficient to examine relationship between the nodes of the graph.

2. Small insignificant details are omitted that, in most cases, are no object edge elements. This feature depends on the size of elements and density of the auxiliary grid. This allows for simultaneous image denoising from other non-essential elements.

3. The amount of data required to represent the significant image edges is rapidly reduced. Taking into account the conclusions from Table 1 and Table 2, we can conclude that the method of graph-based representation is more efficient then the map-based method. It requires average about only 5% of the number of nodes that are needed by the traditional methods. Links between the nodes are not taken into consideration because map-based representation does not contain relations between points.

4. The ability to compress the image edge representation by reducing density of the auxiliary grid. Resulting graph contains less number of nodes what is presented in Table 3 and larger distances between nodes. As we can see in Figure 6, even low-density grids allow to create readable graphs that contain most characteristic edges of the image.

5. Reduced shape detail of edge, depending on the density of the auxiliary grid. It is not possible to read the exact shape of the edge between the nodes. It is also not possible to read the information about nearby gradient of edge.

6. No direct access to the edge node by reference to the position. We need to perform a graph iteration to find the closest node to the position. Optionally the graph can be mapped into an array to speed up the search process.

As we can see, both methods are different from each other. Graph-based methods of edge representation can certainly be applied in areas where approximated description of the detected edges of image, small amount of required data, and where there is no need to focus on the details of the image.

Acknowledgments. The work presented in this paper was supported by a grant from Switzerland through the Swiss Contribution to the enlarged European Union.

References

1. Canny, J.: A computational approach to edge detection. IEEE Trans. Pattern Anal. Mach. Intell. 8(6), 679–698 (1986)
2. Holtzman-Gazit, M., Lihi, Z.-M., Irad, Y.: Salient Edges: A Multi Scale Approach. In: ECCV 2010 Workshop on Vision for Cognitive Tasks (2010)
3. Janakiraman, T.N., Mouli, P.V.S.: Image Segmentation Based on Minimal Spanning Tree and Cycles. In: International Conference on Computational Intelligence and Multimedia Applications, December 13-15, vol. 3, pp. 215–219 (2007)
4. Karande, K.J.: Multiscale wavelet based edge detection and Independent Component Analysis (ICA) for Face Recognition. In: 2012 International Conference on Communication, Information & Computing Technology, ICCICT. IEEE (2012)
5. Ogiela, M.R., Tadeusiewicz, R., Ogiela, L.: Intelligent Semantic Information Retrieval in Medical Pattern Cognitive Analysis. In: Gervasi, O., Gavrilova, M.L., Kumar, V., Laganá, A., Lee, H.P., Mun, Y., Taniar, D., Tan, C.J.K. (eds.) ICCSA 2005. LNCS, vol. 3483, pp. 852–857. Springer, Heidelberg (2005)

6. Scherer, R., Rutkowski, L.: Neuro-fuzzy relational classifiers. In: Rutkowski, L., Siekmann, J.H., Tadeusiewicz, R., Zadeh, L.A. (eds.) ICAISC 2004. LNCS (LNAI), vol. 3070, pp. 376–380. Springer, Heidelberg (2004)
7. Scherer, R., Rutkowski, L.: A fuzzy relational system with linguistic antecedent certainty factors. In: 6th International Conference on Neural Networks and Soft Computing, Zakopane, Poland, June 11-15. Advances in Soft Computing, pp. 563–569 (2002)
8. Scherer, R., Rutkowski, L.: Connectionist fuzzy relational systems. In: Halgamuge, S.K., Wang, L. (eds.) Computational Intelligence for Modelling and Prediction. SCI, vol. 2, pp. 35–47. Springer, Heidelberg (2002)
9. Senthilkumaran, N., Rajesh, R.: Edge detection techniques for image segmentation-A survey of soft computing approaches. International Journal of Recent Trends in Engineering 1(2), 250–254 (2009)
10. Sotak, G.E., Boyer, K.L.: The Laplacian-of-Gaussian kernel: a formal analysis and design procedure for fast, accurate convolution and full-frame output. Computer Vision, Graphics, and Image Processing 48(2), 147–189 (1989)
11. Tadeusiewicz, R., Ogiela, L., Ogiela, M.R.: The Automatic Understanding Approach to Systems Analysis and Design. International Journal of Information Management 28(1), 38–48 (2008)
12. Tadeusiewicz, R., Ogiela, L., Ogiela, M.R.: Cognitive Analysis Techniques in Business Planning and Decision Support Systems. In: Rutkowski, L., Tadeusiewicz, R., Zadeh, L.A., Żurada, J.M. (eds.) ICAISC 2006. LNCS (LNAI), vol. 4029, pp. 1027–1039. Springer, Heidelberg (2006)
13. Wu, Z., Leahy, R.: Image segmentation via edge contour finding: a graph theoretic approach. In: Proceedings of the 1992 IEEE Computer Society Conference on Computer Vision and Pattern Recognition, CVPR 1992, June 15-18, pp. 613–619 (1992)
14. Wei, H., et al.: A novel content-adaptive image compression system. In: 2012 IEEE Visual Communications and Image Processing, VCIP. IEEE (2012)
15. Xu, L., et al.: The rapid method for road extraction from high-resolution satellite images based on USM algorithm. In: 2012 International Conference on Image Analysis and Signal Processing, IASP. IEEE (2012)

A Novel Graph-Based Descriptor for Object Matching

Tomasz Nowak, Patryk Najgebauer, Janusz Rygał, and Rafał Scherer

Institute of Computational Intelligence, Częstochowa University of Technology
al. Armii Krajowej 36, 42-200 Częstochowa, Poland
{tomasz.nowak,patryk.najgebauer,janusz.rygal,
rafal.scherer}@iisi.pcz.pl
http://iisi.pcz.pl

Abstract. Representing images by their interesting points has become recently one of the most effective methods of comparing images. One of the main challenges in image processing is to create a universal descriptor that will be invariant to changes in scale, rotation and illumination. One of the most popular and the most effective algorithm, which generates the key points is currently SURF. The problem discussed in this work concerns the comparison of objects belonging to the same category, but different from each other e.g. two different cars. We propose a new descriptor designed for objects in the image to compare similar objects. It is based on a graph, which was built on the basis of the key points that were generated using SURF algorithm. We present results of experiments which have been conducted for various objects and descriptors generated using the proposed method.

Keywords: object matching, graph-based descriptor, shape representation.

1 Introduction

One of the tasks of image processing is comparison of various images, based on their features such as shapes, colors, keypoints or dependencies between objects [11][13][12][10]. Very crucial issue here is a selection of appropriate feature sets and methods of storing them in databases. Selected features of the image should be invariant to noise, easy to store and process, but also unique. The choice of appropriate features of objects contained within the image contributes to reduction of redundant data, which must be processed during image matching stage. There are many different types of descriptors which allow to describe images in many different ways and comparing with other images located in a database. Content-based image retrieval algorithms usually work in a similar manner: application reads the image, locate and segment objects and processes them. The result is a descriptor, which should include all necessary information about the content of the image.

L. Rutkowski et al. (Eds.): ICAISC 2013, Part I, LNAI 7894, pp. 602–612, 2013.

Currently, there are many different methods based on invariant features which allow comparing pairs of images: objects located on the reference image are compared with other images. Usually the objects are the same. Probably the most efficient algorithm for extracting image features is SIFT [1]. This algorithm uses a scale for keypoint detection - space from a pyramid of difference of Gaussian images. Descriptors, to a certain extent, are resistant to changes in scale, rotation and illumination. Another very popular method of creating descriptors is Harris Corner Detector [2], but this method is not scale invariant. Both of these methods do not work in the case when we search for similar images, containing objects from the same group, but not exactly the same objects. These methods work very well in case of tracking objects (e.g. in the movie), or search for exactly the same object in another picture.

There exists many methods for keypoints detection, e.g. maximally stable extremal regions (MSERs) [3], and Harris-Affine and Hessian-Affine corners [4] or difference-of-Gaussian [1]. Recently image hashing techniques gained popularity for dimensionality reduction. Among them we can highlight the two most popular: SVD [5] and NMF [6], which are robust to blurring, minor noise, and compression, but suffer from brightness changes and large geometric transforms.

Currently, the most frequently descriptors are created using SIFT. An alternative for SIFT algorithm is SURF, which was published by the Bay in 2006[7]. Just like SIFT, SURF creates the keypoints and descriptors of these points. The advantage of the SURF on the SIFT is to significantly reduce the amount of calculation, what is an important factor in more demanding applications. Keypoints are found by using a so called Fast-Hessian Detector that bases on a determinant of the Hessian matrix for a given image point. The responses to Haar wavelets are used for orientation assignment, then keypoint descriptors are formed from the wavelet responses in a certain surrounding of the keypoint.

In this work, a novel region descriptor is proposed for objects contained in the image. The proposed type of descriptors will be used to search for objects belonging to the same class of objects. The descriptor is based on key points which are generated for the image using the SURF algorithm. The graph stretched on key points of an object is a good starting point for a quick comparison of the objects in the image, and allows searching for objects with similar structure, not just limited to identical objects.

The rest of the paper is organized as follows. In Section II we introduce some preliminary concepts, while section III outlines the region descriptor algorithm. Section IV describes experiments and discussion of the proposed descriptor. Section V provides the final conclusions.

2   Existing Methods

SURF (Speeded Up Robust Features) is an algorithm which searches for features resistant to changes in scale, rotation and illumination, and was presented in 2006 by H. Bay. SURF was developed on the basis of the SIFT algorithm, requires much less resources during the operation, and the method of operation is faster

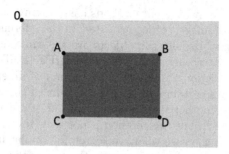

Fig. 1. Thanks to integral images concept, it takes only three additions and four memory accesses to calculate the sum of intensities inside a rectangular region of any size

than SIFT. The main element of the algorithm is the structure named Images, what allows to significantly reduce the number of operations. The next structure is an integral image, which represents the sum of pixels in any rectangular area of the input image I.

$$I_\Sigma(x,y) = \sum_{i=0}^{i\leq x}\sum_{j=0}^{j\leq y} I(x,y) \tag{1}$$

where I - processed image, $I_\Sigma(x,y)$ - the sum of all pixels in the image. Calculation of the sum of the pixels in the selected area of the image (Integral Image) is presented in Fig. 1, and is described by (2).

$$\sum = A - B - C + D \tag{2}$$

where A, B, C, D values are the sum of pixels in the selected point. Using Integral Images, it takes only three additions and four memory accesses to calculate the sum of intensities inside a rectangular region of any size. Calculation time is independent of its size, which translates to the performance of the algorithm. Searching for local extremes is based on determinant of Hessian matrix. Given a point $x = (x,y)$ in an image I, the Hessian matrix $H(x,\sigma)$ in x at scale σ is defined as follows

$$H(x,\sigma) = \begin{bmatrix} L_{xx}(x,\sigma) & L_{xy}(x,\sigma) \\ L_{xy}(x,\sigma) & L_{yy}(x,\sigma) \end{bmatrix} \tag{3}$$

where $L_{xx}(x,\sigma)$ is the convolution of the Gaussian second order derivative $\frac{\delta^2}{\delta x^2}g(\sigma)$ with the image I in point x, and similarly for $L_{xy}(x,\sigma)$ and $L_{yy}(x,\sigma)$. Gaussians are optimal for scale-space analysis. SURF uses other filters (simpler ones) than SIFT. SURF is faster and also somewhat less accurate (Fig. 2) thanks to using less complex filters. However, in many applications high accuracy is not needed, while the execution speed of the algorithm is always important. SURF searches interesting points at different scales. In the SIFT scale-spaces are created of the pyramids consisting from images - the whole picture is resized, which

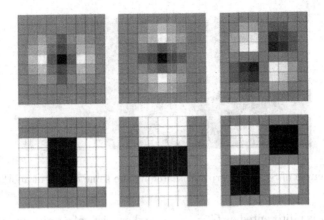

Fig. 2. The filters used in the SIFT (first row) and simplified filters used in the SURF (second row)

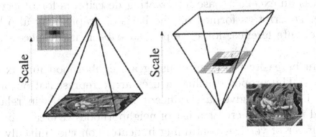

Fig. 3. Iterative reduction in the size of the image (left), the use of integral images allows to scale the filter, what reduces the amount of calculation (right)[7]

requires the use of multiple resources, in SURF only filters are scaled while the image remains unchanged. This approach allowed to substantially speed up calculations (Fig. 3).

In order to precisely locate interest points in the image, values of the determinant are compared with the neighbors, Haar wavelets in conjunction with integral images are used to describe gradients around key points and the direction of the descriptor is determined based on the sum of these wavelets.

SURF is usually applied to search for exactly the same object in another picture, e.g. while tracking an object on a video sequence. The algorithm allows to find the searched object in another image even if it is rotated or partially hidden. Its descriptors are also resistant to some extent to change the lighting and the scale (Fig. 4). Graphs are universal structures, which can represent selected features using vertices, and edges, and can reflects relationships between them. The edge may have a weight, which can specify for example the distance between the vertices.

Fig. 4. Example of SURF algorithm: searching the same object in another image

A graph G is represented as $G = (V, E)$ and consists of a finite and non-empty set of vertices $V = v_1, ..., v_n$, where n is a number of vertexes, collection of edges $E \subseteq V \times V$, where $e \in E, e = (v_i, v_j)$ is the connecting edge of vertices $v_i, v_j \in V$.

Methods of connecting key points using graphs has become very popular recently, and is an excellent base for creating descriptors for objects contained in the image. Descriptors formed on the basis of graphs may also be resistant to all sorts of interference, for example, have been used successfully in face recognition [8].

Graphs can be easily represented using a neighborhood matrix or a list of neighborhoods. The proposed solution uses array representation of the neighborhood list because it gives a significant memory savings in relation to the neighborhood matrix. To create a list of neighborhood we create an array equal to size of number of vertices containing indicators on the (initially empty) list - the subsequent list items mean the next neighbors of the vertex to which the list is allocated.

Let an array is called LS. For each edge (v_i, v_j), to the list pointed to by $LS[i]$ is added vertex index v_j. $LS[i]$ indicates now to a list of containing indexes of all neighbors of the apex v_i. To delete an edge (v_i, v_j) we just remove index v_j from the list $LS[i]$, and index v_i from $LS[j]$.

The array representation of the neighborhood list was presented in Fig. 5.

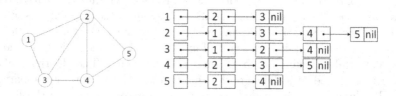

Fig. 5. An example of a graph, and the corresponding neighborhood list

3   Proposed Method

Most of the existing methods for comparing images process the whole picture, but in many cases, a lot of data in the photo is not relevant. The primary elements that characterize the photo are the main objects (e.g., car, animal, man), or relationships of these objects. The proposed solution processes only the objects that are located in the image, without background elements. Objects are cut from the image using the method presented in [9](Fig. 6). In the proposed method we create a descriptor of the area with the object in the image. It is created on the basis of the key points that were generated with the help of the SURF algorithm. This descriptor is resistant to deformation and all sorts of changes to objects. The descriptor is based on the graph which gives the ability to search for similar objects, belonging to the same category e.g. dogs, cars, men. Fig. 7 shows a general block diagram of the proposed method. In order to reduce the amount of data needed to generate the graph, we reduce the amount of key points by removing the points which have the lowest importance. The next step in this solution is to add the point that will determine the center of the object relative to the key points. This is designed to prevent the generation of the graph

Fig. 6. The left side shows the input image, on the right we can see the effects of the algorithm presented in [9]

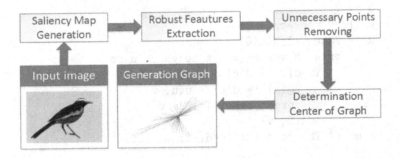

Fig. 7. General flowchart of the proposed method

with randomly selected points, as was done in the some methods presented in the literature. Position of the new point for the object is determined by the following expression:

$$\bar{x} = \frac{\sum_{i=1}^{n} w_i x_i}{\sum_{i=1}^{n} w_i}, \quad \bar{y} = \frac{\sum_{i=1}^{n} w_i y_i}{\sum_{i=1}^{n} w_i} \tag{4}$$

where $[x_1, x_2, ..., x_n]$, $[y_1, y_2, ..., y_n]$ are coordinates of the points and $[w_1, w_2, ..., w_n]$ are weights of the points. If we have the center point and other keypoints of the object, we can proceed to create a graph on them. When the graph is created, we used Dijkstra's algorithm, through which all vertices (points) will be connected by the shortest possible route. The algorithm combines points by choosing the path with the smallest weights (weights cannot be negative). In our solution, the edge weight value is the Euclidean distance between key points. In Dijkstra algorithm, a collection of vertices Q is stored, for which the shortest paths, and vector $D[i]$ distance from vertex S to I are continuously calculated. Initially, the set Q contains all vertices, and vector D is the first row of the matrix edge of weights A.

1. While the collection Q is not empty execute:
2. Take from a collection of Q, vertex v with the smallest value $D[v]$ and remove it from the collection.
3. For every consequent i vertex v perform path relaxation, i.e. check if $D[i] > D[v] + A[v, i]$, i.e. if the current estimation of the distance from the vertex i is greater than the estimation of the distance from the vertex (envy) plus edge (v, i) weight.

   If so, update estimation $D[i]$ by assigning the right side of the inequality (that is the lower value). If so, update the estimate of $D[i]$ by assigning it the right side of the inequality (i.e. lower value).

Dijkstra algorithm pseudocode is as follows:

```
Dijkstra(G,w,s):
    for each vertex v in V [G], do
        d[v] := Infinity
        predecessor [v] := undefined
    d[s] := 0
    Q := V
    While Q non-empty do
    u := Take_Off_Min(Q)
        for each vertex v = a neighbor u do
            if d[v] > d[u] + w(u, v) then
                d[v] := d[u] + w(u, v)
                predecessor [v] := u
            Add(Q, v)
    cout <<"The road is: "<<d[v];
```

Graphs created as a result of the algorithm are relatively easy to store in relational databases.

4   Experimental Results

The proposed descriptor has been tested on the data in the form of images with different objects belonging to different categories (men, cars, dogs, birds, etc.). For each of the classes there were generated at least dozens of descriptors. Objects were extracted from photos using Saliency Detection algorithm [9], as background is redundant data and is not needed in the process of identifying objects. Having only objects, we search them for interesting points using SURF algorithm. In order to reduce the amount of key points we removed those with the smallest weights. Points have been classified on the basis of the average of all weights of points found in the object. All points whose weights were less than the average weight of all the points, were passed over during the experiment. Then we generated a new point, which was the beginning of graph. Such action was intended to avoid a situation in which the graph would be generated from random points. In a situation when graph can start from any point, it can be always different, even for the same set of key points. In the next step we generated graphs according to the algorithm presented in section 3.

In the example below we can see the action of SURF algorithm in order to compare the objects belonging to the same category. In the first case, the objects are identical, they had been compared with each other correctly. In the second and third case, we can see two similar objects that belong to the same class (Fig. 8). As we can see, the objects were not classified correctly (Fig. 9). Next, we present the objects and generated for these descriptors. As we can see,

Fig. 8. Example of objects belonging to the same class. The objects are very similar but not identical.

Fig. 9. The effect of the SURF algorithm: first case shows considered objects in another picture (the same object); the second and third case show searching for similar objects in images

examining only the descriptors, we are able to divide them into certain groups, which really constitute different classes of objects (Fig. 10). The objects that belong to the same group do not have to be identical, to be classified in similar categories, what gives the option to search through collections of objects in order to find a similar but not identical things.

Fig. 10. The result of the algorithm is graph, in which vertices represent key points; edges are the distance between them. As we can notice, the graphs are similar for objects belonging to the same category.

5   Conclusions and Future Work

In this paper we proposed a descriptor based on graphs. The model of graph was created on the basis of the key points which were generated using SURF algorithm. Graphs were generated basing on Dijkstra's algorithm, which creates the shortest possible path between the starting point and the other points. The results of experiments showed that, on the basis of the generated descriptors, we are able to divide objects to different classes. In the future we would like to improve the selection of key points, e.g. we can combine them in groups (clusters) and on the basis of these groups generate the graph.

Acknowledgments. The work presented in this paper was supported by a grant from Switzerland through the Swiss Contribution to the enlarged European Union.

References

1. Lowe, D.: Distinctive Image Features from Scale-Invariant Keypoints. Int'l J. Computer Vision 60(2), 91–110 (2004)
2. Ryu, J., Park, H., Park, J.: Corner classification using Harris algorithm. Electronics Letters 47(9), 536–538 (2011)
3. Matas, J., Chum, O., Martin, U., Pajdla, T.: Robust wide baseline stereo from maximally stable extremal regions. In: British Machine Vision Conference, vol. 1, pp. 384–393 (2002)
4. Mikolajczyk, K., Schmid, C.: Scale and affine invariant interest point detector. Int. J. Comput. Vision 60(1), 63–86 (2004)

5. Kozat, S., Venkatesan, R., Mihcak, M.: Robust perceptual image hashing via matrix invariants. In: Proc. IEEE Int. Conf. Image Processing (ICIP), pp. 2442–2446 (2004)
6. Monga, V., Mhcak, M.: Robust and secure image hashing via non-negative matrix factorizations. IEEE Trans. Inf. Forensics Securit 2(3), 376–390 (2007)
7. Bay, H., Ess, A., Tuytelaars, T., Van Gool, L.: Speeded-Up Robust Features (SURF). International Journal of Computer Vision and Image Understanding (CVIU) 110(3), 346–359 (2008)
8. Kisku, D.R., Rattani, A., Grosso, E., Tistarelli, M.: Face Identification by SIFT-based Complete Graph Topology. In: 2007 IEEE Workshop on Automatic Identification Advanced Technologies, June 7-8, pp. 63–68 (2007), doi:10.1109/AUTOID.2007.380594
9. Achanta, R., Süsstrunk, S.: Saliency Detection for Content-aware Image Resizing. In: IEEE International Conference on Image Processing (2009)
10. Tadeusiewicz, R., Ogiela, M.R.: Why Automatic Understanding? In: Beliczynski, B., Dzielinski, A., Iwanowski, M., Ribeiro, B. (eds.) ICANNGA 2007. LNCS, vol. 4432, pp. 477–491. Springer, Heidelberg (2007)
11. Ogiela, M.R., Tadeusiewicz, R.: Syntactic pattern recognition for X-ray diagnosis of pancreatic cancer. IEEE Engineering in Medicine and Biology Magazine 19(6), 94–105 (2000)
12. Ogiela, L., Tadeusiewicz, R., Ogiela, M.R.: Cognitive Computing in Intelligent Medical Pattern Recognition Systems. In: Huang, D.-S., Li, K., Irwin, G.W. (eds.) ICIC 2006. LNCIS, vol. 344, pp. 851–856. Springer, Heidelberg (2006)
13. Ogiela, M.R., Tadeusiewicz, R., Ogiela, L.: Intelligent Semantic Information Retrieval in Medical Pattern Cognitive Analysis. In: Gervasi, O., Gavrilova, M.L., Kumar, V., Laganá, A., Lee, H.P., Mun, Y., Taniar, D., Tan, C.J.K. (eds.) ICCSA 2005, Part IV. LNCS, vol. 3483, pp. 852–857. Springer, Heidelberg (2005)

Extraction of Objects from Images Using Density of Edges as Basis for GrabCut Algorithm

Janusz Rygał, Patryk Najgebauer, Jakub Romanowski, and Rafał Scherer

Institute of Computational Intelligence, Częstochowa University of Technology
al. Armii Krajowej 36, 42-200 Częstochowa, Poland
{janusz.rygal,patryk.najgebauer,jakub.romanowski,
rafal.scherer}@iisi.pcz.pl
http://iisi.pcz.pl

Abstract. When we think about images, we usually think about that what we can detect by our eyes. It is easy for us, because all of the hard work is already done by our own brain. Human brain extracts from images all information which is currently important. It is not possible to mirror the whole natural process, because now we do not posses enough knowledge about our brain. Nevertheless, a lot of research is devoted to achieve even part of the targets. This is a small steps strategy, so we are not able to do all at once, but we try to test different approaches, combine and develop new digital images processing algorithms. In this paper we present a DOE (Density of Edges) algorithm and its application as a basis for the GrubCut algorithm. We also present the whole preprocessing approach and which algorithms were used. Results of that work will be used and integrated in SIA Semantic Image Analysis project developed by authors.

Keywords: Object extraction, Density of edges, Semantic image analysis, CBIR.

1 Introduction

There are many methods of processing and retrieving images on the basis of their content [15] [16] [12] [13]. The aim of our work was to create a preprocessing mechanism, which will be able to fetch the most important information from an image and to filter out unimportant one. The whole process is composed of a sequence of algorithms, which are integrated into a single preprocessing approach. As a result, we expect to obtain selected parts of the image, which will be a basis for further computing. Figure 1 shows a simplified design of our preprocessing mechanism. The whole structure can be expressed as the following list:

1. Conversion an image into grayscale,
2. Median filtration,
3. Edge detection,
4. DOE (Density Of Edges),
5. GrabCut.

Our preprocessing mechanism is composed of several algorithms. One of them is our new approach, calculating density of edges (DoE) and use of the results to restrict the

L. Rutkowski et al. (Eds.): ICAISC 2013, Part I, LNAI 7894, pp. 613–623, 2013.

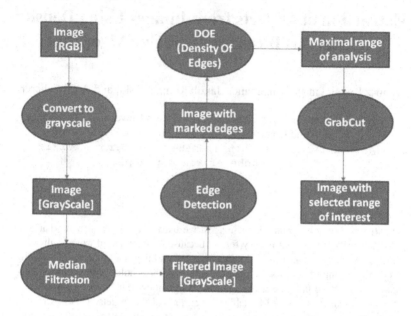

Fig. 1. Structure of our approach in context of preprocessing

range of interest. Almost each part depends on values of parameters; results of using different values of them will be presented in the description of tests. We are going to describe each part of our process, but the main focus is to present the DoE algorithm. There are many of publications about using GrabCut algorithm, but it is very often connected with interaction with human [1] [2] [3]. Interaction with human and manual preprocessing is a popular approach by using iterated graph cuts. Interaction with the user is acceptable in graphics software, this can be also very useful not only in cases, when automatic process failed, but also when we want to influence the program, not always in an obvious, standard way. There are a lot of tools, which support manual way of an extraction of objects, for example "Magic Wand", "Bayes Matte" or "Intelligent Scissors" [5]. In our approach we aim to automate the whole process. We do not need specific, not standard behavior from an algorithm. What we need is to force a process to produce the best results as possible. Of course, the precision is very important, but not at the same level as in the case of work with graphics software. The whole process has to be fully automated.

The paper is organized as follows. Section 2 is a description of the whole preprocessing approach, which was designed as a part of the SIA (Semantic Image Analysis) approach. Section 3 presents in details the DoE (Density of Edges) algorithm. The fourth section was dedicated to a description of our test application. Section 5 contains information about test strategy, results of those tests are presented in the section 6 and finally in the section 7 we have recapitulated an approach presented in this paper, according to further development of the SIA [14].

2   Stages of Preprocessing Approach

Our preprocessing mechanism is composed of several algorithms. One of them is our new approach, i.e. calculating density of edges (DoE) and use results of that computation to restrict the range of interest. Almost each part depends on values of parameters; results of using different values of them will be presented in the description of tests. We are going to describe each part of our process, but the main focus is to present the DoE algorithm.

2.1   Conversion of RGB Image to Grayscale

In digital imaging we use very often a grayscale image. It is caused by the fact that for many of algorithms the information about the intensity is a sufficient value. It is also easier to analyze single channel data. One of the ways to convert an image into grayscale was presented in equation (1) [10] [11].

$$Y = 0.2126R + 0.7152G + 0.0722B \tag{1}$$

where Y is luminance value and R, G and B are values of respectively red, green and blue component.

2.2   Median Filtration

There are several methods of filtration; we have decided to use a median filtration. The main target is to reduce a noise, which is noticeable on almost every image. Median filter gets all pixels in the matrix in a given size, calculates the median value of them and sets all pixels in the matrix with the median value. The most important thing is to establish the proper size of matrix, which will be big enough to remove noise from image and small enough not to remove significant information [10] [11].

$$y\,[m, n] = \text{median}\,\{x\,[i, j]\,,(i, j) \in w\} \tag{2}$$

Where w represents a neighborhood centered around location (m, n) in the image

2.3   Edge Detection

In our approach we have used the Canny edge algorithm invented by John F. Canny in [1986] [7] [8]. This is a more sophisticated way to detect edges than for example, the Sobel operator [6] [4]. But of course this operator is used in the Canny edge algorithm. The kernel of that mechanism uses a multi-stage algorithm. The Canny edge algorithm is often described by three statements: good detection, good localization and minimal number of false alarms [9].

To use Canny edge algorithm we have to approximate gradients, in that operation we use kernels, which are presented in (3) and (4).

$$KGX = \begin{bmatrix} -1 & 0 & 1 \\ 2 & 0 & 2 \\ -1 & 0 & 1 \end{bmatrix} \tag{3}$$

$$KGY = \begin{bmatrix} 1 & 2 & 1 \\ 0 & 0 & 0 \\ -1 & -2 & -1 \end{bmatrix} \tag{4}$$

In the next step we have to compute strength of edge, this can be simply achieved by using the law of Pythagoras (5)

$$|G| = \sqrt{G_x^2 + G_y^2} \tag{5}$$

Where the G_x is the gradient in x direction and G_y is the gradient in y direction. The density of edges can be computed using equation (6).

$$\theta = arctan\left(\frac{|G_y|}{|G_x|}\right) \tag{6}$$

The Canny edges algorithm is known to be very flexible, it could be applied to detect various types of edges by changing parameters of the algorithm. This type of edge detection is also enough robust. The Canny edges algorithm works with two Tresholdolds for detecting weak and strong edges. What is important, a weak edge is only taken into further consideration, when it is connected with a strong edge.

2.4   DOE (Density Of Edges)

This part of the whole process is responsible for restriction of area which will be passed as input to the GrubCut algorithm. Details of DOE algorithm are described in Section 3. In a nutshell, the DOE algorithm analyzes the given image after filtration with detected edges and then divides an image into matrixes with edge pixels. List of matrixes is analyzed and at the output of DOE algorithm we obtain a restricted area, which should contain the most important information about the image and will be the most proper input information for GrubCut algorithm.

2.5   GrabCut Algorithm

The GrabCut algorithm was designed for detection and extraction objects from images. There are many implementations and versions of this algorithm, but the main idea relies on iterative process of classifying pixels as foreground pixels or background pixels [1] [2] [3]. In this paper we will not explain the details of the GrabCut algorithm. It is important that in our process there is no need for human interaction thanks to DOE algorithm. As the input, the GrabCut algorithm expects restricted area of the image, which should be boundary of area with objects. As aforementioned, our approach assumes that this area is determined by DOE algorithm.

3   Design of DOE Algorithm

As already mentioned, the DOE algorithm has to analyze an image in order to establish a subarea of the image, which contains most important information. That area is also known as ROI (Range of Interest). As the input, DOE algorithm required an image with detected and marked edges. The DOE algorithm can be presented as an ordered sequence of activities:

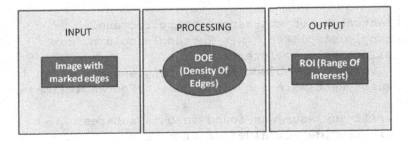

Fig. 2. Position of DOE algorithm in the whole process

1. Dividing a whole image into subareas
2. Computing a density of edges for each subarea, basing on pixels included into each of subarea.
3. Extracting areas, which have the biggest value of density of edges.
4. Fetching the most interesting area of an image. This will be used as ROI for Grab-Cut algorithm.

The best way to show how this process can be realized is to present an excerpt from the computer program. At the beginning, we need to explain some variables, which are the part of the input of the algorithm. One of the most important input values is the size of the singular matrix of density. Number of rows and columns in the matrix of density are expressed as percentage value of width and height of the input image.

Another input value is the level of acceptance, which implicates the filtering step of the algorithm. Only those matrixes of density will be accepted and taken into approximation of the ROI for GrabCut algorithm, which are above level of acceptance in the collection of all significant density matrixes. For example when the level of the acceptance is equal 3, then the sorted collection of matrixes will be divided into three parts; the last most significant two parts will be accepted. The meaning of the level of acceptance is very important, when it is low, then many matrixes will be accepted, which implicates that some of noise will influence computation. On the other hand, when the level is to high, we can lose some of important information.

```
//Height of subarea
int rowInterval = Convert.ToInt32(image.Height *
getDensityMatrixSize());
//Width of subarea
int colInterval = Convert.ToInt32(image.Width *
getDensityMatrixSize());
//Iterating over rows
for (int row = 0; row < (image.Height - rowInterval);
row += rowInterval)
{
   //Iterating over columns
   for (int column = 0; column < (image.Width -
colInterval); column += colInterval)
```

```
{
//Creating an object representing rectangle
Rectangle simpleRec = new Rectangle(column, row,
  colInterval, rowInterval);
  //Creating an object representing subarea of an image
  DensityRectangle rec = new DensityRectangle(image,

    //If any edge was found in this subarea
    if (rec.getSumValue() > 0)
    {
    //Adding to the collection
    densityRecs.Add(rec);
    }
  }
}
}
//When number of significant subareas greater then
//DIVISION_FACTOR default 3
if (densityRecs.Count >= DIVISION_FACTOR)
{
  //Sorting elements ascending
  densityRecs.Sort();
  //Index from them significant subareas
  //will be selected
  int index = Convert.ToInt32(densityRecs.Count /
                                DIVISION_FACTOR);
  //Number of subareas, which will be selected
  int count = densityRecs.Count - index;
  //Selection fo significant subareas
  selectedRecs = densityRecs.GetRange(index, count);
}
```

4 Design of the Test Application

For tests of the DOE algorithm, we have developed an application, which allows easily observing the results of each step of the process. In this process, we have to use several algorithms to achieve expected results. So the ability of observing the results of each of them was one of the main basic use-cases for this program. Another use-case is the possibility of changing input parameters. The next requirement was the possibility of fast developing a new algorithm and getting them easily work consistently in one framework. The diagram in Figure 3 shows the structure of classes, which allows easily adding and implementing new algorithms, which will be automatically included in the framework and provided with standard functionality. The application is written in C# .NET 4.0.30319 with Emgu.CV-2.3.0. The program was tested on the Windows 7.

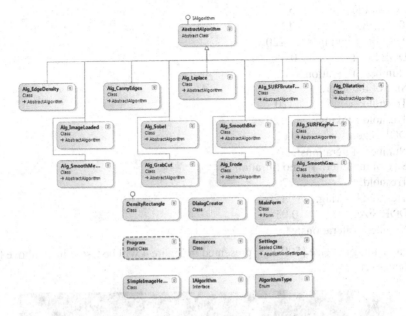

Fig. 3. Class diagram of CBIR 2.0 application

5   Test Strategy

In our tests we have tested several combinations of the input parameters. As already mentioned, our process contains three basic subprocessing algorithms, which require proper input values. In the following list we have presented those parts with values of input parameters, which were tested.
Median filtration:

- Size of the filter {3,5} [pixels]

Canny Edges:

- Tresholdold   {100, 120} [intensity]
- Tresholdold Linking {100, 120} [intensity]

DOE:

- Size of the DOE matrix {0.02, 0.05} [percentage so 2% and 5%]

GrabCut:

- Number of iteration   {10,15} [unit]

Test combinations:

1. Size of the filter: 3
   Tresholdold: 100
   Tresholdold Linking: 100
   DOE Size: 0.02
   Number of iterations: 10

2. Size of the filter: 5
   Treshold: 120
   Treshold Linking: 120
   DOE Size: 0.05
   Number of iterations: 15
3. Size of the filter: 3
   Treshold: 120
   Treshold Linking: 120
   DOE Size: 0.02
   Number of iterations: 10
4. Size of the filter: no filtration
   Treshold: 120
   Treshold Linking: 120
   DOE Size: 0.05
   Number of iterations: 15

The same image of size [500,333] presented in Figure 4 will be tested in all above four combinations.

Fig. 4. Original test image

6   Experimental Results

Images in Figure 5 are results of our tests, which were conducted in accordance with Section 5. Results are grouped in rows, one row for each combination of parameters. First image in each row presents results after combined process of median filtration, edge detection and DOE algorithm. The second image represents the result of the Grub-Cut algorithm, working on data, which had been prepared by DOE algorithm using different combination of parameters.

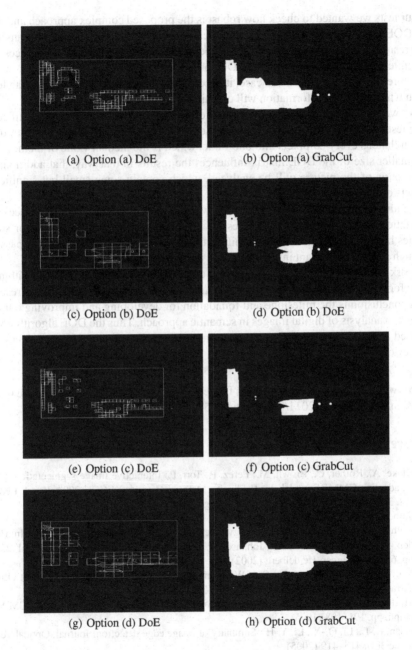

(a) Option (a) DoE

(b) Option (a) GrabCut

(c) Option (b) DoE

(d) Option (b) DoE

(e) Option (c) DoE

(f) Option (c) GrabCut

(g) Option (d) DoE

(h) Option (d) GrabCut

Fig. 5. Images with results of tests, using various combinations of input parameters

7 Conclusions

In our tests we wanted to check how robust is the proposed complex approach and also the DOE algorithm itself. The most significant dependency between input parameters and results is of course filtration. That dependency can be noticed in differences between test b) and test d) in Figure 5. Obviously this behavior strongly depends on the structure of an image, but in our case, it is better to extract more information than less. Even when extracted information will contain some noise.

As we can notice, differences between tests in size of the ROI are not significant, only test b) (Fig. 5) seems to be an exception. It is because of high level of filtration, which flattens every 25 pixels into one value, which is the median value of them.

Smaller size of the DOE matrix influences the results in that way, that additionally those parts of the picture will be analyzed, which contain some small but significant objects or parts of them.

As already mentioned, DOE algorithm was developed to be used in the process of semantic image analysis. In the process of analyzing images and searching for similarities between them, loss of the significant information is more damaging as passing through some unimportant information.

Work presented in the paper proved that our approach of using a DOE algorithm as basis for GrabCut algorithm can be used as automatic alternative with satisfying results. This conclusion is the milestone and foundation for developing and improving our approach to analysis of digital images in semantic approach. Thus the DOE algorithm will be used as one the most important computing parts of SIA (Semantic Image Analysis) framework [14].

Acknowledgements. The project was funded by the National Center for Science under decision number DEC-2011/01/D/ST6/06957.

References

1. Blake, A., Rother, C., Brown, M., Perez, P., Torr, P.: Interactive image segmentation using an adaptive GMMRF model. In: Pajdla, T., Matas, J(G.) (eds.) ECCV 2004, Part I. LNCS, vol. 3021, pp. 428–441. Springer, Heidelberg (2004)
2. Talbot, J.F., Xu, X.: Implementing GrabCut. Brigham Young University (2006)
3. Kolmogorov, V., Zabih, R.: What energy functions can be minimized via graph cuts? In: Heyden, A., Sparr, G., Nielsen, M., Johansen, P. (eds.) ECCV 2002, Part III. LNCS, vol. 2352, pp. 65–81. Springer, Heidelberg (2002)
4. Mai, F., Hung, Y., Zhong, H., Sze, W.: A hierarchical approach for fast and robust ellipse extraction. Pattern Recognition 41(8), 2512–2524 (2008)
5. Mortensen, E., Barrett, W.: Intelligent scissors for image composition. In: Proc. ACM Siggraph, pp. 191–198 (1995)
6. Duan, R.-L., Li, Q.-X., Li, Y.-H.: Summary of image edge detection. Journal, Optical Technique 3(3), 415–419 (2005)
7. Canny, J.: A computational approach to edge detection. IEEE Trans. Pattern Analysis and Machine Intelligence PAMI-8(6), 679–698 (1986)
8. Zeljko, H., Suzana, V., Verica, H.: Improved Canny Edge Detector in Ceramic Tiles Defect Detection. IEEE Industrial Electronics (2006)

9. Meer, P., Georgescu, B.: Edge Detection with Embedded Confidence. IEEE Trans. on PAMI 23(12), 1351–1366 (2001)
10. Gonzalez, R.C., Woods, R.E.: Digital Image Processing, 2nd edn. Pearson Education (2005)
11. Jensen, J.R.: Introduction to Digital Image Processing: A Remote Sensing Perspective. Practice Hall, New Jersey (1996)
12. Ogiela, M.R., Tadeusiewicz, R., Ogiela, L.: Intelligent Semantic Information Retrieval in Medical Pattern Cognitive Analysis. In: Gervasi, O., Gavrilova, M.L., Kumar, V., Laganá, A., Lee, H.P., Mun, Y., Taniar, D., Tan, C.J.K. (eds.) ICCSA 2005, Part IV. LNCS, vol. 3483, pp. 852–857. Springer, Heidelberg (2005)
13. Tadeusiewicz, R., Ogiela, L., Ogiela, M.R.: The Automatic Understanding Approach to Systems Analysis and Design. International Journal of Information Management 28(1), 38–48 (2008)
14. Rygał, J., Najgebauer, P., Nowak, T., Romanowski, J., Gabryel, M., Scherer, R.: Properties and Structure of Fast Text Search Engine in Context of Semantic Image Analysis. In: Rutkowski, L., Korytkowski, M., Scherer, R., Tadeusiewicz, R., Zadeh, L.A., Zurada, J.M. (eds.) ICAISC 2012, Part I. LNCS, vol. 7267, pp. 592–599. Springer, Heidelberg (2012)
15. Górecki, P., Sopyła, K., Drozda, P.: Ranking by K-Means Voting Algorithm for Similar Image Retrieval. In: Rutkowski, L., Korytkowski, M., Scherer, R., Tadeusiewicz, R., Zadeh, L.A., Zurada, J.M. (eds.) ICAISC 2012, Part I. LNCS, vol. 7267, pp. 509–517. Springer, Heidelberg (2012)
16. Sopyła, K., Drozda, P., Górecki, P.: SVM with CUDA Accelerated Kernels for Big Sparse Problems. In: Rutkowski, L., Korytkowski, M., Scherer, R., Tadeusiewicz, R., Zadeh, L.A., Zurada, J.M. (eds.) ICAISC 2012, Part I. LNCS, vol. 7267, pp. 439–447. Springer, Heidelberg (2012)

Computer Vision Based Method for Real Time Material and Structure Parameters Estimation Using Digital Image Correlation, Particle Filtering and Finite Element Method

Marcin Tekieli and Marek Słoński

Institute for Computational Civil Engineering
Faculty of Civil Engineering
Cracow University of Technology
{mtekieli,mslonski}@l5.pk.edu.pl
http://www.l5.pk.edu.pl

Abstract. This paper presents the design and implementation of a novel method for real time material and structure parameters estimation. Digital image correlation (DIC) and particle filtering (PF) are used for obtaining the full-field deformations of a structure or model. In order to take into account all advantages of both methods, new marker design is proposed. Particle filtering method is also used in combination with finite element method (FEM) for estimating material and structure parameters, such as Young's modulus, by solving inverse problems. Main algorithm and all of the above methods are implemented in C++. Experiments are carried out on the model of an aluminum frame, using high resolution industrial camera.

Keywords: computer vision, digital image correlation, finite element method, particle filtering, sequential Monte Carlo method.

1 Introduction and Motivation

The problem of structural material and structure elements identification is an important and difficult class of inverse problems in structural mechanics. Identification is based on a set of measurements on static and dynamic structural responses. Data can be collected by conventional sensors - strain gauges or accelerometers but it requires extensive knowledge of how these sensors work and how they should be mounted on the structure. Connection between each sensor and the data acquisition unit is also required. In this case, data are collected using computer vision methods with high resolution industrial camera, thus the organization of the test stand is much simpler and faster. Optical techniques offer the potential to acquire structure performance data without the need for installation of conventional sensors, lasers or other devices.

The essence of the research is to combine three powerful computational methods - digital image correlation (DIC) for full-field displacement measurements

L. Rutkowski et al. (Eds.): ICAISC 2013, Part I, LNAI 7894, pp. 624–633, 2013.
© Springer-Verlag Berlin Heidelberg 2013

with high accuracy, finite element method (FEM) for structural analysis and particle filtering (PF) for dynamic state estimation and digital image processing.

Digital image correlation is an optical method that is widely used in many areas of science and civil engineering to measure deformation on an object surface [1] and it is relatively easy to use in micro scale for mechanical testing of materials such as steel [2], concrete [3], biomaterials [4] or even paper foils [5].

DIC usage for the displacement measurements in the whole structure or a complex model is rather rare and usually this method is implemented as part of the system for Structural Health Monitoring (SHM) [6]. This is due to difficulties in specifying areas of the specimens because each video frame contains mostly background instead of construction elements. What is more, to ensure the high level effectiveness of this method, the samples would have to have the right texture, which is problematic for some materials used in construction. The proposed method solves this problem by using special markers, very easy to prepare, cheap to manufacture and precede the DIC phase with another step using particle filters to locate markers and use areas that are applicable for monitoring displacement with DIC.

A particle filter, also known as a sequential Monte Carlo method (SMC), is a sophisticated model estimation technique based on simulation. In this method, each distribution is expressed by many of its realizations, and the trajectory of each particle in successive prediction stages is simulated by using the assumed model. At the filtering stage, the resampling with a weight proportional to the likelihood is performed to get a set of particles that represents the filter distribution [7,8]. In this paper, the same particle filtering is used twice but with different types of particles.

Another method used in this research is finite element method (FEM) - a numerical method for solving differential or integral equations. In this method a model or a structure is divided into an equivalent system of many smaller units (finite elements) interconnected to other elements at points called nodes [9]. FEM can be also successful combined with SMC on field of dynamic state estimation, to tackle the problem of structural system parameter identification based on a set of noisy measurements on static or dynamic structural responses. [10]

2   System Design

The central element of the system is the algorithm responsible for displacement measurements and material or structure parameters estimation. Each video frame taken from camera using uEye Software Development Kit [11] is converted to IplImage format from OpenCV Library [12], which was tested during the implementation of the previous project of the computer vision based system for real time traffic sign detection and recognition [13]. Video frames are subjected to preliminary processing in order to prepare it for the next steps of the main algorithm. The application was developed in order to allow its use for different

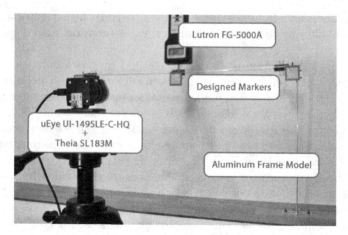

Fig. 1. Test stand with frame model, uEye camera and strain gauge

structures (frames, trusses and beams) with any number of measuring points represented by designed markers. Application is fully object-oriented and it was developed in Microsoft Visual Studio 2010 environment. By introducing a number of improvements in the algorithm, it is also optimized to operate in real-time.

Video frames are collected by industrial high-resolution USB camera uEye UI-1495LE-C-HQ equipped with Theia SL183M Ultra Wide Lens. Due to the limitations of the USB interface and very high resolution of each image (3840 x 2748px), the number of frames processed per second is limited to three. Calculations are performed on a computer with mobile Intel i7 1.86GHz processor and 4GB of RAM.

2.1   Novel Marker Project

Simultaneous use of two different methods - PF and DIC for detection and tracking markers, led to the development of a new marker design, which fully utilizes the advantages of both methods. The marker consists of two elements - single colored frame which allows for rapid searching for a marker using PF and narrows the region of interest only to the area of the marker. Interior of the marker is composed of two kinds of pixels - whites and in the color of the frame. They are set randomly and allow subsequent use of DIC to track the location of the marker and determine its movements. The use of PF allows very fast marker finding, but the tracking of the marker with this method would have relatively small accuracy. The interior of the marker allows to use digital image correlation method, which accuracy is much better. Generation of the described markers is very easy and fast. We can modify the color, size of the markers and change width of the frame. Markers can be adapted to the specific case - the size of the structure and the distance of the object from the camera.

Fig. 2. Different types of proposed marker model

The color of the marker may define its features - whether it is a marker in the node of the structure, or a marker placed inside the element. Tests were carried out with markers of size from 10x10mm to 50x50mm and the frame width from 3 to 10mm. Several patterns of the markers are shown in Figure 2.

2.2 Full-Field Displacement Measurement

The first phase of the algorithm is the detection of the markers. Thanks to the preparation of an application in a fully object-oriented way, work with a different number of markers is comfortable, and each marker is a separate object, which has assigned a set of particles, the position of the marker, the maximum value of the correlation during the displacements measurement and other useful parameters.

Detection of markers is based on a particle filter with particles which are represented by pixels with three main components - the intensity of each color of RGB color space. Reference particle is the pixel with a color similar to the color of the marker e.g. for red markers reference particle can be $p = RGB(255, 0, 0)$.

For each marker a collection of particles covering the entire image is generated with a uniform distribution. To avoid repeated recognition of the same marker, no marker detection is carried out in parallelly, and the occurrance area of next marker's particles is disjointed from the whole area containing marker's particles previously detected. The process of finding the next marker can start only after finding all previous ones.

For image resolution 3840x2748px satisfactory results are obtained already for a population containing only 3000 particles. Searching for markers is a single process and it does not need to be repeated during the algorithm execution. At the test stage, the population of particles for each marker was established at 5000, to ensure the correct detection of each marker.

To calculate the weight of particles, parameters of pixel are used, which are the colors of the three components of the RGB color space. Weight of the particle is higher, if the color of a pixel represented by this particle is more similar to the color of the reference particle. At this stage, the density function for a Gaussian distribution is used, given by following formula:

$$\phi_{\mu,\sigma}(x) = \frac{1}{\sigma\sqrt{2\pi}} e^{\left(-\frac{(x-\mu)^2}{2\sigma^2}\right)} \tag{1}$$

where the parameter σ is the standard deviation of the distribution and the parameter μ is the mean of the distribution (also called *expected value*). Particles resampling was based on a modified method of the roulette wheel. Weight of each particle is calculated at this stage and then all particle weights are normalized to the $[0.0; 1.0]$ interval. After the weights normalization a new population of particles is created. The value w_t is drawn from the $[0.0; 1.0]$ interval using uniform distribution. From a set of particles, also with uniform distribution, one particle is drawn. The weight of a drawn particle is compared with w_t value and if the weight of the particle is larger, particle is moved to a new population of particles. Otherwise, another particle is drawn and compared with w_t. The process takes as long as the new population of particles is just as large as the population of particles subjected to resampling phase.

In addition, to increase the efficiency of the algorithm, and to avoid convergence to a local minimum, the coordinates of particles are slightly modified with the integer value of the interval $[0.0; resRange]$. The above steps are iterated until all particles assigned to the marker will be moved in the area of selected dimensions (condition of the population concentration).

After the detection phase, measurement of displacements for each of the found markers takes place. At this stage, the image correlation method is used. After the detection phase, each marker is represented by the area containing particles assigned to the marker. Marker's area is narrowed to its interior containing two-color pattern in the middle part of the marker which is suitable for digital image correlation method. Narrowed area is now a reference image, which displacements are monitored. To calculate the correlation coefficient between the model f and a sample g of sizes MxN, the method of Zero Mean Normalized Cross Correlation is used. It is given by the following formula:

$$CC^{ZMN} = \frac{\sum\limits_{i=1}^{M}\sum\limits_{j=1}^{N}((f(i,j) - \mu_f) \times (g(i,j) - \mu_g))}{\sqrt{\sum\limits_{i=1}^{M}\sum\limits_{j=1}^{N}(f(i,j) - \mu_f)^2} \times \sqrt{\sum\limits_{i=1}^{M}\sum\limits_{j=1}^{N}(g(i,j) - \mu_g)^2}} \qquad (2)$$

where μ_f and μ_g denote the average luminance of the pattern and the sample. Calculation of average luminance for the pattern and the sample improves the results when measurements are made in variable lighting conditions. Best match sample is determined by the maximum value of the correlation coefficient (CC^{ZMN}).

To optimize the algorithm performance, modifications of standard method of correlation are introduced. Search area is not constant and it moves along with the marker. Thanks to that, it is possible to significantly narrow down the search area width and height. It drastically reduces the number of iterations performed during each searching step. Without the introduction of this modification, the value of parameter $searchRange$, which defines the size of search area, had to be established at 30px. In case of using marker tracking, the value may be reduced up to 5px. In tests the values of 10px and 15px were assumed. The value of this parameter is dependent on the dynamics of changes in the structure and should be inversely proportional to the number of frames processed per second.

2.3   Parameters Estimation

In the second stage, finite element method and particle filtering are used simultaneously to determine structure parameters - in this case Young's modulus of used material. Single particle is represented by finite element method model with particular Young's modulus of the material being used.

Particle filter applied at this stage of the algorithm is very similar to the particle filter used in the markers search phase. The properties of a single particle are represented by a single parameter - Young's modulus, in contrast to a particle represented by the pixel where three values - the intensity of each color of RGB color space, are assigned to a single particle.

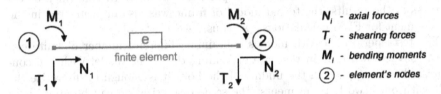

Fig. 3. Frame finite element model

Each particle is a separate structural model, which is solved by the finite element method using frame elements. Schematic model of this type of element is shown in Figure 3.

$$K = \begin{bmatrix} \frac{EA}{L} & 0 & 0 & \frac{-EA}{L} & 0 & 0 \\ 0 & 12\frac{EI}{L^3} & 6\frac{EI}{L^2} & 0 & -12\frac{EI}{L^3} & 6\frac{EI}{L^2} \\ 0 & 6\frac{EI}{L^2} & 4\frac{EI}{L} & 0 & -6\frac{EI}{L^2} & 2\frac{EI}{L} \\ \frac{-EA}{L} & 0 & 0 & \frac{EA}{L} & 0 & 0 \\ 0 & -12\frac{EI}{L^3} & -6\frac{EI}{L^2} & 0 & 12\frac{EI}{L^3} & -6\frac{EI}{L^2} \\ 0 & 6\frac{EI}{L^2} & 2\frac{EI}{L} & 0 & -6\frac{EI}{L^2} & 4\frac{EI}{L} \end{bmatrix}, \begin{matrix} A = bh \\ I = \frac{bh^3}{12} \end{matrix} \quad (3)$$

Stiffness matrix K of this element is given by formula (3), where L is length of the element, E is Young's modulus, A is cross-section area and I is element cross section property. FEM algorithm was programmed using Armadillo C++

linear algebra library [14]. Determination of displacement in the structure via FEM boils down to calculating the nodal displacement vector Q from the giving equation:

$$K_g Q = R \quad \rightarrow \quad Q = K_g^{-1} R \tag{4}$$

where K_g is the assembled stiffness matrix of all elements in global coordinate system, and R is a defined force vector.

Because the expected value (correct value of Young's modulus) is unknown, the filter operating time (the number of generations of a set of particles) is dependent on a modified version of the mean square error. Iterations are performed until all values assigned to the N particles (p_{val}) are not in range based on mean value M_{val} and convergence factor C_{val}:

$$[M_{val} - C_{val}, M_{val} + C_{val}], \quad M_{val} = \frac{1}{N} \sum_{i=1}^{N} p_{val} \tag{5}$$

After reaching established convergence, the return value of Young's modulus is calculated as the average value for all particles. In order to confirm the correctness of the results, the tested model of frame was also implemented in the environment for FEM calculations - Abaqus CAE 6.12 [15].

The tests performed with models containing different number of finite elements have shown that in the case of loading the frame model with the concentrated force applied in the middle of the bolt, it is enough to discretize the bolt with only two finite elements (the same discretization can be applied for frame pillars). The number of elements should be increased in the case where the applied force is located at a different point. This is because the point of force application in FEM must be located on the boundary of finite elements.

3   Experimental Results

Preliminary tests are performed on the model of the aluminum frame with markers placed in characteristic points of the structure. Frame model is stressed with a known load at known position, what causes displacements at each node and inside the structure elements.Strength value was determined using digital force gauge Lutron FG-5000A which measures tension and compression in $0.05oz$ or $1g$ resolution with 0.2% accuracy.

The first set of tests consisted of measuring the displacement at the point where force of the known values was applied. Force value varied from 1 to $10N$. The results were compared with results obtained from computer simulation of the frame model in Abaqus CAE environment. Resolution of the performed measurements f was set to $0.25mm$. It was determined by measuring the width of the marker on the single video frame. Figure 5 shows obtained results.

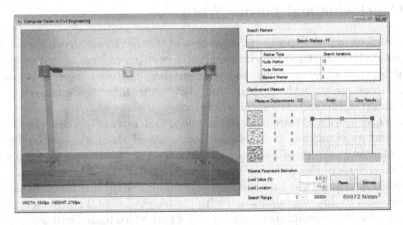

Fig. 4. Application interface

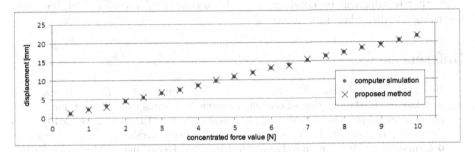

Fig. 5. Vertical displacement in the middle of the frame bolt

The second set of tests was carried out to estimate the value of Young's modulus of the used material during the structure loading in different points with known concentrated force values. Young's modulus for aluminum is $E_{alum} = 69000N/mm^2$. Parameter estimation was tested in $[0, 300000]$ range with no a priori knowledge. The obtained results are presented in Figure 6.

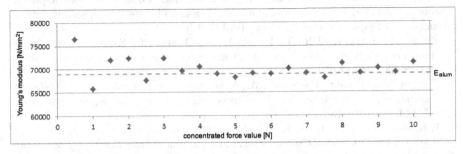

Fig. 6. Young's modulus estimation

For small values of concentrated force (less than $2N$) mean error value is about 6%. With the increasing value of applied force mean error amounts to 3%.

4   Conclusion and Future Work

The results clearly confirm the effectiveness of the developed algorithm combining two methods that require completely different parameters of marker placed on the structure. We managed to design markers that can be used in case of simultaneous use of both methods and allow us to take measurements at the maximum possible accuracy for used camera.

Currently, work and tests have already been underway to increase the number of parameters estimated at the same time - one of them will be the Poisson ratio. Moreover, the possibilities of location detection of the applied force and the effectiveness of the system with measurement noise added are tested.

Work is also underway on communication module implementation in the RS-232 standard to link our application with the usage of digital gauge meter. This will allow for the estimation of parameters for each video frame, without entering the value of the force manually.

Further testing will be conducted on the actual structure of the bridge over the suburb railway line in Cracow.

References

1. Brémand, F., Malesa, M., Szczepanek, D., Kujawińska, M., Świercz, A., Kołakowski, P.: Monitoring of civil engineering structures using digital image correlation technique. In: EPJ Web of Conferences, vol. 6. EDP Sciences (2010)
2. Savic, V., Hector Jr., L., Fekete, J.: Digital image correlation study of plastic deformation and fracture in fully martensitic steels. Experimental Mechanics 50(1), 99–110 (2010)
3. Skarżyński, L., Syroka, E., Tejchman, J.: Measurements and calculations of the width of the fracture process zones on the surface of notched concrete beams. Strain 47, e319–e332 (2011)
4. Milosevic, M., Mitrovic, N., Sedmak, A.: Digital image correlation analysis of biomaterials. In: 2011 15th IEEE International Conference on Intelligent Engineering Systems, INES, pp. 421–425 (2011)
5. Garbowski, T., Maier, G., Novati, G.: On calibration of orthotropic elastic-plastic constitutive models for paper foils by biaxial tests and inverse analyses. Structural and Multidisciplinary Optimization, 1–18 (2012)
6. Kohut, P., Holak, K., Uhl, T., Krupiński, K., Owerko, T., Kuraś, P.: Structure's condition monitoring based on optical measurements. Key Engineering Materials 518, 338–349 (2012)
7. Gordon, N., Salmond, D., Smith, A.: Novel approach to nonlinear/non-Gaussian Bayesian state estimation. In: IEE Proceedings F Radar and Signal Processing, vol. 140, pp. 107–113. IET (1993)
8. Kitagawa, G.: Monte Carlo filter and smoother for non-Gaussian nonlinear state space models. Journal of Computational and Graphical Statistics 5(1), 1–25 (1996)
9. Zienkiewicz, O., Taylor, R., Zhu, J.: The Finite Element Method: Its Basis and Fundamentals, vol. 1. Butterworth-Heinemann (2005)
10. Nasrellah, H., Manohar, C.: Finite element method based Monte Carlo filters for structural system identification. Probabilistic Engineering Mechanics 26(2), 294–307 (2011)

11. IDS-Imaging: uEye Camera Manual (2012), http://www.ueyesetup.com
12. WillowGarage: The OpenCV Library (2012), http://opencv.willowgarage.com
13. Tekieli, M., Słoński, M.: DriastSystem: a computer vision based device for real time traffic sign detection and recognition. In: Rutkowski, L., Korytkowski, M., Scherer, R., Tadeusiewicz, R., Zadeh, L.A., Zurada, J.M. (eds.) ICAISC 2012, Part I. LNCS, vol. 7267, pp. 608–616. Springer, Heidelberg (2012)
14. Sanderson, C.: Armadillo C++ linear algebra library (2012), http://arma.sourceforge.net
15. DassaultSystémesSimuliaCorp.: ABAQUS/Standard User's Manual (2012)

Author Index